Policy Implications on International Financial Economics and Banking

Shakeb Akhtar
https://orcid.org/0000-0003-2069-6669
Department of Business Studies, College of Economics and Business Administration, University of Technology and Applied Science, Ibra, Oman & Department of Business and Communications, INTI International University, Nilai, Malaysia

Mohsin Khan
Department of Commerce, School of Social Science and Language, Vellore, India

Faozi Abduljalil Gazem Almaqtari
https://orcid.org/0000-0002-5625-3643
A'Sharqiyah University, Oman

V. Selvam
Vellore Institute of Technology, Vellore, India

Shilpa Bahl
https://orcid.org/0000-0001-7818-7715
Galgotias University, Greater Noida, India

IGI Global
Scientific Publishing
Publishing Tomorrow's Research Today

Published in the United States of America by
IGI Global Scientific Publishing
701 East Chocolate Avenue
Hershey, PA, 17033, USA
Tel: 717-533-8845 | Fax: 717-533-7115
Website: https://www.igi-global.com E-mail: cust@igi-global.com

Library of Congress Cataloging-in-Publication Data

Names: Akhtar, Shakeb editor
Title: Policy implications on international financial economics and banking / [edited by] Shakeb Akhtar, Mohsin Khan, Faozi A. Almaqtari, Selvam V, Shilpa Bahl.
Description: Hershey, PA : IGI Global Scientific Publishing, [2026] | Includes bibliographical references and index. | Summary: "This book aims to analyze the impact of monetary and fiscal policies on international financial markets and banking systems"-- Provided by publisher.
Identifiers: LCCN 2025019819 (print) | LCCN 2025019820 (ebook) | ISBN 9798337337258 hardback | ISBN 9798337337265 paperback | ISBN 9798337337272 ebook
Subjects: LCSH: Monetary policy | Fiscal policy | International finance
Classification: LCC HG230.3 .P635 2026 (print) | LCC HG230.3 (ebook) | DDC 332.4/6--dc23/eng/20250716
LC record available at https://lccn.loc.gov/2025019819
LC ebook record available at https://lccn.loc.gov/2025019820

British Cataloguing in Publication Data
A Cataloguing in Publication record for this book is available from the British Library.

Table of Contents

Preface xvi

Acknowledgment xx

Introduction xxiv

Section 1
Foundations of International Financial Economics and Banking

Chapter 1
Introduction to International Financial Economics and Banking 1
K. Balaji, Christ University, Bengaluru, India
Mahfooz Alam, University of the People, USA

Chapter 2
The Role of Monetary Policy and Fiscal Policy on Global Finance 29
Bhargavi Rachamadugu, Woxsen University, India
Krunal Purohit, Woxsen University, India
Afzalur Rahman, Woxsen University, India

Chapter 3
Global Financial Crises: Lessons From Policy Failures and Successes 65
Ameya Anil Patil, Dr. Vishwanath Karad MIT World Peace University, India
Mahesh Kumar, Dr. Vishwanath Karad MIT World Peace University, India
Rajeev Sengupta, Dr. Vishwanath Karad MIT World Peace University, India
Rakesh Yadav, Prin. L.N.Welingkar Institute of Management Development and Research, India
Piyush Dixit, Indira University, India

Section 2
Policy, Regulation, and Stability

Chapter 4
Regulatory Frameworks and Their Impact on International Banking 93
Safas V. P., Department of Commerce, School of Social Sciences and Languages, Vellore Institute of Technology, Vellore, India
Mohsin Khan, Department of Commerce, School of Social Sciences and Languages, Vellore Institute of Technology, Vellore, India

Chapter 5
Sustainable Finance and Banking Policy Approaches for Stability 125
Rishikaysh Marotrao Kaakandikar, SaiBalaji International Institute of Management Sciences, India
Swati S. Bhalerao, Indira College of Pharmacy, India

Chapter 6
Managing Financial Distress: The Global Impact of Monetary and Fiscal Policies on Non-Performing Assets 165
Faiz ur Rehman, Aligarh Muslim University, India
Nawab Ali Khan, Aligarh Muslim University, India
Shakeb Akhtar, University of Technology and Applied Science, Ibra, Oman & INTI International University, Nilai, Malaysia
Bilal Asghar, Al Fayha College, Al Jubail, Saudi Arabia

Section 3
Emerging Trends in Digital and Monetary Innovations

Chapter 7
U.S. Strategy to Dominate the Dollar With Stablecoins: Geopolitical and Economic Implications 195
Silvio Andrae, Independent Researcher, Germany

Chapter 8
CBDCs in a High-Evasion Economy: Seigniorage, Tax Collection, and Institutional Tensions 237
Harpreet Kaur, Christ University, India
Surbhi Srivastava, Christ University, India
Shanu Singh, Christ University, India

Chapter 9
Artificial Intelligence Applications in Finance: A Proposed Model................. 265
Vedantam Seetha Ram, Jain University, India
Sukirno Sukirno, Universitas Negeri Yogyakarta, Indonesia
Rama Rao Gangadhara Sakha, GITAM University, India

Chapter 10
Combatting Bank Robbery and E-Banking Theft in North Central Nigeria With Advanced Artificial Intelligence (AI) Technology 297
Basil Osayin Daudu, Kogi State Univerisity, Nigeria

Section 4
Financial Markets and Risks

Chapter 11
Navigating Uncertainty: Global Stock Exchanges in the Age of Policy and Geopolitical Risk 325
Abhishek Sinha, Mahindra University, India
Vikas Maheshwari, Independent Researcher, UAE

Chapter 12
Analysing the Relationship Between Credit Default Swaps and the Financial Sector in G20 Countries: Evidence From Asymmetric Causality Test 355
Niyaz Hasanov, Yelo Bank, Azerbaijan
Mehmet Levent Erdas, Akdeniz University, Turkey

Chapter 13
Climate Risk Assessment and Financial Modelling for Sustainable Enterprises 379
Ekta Saraswat, IILM University, Greater Noida, India

Section 5
Inclusive Finance and Innovations

Chapter 14
Mapping the Landscape: A Bibliometric Analysis of FinTech Innovations in the Banking Industry 411
Mohammad Ammar Ahsan, Aligarh Muslim University, India
Mohd Salim, Woxsen University, India
Parvez Alam Khan, University Technology Petronas, Malaysia
Shakeb Akhtar, University of Technology and Applied Science, Ibra, Oman & INTI International University, Nilai, Malaysia

Chapter 15
Implications of Financial Literacy on Pawnshop Usage 441
José G. Vargas-Hernandez, Financial Literacy Research Center, Universidad Cristóbal Colón, Mexico & Tecnológico Nacional de México, ITS Fresnillo, Mexico
Csongor Czipf, Gyula Kautz Faculty of Economics, Széchenyi István University, Győr, Hungary
Absalón J. Salmerón-Zapata, Financial Literacy Research Center, Universidad Cristòbal Colòn, Mexico
Selene Castañeda-Burciaga, Universidad Politécnica de Zacatecas, Mexico
Omar A. Guirette-Barbosa, Universidad Politécnica de Zacatecas, Mexico

Compilation of References 465

About the Contributors 521

Index 533

Detailed Table of Contents

Preface........ xvi

Acknowledgment........ xx

Introduction........ xxiv

Section 1
Foundations of International Financial Economics and Banking

Chapter 1
Introduction to International Financial Economics and Banking 1
K. Balaji, Christ University, Bengaluru, India
Mahfooz Alam, University of the People, USA

The global financial economics and banking is emerging to be a very important element in an economical setting that becomes increasingly global. The primary objective is to deliberate how the capital flows, foreign exchange markets, interest rate parity and banking regulations have affected financial stability across nations and the economic growth. Background and theoretical structures that define the field of international finance and international banking that interconnect is outlined in the chapter. The chapter sheds some light on the dynamic entanglements between global financial institutions multinationals, central banks, and the overall global capital finance markets, cross-border risk evaluation set ups, and international liquidity indicators for macro-financial connections. The given work can contribute to the main part of the scholarly work by providing a complete image that combines the classical theory with the modern developments, hence, can be of use to scholars, policy makers, and financial professionals dealing with global financial markets.

Chapter 2
The Role of Monetary Policy and Fiscal Policy on Global Finance 29
Bhargavi Rachamadugu, Woxsen University, India
Krunal Purohit, Woxsen University, India
Afzalur Rahman, Woxsen University, India

This chapter explores the evolving landscape of global finance, specifically examining the profound influence of Central Bank Digital Currencies (CBDCs) on monetary and fiscal policy transmission mechanisms. It delineates the foundational principles of traditional monetary and fiscal policies, contrasting them with the transformative potential of CBDCs in achieving economic stability and growth. The analysis delves into CBDC's direct impact on macroeconomic factors, including financial stability, bank profitability, and financial inclusion, from both central bank and public perspectives. Furthermore, the chapter addresses the multifaceted challenges associated with CBDC implementation, such as cybersecurity and digital literacy, proposing strategic frameworks for successful adoption. The findings underscore CBDC's capacity to enhance policy efficacy, transparency, and the efficiency of public fund disbursement, offering critical insights for policymakers and future research in the digital finance era.

Chapter 3
Global Financial Crises: Lessons From Policy Failures and Successes 65
Ameya Anil Patil, Dr. Vishwanath Karad MIT World Peace University, India
Mahesh Kumar, Dr. Vishwanath Karad MIT World Peace University, India
Rajeev Sengupta, Dr. Vishwanath Karad MIT World Peace University, India
Rakesh Yadav, Prin. L.N.Welingkar Institute of Management Development and Research, India
Piyush Dixit, Indira University, India

Financial crisis have always fascinated and concerned acadmicians, finance enthusiasts and policymakers alike. and This article explores the major global financial crises, including the Great Depression, the Latin American Debt Crisis, the Asian Financial Crisis, the Global Financial Crisis and the recent COVID-19 economic shock. The causes, policy responses, and outcomes of these crises, have been discussed to provide policy lessons in the context of financial crisis. T Key policy failures such as rigid monetary policies, austerity, and regulatory gaps exacerbated these economic crisis and the corresponding social damage, while .On the other hand, timely measures such as countercyclical stimulus, financial reforms, and global cooperation have facilitated recoveries during these times. This article synthesizes these insights into actionable principles for future crisis management, emphasizing swift liquidity provision, robust regulation, inclusive policies, and multilateral coordination.

Section 2
Policy, Regulation, and Stability

Chapter 4
Regulatory Frameworks and Their Impact on International Banking 93
Safas V. P., Department of Commerce, School of Social Sciences and Languages, Vellore Institute of Technology, Vellore, India
Mohsin Khan, Department of Commerce, School of Social Sciences and Languages, Vellore Institute of Technology, Vellore, India

Technological enhancements have led to a new world where borders are no longer a criterion for financial transactions, as the number of cross-border financial transactions has increased, the need for regulatory compliance is the need of the hour. This chapter explores such regulatory frameworks on international banking, particularly focusing on major initiatives and the Basel Accords (Basel I, II, and III). It explains the objectives of major international banking regulations by conducting historical analysis and case studies. It also discusses the challenges faced during the implementation, such as the regulatory complexity of having different types of regulations in different nations, and the compliance burden in the increasingly interconnected world. This chapter also looks into the contemporary issues, such as the need for adaptive regulations for technologically changing financial areas like Fintech and digital currency. The chapter concludes by examining the ongoing policy debates and suggesting considerable solutions to overcome the existing hindrances.

Chapter 5
Sustainable Finance and Banking Policy Approaches for Stability 125
Rishikaysh Marotrao Kaakandikar, SaiBalaji International Institute of Management Sciences, India
Swati S. Bhalerao, Indira College of Pharmacy, India

In the face of escalating climate risks, environmental degradation, and socio-economic inequalities, sustainable finance and banking have emerged as critical levers to drive stability and resilience in the global financial system. This chapter explores the evolving landscape of sustainable finance, focusing on how regulatory and policy frameworks are shaping banking practices to align with environmental, social, and governance (ESG) goals. It critically examines various policy approaches ranging from green taxonomy development, disclosure regulations, and central bank interventions to prudential measures and fiscal incentives. Through comparative analysis of global initiatives and national strategies, the study highlights how a cohesive policy environment can enhance risk management, promote long-term investment, and ensure systemic financial stability. The chapter concludes by offering recommendations for policymakers and financial institutions to foster a more sustainable and inclusive financial future.

Chapter 6
Managing Financial Distress: The Global Impact of Monetary and Fiscal Policies on Non-Performing Assets 165
Faiz ur Rehman, Aligarh Muslim University, India
Nawab Ali Khan, Aligarh Muslim University, India
Shakeb Akhtar, University of Technology and Applied Science, Ibra, Oman & INTI International University, Nilai, Malaysia
Bilal Asghar, Al Fayha College, Al Jubail, Saudi Arabia

This chapter explores the global impact of monetary and fiscal policies on the management of Non-Performing Assets (NPAs), emphasizing their role in financial distress and economic instability. It examines the influence of key macroeconomic variables such as Annual GDP growth rate, inflation rate, unemployment rate, Real interest rate, and exchange rates on the rise and resolution of NPAs across different economies. The chapter highlights how elevated NPAs weaken banking systems by constraining credit flow, reducing profitability, and undermining investor confidence. It also discusses policy responses, including debt restructuring, bank recapitalization, and the establishment of asset reconstruction mechanisms like bad banks. Drawing on international literature and empirical insights, the study underscores the need for robust regulatory frameworks, effective risk management, and globally coordinated policy measures to maintain financial stability and support sustainable economic recovery in both advanced and emerging markets.

Section 3
Emerging Trends in Digital and Monetary Innovations

Chapter 7
U.S. Strategy to Dominate the Dollar With Stablecoins: Geopolitical and Economic Implications 195
Silvio Andrae, Independent Researcher, Germany

This chapter thoroughly examines the United States' strategy of intentionally utilizing stablecoins to bolster and extend the dollar's hegemony in the digital era. The objective is to systematically scrutinize the economic logic, political narratives, and geopolitical implications of this strategy. Methodologically, the article integrates political economy, hegemonic currency theories, and empirical analyses of the issuance, use, and regulation of stablecoins, supplemented by case studies in emerging markets. The results demonstrate that stablecoins amplify the demand for U.S. government bonds, streamline international payment flows, and firmly establish the dollar on a global scale through digital platforms. However, this strategic move also introduces new risks. In summary, the analysis reveals that stablecoins are more of a digital extension of dollar hegemony than a replacement, offering opportunities for the US, but also posing significant risks to the stability of the global financial order.

Chapter 8
CBDCs in a High-Evasion Economy: Seigniorage, Tax Collection, and Institutional Tensions 237
Harpreet Kaur, Christ University, India
Surbhi Srivastava, Christ University, India
Shanu Singh, Christ University, India

This chapter investigates the welfare implications of introducing Central Bank Digital Currency (CBDC) in an economy with tax evasion and varying degrees of central bank independence (CBI). The model considers scenarios with and without central bank independence, where the fiscal authority finances its expenditure through sales tax and/or seigniorage revenue from the central bank. The model analyses the equilibrium conditions for the coexistence of cash and CBDC, and it depends on the degree of CBI.

Chapter 9
Artificial Intelligence Applications in Finance: A Proposed Model................. 265
Vedantam Seetha Ram, Jain University, India
Sukirno Sukirno, Universitas Negeri Yogyakarta, Indonesia
Rama Rao Gangadhara Sakha, GITAM University, India

Artificial intelligence is being used across the domains irrespective of its pros and cons highlighted by various stakeholders across the globe. AI is having a decisive role in the finance field in bringing out innovative financial instruments that cater the economic growth. Current chapter is a literature survey driven one, for which research papers covering digital banking, technology applications in banking and finance industry, technology adoption, digital research study reports of governments, monitoring agencies and research organizations are considered. Finally, 43 variables are identified from dimensions as part of factors, like personal, psychological, technical, and policy maker's guidelines that have influence on the adoption of AI technology in finance field such that a model is proposed which helps prospective researchers as a tool. This chapter considers the pros and cons of AI technology in finance field so that a corrective mechanism can be established in enhancing the quality of financial instruments to mitigate risk, such that a sustainable financial growth prevails.

Chapter 10
Combatting Bank Robbery and E-Banking Theft in North Central Nigeria With Advanced Artificial Intelligence (AI) Technology 297
Basil Osayin Daudu, Kogi State Univerisity, Nigeria

Banks are widely trusted as secure places for storing money and valuables, and provide essential services for physical and online transactions. However, despite their successes, the banking sector remains vulnerable to significant robbery and internet fraud losses. In North Central Nigeria, bank robberies occur seasonally despite security measures, while e-banking theft by internet fraudsters happens daily. Thus, this chapter is guided by the following objectives: (i) To investigate the techniques used by bank robbers and internet fraudsters in North Central Nigeria, (ii) To examine the impact of banking robbery and e-banking theft on the Nigerian economy, and (iii) To suggest artificial intelligence technology as a viable means of addressing bank robbery and e-banking theft in North Central Nigeria. With qualitative analysis, the chapter examines bank robbery and e-banking theft as unlawful and dishonest means of livelihood, and endorses advanced artificial intelligence (including robotics and others, for instance) as a potential solution to these problems in Nigeria.

Section 4
Financial Markets and Risks

Chapter 11
Navigating Uncertainty: Global Stock Exchanges in the Age of Policy and Geopolitical Risk 325
Abhishek Sinha, Mahindra University, India
Vikas Maheshwari, Independent Researcher, UAE

The post-COVID era has brought extreme market volatility, fueled by policy divergence, retail trading frenzies, and disruptive technologies. Inflation in developed markets contrasts with China's deflation, while meme stocks, crypto, and algo trading amplify swings—even destabilizing traditionally safe Treasuries. Dark pools, zero-day options, and excessive leverage distort pricing, while geopolitical tensions trigger capital flight. Emerging markets face heightened risks due to weak oversight, but even advanced economies aren't immune. Solutions require coordinated regulation, transparency tools like blockchain, and stress-tested safeguards to prevent systemic crises in an increasingly fragmented financial landscape..

Chapter 12
Analysing the Relationship Between Credit Default Swaps and the Financial Sector in G20 Countries: Evidence From Asymmetric Causality Test 355
Niyaz Hasanov, Yelo Bank, Azerbaijan
Mehmet Levent Erdas, Akdeniz University, Turkey

Credit default swaps (CDS) have an important role in monitoring a country's credit risk. It is essentially accepted as a market-based benchmark for the country's credit risk. CDS spreads are mostly preferred by policy makers as an indicator in economic and financial markets. The purpose of this research is to determine whether there is a relationship between CDS spreads and the financial sector stock market in G20 countries. To this end, the research employs the asymmetric approach to evaluate daily data from 2019 to 2024 using Hatemi-J (2012) test. The findings mostly indicate that there are asymmetric relationships between CDS spreads and financial sector equity markets in G20 countries. Particularly, the findings mostly provide evidence that a positive shock in CDS spreads leads to a negative impact on financial sector stocks markets in developed countries. By helping to understand the relationship between credit risk and equity markets, these findings provide policymakers with important insights for managing financial risks and developing economic strategies.

Chapter 13
Climate Risk Assessment and Financial Modelling for Sustainable Enterprises 379
Ekta Saraswat, IILM University, Greater Noida, India

Climate change has emerged as one of the most pressing challenges of the 21st century, with significant economic, social, and environmental consequences. Financial modelling plays a crucial role in quantifying and mitigating these risks, enabling enterprises to make data-driven decisions that align with sustainability objectives. The rise of environmental, social, and governance (ESG) frameworks has further emphasized the need for sustainable financial planning, making it essential for businesses to adopt innovative tools and methodologies to assess climate-related risks. This chapter aims to explore the intersection of climate risk assessment and financial modelling, focusing on methodologies, tools, and strategies that support sustainable enterprises. By leveraging advancements in data analytics, artificial intelligence, and regulatory frameworks, organizations can integrate climate considerations into financial decision-making, ensuring resilience and long-term value creation.

Section 5
Inclusive Finance and Innovations

Chapter 14
Mapping the Landscape: A Bibliometric Analysis of FinTech Innovations in the Banking Industry 411
Mohammad Ammar Ahsan, Aligarh Muslim University, India
Mohd Salim, Woxsen University, India
Parvez Alam Khan, University Technology Petronas, Malaysia
Shakeb Akhtar, University of Technology and Applied Science, Ibra, Oman & INTI International University, Nilai, Malaysia

In the wake of the 2008 financial crisis, Financial Technology (FinTech) innovations emerged as transformative forces in the banking industry. This bibliometric analysis investigates the integration of FinTech in banking by examining growth in Scopus-indexed publications post-crisis, identifying top contributing journals, authors, countries, and institutions, and exploring emerging research themes. The chapter aims to build a theoretical structure of FinTech adoption in banking and assess how it evolved in response to post-crisis challenges and opportunities. Using scientific mapping and performance analysis through Biblioshiny, this research analyses highly cited documents sourced from Scopus. It provides key publication metrics, visualizes research development, identifies trending topics, and proposes a structured research agenda.

Chapter 15
Implications of Financial Literacy on Pawnshop Usage 441
José G. Vargas-Hernandez, Financial Literacy Research Center, Universidad Cristóbal Colón, Mexico & Tecnológico Nacional de México, ITS Fresnillo, Mexico
Csongor Czipf, Gyula Kautz Faculty of Economics, Széchenyi István University, Győr, Hungary
Absalón J. Salmerón-Zapata, Financial Literacy Research Center, Universidad Cristòbal Colòn, Mexico
Selene Castañeda-Burciaga, Universidad Politécnica de Zacatecas, Mexico
Omar A. Guirette-Barbosa, Universidad Politécnica de Zacatecas, Mexico

This chapter aims to analyze financial literacy implications on pawnshop usage. The analysis departs from the assumption that individuals and micro-organizations lacking financial literacy and lower opportunities to have access to short-term credit provided by formal financing and banking institutions, are more likely to use pawnshops to get easily and fastest financial resources urgently needed for survival, living expenses and other required matters. The method used is the semi-structured interviews to borrowers followed by meta-analysis and meta-cognitive approaches based on conceptual, theoretical and empirical literature review. The chapter concludes that the financial literacy of undeserved individuals and micro-organizations, tend to reduce their access to formal financial and banking institutions to get credit, driving them to use pawnshops.

Compilation of References 465

About the Contributors 521

Index 533

Preface

The global financial system has undergone remarkable transformations over the past few decades, shaped by technological progress, regulatory reforms, economic crises, and the growing need for sustainable development. In today's interconnected world, financial economics and international banking are not simply technical subjects reserved for academics or financial professionals they are central pillars that determine global economic stability, political power balances, and the everyday lives of individuals and businesses.

The book *Policy Implications on International Financial Economics and Banking* emerges against this backdrop of uncertainty, innovation, and reform. The international financial landscape faces profound challenges, including fluctuating monetary and fiscal policies, the rise of digital currencies, climate-induced risks, technological disruptions, and increasing geopolitical volatility. These developments pose both opportunities and threats, making it crucial to analyze the role of policy in shaping financial outcomes.

This edited volume brings together diverse perspectives from scholars and practitioners worldwide to explore the multifaceted implications of financial and banking policies in this dynamic environment. The chapters investigate issues ranging from regulatory frameworks, sustainability approaches, and monetary-fiscal coordination to the disruptive impact of fintech, artificial intelligence, and digital assets. By doing so, the book aims to bridge theory with practice and policy with implementation, offering a comprehensive understanding for policymakers, academics, and financial sector stakeholders.

RATIONALE AND CONTRIBUTION OF THE BOOK

This book is premised on the belief that policy decisions in finance and banking extend far beyond national borders. In a globalized economy, the ripple effects of policy changes in one country can reshape capital flows, exchange rates, and banking systems elsewhere. The U.S. Federal Reserve's interest rate adjustments, the European Central Bank's regulatory measures, or China's experiments with Central Bank Digital Currencies (CBDCs) all reverberate through emerging markets, influencing debt sustainability, investment inflows, and financial inclusion.

The book contributes to the growing body of literature by focusing on policy implications rather than purely descriptive accounts of financial systems. While much research has analyzed financial products, markets, and crises, fewer works systematically connect them to their broader regulatory and political context. By doing so, this volume offers a holistic view of international financial economics and banking, making it relevant for multiple audiences.

STRUCTURE OF THE BOOK

The book is organized into five interconnected parts, each addressing a specific dimension of international financial economics and banking.

Part I: Foundations of International Financial Economics and Banking

The opening part provides readers with the essential conceptual and historical foundations.

- The Introduction to International Financial Economics and Banking outlines the evolution of global finance and situates current challenges within broader economic theories.
- The chapter on Monetary and Fiscal Policy explores the delicate balance governments and central banks must strike in managing inflation, growth, and debt sustainability.
- Finally, the chapter on Global Financial Crises reflects on past policy successes and failures, offering lessons crucial for today's volatile world.

This part sets the tone, reminding readers that the financial sector is never static but continually reshaped by institutional design and macroeconomic strategy.

Part II: Policy, Regulation, and Stability

This section delves into the regulatory and institutional frameworks that govern financial systems.

- The chapter on Regulatory Frameworks investigates how global banking regulations from Basel Accords to local supervisory mechanisms affect financial stability and capital adequacy.
- Sustainable Finance and Banking Policy Approaches highlights the intersection between environmental goals and financial regulation, emphasizing the critical role of green finance and ESG integration.
- The final chapter examines Managing Financial Distress, particularly through the lens of non-performing assets (NPAs), and evaluates how policy responses to distress can determine long-term resilience.

Together, these chapters illustrate how effective policy and regulatory frameworks form the backbone of a stable global banking system.

Part III: Emerging Trends in Digital and Monetary Innovations

This part focuses on disruptive technologies and monetary innovations that are rapidly redefining the financial ecosystem.

- U.S. Strategy to Dominate the Dollar with Stablecoins provides a geopolitical perspective on the intersection of digital currencies and power politics.
- CBDCs in High-Evasion Economies sheds light on the opportunities and challenges of central bank-issued digital currencies, particularly in fragile economies with weak tax systems.
- Artificial Intelligence Applications in Finance offers a model-driven approach to applying AI for decision-making and risk management.
- Finally, the chapter on Combatting Bank Robbery and E-Banking Theft in Nigeria shows how AI can address security risks in vulnerable banking systems.

This part demonstrates that innovations are not merely technological shifts; they carry deep policy and regulatory implications that can redefine financial sovereignty, trust, and stability.

Part IV: Financial Markets and Risks

Global markets are inherently shaped by uncertainty, volatility, and policy direction.

- The chapter on Global Stock Exchanges examines how geopolitical tensions and policy uncertainties ripple across capital markets.

- Credit Default Swaps in G20 Countries explores asymmetric causality relationships, offering valuable insights into systemic risk management.
- Climate Risk Assessment and Financial Modelling brings sustainability into the financial risk discussion, showing how enterprises must adapt their financial models to incorporate climate-related uncertainties.

This part is particularly relevant for investors, regulators, and financial institutions navigating risk management in today's interconnected markets.

Part V: Inclusive Finance and Innovations

The final part emphasizes inclusivity and innovation in the global financial landscape.

- Bibliometric Analysis of FinTech Innovations maps the evolving research trends in fintech, helping scholars and practitioners understand the intellectual terrain.
- Implications of Financial Literacy on Pawnshop Usage highlights the role of literacy and access in determining financial behavior, especially among vulnerable populations.

By concluding with inclusivity, this part underscores that financial policy is not just about stability and innovation but also about accessibility and equity.

SCHOLARLY AND PRACTICAL RELEVANCE

The issues explored in this volume are timely and far-reaching. Policymakers grappling with inflationary pressures, regulators overseeing complex financial institutions, bankers designing sustainable finance models, and researchers analyzing fintech trends will all find valuable insights in these chapters. Moreover, the interdisciplinary nature of this book bridging economics, finance, technology, and sustainability ensures its relevance to multiple disciplines. It can serve as a reference for university courses in international finance, banking policy, and financial economics, as well as a guide for practitioners in the financial industry.

Acknowledgment

The completion of an edited volume is never the effort of a single individual. It is a collective endeavor that requires the intellectual curiosity of contributors, the support of academic institutions, the guidance of mentors, the encouragement of colleagues, the patience of families, and the facilitation of publishers. With immense gratitude and humility, we extend our deepest appreciation to all those whose contributions, both direct and indirect, have made this book Policy Implications on International Financial Economics and Banking a reality.

GRATITUDE TO CONTRIBUTING AUTHORS

First and foremost, we wish to acknowledge the chapter contributors, who form the intellectual heart of this volume. Their rigorous scholarship, empirical insights, and theoretical reflections have enriched the book in ways that a single perspective never could. The breadth of topics from monetary and fiscal policy, regulatory frameworks, and sustainable finance to digital innovations such as CBDCs, AI in banking, and fintech-driven inclusivity speaks to the diversity and depth of expertise represented in this volume.

Each author invested significant time and energy into their chapters, responding to editorial feedback, engaging with peer reviewers, and ensuring that their research aligned with the broader objectives of the book. Their commitment to academic excellence and their willingness to contribute to a collective vision exemplify the spirit of scholarly collaboration. This book is as much theirs as it is mine, and I am deeply grateful for their trust and dedication.

APPRECIATION TO REVIEWERS AND PEER SCHOLARS

Equally important are the reviewers and academic peers who provided thoughtful and constructive feedback. Their critical insights challenged contributors to refine their arguments, strengthen their evidence, and situate their chapters within the larger discourse of international financial economics. Without their intellectual generosity and commitment to academic rigor, the book would not have achieved the same level of clarity, coherence, and impact.

To the anonymous peer reviewers who devoted their time to reading and evaluating the chapters, we extend our sincere gratitude. Their role is often invisible, yet it is foundational to the credibility of academic publishing.

INSTITUTIONAL AND ACADEMIC SUPPORT

This project would not have been possible without the encouragement and resources provided by academic institutions and research organizations. Universities, research centers, and business schools across different countries fostered an environment where knowledge exchange and interdisciplinary collaboration could thrive.

Special acknowledgment is due to the institutions of the contributing authors, which supported their research endeavors and encouraged them to share their findings in this edited volume. Such institutional backing is invaluable for advancing scholarship in financial economics and banking, and it demonstrates the continuing relevance of academic research in addressing real-world challenges.

SUPPORT FROM IGI GLOBAL

A book of this magnitude requires not only intellectual contributions but also the infrastructure of publishing. We are profoundly grateful to IGI Global for their unwavering support throughout the publication process. Their team provided guidance on structure, formatting, and deadlines, ensuring that the manuscript progressed smoothly from draft to final publication.

The professionalism, patience, and responsiveness of the publishing staff were instrumental in transforming a collection of chapters into a coherent volume. Their commitment to disseminating cutting-edge research across disciplines resonates with the objectives of this book.

MENTORS, COLLEAGUES, AND COLLABORATORS

We owe a special debt of gratitude to our mentors and senior colleagues, who have shaped my intellectual journey and instilled in me the curiosity to explore complex questions in international finance and banking. Their mentorship has been a constant source of inspiration, reminding us that academic inquiry must always be guided by both rigor and relevance.

To our colleagues and collaborators both within my institution and across the academic community, we extend heartfelt thanks for their encouragement and dialogue. Informal conversations, conference discussions, and collaborative projects often served as the seeds of ideas that found their way into this book. The academic community thrives on exchange, and this book is a product of that vibrant ecosystem.

GRATITUDE TO POLICYMAKERS AND PRACTITIONERS

While this is an academic volume, it is deeply informed by the work of policymakers, regulators, and practitioners. Their efforts in managing crises, designing monetary and fiscal strategies, experimenting with digital currencies, and integrating sustainability into finance provided much of the real-world context that shaped the chapters.

Although many of these individuals are not direct contributors, their work forms the backdrop against which this book was conceived. To the policymakers who grapple with uncertainty, the regulators who safeguard stability, and the practitioners who innovate daily within the constraints of financial systems this book is also dedicated to you.

FAMILY AND PERSONAL ACKNOWLEDGMENT

No academic endeavor is ever truly possible without the support of one's family and loved ones. Their patience, encouragement, and understanding provided the foundation upon which this project was built. Long hours of reading, writing, and correspondence often come at the expense of family time, and we are deeply grateful to our family for their unwavering support and belief in the value of this work.

Their encouragement reminded me that scholarship is not an isolated pursuit but part of a broader journey of personal and professional growth. To them, we dedicate this acknowledgment with love and gratitude.

THE BROADER SCHOLARLY COMMUNITY

Finally, we wish to acknowledge the broader scholarly community in international financial economics, banking, and policy studies. The debates, conferences, journal articles, and informal networks of scholars across the world provided the intellectual environment within which this book took shape. The book builds upon, dialogues with, and extends the work of countless scholars who have advanced our understanding of financial systems, crises, and innovations.

REFLECTION ON THE JOURNEY

The journey of editing this book has been one of learning, collaboration, and reflection. It reinforced our belief that financial economics and banking cannot be understood solely through numbers or equations but must be contextualized within policy choices, institutional structures, and societal needs. This acknowledgment, therefore, extends not only to the individuals directly involved in the book but also to the countless others whose ideas, work, and inspiration indirectly shaped its direction.

In bringing together scholars from diverse backgrounds, this volume aspires to contribute to both academic discourse and policy debates. While we have served as the editor, the real strength of the book lies in the collective contributions of authors, reviewers, institutions, and the publishing team. To all who have walked this journey with us whether through direct contribution, constructive critique, or quiet support, we extend our deepest gratitude. It is our hope that this book not only informs but also inspires continued dialogue on how financial systems can be governed, innovated, and sustained in ways that promote stability, inclusivity, and prosperity.

Introduction

The twenty-first century has witnessed financial and banking systems undergoing profound transformation, fueled by technological innovations, geopolitical realignments, sustainability imperatives, and regulatory reforms. The world of international finance is no longer confined to monetary policy frameworks or central banking operations alone; it has become an interconnected domain where digital assets, artificial intelligence, environmental risks, and financial inclusion occupy centre stage. Against this backdrop, the edited volume Policy Implications on International Financial Economics and Banking arrives at a critical juncture, offering deep scholarly reflections and policy-oriented insights that are urgently needed.

At its core, this book recognizes that financial systems cannot be studied or regulated in isolation. The ripple effects of financial crises, the volatility of global capital markets, the disruptive rise of central bank digital currencies, and the role of monetary-fiscal coordination transcend national boundaries. A decision taken by the United States Federal Reserve, the European Central Bank, or the People's Bank of China inevitably influences emerging markets in Asia, Africa, and Latin America. Similarly, innovations in fintech and artificial intelligence, often pioneered in one region, rapidly diffuse across borders, reshaping banking services, financial inclusion models, and regulatory frameworks worldwide.

THE RELEVANCE OF POLICY IN GLOBAL FINANCE

Policy both fiscal and monetary remains at the heart of international financial economics. From stabilizing inflation to managing sovereign debt and ensuring banking resilience, policy decisions dictate the trajectory of global finance. However, policies are not merely economic tools; they are political instruments, shaped by domestic priorities and international power dynamics. The COVID-19 pandemic revealed how divergent policy responses could deepen inequalities, while the global financial crisis of 2008 highlighted the importance of timely interventions and coordinated regulation.

This book makes a significant contribution by examining not only the mechanics of financial economics but also their policy implications. By analyzing case studies, empirical evidence, and theoretical insights, the chapters collectively provide a roadmap for understanding how policies interact with markets, institutions, and societies.

STRUCTURE AND FLOW OF THE VOLUME

The book is carefully structured into five parts, each dealing with a crucial dimension of international financial economics and banking:

- Foundations: Here, the readers are introduced to the theoretical underpinnings of global finance and banking. The historical context, coupled with lessons from global crises, provides a robust grounding for subsequent discussions.
- Policy and Regulation: With the Basel framework, sustainable banking, and financial distress management at its center, this section examines the critical role of regulation in maintaining systemic stability.
- Digital and Monetary Innovations: Stablecoins, CBDCs, and artificial intelligence redefine the currency of trust in the twenty-first century. This part explores the technological forces reshaping the global financial order.
- Financial Markets and Risks: From stock exchanges influenced by geopolitical uncertainty to climate risk modeling and credit default swaps in G20 economies, this section bridges market realities with risk management strategies.
- Inclusivity and Innovation: The concluding part turns toward inclusivity, emphasizing financial literacy, fintech adoption, and the importance of equitable access to financial services.

This organization ensures a coherent progression from theory to practice, from regulation to innovation, and from systemic stability to inclusivity. It also reflects the multidisciplinary nature of the subject, where economics, finance, technology, sustainability, and politics converge.

GLOBAL CHALLENGES ADDRESSED

The volume is particularly timely because it addresses several pressing challenges:

- Digital Currency and Monetary Sovereignty

The emergence of stablecoins and CBDCs has reignited debates about sovereignty in monetary policy. For the United States, leveraging stablecoins may reinforce the dollar's global dominance, while for smaller economies, CBDCs present both opportunities for financial inclusion and risks of institutional strain.

- Artificial Intelligence and Financial Security

AI applications promise efficiency, predictive accuracy, and enhanced decision-making. Yet, as highlighted in this volume, AI also raises ethical, regulatory, and security questions ranging from cybercrime to algorithmic bias.

- Sustainability and Climate Risks

Climate change is no longer a peripheral concern but a central determinant of financial stability. Integrating climate risks into financial models is essential for enterprises and regulators seeking to ensure long-term resilience.

- Financial Crises and Policy Lessons

Historical crises from the Great Depression to the 2008 meltdown offer critical lessons. This book revisits these episodes to remind us that financial systems are inherently cyclical and vulnerable, and that proactive policy design remains the best safeguard.

- Financial Inclusion and Literacy

True progress in international finance must be measured not only by GDP growth or capital flows but by inclusivity. The chapters on fintech innovation and pawnshop usage remind readers that financial literacy and access are as important as macroeconomic stability.

BRIDGING ACADEMIA, POLICY, AND PRACTICE

One of the strengths of this book lies in its ability to bridge different worlds:

- For academics, it provides rigorous theoretical insights and bibliometric analysis that contribute to scholarship.
- For policymakers, it offers evidence-based discussions on regulation, crises, and monetary innovation.

- For financial practitioners, it delivers practical frameworks on risk management, sustainability, and technological adoption.

Such a cross-cutting approach is rare, and it underscores the book's importance as a reference text for multiple audiences.

LOOKING FORWARD: THE FUTURE OF GLOBAL FINANCE AND BANKING

As we look to the future, several trends will define international financial economics and banking:

- Decentralization vs. Centralization: Blockchain technologies challenge the authority of central banks, even as states experiment with CBDCs. The tension between decentralized finance (DeFi) and centralized regulation will persist.
- Geopolitical Financial Competition: The weaponization of finance—through sanctions, reserve currency strategies, and cross-border regulatory competition—will shape the global balance of power.
- Technological Convergence: AI, machine learning, and quantum computing will not only disrupt banking but may also redefine financial forecasting, fraud detection, and customer engagement.
- Sustainable Transformation: Green finance, ESG investment, and carbon markets will transition from niche interests to mainstream imperatives.
- Inclusivity as a Policy Priority: Bridging the digital divide, improving financial literacy, and ensuring access to affordable credit will remain essential to global development.

This volume is not just a reflection of where we stand today but also a guide for navigating these emerging complexities.

CONCLUSION

In endorsing this volume, I emphasize its role as a critical reference point in the evolving discourse on international financial economics and banking. It does not simply analyze the past or describe the present; it charts a course for the future. By focusing on policy implications, it compels readers to recognize that financial systems are ultimately shaped by choices made by governments, regulators, institutions, and individuals.

For academics, it enriches the literature; for policymakers, it provides actionable insights; for practitioners, it offers practical relevance. Above all, it serves as a reminder that finance and banking, though technical in form, are profoundly human in impact affecting livelihoods, shaping societies, and determining the trajectory of global development.

We invite readers to engage with the chapters that follow not merely as abstract discussions but as vital contributions to one of the most consequential debates of our time.

Section 1

Foundations of International Financial Economics and Banking

Chapter 1
Introduction to International Financial Economics and Banking

K. Balaji
https://orcid.org/0000-0002-3065-3294
Christ University, Bengaluru, India

Mahfooz Alam
https://orcid.org/0000-0002-9311-5688
University of the People, USA

ABSTRACT

The global financial economics and banking is emerging to be a very important element in an economical setting that becomes increasingly global. The primary objective is to deliberate how the capital flows, foreign exchange markets, interest rate parity and banking regulations have affected financial stability across nations and the economic growth. Background and theoretical structures that define the field of international finance and international banking that interconnect is outlined in the chapter. The chapter sheds some light on the dynamic entanglements between global financial institutions multinationals, central banks, and the overall global capital finance markets, cross-border risk evaluation set ups, and international liquidity indicators for macro-financial connections. The given work can contribute to the main part of the scholarly work by providing a complete image that combines the classical theory with the modern developments, hence, can be of use to scholars, policy makers, and financial professionals dealing with global financial markets.

DOI: 10.4018/979-8-3373-3725-8.ch001

1. INTRODUCTION

International Banking and Finance involves investment, transfer of financial services and transactions across countries. It is engaging foreign exchange markets, international lending, trade financing and global regulatory system. It is an important area of maintaining international trade, investment and economic stability. Its geography is yet to undergo transformations with the transformations of the level of technology, and the ever-evolving financial tools.

1.1. The History of International Banking and Finance

The history of international finance dates back in 19th century when the gold standard was introduced which gave international transaction and exchange rates a solid base. The interwar process was broken by economic depression with its associated protectionism which disrupted the movement of funds and made stark testament to the need of an international coordinated surveillance. The period between the World War and 1944 Bretton Woods conference that came into the creation of the International Monetary Fund (IMF) and the World Bank. These institutions enabled foreign monetary collaboration and reconstruction plan to occur since they controlled the exchange rates against the Bretton Wood system in order to permit stability to ensue until 1971 when collapse occurred (Adekunle, W., & Ndukwe, I, 2018).

The 1980s and the 1970s were the demarcation point because the capital accounts were liberalised as well as bank systems were deregulated and floating exchange rates were born. International banking services were becoming a need to the multinational corporations that assist the activities of its international operation (Agosin, M. R., & Huaita, F, 2011). The emergent offshore financial centres (e.g. London, Singapore and the Cayman Islands) possessed extremely liquid markets and were beyond the reach of old regulation.

1.1.1 Growth of Global Banking and Financial Integration

With the globalization gaining momentum in the 1990s, international financial markets were getting highly integrated with increasing intra-financial consequences. This was because communication technology was improved, trade and freedom of movement of capital were relaxed. A further integration occurred in 1995 in the formation of world trade organization (WTO), regional economic blocks such as EU (European Union) among others (Badarinza, C., & Ramadorai, T, 2018). This is when cross border lending, international bonds issues and derivatives markets were fast developing and global systemically important banks (G-SIBs) came up. The electronic payments systems and digital financial services got popularized and the cost of the transactions be reduced tremendously and efficiency be improved (Alami et al., 2023).

Success of the integration did not come at a free cost though. These were the 1997 Asian Financial Crisis and the 2008 Global financial Crisis (GFC) that exposed the system to weakness when subjected to heavy leverage, regulation arbitrage and turbulence of capital flows. GFC, in its turn, was a cure concerning the dangers of interconnected financial institutions which are operating under ineffective regulation and one of the consequences has to be the slowdown of the global economies (Alami, I, 2018). This is what multilateral efforts have been able to come up with to counter it and it is Basel III norms on capital adequacy, stress testing and liquidity requirements. The regulators and the central banks all over the world began to work well together in trying to monitor the concept of systemic risk and financial contagion.

1.1.2. Growth of Global banking and Fintech

The World Economic Outlook (WEO) April 2025 offers revised real GDP ratio figures of global and regional growth enabling an understanding of the updated dynamics of the economies in various regions of the globe. The projections provide important information on the rate at which economic activity can recover and change as resolutions of the repercussions of shocks that countries have experienced previously and policy changes and structural difficulties still prevail (Balaji, K., 2024). Although it is expected that the world (3.2 percent) will be growing only at a moderate pace (2.8 percent) in 2025 and with a marginal increase (3.0 percent) in 2026, regional distributional gaps are huge.

There is a relatively low growth trend in the advanced economies such as the United States and the Euro Area but emerging and developing Asia remains the growth engine of the world with some slight slowdown due to Asian driven economies such as India and China. The Middle East and Central Asia and sub-Saharan Africa record gradual improvements that indicate resistance to out-of-bound conditions, along with reforms that are still underway (Azubuike et al., 2023). These forecasts emphasize the need of policy interventions in certain areas, fiscal prudence and innovation and international collaborations in promoting inclusive and sustainable growth across regions (Figure 1).

Figure 1. Growth of Global banking and Fintech.

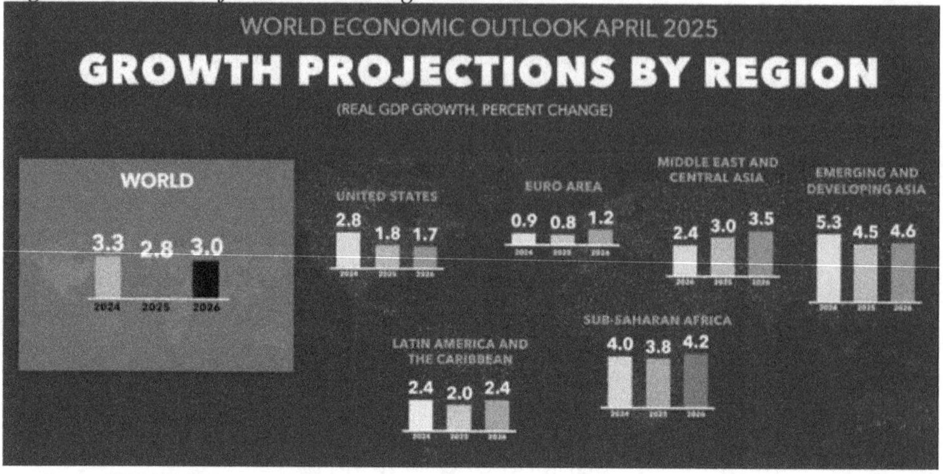

Source: IMF World Economic Outlook 2025.Complied by: Author.

Such regional differences and economic trends overviewed in the figure 1 by world economic outlook April 2025 inform on significant regional differences in the prospects of growth and economic trends defining the global picture. Though the GDP of the world may slightly increase its growth rate in 2026 as compared to 2025, namely 2.8 to 3.0 percent, the rate is still low as compared to the year 2024, which signifies the persistence of certain difficulties, including inflation management, geopolitical conflict (Balaji, K., 2024). The United States depicts a prominent slowdown slowing down over time as it slows down briefly to a mere 1.7 percent in 2026 in 2024 and slowly decreasing in 2026 implying a slowdown in economy maybe in terms of stringent monetary climate, as well as a decrease in consumption (Balaji, 2024). Equally, slow growth remains a concern in the Euro Area as growth is projected to remain below 2% until 2026 due to structural rigidities and consistent efforts to manage fiscal constraints.

On the contrary, Emerging and Developing Asia remains at the forefront of growing across the world with the anticipation of 4.5 percent and 4.6 percent by the year 2025 and 2026 respectively, a fact underscores the high rates of investment flows within Asia. The same can be said about Middle East and Central Asia, and Sub-Saharan Africa who are also experiencing a positive dynamic, and it is projected to reach 3,5 percent and 4,2 percent in 2026, respectively, due to commodity exports, diversification policies, and post-pandemic restorative measures (Bonizzi, B., & Kaltenbrunner, A., 2019). In the meantime, the situation in Latin America and the Caribbean is rather contradictory, as an upswing in the region declined in 2025, and then recovery occurred, which is a sign of a susceptibility to external shocks and fiscal austerity. On the whole, the data highlights the optimistic prospect temporally, as advanced economies struggle to maintain pace, whereas emerging economies were in the forefront on the global stage.

1.2. Theoretical Background

This section provides information about various models and foundations for international banking and finance. The detailed discussion is as follows.

1.2.1. Current Relevance in the Post Pandemic and Digital Age

The international flow of the capital became uncontrollable and liquidity crunch was happening in some regions in need of foreign exchange swap line between bank policies (Balaji, 2025). These events and incidences confirmed again the overriding importance of international financial and bank strength. On a parallel line, the Technologies that changed the provision of services and risk management in the realm of international finance include blockchain and artificial intelligence (AI), and mobile banking. The failure of the Chinese tech giant to actually launch the digital version of Yuan, the attempts of the European Central Bank and the Federal Reserve in the U.S. to do the same have added fuel to this fire (Carpenter, S. B., & Demiralp, S., 2010).

1.2.2. Fundamentals of International Financial Economics

International Financial Economics builds on an assumption of a set of principles and tools of analysis that establish the interactions between economies in terms of flows of trade and investment and means of finance between economies. This section gives the background data which are important in the understanding of cross border economic activities as well as financial relations. These include the state of balance of payments, arrangements of exchange rates, the free movement of capital and the basic theoretical models; such as; interest rate parity (IRP) and the purchasing power parity (PPP). It is the synthesis of the frameworks that forms the foundation of the study of the international monetary relations, the assessment of the macro-economic stability and the policy advice of globalized world (Balaji, 2025).

1.2.2.1. Balances of Payments (BoP)

Balance of Payments (BoP) is a documented list of all the transactions conducted in the economy of one country with the rest of the others at a particular time. It is composed of the current account, capital account and financial account. The current account is an indicator of exchange of services and goods plus earnings that are produced outside the nation and bilateral transfers such as payment of remittances.

The capital and financial account have reports of cross border investments and flow of portfolios and reserves. When the balance of payments is in surplus then the net capital inflow prevails and a balance of payments deficit signifies net capital outflow or reliance on external borrowings (Ergüven, E., 2020). The policymakers on the other hand are very keen on the balance of payments statistics in order to come up with information like economic competitive information, currency stability and viability of external debt.

1.2.2.2. Currency Immune Swaps and Exchange Rates

Central importance in international financial economics is attributed to the price of the currency of one country expressed in terms of the currency of another, the so-called exchange rates. They impact on export competitiveness, prices of imports, inflation and inflows of investments. They are floating system, fixed system, pegged system or managed floats. The exchange rate regime is one adopted by the countries in order to carry out currency exchange. In this system of floating regime, the exchange rate is determined by the market aspect of supply and demand as in the case of the economies including the United States and the Eurozone (Jacob, J. M., & Rosemary, E. A., 2019) pegged regimes or fixed; the government interferes with a view of stabilizing the rate as it was the case in Saudi Arabia peripheral to the U.S. Dollar. Fluctuation of the currency rate can also create uncertainties among the traders and other investors and the measure to protect the uncertainty might be to use the instruments of hedging such as forward contract and options.

1.2.2.3. Global Financial Integration and Capital Mobility

Definition of capital mobility entails the extent to which a financial asset and investment can flow across the borders with ease. Even though capital mobility and mobility enhance efficient allocation and diversification of risk, they can also, on the contrary, increase the volatility of the economy. The mammoth movement of capital may result in the formation of the asset bubbles and the increase of the value or weaken the currency as in the case of the Asian Financial Crisis of 1997 and the Global Financial Crisis of 2008(Kalu et al., 2019). Inspired by the liberalization policies and the growth of technology, the global financial integration has contributed to the height of the capital mobility in most of the economies (Ogunjobi et al., 2022).

1.3. Fundamental Theories

In order to understand the intricacies about international financial interactions, it is important to discuss the theoretical bases which has been is discussed as follows.

1.3.1. *The Interest Rate Parity (IRP) Theory*

Interest rate parity (IRP) is a basic theory, which cuts across the interest rates and the exchange rates of the global finance. It includes two types as discussed as follows.

Covered Interest Rate Parity (CIRP), asserts that interest rate differentials will equalise the forward premiums (or discounts) through arbitrage activity within the forward exchange market. This state of affairs is not available to the investor in the event that CIRP is true and allows him to get risk free returns by shifting funds between countries.

Uncovered Interest Rate Parity (UIRP) asserts that, anticipated future spot rate would act to neutralize the interest rate premiums, but there are possibilities of movements of currencies in such mechanism, as there is no forward cover.

The theoretical model employed in the forecast of the exchange rates and in the derivation of trading strategies of hedging and of analysing returns on investments in the international capital markets is named IRP. According to empirical enquires however, such deviations have in reality turned out to be frequent and it is due to the transaction costs that the capital controls are risk perceptions.

1.3.2. *Purchasing Power Parity (PPP) Theory*

The other major pillars of the global financial economics are the Purchasing power parity (PPP) that lays its focus on the aspect of interaction between prices and exchange rates. There is an assumption in the theory that the goods of same type must be sold at a similar price in any other country of which they use a common currency after stripping all the cost of transport and borders that is involved with trade.

PPP is of two types:

Under absolute PPP, the exchange rate will be at par with price on a standard basket of commodities in a country. Relative PPP means that the exchange rates should be changing at a rate which averages upon itself the difference of the inflation rates of the two countries.

PPP is popular because of making comparisons concerning the living standards and estimation of long-range equilibrating exchange rates. Its instruments have been employed e.g. in a simplified description of currency misalignment within the Big Mac Index published by The Economist. However, in the temporary patterning, the PPP deviations are common and the cause of the deviations is capital market frictions, consumption baskets and speculative flow differences (Oyinbo et al., 2014). But in the long run, PPP may be an acceptable benchmark in the debate of the valuation of currencies and a benchmark to macroeconomic adjustments. The key ideas presented namely, the Balance of Payments, exchange rate dynamics, the capital mobility, and the parity theories are absolutely essential to the nature and the operation of the international financial system.

1.4. Structure and Role of International Banking

The international banking system is a very important part of the global financial infrastructure that is capable of facilitating smooth capital flow, trade financing and monetary stability across nations. It is an organization with a broad mix of banking institutions and systems that are not restricted to the confines of a domestic country, but rather that is meant to fulfil the needs of the multi-faceted international marketplace of trade and investment.

1.4.1. *The Forms of International Banks: Multinational, Offshore and Correspondent Banks*

There are three broad categories of international banks namely multinational banks, offshore banks and correspondent banks. Multinational banks have subsidiaries, branches or joint-ventures in more than one country and provide an entire package of facilities, which are customized to the specific regulatory controls of each nation. They are multinational institutions, like JPMorgan Chase, HSBC, and Citigroup that support cross border trade, investment and foreign exchange activities, and they are very likely to become the avenues in the global economy integration.

The off-shore banks, on the contrary, are located in the jurisdiction of a favourable legal and taxation environment. They mostly serve the non-resident customers and provide them with confidentiality and asset protection as well as tax optimization. These banks are important in international wealth management as well as capital liquidity but they are getting more exposed to transparency standards through schemes such as the OECD Common Reporting Standard (CRS). Correspondent banks are the banks that provides facility to get all facilities of foreign banks.

1.4.2. *Global Finance Roles: Intermediation, Foreign Investment and Liquidity Provision*

International financial institutions promotes global payment ecosystem as follows (Sertoglu et al., 2017).

1.4.3. *Cross-Border Lending and Global Payment Systems*

It plays a key role in global remittances through bodies like the Bank for International Settlements (BIS) and Basel Committee by using international communication protocols.

1.5. Foreign Exchange Markets and Currency Dynamics

The international financial system is anchored by the foreign exchange (forex or FX) market which acts as the place where currencies are bought and sold between countries and where earmarked values are fetched. Being the largest most liquid financial market in the world with an ability that enables convenient conversion of one currency into another with a 24/7 operating nature depending on various major financial centres in the world, would entail such benefits of being able to make money appear out of thin air.

1.5.1. *Mechanisms of Foreign Exchange Markets*

The international bodies like international monetary fund along with worlds top financial institutions promote smooth financial or currency flows in case of cross border remittances.

1.5.2. *Exchange Rate Regimes: Fixed, Floating, and Hybrid Systems*

The exchange rate regime that countries adhere to on maintaining the value of their currency vis-a-vis that of others depends on their economic objectives and the specificities of the external trade. Fixed exchange rate regime means that a particular country fixes its respective currency to a major currency (whether US dollar or euro) at an established rate. It achieves stabilization of international prices and minimizes risks of transactions; however, it may limit the flexibility of monetary policies and necessity of high foreign exchange reserves to intervene in the market.

1.6. Global Financial Institutions and Regulatory Frameworks

International financial and trade institutions like the International Monetary Fund (IMF), World Bank and the World Trade Organization (WTO) are promoting the international banking practices across the world.

1.6.1. *Role of IMF, World Bank, BIS, and WTO*

The International Monetary Fund (IMF) offers policy guidance and financial aid to member countries that experience a balance-of-payments crisis and checks on the worldwide economic conditions by conducting surveillance operations.

The World Bank Group, which also includes the IBRD and the IDA, is an organization that works on the reduction of poverty and development of infrastructure in emerging economies providing long-term finance and technical support. The Bank for International Settlements (BIS) serves as a central bank for central banks, promoting global financial stability and hosting the Basel Committee, which sets international banking standards. Meanwhile, the World Trade Organization (WTO), though primarily a trade body, influences international finance through its rules on trade in financial services and dispute resolution mechanisms that impact capital flows and cross-border investments.

1.6.2. *Basel Accords and International Banking Regulations*

The Basel Accords, Basel I, II, and III are a key pillar in international financial regulations created by the Basel Committee within the BIS to strengthen the health and stability of the international banking system. The Basel I (1988) statements marked the first introduction to the risk-weighted standards of capital adequacy and the need to ensure that the minimum capital positions were abided. This was streamlined by Basel II (2004) and Basel -III.

1.6.3. *Financial Stability and Systemic Risk Management*

Stability of the financial system together with systemic risk management have been of main concern to the global regulators, given the fact that financial markets have been growing in complexity and interconnectedness. Systemic risk is that the collapse of one large financial institution or other segment of the market could branch off like a chain reaction and cause a vertical shock to the rest of the economy. The recent global financial crisis highlighted the benefit of increased macroprudential regulation and accordingly proper tools of crisis management.

The International institutions and national supervisors now focus on stress tests, Recovery and Resolution Frameworks as well as cross-border supervisory cooperation. The Financial Stability Board (FSB) created by G20 is an international body that harmonizes activities of standard-setting bodies and tracks the delivery of regulatory reforms to minimize the systematic weaknesses. Meanwhile, the changes in fintech, crypto-currency and the field of decentralized finance are adding new types of systemic risk, necessitating fresh responses on the part of tectonic, and more coordinated international responses.

1.7. International Financial Markets and Instruments

The international financial markets are the channel where the capital mobilization across international borders take place, where investment in the economy is achieved, and where trading of various goods take place. Financial instruments available in these markets are diverse and allow governments, multinational corporations and investors to cope with funding, investment, risk.

1.7.1. *Eurocurrency Markets, International Bonds, and Syndicated Loans*

The Eurocurrency market is a sensitive part of global finance, and it denotes money taken as a deposit in another currency that is not in its home country but instead in another currency, e.g. USD in European Banks. Such markets offer borrowers across the world with the highly liquid, flexible and efficient sources of capital. Low regulatory burdens and competitive rates of interest.

International bonds, e.g., Eurobonds and foreign bonds, enable the issuers to borrow in foreign markets. Eurobonds are largely priced in a currency that is not indigenous to the issuing country and are usually traded to investors in different countries. By comparison, foreign bonds are sold in a local market by a non-local seller and are controlled by local rules (e.g., in the U.S., "Yankee" bonds and in Japan, "Samurai" bonds). The instruments offer diversification advantages to the investors.

Syndicated loans are a form of financing in which a number of lenders group together to supply large scale funding to one borrower and they are usually used to finance infrastructure projects and merger and acquisition opportunities or to support working capital requirements. The loans help limit the exposure to the individual lenders and allow the borrowers to gain access to large amounts of capital. Risk and return trade-off are a main concept of finance and investment. It is founded on the principle that the greater the risk that an investor is willing to bear, the better are the returns that he/she gets. On the other hand, a risk aversion-type of investment has a smaller reward.

Figure 2. Risk and return trade-off of International Financial Instruments.

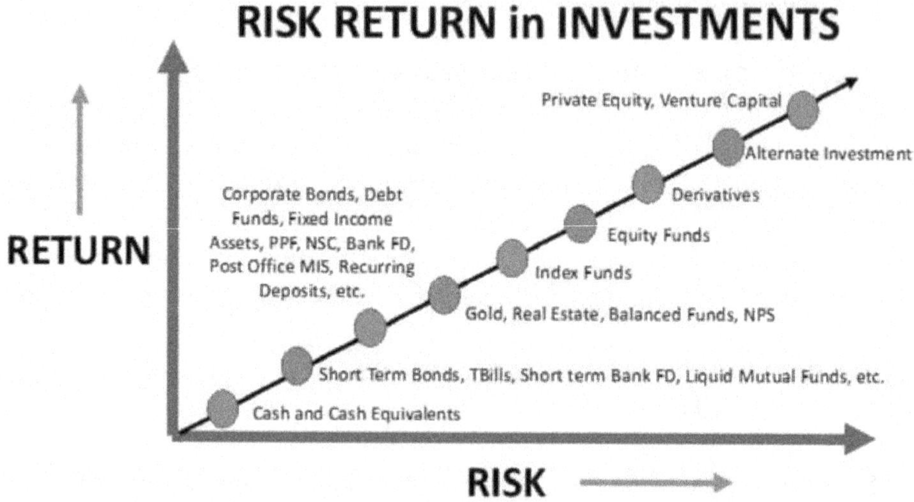

Source: (top10stockbroker.com). Compiled by: Author.

The graph (Figure 2) shows clearly the underlying principle of the risk-return trade-off in the bases of investment decisions. It demonstrates that with greater change in the investment or the shift in it towards high-risk securities such as Common Stocks, the greater is the expected return, but at the same time, the degree of risk. The efficient frontier is represented by the upward-slopping curve that depict investments giving best returns at a defined risk. Yellow star in the diagram is a poor to use the investment because it is below the efficient frontier meaning either it is too risky with too little reward or too rewarding at the perceived risk. In order to render this investing effective, one: risk needs to be minimized or the level of expected return should be higher.

1.7.2. *Derivatives in International Finance: Forwards, Options, and Swaps*

In international finance, financial derivatives are very crucial in managing currency risks, changes in interest rates, and credit risks. The forward, options, and swaps are among the most popular instruments. Forward contract is an agreement between two parties that have been customised to allow them to buy a particular amount of currency at a certain date and rate that has been agreed upon. This enables companies that deal with the international market against fluctuations of currencies. The currency options give the choice to purchase or sell a currency at a given price before a stipulated date but does not give the necessity. Multinational firms make extensive use of swaps, and in particular interest rate and currency swaps in order to balance their asset-liability positions and reduce the cost of funds (Azmi, S., & Akhtar, S. 2024).

1.8. Risks in International Finance and Banking

It is essential to know how to deal with these risks as this is important to the integrity of cross-border transactions, resilience of global banks, and to sustainability of economic growth. An optimum risk management in international finance does not just depend on the internal control mechanisms, but also on adhering to the universal regulatory frameworks as well as synchronised strategies of crisis response.

1.8.1. *Types of Risks: Exchange Rate, Sovereign, Credit, and Operational*

The currency or exchange rate risk occurs as a result of variations in values of foreign currency. This may affect multinational companies that operate in more than one country, investors who have international portfolio, and the banks that do cross-border lending. Rapid fluctuation in value of currencies can drive profits, swell liabilities, or distort values of assets. Normal methods to deal with this risk would include hedging of this with derivatives and matching of revenues and expenditure in same currency.

The risk of default in the debt or imposing capital controls that limit money movement by a foreign government is known as sovereign risk. Sovereign defaults may occur due to political instability or economic mismanagement or because of geopolitical tensions as is the case with Argentina (2001) or Greece (2010s). Credit risk in foreign finance means that a counterparty, either corporation or an institution specialized in finance, might default in meeting its obligations of a financial outlook or a contract promise which is of a derivative nature with respect to a debt. This risk is increased by cross border differences in legal systems, accounting standards and economic conditions. Operational risk covers breakdown in internal systems, the processes, or human error or external circumstances that may interfere with the international banking operations. As cross-border banks depend more on digital infrastructure, they are also susceptible to cyber threats, frauds and compliance breaches.

1.8.2. *Risk Mitigation Strategies and International Compliance Frameworks*

The overall risk mitigation strategies, which international financial institutions incorporate, are diversification, insurance, stress test, usage of derivative securities, such as forwards, swaps, and options.

The frameworks like, Basel Accords, IFRS standards, the directives on AML (Anti-Money Laundering) and Know Your Customer (KYC) regulations bring transparency, accountability and consistency in the banking practices all around the world. Regulators at the national and international level, like the Financial Action Task Force (FATF) and the Financial Stability Board (FSB), also provide state control of the actions of institutions.

1.8.3. *Crisis Management: Case Studies of Global Financial Crises*

Major crises of systemic collapse have marked the history of international finance leading to the lesson that crises should be actively managed. The Asian Financial Crisis (1997-1998) demonstrated the risks of too much foreign borrowing, poor regulation and being prone to exchange rate shocks. Such countries as Thailand, Indonesia, and South Korea were speedily hit by capital flight, currency failures, and shrinking of the economies. The crisis resulted in significant institutional transformation and additional consideration on capital controls and foreign reserve reserves.

When the subprime mortgage markets in the United States collapsed in 2007, this degenerated into a worldwide banking and liquidity crisis, as the Global Financial Crisis (20072008) developed quickly. The case of Lehman Brothers that filed bankruptcy and the consequential freeze in the interbank markets demonstrated the vulnerability of an integrated financial system. It resulted in coordinated efforts among central banks, to deploy quantitative easing, and augment capital and liquidity requirements by deployment of Basel III.

Recently the COVID 19 pandemic caused an unprecedented world financial shock, characterized by high volatility of financial market, broken supply chains, tremendous fiscal monetary stimulus. Moratoriums on debts, liquidity provision, and asset purchasing formats engaged by central banks and governments were launched to help avoid the collapse of the system. The crisis has underlined the relevance of digital infrastructure, adaptability of policy-based structures and the multilateral cooperation in countering financial turmoil.

These crises highlight that it is not sufficient to have well capitalized and diversified resilient international banking and financial systems, but also those that are agile to confront the emerging global risks quickly. Comprehensive international financial conditions would be more secure through enhancing regulatory coordination, increasing data availability, and developing technologies of risk predictability.

1.9. International Taxation and Transfer Pricing

The forces of globalization, digitization and multinational business operations have also rendered international taxation and transfer pricing to be both a lot more complicated and relevant.

1.9.1. *Principles of Cross-Border Taxation*

A mixture of bilateral tax treaties, home country taxation, and international agreements is the rule book of the cross-border taxation. The main philosophy is that income must be taxed where people perform economic activities and they create value. There are normally two main methods through which this can be accomplished; they include residence-based taxation where a nation taxes the incomes of its citizens worldwide and source-based taxation where an income is taxed where it is derived.

Countries sign Double Taxation Avoidance Agreements (DTAAs), granting one party the right to impose taxes, thereby preventing the same tax from collector multiple times; and in many cases, these agreements reduce or completely waive any withholding tax on any payment being made across borders such as dividends, interest, and royalty. Also transfer pricing laws are there to regulate the prices of the transactions between entities that are related in the MNE so as to make sure that the prices are standard.

1.9.2. *OECD's BEPS (Base Erosion and Profit Shifting) Initiative*

The OECD Base Erosion and Profit Shifting (BEPS) project is an unprecedented multilateral initiative against the tax avoidance practices that target the gaps and inconsistencies in the tax regulations. The most common BEPS practices are profit shifting of low-taxed or no-taxable jurisdiction (tax havens) to high-taxed jurisdictions and eroding the tax base of the source country.

BEPS project was launched in 2013 and supported by the G20 by adding 15 Action Plans to attack aggressive tax planning, improve transparency and bring taxation better into line with economic reality. They are country-by-country reporting (CBCR), hybrid mismatch arrangements, limits to interest deductions, and harmful tax practices. Interestingly, Action Plan 13 transfer pricing documentation will ask MNEs to report more detailed financial and operational information by jurisdiction and therefore improve the capacity of tax administrations to evaluate and examine possible transfer pricing risks.

Moreover, the BEPS system has paved the phase upon which a two-pillar approach that has the ability to modernize international taxation rules in line with the digital economy was established. Pillar One divides certain taxing rights to market jurisdictions where users and customers are based, and Pillar Two presents a global minimum rate of the corporate income tax to discourage a harmful effect of tax competition (Jha et al., 2025).

1.10. Regional Financial Integration and Currency Unions

Regional financial integration process is an increasingly important feature in the global financial regime, with an increased level of economic collaboration, augmented transfer or mobility of capital, and consolidation of monetary and fiscal agreement among regional states. Certain regional blocks like the European Union (EU), Association of Southeast Asian Nations (ASEAN) and the emerging blocs like BRICS (Brazil, Russia, India, China, South Africa) have been engaged in financial integration to a certain extent which indicates the common economic interests and strategic aims.

The European Union is the most sophisticated example of regional financial integration and this process led to the formation of the Euro zone, a monetary zone which consists of 20 EU member states which share one single currency, the euro.

It is embarked on the integration of the regional financial systems in a more soft and modest way. Although ASEAN does not run a monetary union, there are certain efforts, like the ASEAN Banking Integration Framework (ABIF), the Asian Bond Markets Initiative (ABMI), to integrate standards and make their finances more compatible and to improve the depth of their capital markets. Such initiatives have enabled the region to experience more financial inclusion, sharing of risks and trade facilitation in Southeast Asia as well as an ability of countries to enjoy monetary sovereignty.

The BRICS states that are rather dissimilar in their economic patterns and political governance, have also made a significant step to the development of regional financial cooperation. Such pushes by BRICS to achieve a limited reliance on western-dominated financial institutions represented in the creation of the New Development Bank (NDB), established and the Contingent Reserve Arrangement (CRA) which aims to achieve intra-block financial stability and financial development financing between historically newer countries. Although the bloc is not a monetary union, it is investigating something to replace the dollar-based system, such as experimenting with digital currency, and trading in domestic currencies rather than the dollar.

The creation of monetary unions and convergence to the use of common currencies, as it is else the case with the euro, creates opportunities and challenges. On the one hand, monetary unions do away with the exchange rate risk, enhance market integration and enhance credibility in the international markets. In contrast, they need powerful institutional arrangements, fiscal discipline and provisions of inter-country transfers in order to deal with asymmetric shocks and keep stability in the economy.

1.11. Role of Technology in Compliance and Surveillance

In an era where the financial systems and flow of capital across borders have become much complex, technology has emerged a groundbreaking device in ensuring the degree of compliance and monitoring of regulation.

1.11.1. *RegTech and SupTech: Enhancing Regulatory Efficiency*

RegTech may be described as a use of technology in the process of making the compliance with financial regulations more efficient and cost-effective. It involves the tools and platforms that can automatically collect data, report, and evaluate risks and digitally verify identities. In the case of financial institutions, RegTech solutions can minimize the cost of compliance, human error and allow real-time compliance with dynamically updated regulations. These are, e.g., automated anti-money laundering (AML) screening platforms, e-KYC (Know Your Customer) systems, and regulatory reporting applications on such standards as Basel III or MiFID II.

Figure 3. RegTech and SupTech in Global scenario.

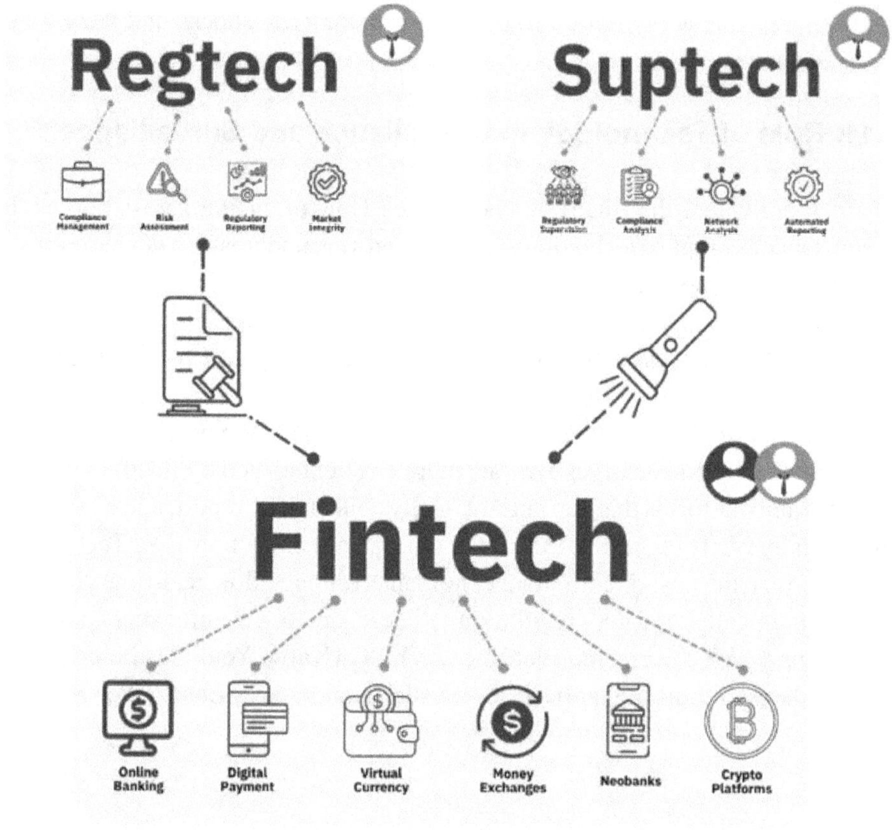

Source: Google.Com. Compiled by Author.

Figure 3 illustrates the interconnected roles of FinTech, RegTech, and SupTech in transforming financial services. FinTech leads innovation through services like digital banking, crypto platforms, and money transfers. RegTech supports financial institutions in managing compliance, risk, and regulatory changes. SupTech empowers regulators with tools for real-time monitoring, analytics, and automated reporting. Together, they create a cohesive ecosystem for secure and efficient financial operations.

The ASEAN Green Bond Standards, based on ICMA guidelines, support regional cooperation and encourage cross-border investment in sustainable projects. A good example is Indonesia's sovereign green sukuk bonds, which combine Islamic finance, green finance, and global investor interest. In Europe, the EU's Digital Finance Strategy uses RegTech to standardize compliance across member countries, making cross-border banking easier. The PSD2 directive also promotes secure open banking within the EU. In Africa, the Pan-African Payment and Settlement System (PAPSS), developed by African EXIM bank, uses blockchain technology to enable cross-border payments in local currencies. This reduces reliance on major global currencies like the USD and EUR, while strengthening regional financial integration under ECOWAS and the African Continental Free Trade Area (AfCFTA), and encouraging innovation and competition across borders (Fernando de Oliveira Santini et.al,2024).

1.11.2. *Blockchain in Anti-Money Laundering (AML) and KYC Processes*

Due to the decentralized ledger, blockchain technology is transforming the matter in which the financial organizations manage the requirements of compliance with anti-money laundering and know your client. Blockchain enables tamper proof transaction record that can conveniently be tracked and confirmed across jurisdictions in AML compliance.

1.11.3. *AI and Big Data in Monitoring Cross-Border Financial Flows*

The blockchain technology is changing the issue of requiring the financial organizations to address the requirements of the compliance with anti-money laundering and know your client as a result of the decentralized ledger. Blockchain allows tamper proof transaction record that can easily be followed and verified across jurisdictions during AML compliance. As compliance rules can be programmed on smart contracts, they can issue alerts and even preventive actions when set limits of risks are exceeded. The possibility of decentralized, shared digital identity infrastructure in KYC processes, investment, and imposing a hold over policy dynamism shall be the most significant in achieving an inclusive and long-lasting economic growth at the respective locales.

The Artificial Intelligence (AI) and the big data analytics are blowing up and changing cross-border financial flows monitoring and analysis. With the daily transactions on global networks reaching billions, the AI algorithms are able to scan and analyse large volumes of data to allow the system to identify anomalies, patterns and violation of financial regulations. Application A machine learning models could be applied at predictive risk modelling, fraud detection and real time tracking of capital movement.

Regulatory authorities and banks can use big data to trace trade based money laundering, tax evasion as well as money manipulation by following the flow of money to match the correlation of transactional data to behavioural, geographic and temporal data. The sanctions screening is also being automated using the AI-based systems to identify beneficial ownership structures that would otherwise be obscured by having multiples of shell companies. Altogether, utilizing technology to improve compliance and regulatory procedures has already stopped being a tendency but turns out to be an obligation in modern finance.

1.12. Contemporary Trends and Innovations

The technological changes, sustainability and consumer demands have added to the revolutionary realignment that is occurring in the global financial and banking environment. The new inventions of the Central Bank Digital Currencies (CBDCs), the breakneck speed of the Financial Technology (FinTech) and Decentralized Finance (DeFi), and the advance of green finance and ESG-friendly investments are shaping a paradigm shift on the foundations of the cross-border financial systems. Besides being the marker of evolution of the old finance, these trends signify a future that is accommodative, transparent and sustainable (Naseema N,et.al; 2025).

1.12.1.Central Bank Digital Currencies (CBDC)

CBDCs are electronic forms of sovereign money which are emitted and regulated by the central banks of the countries, and which are destined to become lawful tender. In contrast to cryptocurrencies, CBDCs have full backing of faith and credit of a government that issues it guaranteeing steadiness and veracities. China (in digital yuan), the Bahamas (Sand Dollar), India and the European Union are also contemplating and/or testing CBDCs.

The adoption of CBDCs has an array of advantages across the world with better financial inclusion being one of them.

1.12.2. FinTech and DeFi Effects on Global Banking.

The innovations of FinTech (Financial Technology) and Decentralized Finance (DeFi) provide a revolution kind by disintermediating the traditional financial facilities and suggesting the innovative and technology-based tips to transform the banking world. Artificial intelligence, blockchains, cloud computing and Big Data are being adopted by FinTech firms to develop agile customer facing services, including digital wallet and robo advisory services, peer-to-peer lending and algorithms trading. More precisely, it is possible to consider DeFi as a paradigm shift since it incorporates financial methods of lending, borrowing, trading, and asset management, enforced as decentralized blockchain protocols without centralized counterparts. Ethereium and other blockchains have been used as the foundation of a new family of smart contracts and decentralized applications (dApps), and, in competition to the traditional banking model.

1.13. Green Finance and ESG-Congruent International Investments.

The growing need of climate change and social responsibility in question has caused the worldwide scramble of green finance and Environmental, Social, and Governance (ESG)-aligned investments. Green finance is believed to be financial transactions with the sustainability of the environment such as renewable energy equipment, sustainable agriculture and clean fuel. DMS solutions like green bonds, sustainability-linked loans etc. and carbon trading platforms have been created. They have drawn both the government and the business investors.

The processes involved in the integration of ESG criteria into investment decision making is being propelled by the institutional investor mandates, regulatory disclosure requirements and stakeholder activism into international capital markets. Multilateral development banks, sovereign wealth funds and other large asset managers are converging portfolios with the global sustainability frameworks, which include UN Sustainable Development Goals (SDGs) and the Paris Agreement. The move towards ESG investing does not only encourage responsible capital allocation but also boosts risk-adjusted returns as it is the one that finds long-term drivers of values. Nevertheless, the sector has some difficulties regarding greenwashing, poor ESG indicators, and non-standardization. The solutions to these problems fall under the international organization to work out unified taxonomies, enhance transparency, and promote accountability culture in sustainable finance.

CONCLUSION

The chapter gives a well-informed and thorough discussion on the complex dynamics that are the governing factor in international finance and banking. It is brilliant in terms of tracking the evolution of the architecture of the global financial system through the course of the history, beginning with the historical gold standard and Bretton Woods and moving into the territories as recent as the introduction of digital currency and decentralized finance. It provides a combination of the adequate theoretical substantiation and empirical knowledge, which enables the reader to grasp the key dynamics of capital mobility, foreign exchange market, regulatory environment, financial innovation, and systemic controls when economies are increasingly becoming interdependent.

This chapter begins by pointing out why international financial economics is becoming significant and more so in a globalized environment and it presents some of the key historical events that have contributed to the design and functioning of financial systems in international environments. It is the cautious record of the manner and the reason as to how the fixed exchange regimes involving the regulation of the flow of capital are changed to liberalized financial markets through floating exchange rates. Special attention is paid to the post-Bretton Woods liberalization, the expansion of the Eurocurrency markets, and the advent of offshore banking because they demonstrate how the developments resulted in more financial integration.

The theoretical underpinnings that are heavily criticized in this chapter include Balance of Payments (BoP), Interest rate parity (IRP) and Purchasing Power Parity (PPP) models whose theories give the important framework of evaluating the action of the exchange rates and capital flows behaviour. These models present a study basis of macro interactions and policy recommendations development in the interdependent world.

Another aspect that the chapter tears apart is the modern structure of the international bank system and the various forms- multinational banking, offshore banking, the explanation of what each type of bank does in regard to cross-border financial intermediation, facilitation of investment and the provision of liquidity. It puts emphasis on the role of institutions such as IMF, World Bank, BIS and WTO in the process of monetary cooperation and fiscal stability.

This other eye-opening aspect of the chapter is the discussion of the systemic financial risks in quite detailed detail and underpinned with the real-life case studies, including the Asian Financial Crisis, the Global Financial Crisis (2007- 2008) and the economic change brought about by the COVID-19 pandemic. These instances once again justify the necessity of a presence of coordinated international surveillance, macro-prudential regulation and shock absorptive financial systems. Another issue that is of importance is the exposition in this chapter about the financial instruments I.e the Eurobonds, syndicated loans, derivatives and their role in the global capital markets as a facilitator of growth as well as source of volatility when left unchecked.

Another prospective idea presented in the chapter is the evaluation of the value of technology in compliance and financial innovation. It discusses the fact that the application of RegTech and SupTech can revolutionize the process of regulatory supervision and ensure its compliance with the complex legal norms in real time. In addition, it covers the functionality of the blockchain in AML/KYC processes, how AI and big data are altering the management of cross-border movement, which strengthened the foundation of more flexible and smart regulatory environment.

Notably, it also discusses the area of green finance, ESG-capable investment, and the implications of such a new trend as Central Bank Digital Currencies (CBDCs) and Decentralized Finance (DeFi). The trends do not simply end at technological disruption, but they also indicate a larger ideological shift to sustainability, inclusion and transparency of international financial systems. The understanding presented in this chapter through the embedded themes is insightful that the stakeholders, such as governments, investors, and consumers, have altered their expectations in the digital world, and in the post-pandemic world.

The chapter implications are profound on the aspect of being a professional. It may lead the policymakers and the regulators to attain the harmonization of the regulatory and monetary regulations across the jurisdictions, the enhancement of the institutional resilience and the enhancement of the cross-border coordination. It provides a cross-disciplinary framework that can be used by scholars to synthesize the traditional theory and recent financial findings to facilitate the further investigation of the specific novel topics in algorithmic trading, risk pricing with the help of artificial intelligence, and climate financial reporting. It will provide practical information to the financial practitioner and the financial institution on how they are supposed to handle this currency exposure, the capital they are supposed to better use, and how they can use financial technology to gain an advantage in the international financial markets.

In conclusion, one can say that the chapter successfully integrates the fundamentals with more contemporary issues, hence giving a wide policy-relevant perspective on international financial economics and banking. This is to imply that, as the geopolitical turmoil, technological disruption, and sustainability pressures remain dominant in the world, the ingrained understanding of the global financial ecosystem, as revealed in this entity becomes obligatory. This literary work is not just a source of information, but also tactical guide to regulators, institutions, and academics in seeking international finance in future. The need to introduce the inclusive-transparent-adaptive financial systems is often urgent, and this chapter contributes positively to the same discussion.

REFERENCES

Adekunle, W., & Ndukwe, I. (2018, June 2). *The Impact of Exchange Rate Dynamics on Agricultural Output Performance in Nigeria* [MPRA Paper]. https://mpra.ub.uni-muenchen.de/87750/

Agosin, M. R., & Huaita, F. (2011). Capital flows to emerging economies: Minsky in the tropics. *Cambridge Journal of Economics, 35*(4), 663–683. DOI: 10.1093/cje/beq047

Alami, I. (2018). On the terrorism of money and national policy-making in emerging capitalist economies. *Geoforum, 96*, 21–31. DOI: 10.1016/j.geoforum.2018.07.012

Alami, I., Alves, C., Bonizzi, B., Kaltenbrunner, A., Koddenbrock, K., Kvangraven, I., & Powell, J. (2023). International financial subordination: A critical research agenda. *Review of International Political Economy, 30*(4), 1360–1386. DOI: 10.1080/09692290.2022.2098359

Azubuike, V. osai, Nwogwugwu, U., & Nwokoye, E. (2023). The Role of Agriculture in Economic Development. *Journal of International Economic Relations and Development Economics, 3*(2), 103–111. https://www.theinterscholar.org/journals/index.php/jierade/article/view/208

Badarinza, C., & Ramadorai, T. (2018). Home away from home? Foreign demand and London house prices. *Journal of Financial Economics, 130*(3), 532–555. DOI: 10.1016/j.jfineco.2018.07.010

Balaji, K. (2024). Exchange-Traded Funds (ETFs): Redefining Financial Instruments in the 21st Century. In Faxing, L., & Kok Loang, O. (Eds.), (pp. 283–310). Advances in Finance, Accounting, and Economics. IGI Global., DOI: 10.4018/979-8-3693-8583-8.ch011

Balaji, K. (2024). Neuromarketing and Sustainable Finance: Real-World Case Studies of Green Investment Promotions. In Taneja, S., Chahal, B. P. S., Johri, A., Ozen, E., & Kumar, P. (Eds.), (pp. 169–204). Advances in Business Strategy and Competitive Advantage. IGI Global., DOI: 10.4018/979-8-3693-9117-4.ch010

Balaji, K. (2025). Revolutionizing High-Frequency Trading: The Impacts of Financial Technology and Data Science Innovations. In Chen, H. (Ed.), (pp. 103–124). Advances in Finance, Accounting, and Economics. IGI Global., DOI: 10.4018/979-8-3693-8186-1.ch004

Bonizzi, B., & Kaltenbrunner, A. (2019). Liability-driven investment and pension fund exposure to emerging markets: A Minskyan analysis. *Environment and Planning A. Environment & Planning A, 51*(2), 420–439. DOI: 10.1177/0308518X18794676

Carpenter, S. B., & Demiralp, S. (2010). Money, Reserves, and the Transmission of Monetary Policy: Does the Money Multiplier Exist? *Finance and Economics Discussion Series, 2010.0*(41), 1–55. DOI: 10.17016/feds.2010.41

Ergüven, E. (2020). The Political Economy of Housing Financialization in Turkey: Links With and Contradictions to the Accumulation Model. *Housing Policy Debate, 30*(4), 559–584. DOI: 10.1080/10511482.2019.1681017

Fernando de Oliveira, S., Lugo, D. B., Ladeira, W. J., Akhtar, S., Luciana da Silva, R., & Sott, M. K. (2024, November 20). Corporate social responsibility as a moderator of loyalty antecedents in the Brazilian banking context. *International Journal of Bank Marketing, 42*(7), 2075–2098. DOI: 10.1108/IJBM-12-2023-0667

Jacob, J. M., & Rosemary, E. A. (2019). Effects of Exchange Rate Fluctuation on Economic Growth in Nigeria 1981-2018. *International Journal of Intellectual Discourse, 2*(2), 1–11. https://ijidjournal.org/index.php/ijid/article/view/105

Jha, P., Akhtar, S., & Rana, P. (2025). The Swift Rise and Sudden Fall: Examining the Collapse of Silicon Valley Bank. *Emerging Economies Cases Journal, 0*(0), 25166042251319596. Advance online publication. DOI: 10.1177/25166042251319596

Kalu, E. U., Ugwu, O. E., Ndubuaku, V. C., & Ifeanyi, O. P. (2019). Exchange Rate and Foreign Reserves Interface: Empirical Evidence from Nigeria. *The Economics and Finance Letters, 6*(1), 1–8. https://ideas.repec.org//a/pkp/teafle/v6y2019i1p1-8id1615.html

Naeem Azmi, S., & Akhtar, S. (2024). Does financial development and economic growth matter for services export? Cross-country evidence from OECD countries. *The Journal of International Trade & Economic Development, 34*(5), 1048–1069. DOI: 10.1080/09638199.2024.2361658

Naseema, N., Akhtar, S., & Jha, P. (2025). Blockchain Disrupting Supply Chain Finance: Transformative Solutions and Emerging Challenges. Transformation of Supply Chain Ecosystems, 33-47.

Ogunjobi, J. O., Oladipo, O. A., Eseyin, O., Opaola, O., & Aransiola, I. J. (2022). Exchange Rate and Agricultural Exports: Evidence From Nigeria (1981-2019). *International Journal of Innovation and Scientific Research, 09*(04), 89–101. DOI: 10.51244/IJRSI.2022.9410

Oyinbo, O., Abraham, F., & Rekwot, G. (2014). Nexus of Exchange Rate Deregulation and Agricultural Share of Gross Domestic Product in Nigeria. *CBN Journal of Applied Statistics, 5*(2), 49–64. https://dc.cbn.gov.ng/jas/vol5/iss2/3

Sertoglu, K., Ugural, S., & Bekun, F. V. (2017). The Contribution of Agricultural Sector on Economic Growth of Nigeria. *International Journal of Economics and Financial Issues*, *7*(1), 547–552. https://www.econjournals.com/index.php/ijefi/article/view/3941

Soni, H. P., Shyamsuder, C., & Prasad, K. (2023). Risk return profile of commodity derivatives: An investors perception. [Management and Administrative Professional Review]. *Revista de Gestão e Secretariado, 14*(7), 12004–12016. DOI: 10.7769/gesec.v14i7.2389

KEY TERMS AND DEFINITIONS

Balance of Payments (BoP): A comprehensive record of a country's economic transactions with the rest of the world, including the current, capital, and financial accounts.

Basel Accords (I, II, III): International regulatory frameworks established to strengthen regulation, supervision, and risk management within the banking sector.

Capital Mobility: The ease with which financial capital or investment can move across international borders.

Central Bank Digital Currency (CBDC): A digital form of a country's official currency, issued and regulated by its central bank.

Currency Swap: An agreement to exchange currency between two foreign parties, often used to hedge against currency fluctuations.

Decentralized Finance (DeFi): A blockchain-based form of finance that does not rely on central financial intermediaries, such as brokerages or banks.

ESG Investments: Investment strategies that consider Environmental, Social, and Governance factors in portfolio selection and management.

Eurocurrency Market: A market for currencies deposited outside their country of origin, e.g., US dollars deposited in a European bank.

Exchange Rate Regime: The method by which a country manages its currency in relation to other currencies, including fixed, floating, pegged, or managed float systems.

Foreign Exchange (Forex) Market: The global marketplace for buying and selling national currencies against one another.

Forward Contract: A customized contract between two parties to buy or sell an asset at a specified future date at a price agreed upon today.

Global Systemically Important Banks (G-SIBs): Large interconnected banks whose failure might trigger a financial crisis.

Green Finance Financial: Investments flowing into sustainable development projects and initiatives that encourage the development of a more sustainable economy.

Interest Rate Parity (IRP): A theory stating that the difference in interest rates between two countries is equal to the expected change in exchange rates between the countries' currencies.

International Monetary Fund (IMF): A global organization that promotes financial stability, facilitates international trade, and provides monetary cooperation and financial assistance.

OECD BEPS Initiative: The OECD's Base Erosion and Profit Shifting project to tackle corporate tax avoidance strategies that exploit gaps and mismatches in tax rules.

Purchasing Power Parity (PPP): A theory that states that in the long term, exchange rates should move toward the rate that equalizes the prices of an identical basket of goods and services in any two countries.

RegTech: Technology used to help financial institutions comply with regulations efficiently and at a lower cost.

SupTech: Technology used by supervisory agencies to support oversight and data-driven regulatory analysis.

Syndicated Loan: A loan offered by a group of lenders (a syndicate) who work together to provide funds for a single borrower.

World Bank: An international financial institution that provides loans and grants to the governments of poorer countries for development projects.

Chapter 2
The Role of Monetary Policy and Fiscal Policy on Global Finance

Bhargavi Rachamadugu
https://orcid.org/0009-0003-8846-532X
Woxsen University, India

Krunal Purohit
https://orcid.org/0009-0004-0092-6732
Woxsen University, India

Afzalur Rahman
https://orcid.org/0000-0002-1561-561X
Woxsen University, India

ABSTRACT

This chapter explores the evolving landscape of global finance, specifically examining the profound influence of Central Bank Digital Currencies (CBDCs) on monetary and fiscal policy transmission mechanisms. It delineates the foundational principles of traditional monetary and fiscal policies, contrasting them with the transformative potential of CBDCs in achieving economic stability and growth. The analysis delves into CBDC's direct impact on macroeconomic factors, including financial stability, bank profitability, and financial inclusion, from both central bank and public perspectives. Furthermore, the chapter addresses the multifaceted challenges associated with CBDC implementation, such as cybersecurity and digital literacy, proposing strategic frameworks for successful adoption. The findings underscore

DOI: 10.4018/979-8-3373-3725-8.ch002

CBDC's capacity to enhance policy efficacy, transparency, and the efficiency of public fund disbursement, offering critical insights for policymakers and future research in the digital finance era.

1. INTRODUCTION

Every country uses diverse economic systems (Capitalism, Socialism, Mixed Economy) and various economic policies (Industrial Policy, EXIM policy, Monetary Policy and Fiscal Policy) to achieve faster economic growth in particular sectors. Among them, monetary Policy is a key strategy employed by the Reserve Bank of India to stimulate economic growth while controlling inflation. To meet these goals, the RBI uses various qualitative and quantitative tools, including but not limited to the Cash Reserve Ratio[1] (CRR), Statutory Liquidity Ratio[2](SLR), Repo Rate[3], and Reverse Repo Rate[4]. On the other hand, fiscal policy is an economic directive established by the government of India that is intended to delineate all sources of revenue (Taxes) and expenditures (Welfare) for the forthcoming financial year. The fiscal policy is typically unveiled annually in February, projecting the anticipated capital account and Revenue Account. Moreover, the Fiscal Policy comprises capital expenditure[5], capital income[6], revenue income[7] and revenue expenditure[8] and their definitions have been shown in the footnotes. Additionally, Global Finance refers to enabling the products and services available to the entire world, and Gen Z[9] leverages technology including but not limited to AI, decentralized technologies, and smart contracts. The Fourth Industrial Revolution[10] has profoundly reshaped Global Finance by introducing new opportunities, including but not limited to AI bonds[11], green bonds[12], Fintech stocks[13], and digital assets like Cryptocurrency[14] and CBDC. Therefore, this chapter deals with how fiscal tools (government spending, taxation and debt) and monetary policies (interest rates and quantitative easing) impact the stability of the global financial system amid the introduction of CBDC. It also explores how CBDCs could transform monetary policy and international payment systems. By examining lessons from events like the 2008 global financial crisis and the COVID-19 pandemic, the chapter offers insights into policy decisions that can strengthen global financial stability and affect international banking.

The content of the chapter will first focus on the traditional ways that monetary and fiscal policies are transmitted to control the inflation and deflation rates. It then examines the economic crisis that has occurred due to the failure of these conventional tools. Following this, it introduces CBDCs, discussing various pilot studies and different models. Finally, it analyses the macroeconomic impact of CBDCs and how monetary and fiscal policy transmission happens with their introduction (depicted in Figure 1).

Figure 1. Transformation of the transaction and effectiveness of Monetary and Fiscal Policy

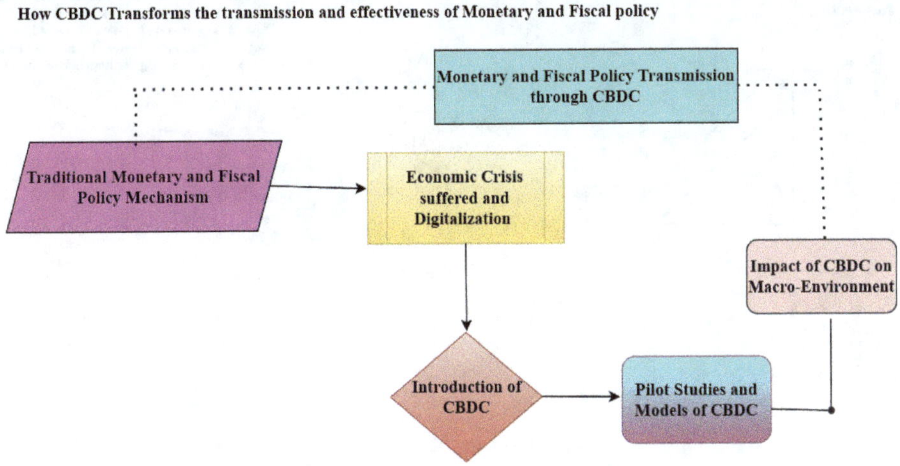

2. TRADITIONAL MONETARY POLICY

This section delves into how conventional monetary policy instruments are employed to manage inflationary pressures. As previously noted, the primary objectives of monetary policy are to control both inflation [15]and deflation[16] typically achieved through adjustments to interest rates.

2.1 Expansionary Monetary Policy (Deflation Control)

The Reserve Bank of India uses Expansionary and Contractionary monetary policies to manage inflation. The choice between these policies is determined by the phase of the business cycle which describes the natural fluctuations in economic activity often measured by how well businesses are doing. Expansionary Monetary Policy is specifically used to stimulate economic growth, particularly during a recession or economic slowdown when business profits are declining, and the essence of this policy has been described below.

Figure 2. Deflation Control

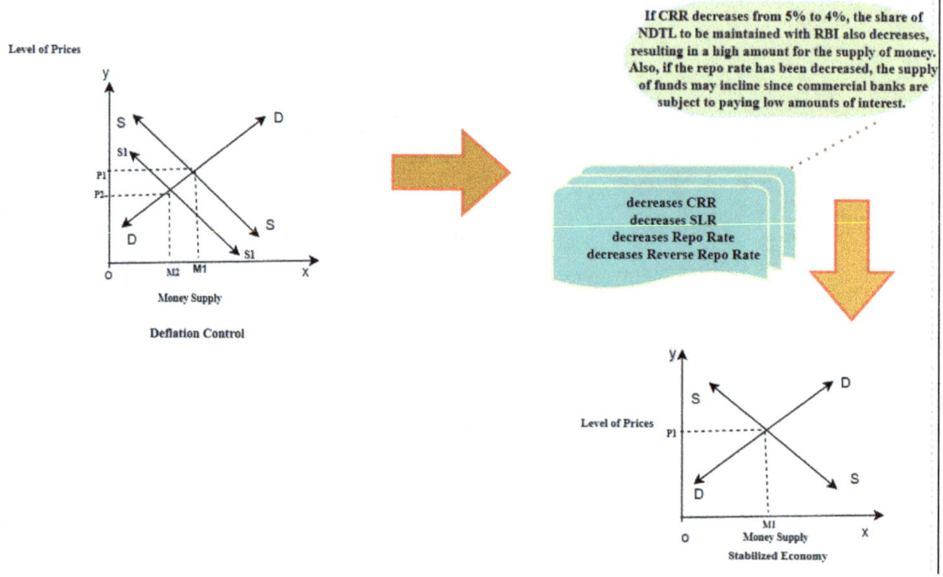

The Reserve Bank of India (RBI) manages deflation, a perilous economic state more damaging than inflation since it is characterized by rising unemployment, declining GDP and Per Capita Income, and a shrinking currency value, posing a severe threat to the entire economic system. The text's accompanying diagram illustrates this by showing that a decrease in money supply from S to S1 leads to a drop in prices from P1 to P2. To counteract this, the RBI implements measures to boost the money supply, which involves decreasing the Cash Reserve Ratio, Statutory Liquidity Ratio (SLR) and Repo Rate. Decreasing the amount of reserves makes more funds available for commercial banks to lend to their customers. On the other hand, there is a reduction in the Reverse Repo Rate, thereby discouraging commercial banks from depositing their surplus funds with the central bank. Thus, it encourages the banks to increase lending to consumers and business houses, which in turn boosts the money supply. Since it helps to counter a deflationary economic decline, we call it Expansionary Monetary Policy.

2.2 Contractionary Monetary Policy: (Inflation Control)

As illustrated in Figure 3, an excess of money in the economy leads to higher prices, thereby directing the central banks to use certain key instruments. As soon as the percentage of CRR increases, it compels the commercial bank to deposit more of its funds. As a result of which, the central bank pools money from banks.

On the other hand, the RBI increases the Repo Rate, making it more expensive for commercial banks to borrow.

Figure 3. Inflation Control

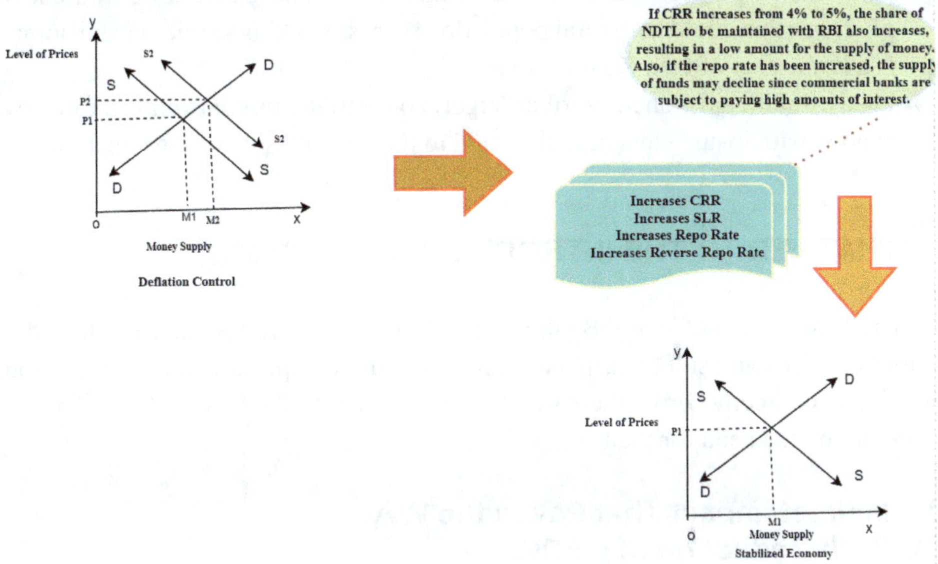

These combined actions shrink the money supply, which is intended to reduce inflationary pressures by slowing down both lending and economic activity. This coordinated action helps to reverse the inflationary trend illustrated by the shift from P2 to P1 by curtailing the expansion of money from S2 to S. The text concludes by emphasizing the importance of also utilizing other instruments like the Marginal Standing Facility, Bank Rate, and Open Market Operations for a comprehensive approach to inflation control (Figure 3).

2.3 Limitations of Monetary Policy

While various monetary policy tools will undoubtedly be employed to manage inflation and deflation, their traditional application in the Gen Z era faces specific limitations.

1. The simultaneous use of multiple instruments like CRR, SLR, Repo Rate, and Reverse Repo Rate can lead to diverse and potentially conflicting results, complicating their overall impact.

2. Traditional monetary policy implementation often overlooks the integration and adoption of emerging technologies, hindering its adaptability in a modern economy.
3. Its primary focus on economic growth and inflation means it generally doesn't prioritize or promote financial inclusion[17], especially concerning awareness programs that could help rural populations access banking services from home, is a key aspect of Gen Z initiatives.
4. Lastly, traditional monetary policy largely concentrates on controlling the money supply, with insufficient attention paid to the demand side of the equation.

3. WHAT LED TO THE INTRODUCTION OF CBDC?

The move towards Central Bank Digital Currencies (CBDCs) isn't a sudden development; it's the result of various factors, some directly pushing for their creation and others indirectly (From the Asian Financial Crisis to the Covid-19 Pandemic), highlighting the need for them.

3.1 Indirect Impact That Paved the Way for the Introduction of CBDC

Major economic crises over the past few decades, like the Asian Financial Crisis, the 9/11 attacks, the Great Recession, the European Debt Crisis, China's stock market crashes, and the COVID-19 pandemic, didn't directly cause CBDCs to be introduced. Instead, they highlighted weaknesses and challenges in our traditional financial systems, which in turn made central banks seriously consider and ultimately adopt digital currencies.

Asian Financial Crisis: Imagine a country, Thailand, whose money (Baht) was tied directly to the strong US dollar. When the US dollar got even stronger, the Baht suffered. At first, some in Southeast Asia thought this might help their exports. But it became too much. Thailand's government tried to keep the Baht stable by spending its savings (foreign reserves). Once those savings ran out, they had to untie their currency from the dollar and let it float, meaning its value can change freely. This caused a huge crash in Thailand - the stock market fell, and banks struggled to get the loans repaid. This shock quickly spread. Other countries in Southeast Asia got scared that their money would also crash. Investors panicked, selling off their local investments and converting their money into safe U.S. dollars. This rush of money caused the crisis. The big lesson here is that tying your currency to another currency can be risky, especially when confidence drops and money starts fleeing the country.

9/11 attack: When the terrible 9/11 terrorist attack happened in the United States, it was not a tragedy for America. It sent ripples across the world. Airlines and tourism immediately suffered because flights were grounded, and people were afraid to travel. The stock market also took a hit, and uncertainty and fear gripped the nation. While the physical damage was in the US, the economic and emotional shock was felt globally.

The Great Recession (2008): After 9/11, the US central bank (Federal Reserve) cut interest rates to help the economy recover. This meant borrowing money became very cheap. At the same time, some financial rules were loosened, leading to a lot of irresponsible lending. Banks and other financial companies started giving out loans, especially for houses, without properly checking the repayment capability. Most complex financial products were created based on these risky loans. Eventually, these bad loans led to massive losses for these countries, billions of dollars. This led to the global financial crisis of 2008, a major worldwide downturn.

European Debt Crisis: After the Great Recession, several European countries, including Iceland and Spain, borrowed a lot of money from other nations. Their economies were not growing well, so they found it harder to pay back their debts. This struggle to manage their debt loads sparked the European debt crisis. It significantly impacted many European countries like Ireland, Portugal, Italy, Greece and Spain, showing how vulnerable the eurozone was.

China Stock Market Crash: China's stock market crash was caused by speculative trading when many investors excitedly bought stocks, expecting prices to just keep going up (often called herding behaviour). This drives stock values to unrealistic levels. But eventually, if people start to worry that prices are too high or something shifts, a huge number of investors sell their shares all at once. This massive selling pressure causes stock prices to drop sharply and quickly, leading to a market crash.

COVID-19 pandemic: The COVID-19 pandemic caused a major global economic crisis, and a lot of wild swings were experienced in the financial markets. At first, stock markets plummeted, and there was a rush to safe investments like gold and US government bonds. Government and Central Banks worldwide reacted with massive spending and money-related policies, which included direct payments to people, unemployment benefits, and help for businesses. Central banks cut interest rates, bought huge amounts of losses (quantitative easing) and made sure there was enough cash flowing in the financial system. All these actions were meant to soften the economic blow, support incomes, and stabilize the markets.

The pandemic exposed weak points in global supply chains, made existing inequalities worse and caused governments to take on much more debt. The long-term effects on global finance are still playing out with ongoing discussions about inflation, interest rates, and sustainability. The crisis also sped up trends like the rise of digital finance and put a stronger focus on making the financial system more resilient.

3.2 Direct Factors That Paved the Way for the Successful Adoption of CBDC

Several social and technological trends beyond the past economic crisis are driving the push for the implementation of CBDCs.

Less use of physical cash: A primary driver is the decreasing use of physical cash. As people grow more comfortable with digital transactions via the usage of apps, online banking and cards, the Central Banks are naturally prompted to explore a digital version of their currency. This change reflects the modern financial system evolving needs and our increasing reliance on digital money.

Embracing New Technologies: Our society has rapidly adopted new technologies across all aspects of life, and finance is no exception. Advances in areas like secure digital ledgers (the tech behind cryptocurrencies) and advanced encryption have made the idea of a digital currency issued by a central bank technically feasible and secure. This technological readiness is a key enabler for CBDCs.

Shortcomings of traditional financial systems: CBDCs are being explored as a solution to key problems in traditional financial systems. One major issue is financial inclusion, as many people lack access to banking services. CBDCs could offer a more affordable and accessible way for everyone to participate in the economy. Additionally, traditional systems face operational and market risks, including cyberattacks and system failures, which a well-designed CBDC could help mitigate by providing a more resilient infrastructure. Finally, the current system is burdened by high costs associated with managing cash and maintaining a complex banking network. CBDCs could streamline these processes, thereby reduce expenses and improve efficiency.

Because of these limitations, policymakers are considering new ways to improve monetary policy and payment systems. CBDCs are seen as a vital innovation that could simplify payments, allow for direct government stimulus to citizens and strengthen the effectiveness of monetary policy.

4. INTRODUCTION TO CBDC

Table 1 highlights the key aspects of introduction to CBDC by highlighting its definition, its types and its three features- Programmability, Centralized power and technology-driven.

Table 1. Introduction to CBDC

Characters	Description
Definition	A modern payment system that leverages technology to promote financial inclusion, backed up by its nation's currency.
Types of CBDC	A Wholesale CBDC is a central bank-issued digital currency intended for financial institutions and commercial banks. It is used to streamline large-scale transactions (interbank settlements) to boost efficiency and reduce risk within the wholesale financial system.
	Retail CBDC is a digital currency issued by a central bank that is made available directly to individuals and the public. It functions like a digital version of physical cash, allowing everyday transactions between consumers and businesses. While the amount might be small per individual transaction, it is meant for widespread use, offering a secure and convenient digital payment method.
Programmable	CBDCs boost transparency because they allow authorized individuals to view transaction details. This means that regulators or other designated parties can monitor financial flows, which can help in areas like combating illicit activities.
Centralization	By design, CBDCs are pegged to their respective national currencies, thereby consolidating their ultimate control under the purview of each nation's central bank. This ensures that monetary sovereignty is maintained.
Technology	Various models have been developed for the maintenance of CBDC, including but not limited to Distributed Ledger Technologies, Smart Contracts and Centralized technologies.

CBDC could offer a solution to the weaknesses in traditional banking systems, such as those that contributed to the collapse of YES Bank. The bank's failure was caused by issues like underreported non-performing assets (Akhtar, Alam, & Khan, 2021). By providing a direct liability of the central bank, CBDCs would reduce the public reliance on commercial bank deposits. Furthermore, the enhanced traceability and transparency of CBDC could improve financial stability and the effectiveness of monetary policy. This shift could help to prevent similar crises and complement existing regulatory frameworks.

(Akhtar, Alam, & Ansari, 2022) looked at how the financial crisis affected Indian Commercial banks from 2015 to 2018. They found that while bank profitability measured by ROA dropped during these crises, public sector banks were able to maintain strong liquidity. In contrast, private sector banks showed better earnings. This suggests that the banking sector has a solid financial stability mechanism in place and that CBDC could further strengthen these systems. The adoption of CBDC gives better tools for managing liquidity and helps them to create new avenues for the adoption of digital financial products, which in turn boost financial stability and profitability.

Even though various shortcomings were identified during the early stage of CBDC adoption, the central banks of various countries have initiated certain pilot projects to test their feasibility and their practical implications, which will be discussed further.

Pilot Study on CBDC

Major central bank, including the reserve bank of India (RBI), the Federal reserve, and the people's bank of china (PBOC), are utilizing programs to assess the viability of central bank digital currencies (CBDCs), This approach offers a flexible way to handle the unpredictable nature f CBDC implementation. The strategy suggests that a country's existing digital infrastructure, legal framework, and institutional capacity should be evaluated in an incremental process. This allows central banks to modify their projects scope and speed based on changing domestic and international circumstances.

An alternative framework, the 5P methodology, provides a structured, research-driven guide for CBDDC development. It outlines five distinct stages:

Preparation: Initial research and planning

Proof of Concept: Testing the core idea

Prototypes: Building a preliminary version

Pilots: Conducting real-world trials

Production: Full-scale implementation

This methodology offers a clear roadmap for projects, emphasizing best practices in key areas such as risk management, stakeholder collaboration, and cybersecurity. The goal is to ensure a seamless transition from a theoretical concept to a fully operational system (Tourpe, 2023).

4.1 E-Digital Rupee

In an October 7, 2022, concept note, the reserve bank of India (RBI) announced its plans for a central bank digital currency (CBDC) pilot program. This followed an earlier statement in the Lok Sabha by Union Minister of State for Finance, Shri Pankaj Chaudhary, who provided preliminary information on the upcoming trial. Known as the e-Digital rupees, this initiative marks India's first pilot study to assess the feasibility and public acceptance of a CBDC within a controlled regulatory environment. All the details related to this pilot study have been represented in Table 2:

Table 2. E-Digital Rupee

Types of CBDC	Launched on	Intermediaries	Participants
Digital Rupee Wholesale (ED-W)	November 01, 2022	SBI Bank, ICICI Bank, Yes Bank and first IDFC bank	Limited to the settlement of secondary market transactions and facilitating inter-bank settlement.
E-Digital Retail (ED-R)	December 01, 2022	Bank of Baroda, Union Bank of India, HDFC, Kotak Mahindra.	Closed User Group (CUG) with merchants and individuals

The e -R (Digital Rupee - Retail) is designed to be used via a digital wallet. This allows for easy peer-to-peer (P2P) payments between individuals and peer-to-merchant (P2M) payments for purchases. Importantly, the e -R is non-remunerative, meaning the central bank won't pay any interest on it. It aims to be a trustworthy option for investments and offers high liquidity, like holding deposits in a bank[18].

4.2 Digital Dollar Project

The Digital Dollar Project, a pilot study launched in 2020 by Accenture and Digital Dollar Foundation, commenced its initial study in May 2021 to assess the feasibility of CBDC in the United States. The Underlying assumptions include simulated currency value, utilizing a two-tier architecture, commercial banks as hosts, and the Federal Bank as Custodian, and allowing both digital and traditional assets to serve as collateral. This pilot investigation has been structured on a two-tier model (Where the central bank issues CBDC to Commercial Banks based on DLT (Distributed Ledger Technology), followed by peer-to-peer payments. The pilot study has identified four significant advantages: Reduced Risk, optimized costs, enhanced Customer experience, improved visibility of transactions, and CBDC acts as a catalyst for financial inclusion[19].

4.3 e-CNY

e-CNY (A digital form of renminbi) is a CBDC issued by the PBOC (People's Bank of China), formulated in 2019 and was officially launched in 2020 in four cities, namely Shenzhen, Suzhou, Chengdu, and Xiong'an, and then, a pilot study was expanded to other cities according to their population and advancement. (El-Almari, 2023) examines whether China's pilot launch of a CBDC improved tax revenues. Using a difference-in-differences approach on provincial data from 2000-2021, the study finds that provinces implementing the CBDC pilot experienced higher tax collection compared to non-pilot regions, with particularly strong effects in smaller provinces. The increase was evident across major tax categories, including

VAT, corporate income tax and the personal income tax. These results suggest that the CBDCs can strengthen tax compliance and enhance government revenue, offering valuable insights for policymakers considering digital currency adoption. Most central banks are exploring CBDC, and China's e-CNY stands out as one of the pioneers in public deployment. E-CNY is currently undergoing extensive pilot programs, facilitating payments for everyday transactions like retail purchases and public transport. Nevertheless, by the end of 2021, 261 million digital wallets had been operated, and by August 2022, the total transaction exceeded RMB 100 billion, showing the successful adoption of e-CNY. Despite being legal tender, e-CNY still faces certain challenges. The recent enhancements, such as offline contactless payment and smart contract capabilities introduced in late 2022 and 2023, are expected to boost its adoption rate. The e-CNY has achieved success in its adoption due to its distinct three features: Tax Payment through CBDC, Programmable CBDC, and risk management with CBDC[20,21].

5. MODELS OF CBDC

The move towards a direct introduction of CBDC has been paved by a combination of factors driven by both the evolving digital landscape and the inherent limitations and challenges within traditional financial systems. This section explores the different models of CBDC, highlighting their key roles.

5.1 Single-Tier Model of CBDC

Figure 4, depicting a single-tier CBDC model, illustrates a direct operational link between the Reserve Bank of India (RBI) and all end customers. In this simplified system, the RBI would directly manage the digital currency for a wide range of users, including individual households, various types of businesses (such as partnerships, private and public companies), and other financial institutions. This structure implies that the central bank itself would be responsible for tasks like account management and transaction verification for every user, creating a direct relationship that bypasses traditional commercial banking intermediaries for the core digital currency function.

Figure 4. One-tier model of CBDC

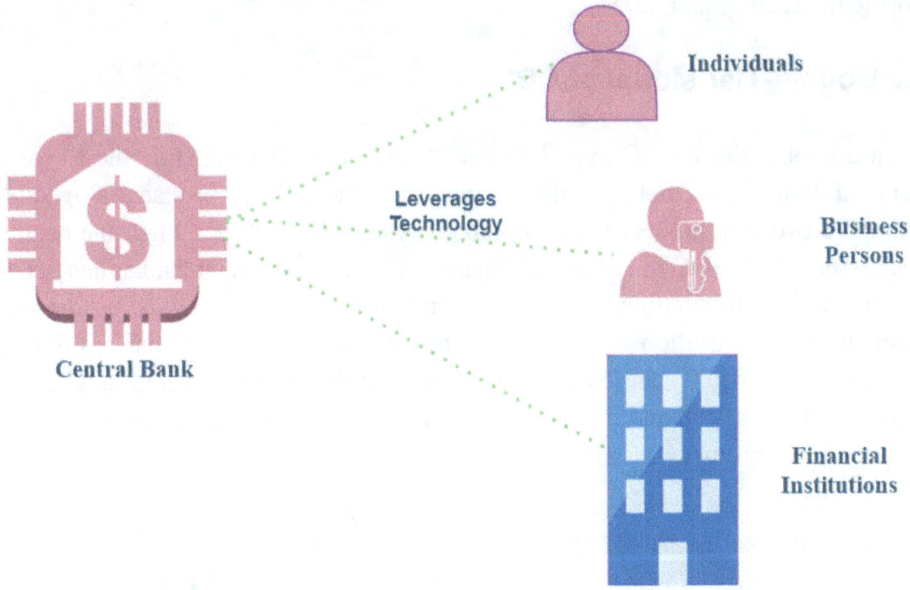

This model empowers the central bank with direct control and oversight over the digital currency's issuance, distribution, and all transactions. Since this model eliminates intermediaries for the core function of CBDC, it may lead to greater efficiency and lower transaction costs as settlements occur directly on the ledger account of the RBI, thereby reducing inter-bank settlements. A key benefit is enhanced financial inclusion as it allows all individuals and business houses, irrespective of illiteracy, Unbanked and underbanked, to directly hold accounts with the central bank, providing a universally accessible, secure, and risk-free digital payment method.

Also emphasizes that CBDCs need not supplement the FPS or e-money but rather can coexist strategically with them. Through thoughtful design, each payment system i.e., CBDCs, FPS and e-money, can contribute distinct benefits such as enhancing payments efficiency, promoting financial inclusion and ensuring continued access to central bank money in an increasingly digital environment, The note advises that central banks should closely monitor all three solutions, assess their evolving roles and craft flexible strategies to adopt as technologies and objectives develop. This direct link also means that CBDC is a direct liability of the central bank, making it a safe and reliable. Furthermore, it offers the central bank new tools for monetary policy implementation, potentially allowing for more precise control over money supply and faster, more direct distribution of funds for government aid or subsidies, as seen during COVID-19. Lastly, the traceability of direct CBDC transactions can significantly aid in combating illicit activities like money laundering and terrorist financing. While also reducing the operational costs associated with printing and storing the cash. (Patel, 2024)

5.2 Double-Tier Model of CBDC

In a double-tier CBDC model (Figure 5), the central bank (like the Reserve Bank of India) does not directly interact with the public. Instead, it operates through a two-step process to get digital currency to customers. First, the central bank issues the CBDC to commercial banks. These commercial banks then act as intermediaries, distributing the CBDC to end customers (households, businesses, other financial institutions). This process involves the commercial bank verifying the customer's identity and authorizing transactions, thereby leveraging existing banking infrastructure and relationships while still ensuring the digital currency's security and legitimacy.

Figure 5. Two-tier model of CBDC

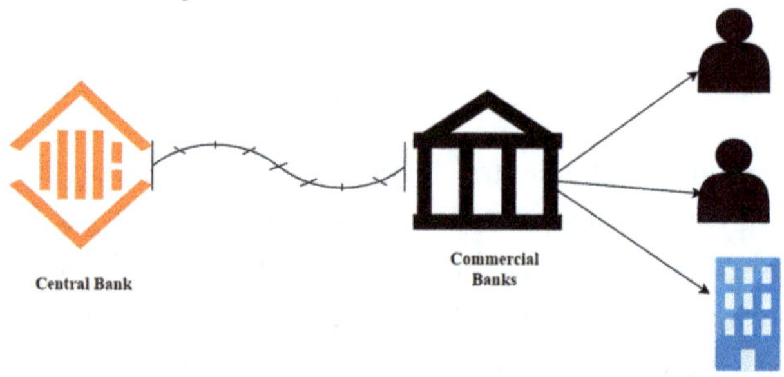

The following section highlights the two-tier model of CBDC and thereby differentiates it from the one-tier model.

- **Preserves the role of commercial Banks:** The two-tier model allows commercial banks to remain the primary point of contact for customers. This means they continue to handle customer onboarding, identity verification (KYC/AML), fraud detection, customer service and a vast array of financial products and services (like loans and mortgages) that underpin the economy. A single-tier model would require the central bank to take on these massive operational responsibilities, which it is neither equipped nor designed to do.
- **No New infrastructure:** Commercial banks already have established payment systems, digital platforms and a vast network of branches and personnel. The two-tier model leverages this existing infrastructure, reducing the

need for the central bank to build an entirely new, massive retail operation from scratch. This makes implementation more efficient and less disruptive.

- **Manages operational Risk:** By delegating customer-facing operations to commercial banks, the central bank can focus on its core mandate of monetary policy and financial stability. This decentralizes operational risks, as individual bank failures would not directly disrupt the entire CBDC system in the same way a central bank system failure might in a single-tier model.
- **Promotes innovation and competition:** Commercial banks and other financial service providers can innovate on top of the CBDC platform, offering new services and features to customers. This fosters competition in the digital payment space, potentially leading to better services and lower costs for consumers.
- **Maintains financial stability:** While CBDC could potentially lead to bank runs (Where people withdraw deposits from banks to hold risk-free CBDC directly with the central bank during the crisis), the two-tier model helps mitigate this. Since customers interact with commercial banks for their CBDC, deposits are less likely to directly flow out of the banking system into the central bank, thus helping to preserve banks' ability to lend and support the economy.
- **Ensures financial inclusion through familiar channels:** while the single-tier model aims for financial inclusion, the two-tier model can achieve it by leveraging the established reach of commercial banks and their familiarity with diverse customer segments, including those in remote or underserved areas.

(Uddin & Akhtar, 2025) States that technological and efficiency gaps between Indian banks have narrowed over the last two decades, a trend that was briefly interrupted by crises like the Global Financial Crisis and Covid-19. This convergence is particularly relevant for the implementation of CBDC. The fact that banks are becoming more technologically simplified simplifies the deployment of CBDC, as it suggests a more uniform infrastructure to handle aspects like interoperability and cybersecurity. However, the study also reveals a significant risk: It can disrupt the efficiency of the banking system. This could lead to some banks lagging in key functions like transaction processing and fraud monitoring during times of economic stress, which could undermine public trust in the CBDC. Therefore, this paper suggests that a hybrid or two-tier model where banks handle wallets and transactions would be a good fit given their convergence of technological capabilities. Policymakers should also incorporate resilience measures into the CBDC framework, such as offline transaction options and contingency plans, to mitigate the risk of efficiency slowdowns during a crisis and ensure the stability and reliability of digital currency.

5.3 Three-Tier CBDC Model

A three-tier model (Figure 6) for CBDC expands upon the more common two-tier structure by introducing an additional layer of service providers between commercial banks and the end customer. In this setup, the central bank remains the sole issuer of CBDC. It then distributes this digital currency to commercial banks and other authorized wholesale financial institutions, who hold it and manage the wholesale ledger.

Figure 6. Three-tier model of CBDC

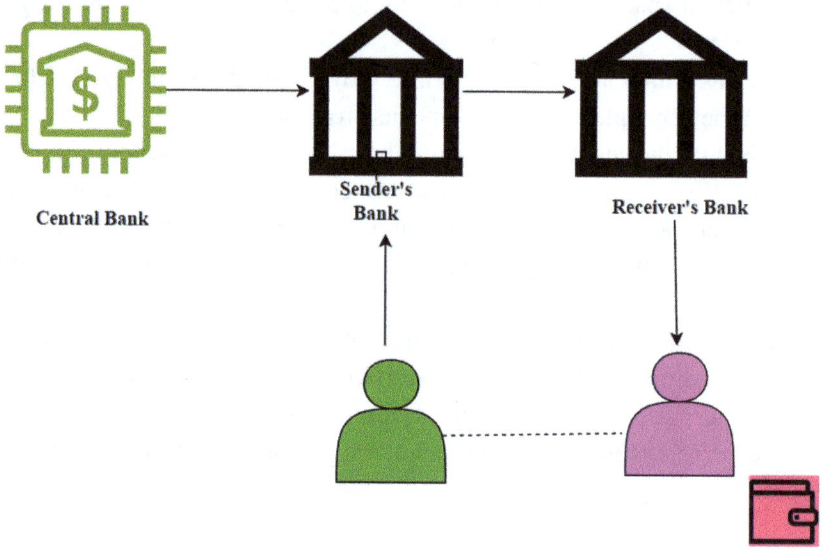

The defining characteristic of the three-tier model is the involvement of a third layer- specialized payment service providers (PSPs), fintech companies, or digital wallet providers (Tier 3). These Tier 3 entities acquire CBDC from the Tier 2 banks and are primarily responsible for providing the customer-facing services, such as digital wallets, payment interfaces, and value-added applications. This model aims to foster greater innovation and competition in retail services, leverage existing fintech expertise, potentially broaden reach for financial inclusion, and allow commercial banks to focus on their core functions while still maintaining a robust and regulated CBDC ecosystem.

6. MONETARY POLICY TRANSMISSION THROUGH CBDC

The introduction of a CBDC could significantly alter and enhance the way monetary policy is transmitted through the economy. Rather than solely depending on commercial banks as the primary conduit, a CBDC provides the central bank with new and more direct channels to influence the money supply and interest rates. This section's main goal is to distinguish between CBDC and Cryptocurrencies, then explain how monetary policy works from both the policymakers' and the customers' perspectives and then discuss the benefits to both parties. (Das, 2023) states that the impact of CBDC on Monetary Policy depends strongly on both the design of CBDC (such as whether it pays interest) and country-specific economic characteristics. CBDCs can enhance financial inclusion, provide a stable digital payment method, and potentially serve as a monetary anchor in increasing cashless economies. While transmission effects are likely small in normal times, the influence of CBDCs grows in environments of low interest rates or financial stress. Overall, CBDCs have complex implications for bank funding, profits, financial stability, wholesale funding and the effectiveness of central banks' policy tools.

(Chen, H., & Siklos, P. L. 2022) distinguishes between a narrow CBDC, which primarily replaces physical cash and a broader CBDC that includes deposit-like features, noting that the narrow version is more likely to be deployed first. Drawing on historical data and cross-country evidence, the paper explores the hypothetical impact of CBDC on inflation and financial stability. The introduction of CBDC has brought changes in all channels of monetary policy, such as interest rate channels, capacity of bank lending, asset prices, and exchange risks. The transmission of CBDC has brought drastic changes in the macro environment, i.e., it acts as a competitor to deposit funding[22], encourages wholesale funding[23], reduces the bank profits and promotes financial inclusion, universal access and encourages de-dollarization[24]. The use of CBDC promotes financial inclusion by providing liquidity[25], lower transaction costs, reducing intermediation, a simple user interface and promoting a two-sided market[26], and advanced privacy and security. The efficiency of CBDC has been improved because of its efficiency, Competition[27] and Resilience[28]. Still, for the successful implementation of CBDC, the central bank should promote awareness and digital literacy programs and other infrastructure required for the advancement. On the other hand, CBDC has been exposed to a broad range of threats since it has been digitalized, and the type of risk exposed associated with it is known as cyber risk, and the way it is withstanding itself in the market is known as cyber resilience- CIA framework- Confidentiality, integrity, and Availability(Das et al., 2023). The author examines the cybersecurity and resilience challenges faced by CBDC ecosystems. With over 100 central banks exploring CBDCs, the authors emphasize the urgent need for a cyber resilience framework before widespread adoption. They highlight that CBDCs not only create new vulnerabilities but also magnify existing risks in national payment systems. (Bharath, 2024). This paper emphasizes that CBDC systems should be built with CFM (Capital Flow Management) by leveraging the programmability of digital payment infrastructures to make policy enforcement more efficient and targeted than traditional methods. These notes highlight that implementing CFM via CBDCs requires strong coordination among central banks to establish common standards and practices. It also stresses that CBDC-enabled CFNs should complement, not replace, existing policy tools, ensuring a balanced approach in the evolving digital era (He et al., 2023). In this paper, the author explores how CBDC can foster financial inclusion, especially in emerging and low-income economies, by providing a risk-free, widely accepted form of digital money that can bridge access gaps. Features like offline payment capability, wide accessibility, and potentially lower transaction costs make CBDC particularly useful in reaching the unbanked and underbanked; when well designed, they serve as entry points into the broader formal financial system. However, the note cautions that CBDCs' practical experience is necessary to fully realize their inclusive potential (Lannquist, 2023).

This note examines how retail central bank digital currencies (CBDCs), designed primarily for households and non-financial firms, can be structured to support and enhance cross-border payment systems. It emphasizes that, much like other payment systems, CBDCs can reduce frictions in cross-border transactions by offering a safe, liquid central bank money and minimizing reliance on multiple intermediaries, thereby lowering settlement risk. While the core design approach is not fundamentally different from conventional systems, the public money nature of retail CBDCs means that central banks may take a more central and active role. Drawing on experiments and empirical work, the note outlines key design and policy considerations to ensure retail CBDCs are compatible with seamless and efficient cross-border transactions. (Reslow, 2024)

Abad et al. (2025) find that introducing a central bank digital currency (CBDC) leads to a contraction in commercial bank deposits. If the decline is large, it causes a reduction in reserves and prompts increased recourse to central bank credit. CBDCs have the potential to change a central bank's operating model, moving it from a floor system to a corridor or ceiling system, which would impact credit markets, investments and overall economic output. While CBDCs are built on technologies like Distributed Ledger Technology (DLT) and smart contracts, more research is needed to determine the best way to implement them and their broader ecosystem, which includes central banks, commercial banks, developers and the regulators. This study also examines how blockchain is revolutionizing supply chain finance. This research indicates that blockchain improves the transparency, security, and efficiency of financial transactions, fostering greater trust among all the participants. However, the study also identifies significant barriers to its adoption, such as technological constraints, difficulties with integration and challenges in managing data governance.

6.1 Monetary Policy Transmission-From the Point of View of the Central Bank

From a central bank's perspective, monetary policy transmission describes how its decisions, such as adjusting interest rates, are passed through the financial system and ultimately influence the broader economy. Monetary Policy Transmission is a way in which the central bank guides the economy towards its primary objectives of keeping prices stable (low inflation) and promoting healthy growth. Essentially, it is the mechanism the central bank uses to translate its policy signals into real-world economic outcomes.

6.1.1 Inflation Control:

Inflation control is generally managed through two main approaches: a traditional method and a modern one. The traditional method directly combats inflation by raising interest rates and increasing bank reserve requirements. This action reduces the amount of money circulating in the economy. As the money supply tightens, inflationary pressures decrease, which promotes greater financial stability and, in the long run run, supports economic growth.

- **Flexible Fund Pooling:** The central bank can gather funds as customers choose to invest, allowing for a more dynamic and responsive approach.
- **Non-Remunerable Nature:** A key advantage of pooling funds using a Central Bank Digital Currency (CBDC) is that the central bank is not required to pay interest on those funds. While the Central bank is still responsible for the original amount, it avoids the expense of interest payments.
- **Direct Control:** CBDC eliminates the need for intermediaries like commercial banks and other financial institutions, enabling the central bank to interact directly with individuals and commercial banks. This direct engagement provides a more streamlined and efficient way to manage monetary policy (Figure 7).

Figure 7. Monetary Policy Transmission through CBDC

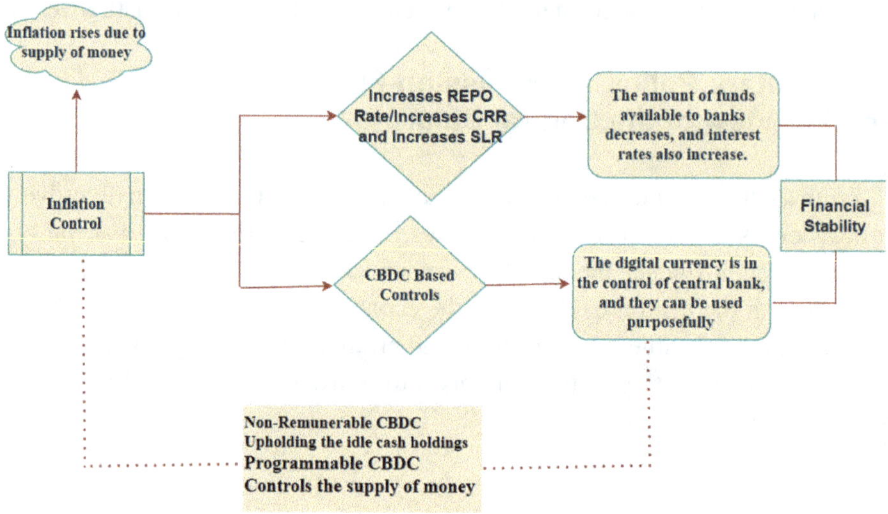

6.1.2 Deflation Control:

Deflation, characterized by a general decline in prices, can be addressed through both traditional and modern methods. The traditional approach to combating deflation involves lowering interest rates and decreasing the percentage of reserves banks are required to hold. This makes it cheaper for commercial banks to borrow money, increasing the funds available to them.

Figure 8. Monetary Policy Transmission through CBDC- Deflation Control

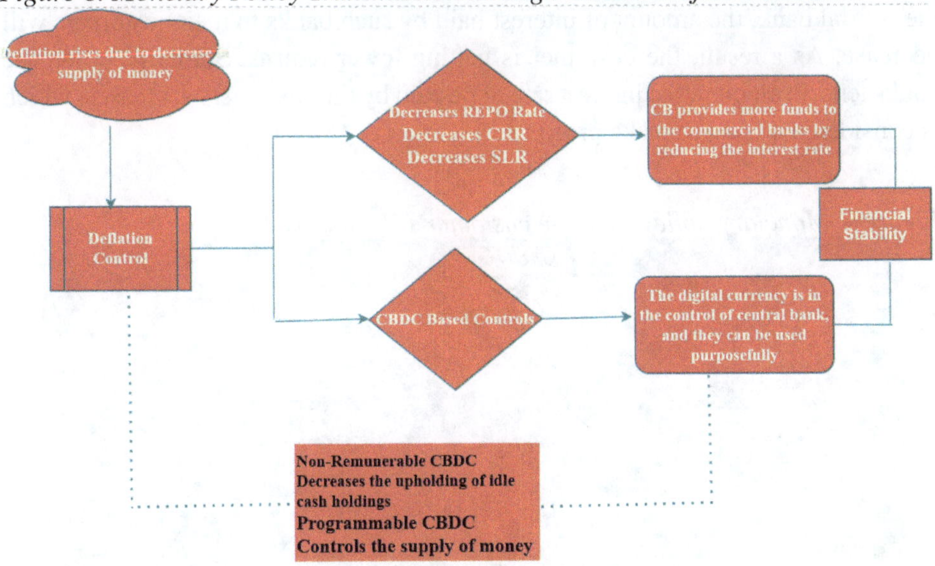

As the supply of funds in the economy expands, it counteracts deflationary pressures. Conversely, the modern method leverages Central Bank Digital Currency (CBDC) as an indirect tool to control deflation. In times of deflation, customers can use their CBDC directly based on their needs. This direct injection of funds into the economy boosts the money supply, fostering financial stability and stimulating economic growth and the same is illustrated in Figure 8.

6.2 Monetary Policy Transmission From the Customer's Point of View

Figure 9 depicts how the end customers will benefit from the introduction of modern monetary policy, i.e., CBDC-based controls. As stated earlier, the primary objectives of a monetary policy include controlling inflation and deflation. Inflation control is considered scenario 1, and deflation control is considered scenario 2. In both scenarios, the central bank has two functions: Accepting deposits and lending loans. Under scenario 1 (Inflation Control), when the small banks accept the deposits from the customers, they may not be able to pay higher interest rates to the depositors. But if a bank is large enough, it may be able to pay the interest rates to attract more deposits, thereby controlling inflation. When the banks provide loans to customers, especially during inflation control, they may charge high interest rates to their customers. So, paying high interest may cause a loss to the customers, whereas under scenario 2, i.e., deflation control, the commercial banks have two functions- accepting deposits and lending loans. When banks accept deposits from the central bank, the amount of interest paid by such banks to their customers will decrease. As a result, the customer is getting lower returns. Similarly, when the banks lend an amount, the interest rate to be paid by the customers decreases, which is considered a boon to make profits.

Figure 9. Monetary policy from the customer's Point of view

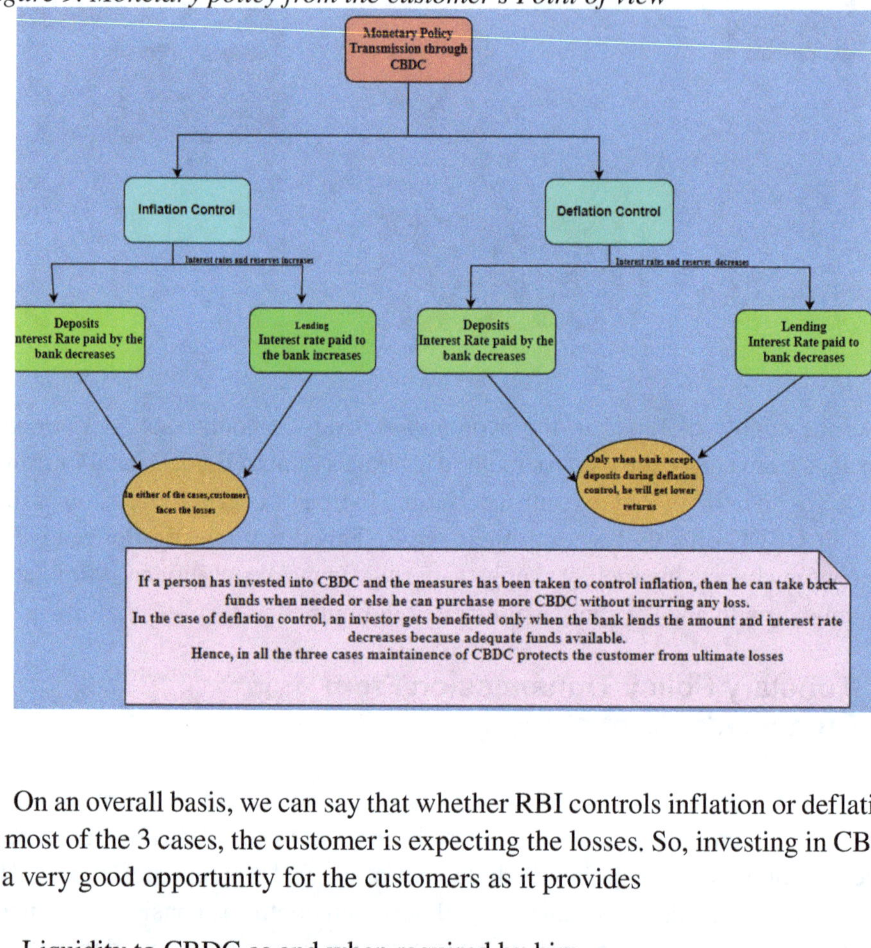

On an overall basis, we can say that whether RBI controls inflation or deflation, in most of the 3 cases, the customer is expecting the losses. So, investing in CBDC is a very good opportunity for the customers as it provides

1. Liquidity to CBDC as and when required by him
2. Safe investment when compared to investment in commercial banks.
3. Bypasses all the limitations of commercial banks.

7. FISCAL POLICY TRANSMISSION THROUGH CBDC

Building upon the preceding discussion of fiscal policy's core components (Revenue Expenditure, Revenue Income, Capital Income, and Capital Expenditure), this section transitions to an examination of the various deficits inherent in fiscal policy. Furthermore, it explores how the distinct characteristics of Central Bank Digital Currency (CBDC) can contribute to mitigating these fiscal imbalances. Table 3 highlights the types of deficits that a fiscal policy possesses.

1. Revenue Deficit = Revenue Expenditure > Revenue Income
2. Fiscal Deficit arises when the government's total spending—which includes both its routine (revenue) and investment (capital) expenditures—is greater than its total earnings, encompassing both revenue and capital income.
3. Capital account deficit = Capital Expenditure > Capital Income

Table 3. Types of Deficits

	Categories:	Formulae:
Expenditures	Revenue Expenditure (A) 1. Pensions 2. Salaries to the government employees 3. Disbursement of funds	• A+B = Total Expenditure(E) • C+D = Total Income(F) • If E>F= Fiscal Deficit • Fiscal Deficit – Interest payments made by the government = Primary Deficit
	Capital Expenditure (B) 1. Army, Defence, and Navy 2. Construction of roads and dams	
Revenue	**Revenue Income (C)** 1. Tax Revenue **2.** Non-Tax Revenue	• A-C = Revenue Deficit • B-D = Capital Account Deficit
	Capital Income(D) 1. Sale of government assets **2.** Revenue from public sector units and other establishment units	

7.1 Characteristics of CBDC That Impact Components of Fiscal Policy

Table 4 details key characteristics of Central Bank Digital Currency (CBDC), specifically Authorization, Efficiency, Inclusion, Programmability, and Universal Access and their potential impact on the transmission of fiscal policy.

Table 4. Fiscal Policy Transmission through CBDC

Characteristics of CBDC	Capital Expenditure	Capital Income	Revenue Expenditure	Revenue Income
Authorization	Optimizes	Enhances	optimize	Enhances
Efficiency	Minimizes	Maximizes	Minimization	Maximizes
Inclusion	No effect	No effect	Maximizes	Maximizes
Programmability	Enhances	Enhances	Enhances	Enhances
Universal Access	No effect	No effect	Maximizes	Maximizes

1. **Authorization:** Just like how public and private keys in cryptocurrency allow the owner to control their digital assets, Central Bank Digital Currency (CBDC) enables the original sender to manage how their digital currency is used. This means the owner of CBDC can set conditions or grant permission for others to use the funds. This built-in control ensures that payments reach only the intended and authorized recipients, thereby guaranteeing that funds are correctly distributed to the right individuals, leading to optimization of capital expenditure and revenue expenditure. On the other hand, since payment through CBDC is authorized, it enhances the capital income and revenue income.
2. **Efficiency**: Undoubtedly, CBDC helps to reduce overall expenditure by enabling direct and authorized fund disbursements, proving cost-effective, and offering a timely, modernized payment method. Conversely, CBDC payments are digital and centralized with the RBI; every transaction is recorded. Moreover, CBDCs enhance financial inclusion by being accessible to all, including those without a conventional bank account or residing in isolated regions, thereby creating a substantial impact.
3. **Inclusion:** A key benefit of a CBDC is its ability to promote financial inclusion. It makes financial services accessible to everyone, including those who don't have a traditional bank account or who live in remote areas, which can have a significant positive on society.
4. **Universal Access:** Central Bank Digital Currencies (CBDCs) provide several advantages for governments and economies. They can increase revenue and efficiency by promoting wider participation in the digital economy, resulting in greater government income and more streamlined, inclusive payments to citizens. Additionally, the stability and central bank of a CBDC make it an ideal tool for international transactions, helping a country increase its capital and optimize its global spending.
5. **Programmability:** One significant benefit of a CBDC is its programmability, which allows the central bank to make targeted economic interventions. By

designating funds for specific uses or individual, the central bank can ensure that money is used effectively to foster long-term economic growth and stability. Additionally, a CBDC can improve a government's tax collection efforts by simplifying the process, making it more efficient, and reducing tax evasion.

A CBDC is designed to boost a government's revenue by making tax collection more efficient and reducing tax evasion. Furthermore, its programmable nature can optimize capital expenditure by allowing funds to be used for specific purposes or under defined conditions, ensuring more targeted and effective spending. Thirdly, a CBDC facilitates the effective and transparent disbursement of funds, which in turn ensures transparent revenue expenditure by making government spending more traceable and accountable. Lastly, the technology behind CBDC enables faster settlement and reduced fraud, which ultimately contributes to optimized capital revenue by enhancing the speed and security of financial flows within the economy.

8. IMPACT OF CBDC ON MACRO-ENVIRONMENT

Business Environment[29] mainly comprises the Internal Environment[30] and External Environment [31] which is again categorized into Micro-Environment and Macro-Environment. Now, in this section, we are going to analyse how the introduction of CBDC impacts the external environment, especially the Macro-Environment. In this section, we are going to analyse how the introduction of CBDC affects the Macro-Environment.

(Cao et al., 2023) states that CBDC primarily replaces bank deposits, with low adoption levels maintaining the existing floor system, while higher adoption can shift operations to corridor or ceiling systems as reserves diminish. The macroeconomic impact operates through two channels: a reduction in average returns on household liquidity, which lowers savings and investment and a decline in bank profitability under corridor systems, which reduces equity and lending. Although GDP effects are modest, around a 0.25% decline at high adoption. The study shows that central bank strategies such as preserving reserve levels or remunerating CBDC can neutralize these outcomes, making its introduction largely macro-neutral.

Figure 10. Impact of CBDC on Macro-Environment

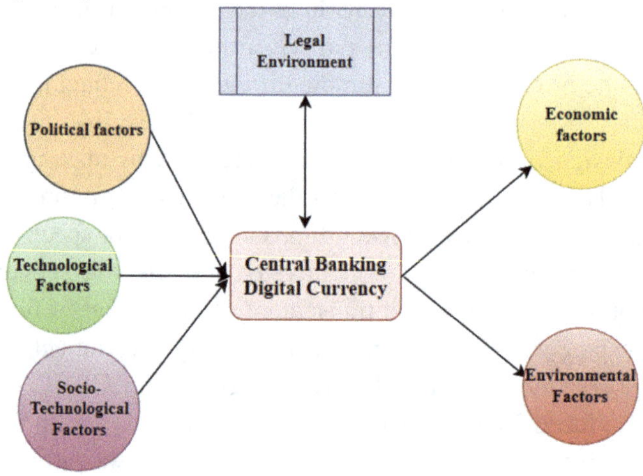

Figure 10 delineates the complex interplay between a Central Bank Digital Currency (CBDC) and the broader macro-environment. It illustrates a two-way influence: certain macro-environmental factors shape CBDC's introduction, while CBDC, in turn, impacts others. Specifically, political, socio-cultural, and technological factors (PST) are depicted as influencing the implementation of a CBDC. Conversely, the introduction of a CBDC is shown to affect economic and environmental factors. Furthermore, the legal environment presents a reciprocal relationship: it both influences the launch of a CBDC and is subsequently impacted by its introduction.

1. **Political factors:** The Reserve Bank of India (RBI) and the government generally collaborate to foster economic growth and ensure financial stability. In this partnership, the RBI often functions as the government's agent for tasks such as fund disbursement and managing treasury bills. Given that the RBI acts in this capacity and that a Central Bank Digital Currency (CBDC) would be centrally controlled by the central bank, it logically follows that the government, representing political factors, would exert significant influence over the CBDC's design and implementation. This influence may shape its regulatory framework, technological infrastructure adoption strategies, cross-border compatibility, and overall alignment with the national economic and political objectives of a country.
2. **Technological Factors:** As previously established, a Central Bank Digital Currency (CBDC) represents a modern payment system fundamentally reliant on technological infrastructure like Centralized Ledger Technology (CLT) or Distributed Ledger Technology (DLT). As the technologies underpinning

central bank digital currencies (CBDCs) are constantly changing, any CBDC system must be highly adaptable to these developments. Therefore, technological considerations will have a major on a CBDCs design, features, and continuous evolution.

3. **Socio-Technological Factors:** Public acceptance is crucial for the successful implementation of a central bank digital currency (CBDC). People who are comfortable with technology and open to new advancements are more likely to adopt a CBDC. In contrast, those resistant to change, often called "laggards," may be hesitant to trust and use digital money. This means that the broad adoption of a CBDC depends heavily on what consumers think and how behaviour changes over time, underscoring the vital role of socio-technological factors in its introduction.
4. **Economic factors:** The reserve bank of India (RBI) intends to use a central bank digital currency (CBDC) to foster economic growth and stability. As a result, introducing a CBDC is expected to have a notable impact on the country's economy.
5. **Environmental Factors:** A central bank digital currency (CBDC) has several benefits as a digital asset. It indirectly helps the environment by reducing the need for physical cash, which lowers the ecological footprint of producing, transporting, and disposing of it. Additionally, because all CBDC transactions are legally recorded, the currency promotes a healthier financial environment by deterring illegal activities, thereby fostering greater transparency between the government and its citizens.
6. **Legal Environment:** The legal framework for a central bank digital currency (CBDC) in India is shaped by the constant interaction between the reserve bank of India's (RBI) efforts to promote its use and the ultimate authority of the constitution. This dual influence means the legal environment is not just a reaction to public interest but is a dynamic system defined by both regulatory changes and constitutional limits. Furthermore, because all CBDC transactions are legally recorded, it helps create a more transparent and trustworthy financial system, which in turn aids in the fight against illegal activities.
7. **Align with sustainable goals:** The legal framework for a central bank digital currency (CBDC) in India is a dynamic system shaped by the interaction between the reserve bank of India's (RBI) regulatory authority and constitutional constraints. While the RBI can issue regulations to promote CBDC use, its power is not limitless. This ongoing balance means the legal environment is an evolving system defined by both new regulations and established constitutional boundaries, rather than simply a response to public interest. Furthermore, because all CBDC transactions are officially recorded, the currency helps create a more transparent and reliable financial system, which in turn aids in combating illegal activities. (Jan et al., 2022).

8. **Challenges and Future Trajectories of CBDC Implementation:** Launching a central bank digital currency (CBDC) is a complex undertaking that could reshape global finance, but it faces significant hurdles. These interconnected challenges include technical, economic and social issues, such as concerns about financial stability, operational difficulties for banks, and the need to create new regulations. Although many pilot programs are underway, the slow pace of widespread CBDC implementation highlights the need for a comprehensive and collaborative strategy to address these multifaceted problems.
    1. **Cybersecurity and Public Trust:** As a digital asset, a CBDC's cybersecurity is a top priority. Due to its high vulnerability to sophisticated cyberattacks, a CBDC system must be designed with Cyber resilience. The ability to anticipate, withstand, and recover from threats. This is not only a technical requirement but also essential for gaining public trust. A single security breach could severely damage confidence in the CBDC, making robust security a core operational necessity.
    2. **Digital Literacy and adoption:** For a central bank digital currency (CBDC) to succeed, public awareness and digital literacy are essential. Central banks must educate the public and create user-friendly systems to encourage adoption. A strategic guide for this process is the REDI framework, which outlines four key elements for a successful rollout.
    3. **REDI Framework for adoption:** The REDI framework is a strategic guide for a successful central bank digital currency (CBDC) rollout, consisting of four interconnected elements.
        - Regulation – Creating clear rules to govern the operations
        - Education- Promoting adoption through effective awareness campaigns.
        - Design- Develop a user-friendly and technically robust CBDC tailored to specific needs.
        - Incentives: Offering incentives to the people (Public and business houses) for the usage of CBDC.

9. FUTURE SCOPE AND DIRECTIONS

Current research on CBDC is exploring several key areas. A major focus is on improving efficiency by using new technologies like Distributed Ledger Technology and Smart Contracts.

1. **Cross-border payments:** An additional significant trend in CBDC design is the focus on cross-border payments. To facilitate seamless international transactions,

central banks must incorporate interoperability from the outset, addressing key factors such as access, currency exchange, and regulatory compliance.

2. **Trade-off between data and privacy:** There is a crucial research area focused on the balance between data collection and privacy. While a CBDC can produce useful data for economic policy, this digital trail also raises significant privacy issues. Central banks must address these concerns to keep the public's trust in the new currency.
3. **Credit Creation and User Adoption Patterns:** Further research on central bank digital currencies (CBDC) should focus on several key areas. Further investigation is needed into the disintermediation risk, which is the potential for a CBDC to bypass traditional commercial banks. Researchers also need to explore the risk of bank runs, where large numbers of people might quickly withdraw their money from banks and convert it into a CBDC during a financial crisis. Another vital area of study is the overall impact a CBDC could have on credit creation. Additionally, a better understand of user adoption patterns and the factors that influence them I crucial for a successful rollout.
4. **Socio-economic implications:** Our understanding of the full implications of a central bank digital currency (CBDC) is still evolving, which means that policy in this area must be adaptive and iterative. Policymaking should be informed by ongoing research and real-world pilot results. Future research should focus not only on technical advancements but also on the socio-economic impacts, cross-border interoperability, and the delicate balance between data utility for policy and individual privacy. This underscores the dynamic nature of the CBDC landscape and the continuous need for scholarly inquiry to guide effective policy.

A paper by Singh & Yadav (2025) offers a thorough review of existing literature to understand the factors affecting the adoption of digital currencies. The study analyses major drivers, including institutional trust, the regulatory environment, and the usability and security of the technology. The authors point out gaps in current research and suggest future directions, advocating for the exploration of new contexts and the use of more diverse research methods. Ultimately, the paper serves as a guide for policymakers and researchers aiming to increase the adoption of digital currencies.

10. CONCLUSION

Interest in central bank digital currencies (CBDCs) is rapidly increasing among policymakers, researchers, and financial institutions globally. However, this progress is fuelled by advanced technologies such as DLT, and smart contracts and these tools are being explored to make CBDC systems more efficient, transparent and resilient. They have the potential to reduce the transaction time and cost while increasing security, which will entirely change the way payments are made within and across borders.

A significant focus of this research is the cross-border implications. Since the global economy is so interconnected, interoperability must be a priority from the very beginning of a CBDC's design. This means creating effective ways to convert currencies, ensuring fair access to everyone and following strict rules like AML (Anti-Money Laundering) and Counter-terrorism financing (CTF). Without these measures, CBDCs could create a fragmented system that harms rather than helps in global financial integration.

CBDCs inherently create a digital record of all the transactions, which can generate valuable real-time economic data. This information could help the central banks improve monetary policy by providing better insights into economic trends. However, it suffers from several concerns, such as individual privacy and data security. Finding the right balance between using this data is crucial for building public trust, widespread adoption, transparent governance, robust encryption and clear data protection laws will be essential.

In short, CBDC research is advancing on three main pillars- technology, cross-border functionality and privacy. The progress in each of these areas will ultimately determine not only the effectiveness of CBDC but also its legitimacy and public acceptance. As countries move from pilot projects to full-scale launches, addressing these challenges comprehensively will be key to shaping the future of money in this digital age.

REFERENCES

Abad, J., Nuño, G., & Thomas, C. (2025). CBDC and the operational framework of monetary policy. *Journal of Monetary Economics*, *151*, 103762. DOI: 10.1016/j.jmoneco.2025.103762

Akhtar, S., Alam, M., & Ansari, M. S. (2022, November 24). Measuring the performance of the Indian banking industry: Data envelopment window analysis approach. *Benchmarking*, *29*(9), 2842–2857. DOI: 10.1108/BIJ-03-2021-0115

Akhtar, S., Alam, M., & Khan, M. M. (2021). YES Bank Fiasco: Arrogance or Negligence. Emerging Economies Cases Journal, 3(2), 95-102. (Original work published 2021)DOI: DOI: 10.1177/25166042211061003

Bharath, A. (2024). Cyber Resilience of the Central Bank Digital Currency Ecosystem. *Fintech Notes*, *2024*(003), 1. DOI: 10.5089/9798400286995.063

Cao, H., Huang, Y., Huang, Y., Yeung, B., & Zhang, X. (2023). Fintech, financial inclusion, digital currency, and CBDC. *The Journal of Financial Data Science*, *9*, 100115. DOI: 10.1016/j.jfds.2024.100115

Chen, H., & Siklos, P. L. (2022). Central bank digital currency: A review and some macro-financial implications. *Journal of Financial Stability*, *60*, 100985. DOI: 10.1016/j.jfs.2022.100985

Das, M. (2023). Implications of Central Bank Digital Currencies for Monetary Policy Transmission. *Fintech Notes*, *2023*(010), 1. DOI: 10.5089/9798400252792.063

el Armali, J. (2023). Central bank digital currency and fiscal policy in a Diamond-Dybvig Model. *Journal of Government and Economics*, *12*, 100089. DOI: 10.1016/j.jge.2023.100089

Jan, A. A., Lai, F. W., Asif, M., Akhtar, S., & Ullah, S. (2022). Embedding sustainability into bank strategy: Implications for sustainable development goals reporting. *International Journal of Sustainable Development and World Ecology*, *30*(3), 229–243. DOI: 10.1080/13504509.2022.2134230

Lannquist, A. (2023). Central Bank Digital Currency's Role in Promoting Financial Inclusion. *Fintech Notes*, *2023*(011), 1. DOI: 10.5089/9798400253331.063

Patel, M. (2024). Positioning Central Bank Digital Currency in the Payments Landscape. *Fintech Notes*, *2024*(006), 1. DOI: 10.5089/9798400289118.063

Reslow, A. (2024). Cross-Border Payments with Retail Central Bank Digital Currencies. *Fintech Notes*, *2024*(002), 1. DOI: 10.5089/9798400272035.063

Singh, V., & Yadav, M. (2025). User adoption of digital currency: A systematic review and future agenda using TCCM approach. *Central Bank Review*, *25*(1), 100183. DOI: 10.1016/j.cbrev.2024.100183

Tourpe, H. (2023). A Guide to Central Bank Digital Currency Product Development. *Fintech Notes*, *2023*(007), 1. DOI: 10.5089/9798400253690.063

Uddin, S. M. M., & Akhtar, S. (2025). Convergence in efficiency and technology gap of Indian banks: Implication of GFC and COVID-19. *Quality & Quantity*. Advance online publication. DOI: 10.1007/s11135-025-02195-7

ENDNOTES

1 **Cash Reserve Ratio:** A share of NDTL that a bank maintains with its central bank in the form of cash on a daily basis is known as the Cash Reserve Ratio.

2 **Statutory Liquidity Ratio:** A share of NDTL that a commercial bank maintains itself in the form of gold and government securities is known as Statutory Liquidity Ratio.

3 **Repo Rate:** The Interest rate charged by the RBI to commercial banks at the time of lending is called as Repo Rate.

4 **Reverse Repo Rate:** The Interest rate charged by the commercial banks from RBI is called as Reverse Repo Rate.

5 **Capital Expenditure:** Capital Expenditure is the money that a government spends on long-term projects and assets. Think of large-scale investments like building roads, dams and purchasing Défense equipment. These are typically heavy, one-time investments that are not expected to be repaid directly in the future, but they are crucial for providing long-term benefits and improving the welfare of citizens.

6 **Capital Income:** Capital receipts are funds the government receives that either create a liability (They have to be repaid) or reduce its assets. A common example is taking out a loan. Another is selling off shares in a public sector company, which reduces the government's financial assets. These are different from the recurring income the government generates from its day-to-day operations.

7 **Revenue Income:** Revenue receipts are the government's regular and recurring sources of income. They do not create a liability or decrease the government's

assets. This includes tax revenue (Money collected from direct taxes) and indirect taxes (like GST) and Non-tax revenue (Income from rendering government services (fees), profits from state-owned entities, interest on government loans, and penalties on traffic lines.

8 **Revenue Expenditure:** Revenue Expenditure is the government's recurring day-to-day spending. This type of spending is smaller than the capital expenditure and includes things like paying salaries to government employees and providing monthly pensions to senior citizens. It is the kind of spending that happens regularly to keep the government running.

9 **Gen Z**: Demographic group of people born between 1997-2012:

10 **Fourth Industrial Revolution** refers to a transformative era characterized by the fusion of various technologies, and this revolution has brought tremendous changes in the financial sector, focusing more on the digitalization of financial markets, financial institutions, financial services, and financial products.

11 **AI Bonds:** AI stocks refer to the stocks that have been issued by the companies engaged in the development of Gen AI tools in distinct fields including but not limited to health care, finance, and agriculture.

12 **Green Bonds:** Green stocks refer to the stocks issued by the CESC (Clean Energy Stock Companies), i.e., the companies whose objective is the profit maximization without harming society.

13 **Fintech Stocks:** Fintech refers to leveraging technology to provide financial services to the end users and shares issued by such companies are referred to as fintech stocks. Examples include stocks issued by Paytm, Master card Inc.

14 **Cryptocurrency:** Cryptocurrency has been defined as a digital asset leveraged on Blockchain Technology- Distributed Ledger Technology. Various cryptocurrencies have emerged, and nearly 82% of the market has been occupied by Bitcoin. Due to the tax advantage provided by cryptocurrency, a huge market has emerged, and hence it is subject to volatility.

15 **Inflation:** Inflation is characterized by a sustained decrease in the purchasing power of money, which manifests as a general increase in the prices of goods and services. This often leads to a higher demand for nominal money balances.

16 **Deflation:** Deflation, while increasing the purchasing power of money, is often considered more detrimental to an economy than inflation. It typically results in a decline in GDP growth rates and an escalation in unemployment figures.

17 **Financial inclusion:** Financial inclusion refers to making the financial services available to the people, even in rural and remote areas, by building awareness programmes for the illiterates and by providing proper technological infrastructure for its development.

18 https://www.pib.gov.in/PressReleaseIframePage.aspx?PRID=1882883

19 https://digitaldollarproject.org/wp-content/uploads/2023/08/Digital-Dollar-Project-Cross-Border-Remittance-Pilot-Paper.pdf

20 https://www.atlanticcouncil.org/blogs/econographics/a-report-card-on-chinas-central-bank-digital-currency-the-e-cny/

21 https://www.capco.com/intelligence/capco-intelligence/e-cny-and-cbdc

22 **Deposit Funding:** Because a Central Bank Digital Currency (CBDC) is directly backed by the central bank, individuals can deposit funds directly with the central bank. This could reduce the number of deposits held by commercial banks.

23 **Wholesale Funding:** Wholesale funding" refers to a significant source of capital for financial institutions, often in large amounts, used for purposes like inter-bank settlements, lending, and managing liquidity. While valuable, it also presents challenges and risks.

24 **De-dollarization:** Introduction to CBDC discourages the dependency on the foreign currency, which we refer to as de-dollarization.

25 **Liquidity:** Liquidity refers to the free conversion of physical cash into CBDC and vice versa

26 **Two-sided market-** In the circular flow of money, both individuals and business houses are interested in the adoption of CBDC, i.e., business houses are encouraging the payments and individuals are also interested because CBDC is considered a legal tender.

27 **Competition:** This refers to the unique features and benefits that make a CBDC a compelling alternative to existing forms of money (cash, commercial bank deposits, or other digital payment systems). These features aim to address shortcomings in current payment systems or offer new functionalities.

28 **Resilience:** Resilience refers to the dynamic nature of CBDC to stand out across various disruptions, including but not limited to operational disruptions, cyber disruptions, and technical disruptions.

29 **Business Environment:** Business environment comprises all external and internal factors that influence an organization's operations and profitability.

30 **Internal Environment:** The internal environment consists of elements entirely within an organization's control, such as its management, employees, and leadership style. These factors are considered unsystematic risks because they are manageable through policies and regulations and do not affect an investor's overall risk.

31 **External Environment:** The external environment encompasses factors largely beyond the organization's direct control. This includes a micro-environment, where organizations have some influence through stakeholder relationships, and a macro-environment, which significantly impacts investor risk. To mitigate risks associated with these uncontrollable macro factors, organizations commonly employ PESTLE analysis, examining Political, Economic, Socio-cultural, Technological, Legal, and Environmental influences.

Chapter 3
Global Financial Crises:
Lessons From Policy Failures and Successes

Ameya Anil Patil
https://orcid.org/0000-0002-4920-7630
Dr. Vishwanath Karad MIT World Peace University, India

Mahesh Kumar
https://orcid.org/0000-0003-3819-7868
Dr. Vishwanath Karad MIT World Peace University, India

Rajeev Sengupta
https://orcid.org/0000-0001-7451-239X
Dr. Vishwanath Karad MIT World Peace University, India

Rakesh Yadav
https://orcid.org/0000-0001-7872-3100
Prin. L.N.Welingkar Institute of Management Development and Research, India

Piyush Dixit
https://orcid.org/0009-0001-7960-1639
Indira University, India

ABSTRACT

Financial crisis have always fascinated and concerned acadmicians, finance enthusiasts and policymakers alike. and This article explores the major global financial crises, including the Great Depression, the Latin American Debt Crisis, the Asian Financial Crisis, the Global Financial Crisis and the recent COVID-19 economic shock. The causes, policy responses, and outcomes of these crises, have been discussed to provide policy lessons in the context of financial crisis. T Key

DOI: 10.4018/979-8-3373-3725-8.ch003

policy failures such as rigid monetary policies, austerity, and regulatory gaps exacerbated these economic crisis and the corresponding social damage, while .On the other hand, timely measures such as countercyclical stimulus, financial reforms, and global cooperation have facilitated recoveries during these times. This article synthesizes these insights into actionable principles for future crisis management, emphasizing swift liquidity provision, robust regulation, inclusive policies, and multilateral coordination.

1. INTRODUCTION

The trajectory of global financial crises tells a compelling story of human ambition colliding with economic reality. These episodes have been characterized by market collapses, mass unemployment, and shattered public confidence. Global financial crisis highlight the vulnerabilities inherent in interconnected financial systems and the critical role that governance plays in determining economic outcomes. From the devastating Great Depression of the 1930s through the Global Financial Crisis (GFC) of 2007–2008, to the more recent economic disruption precipitated by the COVID-19 pandemic, financial crises have repeatedly tested national resilience and challenged policymakers' capacity for innovative response. Each crisis emerges from distinct circumstances and unfolds through unique dynamics. These are characterized by the complex interaction between market failures and policy missteps, alongside the arduous process of rebuilding stability. This analysis examines these defining moments, scrutinizing both the policy failures that intensified economic devastation and the strategic successes that illuminated pathways to recovery. The authors seek to distill enduring insights that can apprise future responses to economic turbulence.

Financial crises are not a mere economic disruption, but profound human catastrophes that ripple through the fabric of society. The Great Depression rendered millions unemployed, catalyzing social upheaval and fundamentally altering political landscapes across nations. The Asian Financial Crisis of 1997–1998 transformed thriving economies into scenes of chaos, revealing critical weaknesses in rapidly globalizing markets. The GFC precipitated a worldwide recession that eliminated trillions in wealth while fostering deep institutional distrust. COVID19 pandemic highlighted the cascading effect of non-financial shocks through economic systems, compelling policymakers to respond with unprecedented speed and scale. These crisis have reinforced the profound consequences of policy choices . The decisions made by central banks, governments, and international institutions have the power to alleviate or compound suffering caused by crisis. These decisions determine whether a crisis becomes a temporary disruption or an enduring catastrophe.

This chapter focusses on three pivotal crises, viz.the Great Depression, the Asian Financial Crisis, and the GFC,while drawing instructive parallels to the COVID-19 economic shock and other recent disruptions. Each crisis investigates the intricate interplay among monetary, fiscal, and regulatory policies, exploring the factors that enabled certain interventions to succeed while others failed dramatically. The Great Depression, for instance, was prolonged by inflexible adherence to the gold standard and counterproductive fiscal austerity, yet its eventual recovery was catalyzed by the bold reforms of the New Deal. The Asian Financial Crisis demonstrated the hazards of maintaining fixed exchange rates and implementing overly rigid international bailout conditions, while simultaneously revealing the effectiveness of carefully tailored reforms and regional cooperation. The GFC exposed the risks inherent in unchecked financial complexity, yet its resolution underscored the power of coordinated global action. The COVID -19 response, meanwhile, showcased the potential of massive stimulus measures while also highlighting the risks of subsequent inflationary pressures.

The authors make an attempt to draw lessons by exploring the underlying causes of each crisis, the policy responses that shaped their evolution, and the insights they offer for future practice. They key considerations involve monetary policy's role in market stabilization, fiscal interventions impacting aggregate demand, and robust regulatory frameworks in preventing systemic collapse. Further, the global dimensions of crises have been investigated. Interconnected economies do necessitate coordinated responses, while tking due care ofdistinctive national circumstances. By synthesizing these insights, authors aim to construct a framework for navigating future crises that balances decisive action with adaptability, and strategic foresight with appropriate humility.

As financial systems evolve in complexity and global integration deepens, the potential for systemic shocks continues to expand. However, history demonstrates the potential of crisis to create opportunities for meaningful reform and institutional renewal, despite their hazardous nature(Kolte et al.,2021). The Glass-Steagall Act, the Basel accords, and regional financial safety nets have their roots in the lessons learned during past crises. Such measure have strengthened the global economic architecture. By understanding these historical experiences, policymakers can be in a better position to prevent crises where feasible, mitigate their impact when they occur, and foster sustainable recoveries.

2. HISTORY OF FINANCIAL CRISIS - THE DIFFERENT EPISODES

Financial crises, though varied in their triggers and contexts, expose the vulnerabilities of economic systems and the critical role of policy in shaping outcomes. This section examines four pivotal crises,viz.the Great Depression (1929–1939), the Latin American Debt Crisis (1980s), the Asian Financial Crisis (1997–1998), and the Global Financial Crisis (2007–2008).The authors aim to uncover the causes, policy responses, and lessons that inform modern crisis management. Each case of crisis highlights the interplay of market failures, governance decisions, and global interconnections, offering insights into how policymakers can mitigate future disruptions.

2.1 The Great Depression (1929–1939): A Cascade of Policy Missteps

The Great Depression, ignited by the U.S. stock market crash of October 1929, was a global economic catastrophe that reshaped societies and policy frameworks. While the crash—wiping out $30 billion in market value—was a trigger, deeper structural flaws fueled the crisis. Speculative excesses in the 1920s, driven by margin lending (90% loan-to-value ratios), inflated stock prices. Weak banking systems, with 20,000 U.S. banks holding fragmented reserves, were prone to runs. *Global imbalances, as Eichengreen (2015) notes, exacerbated vulnerabilities: U.S. capital exports to Europe and Latin America fueled unsustainable borrowing, while agricultural distress—wheat prices fell 50% from 1925–1929—eroded rural incomes.* Income inequality, with the top 1% holding 24% of U.S. income by 1928, concentrated wealth and fueled speculative bubbles, reducing aggregate demand as middle-class purchasing power waned. Internationally, the gold standard constrained monetary flexibility, tying currencies to finite gold reserves. By 1933, U.S. GDP had contracted by 30%, industrial production plummeted 47%, and unemployment hit 25%. Global trade collapsed, with exports falling 66% by 1934, as nations turned inward.

Policy Failures

The Great Depression's severity was amplified by flawed policy responses, showcasing profound mismanagement. The U.S. Federal Reserve, constrained by the gold standard, tightened monetary policy to defend the dollar's peg, reducing liquidity as banks collapsed. Between 1930 and 1933, over 9,000 U.S. banks failed, erasing $7 billion in deposits. Friedman and Schwartz (1963) argue the Fed's failure to counter deflation, which reached 10% annually, crushed real wages and deepened debt burdens. By not acting as a lender of last resort, the Fed allowed bank runs to spiral, eroding public trust. Governments pursued fiscal austerity, cutting spending and raising taxes amid collapsing demand. The U.S. Revenue Act of 1932 raised taxes, stifling consumption, while deflation, with prices falling 25% by 1933, crushed debtors and businesses as real debt burdens soared. The Smoot-Hawley Tariff Act of 1930 raised tariffs on 20,000 goods, prompting retaliatory tariffs worldwide, causing a 66% decline in global trade and strangling export-dependent economies like Canada and Argentina. The gold standard also fostered competitive devaluations and gold hoarding, exacerbating global financial instability. The 1931 collapse of Germany's banking system, following Austria's Creditanstalt failure, spread panic across Europe, with German industrial output dropping 40%. The lack of international coordination worsened this contagion.

Policy Successes

Recovery began in 1933 with President Franklin D. Roosevelt's New Deal, marking a shift to bold intervention. The U.S. suspended the gold standard in 1933, devaluing the dollar by 40%, which boosted exports, enabled monetary expansion, stabilized prices, and eased debt burdens. The Banking Act of 1933 established the Federal Deposit Insurance Corporation (FDIC), insuring deposits and restoring public confidence, while the Glass-Steagall Act separated commercial and investment banking to curb speculation. New Deal programs, such as the Works Progress Administration (WPA), employed 8 million people, constructing 650,000 miles of roads and 125,000 public buildings. Roosevelt's fireside chats, reaching 80% of U.S. households, rebuilt trust, countering Keynes's "animal spirits" of fear. The Civilian Conservation Corps provided jobs to 3 million young men, helping reduce unemployment from 25% to 14% by 1937. The Reciprocal Trade Agreements Act of 1934 lowered tariffs with 20 countries, increasing U.S. exports by 40% by 1939 and aiding global recovery. The 1936 Tripartite Agreement between the U.S., UK, and France stabilized currencies, easing trade tensions and fostering modest global growth.

Lessons

The Great Depression highlighted the perils of rigid monetary policies, austerity during downturns, and protectionism. It underscored the need for central banks to act as lenders of last resort and for countercyclical fiscal policy to boost demand. *The crisis also revealed the role of psychological factors, with public confidence critical to recovery, and the need to address inequality to sustain demand.* The gold standard's collapse paved the way for flexible exchange rate regimes, a cornerstone of modern monetary policy.

2.2 The Latin American Debt Crisis (1980s): Sovereign Debt and External Shocks

The Latin American Debt Crisis, beginning with Mexico's default in August 1982, was a pivotal episode of sovereign debt distress that engulfed countries like Brazil, Argentina, and Venezuela. Fueled by the 1970s oil shocks, petrodollar recycling saw Western banks lend $327 billion to Latin America by 1982, often at variable interest rates. *High U.S. interest rates, raised to 20% by 1981 to curb inflation, increased debt servicing costs, with Mexico's debt rising from 30% to 50% of GDP.* Commodity price collapses—oil fell 40% from 1980–1982—slashed export revenues for oil-dependent economies. Weak governance and overborrowing, often for unproductive projects, exacerbated vulnerabilities. By 1983, 16 Latin American countries had defaulted or rescheduled debts, with regional GDP contracting 2.8% and unemployment rising to 12%.

Policy Failures

Governments in Latin America borrowed heavily without hedging against interest rate or commodity price risks, leading to severe economic vulnerabilities. Argentina's debt doubled to $45 billion by 1982, with much of it misallocated to military spending. IMF bailouts, such as Mexico's $3.9 billion package, imposed austerity measures that required cutting public spending and devaluing currencies. In Brazil, these measures slashed real wages by 20%, triggering riots, while the IMF's emphasis on fiscal discipline overlooked social costs, causing poverty rates to rise 10% across the region. The U.S. Federal Reserve's interest rate hikes further strained economies, as 70% of Latin American loans were dollar-denominated, creating an external shock beyond regional control and exposing global interdependence. Early responses also failed to address debt restructuring, delaying relief and prolonging stagnation. Banks resisted write-offs to avoid losses, while governments grappled with capital flight, exacerbating the crisis.

Policy Successes

The 1989 Brady Plan, supported by the U.S., restructured $191 billion in debt by offering bonds with reduced principal or interest, significantly easing financial pressures. Mexico's debt service costs dropped 30%, freeing resources for economic growth, and by 1994, regional GDP growth reached 4%. Countries like Chile adopted market-oriented reforms, privatizing state-owned firms and boosting exports, which drove Chile's GDP growth to 6% annually by the late 1980s. Regional cooperation through the 1984 Cartagena Group enhanced Latin America's bargaining power in debt negotiations with creditors, fostering collective resilience. Argentina's 1991 Convertibility Plan pegged the peso to the dollar, taming hyperinflation that had reached 3,000% in 1989 and restoring investor confidence, stabilizing the economy.

Lessons

The Latin American Debt Crisis underscored the dangers of unhedged foreign debt and external shocks like U.S. monetary policy shifts. *It highlighted the social costs of austerity, with IMF programs often exacerbating inequality.* The Brady Plan showed the value of debt restructuring, while regional cooperation offered a model for collective action. The crisis emphasized the need for prudent debt management and diversified economies to reduce commodity dependence.

2.3 The Asian Financial Crisis (1997–1998): Contagion and Structural Flaws

The Asian Financial Crisis erupted in July 1997 when Thailand devalued the baht, unable to defend its dollar peg. The crisis spread to Indonesia, South Korea, Malaysia, and the Philippines, driven by speculative attacks, capital flight ($100 billion exited in 1997), and collapsing asset prices. *Radelet and Sachs (1998) highlight "herd behavior," with investors fleeing emerging markets indiscriminately.* GDP contracted 5–15% across affected countries, and 20 million jobs were lost. Structural weaknesses fueled the crisis: overreliance on short-term foreign debt ($200 billion in Southeast Asia), weak financial regulation, and crony capitalism. *Thailand's real estate bubble, absorbing 30% of GDP in loans, collapsed as vacancies soared.* Rapid 1990s capital inflows fueled asset bubbles, while fixed exchange rates encouraged unhedged borrowing. *Urban migration strained financial systems, with 50% of Thailand's population urban by 1997, increasing credit demand.* Falling export growth, as China's devalued yuan undercut competitors, triggered investor panic.

Policy Failures

Fixed exchange rate policies in Asia encouraged excessive foreign borrowing, but central banks struggled to maintain them. Thailand's central bank exhausted $24 billion in reserves defending the baht, and forced devaluations, such as Indonesia's rupiah plummeting 80%, triggered widespread debt defaults. IMF bailouts totaling $110 billion to Thailand, Indonesia, and South Korea imposed high interest rates and austerity measures. Stiglitz (1999) criticized these policies, highlighting how Indonesia's bankruptcy rate surged 50% as interest rates reached 70%, leading to a 13.1% GDP decline and riots that killed 1,200 people. Weak financial oversight exacerbated the crisis, with lax regulations allowing banks to accumulate non-performing loans, which accounted for 20% of Thai bank assets. South Korea's chaebols amassed $150 billion in foreign debt with debt-to-equity ratios of 500%, amplifying vulnerabilities. Policymakers underestimated the risk of contagion, as panic-driven investor withdrawals caused Malaysia's ringgit to fall 40% despite stronger economic fundamentals. Malaysia's rejection of IMF bailouts in favor of capital controls reflected regional distrust of external solutions.

Policy Successes

Adopting flexible exchange rates helped restore competitiveness in countries like Thailand and South Korea. South Korea's exports increased 12% by 1999, contributing to a 10.9% GDP growth rate. Financial restructuring efforts stabilized economies, with South Korea reducing chaebol debt ratios to 200% and injecting $130 billion to recapitalize banks. Thailand's TAMC bad bank absorbed $30 billion in non-performing loans, strengthening the financial sector. Regional cooperation through the Chiang Mai Initiative (2000) established a $120 billion currency swap network, reducing dependence on the IMF, while ASEAN's trade integration increased intra-regional exports by 20% by 2000. Malaysia's 1998 capital controls, which pegged the ringgit and restricted capital outflows, enabled lower interest rates, resulting in a GDP contraction of only 7.4%, significantly less severe than Indonesia's 13.1%.

Lessons

The Asian Financial Crisis exposed the risks of fixed exchange rates, short-term foreign debt, and weak regulation in open capital markets. *It highlighted the social costs of austerity, with Indonesia's poverty rate rising 20% due to weak safety nets.* The IMF's one-size-fits-all approach often failed, while Malaysia's controls showed tailored policies could succeed. Regional cooperation and financial restructuring offered models for resilience, emphasizing diversified exports and social protections.

2.4 The Global Financial Crisis (2007–2008): Systemic Risk and Global Response

The Global Financial Crisis (GFC), sparked by the U.S. subprime mortgage collapse in 2007, was the most severe crisis since the Great Depression. Global markets froze by 2008, with U.S. GDP contracting 4.3% and world trade falling 10% in 2009. The crisis stemmed from excessive risk-taking: subprime lending ($1.5 trillion in loans), complex mortgage-backed securities (MBS), and over-leveraged banks. *Rajan's (2010) "fault lines" highlight U.S. household debt (130% of income by 2007) and global imbalances (China's $400 billion trade surplus).* Shadow banking, with $10 trillion in unregulated assets, amplified risks. Regulatory gaps, misaligned incentives (e.g., banker bonuses tied to short-term gains), and rating agencies' AAA ratings on toxic MBS misled investors. *The crisis hit hardest in low-income U.S. communities, where 20% of subprime borrowers were minorities.*

Policy Failures

Regulatory oversights significantly contributed to the 2008 financial crisis. The SEC's 2004 rule permitted banks like Lehman Brothers to operate with leverage ratios as high as 30:1, amplifying risks. The 1999 repeal of Glass-Steagall enabled speculative banking practices, blurring lines between commercial and investment activities. Rating agencies misjudged mortgage-backed securities (MBS), with 90% of AAA-rated securities downgraded by 2009, undermining market trust. The Federal Reserve's decision to maintain 1% interest rates from 2002 to 2004 fueled a housing bubble, driving U.S. home prices up 80% and encouraging risky subprime lending. Inconsistent crisis responses further destabilized markets; the 2008 collapse of Lehman Brothers, following the bailout of Bear Stearns, triggered $12 trillion in global market losses due to the absence of a clear "too big to fail" policy, sparking widespread panic. In the Eurozone, the single currency restricted monetary flexibility, exacerbating crises in countries like Greece, where debt reached 120% of GDP by 2010. Austerity measures deepened Greece's recession by 25%, while delays by the ECB and IMF allowed contagion to spread to Ireland and Spain.

Policy Successes

Coordinated monetary easing helped stabilize the global economy. The Federal Reserve cut interest rates to near zero and injected $2 trillion in liquidity through the Term Auction Facility, while swap lines with 14 central banks alleviated dollar shortages. The ECB and Bank of England expanded asset purchases, further calming markets. Bank bailouts and stress tests restored financial stability; the U.S. TARP program, allocating $700 billion, recapitalized banks, with 95% repaid by 2014. Stress tests in 2009 enhanced transparency, boosting investor confidence. Europe's EFSF, established in 2010, provided support to struggling peripheral economies. Fiscal stimulus measures mitigated economic decline, with the U.S. Recovery Act ($787 billion) and China's $586 billion package, which included building 20,000 km of high-speed rail, sustaining global demand. The G20's 2009 commitment of $1 trillion to the IMF bolstered global financial safety nets, helping limit U.S. unemployment to a peak of 10%, lower than anticipated. Regulatory reforms, including the Dodd-Frank Act of 2010, raised capital requirements and established the Consumer Financial Protection Bureau, while Basel III mandated 7% bank capital ratios, reducing systemic risks.

Lessons

The GFC emphasized robust regulation, coordinated global responses, and decisive intervention to prevent systemic collapse. *It highlighted inequality, with low-income households losing 30% of wealth, necessitating inclusive recoveries.* Shadow banking and complex instruments underscored the need for transparency and macroprudential oversight. The Eurozone's struggles showed the limits of monetary unions without fiscal integration, while G20 coordination set a model for global action.

3. RECENT CRISES: THE COVID-19 PANDEMIC (2020–2022)

The COVID-19 pandemic, which began in early 2020, triggered an unprecedented economic crisis, distinct from prior financial crises due to its origin in a non-financial, exogenous shock—a global health emergency. Unlike the Great Depression or the Global Financial Crisis (GFC), which stemmed from financial imbalances or market failures, the pandemic's economic impact was driven by government-imposed lockdowns, supply chain disruptions, and shifts in consumer behavior. Global GDP contracted by 3.4% in 2020, marking the deepest global recession since World War II (IMF, 2021). The crisis exposed vulnerabilities in interconnected economies, particularly in sectors reliant on physical proximity, such as tourism, hospitality, and retail, which saw revenue declines of up to 50% in some regions (Yu et al.,2021) .Supply chain bottlenecks, notably in semiconductors and shipping, disrupted manufacturing, with global trade volumes falling 8.2% in 2020 (World Bank, 2021).

The crisis's roots lay in the rapid spread of the SARS-CoV-2 virus, which prompted governments to impose lockdowns to curb infections. By April 2020, over 90% of the world's population lived under some form of mobility restriction (Hale et al., 2021). These measures halted economic activity, slashing demand and supply simultaneously. In the U.S., retail sales fell 16.4% in April 2020, while global air travel plummeted 94% (IATA, 2020). Labor markets bore a severe brunt: the International Labour Organization (2020) estimated a loss of 255 million full-time-equivalent jobs globally, with low-income and informal workers—often women and minorities—disproportionately affected. Unlike financial crises driven by speculative bubbles or debt, the pandemic's economic shock was a direct result of policy choices to prioritize public health, revealing the delicate balance between human welfare and economic stability.

Global interconnections amplified the crisis. Just-in-time supply chains, optimized for efficiency, faltered as factory closures in China rippled through global production. Semiconductor shortages delayed automobile production, reducing global car output by 16 million units in 2021 .Commodity prices, initially depressed by falling demand (oil prices briefly turned negative in April 2020), surged as economies reopened, with natural gas prices in Europe rising 400% by late 2021 (IEA, 2022). Financial markets, initially resilient due to pre-existing liquidity, faced volatility: the S&P 500 fell 34% in March 2020 before recovering, driven by unprecedented policy interventions (Bloomberg, 2020). The crisis also exposed inequalities, as wealthier households, able to work remotely, accumulated savings, while low-income groups faced job losses and food insecurity, with global extreme poverty rising for the first time in decades by 88 million people (World Bank, 2020).

3.1 Policy Responses

Policymakers responded with extraordinary speed and scale, deploying monetary, fiscal, and regulatory measures to prevent a financial collapse and cushion economic losses. These interventions, while unprecedented, drew on lessons from past crises, particularly the GFC's emphasis on liquidity and coordinated action.

Monetary Policy, which witnessed Unprecedented Liquidity was a major response .Central banks acted decisively to stabilize financial markets and support lending. The U.S. Federal Reserve cut interest rates to near zero (0–0.25%) in March 2020 and launched unlimited quantitative easing, expanding its balance sheet from $4.2 trillion in 2019 to $8.9 trillion by 2022 (Federal Reserve, 2022). Programs like the Main Street Lending Facility and Corporate Credit Facilities supported businesses and municipalities, injecting $2.3 trillion into markets. The European Central Bank (ECB) expanded its Pandemic Emergency Purchase Programme (PEPP) by €1.85 trillion, while the Bank of Japan and Bank of England scaled up asset purchases (ECB, 2021). Currency swap lines, extended to 14 central banks, eased dollar shortages in emerging markets, preventing a repeat of the Asian Financial Crisis's capital flight (BIS, 2020).These measures stabilized markets but had limits. Low interest rates fueled asset price inflation, with U.S. home prices rising 18% in 2021, exacerbating affordability issues (Case-Shiller, 2022). Emerging markets, reliant on dollar-denominated debt, faced pressures as the dollar strengthened, with countries like Turkey seeing currency depreciations of 40% (Tsang, 2023).Central banks also faced a dilemma: prolonged loose policy risked inflation, yet premature tightening could choke recovery, a tension that became evident in 2022.

In tune with monetary policy, even fiscal policies saw historic stimulus.Governments unleashed massive fiscal packages, dwarfing GFC-era interventions. The U.S. passed the $2.2 trillion CARES Act in March 2020, providing $1,200 direct payments to individuals, enhanced unemployment benefits (adding $600 weekly), and $500 billion for businesses via the Paycheck Protection Program (PPP). Subsequent packages, including the $1.9 trillion American Rescue Plan (2021), pushed U.S. fiscal support to 25% of GDP (CBO, 2021). The European Union launched the €750 billion NextGenerationEU fund, focusing on green and digital transitions, while Japan's ¥117 trillion package supported wages and healthcare (IMF, 2021). Globally, fiscal measures totaled $16 trillion, or 15% of global GDP, by mid-2021 (IMF, 2021).These programs mitigated economic collapse. U.S. unemployment, peaking at 14.7% in April 2020, fell to 3.9% by late 2021, aided by stimulus (BLS, 2022). In Germany, the Kurzarbeit program preserved 10 million jobs, limiting unemployment spikes. However, fiscal largesse fueled demand amid supply constraints, contributing to inflation. By mid-2022, U.S. consumer prices rose 8.5%, the highest in 40 years, driven by energy, food, and housing costs (BLS, 2022). Uneven distribution also widened inequality: wealthier households saved stimulus checks, boosting stock and real estate markets, while low-income groups faced rising costs (Chetty et al., 2020).

Regulators adopted flexible measures to maintain financial stability. The Basel Committee eased bank capital requirements, allowing banks to lend $5 trillion more globally (FSB, 2020). Loan moratoria and debt repayment pauses prevented widespread defaults, particularly in small businesses, with 60% of U.S. small firms receiving PPP loans .Governments also supported supply chains, with the U.S. invoking the Defense Production Act to boost medical supply production (FEMA, 2020). Vaccine rollouts, accelerated by public-private partnerships, restored economic confidence, with 60% of the global population vaccinated by mid-2022 (WHO, 2022).However, regulatory forbearance risked masking underlying weaknesses. Non-performing loans in Europe rose to €400 billion by 2022, as moratoria ended (EBA, 2022). Supply chain interventions were often reactive, failing to address structural vulnerabilities like reliance on single-source suppliers. Vaccine inequities, with low-income countries receiving only 10% of doses by 2021, prolonged global recovery (UNICEF, 2021).

The response to the COVID-19 pandemic prevented a deeper economic crisis through swift and large-scale interventions. Monetary and fiscal measures stabilized financial markets, enabling the S&P 500 to recover its March 2020 losses by August and keeping global banking systems intact, unlike the bank failures during the Global Financial Crisis (Bloomberg, 2020). Unemployment spikes were less prolonged than in previous crises, and global growth rebounded by 6.1% in 2021 (IMF, 2021). Enhanced unemployment benefits and direct payments cushioned household incomes, reducing U.S. poverty rates from 11.8% in 2019 to 8.8% in 2021 (Census Bureau, 2021). Programs like India's PM Garib Kalyan Yojana delivered food and cash to 800 million people, mitigating hunger (World Bank, 2021). The G20's Debt Service Suspension Initiative (DSSI) paused $12.9 billion in debt payments for 48 low-income countries, easing fiscal pressures, while COVAX aimed to distribute 2 billion vaccine doses, though delivery fell short. These efforts reflected the multilateralism seen during the Global Financial Crisis but highlighted gaps in equitable access. Public-private partnerships accelerated vaccine development, with mRNA vaccines achieving 95% efficacy (Pfizer, 2020), and a 25% surge in global e-commerce sustained economic activity (UNCTAD, 2021).

3.2 Policy Challenges

Despite these achievements, the response faced significant obstacles and unintended consequences. Prolonged monetary and fiscal stimulus, coupled with supply chain disruptions, drove global inflation to 8.8% by 2022, eroding real wages and triggering cost-of-living crises (IMF, 2022). Central banks, including the Federal Reserve, faced criticism for initially dismissing inflation as "transitory" and delaying rate hikes, with U.S. rates reaching 4.5% by early 2023 (Federal Reserve, 2023). The crisis disproportionately affected vulnerable groups, with women, who made up 70% of global healthcare and informal workers, experiencing higher job losses . In the U.S., Black unemployment peaked at 16.7% compared to 12.9% for white workers (BLS, 2020), and the top 1% captured 50% of U.S. stock market gains, widening wealth gaps (Oxfam, 2022). Just-in-time supply chains proved fragile, with port congestion and chip shortages persisting into 2022, reducing U.S. imports by 20% in Q2 2020 and disrupting retail and manufacturing (Census Bureau, 2020). Subsidies for domestic production were slow and costly. Fiscal stimulus pushed global public debt to 100% of GDP by 2021, the highest since World War II (IMF, 2021), leading to defaults in countries like Zambia and rising borrowing costs for others (World Bank, 2022). The DSSI offered only temporary relief, failing to address structural debt issues. High-income countries recovered faster due to vaccine access and fiscal capacity, with U.S. GDP surpassing pre-crisis levels by 2022, while sub-Saharan Africa's output lagged 4% below 2019 levels, underscoring vaccine inequity and limited stimulus capacity in low-income nations (IMF, 2022).

3.3 Lessons for Future Crises

The COVID-19 economic crisis provides valuable insights for managing future disruptions, combining successes with cautionary lessons. Rapid and substantial monetary and fiscal interventions averted systemic collapse, reinforcing the importance of decisive action seen in the Global Financial Crisis. Central banks should prioritize liquidity, and governments must deploy countercyclical stimulus tailored to national contexts to sustain demand. However, prolonged loose policies fueled inflation, emphasizing the need for central banks to closely monitor supply-demand imbalances. Early warning systems incorporating supply chain data could guide timely policy adjustments to prevent derailing recovery. The crisis highlighted the importance of inclusive policies to address inequality. Targeted support for low-income households, women, and minorities through cash transfers, job retention schemes, and affordable childcare can reduce disproportionate impacts, while wealth taxes or progressive fiscal measures could narrow wealth gaps. Supply chain resilience requires diversification and strategic reserves for critical goods like semiconductors and medical supplies, supported by regional trade agreements and public-private partnerships to reduce reliance on single-source suppliers. The uneven global recovery exposed weaknesses in multilateral frameworks. Strengthening initiatives like COVAX and the DSSI with binding commitments for equitable vaccine and debt relief distribution is crucial, alongside greater access to concessional financing for low-income countries to prevent debt traps. Temporary regulatory flexibility preserved financial stability but risked concealing weaknesses, so macroprudential oversight must evolve to monitor post-crisis risks, such as non-performing loans, and stress-test supply chain vulnerabilities. The pandemic underscored the need for contingency plans for non-financial shocks, with scenario planning that integrates health, climate, and technological risks. Investments in public health and digital infrastructure can further enhance resilience to diverse crises.

4. SYNTHESIS: COMMON THEMES AND POLICY PRINCIPLES

The history of global financial crises reveal recurring patterns in their causes, impacts, and resolutions. These episodes, spanning nearly a century, underscore the fragility of interconnected economic systems and the pivotal role of policy in shaping outcomes. By synthesizing insights from the Great Depression (1929–1939), the Latin American Debt Crisis (1980s), the Asian Financial Crisis (1997–1998), the Global Financial Crisis (GFC, 2007–2008), and the COVID-19 pandemic (2020–2022), this section identifies common themes and distills actionable policy principles. The synthesis draws some insights from research and contemporary economic literature to help policymakers in preventing, mitigating, and recovering from future crises. The analysis emphasizes not only economic mechanisms but also the human and societal dimensions of crises, recognizing that effective policy must address both systemic stability and social welfare.

4.1 Common Themes Across Crises

Financial crises repeatedly reveal the fragility of interconnected economic systems, the amplifying effect of policy missteps, the role of inequality as both cause and consequence, the power and limits of interventions, and the double-edged nature of global coordination.

Interconnected economies are highly vulnerable to systemic shocks. The Great Depression's global trade collapse, driven by protectionist measures like the Smoot-Hawley Tariff Act, showed how linked markets can magnify disruptions (Irwin, 2011). The Asian Financial Crisis saw $100 billion flee Southeast Asia in 1997, destabilizing the region through capital flight and contagion (Radelet & Sachs, 1998). The Global Financial Crisis exposed the risks of globalized finance, with toxic mortgage-backed securities causing $12 trillion in market losses worldwide (Reinhart & Rogoff, 2009). The COVID-19 crisis highlighted supply chain weaknesses, as semiconductor shortages cut global car production by 16 million units in 2021 (McKinsey, 2021). Globalization fosters growth but creates structural dependencies that amplify risks, as seen in the cascading failures during the Global Financial Crisis triggered by Lehman Brothers' collapse or the fragility of just-in-time supply chains during COVID-19 (Acemoglu et al., 2015; Baldwin & Tomiura, 2020). These examples underscore the need for coordinated governance to manage systemic risks effectively.

Policy missteps consistently worsen crises. During the Great Depression, adherence to the gold standard led to monetary contraction, causing over 9,000 U.S. bank failures by 1933 (Friedman & Schwartz, 1963). The Latin American Debt Crisis was deepened by IMF austerity measures that cut Brazilian real wages by 20%, sparking unrest (Pastor, 1987). The Asian Financial Crisis saw IMF-imposed austerity drive Indonesia's GDP down 13.1%, fueling deadly riots (Stiglitz, 1999). The Global Financial Crisis suffered from inconsistent responses, such as Lehman Brothers' failure after Bear Stearns' bailout, triggering global panic (Bernanke, 2015). The COVID-19 response, though largely effective, faced challenges from delayed monetary tightening, contributing to 8.8% global inflation by 2022 (IMF, 2022). Behavioral economics highlights why such errors occur: policymakers, swayed by short-term pressures, often favor reactive measures like austerity or protectionism, as seen with the Smoot-Hawley Tariff Act, or misjudge risks, like dismissing COVID-19 inflation as "transitory" (Kahneman & Tversky, 1979). These patterns emphasize the need for evidence-based, forward-looking policies to counter human biases.

Inequality drives and results from crises. In the Great Depression, the top 1% held 24% of U.S. income by 1928, weakening demand and fueling speculative bubbles (Piketty & Saez, 2003). The Global Financial Crisis was exacerbated by U.S. household debt reaching 130% of income by 2007, particularly among low-income groups targeted by subprime lenders (Rajan, 2010). The COVID-19 crisis hit vulnerable groups hardest, with women, comprising 70% of global healthcare and informal workers, facing disproportionate job losses. Recoveries often widen gaps: low-income households lost 30% of their wealth post-Global Financial Crisis, while the top 1% captured 50% of U.S. stock market gains after COVID-19 (Oxfam, 2022). Rising inequality increases financial fragility as lower-income households borrow to sustain consumption, a dynamic evident in the subprime crisis and COVID-19's uneven recovery, where wealthier households boosted asset prices while low-income groups faced rising costs (Kumhof et al., 2015; Chetty et al., 2020). Crises amplify pre-existing disparities, necessitating equitable recovery policies.

Policy interventions can mitigate crises but come with trade-offs. The New Deal's fiscal stimulus reduced U.S. unemployment from 25% to 14% by 1937, and the Global Financial Crisis's $787 billion U.S. Recovery Act, paired with G20 coordination, capped unemployment at 10% (CBO, 2014). The COVID-19 response, with $16 trillion in global fiscal measures, drove a 6.1% growth rebound in 2021 (IMF, 2021). However, the Latin American Debt Crisis's Brady Plan, restructuring $191 billion in debt, took years, prolonging stagnation (Eichengreen, 2015), and COVID-19 stimulus fueled 8.5% U.S. inflation by mid-2022, eroding real wages (BLS, 2022). Aggressive, early stimulus is more effective, as seen with the rapid CARES Act compared to the Eurozone's delayed Global Financial Crisis response, but must include exit strategies to avoid overheating (Blanchard & Summers, 2017). Bold action is essential, yet policymakers must anticipate secondary effects and adapt dynamically.

Global coordination is critical but often falls short. The Global Financial Crisis's G20-led $1 trillion IMF pledge and monetary easing stabilized markets, and the COVID-19 crisis's Debt Service Suspension Initiative paused $12.9 billion in payments for low-income countries. However, the Great Depression suffered from absent cooperation, with competitive devaluations worsening trade collapses (Eichengreen & Sachs, 1985). The Asian Financial Crisis's IMF bailouts were criticized for rigidity, and COVID-19's COVAX delivered only 10% of promised vaccines to low-income countries by 2021 (UNICEF, 2021). National priorities often undermine multilateral efforts, as seen in COVID-19 vaccine nationalism, while institutional trust, strong in the Global Financial Crisis but weak in the Great Depression, shapes outcomes (Rodrik, 2011; Keohane & Nye, 1973). Effective coordination demands enforceable agreements and equitable implementation to succeed.

4.2 Policy Principles for Future Crises

Drawing on historical crises and contemporary research, the following principles provide a framework for managing future financial crises, balancing decisive action with adaptability to ensure economic stability and social equity.

Central banks must prioritize swift liquidity provision as lenders of last resort to stabilize markets, as demonstrated by the Global Financial Crisis's $2 trillion Federal Reserve injections and the COVID-19 crisis's $4.7 trillion balance sheet expansion (Federal Reserve, 2022). Flexible exchange rates, adopted after the Great Depression and during the Asian Financial Crisis, enhance monetary autonomy, allowing tailored responses (Obstfeld & Rogoff, 2002). However, low interest rates can fuel asset bubbles, as seen with post-COVID housing inflation (Case-Shiller, 2022). Early warning systems, integrating real-time financial and supply chain data, can guide timely policy adjustments to prevent overheating (Borio, 2014). Also, efficient use of ICT tools can help firms to optimize the use of internal funds, thereby reducing liquidity risks(Quarshie et al.,2025).

Fiscal policy should deploy countercyclical stimulus to counteract demand collapses, as evidenced by the New Deal's job programs and the $2.2 trillion CARES Act during COVID-19. Research shows fiscal multipliers are higher in recessions, justifying bold action (Romer, 2012). Stimulus must be targeted to avoid inflation and paired with exit strategies to manage debt, which reached 100% of global GDP post-COVID (IMF, 2021). Progressive taxation or wealth taxes can fund stimulus while reducing inequality, addressing disparities exacerbated by crises (Saez & Zucman, 2019).

Robust macroprudential regulation is essential to prevent systemic risks. Post-Global Financial Crisis reforms like Dodd-Frank and Basel III curbed bank leverage, but shadow banking and fintech, holding $218 trillion in assets by 2020, pose new threats (FSB, 2021; Adrian & Ashcraft, 2012). Stress tests and capital buffers should extend to supply chains and climate risks, reflecting their growing impact (Battiston et al., 2017). Regulatory flexibility, like COVID-19's loan moratoria, supports stability without stifling growth.

Crises amplify inequality, necessitating inclusive policies. COVID-19's cash transfers and job retention schemes, such as Germany's Kurzarbeit, reduced poverty .Prioritizing vulnerable groups—women, minorities, and low-income households—through childcare, wage subsidies, and progressive benefits fosters equitable recoveries, which sustain long-term growth (Stantcheva, 2022). Addressing structural gaps, like digital infrastructure access, is vital in a post-COVID world (World Bank, 2022).

Global crises require multilateral responses. The Global Financial Crisis's G20 coordination and COVID-19's Debt Service Suspension Initiative demonstrate collective action's value, but equitable outcomes demand stronger commitments.

Low-income countries, facing $400 billion in debt service costs in 2021, need concessional financing and relief (World Bank, 2022). Strengthening institutions like the IMF and WHO with binding resource-sharing agreements can address inequities, such as vaccine access gaps. Regional frameworks, like the Chiang Mai Initiative, provide resilience models (Sussangkarn, 2011).

The COVID-19 crisis underscored the need to prepare for non-financial shocks. Scenario planning for health, climate, and technological risks can guide contingency measures (FSB, 2020). Investments in public health, digital infrastructure, and green technologies, like the EU's €750 billion NextGenerationEU fund, enhance resilience (European Commission, 2021). Diversifying supply chains and maintaining strategic reserves for critical goods, such as semiconductors, reduce vulnerabilities (Shih, 2020).

Public confidence drives recovery, as seen in Roosevelt's fireside chats during the Great Depression and stress tests post-Global Financial Crisis (Bernanke, 2015). Behavioral economics emphasizes transparent communication and credible policies to counter fear-driven reactions (Akerlof & Shiller, 2009). Data-driven nudges, leveraging real-time economic indicators, can guide public behavior and sustain demand during crises (Thaler & Sunstein, 2008).

5. CONCLUSION

Global financial crises are an enduring feature of interconnected economies, reflecting the intricate interplay of human behavior, market dynamics, and policy decisions. From the Great Depression's devastating collapse to the Asian Financial Crisis's regional contagion, the Global Financial Crisis's systemic shock, and the COVID-19 pandemic's exogenous disruption, these episodes reveal both the fragility and resilience of global economic systems. Each crisis, while distinct in its origins, underscores a universal truth: the choices made by policymakers—whether central banks, governments, or international institutions—profoundly shape the trajectory of recovery and the extent of human suffering. This chapter has dissected these pivotal moments, extracting lessons from policy failures and successes to offer a roadmap for navigating future crises. As financial systems grow more complex and new risks emerge, these lessons are not merely historical reflections but urgent imperatives for building a more robust and equitable global economy.

The Great Depression taught us the catastrophic consequences of policy inaction and rigidity. Adherence to the gold standard and fiscal austerity deepened a crisis that left 25% of the U.S. workforce unemployed and global trade in tatters. Yet, the New Deal's bold interventions—abandoning the gold standard, implementing banking reforms, and launching massive public works—demonstrated the power of decisive, countercyclical action to restore confidence and demand. The Asian Financial Crisis exposed the vulnerabilities of fixed exchange rates and unchecked capital flows, with Thailand's baht devaluation triggering a $100 billion capital flight. The IMF's austerity measures exacerbated social unrest, but tailored responses, like Malaysia's capital controls and South Korea's financial restructuring, highlighted the efficacy of context-specific policies. The Global Financial Crisis revealed the perils of financial innovation run amok, as subprime mortgages and complex securities erased $12 trillion in global wealth. Coordinated G20 action and robust regulatory reforms, such as Dodd-Frank and Basel III, mitigated the damage, underscoring the value of global cooperation and macroprudential oversight. The COVID-19 pandemic, a non-financial shock, tested policymakers' ability to respond at unprecedented speed and scale. The $16 trillion in global fiscal stimulus and rapid monetary easing averted a deeper collapse, but inflationary pressures and unequal recoveries exposed the challenges of sustaining long-term stability.

These crises collectively illuminate several enduring lessons. First, liquidity is the lifeblood of crisis management. Central banks must act swiftly as lenders of last resort, as seen iduring the GFC and COVID-19. Second, countercyclical fiscal policy is critical to sustaining demand, as evidenced by the New Deal's job programs and the CARES Act's $2.2 trillion package. However, these interventions must be paired with exit strategies to manage debt and inflation, as the 8.8% global inflation rate in 2022 painfully demonstrated. Third, robust regulation is essential to prevent systemic risks. Yet, regulators must remain agile, adapting to new threats like shadow banking, fintech, and supply chain vulnerabilities. Fourth, global coordination can amplify the impact of national policies, as seen in the GFC's G20 pledges and the COVID-19 Debt Service Suspension Initiative, but equitable implementation remains a persistent challenge, exemplified by the COVAX initiative's vaccine delivery shortfalls.

Beyond these technical lessons, crises reveal the human and societal dimensions of economic turmoil. Inequality, both a cause and consequence of crises, demands targeted policies to protect vulnerable groups. The Great Depression's income concentration fueled speculative bubbles, while the GFC and COVID-19 crises disproportionately harmed low-income households, women, and minorities. Inclusive recoveries, supported by cash transfers, job retention schemes, and progressive fiscal measures, are not only moral imperatives but also economic necessities, as sustained demand drives long-term growth. Behavioral insights, from Roosevelt's fireside chats to GFC stress tests, underscore the role of public confidence in stabilizing markets. Transparent communication and credible policies can counteract fear-driven "animal spirits," fostering trust in institutions.

Looking forward, the global economy faces unprecedented challenges that will test the resilience of these lessons. Climate change poses systemic risks, with potential losses from natural disasters estimated at $200 billion–$300 billion annually by 2050 (IPCC, 2022). Technological disruptions, including artificial intelligence and cyber threats, could destabilize financial systems, with cyberattacks costing $6 trillion globally in 2021 (Cybersecurity Ventures, 2021). Geopolitical tensions, such as trade wars and regional conflicts, threaten supply chains and economic cooperation, as seen in the 400% surge in European natural gas prices amid the 2022 Russia-Ukraine conflict (IEA, 2022). These emerging risks demand proactive measures: stress-testing financial systems for climate and cyber shocks, diversifying supply chains to reduce single-source dependencies, and strengthening multilateral frameworks to counter fragmentation.

Crises, while painful, are also catalysts for reform and renewal. The Glass-Steagall Act, the Basel accords, the Chiang Mai Initiative, and the EU's Next GenerationEU fund all emerged from the ashes of past turmoil, fortifying the global economic architecture. Policymakers must seize these opportunities to address structural weaknesses, from inequality and regulatory gaps to supply chain fragility and climate vulnerability. This requires a delicate balance: decisive action to stabilize markets, flexibility to adapt to unique contexts, and foresight to anticipate secondary effects like inflation or debt sustainability. It also demands humility, recognizing the limits of economic models and the unpredictability of human behavior.By prioritizing liquidity, countercyclical fiscal policy, robust regulation, and inclusive global cooperation, policymakers can mitigate the human and economic toll of future disruptions. As financial systems evolve and new threats emerge, the tools to manage them must evolve in tandem.

REFERENCES

Acemoglu, D., Ozdaglar, A., & Tahbaz-Salehi, A. (2015). Systemic risk and stability in financial networks. *The American Economic Review, 105*(2), 564–608. DOI: 10.1257/aer.20130456

Adrian, T., & Ashcraft, A. B. (2012). Shadow banking: A review of the literature. *Federal Reserve Bank of New York Staff Reports*, No. 580. https://www.newyorkfed.org/research/staff_reports/sr580.html

Akerlof, G. A., & Shiller, R. J. (2009). *Animal spirits: How human psychology drives the economy, and why it matters for global capitalism.*

Baldwin, R., & Tomiura, E. (2020). Thinking ahead about the trade impact of COVID-19. In Baldwin, R. E., & Evenett, S. J. (Eds.), *COVID-19 and trade policy: Why turning inward won't work* (pp. 59–71). CEPR Press.

Battiston, S., Mandel, A., Monasterolo, I., Schütze, F., & Visentin, G. (2017). A climate stress-test of the financial system. *Nature Climate Change, 7*(4), 283–288. DOI: 10.1038/nclimate3255

Bernanke, B. S. (2015). *The courage to act: A memoir of a crisis and its aftermath.* W. W. Norton & Company.

Blanchard, O., & Summers, L. H. (2017). Rethinking stabilization policy: Evolution or revolution? *NBER Working Paper No. 24179.* National Bureau of Economic Research. https://www.nber.org/papers/w24179

Bloomberg. (2020). S&P 500 index data. Retrieved from https://www.bloomberg.com/quote/SPX:IND

Borio, C. (2014). The financial cycle and macroeconomics: What have we learnt? *Journal of Banking & Finance, 45*, 182–198. DOI: 10.1016/j.jbankfin.2013.07.031

Case-Shiller. (2022). S&P CoreLogic Case-Shiller U.S. National Home Price Index. Retrieved from https://www.spglobal.com/spdji/en/indices/indicators/sp-corelogic-case-shiller-us-national-home-price-nsa-index/

Census Bureau. (2021). Income and poverty in the United States: 2020. U.S. Census Bureau. https://www.census.gov/library/publications/2021/demo/p60-273.html

Chetty, R., Friedman, J. N., Hendren, N., Stepner, M., & the Opportunity Insights Team. (2020). The economic impacts of COVID-19: Evidence from a new public database built using private sector data. *NBER Working Paper No. 27431.* National Bureau of Economic Research. https://www.nber.org/papers/w27431

Congressional Budget Office (CBO). (2014). The effects of the American Recovery and Reinvestment Act of 2009. https://www.cbo.gov/publication/49958

Congressional Budget Office (CBO). (2021). The budget and economic outlook: 2021 to 2031. https://www.cbo.gov/publication/56970

Eichengreen, B. (2015). *Hall of mirrors: The Great Depression, the Great Recession, and the uses—and misuses—of history*. Oxford University Press.

Eichengreen, B., & Sachs, J. (1985). Exchange rates and economic recovery in the 1930s. *The Journal of Economic History*, *45*(4), 925–946. DOI: 10.1017/S0022050700035178

European Banking Authority (EBA). (2022). Risk dashboard: Q2 2022. https://www.eba.europa.eu/risk-analysis-and-data/risk-dashboard

European Central Bank (ECB). (2021). Pandemic Emergency Purchase Programme (PEPP). https://www.ecb.europa.eu/mopo/implement/pepp/html/index.en.html

European Commission. (2021). NextGenerationEU: Recovery plan for Europe. https://ec.europa.eu/info/strategy/recovery-plan-europe_en

Federal Emergency Management Agency (FEMA). (2020). Defense Production Act. https://www.fema.gov/disasters/defense-production-act

Federal Reserve. (2022). Balance sheet trends. https://www.federalreserve.gov/monetarypolicy/bst_recenttrends.htm

Federal Reserve. (2023). Monetary policy reports. https://www.federalreserve.gov/monetarypolicy/2023-03-mpr-summary.htm

Financial Stability Board (FSB). (2020). Holistic review of the March market turmoil. https://www.fsb.org/2020/11/holistic-review-of-the-march-market-turmoil/

Financial Stability Board (FSB). (2021). Global monitoring report on non-bank financial intermediation 2021. https://www.fsb.org/2021/12/global-monitoring-report-on-non-bank-financial-intermediation-2021/

Friedman, M., & Schwartz, A. J. (1963). *A monetary history of the United States, 1867–1960*. Princeton University Press.

Hale, T., Angrist, N., Goldszmidt, R., Kira, B., Petherick, A., Phillips, T., Webster, S., Cameron-Blake, E., Hallas, L., Majumdar, S., & Tatlow, H. (2021). A global panel database of pandemic policies (Oxford COVID-19 Government Response Tracker). *Nature Human Behaviour*, *5*(4), 529–538. DOI: 10.1038/s41562-021-01079-8

International Air Transport Association (IATA). (2020). Air passenger market analysis. https://www.iata.org/en/publications/economics/

International Energy Agency (IEA). (2022). Gas market report, Q1 2022. https://www.iea.org/reports/gas-market-report-q1-2022

International Monetary Fund (IMF). (2021). World Economic Outlook: Recovery during a pandemic. https://www.imf.org/en/Publications/WEO/Issues/2021/10/12/world-economic-outlook-october-2021

International Monetary Fund (IMF). (2022). World Economic Outlook: War sets back the global recovery. https://www.imf.org/en/Publications/WEO/Issues/2022/04/19/world-economic-outlook-april-2022

Irwin, D. A. (2011). *Peddling protectionism: Smoot-Hawley and the Great Depression*. Princeton University Press.

Kahneman, D., & Tversky, A. (1979). Prospect theory: An analysis of decision under risk. *Econometrica*, *47*(2), 263–291. DOI: 10.2307/1914185

Keohane, R. O., & Nye, J. S.Jr. (1973). Power and interdependence. *Survival*, *15*(4), 158–165. DOI: 10.1080/00396337308441409

Kolte, A., Patil, A., & Mal, H. (2021). Monetary policy in tough times-case study approach. *International Journal of Intelligent Enterprise*, *8*(1), 105–122. DOI: 10.1504/IJIE.2021.112323

Kumhof, M., Rancière, R., & Winant, P. (2015). Inequality, leverage, and crises. *The American Economic Review*, *105*(3), 1217–1245. DOI: 10.1257/aer.20110683

Oxfam. (2022). Inequality kills: The unparalleled action needed to combat unprecedented inequality in the wake of COVID-19. https://www.oxfam.org/en/research/inequality-kills

Pastor, M.Jr. (1987). The effects of IMF programs in the Third World: Debate and evidence from Latin America. *World Development*, *15*(2), 249–262. DOI: 10.1016/0305-750X(87)90080-5

Piketty, T., & Saez, E. (2003). Income inequality in the United States, 1913–1998. *The Quarterly Journal of Economics*, *118*(1), 1–41. DOI: 10.1162/00335530360535135

Quarshie, M. A., Djimatey, R., Akhtar, S., & Nawaah, D. (2025). Maximizing financial efficiency through technological synergy: Unleashing ICT for enhanced cash management in SMEs. Journal of the International Council for Small Business, 1–31. DOI: 10.1080/26437015.2025.2461025

Radelet, S., Sachs, J. D., Cooper, R. N., & Bosworth, B. P. (1998). The East Asian financial crisis: Diagnosis, remedies, prospects. *Brookings Papers on Economic Activity, 1998*(1), 1–90. DOI: 10.2307/2534670

Rajan, R. G. (2010). *Fault lines: How hidden fractures still threaten the world economy*. Princeton University Press.

Reinhart, C. M., & Rogoff, K. S. (2009). *This time is different: Eight centuries of financial folly*. Princeton University Press.

Rodrik, D. (2011). The globalization paradox: Democracy and the future of the world economy. *World Trade Review, 10*(1), 409–417.

Romer, C. D. (2012). Fiscal policy in the crisis: Lessons and policy implications. *IMF Fiscal Forum*. https://www.imf.org/external/np/seminars/eng/2012/fiscal/

Saez, E., & Zucman, G. (2019). *The triumph of injustice: How the rich dodge taxes and how to make them pay*. W. W. Norton & Company.

Stantcheva, S. (2022). Inequalities in the times of a pandemic. *Economic Policy, 37*(109), 5–41. DOI: 10.1093/epolic/eiac006

Stiglitz, J. E. (1999). Lessons from East Asia. *Journal of Policy Modeling, 21*(3), 311–330. DOI: 10.1016/S0161-8938(99)00005-8

Sussangkarn, C. (2011). Chiang Mai Initiative Multilateralization: Origin, development, and outlook. *Asian Economic Policy Review, 6*(2), 203–220. DOI: 10.1111/j.1748-3131.2011.01196.x

Thaler, R., & Sunstein, C. (2008). Nudge: Improving decisions about health, wealth and happiness. In *Amsterdam Law Forum; HeinOnline: Online* (p. 89).

Tsang, M. (2023). Currency crisis: Turkey in 2021. *The CASE Journal, 19*(5), 679–698. DOI: 10.1108/TCJ-08-2022-0140

UNICEF. (2021). COVID-19 vaccine delivery: Challenges and opportunities.

United Nations Conference on Trade and Development (UNCTAD). (2021). Digital economy report 2021. https://unctad.org/publication/digital-economy-report-2021

World Bank. (2020). Poverty and shared prosperity 2020: Reversals of fortune. https://www.worldbank.org/en/publication/poverty-and-shared-prosperity-2020

World Bank. (2021). Global economic prospects. https://www.worldbank.org/en/publication/global-economic-prospects

World Bank. (2022). Global economic prospects. https://www.worldbank.org/en/publication/global-economic-prospects

World Health Organization (WHO). (2022). Global vaccination coverage. https://www.who.int/news-room/fact-sheets/detail/immunization-coverage

Yu, Z., Razzaq, A., Rehman, A., Shah, A., Jameel, K., & Mor, R. S. (2021). Disruption in global supply chain and socio-economic shocks: a lesson from COVID-19 for sustainable production and consumption. *Operations Management Research*, 233–248. DOI: 10.1007/s12063-021-00179-y

Section 2

Policy, Regulation, and Stability

Chapter 4
Regulatory Frameworks and Their Impact on International Banking

Safas V. P.
https://orcid.org/0009-0003-5070-2836
Department of Commerce, School of Social Sciences and Languages, Vellore Institute of Technology, Vellore, India

Mohsin Khan
https://orcid.org/0000-0001-7986-9478
Department of Commerce, School of Social Sciences and Languages, Vellore Institute of Technology, Vellore, India

ABSTRACT

Technological enhancements have led to a new world where borders are no longer a criterion for financial transactions, as the number of cross-border financial transactions has increased, the need for regulatory compliance is the need of the hour. This chapter explores such regulatory frameworks on international banking, particularly focusing on major initiatives and the Basel Accords (Basel I, II, and III). It explains the objectives of major international banking regulations by conducting historical analysis and case studies. It also discusses the challenges faced during the implementation, such as the regulatory complexity of having different types of regulations in different nations, and the compliance burden in the increasingly interconnected world. This chapter also looks into the contemporary issues, such as the need for adaptive regulations for technologically changing financial areas like Fintech and digital currency. The chapter concludes by examining the ongoing policy debates and suggesting considerable solutions to overcome the existing hindrances.

DOI: 10.4018/979-8-3373-3725-8.ch004

1. INTRODUCTION

In the always evolving financial sector, international banking regulations play a crucial role in bringing stability, integrity, and security. As the bank plays a major role in the development of the economy (Akhtar et al., 2021). With the increasing number of cross-border transactions, it is highly required to protect the customers from risks such as credit, market, and operational risks. The lack of proper international banking regulations can lead to disasters, as seen in the global financial crisis 2007-2008, where banks took risks which was not controllable by themselves, also the recent collapse of Silicon Valley Bank (SVB) was also linked to lack of proper regulations or due to regulatory loopholes (Jha et al., 2025). To eliminate such issues, it is made compulsory for all banks to follow the international regulatory frameworks formulated by the Basel Committee on Banking Supervision, which explain the capital adequacy requirement and how they are expected to work in a way that will not affect the global financial economy (Basel Committee on Banking Supervision, 2006). For example, the BASEL III provided a set of standards that ensures all banks keep adequate capital, liquidity, and leverage, so that we can avoid a future crisis by making banks stronger by holding a proper amount of capital to manage liquidity risk (Basel Committee on Banking Supervision et al., 2021). Moreover, the financial stability of international regulations plays a role in global security by identifying and destroying activities leading to money laundering and terrorist financing (Aluko & Bagheri, 2012). To deal with this, we have other international standards like Anti-Money Laundering (AML) and Counter Terrorism Financing (CTF) set by bodies like the Financial Action Task Force (Pavlidis, 2020). These standards monitor all financial activities and report suspicious activities so that authorities can take proper measures. In addition, international regulations are important in preventing regulatory arbitrage, which means banks exploit the differences in the regulations of different nations for their advantage and undergo unethical practices (Houston et al., 2012). To face such cross-border challenges, the Financial Stability Board (FSB) and the Basel Committee facilitate cooperation and share information among different nations' regulators to ensure that no regulatory arbitrage occurs (Brummer, 2012). Moreover, the regulations also serve the investors and customers by enhancing the banking sector's transparency by setting standards on disclosures and fair treatment, which increases confidence in the aforementioned parties (De Mendonça et al., 2012). In summary, the international banking regulations are paramount for protecting the economy from financial crisis, global security, preventing regulatory arbitrage, and protecting the investors and customers of banks. Without international banking regulations, conducting cross-border banking is an invitation to total disruptions for economies and societies all around the world.

The international banking regulation has four key objectives: Financial stability, Risk mitigation, Consumer protection, and System risk reduction. All these objectives collectively serve the same purpose of safeguarding the global financial system. A Stable Banking sector is vital for economic growth as well as for individuals and businesses (Jokipii & Monnin, 2012). To achieve financial stability, there are various components of banking regulations, such as Liquidity management, Capital adequacy requirements, Risk management, Governance, Supervision, and Regulatory enforcement (Caprio & Honohan, 1999). This measure promises that it will mitigate systematic risk by capital requirements, which will withstand financial shocks, and enhance market confidence by becoming more transparent, and minimizing moral hazard by discouraging risky banking behaviours.

Risk mitigation is the next objective. In a dynamic environment, banks are exposed to numerous risks like credit, market, operational, liquidity, and compliance risks. Mitigating these risks is crucial, and an effective mitigation process includes identifying, measuring, monitoring, and controlling risks. Banks use credit scoring models, stress testing, value at risk (VaR) models, scenario analysis, and operational risk management (ORM) tools to measure the risk. Monitoring tools like real-time monitoring systems, dashboards, reporting tools, and early warning systems are used. For controlling the risk, hedging instruments, credit derivatives, and capital adequacy requirements are commonly used methods. Regulatory requirements also make sure these measures are carried out by mandating internal control, sound corporate governance, and independent oversight, which combined bring financial stability to the organization (Mba, 2024).

Consumer protection is another important part of banking regulations (Akinbami, 2011), as they are the main source of banks' revenue; their satisfaction plays a vital role in a bank's success. In this context, the regulation’s target is promoting fair and transparent transactions between customers and their banking partner. To fulfil this, the regulation mandates the banks to disclose proper information regarding all the fees and charges, interest rate, and terms and services, which will make customers more aware of banking tools and enable them to make adequate decisions. In the European Union, they have defined set rules to protect customers, such as basic payment accounts, transparent fee disclosures, and protection of deposits up to a specified level in case of bank collapse. Additional safeguards include limits on consumer liability in the event of fraud and enhanced security measures for online payments. These regulations not only help customers but also help banks attract more loyal customers and ensure smooth operations (*Bank Regulation Definition, Importance & Examples - IDnow*, n.d.).

The last objective, systematic risk reduction, is another important and widely applicable objective, as it solves the problems of the individual banks or local market and stops it from escalating to broader markets and paving the way for a financial crisis. Systematic risk is seen as a negative externality with two dimensions. The first one is cross-sectional, where we should try to reduce the damage that can arise because of the interlinkages between institutions and their common exposures. Second is the time dimension, which seeks to address issues that can arise when the market is not in good condition because most of the financial systems will work smoothly during good market conditions, and based on that, we should never set our standards because they will not be sufficient in the case of a market shock. The BASEL III framework, in fact, addresses systematic risk with its strict capital requirements and liquidity controls, which enhanced the banking sector, making it stronger to face any market condition and controlling domestic issues itself (Caruana, 2010).

The emergence of the regulatory frameworks is a reaction to the effects of the financial crisis to address the vulnerabilities of the current financial system to prevent the economy from another crisis. The 1980s banking crisis led to the creation of the Basel I Accord (1988) as the first international regulation that standardized the capital requirements for banks to keep a minimum of an 8% capital ratio against risk-weighted assets (Panico et al., 2014). However, these regulations were not enough; the 2007-2008 crisis opened our eyes towards more vulnerabilities, like excessive risk-taking and inadequate liquidity buffers, which further led to more comprehensive regulations.

In 2010, the Basel III framework came into existence and became a major cornerstone in the post-crisis reforms. It fortified capital adequacy by increasing Tier one capital requirements, implemented liquidity standards like Net Stable Funding Ratio (NFSR) and Liquidity Coverage Ratio (LCR), and added a leverage ratio to control excessive dependence on borrowed funds (Basel Committee on Banking Supervision, 2017). The mentioned changes are targeted to make banks withstand any crisis or financial shocks without a government bailout ("Global Financial Stability Report, October 2018: A Decade After the Global Financial Crisis: Are We Safer?," 2018). At the same time different nations implemented their own reforms to face such challenges, the Dodd Frank Act (2010) in the US established the Consumer Financial Protection Bureau (CFPB) and Volcker Rule to limit speculative trading, similarly EU created the European Systematic Risk Board (ESRB) to monitor the risk that can affect the entire financial system and bring peace among member states (Reetu & Devi, 2025).

Post-crisis regulation is more focused on systematic monitoring, assessment, and regulation of the entire financial system to identify systemic risk and mitigate it. The G20 and Financial Stability Board brought global efforts together, mandating higher capital buffers for major financial institutions and stress testing to evaluate how banks withstand these circumstances. For instance, to mitigate procyclicality, the BASEL III's countercyclical capital buffers allow regulators to adjust capital requirements during credit boom periods (*Financial Regulation After the "Subprime" Crisis: What Lessons Can Be Learned and What Reforms Undertaken?*, n.d.).

Even though measures have been taken, still many challenges persist, as the global market gets complex each day and the introduction of shadow banking and fintech innovations thrives in the market, we still need more regulations to curb the financial system from reaching another crisis. The IMF states that even though measures have been taken to regulate non-banking financial intermediaries and sovereign exposures remain.

2. CONCEPTUAL FOUNDATIONS

2.1 Key Terminologies

Understanding key terms is important to understand the concepts related to international banking regulations

2.1.1 Regulatory Framework

A set of rules and standards framed to make sure banks operate in a safe and transparent manner, such as capital adequacy requirements, to ensure the safety of consumers and the financial system as a whole.

2.1.2 Risk Sensitivity

Different assets possess different levels of risk, and risk sensitivity is assigning proper regulatory requirements for them. The BASEL III framework followed risk-weighted asset calculations and stress testing in relation to this (*Basel III: International Regulatory Framework for Banks*, 2017).

2.1.3 Simplicity

It is a feature of a framework that focuses on making the capital standard and capital calculation process simple (*Basel III: International Regulatory Framework for Banks*, 2017).

2.1.4 Comparability

This is an outcome of a framework that is expected to deliver comparability between banks, comparable over time, and comparable information (*International and National Regulatory Frameworks - Oesterreichische Nationalbank (OeNB)*, n.d.).

2.1.5 Systemic Risk

This is the risk that can spread from individual units or local markets to a wider market.

2.2 Core Principles for Effective Banking Supervision

The core principles established by the Basel Committee on Banking Supervision are considered the international standard for banks and banking systems. It was first introduced in the year 1997, and during the following years, it was updated. The following are the 29 core principles based on the 2019 December 15 version of Core Principles for effective banking supervision by the Basel Committee on Banking Supervision(2019). These principles address all the essential elements required for a well-governed banking system, ranging from powers and independence of supervisory authority to individual banking requirements that themselves should meet.

2.2.1 Principle 1: Responsibilities, Objectives, and Powers

This principle states that the supervisory roles, goals, and the legal authority to oversee the banks should be defined in a clear manner, starting from granting a licence to intervening during the required time. This can clear a lot of complexity, and the supervisors will know what they are responsible for and what they are supposed to do.

2.2.2 Principle 2: Independence, Accountability, Resourcing, and Legal Protection for Supervisors

To make supervisors act impartially for the protection of the banking system, they should be provided with operational independence from political and industrial pressures, alongside the need for resources (staff, technology, and funds).

2.2.3 Principle 3: Cooperation and Collaboration

In today's interconnected cross-border financial market, supervisors from different regions should work together with domestic and international regulatory bodies, so that they can understand and address cross-border risks.

2.2.4 Principle 4: Permissible Activities

Banks are major pillars of our financial system; anything that affects banks will affect the financial system itself. Due to this, we will not allow banks to enter risky business. Therefore, it is defined what activities banks are entitled to do and not to do. Controlling the usage of the term "bank" helps gain trust among common citizens.

2.2.5 Principle 5: Licensing Criteria

Banking licensing should be provided after going through a rigorous licensing standard procedure in which the following factors to be assessed properly: ownership, governance, business plans, risk management, and financial strength. This way, we can eliminate unfit institutions from getting into banking.

2.2.6 Principle 6: Transfer of Significant Ownership

The supervisors should stay vigilant during the transfer of ownership of banks, because when unsuited entities enter, they might jeopardize the bank's functionality.

2.2.7 Principle 7: Major Acquisitions

Similarly, the supervisors should oversee what assets the banks are investing in; acquiring highly risky assets is not suitable for a bank.

2.2.8 Principle 8: Supervisory Approach

A proactive and forward-looking supervisory approach is a must for identifying and addressing risks before they escalate into broader markets. This includes understanding a bank's risk profile, having mechanisms for early intervention, and planning for the orderly resolution of failing banks to reduce systemic impact.

2.2.9 Principle 9: Supervisory Techniques and Tools

Supervisors should use different techniques and tools for overviewing the banks, tools like on-site inspections and off-site monitoring can be used and such tools should be allocated based on the risk level of the banks, i.e. banks exposed to higher level of risks need more attention when compared to a low-risk category bank.

2.2.10 Principle 10: Supervisory Reporting

The banks are required to submit an accurate report on proper timings, which is crucial for supervisors to identify vulnerabilities, and supervisors should verify them individually.

2.2.11 Principle 11: Corrective and Sanctioning Powers of Supervisors

For the smooth functioning and integrity in supervising, supervisors should take timely decisions on banks when they are found to fail to work according to the guidelines or engage in unsafe practices. Also, they should revoke the license in the ultimate situation.

2.2.12 Principle 12: Consolidated Supervision

Supervision is required on all the banking group, including its subsidiaries and affiliates, because the failure of one of these can spread to it and jeopardize the stability of the whole.

2.2.13 Principle 13: Home-Host Relationships

In a highly interconnected globalized banking world, the coordination between the home country and the host country is crucial for consistent supervision. With proper rules and communication standards.

2.2.14 Principle 14: Corporate Governance

The banks should have efficient corporate governance to make sure that the bank is managed efficiently. It should provide clear-cut information regarding the roles and responsibilities of the board and management, logical internal control, and appropriate compensation policies. This will reduce the risk as well as improve the ethical behaviour of the banks. Alam et al. (2023) links board accountability is significantly influence the profitability of banks in terms of return on assets, return on equity and Tobin's Q.

2.2.15 Principle 15: Risk Management Process

Each bank should have a risk management framework that covers the identification, measurement, evaluation, monitoring, and control of all the risks that the bank might face. This is the backbone of an effectively managed banking operation, interlinked with capital adequacy and liquidity.

2.2.16 Principle 16: Capital Adequacy

Capital requirement is the backbone of a bank's ability to overcome unexpected shocks (Teglio et al., 2012) that happen in the market, and it can also help the regulators to control the bank's unwanted risk-taking behaviour (Wang et al., 2021). Setting sensitive capital adequacy requirements is important so that banks have sufficient financial buffers to manage potential shocks.

2.2.17 Principle 17: Credit Risk

Lending credit is the main function of any bank. Effective credit management is highly required for mitigating losses. They should evaluate the borrowers, develop proper policies for approving loans, and manage the loan portfolio are must for preventing NPAs

2.2.18 Principle 18: Problem Assets, Provisions, and Reserves

The early identification of problem assets and their proactive management is necessary to stop them from creating huge losses. To meet such assets, proper provisions and reserves are required.

2.2.19 Principle 19: Concentration Risk and Large Exposure Limits

Banks are not allowed to allow a single borrower or a sector to be the major borrower; such a scenario can end up as a big mess. To avoid it, banks should always focus on diversifying their borrowers.

2.2.20 Principle 20: Transactions With Related Parties

Strict oversight is mandatory when transactions are occurring between the bank and its related parties. Prior to making any such transactions, banks should ensure that these transactions do not violate the conflict of interest or harm the depositors.

2.2.21 Principle 21: Country and Transfer Risks

For banks engaged in international lending and investment, it is important to understand and manage the country-specific risks (e.g., political instability, economic downturns) and the risk of funds being blocked (transfer risk), which are important for protecting their international operations.

2.2.22 Principle 22: Market Risks

Banks that are trading in the financial markets need to be equipped to face the risk associated with them, like market prices, such as interest rates, exchange rates, and equity prices, to eliminate significant losses that can arise from it.

2.2.23 Principle 23: Interest Rate Risk in the Banking Book

As interest is a bank's major revenue source, the changes to interest will directly affect the bank's profitability and the value of the assets, so it must be managed properly for the long-term stability of the bank.

2.2.24 Principle 24: Liquidity Risk

To prevent the bank from getting a liquidity crisis, banks should ensure sufficient liquid assets are kept.

2.2.25 Principle 25: Operational Risk

Operational risks related to process, people, and system are exposed to a wide range of risks like errors, fraud, and system failure; managing them is essential to reduce losses.

2.2.26 Principle 26: Internal Control and Audit

In continuation with operational risk, each bank should conduct internal control, ensuring that no errors, fraud, or system failures occur. Along with that, banks should have an external audit to review that the internal controls are functioning properly.

2.2.27 Principle 27: Financial Reporting and External Audit

Disclosure of the financial report is mandatory for the stakeholders to understand the financial strength and weaknesses. Such reports needed to undergo external audits to validate their genuineness.

2.2.28 Principle 28: Disclosure and Transparency

Banks are expected to provide sufficient information to the stakeholders, especially investors, so that they can make proper decisions.

2.2.29 Principle 29: Abuse of Financial Services

Supervisors should monitor the activities of the financial institutions and make sure they do not enter into any unethical practices such as money laundering and terrorist funding activities.

3. EVOLUTION OF INTERNATIONAL BANKING REGULATION

The international banking regulation evolution is based on the crisis that has led the world to come up with some rules and standards so that the financial system can withstand another crisis efficiently. This section will explain the same in the following segments: Pre-Basel era, Basel Accords (I, II, III), and Major regulatory milestones and their triggers.

3.1 Pre-Basel Era

Prior to 1970, international banking operated under individual nations' regulations with comparatively less coordination with foreign countries. Individual nations set their own standards, supervisory protocols, and crisis management practices. This individualised approach didn't go well when the banks expanded their business in foreign nations, which resulted in complex issues that spread across countries. The failure of Bankhaus Herstatt of Germany is a clear example that the financial mistakes or financial crisis of one country can easily spill over to others, as the markets are highly interconnected. This event, along with other problems that occurred during the period, highlighted the need for international coordination and unified standards to prevent the system from regulatory arbitrage. To address this issue, the Bank for International Settlements (BIS) in Basel, Switzerland, hosted a summit of the central bank governors of the Group of Ten(G10) countries, which created the Basel Committee on Banking Supervision (BCBS) in 1974. The initial objective of the committee was to set guidelines on information sharing and define the responsibilities of the home and host countries in supervising (Ams et al., 2018).

3.2 Basel Accords

The Basel Accords are a series of international banking regulations formed by the BCBS to regulate banking activities all over the world. These accords will provide operational standards for banks and supervisory guidelines for national supervisors.

3.2.1 Basel Accord I

The first Basel Accord was introduced in the year 1988, which was known as Basel I. It was the foremost attempt to establish a global standard for capital adequacy, primarily focused on making the banks keep a minimum amount of capital at their disposal to meet any uncertain losses and protect the depositors. One of the key feature of Basel I was its concept of Risk weighted assets (RWAs), were different assets were assigned different weights according to their riskiness like government bonds are given a weight of zero while corporate loans were given 100% weight, and based on RWA banks should keep their minimum amount of capital. Even though Basel I was a major step in banking regulations, it was criticized for two factors: oversimplification and a focus on a single risk, while banks were exposed to multiple risks, such as market risk and operational risk. However, along with its limitations, Basel I received global acceptance and became an international standard for capital adequacy (BASEL COMMITTEE ON BANKING SUPERVISION et al., 1999).

3.2.2 Basel Accord II

As it was already explained, the Basel I faced some limitations to address this, the committee introduced a new accord, Basel II, in the year 2004, which was more complex and risk sensitive. Its major objectives were to align capital requirements with underlying risk faced by the banks, promote enhanced stability for the financial system, and increase competitive equality. Basel II followed a three-pillar approach:

- **Pillar 1 (Minimum Capital Requirement):** Enhanced the approach to credit risk, along with the introduction of capital requirements to address operational risk. It made banks adopt more innovative internal models to evaluate their risk, leading to customised capital requirements.
- **Pillar 2 (Supervisory Review Process):** This pillar focuses on supervising the bank's risk assessment process and capital adequacy. Because setting a standard is not enough, there should be proper monitoring; only then will banks have the motivation to implement them properly.
- **Pillar 3 (Market Discipline):** This pillar gave importance to transparency and disclosure requirements of banks, which will, in turn, create awareness among market participants regarding the bank's financial health.

Compared to Basel I, Basel II made significant changes, but it was still criticized for its complexity and procyclicality, and it was not able to protect the financial system from the 2008 financial crisis. Basel II was adopted by many countries with variations in implementation (History of the Basel Committee, 2014).

3.2.3 Basel Accord III

The 2007-08 global financial crisis unveiled major weaknesses of Basel II, specifically liquidity risk, excessive leverage, and inadequate capital buffers. This leads to the creation of a new regulation, Basel III, by the BCBS. The Basel III aimed to nourish the bank and banking system by improving banks' capacity to face financial shocks and economic stress, and minimize the spread of risk from the financial sector to the real economy. The key features of these regulations are:

- Higher and better-quality capital requirements, with a target on Common Equity Tier 1 capital.
- Introduction of a leverage ratio to supplement risk-weighted capital requirements.
- Introduction of liquidity standards, including the Net Stable Funding Ratio (NSFR) and Liquidity Coverage Ratio (LCR).
- Measures to address systemic risk, such as higher capital requirements for systemically important financial institutions (SIFIs).
- Countercyclical capital buffers to dampen procyclicality.

Basel III plays an important role in regulating international banking and protecting the financial system. Its implementation began in 2013, and it is still ongoing in various regions. The EU's Capital Requirement Regulation and the US Dodd-Frank Act are a part of this at the national level (*History of the Basel Committee*, 2014).

3.3 Major Regulatory Milestones and Their Triggers

The evolution of international banking regulation was a product of the financial crisis that occurred all over the world. Initially, it led to the creation of the first Basel I regulation, and the following events led us to understand the weaknesses in the existing regulations and prompted their renewal.

3.3.1 1980s Debt Crisis

The Latin American debt crisis highlighted the sovereign default risk, which proved the necessity of a common regulation and created the Basel I, and strengthened the banks' capital (Ams et al., 2018).

3.3.2 1997 Asian Financial Crisis

The Asian financial crisis started in Thailand, and later it spilled over to other Asian countries, affecting their stock market. This crisis displayed the vulnerabilities in existing regulations, leading to the creation of the Basel Core Principles for Effective Banking Supervision. This became the best practice for national regulators (BASEL COMMITTEE ON BANKING SUPERVISION et al., 1999).

3.3.3 2007–2008 Global Financial Crisis

This crisis began in the US when the banks issued more mortgage loans to people without verifying their eligibility. It is also known as the subprime crisis which is directly pointed out the reckless lending behaviour of the major banks in the US (Ansari et al., 2023), this seems like a national problem but when people started not paying loans it made bank loans lose its value and all those investments made on such assets also started losing its value and it affected all the economies because these investments were made from everywhere. This issue opened the eyes of BCBS. They introduced many regulatory controls on banks involving risky business, and that became the third Basel Accord (*History of the Basel Committee*, 2014).

3.3.4 Post-2010 Developments

As the world goes forward, the financial system still faces challenges in new forms like shadow banking and fintech. Thus, the regulators are framing rules and standards so that one day this will not lead to another crisis (European Central Bank, 2024).

4. COMPARATIVE ANALYSIS OF INTERNATIONAL BANKING REGULATIONS: DEVELOPING VS DEVELOPED NATIONS

So far, we have seen how the international banking regulations, specifically the Basel Accords, formed and shaped the banking ecosystem that we use; however, the effectiveness and efficiency of the regulations differ hugely between developing and developed nations (Brownbridge & Kirkpatrick, 2000) because of their variations in market maturity, supervisory capacity, and economic integration. A recent study found different patterns in this when comparing the BRICS and G7 economies, where the former is considered a developing nation and the latter includes major advanced economies.

- **Activity Restrictions:** When compared with G7 countries, BRICS (developing) nations imposed more restrictions on banking activities (Yin, 2021). This looked like a conservative approach by the regulatory authorities of the developing nations to tackle unexpected volatility and safeguard from financial crisis. But at the same time, stricter restrictions can affect the banks' diversification strategies (Gulati, 2020).
- **Entry Requirements:** In case of entry requirements, both categories imposed strict requirements to enter their territory for new banks, emphasizing that only properly licensed and fit banks are allowed to maintain the integrity of the sector.
- **Foreign Bank Entry:** comparatively, the BRICS nations of developing economies have more stringent policies on foreign bank entry, but a study found that over the course of 2000-2019, there has been a gradual convergence of the BRICS nations, aligning closer to the G7 nations (Li, 2021). Although the developed nations are seen as a more liberal environment for foreign banks.
- **Capital requirement:** In BRICS nations, the capital requirements have tightened effectively after 2003 to align their regulations with the Basel standards. However, G7 nations have already tightened their capital requirement that evolved over a course of period.
- **Deposit Insurer Power:** both BRICS and G7 nations face ongoing issues pertaining to this area. Enhancing deposit insurer authority, along with reforming the deposit insurance mechanisms, is a must to reduce the systemic risk (Ahmad et al., 2021).

Similarly, when we look into the performance and competition of banks in developed nations and developing nations, we can also find differences: in developed nations like G7 countries, they support the higher pressurized competition and good resource allocation, along with efficiency improvements. And in these countries, the regulators are advanced; they have enough resources to both implement and monitor the regulations that they mandate in their territory effectively (Ahmad et al., 2021). While in developing nations like BRICS countries, the situations are different; here, when they go for strict regulations, it will raise the compliance costs and lead to restrictions on access to finance for smaller banks and clients. In these countries, the alignment of their regulation is seen as a reputational factor that can attract foreign investments (Ahmad et al., 2021), and the competitiveness is affected due to the lack of financial freedom (Moudud-Ul-Huq, 2020). And when it comes to adaptations the developed countries had benefit of influence over the formulations all major standards and along with that they posses a mature and capable banking sector which made them easily adapt to major regulations, but on the other side the developing countries with limited supervisory and uncapable, unmature financial market made it more difficult for them to adapt the global regulations, even though they aligned their regulations with Basel purely due to external pressures such as reputation and cross border coordination. And in these nations, it would be better if they use a tailored version of the global regulations as their market is entirely different from a global scenario (Ahmad et al., 2021).

5. CASE STUDIES: EU BANKING UNION, US DODD-FRANK ACT

These two case studies can provide insight into how regulatory frameworks are designed and implemented in the European Union and the United States.

5.1 EU Banking Union

The EU Banking Union was established as a reaction to the sovereign debt crisis to safeguard financial stability and protect taxpayers' money from bank bailouts. It operates on three pillars

- **Single Supervisory Mechanism (SSM)**

The European Central Bank (ECB) directly administers the eurozone's 115 big banks (holding ~82% of EU banking assets) and implements supervisory standards for other banks (small banks) (European Central Bank, 2024). This centralized control helps the European Union to safeguard its banks from numerous risks.

- **Single Resolution Mechanism (SRM)**

This resolution is created to handle the banks that are failing in the European Union. Under this, they will collect a reserve amount from banks, which is known as the Single Resolution Fund (SRF), and this money is given back to them when they are in need of it. This way, the bank failures do not cost the public (Single Resolution Board, 2024).

- **Deposit Guarantee Schemes (DGS)**

This scheme is like providing insurance for the depositor's money. When any bank fails, the customers will receive their deposits up to a certain limit under this scheme. This way, the public can trust the banks for depositing money (European Banking Authority, 2024).

5.1.1 Impact and Challenges:

The Banking Union improved supervision quality, crisis management, and bank resilience, which is why the banks were able to stay stable during the COVID-19 global pandemic when the economy was going through a shock (Oliver Wyman, 2023). Even though there is only limited integration with other countries, which affects the broader cross-border transactions (Eurofi, 2024).

5.2 US Dodd-Frank Act

This Act came into existence in the year 2010 to prevent crises like the 2008 financial crisis, to regulate banks and financial companies more rigidly, to protect customers, and to reduce systemic risk. The following are the key components of this act.

- **Financial Stability Oversight Council (FSOC)**

This is a group that monitors the entire financial system and identifies risks, regulates non-banking financial institutions, coordinates between agencies, and advises the government (U.S. Department of the Treasury, 2024).

- **Consumer Financial Protection Bureau (CFPB)**

This bureau regulates financial products and protects consumers from potential threats (Consumer Financial Protection Bureau, 2024).

- **Volcker Rule**

This is a key part of the act that restricts banks from getting into risky investments (Federal Reserve, 2023).

- **Derivatives Regulation**

Mandates centralized clearing and transparency for swaps trading to mitigate counterparty risks (U.S. Commodity Futures Trading Commission, 2024).

5.2.1 Impact and Criticisms

The Dodd-Frank Act strengthened the banks' capital buffers and improved banks' capacity to face stress and shocks in the market, like the COVID-19 pandemic (Council on Foreign Relations, 2023). At the same time, the critics argued that this act favoured bigger banks and overburdened the smaller banks, which reduced their market share from 40% in the year 1994 to 15% in 2024.

5.3 Comparative Analysis

Table 1. Comparative Analysis

Feature	EU Banking Union	US Dodd- Frank
Primary Goal	Centralized supervision/resolution in the eurozone	Prevent systemic risks and protect consumers
Key Tools	SSM, SRM, DGS	FSOC, CFPB, Volcker Rule, derivatives regulation
Successes	Improved crisis resilience and supervision	Reduced "too-big-to-fail" risks
Challenges	Limited cross-border integration	High compliance costs for small banks

6. IMPACT ON INTERNATIONAL BANKING

6.1 Effects on Bank Behaviour: Capital Structure, Risk-Taking, Innovation, and Business Models

Regulatory frameworks significantly influence banks ' risk-taking and capital structure when they impose higher capital requirements and strict oversight. Empirical evidence proved that when strict capital requirements are mandated, the banks keep larger reserves, which reduces their engagement in risky investments and focuses them more on conservative lending strategies (Agoraki et al., 2011; Hellmann et al., 2000). For example, higher capital requirements under Basel III mandate banks to prioritize consistent funding over speculative investments (Repullo, 2004). Regulatory measures also shape banks' innovation strategies, because often innovative banks that are better at operations and risk management systems meet the capital adequacy requirement and may choose regulatory frameworks that align with their strengths (Yang et al., 2025).

6.2 Impact on Large, Complex Financial Institutions (LCFIs)

Large complex financial institutions play a crucial role in an economy, as any impact on such institutions will directly impact that nation itself, and it will spread quickly. Due to this, LCFIs face unique regulatory challenges, the regulation focuses on enhancing capital and liquidity buffers, strengthening risk assessment, and improving supervisory oversight to reduce systemic risk. However, LCFIs often find ways to adjust their strategies to reduce the impact of new regulations, and for the regulation to work smoothly, there should be coordination between all countries (IMF, 2010; Ötker-Robe et al., 2010). LCFIs are often considered "too big to fail," making them require special regulatory attention to mitigate systemic risk.

6.3 Influence on Cross-Border Banking, Financial Inclusion, and Emerging Markets

International regulations had a mixed effect on cross-border banking and financial inclusion in the emerging markets. On one side, the enhanced information disclosure requirement supported financial inclusion by providing transparent information; on the other side, the strict capital requirement and macroprudential requirements made banks more risk-averse, resulting in less lending of money to the underdeveloped or low-income class (CIGI, 2013).

6.4 Unintended Consequences: Complexity, Reduced Comparability, Compliance Costs

When the regulations became complex and too strict, it led to problems like Higher compliance costs, Less comparability, and Regulatory arbitrage. While what is actually required is proportionality, where the rules are different for different banks based on their size, this way it eliminates unnecessary regulatory burden from the smaller banks. But implementing such regulation is a bit challenging, as any mistake in the classification of banking can lead to fraud, and such an act can end up in disaster (BIS, 2019).

7. CONSEQUENCES OF INTERNATIONAL BANKING REGULATORY FRAMEWORKS

A critical assessment of international banking regulations conducted revealed unexpected realities; instead of the expected or intended objectives, the outcomes revealed major consequences. One of the major reforms of Basel III was setting stricter and higher capital as well as liquidity requirements enhanced the banks' strength and reduced systemic risk and greater financial stability (Yan et al., 2012). But this effect is uneven around the world, especially between the developed and developing nations. The advanced nations strengthened their capital positions but, they reduce capital flow towards the developing nations or they made it more expensive to meet the new compliances, thus it has led a slow financial growth in the developing nations and it became more costly for them to gather consistent funding, mainly in the short term (Ghosh et al., 2011). In the era of banks taking unwanted risks, Basel III's oversight and tight regulations protected the system, especially with the increased loss absorption capacity and leverage ratios, which have made the banks safer. These changes have reduced the chances of systemic risk and future crises and reduced the drawbacks of the earlier regulations (King, 2013; Yan et al., 2012). However, the calculation of risk weighted assets of Internal Rating Based (IRB) suggested by the Basel III can lead to a regulatory arbitrage situation, were the large banks might underreport their risk exposure or maybe change their activities to a less regulated area like "shadow banking" to reduce capital charges which might result making the system less transparent and having vulnerabilities (Plotnikova, 2018). Theoretically, and as confirmed by empirical modelling, these strict rules of Basel III have benefited in two ways: one is that it has lowered the exchange rate fluctuations or volatility by making the banking sector less vulnerable to shocks that transmit across borders (Basel Committee on Banking Supervision, 2021). Basel III's architecture has enhanced the resilience of the international banking system and improved its ability to manage systemic risk, but policy challenges persist, including issues with regulatory arbitrage, uneven global implementation, and the ongoing moral hazard associated with systemically important banks, which necessitate continued adjustments and increased international cooperation.

8. CURRENT CHALLENGES AND FUTURE DIRECTIONS

8.1 Complexity vs. Simplicity and Comparability in Regulation

The regulations that came after the crisis were well-built, but at the same time, they were complex in nature. The intention of the regulation was to address the vulnerabilities exposed during the financial crisis, like capital adequacy and liquidity buffers, but that has become a burden for the banks. For example, the United States is implementing Basel III in different phases and which is to be completed in 2028, and similarly, delays and modifications are happening in the UK and European Union, making it more complicated for international banks (Moody's, 2024).

The Bank of Spain notes that the Basel III framework will standardise risk-weighted asset calculation and transparency, but at the same time, it makes it difficult for small banks because of reduced lending capacity and sector consolidation. Over the past three decades in the United States, a substantial decrease has occurred in the number of community banks, which is a result of the disproportionate regulatory compliance (Stanton Chase, 2025). Proportionality is the key to addressing such challenges by customising the regulations based on the size and risk profile of the institution (GFM Review, 2025).

8.2 Regulatory Gaps and Emerging Risks

8.2.1 Fintech and Digital Currencies

The rise of Fintech, decentralized finance (DeFi), and digital currencies was not properly addressed in the regulations, which shows a significant gap that requires attention. There are many fintech innovations that work all around the world without border restrictions, which leave the offenders to exploit the regulatory arbitrage in countries where regulations are not so strong (Stanton Chase, 2025).

8.2.2 Cybersecurity Risks

As banks depend more on digitalization for running the business, which opens the door for another threat, "cybersecurity risks", the diversity of different institutions depending on different partners to address this issue also complicates the coordinated move to address this problem (Stanton Chase, 2025).

8.2.3 Climate Risk

Climate risk is another issue that is to be addressed along with this, because Fintech applications have the potential to gather green finance, but to do so, they require standardized data and digital infrastructure, which are not currently available in emerging markets. The International Monetary Fund (IMF) depicted that 60% of the emerging markets do not possess the required digital tools to verify climate metrics, which hinders the scaling up of sustainable finance (IMF, 2024).

8.3 Ongoing Reforms and Policy Debates

8.3.1 Basel III Finalization

The Basel III committee's standardized approach to reduce the variability got the attention of critics as making it oversimplified will not be able to capture all the risks, especially complex risks (Bank of Spain, n.d.).

8.3.2 Macroprudential Tools

Similarly, there is a debate going on about the effectiveness of the macroprudential tools like countercyclical capital buffers and total loss-absorbing capacity (TLAC) requirements. The Financial Stability Board (FSB) believes TLAC is the right tool for addressing "too big to fail" risks, but at the same time, the disproportionality created by this is affecting smaller banks, and they argue that these rules are favouring large institutions (Bank of Spain, n.d.).

8.3.3 Regulatory Technology (RegTech)

The usage of regtech or artificial intelligence is one of the way to automate compliance and risk monitoring. However, the implementation of such technology is not that progressive, for instance, only 15% of Swiss banks had implemented enterprise-wide AI solutions by early 2025, which clearly indicate a gap between regulatory ambition and practical execution (Stanton Chase, 2025).

8.4 Future Directions

- Harmonization: Strengthening international coordination through bodies like the Financial Stability Board is a way to reduce regulatory arbitrage and fragmentation.

- Proportionality: Usage of a tailored regulation framework is a way to reduce regulatory burdens on smaller banks and foster competition (GFM Review, 2025).
- Climate Finance Infrastructure: There is a need for investing in digital tools and standardized data to support the growth of sustainable finance, especially in emerging markets (IMF, 2024).

9. CONCLUSION

International banking regulation has evolved a lot in the last few decades due to a series of financial crises exposing the vulnerabilities in the existing regulation and leading to a newer one. The journey from the initial Basel framework, which mandated the capital requirement, to comprehensive internationally coordinated regulations of today, the Basel Committee and its accords and establishments like the Financial Stability Board played a crucial role in building a regulation that protects the consumers, reduces systemic risk, and smoothens international banking. However, the evolving financial environment again challenges the regulation in different ways, requiring it to be fortified again.

The regulatory frameworks that have been introduced in the last decades, namely Basel III, the EU Banking Union, and the US Dodd-Frank Act, have strengthened the banking system. Currently, banks run with adequate capital requirements, liquidity buffers, and transparency. These measures have proven their potential, especially during the COVID-19 pandemic period, when the entire economy was going through stress, the banking sector stood still, and faced the shock. The EU's centralized supervision and resolution mechanism has improved its crisis management and reduced the chances of bailing out with taxpayers' money (Oliver Wyman, 2023; Bank of Spain, n.d.). Similarly, the Dodd-Frank Act worked on mitigating systemic risk and protecting consumers, making their financial system robust. However, it is still criticised for putting more regulatory burden on small institutions.

However, the complexity of the new regulations has created new issues. The high-risk sensitivity requirement and precision capital adequacy made things more complicated, but at the same time, they provided comparability and supervisory effectiveness. The Basel Committee on Banking Supervision (2017) acknowledges that the distribution of risk-weighted asset calculation and dependence of advanced internal models can make it difficult to compare banks' positions in different regions. This problem can not only stress the supervisory team, but also affect the market confidence if the stakeholders consider the regulations to be unreliable.

Moreover, the rise of fintech, digital currencies, and decentralized finance has exposed significant gaps in the regulatory framework. These new technologies often work across borders and traditional banking structures fail to control them, leading to a challenge to the existing regulations and creating a regulatory arbitrage situation (Stanton Chase, 2025). Cybersecurity risks have also increased as banks depend more on digital infrastructure, requiring the need for coordinated, cross-border responses to emerging threats. Similarly, climate risk is also another issue to be addressed, as financial institutions and regulators understood the need for standardized data and robust frameworks to back up climate finance, yet there is a downtrend in achieving it, adding to this the IMF (2024) has quoted that there is lack of digital tools and infrastructure to verify climate metrics, which resisting the effectiveness of sustainable finance initiatives.

In the future, international banking regulations should be careful, leaving no space for regulatory arbitrage. At the same time, they should strengthen the capacity to face challenges and crises of the financial system and make sure the regulation focuses on proportionality, transparency, and is adaptable to new risks. The principle of proportionality, which sets regulations for institutions based on their size and risk, offers a smooth path as it reduces unwanted regulatory burden from small banks (GFM Review, 2025). At the same time, international coordination is essential to address cross-border challenges and prevent regulatory fragmentation.

The ongoing debate over macroprudential tools, such as countercyclical capital buffers and total loss-absorbing capacity requirements, highlight the requirement of a sophisticated approach to systematic risk, however these measurements helped to reduce the chances of "too big to fail" situations but they should be implemented in way that should not unfavour the small banks. The use of regulatory technology (RegTech) and artificial intelligence will play a major role in automating compliance and monitoring risk. However, the adoption is still not that progressed, only a small group of banks have fully implemented these tools into their operation (Stanton Chase, 2025).

Ultimately, the effectiveness of international banking regulation highly depends on its ability to evolve according to the dynamic financial landscape. Regulators must remain vigilant, proactive, and open to feedback from all the stakeholders of the financial system. The vulnerabilities of the earlier framework- crisis, regulatory arbitrage, and complexity of the rule are to be remembered while designing future regulations. The Basel Committee on Banking Supervision (2017) notes that the need for balance between risk sensitivity, simplicity, and comparability is a fundamental requirement to create confidence among the public in our financial system. Also the involvement of government as a regulator can improve the synergy between banks and uphold against crisis (Akhtar et al., 2024).

In sum, international banking regulation is a dynamic, ongoing process that reflects the relationship between innovation and risk and the demands of stability. The progress from the global financial crisis has been enormous, but there is still a long way to go. Through embracing the spirit of proportionality, international co-operation, and the opportunities provided by technology, regulators can help to support a banking system that is resilient, inclusive, and able to support sustainable growth in a world that is becoming ever more uncertain.

REFERENCES

Agoraki, M. E. K., Delis, M. D., & Pasiouras, F. (2011). Regulations, competition and bank risk-taking in transition countries. *Journal of Financial Stability*, *7*(1), 38–48. https://mpra.ub.uni-muenchen.de/121587/1/MPRA_paper_121587.pdf. DOI: 10.1016/j.jfs.2009.08.002

Ahmad, A., Khan, A., Akhtar, S., & Akram, H. W. (2021). Examining the Development of Banking Sector Regulations and Supervision Practices across BRICS and G7 Countries. *Complexity, 2021*(1). DOI: 10.1155/2021/1192829

Akhtar, S., Alam, M., & Khan, M. M. (2021). YES Bank fiasco: Arrogance or negligence. *Emerging Economies Cases Journal*, *3*(2), 95–102. DOI: 10.1177/25166042211061003

Akhtar, S., Azmi, S. N., Khan, P. A., Jan, A. A., & Ansari, Z. (2024). Unveiling the financial landscape: Analyzing profitability, productivity, and efficiency of banks in an emerging economy using the CAMELS framework and panel analysis. *Cogent Business & Management*, *11*(1), 2399747. Advance online publication. DOI: 10.1080/23311975.2024.2399747

Akinbami, F. (2011). Financial services and consumer protection after the crisis. *International Journal of Bank Marketing*, *29*(2), 134–147. DOI: 10.1108/02652321111107620

Alam, M., Akhtar, S., & Al-Faryan, M. S. (2023). Do Indian banks perform better in corporate governance than other SAARC nations? An empirical analysis. *Corporate Governance (Bradford)*, *24*(4), 799–830. DOI: 10.1108/CG-02-2023-0059

Aluko, A., & Bagheri, M. (2012). The impact of money laundering on economic and financial stability and on political development in developing countries. *Journal of Money Laundering Control*, *15*(4), 442–457. DOI: 10.1108/13685201211266024

Ams, J., Asonuma, T., Bergthaler, W., DeLong, C., Mehdi, N. E., Flanagan, M., Hagan, S., Liu, Y., Lundgren, C., Mühleisen, M., Pienkowski, A., Pinto, G., & Robert, E. (2018). *Prevention and resolution of sovereign debt crises.* Selected Legal and Institutional Papers Series., DOI: 10.5089/9781484371329.009

Ansari, M. S., Akhtar, S., Khan, A., & Shamshad, M. (2023). Consequence of Financial Crisis on liquidity and profitability of commercial banks in India: An empirical study. *Studies in Economics and Business Relations*, *3*(2), 36–50. DOI: 10.48185/sebr.v3i2.367

Bank for International Settlements. (2019). Proportionality in bank regulation and supervision – a joint global survey. https://www.bis.org/bcbs/publ/d523.pdf

Bank regulation definition, importance & examples – IDnow. (n.d.). IDnow. Retrieved June 2, 2025, from https://www.idnow.io/glossary/bank-regulation/

Basel Committee on Banking Supervision. (1999). Supervisory lessons to be drawn from the Asian crisis (Working Paper No. 2). https://www.bis.org/publ/bcbs_wp02.pdf

Basel Committee on Banking Supervision. (2006). Core principles methodology. https://www.bis.org/publ/bcbs130.pdf

Basel Committee on Banking Supervision. (2017). Basel III: Finalising post-crisis reforms. https://www.bis.org/bcbs/publ/d424.htm

Basel Committee on Banking Supervision. (2017, December 7). Basel III: International regulatory framework for banks. https://www.bis.org/bcbs/basel3.htm

Basel Committee on Banking Supervision. (2019). Core principles for effective banking supervision.

Basel Committee on Banking Supervision. (2021). Assessing the impact of Basel III: Evidence from macroeconomic models: literature review and simulations. In *Working Paper 38*. https://www.bis.org/bcbs/publ/wp38.pdf

Basel Committee on Banking Supervision. (2021). Basel III monitoring report September 2021 (by Birn, M., Martiarena, G. A., Yen, G., et al.). https://www.bis.org/bcbs/publ/d524.pdf

Brownbridge, M., & Kirkpatrick, C. (2000). Financial regulation in developing countries. *The Journal of Development Studies*, *37*(1), 1–24. DOI: 10.1080/713600056

Brummer, C. (2012). Financial Stability Board Charter. *International Legal Materials*, *51*(4), 828–839. DOI: 10.5305/intelegamate.51.4.0828

Caprio, G., & Honohan, P. (1999). Restoring banking stability: Beyond supervised capital requirements. *The Journal of Economic Perspectives*, *13*(4), 43–64. DOI: 10.1257/jep.13.4.43

Caruana, J. (2010, February 12). Systemic risk: How to deal with it? https://www.bis.org/publ/othp08.htm

CIGI. (2013). Financial inclusion and global regulatory standards (CIGI Papers No. 7). https://www.cigionline.org/static/documents/new_thinking_g20_no7.pdf

Consumer Financial Protection Bureau. (2024). About us. https://www.consumerfinance.gov/about-us/the-bureau/

Council on Foreign Relations. (2023). What is the Dodd-Frank Act? https://www.cfr.org/backgrounder/what-dodd-frank-act

De Mendonça, H. F., Galvão, D. J. C., & Loures, R. F. V. (2012). Financial regulation and transparency of information: Evidence from banking industry. *Journal of Economic Studies (Glasgow, Scotland), 39*(4), 380–397. DOI: 10.1108/01443581211255602

Eurofi. (2024). Banking union challenges [PDF]. https://www.eurofi.net/wp-content/uploads/2024/12/the-eurofi-financial-forum_budapest_banking-union-challenges_summary_september-2024.pdf

European Banking Authority. (2024). Deposit guarantee schemes data. https://www.eba.europa.eu/activities/single-rulebook/regulatory-activities/depositor-protection/deposit-guarantee-schemes-data

European Central Bank. (2024, September 18). Milestones. https://www.bankingsupervision.europa.eu/about/thessm/milestones/html/index.en.html

European Central Bank. (2024). Understanding the banking union and ESFS. https://www.bankingsupervision.europa.eu/about/thessm/bankingunion/html/index.en.html

Federal Reserve. (2023). Volcker Rule: Final amendments. https://www.federalreserve.gov/newsevents/pressreleases/bcreg20230728a.htm

Financial regulation after the "Subprime" crisis: What lessons can be learned and what reforms undertaken? (n.d.). Retrieved June 2, 2025, from https://www.robert-schuman.eu/en/european-issues/246-financial-regulation-after-the-subprime-crisis-what-lessons-can-be-learned-and-what-reforms

Ghosh, S., Sugawara, N., & Zalduendo, J. (2011). Bank Flows and Basel III—Determinants and regional differences in emerging markets. In *World Bank, Washington, DC eBooks*. DOI: 10.1596/10099

Global Financial Stability Report. (2018, October). A decade after the global financial crisis: Are we safer? DOI: 10.5089/9781484375594.082

Gulati, R. (2020). Demystifying gaps and testing for convergence in bank regulations impacting the competitive environment: A case of India and its peers in BRICS. *Journal of Financial Regulation and Compliance, 29*(1), 15–43. DOI: 10.1108/JFRC-01-2020-0005

Hellmann, T. F., Murdock, K. C., & Stiglitz, J. E. (2000). Liberalization, moral hazard in banking, and prudential regulation: Are capital requirements enough? *The American Economic Review, 90*(1), 147–165. DOI: 10.1257/aer.90.1.147

History of the Basel Committee. (2014, October 9). Retrieved June 2, 2025, from https://www.bis.org/bcbs/history.htm

Houston, J. F., Lin, C., & Ma, Y. (2012). Regulatory arbitrage and international bank flows. *The Journal of Finance*, *67*(5), 1845–1895. DOI: 10.1111/j.1540-6261.2012.01774.x

IMF. (2024). Fintech applications for boosting climate finance in emerging markets. https://www.elibrary.imf.org/view/journals/066/2024/008/article-A001-en.xml

International and national regulatory frameworks – Oesterreichische Nationalbank (OeNB). (n.d.). Retrieved June 2, 2025, from https://www.oenb.at/en/financial-market/banking-supervision/regulatory-frameworks.html

International Monetary Fund. (2010). Impact of regulatory reforms on large and complex financial institutions. https://www.imf.org/external/pubs/ft/spn/2010/spn1016.pdf

Jha, P., Akhtar, S., & Rana, P. (2025). *The swift rise and sudden fall: Examining the collapse of Silicon Valley Bank*. Emerging Economies Cases Journal., DOI: 10.1177/25166042251319596

Jokipii, T., & Monnin, P. (2012). The impact of banking sector stability on the real economy. *Journal of International Money and Finance*, *32*, 1–16. DOI: 10.1016/j.jimonfin.2012.02.008

King, M. R. (2013). The Basel III Net Stable Funding Ratio and bank net interest margins. *Journal of Banking & Finance*, *37*(11), 4144–4156. DOI: 10.1016/j.jbankfin.2013.07.017

Li, S. (2021). Bank Competition, Regulation, and efficiency. In *Contributions to finance and accounting* (pp. 133–178). DOI: 10.1007/978-981-16-3509-0_5

Mba, C. F. (2024, July 8). Risk mitigation in banking: Tools, techniques, and best practices. Retrieved June 2, 2025, from https://www.linkedin.com/pulse/risk-mitigation-banking-tools-techniques-best-cristina-firica-mba-zniif/

Moudud-Ul-Huq, S. (2020). Does bank competition matter for performance and risk-taking? empirical evidence from BRICS countries. *International Journal of Emerging Markets*, *16*(3), 409–447. DOI: 10.1108/IJOEM-03-2019-0197

Oliver Wyman. (2023). The EU banking regulatory framework and its impact on banks and the economy. https://www.ebf.eu/wp-content/uploads/2023/02/The-EU-banking-regulatory-framework-and-its-impact-on-banks-and-the-economy_30Jan-1.pdf

Panico, C., Pinto, A., Anyul, M. P., & Suarez, M. V. (2014). The evolution of financial regulation before and after the crisis. *Revista Economica, 15*(1). Advance online publication. DOI: 10.22409/economica.15i1.p54

Pavlidis, G. (2020). Financial action task force and the fight against money laundering and the financing of terrorism. *Journal of Financial Crime, 28*(3), 765–773. DOI: 10.1108/JFC-09-2019-0124

Plotnikova, M. (2018). *Too Big to Fail or Too Small to Compete? The Impact of Basel III on Risk Taking of Large and Small Bank* [Master's Thesis, Radboud University]. https://theses.ubn.ru.nl/handle/123456789/5873

Reetu, & Devi, M. (2025). The evolution of financial regulation: A historical overview. International Journal of Creative Research Thoughts (IJCRT), 13(3), J728–J729. https://www.ijcrt.org/papers/IJCRT25A3128.pdf

Repullo, R. (2004). Economic and regulatory capital in banking: What is the difference? *International Journal of Central Banking, 3*(3), 87–117.

Review, G. F. M. (2025, May 15). The complexity of clarity: Why banking needs more than simple rules. https://www.gfmreview.com/banking/the-complexity-of-clarity-why-banking-needs-more-than-simple-rules

Single Resolution Board. (2024). Single Resolution Mechanism. https://www.srb.europa.eu/en/content/single-resolution-mechanism

Teglio, A., Raberto, M., & Cincotti, S. (2012). THE IMPACT OF BANKS' CAPITAL ADEQUACY REGULATION ON THE ECONOMIC SYSTEM: AN AGENT-BASED APPROACH. *Advances in Complex Systems, 15*(supp02), 1250040. DOI: 10.1142/S0219525912500403

U.S. Commodity Futures Trading Commission. (2024). Dodd-Frank Act Title VII. https://www.aima.org/asset/3C46E7C1-08D2-49DD-A82E9317C3EF04D7.9BDBBD0D-30E5-4C87-BF4C78D94207928E/

U.S. Department of the Treasury. (2024). Financial Stability Oversight Council. https://home.treasury.gov/policy-issues/financial-markets-financial-institutions-and-fiscal-service/fsoc

Wang, W., Zhang, J., & Wang, Y. (2021). Capital Supervision, Information Disclosure and Risk-taking—Evidence from Rural Commercial Banks in China. *Emerging Markets Finance & Trade, 58*(8), 2273–2289. DOI: 10.1080/1540496X.2021.1971076

Yan, M., Hall, M. J., & Turner, P. (2012). A cost–benefit analysis of Basel III: Some evidence from the UK. *International Review of Financial Analysis*, *25*, 73–82. DOI: 10.1016/j.irfa.2012.06.009

Yang, X., ... (2025). The impact of community banks' innovation on regulatory choices. Edinburgh Research Explorer. https://www.research.ed.ac.uk/files/509090128/YangEtal2025EAPTheImpactOfCommunityBanks_Innovation.pdf

Yin, H. (2021). The impact of competition and bank market regulation on banks' cost efficiency. *Journal of Multinational Financial Management*, *61*, 100677. DOI: 10.1016/j.mulfin.2021.100677

ADDITIONAL READING

Avgouleas, E. (2015). *Governance of global financial markets: The law, the economics, the politics*. Cambridge University Press.

Barth, J. R., Caprio, G., & Levine, R. (2013). *Guardians of finance: Making regulators work for us*. MIT Press.

Borio, C. (2014). The financial cycle and macroeconomics: What have we learnt? *Journal of Banking & Finance*, *45*, 182–198. DOI: 10.1016/j.jbankfin.2013.07.031

Claessens, S., Kodres, L., & Narain, A. (2012). Macroprudential policy: What instruments and how to use them? International Monetary Fund. https://www.imf.org/external/pubs/ft/sdn/2012/sdn1205.pdf

Dewatripont, M., Rochet, J.-C., & Tirole, J. (2010). *Balancing the banks: Global lessons from the financial crisis*. Princeton University Press.

Goodhart, C., & Lastra, R. M. (2018). Populism and banking regulation: After Basel III. *International Journal of Constitutional Law*, *16*(2), 391–417. DOI: 10.1093/icon/moy030

Herring, R. J., & Carmassi, J. (2009). The structure of cross-sector financial supervision. *Financial Markets, Institutions and Instruments*, *18*(1), 49–76. DOI: 10.1111/j.1468-0416.2008.00130.x

Lastra, R. M. (2015). *International financial and monetary law* (2nd ed.). Oxford University Press. DOI: 10.1093/law/9780199671090.001.0001

Schwarcz, S. L. (2016). Systemic risk. *The Georgetown Law Journal*, *97*(1), 193–249. https://scholarship.law.duke.edu/faculty_scholarship/193

Tucker, P. (2018). *Unelected power: The quest for legitimacy in central banking and the regulatory state*. Princeton University Press.

Chapter 5
Sustainable Finance and Banking Policy Approaches for Stability

Rishikaysh Marotrao Kaakandikar
https://orcid.org/0000-0003-0349-6788
SaiBalaji International Institute of Management Sciences, India

Swati S. Bhalerao
Indira College of Pharmacy, India

ABSTRACT

In the face of escalating climate risks, environmental degradation, and socio-economic inequalities, sustainable finance and banking have emerged as critical levers to drive stability and resilience in the global financial system. This chapter explores the evolving landscape of sustainable finance, focusing on how regulatory and policy frameworks are shaping banking practices to align with environmental, social, and governance (ESG) goals. It critically examines various policy approaches ranging from green taxonomy development, disclosure regulations, and central bank interventions to prudential measures and fiscal incentives. Through comparative analysis of global initiatives and national strategies, the study highlights how a cohesive policy environment can enhance risk management, promote long-term investment, and ensure systemic financial stability. The chapter concludes by offering recommendations for policymakers and financial institutions to foster a more sustainable and inclusive financial future.

DOI: 10.4018/979-8-3373-3725-8.ch005

INTRODUCTION

Finance and Banking Overview

The movement towards responsible investment and long-term value appreciation is proven by the fact that the ESG investment and sustainable finance are developing into a fundamental constituent of the modern financial system. Modern environmental, social, and governance (ESG) investing and sustainable finance have brought a paradigm shift in the world of finances over the recent years.

This shift of thinking could be seen in an increasing awareness by politicians, businessmen and investors that governance, social and environmental issues should be taken into account in the decision making process on investments and process-designing. This introductory part will focus on the key concepts of ESG investing and sustainable finance, their applicability, general principles, and what it may suggest to the global days in the field of the financial system.

There is an increase in the awareness by people that the sustainability of banking and finance are important in addressing the issue of climate change and driving sustainable growth in the economy.

Sustainable Finance

Sustainable finance is a type of financial decision that takes into account environmental, social and governance (ESG) impacts. Green Eye focuses on backing efforts and initiatives to promote a more sustainable economy. Important features are:

- **Green finance** supports projects that help the environment, such as making energy use more efficient and inventing renewable energy.
- **Socially Responsible Investing (SRI):** Means choosing investments that consider ethics, social values and the environment.
- **Impact Investing**: Steers investments toward options that positively affect communities and the environment as well as give financial benefits.

Sustainable Banking

The practice of using methods that support sustainability is called Sustainable Banking. This comprises:

- A green loan is for financing projects that are better for the environment.
- Applying environmental, social and governance rules to decisions about where to invest and lend.

- Sustainable products refer to products in the financial sector that promote the Sustainable Development Goals (SDGs).

Defining What Sustainable Finance is and the Ways it has Changed Over Time

According to the European Commission, sustainable finance implies taking environmental, social and governance (ESG) factors into account in decisions about the financial sector hence ensuring that more investments are placed in activities that are more environmentally and socially beneficial in the long-term.

Sustainable finance happens when investments in the financial sector are introduced to environmental, social and governance (ESG) considerations. Such method of operation implies an increase in large-scale spending on long term projects of companies which positively influence environment and economy as the the European Commission on comments. It has turned into a significant trend that regulators, big investors and asset managers across the world embrace.

Central Banks & Sustainable Finance

Central banks are becoming central providers of sustainable finance by incorporating environmental and social needs into regulation and monetary regulations. Faruq and Huq (2024) highlight the proactive functions that the central banks can assume to align the financial sector with sustainability agendas. In the same way, Pfister and Valla (2021) expose that although greening monetary policy has its set of difficulties, the financial stability goals are a more viable channel of dealing with climate crises. To reinforce this, Turek (2022) introduces a new paradigm of sustainable financial stability which has two prongs that include the adoption of environmental and macroeconomic resilience. Moreover, as Tkachenko (2024) emphasises, the carbon footprint impact of AI should be included in the risk models as well since sustainability planning must be fully technology-oriented.

Importance of Financial Stability in Sustainable Development

Financial stability is associated with the achievement of sustainable development goals (SDGs). It helps stabilize the banking environment, builds confidence among investors, accelerates capital gathering in the long run and raises the support of programs that safeguard the environment and the society. Before development can be sustainable, it is required to have a stable financial system. That is why, green transitions, helping the population in poverty and equitable economic development can neither be funded nor sustained. A successful sustainable development is based on financial stability.

Foundation for Long-Term Investment

To support long-term sustainable development, we should place long term investments on renewable energy, roads as well as bridges, healthcare and education. The financial system is well established to lessen the risk of the investors both at home and abroad, and this makes money available in the long run. A more stable banking system leads to increased international resources of climate finance and green investment in a country (World Bank, 2022).

Effective Resource Allocation

Whenever there is stability in the financial sector, capital money can be channelled effectively towards essential activities, e.g. sustainable agriculture, healthcare and education. It facilitates the easier access of small business and marginalised groups to credit and finance, in line with inclusive growth.

Poverty Reduction and Social Inclusion

Sturdy financial systems help avoid frequent economic trouble that mostly hits people earning a lower income. When there are inclusive financial services and a health financial support system, everyone can become part of the economy.

Crisis Prevention and Mitigation

If an economy is stable, it is better able to recover from unforeseen shocks (such as pandemics, disasters and drops in the global economy) without losing much progress. Bailout Cost Effects Are Alleviated: This policy means that the government does not have to spend as much to bail out a business, which saves money that could go toward building the country.

Support for Policy Implementation

The stable financial institutions allow the Government to exercise financial, environmental and social policies in a manner that is stable and reliable. In stable economies the rate of interest is low, so there is more funding in the government hands to support the sustainable development. The development must be sustainable such that a financial base must be established. In so doing, resources would enjoy an equal opportunity to be used and economically be used efficiently, economical growth is futuristic, justice among human beings is achieved and the country is resistant to crisis. Without financial stability, it is highly inefficient and not easy to achieve the state of sustainable development.

Evolution of Sustainable Finance

The banking and payments sector is propelled by sustainable finance, which is leading to major changes and innovations. Looking at its past and making forecasts about its future is very important. Seeing the history of sustainable finance makes it easier to understand its ability to change and influence the world of finance.

UNEP Financial Initiative started operating in 1991.

With the help of UNEP, a collective of banks formed the UNEP Finance Initiative in the year 1991. The main goal of this collaboration was to encourage better sustainability in various places and secure strong financial support for these projects.

In 1992, a settlement was reached.

In less than two years of its inception, the goals and objectives of the UNEP Finance Initiative were accomplished. The commercial banks launched an information campaign to attract more financial institutions, agencies, venture capital firms and others to the sustainable finance topic.

During 1993 to 2005, energy toward reform increased.

Given the growing interest in the green finance, starting with a growing interest in green finance, UNEP Finance Initiative answers by establishing three key frameworks designed to advise how financial institutions are to conduct their operation.

Examples of such frameworks include: An example of such frameworks is the emphasis placed by the Principles for Responsible Investment (PRI) that considering environmental, social and governance factors (ESG) needs to be incorporated when making investment decisions.

The Principles for Responsible Banking (PRB) tie together the Sustainable Development Goals with the plans of banks. The Principles of Sustainable Insurance (PSI) have appealed to the use of sustainability in insurance industry when choosing risks.

In 2019, banks began to participate in sustainable finance movement.

In the same year 2019, 197 banks had joined the Responsible Banking Initiative as feasible due to the data collected by NatWast by that time, and a proportion of one-third of the total number of banks globally was participated by these banks in the Responsible Banking Initiative. The signatory banks must comply with three main targets to make their services more sustainable. They must:

1. Examine how they have begun affecting the environment.
2. Identify and implement specific goals.
3. Make publicly known what they have accomplished.

Sustainable bank companies have observed significant alteration of lending regulations in 2021. Later, in May, the expectations of Sustainability-Linked Loan Principles (SLLPs) have been simplified even more, in order to align with core performance indicators supporting both the success of borrower and the missions of sustainable banking.

Beyond 2023

With banks across different sectors coming out with new offerings for sustainability, sustainable finance is on the verge of being accepted by more people. At this level, people can decide if they want to use products that give custom suggestions related to what they buy and their environmental impact. These qualities are supposed to make people select sustainable products and services instead. Still, the use of personalised recommendations will collect data about individuals, leading to privacy issues.

BANKING HELPS ENCOURAGE SUSTAINABLE PRACTICES (RBI BULLETIN, RESERVE BANK OF INDIA)

Banks play a big role in supporting sustainability by lending to green projects, acting environmentally responsibly and assisting in the switch to a low-carbon world.

Investment and Financing Within Green Finance

Banks are now using green finance more, which consists of financial services to help environmentally friendly projects. Spending on clean energy programs, using green bonds and containing greenhouse gas emissions are all aspects of this.

Money that banks commit to sustainable ventures is important for the advancement of global sustainability.

Green Bonds: Debt securities called Green Bonds are issued mainly to raise money for initiatives that benefit the environment. Banks take part in green bond issuance as well as in investing in them to fund green energy, farming, and improving energy use. Financial institutions are now using Environmental, Social and Governance (ESG) criteria when making investment decisions. The evaluation process looks at finances as well as the environmental and social results of different projects.

Adopting Ethics in Business

When a bank acts sustainably, it is ethical and acknowledges how its financial activities shape things as a whole. More and more, banks are realising how their lending and investment actions play a key role in developing a sustainable economy. This period is defined by a number of main components.

Risk management is being changed to include sustainability by an increasing number of banks. They can determine the environmental risks of each project so that they can decrease possible losses and build a more reliable financial system. Successful Banks: To help the environment, banks have begun using green energy in their offices and creating less waste. As well as cutting their carbon emissions, these actions prove that these companies are serious about sustainability.

Provides Help in Creating Regulations and Frameworks

It is the Reserve Bank of India and other such regulatory organisations that help promote sustainable banking. They build rules that motivate banks to pick eco-friendly lending approaches and invest in green projects. Prominent examples are: For Priority Sector Lending, the rules say to focus on green projects.

Backing Green Initiatives: Banks in the UN are advised to increase their lending to environmentally friendly ventures. Communities need to have sound finances for sustainable development. Financial stability is necessary for sustainable development goals (SDGs) to be reached. This helps the stability of the banking sector, improves confidence among investors, makes it possible to form capital for the long term and encourages environmental and social work.

First we need financial stability, because only then can a country work towards achieving sustainable development. It is necessary for green transitions, reduced poverty and inclusive growth if they are to be financed or sustained. For sustainable development, financial stability is very important in many ways.

Long-Term Investment is the Core

Investing continuously in renewable energy, infrastructure, healthcare, and education supports sustainable growth. A well-balanced financial system lowers risk for both local and foreign investors which encourages more capital to come in the long run. Countries that have stable banks attract more green investment and climate finance, according to the World Bank (2022).

Global Policy Frameworks and Initiatives

Updating global policies and pushing for new initiatives helps to develop sustainable finance and banking. Some major examples of these frameworks and initiatives are listed here.

1. The United Nations Environment Programme Finance Initiative (UNEP FI).

UNEP FI was established in 1992 as the result of cooperation between the United Nations Environment Programme and the international financial sector. It will target to ensure that financial institutions take social and environmental determinants in their operations to enhance sustainable finance.

2. Principles for Responsible Investment (PRI)

Created in 2005, the PRI asks investors to include environmental, social and governance (ESG) factors in their investment portfolios. It aims to strengthen and increase the sustainability of the world's financial system.

Figure 1. shows the Principles for Responsible Investment (PRI).

3. Paris Agreement (concluded in 2015)

Countries have under this agreement established climate targets that are significant at the international level. Due to it, there has been a plea to countries to match their financial aid with climate-resistant development.

The Paris agreement and the consequences it will bring to the financial issues

In 2015, the inking of the Paris Agreement indicated that countries were serious in tackling climate change. it emphasizes the significance of money to climate objectives and maps out a framework over which countries can cooperate in curbing warming.

The second clause of article 2.1(c) of the Paris Intent lays emphasis on the need to align the finance with a strategy to reduce greenhouse gas (GHG) emissions and promote climate-resilient growth. Therefore, the public and the private financial systems should act in order to support the climate and sustainability objectives.

The Paris Agreement is an international treaty on dealing with climate change which was ratified in COP21. It aims at ensuring that global warming does not exceed 2 C, although, 1.5 C is an optimum target. This treaty is endorsed by majority of countries.

Development Status is a Requirement in Finances: Financial pledges in the Paris treaty that take into consideration whether the countries are developed or not is extremely crucial. It urges the developed countries to invest capital in helping in the fight against climate in developing countries. Having the Green Climate Fund and other similar sources of funds will be significant to collect and distribute climate funds required in the agreed goals.

4. The Principles for Responsible Banking (PRB)

The PRB was created by the UN Environment Programme Finance Initiative (UNEP FI) so that banks could integrate their sustainability strategies with sustainability development visions, such as UN SDGs and the Paris Climate Accord.

In 2019 the PRB was established to check that the banks embrace the element of working sustainability into its business operations in a bid to serve not only the environment but also the community.

Six Principles for Responsible Banking (PRB) are called Responsible Banking Principles.

1.Relate the business strategy to the aims defined in the SDGs and Paris Agreement as well as to the demands and objectives of individuals and society.
2.Establish measures to avoid or minimize the damage that the bank is causing as they look to find more ways of doing good. At least have your goals somewhere visible to most people such that your efforts count.
3.Customers and Clients: Enroll in sustainable practices and ensure that the business they partner will result to present and future prosperity by behaving ethically.
4.Find the right people to ensure that the bank strives to pursue the aspirations of the society.
5.Culture & Governance: Train bankers about the responsible behaviour and strategise governance framework.
6.Accountability & Transparency: Compare and report the successes and difficulties that the bank faces in managing the principles and publicize the results on timely basis.

5. *Task Force on Climate-Related Financial Disclosures (TCFD)*

TCFD has been established in 2015 and it is involved in the reinvention of the practices to enhance the information on climate change within financial statements. Consequently, the investors may make improved decisions as they will know of the fiscal climate change effects on the climate.

6. *The Network for Greening the Financial System (NGFS)*

In 2017, the NGFS was founded to include supervisors and central banks who are dedicated to improving how financial systems face environmental and climate risks. It suggests ideas for central banks to consider climate-related risks when checking financial stability.

7. *The Sustainability-Linked Loan Principles (SLLPs)*

SLLPs, which debuted in 2019 and were revised in 2021, set rules for loans that help ensure borrowers follow certain sustainable goals. They make sure the terms of the loan suit the sustainability aims of the organisation taking the loan.

8. *Europe is Aiming to Reach the European Green Deal.*

The European Commission launched the European Green Deal, a wide set of actions, to achieve climate neutrality for the EU by 2050. Creating the EU Taxonomy for Sustainable Activities is an important part of its effort to make finance more sustainable.

Using these frameworks and programs, which create standards, offer guidance and promote teamwork, is vital for moving toward a more sustainable world economy.

UNITED NATIONS SUSTAINABLE DEVELOPMENT GOALS (UN SDGS)

Sustainable Development Goals (UN SDGs) formulated at the United Nations and the work of the financial sector (THE 17 GOALS | Sustainable Development)

Through the Sustainable Development Goals (SDG) the United Nations is challenging all people to end poverty, conserve the environment and make sure that all people live in peace and prosperity all by 2030. In 2015 they were adopted by all the countries who were members of the United Nations as part of the 2030 Agenda for Sustainable Development.

The process focuses on the 17 Sustainable Development Goals (SDGs), that are meant to challenge countries all over the world to work timely when it comes to resolving international issues. There are 169 distinctive goals to every goal and 232 indicators of measuring the progress.

The UN Sustainable Development Goals (SDGs) and the financial sector are becoming interconnected due to the fact that the goals will require a lot of money; they will also be associated with systemic change that the financial world can contribute to. When introducing SDGs into finance, they will act as priorities during risk review, investment decisions, and capital utilization on sustainable successes.

This is the way the financial industry supports the SDGs.

1. Using Capital for the Development of the SDGs

It is estimated by the UN that achieving the SDGs will require \$5–7 trillion a year, and the developing world would be responsible for \$2.5 trillion. The movement of private funds towards goals set by the SDGs will depend mainly on banks, insurers and asset managers. Examples are impact investing, sustainability-linked loans, green bonds and blended finance, which brings together public funds with private ones.

2. Joining the ESG and SDG America Data Challenge

A large number of organisations consider Environmental, Social and Governance (ESG) criteria when making investment and lending choices as proxies for achieving the SDGs. Specific goals like achieving gender equality or combating climate change (SDG 5 or SDG 13) can be supported in portfolios by adopting proven standards like the UNEP FI SDG Impact Standards, which connect investments to SDGs.

3. New Strategies in Banking and Insurance

Companies are encouraged by PRB and PSI to set strategies that contribute positively to the SDGs. Many banks set targets to support more women entrepreneurs (SDG 5) or projects powered by renewable energy (SDG 7).

4. Stock Exchanges and Reporting Aligned With the Sustainable Development Goals

In different parts of the world, more than 100 stock exchanges have programs in place to promote sustainable reporting and SDGs (such as the Sustainable Stock Exchanges Initiative). Companies are urged to share their support of the SDGs so that transparency increases and they can attract impact investors.

5. Financial Products Made to Support the SDGs

The name green bonds or SDG bonds describes investments that can be used for projects supporting certain SDGs (such as setting up affordable housing or clean water systems). You may invest your money in businesses that work on improving health or education. SDGs like reducing poverty (SDG 1) and promoting decent work (SDG 8) can be achieved thanks to microfinance and inclusive finance.

THE RELEVANCE OF BASEL III TO SUSTAINABILITY

Basel III is a new rule proposed by the Basel Committee on Banking Supervision (BCBS) implementing a new global rule on banking supervision and regulations to ensure better handling of risk, supervision and regulations by the world banks. Basel III was caused by the global financial crisis experienced in the year 20072009 which indicated that Basel II was highly flawed. Because Basel II failed to satisfy the required standards, there emerged the Basel III. Important standards provided through Basel III framework establish new liquidity guidelines, establish higher and higher quality capital, greater risk coverage, leverage ratios as hedge against emerging needs in the future, and means of accumulating capital that can be accessed in the course of a crisis.

Basel III Component Details: its relationship with Sustainability

It is stipulated that the banks should store adequate capital to mitigate losses (Pillar 1)

Environmental risk lens can assist in reducing the threat of putting much in high-emitting industries. The liquidity standards (LCR, NSFR) are important to assist in the management of the short-run and long-term cash needs of the banks. Out-of-budget expenses are inevitable when natural calamities such as flood and wild fires strike; funding green can be the safer option. Internal risk management and capital adequacy assessment (ICAAP) - The effectiveness of managing climate-related financial risks in the stress tests and supervisory expectations of this pillar is being increased. It is through transparency that disclosure (Pillar 3) assists the market to better identify and evaluate sustainability risks by banks.

System-Wide Risk Monitoring Watching to protect the risks that interconnect the distinct regions of the financial system. It may entail system wide climate risk and regulators can employ Basel III regulations to avert instability within the financial system.

Risk sensitivity & calibration There is an increased tendency to increase the identification of risks (including operational, market and credit risks), particularly the consideration of climate risks in the risk weighting scores, as the existing ones may not reflect climate risk, possibly leading to failure of traditional analysis.

Stress testing & scenario analysis Immune to adverse situations and change in a climate over time are measured by how banks are affected.

Table 1. The parts of Basel III and why they matter in sustainable finance

Basel III Component	Description	Relevance to Sustainability
Capital Requirements (Pillar 1)	Minimum capital ratios to absorb losses	Recommendations for "Green Supporting" or "Brown Penalising" factors to align capital punishment with environmental risks
Leverage Ratio	Non-risk-based backup to prevent over-leveraging	Taking climate risk-adjusted assets into consideration could discourage overexposure to high-carbon industries.
Liquidity Standards (LCR, NSFR)	Ensure that banks are able to meet both short-term and long-term liquidity requirements.	Climate events such as floods and wildfires can result in unexpected cash outflows; green portfolios may offer greater resilience.
Supervisory Review (Pillar 2)	Internal risk management and capital adequacy assessment (ICAAP)	Stress testing and supervisory expectations are increasingly taking climate-related financial risks into account.
Disclosure (Pillar 3)	Promotes market discipline through transparency	supports the TCFD/ISSB-aligned disclosures on climate change to educate stakeholders about banks' sustainability risks.
Systemic Risk Monitoring	Macro prudential monitoring of interrelated hazards	Systemic climate risk may exist, and regulators may employ Basel III tools to stop financial instability throughout the system.
Risk Sensitivity & Calibration	Improved risk identification (e.g., operational, market, and credit risks)	There is a growing movement to better integrate climate risk into risk weights because traditional models may understate climate risks.
Stress Testing & Scenario Analysis	Assess resilience under adverse conditions	used to assess banks' susceptibility to physical hazards and climate-related transitions over both short- and long-term timeframes.

ROLE OF TRANSPARENCY

Transparent environmental disclosures catalyse sustainable investing. Kenyon, Berrahoui, and Macrina (2022) propose a principle of carbon emission transparency to ensure better decision-making and accountability across the financial sector. Enhanced reporting requirements not only shift investor behaviour but also incentivise institutions to adopt greener operational practices, laying the groundwork for credible, sustainable finance practices

Task Force on Climate-related Financial Disclosures (TCFD) and the use of ESG

To encourage banks, investors, and companies to make consistent disclosures about financial risks related to climate change to the stakeholders, in 2015 the Financial Stability Board (FSB) established the Task Force on Climate-Related Financial Disclosures (TCFD).

In order to help companies provide reliable data that can be used to responsibly use their capital, in 2017 the TCFD published its final recommendations of disclosures related to climate.

The TCFD has over 1600 companies and organisations representing a total market value of nearly 16 trillion in most parts of the globe and the six continents. It has been used in the past few years to enable people make judgments as to how well their investments are going.

Milestone TCFD reporting was this year made mandatory in the G7 group (Canada, France, Germany, Italy, Japan, the United Kingdom and the United States).

The participants in TCFD consent to disclose their management of some of the critical sections of their business, and they are:

Figure 2. Taking lessons from TCFD to incorporate ESG

It has been suggested that firms should focus on or apply some of the TCFD recommendations about governance, strategy, risk management, measurement and goals.

Thematic Area What This Areas Emphasizes What's Important

1. The importance of climate risk supervision by management and the board and how they make the board and leadership take note of climate change
2. Corporate strategy can be modified based on how climate affects a business by considering risks in the near, medium and long term and preparing different scenarios.
3. Risk Management - Assessing risks related to climate change, using techniques from risk management and fitting them into the overall risk management of the company- Adjusts investment, credit or underwriting procedures to deal with climate risks properly
4. Climate monitoring and reporting involves choosing certain measures (e.g., greenhouse gas emissions) and setting goals for progress.

ROLE OF CENTRAL BANKS IN SUSTAINABLE FINANCE

Central banks work to shape the financial world so that development is sustainable. This role of supervisors, regulators and monetary authorities gives them influence over the financial sector's actions on environmental, social and governance (ESG) matters. These are the key activities central banks carry out to help promote sustainable banking and finance:

1. Central Banks

Central banks are now factoring in the economic repercussions of climate change when they predict inflation and growth which might guide them on interest rates. Several central banks are examining or applying green refinance or quantitative easing to help lend money to businesses that protect the environment.

2. Organizing Regulation and Supervision (of Finance)

As outlined by the Task Force on Climate-related Financial Disclosures (TCFD), central banks have the ability to make financial firms assess and report on any risks due to climate change. Reflected in Sustainability Reporting Standards, banks are asked to include ESG factors in their regular reports and risk assessments.

3. Encouraging Financial Stability

Systemic Threats – Uncontrolled habits and climate change put society's stability at risk in the future. Financial stability is ensured when central banks look at and manage these risks. Testing banks in various financial and economic situations to help them discover and fix weaknesses and become stronger.

4. Encouragement for Green Finance

Banks that finance environmentally friendly projects may be given better re-financing terms or different regulations by central banks. They may want to help expand confidence in market activities by contributing to setting up green bond frameworks and offering to participate as green bond investors.

5. Putting Together Sustainable Finance Policies

Central banks can work with governments and international groups to set up and implement sustainable finance strategies. Enhancing Skills: Consulting companies can provide libraries, workshops and ideas for the banking industry to develop sustainable technology.

6. ESG Standards

Many central banks are putting into place ESG standards when they supervise their foreign exchange reserves and investment advisers.

7. Internal Combined Efforts

When a financial institution uses green practices in its own operations, it inspires others in the sector.

CONTRIBUTION OF FINANCIAL INSTITUTIONS TO SUSTAINABLE DEVELOPMENT

The way capital flows move and the amount involved are affected by financial institutions. Part of their role is:

- Spend directly on green infrastructure and actions for climate control
- Using environmental, social and governance factors when making choices

Promoting more financial services available to people. Making sure companies are held responsible and transparent in what they do. They contribute to the move towards a world economy that is both low in carbon, fair and able to handle changes. The part that commercial banks play in organizing green funds. One of the ways commercial banks help is by encouraging private capital to be used in environmentally and sustainability focused projects.

Key Functions:

Green Financing Instruments: issuing and underwriting Green loans and bonds, using Sustainability-linked loans connected to ESG (environmental, social and governance) key performance indicators

Retail and Corporate Advisory: Directing clients how to implement ESG and green design in their projects. Guiding corporations through restructuring using customized financing

Checking ESG performance before approving any loan applicants. Having flexibility in setting interest rates for sustainability aims. HSBC, BNP Paribas and Standard Chartered are investing billions into green lending. Among the steps they take is joining groups such as the Net-Zero Banking Alliance (NZBA).

Fintech Innovations Supporting Sustainable Banking

The adoption of technology is enabling fintechs to change how sustainable finance operates.

Key Innovations:

1. The use of green digital banking means people can do transactions without paper and view their carbon usage.
2. Community crowdfunding for clean energy and solar power.
3. The use of blockchain for transparent trading and reporting related to environmental, social and governance.
4. ESG risk analysis and determining impacts make use of AI and big data.
5. Rural people are now more included in the financial system due to mobile micro-loans and digital wallets.

Examples:

Tandem Bank (UK) ensures its banking activities are environmentally friendly.

Doconomy (Sweden) supplies a credit card that keeps track of your environmental impact.

Sun Exchange (South Africa) is a platform where people can support solar panel projects using blockchain.

Benefits:

Making sustainable financing available to more people
Knowing the company's ESG picture at any moment
Solutions that can serve large numbers of underserved people.

REGULATIONS FOR GREEN AND SUSTAINABLE FINANCE

Governments and financial regulators have implemented regulations, frameworks and supervisory steps to ease the shift to a low-carbon economy and promote environmental care. They are sometimes called regulatory methods for addressing sustainable and green finance. The purpose of these strategies is to ensure that financial markets support goals like the Paris Agreement and the UN's Sustainable Development Goals (SDGs).

Lists of sustainable projects, also known as green finance taxonomies or classification standards (such as the EU Taxonomy).

Green Finance Taxonomies and Classification Standards allow companies to choose green options that are profitable as well. These rules intend to lessen fake claims about being eco-friendly by clearly highlighting how to be green.

A method of classifying financial data called a "green taxonomy" works by:

1. finds out what economic actions are not harmful to the environment.
2. Guides companies, financial investors and regulators.
3. helps put into action policy plans such as the European Green Deal and reaching net-zero.
4. helps get resources to projects that are focused on sustainability.

Key Regulatory Approaches to Green and Sustainable Finance

Table 2. Key Regulatory Approaches to Green and Sustainable Finance

Approach	Description	Examples/Practical Implementation
1. Taxonomies	Schemes for categorizing what makes up green or sustainable economic activity	- European Union Taxonomy Regulation: China's Green Bond-Endorsed Project Catalog
2. Disclosure Requirements	Requiring information about ESG and climate change for regulators and investors	- Reporting in compliance with EU SFDR, ISSB standards (IFRS S1 & S2), and TCFD
3. Prudential Regulation	Integrating climate risk into frameworks for banking supervision and capital adequacy	- Guidelines on climate risk supervision by the Basel Committee: ECB and BoE climate stress tests

continued on following page

Table 2. Continued

Approach	Description	Examples/Practical Implementation
4. Green Bonds & Labeling	Standards and certification programs for green financial products	- EU Green Bond Standard: Green Bond Principles (ICMA)
5. Sustainable Finance Strategies	Initiatives to assist national or regional green finance ecosystems	- The ASEAN Sustainable Finance Roadmap and the EU Sustainable Finance Action Plan
6. Central Bank Involvement	Central banks' efforts to integrate sustainability into their monetary policy and operations	- Network for Greening the Financial System (NGFS)- Green asset collateral or purchasing rules
7. ESG Integration in Investment	Incentives or requirements for institutional investors to consider ESG risks in their decision-making	- Stewardship Codes: ESG requirements for pension funds (e.g., in the UK, Japan, and Netherlands)
8. Climate Stress Testing	Assessing the financial system's resilience in scenarios related to climate change	- BoE Biennial Exploratory Scenario - ECB's climate stress exercises

EU Taxonomy acts as a Global Benchmark.

The EU Taxonomy Regulation (EU) 2020/852 provides a framework to help companies and investors find sustainable practices that meet six major environmental goals, such as biodiversity preservation, climate change adaptation, and mitigation. For an activity to be eligible, it must meet minimal social safety requirements, make a substantial contribution to at least one of these aims, and not seriously impair other goals. The rule affects ESG reports, sustainable investment labels, and the issue of green bonds, and it affects corporate sustainability reporting under the CSRD, affecting industries such as manufacturing, transportation, and energy. It improves openness and encourages prudent investing choices by establishing explicit standards.

Other Taxonomies Around the World

Global initiatives to create green taxonomies are influencing sustainable finance systems in different parts of the world, each of which adjusts to regional concerns while staying in line with more general climate objectives. Through the Common Ground Taxonomy, China's Green Bond Endorsed Projects Catalogue keeps in sync with the EU taxonomy while highlighting green bonds. The RBI and SEBI are still working on India's Draft Green Taxonomy, which incorporates sustainability goals related to the SDGs. Launched in 2022, South Africa's Green Finance Taxonomy focuses on efforts related to the circular economy, pollution avoidance, biodiversity conservation, and climate change. Using a principles-based methodology, ASEAN's Sustainable Finance Taxonomy focuses especially on transition finance.

In the meanwhile, the UK is seeking input on its Green Taxonomy to make sure it complies with EU laws while taking regional factors into account.

POLICY & REGULATORY DISCOURSE

The evolving role of regulations, especially Basel norms, in climate risk management has sparked debate. Llewellyn and Yan (2025) argue that downplaying Basel's role in climate regulation is misguided, as capital adequacy frameworks can indeed be adapted to climate-related risks. News coverage by Reuters (2025) supports this by highlighting the G20's push for broader climate transition plans among financial institutions. These developments underscore the rising significance of integrating climate risks into mainstream financial regulation and governance.

Stress Testing for Climate Risks

Testing the company's ability to handle climate-related risks.

In Stress Testing for Climate Risks, you check how economies, businesses or financial organisations may face problems brought about by climate-related events or changes. It is important for dealing with the financial risks from climate change and now central banks, regulators and businesses turn to it frequently.

The Most Important Aspects of Climate Stress Testing:

1. List of Climate Risks: These risks can arise from gradual changes (such as increased sea level or hotter weather) or sudden weather patterns (such as flooding, droughts or hurricanes). These are what occur during the change to a low-carbon economy, such as different choices by the market, new technology and alterations in laws.
2. To study different outcomes, climate stress testing creates scenarios that may or may not happen. The examples used are often the same as those found in groups such as the IPCC or NGFS. Examples of such scenarios are the "Net Zero by 2050" path or the "Delayed Transition" one.
3. Sectors Affected: Banks handle banking and insurance activities (related to credit risks and underwriting). Sectors like energy and heavy industries also face risks linked to new government regulations and the stranding of assets (for example, older coal plants having stranded value). Flood or fire damage to buildings (real estate), and Agriculture includes issues such as unreliable yield, water shortages.

4. Part of climate risk disclosure and prudential control, regulatory bodies (such as the Bank of England and the European Central Bank) now often ask for stress testing. Climate stress tests are common features in regulatory guidelines provided by the Task Force on Climate-related Financial Disclosures (TCFD) and the new International Sustainability Standards Board (ISSB).
5. Challenges: Many risks have not occurred in the past, which makes it harder to study them. Frequently, such risk models only take into account sudden shocks that last a short period. Doubt about future climate change policies and the growth of new technologies.
6. Use Cases: Guiding the way companies choose where to invest their funds. Making sure businesses tell people about possible climate risks they might face. Helping businesses with both regulatory compliance and strategic planning.

ESG Risk Management & Green Banking

Financial institutions and regulators are transitioning toward green banking models to mitigate ESG-related risks. Kim (2020) explores how financial regulators can set standards that guide banks toward greener portfolios. Malik, Irfan, and Munir (2024) propose a sustainable finance index that measures banks' ESG performance, which is critical for tracking progress within and across banking sectors. Tan (2022) further models sustainability efficiency in banking operations, showing how quantitative tools can aid in assessing green performance. Ferrer, Benitez, and Bolos (2024) use wavelet-based network analysis to study the interaction between green and conventional financial instruments, offering insights into risk spill-overs in sustainable investment markets.

Climate Risk, Green Loans & Public Discourse

Climate events labelled as "Green Swans" pose serious threats to financial stability, prompting urgent preparedness among banks (Time, 2021). Public scrutiny is growing over whether banks are doing enough to tackle climate change. A Financial Times (2024) article questions whether financial institutions are capable of truly solving the climate crisis or merely greenwashing their actions. AP News (2025) reveals how some mega-polluters exploit green loans, casting doubt on the efficacy of current systems. These insights suggest that while the momentum for sustainable finance is growing, vigilance, transparency, and accountability remain crucial.

Mandating ESG Disclosures and Sustainability Reporting

Since 2025, organisations have seen greater attention on sustainability reporting and ESG (Environmental, Social and Governance) disclosures, mainly thanks to new regulations in important countries. To show how they are doing and respond to stakeholders, businesses everywhere are being urged to adopt ESG and sustainability reporting. Some issues have not been resolved, mainly around harmonisation and enforcement, but ESG disclosure systems are still moving toward being necessary, harmonised and significant.

Examples of ESG Disclosures are Providing Information on:

These have environmental effects that include changes in the climate, using too much water, too much energy, too many carbon emissions, etc. Things focused on health and safety, how groups are represented, engaging the community and the treatment of workers. Governance: setting executive salaries, ethics in business, combating corruption and including people from various demographics on the board.

In the EU, ESG reporting by using the European Sustainability Reporting Standards (ESRS) will be required by the Corporate Sustainability Reporting Directive (CSRD) which comes into force in 2024.

In 2024, the SEC is still planning to get public feedback about its proposals for green disclosures by listed companies. UK: Privately-held and listed companies in the UK have to report on climate change following TCFD guidelines. ESG disclosure laws exist in countries like Singapore, India and Japan in Asia. Major frameworks used for Environmental, Social and Governance (ESG) reporting

1. The Global Reporting Initiative (GRI)

The Global Reporting Initiative (GRI) is the most popular framework used to measure sustainability at global and sector levels. By including governments, investors and civil society, GRI focuses on impact materiality which means considering how a company's actions influence the environment. Its modular setup allows it to be used in many types of organizations and industries since it can include sector-specific standards. Organizations inside and outside the public sector, NGOs and public enterprises regularly use GRI to enhance how they report and manage sustainability issues.

2. The Sustainability Accounting Standards Board (SASB)

The Sustainability Accounting Standards Board (SASB) provides a guide for understanding important ESG matters that are specific to each of the 77 industries, mainly to answer investors' interests. SASB was made in the United States, although the importance of ESG and its impact on company value has made it important around the globe. Because of its focus on financial materiality, the framework helps companies decide which ESG matters are likely to affect their income. Public companies that stress the need for following regulations and informing investors use it a lot.

3. The Task Force on Climate-related Financial Disclosures (TCFD)

The Task Force on Climate-related Financial Disclosures (TCFD) has designed a way to disclose climate-related risks and opportunities that is appropriate for investors and regulators. The task covers risk management, making long-term plans, handling climate matters and setting and using important measurement goals. The TCFD which focuses on governance, strategy, risk management and targets, asks companies to review the impacts of climate risks by doing scenario analysis. Due to its role in promoting transparency on climate matters, about 3,000 organizations worldwide now produce TCFD-aligned reports and the UK, EU and other countries have made it mandatory.

4. The International Sustainability Standards Board (ISSB).

The IFRS Foundation launched the International Sustainability Standards Board (ISSB) to unify and standardize what businesses should report about climate change and sustainability, especially to influence financial markets and investors. The ISSB aims to ensure that sustainability reporting is done under the same standards and in a way that is trusted by building on the work of TCFD and SASB. To easily become part of financial reporting systems, IFRS set up IFRS S1 for general sustainability rules and IFRS S2 for climate-related disclosures. The ISSB standards are being introduced in early 2024–2025 and are gaining backing from worldwide businesses, financial sectors and regulatory agencies.

5. The Carbon Disclosure Project (CDP)

Carbon Disclosure Project (now the CDP) is an environmental disclosure system many people use to report on climate change, water problems, deforestation and sustainability in supply chains. CDP focus on collecting data by sending questionnaires to investors, companies and governments and then scores each company on its honesty and the results it reaches on the environmental side. The findings are put to use by financial organisations and investors to examine environmental issues and how sustainable a company is. Currently, more than 18,000 companies from all over the world use CDP, which makes it a major force in environmental disclosure.

6. The Whole Purpose of <IR> is to Give a More Complete Account of a Company

The Integrated Reporting (-IR-) Framework says that by using both financial and non-financial data from six kinds of capitals, companies create value over time. Because the framework makes ESG considerations part of a company's business strategy, it brings about integrated thinking for investors and other stakeholders. This helps firms explain their entire business and its impacts, putting greater priority on creating lasting worth than getting quick cash profits. Following the merger with SASB, the IFRS Foundation is in charge of the framework that encourages companies to report more consistently and strategically

PRACTICES FOR FINANCIAL INSTITUTIONS THAT ARE SUSTAINABLE

Practices in sustainable banking help the environment, support society and maintain the financial health of the institution. Banks that make use of these practices strive to help create a sustainable future by using environmental, social and governance (ESG) principles in their operations.

Some Ways Banks Support Sustainability: Green businesses can take out loans and credit for renewable energy, sustainable farming, eco-friendly buildings and clean transport. Financing the growth of green projects via green bonds.

Inclusion of ESG Factors – Credit risk models now consider ESG factors in their analysis and so do investment decisions. Prevent projects that could cause harmful problems for the environment or society such as deforestation and coal mining. These options supply ethical funds or investment portfolios that focus on businesses that follow ESG rules. Encouraging impact investing which involves choosing investments that provide both profits and help in areas like the environment or community. Expanding Financial Inclusion - Giving banking services to people in places where they are not widely available. Helping to fund microfinance and small businesses, especially in places where they are needed most.

Measure taken by the bank to reduce its effect on the environment such as being more energy efficient and using renewable energy sources, as well as cutting down on waste. Promote digital banking because it lowers the need for paper and waste of resources. Global standards, including the Global Reporting Initiative (GRI) and the Task Force on Climate-related Financial Disclosures (TCFD), should be used for transparency and reporting. Releasing sustainability or ESG reports showing how the bank is performing and what it aims to achieve. Taking action through Stakeholder Engagement means partnering with governments, non-governmental organisations (NGOs), investors and customers to help achieve the Sustainable

Development Goals. Being a part of global initiatives like the UN Principles of Responsible Banking (PRB).

Pros of Sustainable Banking

More people are trusting the brand and feeling devoted to it. Better risk assessment by foreseeing future environmental and social risks. Interest ESG-conscious people in buying your products. Their influence on the United Nations Sustainable Development Goals (SDGs). Using environmental, social and governance criteria before granting loans or making investments, Banks need to consider environmental, social and governance (ESG) criteria when deciding how to lend and invest to be sustainable. It makes certain that financial organisations assess both finances and the effect their actions have on society and the environment.

What Does ESG Integration Refer to?

By adopting ESG integration, one systematically combines environment (like emissions), social (such as how people are treated and paid) and governance (e.g., diversity in the board, anti-corruption) factors into how risks are analysed, how loans are considered and what investments are made. ESG is taken into account when making lending choices.

Banks check if borrowers are respecting and complying with environmental and sustainability standards as part of their risk assessment. Industries with high-risk factors (like oil, mining and tobacco) are examined more closely by ESG watchers. An ESG-linked loan may require companies to meet sustainability performance targets, and the rates are arranged based on those results. Lenders might enforce measures on borrowers to bring their operations into line with ESG standards. Exclusion Policies -Certain banks use negative screening and will not grant loans to businesses involved in fossil fuels, deforestation, child labour or human rights violations.

Using ESG as Part of Making Investment Decisions

Strategies - Focus on investing in companies that excel in environmental, social and governance areas. Negative screening means avoiding investments in companies/sectors that do not meet environmental, social and governance standards. ESG Ratings and analysis– Banks and asset managers use companies such as MSCI and Sustainalytics to carry out their ESG analysis. Traditionally used metrics and ESG data are both used in financial modelling. Renewable energy, protecting water resources and gender equity are among the impact investing themes. With impact investing, returns and their positive effect on society and nature are examined.

Tools and Frameworks

1. The United Nations Principles for Responsible Investment (PRI)
2. The Equator Principles used for project financing
3. The Sustainability Accounting Standards Board (SASB).
4. Task Force on Climate-related Financial Disclosures (TCFD)

Why It Matters to Include ESG in Management

Risk mitigation requires you to anticipate risks from the government, society and the environment. Firms that focus on ESG often do better than others over time. Investor Trust: More people are seeking ethical and sustainable places to put their money. Following new ESG regulations and rules as they appear. Funds raised by green bonds and sustainability-linked loans

Green Bonds and Sustainability-Linked Loans

Projects and businesses can receive sustainable finance through green bonds as well as sustainability-linked loans (SLLs). The structures and purposes for these systems are not exactly the same, but sustainability is supported in both cases.

1. Green Bonds

Green bonds are used to raise money for tasks that help the environment.

Key Features: Where the Money Goes: Funds are limited to use on green projects (e.g., renewable energy, energy saving, clean transportation, eco-friendly water management).

Issuers are required to explain what green means, report on where the money is used and reveal any effects on the environment.

The standards and guidelines involved: The International Capital Market Association (ICMA) developed the Green Bond Principles (GBP).

Guidelines for how the EU can issue green bonds A company can be certified by the Climate Bonds Initiative.

Some Examples of Green Bonds: There are solar and wind farms. Buildings awarded LEED certification for being environmentally friendly. Infrastructure that uses less carbon and other resources. Solution for pollution and recycling plants

2. Sustainability-Linked Loans (SLLs)

Definition: An SLL is a flexible loan that depends on how sustainable the borrower is rather than assigning terms to one particular eco-friendly project.

Key Features: For this kind of pricing, interest is adjusted when a borrower meets certain Sustainability Performance Targets (SPTs). Without making specific commitments, SLLs let issuers use the funds they raise in a flexible manner.

Key performance indicators (KPIs) are connected to targets and measure outcomes. Lessening the amount of carbon used, Using renewable energy. Greater diversity between men and women.

Social Impact Banking

Social Impact Banking includes financial offerings that work to produce positive social effects as well as profits for the users. It gives attention to areas with less financial support, social business and projects that deal with social matters. Social enterprises can use the bank's loan and advisory services. The goal of impact measurement is to notice whether social factors are changing (like more employment or higher rates of schooling). Partners are brought together by teaming up with non-governmental organizations, governments and community organizations.

Microloans for cooperatives by women, grants for building social housing, Support for funding education and health for the community

Advantages: Includes those who might not have bank accounts, supports sustainable growth and makes socially aware customers trust and return to the brand.

Inclusive Finance

Inclusive Finance (Financial Inclusion) aims to provide those who do not normally have access with useful and reasonably priced financial offerings.

Access to services like saving, borrowing money, taking out insurance and making payments is included. The target customer groups are low-income households, residents of rural areas, women and small businesses. mobile banking, fintech solutions and agent banking are part of digital financial services. Tools and rules created by governments that push for equal treatment

Examples can be found in mobile money like M-Pesa in Kenya and Jan Dhan Yojana in India (giving access to banking for people without accounts). MFIs offer small loans to people who do not require any type of collateral as security.

Reducing poverty, reducing inequality, raising the voices of neglected groups and growing the local economy are some of the main benefits achieved through development.

Monitoring and Managing Risks to Environmental and Social Issues

Banks and financial institutions rely on environmental and social (E&S) risk assessment and management to identify and control the probable adverse effects of their investments and loans. managing E&S risks helps financial institutions avoid harm to their reputations, deal with legal issues and lose credit.

What Is the Term Environmental and Social Risks?

Environmental Risk elements are:

1. Appropriating funds for measures against Climate Change and Carbon emissions
2. Destruction of forests and loss of biodiversity.
3. Water is being polluted, which also causes scarcity.
4. Air and soil pollution
5. Dealing with waste disposal

Social Risks deal with issues like:

1. When labour rules, like those against child and forced labour, are violated
2. Communities are being pushed to new areas.
3. Health and safety issues
4. Problems with Inequality and Lack of Diversity
5. Abuse of people's human rights

The Process of Identifying Risks.

The first step is to spot sectors, clients or projects that are at high risk of having environmental or social issues (e.g., mining, oil and gas, large-scale farming). An exclusion list helps companies avoid getting involved in financing illegal practices (like unlawful harvesting of trees and arms trading).

Step 2: Create Risk Groups. Group the client by risk level (low, medium or high), determined by their E&S impact and their specific circumstances such as location, industry and past behaviour.

Example:

Category A (High Risk) includes projects that cause serious and lasting negative effects on the environment and society.

Category B (Medium Risk): Some problems which usually affect the site only

Category C (Low Risk): Little or no harm to the environment

In step 3, you should carry out detailed studies using Environmental and Social Impact Assessments (ESIs). Evaluate how the client deals with environmental, social and governance (ESG) issues and their compliance history. Whenever it is helpful, bring in specialised consultants or professionals from different fields.

The fourth step includes making decisions and planning how to address the risks. Once the E&S review is done, approval or disapproval for the financial support can be given based on the level of risk found. You can incorporate Environmental and Social Action Plans (ESAPs) or covenants that require risk management into the loan. Pricing, terms and the amount of credit available should change based on the level of risk.

Frameworks and Tools That Help With Risk Management

Many organizations use the Equator Principles to identify and handle environmental and social risks in project finance.

IFC Performance Standards: Directives for Dealing with Environmental and Social Risks in Developing Economies. The set of guidelines developed by the Organization for Economic Cooperation and Development (OECD) for regulating multinational companies. The United Nations Guiding Principles on Business and Human Rights.

Tools That Help Manage ESG Risks in a Business

Risk scores and scorecards. Examining how a company will be impacted by climate risks, for example, transition and physical risks. Maps that indicate where and what kind of risks exist. Clients fill out self-assessment questionnaires on environmental, social and governance factors.

Tracking and Reporting Regularly

1. Clients have to provide reports on their environmental and safety compliance on a regular schedule.
2. Supervise audits on-site for the riskiest projects.
3. Follow news about new threats and changes in rules.

Include details about environmental and safety into your company's internal risk dashboard reporting. Proper E&S Risk Management allows a company to avoid penalties from the law and regulation and improves the firm's reputation, credit risk rating and portfolio quality. Greater trust from stakeholders and conformity with global environmental, social and climate goals.

What Financial Institutions Do. - This breaks down the role of financial institutions in sustainable development and discusses the various means they use to mobilize environmentally-friendly money and aid in inclusive and sustainable growth.

How Financial Institutions Help with Sustainable Development. The management of capital flows depends on actions by financial institutions. Primary care providers are responsible for:

1. Defend funding for climate solutions and green infrastructure.
2. Adding ESG factors to the way decisions are made
3. Helping people gain access to financial services
4. Encouraging companies to be more interested in accountability and transparency.

They assist in making the economy healthier, more just and more resilient. The ways commercial banks facilitate the use of green capital. Directing capital toward eco-friendly causes is a main role for commercial banks.

Key Functions:

Green loans and Green bonds (when offering or underwriting) and loans that link their terms to ESG goals. Guiding clients in handling ESG requirements and making green project plans in retail and Corporate Advisory. Providing custom financing to support corporate changes

ESG Consideration: Looking at ESG records before offering loans to borrowers. Balancing interest rates according to sustainability aims

HSBC, BNP Paribas and Standard Chartered have invested billions in green lending. Banks have also joined organisations like the Net-Zero Banking Alliance (NZBA).

Developing Country Perspectives

The implementation of green banking in developing countries presents both opportunities and challenges. Rahman et al. (2022) conducted a systematic review of green finance practices in developing economies, showing that while there is growing awareness, policy and infrastructure gaps hinder effective execution. Their findings underline the importance of capacity-building and international cooperation in advancing sustainability in the global South.Alam, Akhtar, and Al-Faryan (2023) investigated the comparative corporate governance performance of Indian banks within the SAARC region. Similarly, Azmi and Akhtar (2023) explored the dynamic interplay between services exports, financial development, and economic growth in India. In a broader services context, Ladeira et al. (2024) conducted a meta-analysis on the role of big data analytics and artificial intelligence in enhancing the efficiency of the service industry. Akhtar et al. (2024) analyzed key financial indicators—profitability, productivity, and efficiency—of Indian banks using the CAMELS framework, while Khan, Akhtar, and Alam (2024) employed stochastic frontier analysis to evaluate the overall efficiency of Indian banks.

Development Banks and Programs Involving Public and Private Organisations

Development Banks (like the World Bank, ADB and AfDB) loan out funds at low interest rates for building infrastructure, climate protection and helping the poor. Reduce risks in private sector investment using guarantees, technical support and mixed financing. Invest heavily in clean and renewable energy, transportation and access to clean water to help the region.

Public-Private Partnerships (PPPs): Use public money to get private businesses to invest in sustainable infrastructure. Such projects often appear when high startup expenses and a long wait for benefits are involved (as with solar parks and water treatment plants). Help from shared risk groups and better systems for running banks.

Advantages: Fill the gaps in opportunities for investment in developing countries. Support new ideas and effective ways to finish projects. Ask private companies to contribute their expertise to national plans against climate change.

Microfinance Institutions and Rural Areas

MFIs support sustainability at the local level and encourage everyone's participation.

Contributions:

1. Give rural residents, with special emphasis on women, access to small loans, savings and insurance.
2. Encourage soil-smart farming, smart watering and clean forms of energy (such as solar lanterns and biogas units).
3. Try to encourage people to gain different incomes and start local businesses.

Areas Where Sustainability Counts: - Agro ecology and Organic Farming, - Supplies of safe water and proper sanitation in remote areas, - Off-grid ways to generate energy by using renewables

Impact:

Using music to empower those who feel underprivileged

1. Helping communities in climate-risk areas become more resilient
2. Having financial control supports both gender equality and access to education.

Innovation that helps realizes the goals of sustainable banking

Fintech companies are creating technology-powered changes in sustainable finance.

Key Innovations:

1. Paperless transactions are supported by green digital banking and the trackers notify the carbon impact.
2. Raising funds in the community for clean technology and solar energy programs.
3. Employing block chain for clear transactions of carbon credits and reporting on environmental, social and governance issues
4. AI and big data are used to check ESG risks and measure outcomes.

Today, more people in rural areas are included in the financial system by means of digital wallets and mobile micro-loans.

Examples:

Tandem Bank (UK) is known for its environmentally friendly banking policies.

Doconomy (Sweden): Gives you a credit card that helps you monitor your effect on the environment.

Sun Exchange (South Africa) allows people to back solar panel projects through blockchain.

Benefits: Providing more businesses with chances to access green finance

1. More openness and instant ESG information
2. Programs that can be used to help people in underserved areas.

Challenges in Implementing Sustainable Finance Policies

Even though more people are interested in sustainable finance, putting related policies into action is still very challenging. These difficulties stop financial systems from meeting environmental and social targets in the long term.

1. Lack of Standardised Sustainability Metrics

Problem: No standard way exists to evaluate and present ESG results. Because the approaches of ESG rating agencies differ, their rankings of a company may be different. Various opinions about what green or sustainable really means make it difficult to directly compare different markets and products.

Impact:

1. Both investors and lenders have problems comparing and wisely choosing among different projects.
2. The risk of "ESG-washing" appears when companies share inconsistent or unreliable details about ESG issues.
3. Factors that make it hard for different nations to work together and move money across borders for sustainable finance.

Example:

Because every ESG rating uses different approaches and sources of information, a company might score well on some but poorly on others.

2. Greenwashing and Reputational Risks

Problem: Organizations that overplay or lie about their care for the environment or society to gain resources or public approval are engaging in greenwashing. There is no guarantee that financial products listed as sustainable will result in sustainable behaviour.

Impact:

1. People no longer find sustainable finance products attractive.
2. Financial organisations have to handle both legal and reputation risk.
3. Capital investments that are not used wisely go against efforts for a better environment and society.

Example: In 2022, many large fund managers came under investigation for lying about how sustainable their ESG funds are.

3. Inadequate Regulatory Enforcement Mechanisms

Problem: Even if rules for sustainable finance are written, regulators are not always effective and tend to vary in enforcement. Many places do not have what is needed to properly enforce rules related to ESG issues.

Impact: Laws and frameworks are not always followed in the same way everywhere.

There is not much to stop companies from breaking rules or misleading people.

The industry is moving forward with ESG integration, but it is happening more slowly.

Example: Countries don't all implement the TCFD (Task Force on Climate-related Financial Disclosures) recommendations in similar ways.

4. Limited Awareness and Capacity-Building Needs

Problem: Most financial experts in developing and smaller countries as well as in lesser-known companies are yet to get educated in ESG analysis and sustainable finance.

- The firm has trouble with analyzing and using sustainability information for decision-making.

Impact: The lack of long-term investing and ways to manage risk stands out.

Putting too much faith in the opinions of or scores provided by, ESG rating agencies.

difficulty accepting new, environmental-friendly products.

Solution Needs: Specifically designed courses, additional support and environmental, social and governance (ESG) policies for particular industries. Including sustainability education within business and finance classes.

Empirical Evidence & Bank Performance

Empirical studies suggest a strong link between sustainability practices and financial stability. Adebambo, Olayemi, and Adeyemi (2025) provide evidence from Nigeria showing that sustainable banking enhances the stability of deposit money banks. Earlier research by Weber (2016) found that social banking in Europe led to reduced financial risk and improved performance. Jeucken (2001) and Scholtens (2009) emphasize that the financial sector, by embedding sustainability in its core operations, can significantly influence corporate responsibility and long-term profitability. Schoenmaker and Schramade (2019) consolidate these ideas into a comprehensive framework for sustainable finance principles.

CONCLUSION

Sustainable finance is about making sure financial activities take governance, social and environmental factors (known as ESG) into consideration. Ethical investing which once was a niche field, is now being widely used around the world. When banks set aside money for sustainability and apply ESG, they take a major role. Financial stability ensures the country's development helps all groups, long-term planning and the ability to withstand sudden changes.

Watching over the environment and helping society requires steps found in sustainable banking and finance. Agencies in the financial industry should not just convey change; they should drive it as countries make efforts to become more sustainable and equal. Working in partnership, policymakers, financial institutions, regulators and civil society can ensure a fair and reliable financial system that supports sustainability in the long run. Making sure institutions have the necessary skills, raising transparency and shoring up frameworks are crucial steps to bringing about the change.

Examples of international agreements that have urged the financial sector to meet sustainability goals are the UN Sustainable Development Goals (SDGs) and the Paris Agreement. The Basel III regulations and schemes such as the Task Force on Climate-related Financial Disclosures (TCFD) incorporate climate and ESG factors into risk management and financial decisions.

By considering the risks of climate, central banks and their regulatory bodies are beginning to get involved. Climate stress testing, the process of providing required ESG details and green taxonomies (like the EU Taxonomy) are all meant to make financial systems responsible and understandable for sustainability.

Banks depend on green bonds, sustainability-linked loans and inclusive finance to assess how they make their lending and investment decisions. Besides ensuring institutions are safe in the long term, checking risks to the environment and society helps make sure that their financial actions are sustainable.

Several obstacles keep sustainable finance from becoming mainstream such as not having definite sustainability standards, greenwashing, the absence of strict regulatory enforcement and not helping stakeholders build the right skills. Because of them, public trust is lowered and the process becomes harder to compare and track.

REFERENCES

Adebambo, S., Olayemi, A., & Adeyemi, O. (2025). Sustainable banking and bank stability in Nigeria: Empirical evidence from deposit money banks. *Journal of Sustainable Finance & Investment*, *15*(2), 123–140.

Akhtar, S., Azmi, S. N., Khan, P. A., Jan, A. A., & Ansari, Z. (2024). Unveiling the financial landscape: Analyzing profitability, productivity, and efficiency of banks in India using the CAMELS approach. *Cogent Business & Management*, *11*(1), 2399747. DOI: 10.1080/23311975.2024.2399747

Alam, M., Akhtar, S., & Al-Faryan, M. A. S. (2023). Do Indian banks perform better in corporate governance than other SAARC nations? *Corporate Governance (Bradford)*. Advance online publication. DOI: 10.1108/CG-02-2023-0059

Azmi, S. N., & Akhtar, S. (2023). Interactions of services export, financial development and growth: Evidence from India. *Quality & Quantity*, *57*(5), 4709–4724. Advance online publication. DOI: 10.1007/s11135-022-01566-8

Faruq, A. T. M. O., & Huq, M. T. (2024). The role of central banks in advancing sustainable finance. *arXiv*. https://arxiv.org/abs/2411.13576

Ferrer, R., Benitez, R., & Bolos, V. J. (2024). Interdependence between green financial instruments and major conventional assets: A wavelet-based network analysis. *arXiv*. https://arxiv.org/abs/2410.15751

Financial Times. (2024, December 10). Can banks really fix the climate crisis? Financial Times. https://www.ft.com/content/af604f2f-aa1d-486d-85c1-c5cdfc73999e

Jeucken, M. (2001). *Sustainable finance and banking: The financial sector and the future of the planet*. Earthscan Publications.

Kenyon, C., Berrahoui, M., & Macrina, A. (2022). Transparency principle for carbon emissions drives sustainable finance. *arXiv*. https://arxiv.org/abs/2202.07689

Khan, A., Akhtar, S., & Alam, M. (2024). How efficient are Indian banks? An application of stochastic frontier analysis. Journal of Financial Economic Policy. DOI: DOI: 10.1108/JFEP-11-2023-0338

Kim, J. D. (2020). Transition towards green banking: Role of financial regulators and financial institutions. *Asian Journal of Sustainability and Social Responsibility*, *5*(5), 5. Advance online publication. DOI: 10.1186/s41180-020-00034-3

Ladeira, W. J., Santini, F. O., Rasul, T., Cheah, I., Elhajjar, S., Yasin, N., & Akhtar, S. (2024). Big data analytics and the use of artificial intelligence in the services industry: A meta-analysis. *Service Industries Journal*, *44*(15-16), 1117–1144. Advance online publication. DOI: 10.1080/02642069.2024.2374990

Llewellyn, D. T., & Yan, M. (2025, May 14). It is wrong to downgrade Basel's role in climate risk. Financial Times. https://www.ft.com/content/f5d55610-7798-48bb-ab34-2f92f85de15d

Malik, M. S., Irfan, M., & Munir, S. (2024). Developing a sustainable finance index and its implications on inter-intra banking sector. *SAGE Open*, *14*(1), 21582440241271232. Advance online publication. DOI: 10.1177/21582440241271232

News, A. P. (2025, January 20). How mega-polluters take advantage of billions in green loans. AP News. https://apnews.com/article/a28e03c7421222c58025b31ab8185272

Pfister, C., & Valla, N. (2021). Financial stability is easier to green than monetary policy. *Inter Economics*, *56*(3), 154–159. DOI: 10.1007/s10272-021-0972-y

Rahman, S., Moral, I. H., Hassan, M., Hossain, G. S., & Perveen, R. (2022). A systematic review of green finance in the banking industry: Perspectives from a developing country. *Green Finance*, *4*(3), 347–363. DOI: 10.3934/GF.2022017

Reuters. (2025, January 14). G20 financial stability watchdog urges broader adoption of climate transition plans. Reuters. https://www.reuters.com/sustainability/sustainable-finance-reporting/g20-financial-stability-watchdog-urges-broader-adoption-climate-transition-plans-2025-01-14/

Schoenmaker, D., & Schramade, W. (2019). *Principles of sustainable finance*. Oxford University Press.

Scholtens, B. (2009). Corporate social responsibility in the international banking industry. *Journal of Business Ethics*, *86*(2), 159–175. DOI: 10.1007/s10551-008-9841-x

Tan, Y., & Tsionas, M. G. (2022). Modelling sustainability efficiency in banking. *International Journal of Finance & Economics*, *27*(3), 2349–2367. DOI: 10.1002/ijfe.2349

Time. (2021, October 15). 'Green Swan' climate events can rock the world's economies. How banks prepare for them could save more than dollars. Time Magazine. https://time.com/6109448/world-economy-climate-change/

Tkachenko, N. (2024). Integrating AI's carbon footprint into risk management frameworks: Strategies and tools for sustainable compliance in banking sector. *arXiv*. https://arxiv.org/abs/2410.01818

Turek, M. (2022). A new approach to sustainable financial stability and its prospects. *WSB Journal of Business and Finance*, *56*(1), 64–71. DOI: 10.2478/wsbjbf-2022-0007

Weber, O. (2016). The impact of social banking on bank performance and risk: Evidence from Europe. *Journal of Sustainable Finance & Investment*, *6*(1), 1–18. DOI: 10.1080/20430795.2014.887345

Chapter 6
Managing Financial Distress:
The Global Impact of Monetary and Fiscal Policies on Non-Performing Assets

Faiz ur Rehman
https://orcid.org/0009-0004-2722-1871
Aligarh Muslim University, India

Nawab Ali Khan
Aligarh Muslim University, India

Shakeb Akhtar
https://orcid.org/0000-0003-2069-6669
University of Technology and Applied Science, Ibra, Oman & INTI International University, Nilai, Malaysia

Bilal Asghar
https://orcid.org/0000-0002-7092-1222
Al Fayha College, Al Jubail, Saudi Arabia

ABSTRACT

This chapter explores the global impact of monetary and fiscal policies on the management of Non-Performing Assets (NPAs), emphasizing their role in financial distress and economic instability. It examines the influence of key macroeconomic variables such as Annual GDP growth rate, inflation rate, unemployment rate, Real interest rate, and exchange rates on the rise and resolution of NPAs across different economies. The chapter highlights how elevated NPAs weaken banking systems by

DOI: 10.4018/979-8-3373-3725-8.ch006

constraining credit flow, reducing profitability, and undermining investor confidence. It also discusses policy responses, including debt restructuring, bank recapitalization, and the establishment of asset reconstruction mechanisms like bad banks. Drawing on international literature and empirical insights, the study underscores the need for robust regulatory frameworks, effective risk management, and globally coordinated policy measures to maintain financial stability and support sustainable economic recovery in both advanced and emerging markets.

1. INTRODUCTION

The 2007 to 2008 World Economic Crisis, widely viewed as the record unembellished economic shock since the Great Depression, left a lasting impression on the financial systems of the world. A US housing market crisis became a global banking and credit crisis in no time, exposing severe vulnerabilities in financial intermediaries, regulation, and monetary systems. The crisis led to a severe credit contraction, steep falls in asset prices, and broad-based economic recessions among both advanced and developing economies. As per the International Monetary Fund, nations that contribute to nearly 75% of world GDP saw a decline in per capita output during the crisis, which highlights the pervasive extent of economic decline (IMF., 2009). Banks, especially commercial banks, saw increases in loan defaults and write-offs, with many US and European banks having charge-off levels above those of the 1991 to 1992 recession. Although efforts were made to prevent a repeat of the Major Depression, the systemic nature of the disaster prompted urgent reassessments of financial sector resilience (Chaturvedi et al., 2021). One of the central risks that emerged from the crisis was counterparty risk, the possibility that one party in a financial transaction might default on its obligations, thereby triggering a chain reaction of losses across interconnected institutions. This risk was closely linked to the mounting volume of Non-Performing Assets (NPAs) on bank balance sheets. NPAs, which reflect loans that are in nonpayment or close to being in default, began to accumulate rapidly, particularly in economies with weak underwriting standards, poor supervision, and high credit expansion during the pre-crisis boom. The financial crisis underscored the fact that NPAs are not merely accounting anomalies, they are systemic threats with the potential to destabilize the broader economy. A build-up of NPAs weakens banks' balance sheets, limits their ability to extend new credit, and ultimately chokes investment, consumption, and growth. If left unaddressed, they can trigger a vicious cycle of credit tightening, low growth, and financial distress, a phenomenon observed not only during the GFC but also in subsequent episodes such as the Eurozone crisis and the economic outcome from the COVID-19 pandemic.

Indeed, as noted in the IMF's Global Financial Stability Report (2009), the two critical concerns surrounding NPAs are

(a) The need for swift identification and management of impaired assets, and
(b) The recapitalization of viable but capital-starved institutions.

In several countries, particularly those with developing financial markets and weak asset classification systems, delays in recognizing bad loans only served to deepen the crisis. Thus, the timely resolution of NPAs emerged as a cornerstone for restoring confidence and ensuring financial system recovery. What complicates the management of NPAs is their strong linkage to macroeconomic variables. The levels of NPAs are influenced by and in turn influence factors such as Gross Domestic Product growth, inflation, unemployment, exchange rates, and interest rates. For example, economic downturns typically increase default rates, while higher inflation and interest rates may reduce borrowers' repayment capacity. These macroeconomic shocks not only influence the quality of banking assets but also determine the policy responses needed to combat them. Globally, the NPA issue moves beyond local borders and captures systemic vulnerabilities in private credit markets and public regulatory frameworks. All countries, such as India, Italy, Brazil, and Russia, for example, have faced long-standing NPA issues, though with different causes and impacts. In India, for example, over-leveraged corporate borrowers combined with stalled project clearances triggered a steep rise in NPAs of public sector banks. By contrast, Southern European economies faced real estate bubbles and government debt problems that weakened their banking sectors (Jan et al., 2023).

Within this frame of reference, the present study has attempted to provide an extensive and internationally framed examination of NPAs and their macroeconomic consequences. It seeks to address key questions such as

1. What are the common macroeconomic triggers of NPAs across different economies?
2. How do NPAs, once accumulated, affect financial stability and economic performance?
3. How can monetary and fiscal policies be effectively designed to manage and mitigate the impact of NPAs in both advanced and emerging economies?

This study thus presents a multi-dimensional investigation into the causes, effects, and policy responses surrounding non-performing assets. It explores international experiences, surveys existing literature, and evaluates a range of strategies from debt restructuring and asset securitization to central bank interventions and fiscal recapitalization (Akhtar et al., 2022). Particular emphasis is placed on the role of robust regulatory frameworks, early warning systems, and coordinated fiscal-monetary responses in managing NPAs and maintaining systemic resilience. Indeed, so the study aims to contribute meaningfully to the global discourse on financial distress management and provide policymakers, regulators, and researchers with actionable insights for strengthening the foundations of the banking sector (Rehman & Muslim, 2025).

2. LITERATURE REVIEW

Table 1. Empirical Studies on Financial Distress, NPAs, and Macroeconomic Determinants: A Systematic Literature Review

Author(s) & Year	Objective / Focus	Methodology	Key Findings	Implications
Quarshie et al. (2025)	Study ICT's moderating role on SME cash management and financial performance in Ghana.	SmartPLS 4 survey analysis of 212 Ghanaian SMEs.	ICT enhances financial control and reduces risk in SMEs.	ICT can indirectly curb NPAs by improving financial resilience and liquidity forecasting.
Akhtar et al. (2023)	Measure Indian banks' technical efficiency around demonetization via CAMELS.	DEA efficiency + Tobit regression on CAMELS indicators.	Post-demonetization saw gains in efficiency, NPAs had lower technical efficiency.	Demonetization served as a filter for inefficiency, reforms needed to sustain gains.
Akhtar et al. (2021)	Investigate governance failure and NPA misreporting in YES Bank's collapse.	Qualitative case study with RBI AQR and forensic audit findings.	Hidden NPAs and poor governance caused the YES Bank collapse.	Governance lapses and data manipulation lead to underreported NPAs, an urgent need for audit reform.
Das & Uppal (2021)	Investigate the relationship between NPAs and profitability in Indian banks.	Panel data analysis over 14 years for 39 Indian banks.	NPAs significantly reduce profitability and loan growth.	Regulatory strength and credit discipline are central to asset quality.
Syed (2019)	Explore macroeconomic determinants of NPLs in BRICS using cointegration methods.	Fully Modified OLS and cointegration for BRICS economies.	Unemployment and instability raise NPLs, inflation/savings can help if policy is coordinated.	Coordinated macro-policy is essential to tackle systemic banking fragility.
Pasha & Khemraj (2009)	Identify macroeconomic causes of NPLs in Guyana's banking sector.	Panel fixed-effects regression on macroeconomic and lending variables.	Currency overvaluation and liberal lending cause NPAs, GDP growth helps.	Currency mismatches and lax monitoring amplify credit risk volatility.
Türsoy & Günsel (2008)	Analyze macroeconomic indicators' impact on stock returns in Turkey.	Arbitrage Pricing Theory model for stock-market analysis.	Macroeconomic shocks impact both stock returns and bank health.	Macroeconomic variables shape credit risk patterns, policy must anticipate them.
Aver (2008)	Study the macroeconomic correlates of credit risk in Slovenia.	Macroeconomic correlation analysis specific to Slovenia.	Unemployment and interest rates drive NPAs, GDP/FX less impactful.	No universal model for NPA drivers, localized policy crucial.

continued on following page

Table 1. Continued

Author(s) & Year	Objective / Focus	Methodology	Key Findings	Implications
S. Barr et al. (1994)	Evaluate how managerial inefficiency contributes to bank failures using DEA.	DEA model for banking efficiency evaluation.	Management inefficiency is predictive of bank distress.	Managerial inefficiency is a silent driver of NPA buildup, needs early correction.
Demirgüç-Kunt (1989)	Assess how banking structure supports business creation in urban U.S. areas.	Empirical banking structure analysis in metropolitan economies.	Competitive, well-structured banks foster entrepreneurship and growth.	Stable, accessible credit promotes resilience in the broader economy.

Systematic worldwide literature review suggests that combating financial stress caused by Non-Performing Assets (NPAs) needs a two-fold strategy of institutional efficiency and macroeconomic stability. It is anticipated that managerial effectiveness, more especially, internal governance, will be predicted by micro-level analysis as a sign of financial difficulty. It is clear from studies by (Akhtar et al., 2021) that data manipulation and management policy falsification, like in the case of YES Bank's crisis, can conceal the true extent of non-performing assets (NPAs) and cause system failure.

A specific set of fiscal and monetary variables, such as GDP growth, inflation, unemployment, interest rates, and exchange rate valuation, is mentioned in the literature at the macroeconomic level. These variables have varying effects on the creation of Non-Performing Assets (NPAs) depending on the region and the state of the economy. In general, the literature substantiates a comprehensive approach to NPAs, one that brings together initiative governance reforms with flexible macroeconomic and technological responses to counter both overt and underlying risks (Ramasamy et al., 2015).

3. COMPARATIVE GLOBAL CASE STUDY, CROSS-COUNTRY APPROACHES TO MANAGING NON-PERFORMING ASSETS

The global financial landscape exhibits striking contrasts in the way countries respond to the issue of Non-Performing Assets (NPAs). Such contrasts exist on the basis of national policy responses, regulatory development, institutional capacity, and each nation's unique macroeconomic conditions. Although NPAs are an inherent part of banking systems during economic recessions, the magnitude of their effects and the response effectiveness differ greatly between developing and advanced economies. This section includes a comparative study of important economies India and China, the United States and Eurozone, and emerging vs. developed markets featuring critical lessons and successful policy models (Uddin & Akhtar, 2025).

a) India vs. China, Contrasting Approaches in Asia's Giants

i) India, A Slow but Evolving Response

India's NPA crisis has been particularly severe in the public sector banking system. Between 2010 and 2018, the gross NPA ratio of Indian banks rose sharply, reaching a peak of over 11% for public sector banks in 2018. The crisis was fueled by excessive credit growth during the infrastructure boom of the mid-2000s, delays in project implementation, weak risk assessment, and political interference in lending decisions. Recognizing the systemic risk, Indian authorities initiated a series of corrective measures

- Asset Quality Review (AQR) by the Central Bank of India in 2015 to uncover hidden NPAs.
- Introduction of the Insolvency and Bankruptcy Code (IBC) in 2016 to streamline resolution and recovery.
- Capital structure transaction of Public Sector Banks with government funding.
- Formation of a "bad bank" model in 2021 through the National Asset Reconstruction Company Ltd. (NARCL), though its effectiveness is still under evaluation.

Despite these steps, India has struggled with implementation delays, judicial bottlenecks, and a lack of investor interest in distressed assets. Nevertheless, these reforms mark a shift toward a more institutionalized resolution framework.

ii) China, State-Led Stability Through Asset Management Companies

In contrast, China adopted a state-driven approach to NPAs in the late 1990s and again during more recent downturns. The China government has established four large Asset Management Companies (AMCs), Huarong, Cinda, Great Wall, and Orient, to buy bad loans from state-owned banks at book value. These AMCs were funded with government capital and permitted to restructure, manage, or dispose of the impaired assets. Moreover, China employed credit controls, state guarantees, and administrative measures to contain the contagion of bad loans. Although transparency is a problem, the sheer scale and speed of intervention in China served to uphold short-term stability. The Chinese model demonstrates the advantages of rapid centralized action and capital buffers but creates concerns about long-run transparency, moral hazard, and true recovery rates(Walter, 2022).

b) United States vs. Eurozone, Policy Innovation vs. Political Fragmentation

i) United States, A Model of Rapid and Decisive Action

The U.S. handling of the 2007-2008 financial crisis is usually used as a textbook example of successful NPA resolution. The Troubled Asset Relief Program (TARP), passed into law in 2008, allowed the U.S. Treasury to take over or insure as much as $700 billion of toxic assets that banks and financial institutions had on their books.

Key features of the U.S. model included

- Swift implementation and bipartisan support during crisis conditions.
- Direct capital injections into banks to restore confidence.
- Establishment of the Public-Private Investment Program (PPIP) to dispose of legacy assets.
- Transparent reporting and an eventual recovery of most bailout funds with a positive return for taxpayers.

The TARP program, combined with aggressive monetary easing by the Federal Reserve, stabilized the banking system, restored liquidity, and led to a relatively fast recovery. By 2012, most major banks had repaid their TARP funds.

ii) Eurozone, Delayed Response and Sovereign-Bank Loops

Alternatively, the Eurozone had a more protracted and asymmetric reaction to NPAs, largely due to institutional fragmentation. Greece, Italy, Spain, and Portugal have witnessed sharp growth in NPAs following the global financial crisis and the sovereign debt crisis.

Spain's strategy is unique in its eventual success

- Spain established SAREB (Tam & Fulmer, 2021) as a “bad bank” to take in €50 billion of real estate-linked NPAs.
- Backed by the European Stability Mechanism (ESM), Spain shunned a complete bailout and normalized its banks by 2015.

Italy and Greece, though, were plagued by lingering reforms, political opposition, and a deficiency of centralized resolution powers. In Italy, the establishment of a state-supported guarantee scheme (GACS) helped encourage NPA securitization, but elevated NPA ratios persisted for years. The Eurozone experience defines the prices of delayed coordination and the necessity for institutional congruence in dealing with NPAs in a multi-country structure.

c) Emerging Markets vs. Developed Economies, Structural Challenges and Institutional Depth

Emerging markets tend to experience higher and more persistent levels of NPAs due to structural weaknesses, including

- Poor credit appraisal systems
- Political interference in lending
- Weak legal frameworks for insolvency
- Shallow capital markets limiting distressed asset sales

Brazil, Russia, South Africa, and Turkey have witnessed episodic increases in NPAs instigated by currency crises, commodity price shocks, or local political turbulence. In contrast, developed economies, especially those with robust regulatory and legal systems, tend to contain NPAs more efficiently. For instance, Canada and Australia emerged from the global financial crisis with relatively stable asset quality, due in part to conservative lending practices and strong regulatory oversight (Zafar, 2023).

d) The Role of International Financial Institutions

International institutions have played a major role in guiding, backup, and funding NPA management efforts globally

i) IMF (International Monetary Fund)

The IMF's Financial Sector Assessment Programs (FSAPs) assist nations in strengthening their banking systems and determining NPA weaknesses. In times of crisis, technical assistance and conditionality have been provided by the IMF to facilitate asset clean-up in nations such as Ukraine, Pakistan, and Greece (Kupiec, 2005).

ii) World Bank

The World Bank supports regulatory reforms and capacity building in emerging markets to strengthen credit infrastructure and insolvency regimes. By programs like the Financial Sector Reform and Strengthening (FIRST) Initiative, the World Bank promotes best global practices in NPA management.

iii) Bank for International Settlements (BIS)

The BIS provides research, guidelines, and cross-country statistics on financial stability issues, including NPAs. Its Basel Accords (Basel II and III) have been instrumental in shaping capital adequacy requirements, provisioning standards, and risk-weighting guidelines that affect NPA recognition and resolution (Khiaonarong et al., 2023).

Collectively, these institutions are instrumental in establishing global financial standards, coordinating policy, and offering technical and financial assistance in times of financial stress.

4. SOME FACTS AND FIGURES ON NON-PERFORMING ASSETS (NPAS)

Asset quality is a key pillar of stability in the financial sector and is still one of the most effective early-warning signs of looming financial stress in banks. It has been well-documented through academic and policy-driven studies that an NPA surge has systemic threat potential not only for specific financial institutions, but also for economic activity in general. Highlighted by Siems and Barr (1994) was the fact that NPAs form a crucial variable in forecasting bank failures. The research placed strong emphasis on internal governance and asset quality as determining factors in banking resilience. Consequently, Demirgüç-Kunt (1989) discovered weaknesses in the quality of assets, if left uncorrected, to lead to deposit flight, freezes in lending, and eventually institutional insolvency, and hence unearth the far-reaching macroeconomic implications of a credit portfolio deterioration (Ansari et al., 2023).

Hou and Dickinson (2007) strengthened this link by showing that increased NPA reduces banks' operational efficiency, inhibits intermediation, and ultimately impedes economic growth. The adverse impacts don't end at profitability, NPAs also lower the capital cushions, increase risk aversion, and reduce the ability and willingness of banks to lend. As a result, credit availability is restricted, especially in sectors that are more susceptible to economic shocks and rely significantly on bank funding, such as infrastructure, MSMEs, and agriculture.

a) India, A Case of Rapid Deterioration Amid High Growth

Indian banking offers a clear example of how non-performing assets (NPAs) can grow covertly and reach systemic proportions if they are not actively addressed. India saw historically high GDP and investment growth in the years following 2008, particularly in capital-intensive sectors like steel and infrastructure. However, it was followed by late regulatory action, politically influenced lending, especially from state-owned banks, and weak credit evaluation. From 2007 to 08 and 2016 to 17, the gross NPA ratio of SCBs in India rose from 2.2% to 9.3%, reflecting not only cyclical stress but underlying structural vulnerabilities.

A crisis in bank liquidity and confidence was shown by the drop in credit growth over the same time period, which went from over 23% to less than 4.2%. Banks started concentrating on retail loans instead of project lending as risk aversion became the norm. This sudden reduction in credit availability affected capital formation as well as macroeconomic momentum. The Economic Survey of India (2016-17) claims that the increase in non-performing assets (NPAs) is the cause of the "twin balance sheet problem," which refers to financial hardship on both lenders and borrowers. which showed a clear negative correlation between rising NPA levels and profitability ratios such as ROA and NIM. One such problem was that the government had to regularly recapitalise public sector banks at the expense of fiscal resources due to the rising provisioning costs caused by significant non-performing assets (NPAs), which decreased bank profitability and impaired capital adequacy (Akhtar et al., 2021).

b) NPAs as a Share of National Output

The fact that non-performing assets (NPAs) account for a startling 11.5% of India's GDP serves as a clear example of the country's NPA issue. The figure puts the extent to which nonperforming loans were causing credit market distortion, eroding investor confidence, and obstructing economic recovery in perspective. The presence of several non-performing assets in a country's banking system suggests serious inefficiencies in the frameworks for risk management and credit distribution (Akhtar et al., 2023).

c) India in the Global Context

A 2017 analysis by CARE Ratings indicated that India ranked fifth among 39 countries around the world in absolute NPA volume and possessed the highest NPA ratio among BRICS nations. This irony occurred with India's flourishing GDP stats and robust investment climate. It revealed fundamental issues within the banking system, such as

- Inadequate due diligence in loan disbursement
- Lack of robust post-disbursal monitoring
- Weak insolvency resolution mechanisms before the application of the Insolvency and Bankruptcy Code (IBC) in 2016

Conversely, China, characterized by a state-dominated financial industry, has maintained relatively consistent reported non-performing asset (NPA) levels through early resolution mechanisms such as Asset Management Companies (AMCs), despite concerns over transparency expressed by certain analysts. Other emerging nations, such as Brazil and South Africa, experienced elevated non-performing assets during downturns in commodities prices. Nevertheless, India's persistent level of bad loans elicited heightened global apprehension due to the magnitude, complexity, and strategic significance of its economy

d) Policy Implications and Need for Reform

The Indian experience and similar tendencies observed in other high-NPA nations underscore the necessity of early warning systems, prompt regulation, and coordinated policy measures to manage asset quality. Attention must be directed not just towards the resolution of existing non-performing assets (NPAs) through mechanisms such as asset reconstruction companies (ARCs) and bankruptcy legislation, but also towards preventing the emergence of new NPAs

- Enhanced credit appraisal techniques
- Real-time loan monitoring systems
- Data-driven risk modeling
- Improved governance and accountability in bank management

Additionally, macroeconomic coordination plays a key role. Monetary policy must ensure adequate liquidity to allow for credit expansion, while fiscal policy must not excessively rely on bank-funding of public projects in the absence of adequate risk-sharing mechanisms. Internationally, India's experience is a good case study for the emerging economies facing similar structural issues. With economies becoming more interconnected, the risk of financial sector distress, were it left unresolved, can have spill-overs across borders, especially in economies that are extremely exposed to global trade and international capital (Jan et al., 2023).

5. MACROECONOMIC VARIABLES INFLUENCING NON-PERFORMING ASSETS (NPAS)

Non-Performing Assets (NPAs) are also very sensitive to the movements in macroeconomic variables. The state of an economy is well indicated in the asset quality of its economic sector. Different macroeconomic factors like GDP growth, inflation, unemployment, volatility in the exchange rate, and real interest rates determine the capability of debtors to repay and impact the risk profiles of loan portfolios. These variables also interact among themselves, making their independent impacts on NPAs even more complicated. This section discusses how each one of these factors affects NPAs based on cross-country and international empirical evidence.

a) Annual GDP Growth Rate

GDP growth is generally accepted as an indicator of the overall performance of the economy. There is a strong positive connection between GDP growth and bank performance. During times of economic growth, companies witness better revenues, employment levels improve, and borrowers' repayment potential increases. In times of recession or slowdowns in the economy, default risk would increase because of lowered incomes, weak business cycles, and curtailed liquidity. Empirical evidence is in favor of this reverse relationship. For example, Non-performing loans (NPLs) in the Spanish banking industry decrease when there is strong economic growth. The adverse relationship between GDP growth and NPAs in emerging economies indicates that macroeconomic success lessens credit risk. The banking industry in Hong Kong supported economic growth, lowering NPA ratios through enhanced borrower cash flows. Contrarily, documented a constructive correlation between GDP growth and NPAs in certain developing nations, which they explained as pro-cyclicality of lending by banks, where aggressive lending during a boom can result in the degradation of credit quality in the long term. also highlighted that the correlation tends to be nonlinear and context-specific and needs to be analyzed cautiously within each nation's financial environment (Lakštutienė, 2008).

b) Inflation Rate

Inflation influences NPAs primarily through its impact on business input costs, consumer purchasing power, and the real value of debt. When inflation rises moderately, it can help reduce the real burden of outstanding debts. However, sustained or hyperinflation can erode real incomes, reduce firms' profit margins, and adversely affect loan repayment capacity. Established a straight link between inflation and NPLs, arguing that rising prices increase operational costs and uncertainty, especially for small and medium enterprises (SMEs), leading to greater loan delinquencies. The observed inflation is a destabilizing factor for banking sector performance in Turkey and India, respectively. However, the evidence is not entirely uniform. In Slovenia, inflation did not significantly affect NPLs, highlighting that the degree of inflation pass-through and monetary policy credibility influence the relationship between inflation and NPA. In countries with stable monetary frameworks, inflation typically has a muted impact on credit quality.

c) Unemployment Rate

Unemployment is one of the most direct socio-economic indicators influencing loan repayment behavior. Higher unemployment reduces disposable income, weakens household consumption, and limits the ability of borrowers to meet loan obligations. This leads to a rise in individual and household loan defaults, especially in unsecured loan segments. Espinoza and Prasad (2010) studied banks in the Gulf Cooperation Council (GCC) region and concluded that unemployment had a strong positive correlation with NPLs. These previous studies underline the fact that labor market dynamics are critical to asset quality. Unemployment can have a lagging effect, where its influence on NPAs becomes more pronounced a few quarters after initial job losses, particularly in sectors like manufacturing, construction, and retail. Hence, unemployment must be factored in not just as a static economic indicator but also in predictive models of credit risk.

d) Exchange Rate Volatility

Another crucial factor is the exchange rate, especially in open economies with high levels of external borrowing or trade vulnerability. Depreciation of the domestic currency raises the cost of servicing foreign-denominated loans, while appreciation can reduce the competitiveness of export-oriented firms, affecting their ability to repay. In nations with export-driven economies, according to previous research, companies that depend on international demand have a harder time repaying debt since currency appreciation reduces export margins. Exchange rate fluctuations increase credit risk, especially for sectors with currency mismatches between income and liabilities. In contrast, Egypt suggests that currency depreciation can lead to a surge in NPAs when borrowers, particularly those holding loans in foreign currencies, struggle to meet inflated repayment obligations in domestic currency. Thus, the impact of exchange rate volatility on NPAs is context-sensitive, depending on trade balances, foreign debt levels, and the nature of economic exposure (Umeaduma & Dugbartey, 2023).

e) Real Interest Rates

The real interest rate, i.e., the nominal interest rate adjusted for inflation, plays a critical role in determining the cost of borrowing. When interest rates rise, debt servicing becomes more difficult, especially for borrowers with floating-rate loans. This increases the likelihood of defaults, especially among SMEs and highly leveraged corporations. Many studies validate this perspective. In the case of India, contended that elevated real interest rates drain borrower liquidity and drive repayment distress. Interest rate hikes ought to disproportionately affect long gestation projects such as housing and infrastructure. It noted that monetary tightening policy, although necessary to quell inflation, must be balanced with careful consideration of its adverse impact on asset quality.

6. NPAS AND FINANCIAL STABILITY

Non-Performing Assets (NPAs) are more than a matter of accounting are a critical threat to financial system stability. NPAs at very high levels erode banks' profitability, their capital base, and credit supply, ultimately affecting investment, economic growth, and the public's confidence in the financial system. The regulatory environment, banking rivalry, resource allocation efficiency, and general institutional concerns all play a part in the intricate and multidimensional relationship between non-performing assets (NPAs) and financial stability. This section describes how non-performing assets (NPAs) impact banking system stability and how they are linked to more general macroeconomic and structural elements that impact bank resilience (Kadanda, Raj, & Development, 2018).

a) NPAs and Banking Sector Stability

The idea that excessive risk-taking, particularly in a competitive environment, might lead to financial fragility is fundamental to banking regulation. Under the franchise value hypothesis, banks with greater franchise value, i.e., long-run reputation and profitability concerns, are most likely to behave prudently in lending. Greater competition in the banking system, however, can destabilize franchise value and encourage banks to pursue market share by relaxing credit standards and engaging in excessive risk-taking. The contradictory effect of competition on bank risk-taking. Their study concluded that while competition increases, banks tend to relax lending criteria to gain more borrowers, thus exposing themselves to more non-performing loans. This augments systemic risk, particularly when capital buffers are weak or asset growth is valued above asset quality. They also touched upon the aspect of how low franchise value could prompt banks to invest in riskier portfolios, thus increasing the risk of default and hence insolvency.

(Bosiu), nonetheless, proposed the risk-shifting paradigm, positing that competition can bring down loan interest rates and consequently mitigate adverse selection and moral hazard issues. With this perspective, more competition will enhance asset quality by opening banking services and minimizing excessive profit-making motives. The interlinkage among competition and financial stability is therefore nonlinear and contingent on institutional environments, the quality of governance, and regulatory compliance. Hasan (2011) went on to substantiate this notion by placing special emphasis on how heightened competition, unless coupled with robust prudential regulation, would enhance credit risk. Particularly in the context of developing economies, where supervisory regimes are weak or uneven, this would result in the multiplication of NPAs and banking crises.

b) Regulatory Frameworks and NPA-related Risks

The regulatory structure's efficacy and architecture are important in guaranteeing the extent to which NPAs are managed, ranked, and settled. A robust framework of bank regulation not only comprises risk-weighted capital adequacy requirements such as those under Basel III requirements, but also emphasizes liquidity requirements, leverage requirements, and stress tests for the development of financial system resilience. The risk-weighted assets (RWA) approach is a crucial element of this system, as it measures the capital that banks must maintain against diverse exposures. As regulation gets increasingly sophisticated, achieving a balance among risk sensitivity, simplicity, and comparability becomes more challenging. Highly advanced models may lead to regulatory arbitrage, enabling banks to utilise internal ratings to satisfy minimum capital requirements without improving asset quality.

This matter is especially crucial regarding the identification of NPAs. The occurrence of failures in asset classification systems, marked by delayed stress identification, insufficient provisioning requirements, and shortcomings in judicial-regulatory collaboration, is common in many emerging countries. Since 2015, India's financial sector reform has sought to improve NPA recognition via Asset Quality Reviews (AQRs) and stricter provisioning requirements; nevertheless, enforcement and recovery are impeded by institutional delays and capacity limitations. Moreover, an effective resolution process must be implemented. Without adequate bankruptcy frameworks or asset reconstruction alternatives, non-performing loans remain on banking balance sheets, leading to "zombie banks" that endure due to regulatory forbearance but do not promote economic growth. This results in a low-credit, low-growth situation that ultimately jeopardises financial stability..

c) Distorted Capital Allocation and Decline in Productivity

The existence of large NPAs skews the economy's capital allocation. When banks are saddled with bad loans, they become risk-averse and channel funds from potentially productive but risky investments, startups, small firms, and infrastructure ventures, to safer but less productive ones. This results in a misallocation of financial resources, where funds still go to finance unproductive or politically connected companies at the cost of innovative and efficient firms. Hsieh and Klenow (2009) discovered that misallocation of capital within firms greatly lowers aggregate Total Factor Productivity (TFP), especially in developing economies. In such systems plagued by high NPAs, inefficient firms tend to keep accessing credit because of ties, public sector directives, or the absence of risk-based pricing. Consequently, "creative destruction", the mechanism whereby inefficient firms are weeded out and replaced by more efficient ones, is disordered (Mohan & Ray, 2022).

Financial systems do not reallocate resources effectively, innovation declines, and economic dynamism weakens. They demonstrated that ineffective financial intermediation, usually caused by unaddressed NPA overhangs, operates as a restraint to productivity-boosting structural change. This is most evident in state-led banking systems where politically directed lending tends to lead to "evergreening" of loans (i.e., reworking bad loans so that they are not recognized as NPAs). The long-run effect is a moribund banking system that is unable to finance economic growth, resulting in financial repression and impaired policy transmission channels.

7. NPAS AND MONETARY POLICY

Non-Performing Assets (NPAs) have a significant role in determining the effectiveness of monetary policy, especially in countries like India, where banks are the major vector for financial intermediation. The prevalence of high NPAs not only distorts bank balance sheets but also weakens policy rate transmission to the rest of the economy. When credit quality is low, it inhibits banks' capacity to provide credit, curtailing the pass-through of rate of interest changes to industry and consumers. This section discusses how NPAs affect financial accounts, liquidity situations, interest rate channels, and central bank intervention for protecting monetary stability.

a) International Central Bank Strategies

In the world at large, central banks have reacted to NPAs not merely through traditional monetary measures but also focused regulatory actions and liquidity enhancement facilities. These policy initiatives aim to restore banking stability, enhance monetary transmission, and improve macro-financial stability. The Reserve Bank of India employed mechanisms like Prompt Corrective Action (PCA) and Asset Quality Reviews (AQRs), whilst other central banks adopted diverse and, at times, more aggressive measures to mitigate the dual threats of distressed assets and diminishing credit growth.

Following the 2008 crisis, the ECB implemented targeted longer-term refinancing operations (TLTROs), allowing banks to borrow at favourable interest rates contingent upon achieving specified lending levels. This was succeeded by systemic stress tests and asset quality assessments to compel banks to recognise losses and build capital reserves. In 2017, the ECB promulgated comprehensive recommendations for the management of non-performing loans (NPLs) and advised banks to implement prompt provisioning and resolution strategies. National central banks inside the Eurozone, particularly those of Italy and Greece, have collaborated with supranational entities to create government-supported Asset Management Companies (AMCs). The overarching message from the eurozone is that openness, collaborative regulation, and preventative measures to avert severe credit crises are crucial.

The Bank of England (BoE) promptly addressed the global financial crisis by integrating asset quality concerns into the macroprudential framework of its Financial Policy Committee. The Bank of England emphasized the need to monitor systemic risk and urged banks to proactively increase their capital reserves. Recently, the Bank of England commenced the integration of climate risk into banking supervision and emphasized that both physical and transition risks must be included in credit analysis. Climate scenario stress tests have emerged as a standard practice, showcasing the institution's proactive strategy in asset quality management (Morgan, 2022).

The United States Federal Reserve is renowned for its decisive measures amid financial crises. Alongside traditional monetary easing, the Fed initiated programs like the Troubled Asset Relief Program (TARP) and the Term Asset-Backed Securities Loan Facility (TALF), which were only designed to manage distressed assets and provide liquidity. The Main Street Lending Facility of the Federal Reserve, launched during the COVID-19 pandemic, was meant to facilitate credit availability to mid-sized businesses and restrict NPA accumulation. Importantly, U.S. government regulatory agencies like the Office of the Comptroller of the Currency (OCC) and Federal Deposit Insurance Corporation (FDIC) have released tight NPA monitoring and resolution regulations in conjunction with loan grading, capital adequacy, and disclosure guidelines (Lastra, 2025).

On the Asian side, nations like Japan and South Korea also moved systematically. The Bank of Japan, with the experience of enduring banking stress throughout the 1990s, financed recapitalization and asset carve-outs via Resolution and Collection Corporations. The Bank of Korea financed the Korean Asset Management Corporation (KAMCO), a key institution that resolved NPLs in the aftermath of the Asian financial crisis. These incidents highlight the need for state-central bank coordination, particularly in dealing with mass impaired assets in times of systemic deterioration.

Finally, the success of central bank measures depends on timeliness, transparency, and coordination with fiscal authorities. Monetary policy may still be a powerful lever, but it is far more effective when combined with well-designed asset quality measures and regulatory clarity. These global experiences provide useful lessons for developing economies, particularly in creating strong central bank institutions to anticipate NPA cycles in advance without jeopardizing long-term financial stability (De Haan, Eijffinger, & Waller, 2005).

b) NPA-Related Challenges for Monetary Policy Formulation

The existence of high NPAs erodes banks' credibility and effectiveness, resulting in a loss of confidence by investors, depositors, and other stakeholders. As Singh (2013) asserts, NPAs have a direct impact on a bank's financial statements, impacting profitability, as well as capital adequacy and liquidity positions. Investors, who are greatly dependent on financial disclosures to determine the viability of financial institutions, can withdraw money or scale back exposure to poorly performing assets. NPA reduces Return on Assets (RoA), Return on Equity (RoE), and increases provisioning needs, thus reducing the net worth of the banks. This deteriorates their capacity to finance the credit cycle and weakens their capacity to finance new investment, which is crucial in monetary policy-induced growth phases. Additionally, high NPAs cause balance sheet stress, curtailing the effectiveness of monetary easing. Even if the central bank lowers policy rates, risk-averse and capital-starved banks carrying high NPAs might not wish or be able to transmit these cuts to borrowers. This incident, commonly referred to as "credit channel impairment", is a recurring phenomenon in economies with heavy NPA burdens.

c) Market Liquidity and Interbank Lending

High NPAs also have liquidity consequences for the financial system as a whole. Banks with high loan defaults tend to restrict interbank lending or raise risk premiums. According to Bank (2023), these restrictions can cascade through the financial system, affecting mutual funds, insurance companies, and corporate bond markets. The erosion of confidence in interbank operations can lead to systemic liquidity shortages, forcing central banks to inject large volumes of emergency liquidity to stabilize the financial markets. When bank liquidity is impaired due to rising NPAs, the multiplier effect on the economy can be substantial. Consumers face tighter lending conditions, small businesses struggle with working capital shortages, and investment cycles slow down. This puts additional pressure on central banks to balance inflation-targeting mandates with financial stability concerns, often leading to policy trade-offs (al, 2009).

d) Transmission Mechanism and Interest Rate Channels

The effectiveness of monetary policy is heavily reliant on the smooth transmission of interest rate signals from the central bank to the real economy. This occurs through various channels, including interest rates, credit, exchange rates, and expectations. Of these, the interest rate channel remains the most direct and widely used. The IS-LM model, originally developed by Sir John Hicks, illustrates how monetary policy affects aggregate demand via changes in interest rates. In India, the Reserve Bank of India (RBI) primarily uses the repo rate to influence short-term market rates like the call money rate (CMR) and the weighted average lending rate (WALR). When these short-term rates change, they eventually impact long-term rates, which in turn influence consumption, investment, and overall demand in the economy (GLIMS Journal of Management Review and Transformation, n.d.). However, in a high-NPA environment, the transmission of repo rate cuts is frequently muted. Banks prefer to use surplus liquidity to build reserves or invest in safer instruments like government securities rather than expanding risky lending portfolios. This weakens the monetary policy transmission mechanism, reducing its effectiveness in achieving price and output stability.

e) Central Bank Interventions to Address NPAs

Recognizing the risks posed by NPAs, central banks, particularly the RBI, have taken active measures to strengthen asset quality management and enforce transparency in the classification of bad loans. Current RBI regulations have laid stress on internal surveillance systems and early warning mechanisms to facilitate the prompt detection of stress.

As outlined by Adityashendye (n.d.), the RBI mandates banks to

- Establish effective internal controls for identifying large exposures destined to become NPAs.
- Prepare uniform cut-off levels for high-value accounts during a financial year.
- Establish responsibility frameworks assigning culpability for delayed or erroneous classification.

These are a reversal of post-clean-up to pre-emptive monitoring. The idea is that credit risk would be identified and addressed in advance, preventing it from developing into a systemic crisis. Furthermore, tools like Prompt Corrective Action (PCA) templates and Stressed Asset Resolution Mechanisms have been utilised to tackle long-term sustainability challenges. The RBI has advocated for the operationalisation of bad banks, such as the National Asset Reconstruction Company Ltd. (NARCL), to segregate toxic assets from standard banking activities, thereby enabling credit normalisation. The RBI strategically aligns monetary policy measures with liquidity operations and macro-financial oversight to address NPA-induced shocks and uphold financial stability. This integrated strategy acknowledges that monetary policy cannot be established in isolation amid significant balance sheet vulnerabilities (Welford, 2022).

8. NPAS AND FISCAL POLICY, RESOLUTION STRATEGIES AND BUDGETARY IMPLICATIONS

The resolution of Non-Performing Assets (NPAs) constitutes not merely a banking concern but also a significant fiscal policy challenge. Elevated non-performing assets (NPAs) immediately impact government finances through the necessity for recapitalisation of public sector banks, a deceleration in credit expansion, and a decline in tax collection resulting from subdued economic activity. In such economies where the majority of banks are government-owned or heavily regulated, such as India, the fiscal implications of having to deal with NPAs are even more intense. This section addresses how fiscal policy instruments are deployed in NPA resolution and analyzes their budgetary and economic effects.

a) Bank Recapitalization, Fiscal Burden, or Economic Stimulus

Recapitalization of banks is among the most commonly applied fiscal mechanisms to manage NPA-induced stress in public sector banks. The aim is to invest capital in undercapitalized banks, allowing them to withstand losses, achieve regulatory capital requirements, and return to normal lending activities. Following the COVID-19 pandemic, the Government of India allocated 20,000 crore (approx. $2.6 billion) in its 2021 to 22 budgets to recapitalize public sector banks (Ministry of Finance, 2021). While recapitalization is critical to preserving banking sector stability, it comes at a fiscal cost. It often leads to increased government debt and may divert resources away from essential public services. However, if implemented as part of a broader financial reform strategy, recapitalization can act as a counter-cyclical stimulus by restoring the credit cycle and stimulating private investment. Internationally, countries like the United States used similar tools during the Global Financial Crisis through the TARP (Troubled Asset Relief Program). Unlike unconditional capital infusion, TARP combined capital injection with governance reform and asset clean-up, yielding a net positive return for taxpayers. This model underscores the importance of conditionality and accountability in public recapitalization programs (Ghansham & Sriwastaw).

b) Establishing Bad Banks, Asset Resolution, and Fiscal Exposure

The creation of "bad banks" or Asset Management Companies (AMCs) has become an increasingly popular strategy for NPA resolution. These institutions purchase bad loans from banks, often at a discount, enabling banks to clean their balance sheets and focus on new lending. India's formation of the National Asset Reconstruction Company Ltd. NARCL is tasked with acquiring stressed assets worth 2 lakh crore (approx. $25 billion), with partial government guarantees provided for security receipts issued by the AMC. While the idea is to facilitate market-driven asset resolution, government guarantees imply contingent fiscal liabilities. The effectiveness of a bad bank depends on transparent valuation methods, independent governance, and time-bound resolution. Models like SAREB in Spain and Danaharta in Malaysia demonstrated the value of AMCs in restoring banking stability, though fiscal costs vary depending on asset quality and recovery rates.

c) Easing NPA Classification Norms vs. Maintaining Prudential Standards

A controversial yet frequently debated fiscal measure is the relaxation of NPA classification norms. The Indian government has periodically considered extending the classification window from the standard 90 days to 120 or even 180 days, particularly during economic downturns. While such a move may temporarily reduce reported NPAs and avoid panic, it carries the risk of regulatory forbearance and asset quality opacity. As observed during the post-2008 period, extended forbearance often leads to "evergreening" of loans, where borrowers are given fresh loans to pay off older ones, thereby masking the true extent of financial distress (Basu, 2020). From a budgetary point of view, deferral of NPA identification can delay resolution and raise the cost of interventions in the future. Hence, any relaxation in NPA classification windows must be linked to time-bound recovery strategies, borrower viability tests, and regulatory supervision.

d) Loan Restructuring Schemes, Balancing Support and Fiscal Sustainability

Loan restructuring programs like the Corporate Debt Restructuring (CDR) mechanism, Strategic Debt Restructuring (SDR), and the Joint Lenders' Forum (JLF) have been extensively employed by the Reserve Bank of India to manage NPAs. Under the COVID-19 crisis, the RBI had a one-time window of restructuring under its Resolution Framework 2.0, permitting banks to restructure bank loans of borrowers who were standard as of March 1, 2020, without sending them to NPAs (RBI, 2020). Though it relieved stress for stressed borrowers, it came with fiscal implications, particularly when loans were restructured in government-guaranteed industries or where public sector banks were involved. Although restructuring does not require immediate fiscal outflows, it often results in delayed revenue realization and, in some cases, contingent liabilities if borrowers default after restructuring. Thus, fiscal authorities must coordinate closely with monetary and financial regulators to ensure that such schemes are used judiciously and transparently, avoiding long-term risks to taxpayer funds (Aggarwal & Bajaj, 2016).

e) Digitalization and e-Mediation in Debt Recovery

The electronic shift of NPA resolution mechanisms offers great potential to improve fiscal efficiency and transparency. The use of e-mediation platforms and electronic debt recovery systems reduces human error, speeds up resolution, and limits unethical recovery methods.

Digital platforms can facilitate,

- Real-time borrower tracking
- AI-based credit scoring and risk profiling
- Online auctions for distressed assets
- Blockchain-enabled loan records for authenticity and fraud prevention

As per the World Bank (2022), technology-driven innovations in financial resolution not only enhance recoveries but also reduce the administrative cost and cost of litigation for governments engaged in public banking (Naseema et al., 2025). Estonia and South Korea have leveraged digital platforms to make insolvency processes more efficient, with tangible gains to NPA recoveries as well as finances. Projects such as the Central Registry of Securitization Asset Reconstruction and Security Interest (CERSAI) and Public Credit Registry (PCR) in India are foundation stones of a digitally empowered recovery framework.

f) The Role of AI and Climate Risk in Asset Quality

The evolution of banking technology has significantly enhanced the ability to assess asset quality and detect stress in portfolios at an early stage. Artificial Intelligence (AI) and Machine Learning (ML) are highly effective instruments, demonstrating exceptional capability in forecasting borrower behaviour, detecting early signs, and minimizing classification errors. AI-driven algorithms can evaluate vast amounts of both structured and unstructured data, including payment histories, sector-specific risk exposures, and social indicators, to calculate dynamic credit scores and predict the likelihood of loan defaults. Financial institutions in affluent regions are systematically adopting these approaches to improve conventional risk modelling, whereas developing markets are increasingly evaluating their viability. The proper implementation of AI solutions is crucial, as obscure algorithms and biased training data might sustain prejudice and exploit regulatory deficiencies. Consequently, organizations like the European Banking Authority and the Reserve Bank of India are increasingly promoting the implementation of Explainable AI (XAI) to improve transparency, auditability, and accountability in credit decision-making.

Meanwhile, climate risk has also become an untapped but mounting cause of NPAs. With the increasing number of climate-driven disruptions, such as floods, droughts, and heatwaves, the capacity of borrowers in agriculture, infrastructure, and micro-enterprises to repay loans is under threat. For instance, loan defaults increase after weather shocks in locations with poor insurance penetration or credit absorption capacity. According to the Network for Greening the Financial System (NGFS), financial stress triggered by climate is likely to affect developing economies disproportionately, as bank portfolios in these economies are heavily invested in exposed segments. Banks with high exposure in carbon-scarce or disaster-prone segments are subjected to twin risks of stranded assets and high NPAs. Climate stress testing and green asset classification have thus become essential components of prudential banking regulation. Integration of climate risk into the NPA framework, through scenario modeling, disclosure norms, and adaptive provisioning, is no longer a choice but a necessity to realize long-term financial stability (Southall, 2016).

9. POST-COVID GLOBAL INNOVATIONS IN NPA RESOLUTION

The COVID-19 shock was an unexpected economic shock, and governments and central banks around the world were forced to turn to speedy and sometimes unconventional measures to prevent a banking crisis. The combination of systemic defaults, business closures, unemployment, and supply chain disruptions increased the likelihood of a revival in Non-Performing Assets (NPAs). To do this, governments utilised a combination of regulatory forbearance, guarantee agreements, restructuring mechanisms, and digital recovery systems to rescue financial institutions and borrowers from extended hardship. The efforts prompted by the crisis have created new frameworks for managing NPAs and improving financial resilience.

The Reserve Bank of India launched the Resolution Framework 2.0, granting banks a unique opportunity to restructure loans for borrowers affected by COVID without reclassifying these loans as non-performing assets (NPAs). The government launched the Emergency Credit Line Guarantee Scheme (ECLGS), providing collateral-free loans to MSMEs and other sectors affected by COVID-19, supported by a sovereign guarantee. These instruments mitigated a substantial increase in non-performing assets and assisted banks in maintaining asset quality during the recession. The amalgamation of monetary easing, regulatory leniency, and targeted fiscal assistance resulted in a synchronised policy shift favouring resilience over stringent compliance in times of crisis.

The European Banking Authority (EBA) of the European Union temporarily halted non-performing loan (NPL) categorisation standards and instructed banks to provide moratoria and restructuring options to distressed borrowers. The Pandemic Emergency Purchase Programme (PEPP) of the European Central Bank (ECB) supplied liquidity to the financial system and indirectly aided banks in maintaining capital adequacy and averting asset deterioration. Moreover, electronic reporting portals were established to monitor portfolios' stress in real-time, especially in SME lending. They have already integrated into the majority of national banking systems, facilitating early warning and proactive management of non-performing assets (NPAs) (Shampa, Shimu, Chowdhury, Islam, & Ahmed, 2023).

The United States implemented several measures under the Coronavirus Aid, Relief, and Economic Security (CARES) Act, namely the Paycheck Protection Program (PPP) and the Main Street Lending Program. These measures were designed to maintain cash flows while also reducing the potential for non-performing assets by facilitating liquidity and credit availability. The PPP, through its loan forgiveness provisions, effectively averted a widespread default among small industries, hence maintaining asset quality for banks. The US reaction included rapid electronic payment and data centralization to oversee loan performance within these crisis programs.

Singapore and South Korea, among others, have enhanced digital infrastructure for managing NPAs. KAMCO of South Korea increased its acquisition of distressed assets, whilst Singapore's Monetary Authority endorsed digital arbitration systems to expedite and clarify debt recovery conflicts. Moreover, AI-driven credit scoring and instantaneous risk assessment of borrowers have become enduring developments following the epidemic.

The post-COVID era has transformed policymakers' views on addressing NPAs. Governments increasingly employ proactive, technology-driven, and inclusive approaches instead of exclusively depending on traditional recapitalization and asset reconstruction. These modifications emphasize borrower sustainability, economic recovery, and financial system resilience. The pandemic served both as a stress test and a catalyst for the rapid transformation of regulatory and fiscal structures. For emerging economies, such international innovations serve as templates for developing more resilient and progressive strategies to address economic challenges (Stoner).

10. CONCLUSION

The analysis highlights that non-performing assets are not merely banking aberrations but are fundamentally linked to macroeconomic conditions and governance structures. In both developed and developing nations, non-performing assets (NPAs) have emerged as both a catalyst and an indicator of financial trouble. The Indian example demonstrates how delays in detection, inadequate resolution strategies, and regulatory inaction can push non-performing assets to the edge of systemic risk, impacting credit flow, monetary transmission, and fiscal stability. Global examples, like as the US TARP program and the Chinese state-owned AMC model, demonstrate that coordinated, timely, and transparent actions are crucial for preserving sustainable asset quality. Macroeconomic variables, including GDP growth, interest rates, inflation, and unemployment, profoundly affect credit risk, requiring adaptive and data-driven policies from central banks and governments. Post-COVID trends, including AI-driven risk assessment and the use of digital technology, indicate a fundamental shift in NPA resolution tactics. The evidence supports a unified paradigm that integrates early warning systems, ethical technology implementation, and cross-sector collaboration. Managing NPAs requires more than simple repair; it necessitates a proactive policy framework that combines prudence with creativity and rigour with flexibility to ensure enduring fiscal stability and holistic economic recovery.

REFERENCES

Aggarwal, P., & Bajaj, R. J. P. J. B. L. (2016). The Strategic Debt Restructuring Regime in India. *Does It Need Strategic Restructuring., 12*, 45.

Akhtar, S., Alam, M., & Ansari, M. S. (2022). Measuring the performance of the Indian banking industry: Data envelopment window analysis approach. *Benchmarking, 29*(9), 2842–2857.

Akhtar, S., Alam, M., Khan, A., & Shamshad, M. (2023). Measuring technical efficiency of banks vis-à-vis demonetization: An empirical analysis of Indian banking sector using CAMELS framework. *Quality & Quantity, 57*(2), 1739–1761. DOI: 10.1007/s11135-022-01431-8

Akhtar, S., Alam, M., & Khan, M. M. (2021). YES Bank Fiasco: Arrogance or Negligence. *Emerging Economies Cases Journal, 3*(2), 95–102. DOI: 10.1177/25166042211061003

al, H. e. (2009). Systemic risk in the financial sector: An analysis of the subprime-mortgage financial crisis. *157*(2), 129-207.

Ansari, M. S., Akhtar, S., Khan, A., & Shamshad, M. (2023). Consequence of Financial Crisis on Liquidity and Profitability of Commercial Banks in India: An Empirical Study. *Studies in Economics and Business Relations, 3*(2), 36–50. DOI: 10.48185/sebr.v3i2.367

Bosiu, T. The impact of competition on bank risk-taking in sub-Saharan Africa.

Chaturvedi, K., Akhtar, S., Azhar, N., & Shamshad, M. (2021). Impact Of Corporate Social Responsibility On Financial Performance Of Selected Banks In India: Based On Camel Model. *Studies in Economics and Business Relations, 2*(2), 17–31. https://sebr.sabapub.com

De Haan, J., Eijffinger, S. C., & Waller, S. (2005). *The European Central Bank: credibility, transparency, and centralization.* MIT press. DOI: 10.7551/mitpress/2847.001.0001

Demirguc-Kunt, A. (1989). Deposit-institution failures: a review of empirical literat. Economic review-federal reserve bank of cleveland, 25(4), 2.

Espinoza, M. R. A., & Prasad, A. (2010). Nonperforming loans in the GCC banking system and their macroeconomic effects. International Monetary Fund.

Ghansham, A. S., & Sriwastaw, S. K. Trust in Turbulent Times: Effects of NPAs on SBI Depositors During the Pandemic Years.

Jan, A. A., Lai, F. W., Asif, M., Akhtar, S., & Ullah, S. (2023). Embedding sustainability into bank strategy: Implications for sustainable development goals reporting. *International Journal of Sustainable Development and World Ecology*, *30*(3), 229–243. DOI: 10.1080/13504509.2022.2134230

Kadanda, D., Raj, K. J. J. o. S., & Development, E. (2018). Non-performing assets (NPAs) and its determinants: a study of Indian public sector banks. *20*(2), 193-212.

Khiaonarong, T., Das, B., Zhang, C., Gersl, A., Goh, T., Lohmus, P., & Wilson, C. (2023). *Financial sector stability review*. Retrieved from.

Kupiec, P. (2005). The IMF–World Bank financial sector assessment program: A view from the inside. In *Systemic Financial Crises: Resolving Large Bank Insolvencies* (pp. 69-81): World Scientific. DOI: 10.1142/9789812569479_0006

Lakštutienė, A. J. E. e. (2008). Correlation of the indicators of the financial system and gross domestic product in European Union countries. (3 (58)), 7-18.

Lastra, R. M. J. W. I. L. (2025). Central Banking in a Time of Crisis. *The Bank of England.*, *42*, 143.

Mohan, R., & Ray, P. (2022). *The roller coaster ride of non-performing assets in Indian banking*. Centre for Social and Economic Progress.

Morgan, J. (2022). Macroprudential institutionalism: The Bank of England's Financial Policy Committee and the contemporary limits of central bank policy. In *Monetary Economics, Banking and Policy* (pp. 9-25): Routledge.

Naseema, N., Akhtar, S., & Jha, P. (2025). Blockchain Disrupting Supply Chain Finance: Transformative Solutions and Emerging Challenges. In Anamika Pandey and Fadi Al-Turjman, Transformation of Supply Chain Ecosystems, 33-47.

Quarshie, M. A., Djimatey, R., Akhtar, S., & Nawaah, D. (2025). Maximizing financial efficiency through technological synergy: Unleashing ICT for enhanced cash management in SMEs. *Journal of the International Council for Small Business*, *00*(00), 1–31. DOI: 10.1080/26437015.2025.2461025

Ramasamy et al. (2015). Influence of macroeconomic variables on exchange rates. *3*(2), 276-281.

Rehman, F. U., & Muslim, A. (2025). From Growth to Grime : How Macroeconomic Shifts Shape Bad Loans in India " Faiz Ur Rehman, Research Scholar, Department of Commerce, Aligarh Prof. *Nawab Ali Khan, Professor, Department of Commerce, Aligarh Muslim International Journal of Research.*, *12*(05), 71–88.

Shampa, M. T. A., Shimu, N. J., Chowdhury, K. A., Islam, M. M., & Ahmed, M. K. J. H. (2023). A comprehensive review on sustainable coastal zone management in Bangladesh: Present status and the way forward. *9*(8).

Southall, R. J. R. o. A. P. E. (2016). The coming crisis of Zuma's ANC: the party state confronts fiscal crisis. *43*(147), 73-88.

Stoner, H. NGOs in Transition: Exploring Organizational Changes and Online Work Strategies Post-COVID-19.

Tam, D., & Fulmer, S. J. T. J. F. C. (2021). Spain. *Sociedad De Gestión De Activos Procedentes De La Reestructuración Bancaria (Sareb)*, *3*(2), 726–756.

Uddin, S. M. M., & Akhtar, S. (2025). Convergence in efficiency and technology gap of Indian banks: Implication of GFC and COVID-19. *Quality & Quantity, 0123456789*. Advance online publication. DOI: 10.1007/s11135-025-02195-7

Umeaduma, C. M.-G., & Dugbartey, A. N. J. I. J. C. A. T. R. (2023). Effect of exchange rate volatility on export competitiveness and national trade balances in emerging markets. *12*(11), 57-71.

Walter, C. E. (2022). *The red dream: the Chinese Communist Party and the financial deterioration of China*. John Wiley & Sons.

Welford, H. E. (2022). Revisiting the thermophilic bacterial genus Venenivibrio; physiological, phenotypic, and genotypic (re) characterisation the type strain and novel Venenivibrio isolates.

Zafar, A. (2023). Emerging markets: Anatomy, characteristics, and history. In *Emerging markets in a world of chaos: Pathways for economic growth and development* (pp. 23–110). Springer. DOI: 10.1007/978-3-031-29949-0_3

Section 3
Emerging Trends in Digital and Monetary Innovations

Chapter 7
U.S. Strategy to Dominate the Dollar With Stablecoins:
Geopolitical and Economic Implications

Silvio Andrae
https://orcid.org/0000-0002-8586-7812
Independent Researcher, Germany

ABSTRACT

This chapter thoroughly examines the United States' strategy of intentionally utilizing stablecoins to bolster and extend the dollar's hegemony in the digital era. The objective is to systematically scrutinize the economic logic, political narratives, and geopolitical implications of this strategy. Methodologically, the article integrates political economy, hegemonic currency theories, and empirical analyses of the issuance, use, and regulation of stablecoins, supplemented by case studies in emerging markets. The results demonstrate that stablecoins amplify the demand for U.S. government bonds, streamline international payment flows, and firmly establish the dollar on a global scale through digital platforms. However, this strategic move also introduces new risks. In summary, the analysis reveals that stablecoins are more of a digital extension of dollar hegemony than a replacement, offering opportunities for the US, but also posing significant risks to the stability of the global financial order.

DOI: 10.4018/979-8-3373-3725-8.ch007

INTRODUCTION

Dollar Hegemony in the Digital Age

Since the end of World War II, the global economic order has been primarily shaped by the unprecedented hegemony of the U.S. dollar. The dollar not only holds a dominant position in international trade but also serves as a central investment and hedging instrument for governments, financial institutions, and companies. According to Bertaut et al. (2025), approximately 58% of global currency reserves are invested in U.S. dollars. In addition, nearly 90% of all transactions on global foreign exchange markets are conducted in dollars, underscoring its function as the dominant currency (Chatham House, 2025). This position showcases the economic and military power of the US, which stems from institutional agreements such as the Bretton Woods system and the U.S. financial market's role as a 'haven.'

However, with the ongoing digitalization of financial markets and the emergence of new forms of money, the dollar faces new challenges. In this context, stablecoins can be seen as a revolutionary innovation that combines the stability of traditional currencies with the flexibility and innovative power of digital technologies. In contrast, Bitcoin and other cryptocurrencies are considered volatile and should be viewed primarily as speculative assets. In contrast, stablecoins have established themselves as a promising medium for international payment flows, trade, and decentralized financial applications, heralding a new era of financial opportunities. Stablecoins are digital assets designed to maintain a constant value. Typically, this value is pegged to a fiat currency such as the dollar or a basket of assets. Their development was aimed at counteracting the volatility of cryptocurrencies (Catalini, 2025).

The US has identified this potential and increasingly views stablecoins as a geopolitical tool to secure and expand its dollar hegemony in the digital age. In view of increasing competition from the digital yuan, European initiatives under the MiCAR regulation, and discussions about new currency areas in the context of the BRICS+ countries, the U.S. strategy aims to actively shape the digital transformation of the monetary system and structurally anchor the dollar in this new environment. The goal is therefore not only to maintain the dollar's hegemony, but to deepen it globally through digital infrastructures.

Research Questions and Objectives of the Chapter

This problem statement gives rise to key research questions that guide the chapter:

RQ1: The role of stablecoins in the current U.S. strategy to secure the hegemony of the dollar will be examined. This analysis will underscore the strategic importance of stablecoins, focusing on the political and economic logic that positions them as a bridge between traditional financial systems and digital economies.

RQ2: The aim is to examine the intricate economic mechanisms that stablecoins use to increase demand for U.S. dollars and U.S. government bonds. This study will examine the strategic implications of stablecoins, analyzing the design of digital dollar tokens that aim to enhance the liquidity of U.S. capital markets and facilitate international capital flows.

RQ3: The question of which political and regulatory measures support the aforementioned strategy needs to be answered. A particular focus is on the GENIUS Act as a new regulatory basis, supplemented by the role of the SEC, the CFTC, the Federal Reserve, and the Treasury Department.

RQ4: The potential risks and side effects of the U.S. strategy for the stability of the international financial system need to be discussed. This study aims to provide a comprehensive understanding of the potential influencing factors, including possible disintermediation processes within the banking system, regulatory fragmentation, and geopolitical tensions.

RQ5: The question arises as to what impact the current situation will have on the global monetary order. In the long term, the question arises as to whether a 'digital Bretton Woods order' will emerge that secures the dollar's hegemony, or whether new, multipolar structures will emerge.

This chapter systematically analyzes the U.S. strategy for the use of stablecoins. The aim is to highlight the geopolitical and economic implications of this strategy. The focus is on a dual perspective: on the one hand, the stabilization and expansion of dollar hegemony through digital innovations is examined; on the other hand, the potential risks, systemic instabilities, and political conflicts arising from this strategy are analyzed.

Methodological Approaches

This analysis is based on an interdisciplinary methodological approach that combines three levels: In the context of international political economy, stablecoin policy is viewed as an instrument for projecting national power. In this context, the institutional and regulatory framework, the power asymmetries between states, and the interactions between state and private actors are taken into account.

In economic theory, stablecoin policy is interpreted as a further development of traditional mechanisms for securing reserve currencies. This interpretation is based on hegemonic currency theories (including Kindleberger and Eichengreen) and the theory of endogenous money creation. The focus here is on examining the effect of stablecoins on the demand for government bonds and the significance of network effects in platform economies.

The empirical analysis is based on data on the issuance, market capitalization, and use of stablecoins (including Chainalysis and CoinDesk Data). Additionally, case studies examine the use of stablecoins in specific contexts, such as international remittances or in countries with weak national currencies. This study compares the empirical findings with regulatory developments in the US, the EU, China, and the BRICS+ context.

The combination of these methodological approaches provides a comprehensive picture that covers both the theoretical and practical dimensions of the stablecoin strategy.

Structure of the Chapter

The chapter is divided into nine sections. The second section is devoted to the historical and theoretical development of dollar hegemony, analyzing the classification of stablecoins within this context. The third section analyzes stablecoins as a strategic instrument of the US, describing their functioning, typology, and market dynamics. The fourth section is devoted to the regulatory environment in the US, with a particular focus on the GENIUS Act and the role of central authorities. The fifth section is devoted to the economic logic of the stablecoin strategy, while Chapter 6 deals with its risks and potential unintended consequences. The seventh section is devoted to the geopolitical implications, particularly about competition with alternative currency areas and the projection of American power. Section 8 develops scenarios for the future development of dollar hegemony in the digital age and discusses possible policy options. Finally, Section 9 provides a summary assessment and an outlook on the digital future of the global financial order.

HISTORICAL AND THEORETICAL BACKGROUND

The Dollar as a Reserve Currency: From Bretton Woods to the Present Day

The current dominance of the U.S. dollar is the result of a long historical development that began at the end of World War II. The Bretton Woods Agreement of 1944 marked a decisive turning point in global monetary history. It established the dollar as the central anchor currency of the international financial system. In this system, other currencies were pegged to the dollar, while fixed convertibility backed the dollar itself with gold (USD 35 per ounce). The International Monetary

Fund (IMF) and the World Bank supported this architecture by relying on the US as the cornerstone of economic stability.

Despite the collapse of the Bretton Woods system in 1971, the dollar has maintained its dominant position in global trade. This 'exorbitant privilege' is upheld by three crucial factors: the depth and liquidity of U.S. financial markets, confidence in U.S. political and institutional structures, and the significant geopolitical and military leadership role of the US, particularly during the Cold War.

Since the 1980s, the dollar's central role has been reinforced by the globalization of capital markets. The majority of transactions by international banks and multinational companies were conducted in dollars. Commodity markets—especially the oil market—were also quoted in dollars, leading to the emergence of the term 'petrodollar.' Despite repeated crises, such as those in Latin America and Asia, as well as the global financial crisis of 2008, the dollar remained the preferred safe haven in times of uncertainty. This was particularly evident during the euro crisis and the pandemic, when demand for dollar liquidity remained strong.

The historical dominance of the dollar must therefore be viewed in the context of increasing geo-economic fragmentation. Trade conflicts, the trend toward national production, and the formation of geopolitical blocs are eroding the foundations that have underpinned the dollar's role as a reserve currency since the Bretton Woods Agreement. In this study, a transformation of the traditional Triffin dilemma becomes evident. A key aspect of this phenomenon was that global demand for dollar liquidity caused the US to run current account deficits. This resulted in a long-term erosion of the currency's credibility. Stablecoins change this dynamic: the issuance of each new unit immediately leads to increased demand for short-term U.S. government bonds without necessarily creating a current account deficit. Stablecoins thus act as a short-term relief mechanism by stabilizing demand for U.S. assets. At the same time, however, they structurally exacerbate the existing dilemma, as they deepen the global economy's dependence on dollar liquidity without forcing the US to offset these obligations through external economic adjustments. The result is a digital Triffin dilemma: global demand for digital dollar tokens can provide fiscal relief for the US, but at the same time creates new systemic risks if confidence in the backing or liquidity of stablecoins erodes (Lane, 2025).

As the leading currency, the dollar currently forms the foundation of the global financial architecture, which underscores its resilience (Rogoff, 2025). However, the foundations of its historical dominance have gradually weakened over the past two decades. The dollar's share of official foreign exchange reserves currently stands at around 58%, down from approximately 70% at the beginning of the 2000s (Bertaut et al., 2025). The figures presented illustrate not only the stability but also the path dependency of dollar hegemony. This path dependency could take on new forms as a result of digital innovations such as stablecoins.

Theories on the Hegemonic Currency

The classic literature on hegemonic currencies—in particular works by Kindleberger (1973), Eichengreen (2011), and Minsky (1992)—provides key reference points for understanding the dominance of the dollar. On closer inspection, however, it becomes apparent that their explanatory power is limited in the digital age. According to Kindleberger, monetary hegemony is characterized by a dominant power's ability to act as a lender of last resort, thereby guaranteeing systemic stability. The concept proves viable in relation to the postwar order and the role of the US in the Bretton Woods system. However, it overlooks the central question of today: how technological infrastructures—such as blockchain-based stablecoins—can themselves become vehicles of hegemonic stability. The present analysis concludes that the reproduction of hegemony is no longer exclusively carried out by state institutions, but increasingly by platform-based liquidity systems.

With his emphasis on network effects and institutional credibility, Eichengreen has laid important foundations for explaining dollar hegemony in a multipolar world. However, his argument focuses in particular on network effects in the context of state currencies. Stablecoins fundamentally change this logic by developing network effects not between nation-states, but within digital platform economies such as PayPal, Visa, or DeFi ecosystems. These create a digital lock-in dynamic that structurally anchors the dollar as a reference currency—independent of traditional geopolitical institutions. This chapter contributes to the expansion of Eichengreen's approach by positing that digital infrastructure networks have become independent carriers of monetary hegemony.

Finally, Minsky's hypothesis of financial instability opened up an influential perspective on endogenous crisis dynamics. His analysis was based on an examination of the cyclical developments of credit expansion and contraction within the banking system. Stablecoins establish a new level of endogenous money production that does not occur through bank balance sheets, but rather through capital markets, programmable tokens, and algorithmic mechanisms. In this context, instability can arise from run dynamics, smart contract automations, or interactions between crypto and bond markets. This chapter, therefore, refines and nuances Minsky's approaches through a detailed analysis of the potential risks of algorithmically amplified liquidity crises and the blurring of boundaries between private innovation and state monetary sovereignty.

The analysis shows that stablecoins neither fit completely into existing theories nor render them obsolete. Instead, a reconfiguration of central concepts is necessary. Kindleberger's concept of hegemonic stability should be expanded to encompass technological dimensions. Eichengreen's network effects primarily apply in platform economies today, and Minsky's instability hypothesis must take digital liquidity dynamics into account. The perspective proposed in this paper, therefore, understands stablecoins as a hybrid phenomenon that, on the one hand, aligns with classic hegemonic logics, but on the other hand, also introduces new power-political and systemic challenges. Figure 1 illustrates the current hierarchy in the international monetary system. At the top of the monetary system is the reserve currency, the dollar, which dominates central functions such as reserve holding, trade settlement, and capital market liquidity. The currencies examined include the key currencies: the euro, yen, pound sterling, renminbi, and Swiss franc. These currencies play an important role in regional or sectoral markets, but do not exert global hegemony. The third level comprises peripheral currencies, which are highly dependent on convertibility and external anchors. Stablecoins cannot be clearly classified within this structure; instead, they operate across the hierarchy. They are predominantly pegged to the dollar, thereby reinforcing its role as the reserve currency, but at the same time creating new channels through which key and peripheral currencies could also be digitized. The present discussion shows a shift from traditional institutional arrangements to technological infrastructures as the bearers of monetary hegemony (Sachdeva & Saravelos, 2025). In view of advancing digitalization, the question arises as to whether stablecoins represent a new form of hegemonic monetary power that transforms these mechanisms or merely reproduces them digitally.

Figure 1. Current currency hierarchy and stablecoins

Figure 1: Current currency hierarchy and stablecoins

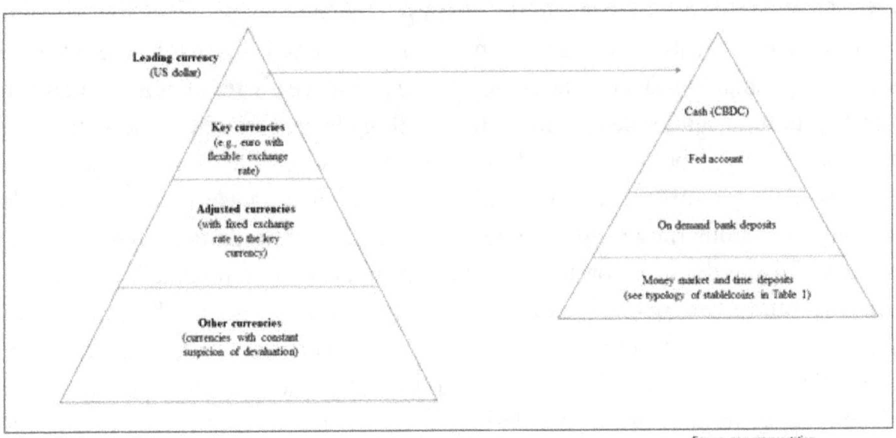

Source: own representation.

Digitalization and Monetary Theory: Stablecoins as 'Hybrid Forms of Money'

The advancing digitalization of financial markets has led to a significant shift in the boundaries between state fiat money and private payment instruments. Cryptocurrencies such as Bitcoin have sparked a debate about the denationalization of money, but have so far been unable to play a systemic role due to their high volatility and limited scalability. Stablecoins, on the other hand, serve as a bridge between the price stability of traditional currencies and the technological advantages of public and private blockchain systems.

In theory, stablecoins can be understood as hybrid forms of money:

- They are issued privately but are often pegged to government currencies.
- They fulfill payment functions without being controlled by central banks.
- They combine asset and transaction characteristics, as they serve both as a means of payment and as digital assets in DeFi ecosystems.

In the monetary theory debate, stablecoins therefore constitute a new level of endogeneity in the concept of money. Traditional theories suggest that the banking system creates money based on deposits and loans. Stablecoins, on the other hand, enable money creation via digital platforms that are also linked to the logic of capital markets. This hybrid form creates a new dynamic: on the one hand, the peg to the dollar stabilizes demand for U.S. government bonds, while on the other hand, control over liquidity is increasingly shifting to private actors.

A significant feature of stablecoins is their endeavor to ensure credible price stability, comparable to a currency pegged to a reserve currency within a currency board system. In academic literature, this analogy is explored in models such as the quasi-target zone model, which is based on classical flexible money price theories. These models demonstrate that the stability of the peg increases with a narrow definition of the trading range and sufficient stabilization of fundamental market forces, in particular the demand for stablecoins, through effective feedback mechanisms. Empirical studies, particularly using the example of Tether, suggest that price stability is indeed supported in practice by a mean reversion effect. The level of liquidity in the stablecoin market and the volatility of other cryptocurrencies, such as Bitcoin, influence the strength of the stabilizing force. At the same time, the migration of stablecoins to various blockchains with a more extensive user base demonstrates that network effects further ensure the prediction of price stability (Hui et al., 2025).

Furthermore, the programmability of stablecoins opens up new perspectives: transactions can be linked to conditions, smart contracts, and compliance rules. This enables closer integration between financial and data flows. From a geopolitical perspective, this is a highly relevant aspect, as it creates new channels for surveillance and control. The present hybrid structure has significant consequences. On the one hand, the stability of stablecoins is determined not only by the quality of their reserve holdings but also by market liquidity and network effects.

On the other hand, it illustrates that stablecoins must increasingly be viewed as monetarily relevant variables, rather than just technological innovations. For regulatory purposes, it is worth noting that questions regarding the permissible price fluctuation range, market depth, and the composition of collateral are of central importance in assessing systemic risks. Stablecoins are not only an economic innovation, but also function as a power-political instrument that mediates between private dynamics and state regulation.

Comparison: Reserve Currency Strategies of Other Countries

The U.S. strategy for the use of stablecoins is relevant in this context, as other players are simultaneously attempting to consolidate their positions in the global monetary system.

The People's Republic of China is pursuing a dual strategy with the implementation of the digital yuan (e-CNY). On the one hand, the e-CNY serves to control domestic payment transactions. On the other hand, it aims to establish itself as an alternative to the dollar in foreign trade, for example, in the Belt and Road Initiative or in commodity trading. The international use of the e-CNY has been limited so far, but the foundation for potential future expansion has been laid with the appropriate infrastructure.

The European Union is pursuing a policy strategy aimed at regulation. With the Markets in Crypto-Assets Regulation (MiCAR) and preparations for a digital euro, it is attempting to create stability and trust in digital markets. In contrast to the U.S. strategy, the EU is focusing less on geopolitical power projection and more on creating a regulatory framework. Nevertheless, a digital euro embedded in the single market could contribute to the long-term diversification of the global monetary system. In addition, the perceived threat to European sovereignty posed by dollar stablecoins is seen as a welcome opportunity for the ECB to develop the digital euro.

With its planned Swiss Bank Deposit Token, Switzerland is pursuing the goal of creating a legally secure, bank-based alternative to privately issued stablecoins. Under the leadership of the Swiss Bankers Association, Postfinance, UBS, and Sygnum Bank are working on a digital franc that could be used as a tokenized bank deposit via public blockchains. Unlike stablecoins from private providers, the deposit token would represent a direct liability on the bank's balance sheet and thus be subject to the exact protective mechanisms as traditional customer deposits, including deposit insurance.

The BRICS countries have been discussing the establishment of alternative currency arrangements for some time, an issue that has gained relevance due to geopolitical tensions with the West. The proposals include a range of options, including commodity-backed currencies and multilateral payment systems based on blockchain technology. Although concrete implementations are currently limited, this reflects the growing need to break away from dependence on the U.S. dollar.

In the context of this comparison, it becomes evident that the strategies of the key players follow different institutional logics. The US focuses on close integration between the private sector and the state. Stablecoins emerge from entrepreneurial innovation, but are politically influenced through the GENIUS Act and their integration into the infrastructure of large platforms. The combination of market-based dynamics and geopolitical control gives stablecoins the characteristics of a flexible instrument that is both economically efficient and politically effective. In contrast, China pursues a more statist logic, with the e-CNY primarily serving as an instrument of state control of the domestic market, but also possessing geopolitical potential. However, its international reach has been limited so far, as its use in global trade chains is politically desirable, but there is only limited demand for it on the market. In this context, a tension exists between the domestic political control function and the foreign policy expansionist agenda. With MiCAR and the digital euro, the European Union is pursuing a regulatory logic that focuses less on geopolitical projection and more on market stability and domestic market sovereignty. The EU views itself less as a hegemonic actor and more as a standard-setter, whose goal is to foster trust through regulation. This strategy can also have an impact at the geopolitical level by reducing dependence on U.S. stablecoins and establishing alternative standards.

STABLECOINS AS A STRATEGIC TOOL

Definition, Functioning, and Typology of Stablecoins

Stablecoins offer a legally secure alternative for companies and private individuals to store, invest in, and process payments. Their issuers do not require a banking license and operate as independent companies. The basic structure of these companies' business models differs significantly from that of traditional banks. An issuer—whether a company or a decentralized autonomous organization (DAO)—issues tokens that are backed 1:1 by reserves, such as bank deposits or government bonds, or by algorithmic rules. Users have the option to exchange fiat money or cryptocurrencies for stablecoins and transfer them to blockchains. Redemption should be possible at par value at any time. While the stablecoins issued are not subject to any interest obligations, the underlying assets—such as government bonds—generate ongoing income that flows entirely to the providers. This results in a profitable model in which the users of digital money effectively provide the capital without sharing in the returns themselves.

This paper examines the variety of classifications of stablecoins. The most common form is fiat-pegged stablecoins, which are backed by traditional assets such as dollar deposits or short-term U.S. government bonds. The most prominent examples include Tether (USDT), USD Coin (USDC), and PayPal USD (PYUSD), with Tether and USDC alone accounting for around 90% of the market share. A significant advantage of this method is its comparatively high stability; however, a disadvantage is its dependence on centralized custodians and the associated regulatory issues.

Algorithmic stablecoins such as TerraUSD (UST), on the other hand, aim to ensure stability through automated mechanisms and arbitrage incentives. However, the collapse of the Terra Luna ecosystem in May 2022 highlighted the inherent risks of these constructs. When UST lost its peg, the value of the fund suffered a significant loss. Algorithmic stablecoins are associated with particular risks due to their complexity (Martino & Roos, 2024). In this study, the market interactions and protocol mechanisms that triggered the collapse are reconstructed in a specially developed simulation environment. This reconstruction reveals the structural weaknesses of the dual-token seigniorage model of algorithmic stablecoins (Calandra et al., 2025). Although these constructs theoretically promise a high degree of decentralization, they are nevertheless fraught with considerable instability and systemic risks.

A third group consists of crypto-based stablecoins that are overcollateralized with volatile cryptocurrencies. The best-known example is DAI in the MakerDAO system, which is secured by overcollateralization. The advantage of this strategy lies in decentralization, while the disadvantage lies in significant capital efficiency and dependence on highly volatile underlying assets. Recently, a new project called 'dEuro' was presented within the European Union, aiming to serve as a savings and credit currency for consumers. Unlike Tether or USDC, the dEuro is backed by cryptocurrencies that users can deposit to borrow stablecoins or lock up for double-digit interest rates. Finally, there are also CBDC-backed stablecoins, a hybrid form that combines private tokens with central bank digital currencies issued by governments. These are currently still mostly theoretical concepts or pilot projects, such as so-called 'synthetic CBDCs.' However, they point to a potential future path of integration between public and private money creation.

The typology of stablecoins presented in Table 1 provides insight into the different types of these cryptocurrencies. Fiat-backed stablecoins are a crucial component of the U.S. strategy, as they generate immediate demand for U.S. dollar liquidity and facilitate a direct connection to U.S. financial markets.

Table 1. Typology of stablecoins

Type	Function	Examples	Strength	Weaknesses
Fiat-backed stablecoins	1:1 backed by fiat reserves (bank deposits, U.S. government bonds)	Tether (USDT), USD Coin (USDC), PayPal USD (PYUSD)	High price stability, simple mechanisms, broad acceptance	Dependence on centralized issuers; trust in reserves required; regulatory risks
Crypto-backed stablecoins	Overcollateralization by volatile crypto assets (e.g., ETH), feedback via smart contracts	DAI (MakerDAO), sUSD	Decentralized, more transparent due to on-chain collateral, less dependence on banks	Capital inefficiency (overcollateralization required), indirect dependence on fiat stablecoins, volatility risk
Algorithmic stablecoins	Stabilization through algorithms and arbitrage models (minting/burning)	TerraUSD (UST, collapsed), Ampleforth	Claim of true decentralization, no dependence on collateral	Highly unstable, prone to market panic and death spirals, low confidence following the collapse of UST
CBDC-backed stablecoins	Private tokens based on central bank digital currencies (CBDCs)	Pilot projects ('synthetic CBDCs'), theoretical concepts	Combination of government stability and private innovation, easier to integrate from a regulatory perspective	Still in the pilot phase, unclear legal and technical implementation, risk of government dominance

Source: Own representation

Stablecoins can therefore be understood not only as 'hybrid forms of money,' but also as different institutionalizations of payment architectures. In this context, Bofinger (2025) differentiates between bond-based stablecoins, which are backed by government bonds such as U.S. Treasuries, and bank-based stablecoins, which are closely linked to the traditional banking system, for example, within the framework of MiCAR. Bond-based stablecoins primarily serve as a digital extension of money market funds by increasing the global reach of the dollar through the purchase of bonds. Bank-based stablecoins, on the other hand, reinforce the interdependence between the banking and cryptocurrency markets.

Overview of the Stablecoin Market

The stablecoin market has experienced an unprecedented boom in recent years, rapidly expanding from approximately 60 active stablecoins in mid-2024 to over 170 within a short period. A significant increase in market capitalization has accompanied this rapid quantitative expansion. In less than two years, the total volume nearly doubled, reaching approximately $280 billion in mid-2025 (compared to approximately $140 billion at the end of 2023). Although cryptocurrencies currently account for only 4% of the total capital in the cryptocurrency market ($300 trillion, Kutler, 2025), they account for over 40% of trading volume. According to calculations by Sachdeva and Saravelos (2025), stablecoins accounted for more than two-thirds of all crypto transactions, with a transaction volume of $27.6 trillion in the previous year, exceeding the total volume of the Visa and Mastercard networks. This significant growth underscores the potential of stablecoins in the digital financial landscape.

Stablecoins have become a significant sector within the global cryptocurrency ecosystem, whose dynamics are increasingly impacting traditional financial markets. A notable trend is evident, characterized by the near-complete dominance of the dollar in the stablecoin sector. An empirical analysis of the correlation between stablecoin volumes and the world's leading currencies, such as the U.S. dollar, reveals a significant association, while other currencies, including the euro, yen, and renminbi, play a minor role. Euro stablecoins, for example, have a capitalization of less than $500 million. It is also worth noting that the market is highly concentrated. An empirical analysis of market capitalization reveals that approximately 90% is accounted for by just two issuers, Tether and USDC, which dominate the market (Aldasoro et al., 2025a). The two dominant stablecoins, which users prefer due to their liquidity, have shares of more than 60% and just under 25%, respectively. Empirical evidence indicates that approximately four-fifths of all stablecoin transactions occur outside the US.

In addition to Tether (USDT) and USD Coin (USDC), the most important players in the stablecoin market include USDS, PayPal USD (PYUSD), and DAI. According to current estimates, Tether is expected to have a market share of around 65% in 2024, thereby achieving the status of the largest stablecoin. Despite ongoing criticism of its lack of transparency regarding its reserves, USDT remains the dominant instrument in crypto trading and is also becoming increasingly important for cross-border payments (Auer et al., 2025). USD Coin, issued by Circle in collaboration with Coinbase, on the other hand, is positioning itself more strongly as a compliant and transparent stablecoin. USDC is a cryptocurrency dollar characterized by its focus on compliance, institutional use, and integration into payment networks. These characteristics make USDC a preferred choice for regulated players. PayPal USD, launched in 2023, is expanding its reach through integration into one of the world's largest payment platforms, particularly in the areas of consumer payments and e-commerce. Finally, DAI occupies a special position as a decentralized stablecoin: from a technical perspective, the object under investigation can be considered innovative, although its market volume is limited in comparison. Another significant aspect is that a substantial portion of the collateral mentioned is based on USDC, which relativizes the desired independence.

An analysis of current usage trends highlights the complexity of the stablecoin economy. In the US and Europe, stablecoins are primarily used as a liquidity instrument in crypto trading, where they serve as a central anchor for trading and arbitrage strategies. In emerging and developing countries, on the other hand, they are increasingly serving as a means of 'dollar access' for households and businesses that have limited or uncertain access to foreign currencies. The remittance sector is currently undergoing remarkable development. Transactions to countries such as the Philippines, Nigeria, or Latin America can be processed much faster and more cost-effectively with stablecoins than through traditional providers such as banks or Western Union. Demographic analyses show that users of stablecoin remittances are predominantly younger and better educated and tend to transfer higher amounts. Among the 26% of remittance users who already use stablecoins, satisfaction and perceived usefulness are the most important drivers for future use. This observation suggests a cyclical dynamic. It has been found that meeting expectations is closely tied to an increase in satisfaction. This, in turn, has a positive impact on perceived usefulness (Ante, 2025). At the same time, institutional investors are also discovering stablecoins, which they increasingly view as a type of digital money market fund, as they directly reference U.S. government bonds through their reserve holdings.

This development suggests that stablecoins have evolved into a product that goes beyond niche applications for crypto enthusiasts. They are establishing themselves as independent infrastructures that operate in parallel with—and in some cases, in competition with—traditional banking channels. A BIS bulletin published in July states that the rising market capitalization of stablecoins and their increasing interconnection with the traditional financial system have reached a stage where potential impacts on that system can no longer be ruled out (Aldasoro et al., 2025a).

Stablecoins as a Bridge Between Fiat Money and Digital Assets

Stablecoins act as a bridge between the traditional monetary system and the new digital economy. In the traditional financial system, they represent dollar deposits. The available financial resources are closely linked to the financial architecture of the US through collateral such as bank deposits or U.S. government bonds. This development has the effect of increasing both the demand for dollars and the demand for safe investments such as treasury bills. In the digital economy, on the other hand, stablecoins serve as the preferred unit of account and form the basis for almost all decentralized finance applications, from lending to staking to derivatives. Without these tokens, the functioning of the DeFi sector would be virtually unthinkable (Aquilina et al., 2024).

Their bridging function also opens up new channels for capital flows. The transition from fiat to crypto initially manifests itself in investors exchanging dollars for stablecoins to gain access to digital assets. In the opposite direction, it is possible to convert profits from DeFi applications or cryptocurrency trading back into dollars via stablecoins. Ultimately, stablecoins present new opportunities in the realm of global payment flows. In so-called emerging markets, residents and companies use stablecoins for trading, saving, and cross-border transfers. In doing so, they bypass local banks. This study concludes that this creates a link between two financial worlds. It also expands the reach of the dollar in an increasingly digitalized global economy.

Although stablecoins are often used in practice as a stable link between fiat money and digital assets, their actual role as a stabilizing force in the volatile cryptocurrency ecosystem is a matter of controversy. A recent empirical study analyzed this potential using a novel conceptual framework that defines three dimensions—stability, independence, and resilience—in relation to other assets (Baptista Palazzi et al., 2025). The study employed methods such as Granger causality, ADCC-GARCH, and transfer entropy to analyze the relationships between leading stablecoins (USDT, USDC, BUSD), the most significant unpegged cryptocurrencies (Bitcoin, Ethereum, Binance), and the largest fiat currencies after the US dollar (EUR, JPY, GBP). Analysis of the results reveals that stablecoins are perceived as a safer alternative in specific market phases. However, they do not consistently exhibit greater stability or independence than other assets. In particular, their resilience is highly dependent on market liquidity, which is why they are exposed to shocks in both the crypto and fiat sectors (Fernandez-Mejia, 2024). These results suggest that the hypothesis that stablecoins could serve as a robust medium of exchange or private substitute for fiat money in the long term is not accurate. At the same time, they illustrate that the bridging function of stablecoins is more ambivalent than their name suggests: they stabilize access to the dollar and strengthen the structural role of the dollar. Stablecoins should therefore be viewed not as competitors, but rather as amplifiers or 'dollar expanders' of hegemony. The U.S. currency is expanding its reach in markets and population groups that were previously excluded from the traditional banking system. However, this does not represent an independent alternative to the dollar. In this function, they stabilize the hegemonic position of the U.S. currency in the digital space and extend the existing path of dollar dominance (Lane, 2025). At the same time, they open up new opportunities for the U.S. government to pursue monetary and fiscal policy in the digital space as well. Nevertheless, there is a possibility of independent instability transmission if their market mechanisms fail to function correctly.

Political Narratives

The strategy pursued by the US of promoting privately issued stablecoins instead of a government-issued digital dollar can be interpreted as a deliberate political calculation. Rather than restricting the innovative power and global reach of the private sector with a centralized CBDC solution, the US is focusing on integrating private stablecoins into the dollar ecosystem. Their economic contribution lies less in directly expanding demand for government bonds and more in securing the global private sector's commitment to dollar-based infrastructures. The result is a digital 'dollar expander' that secures the hegemony of the dollar without the Federal Reserve itself having to actively intervene in the payment infrastructure for private or wholesale customers (Sachdeva & Saravelos, 2025).

Stablecoins are presented in the US not only as a technical financial product, but also as a politically charged narrative. In this study, three strands were identified as particularly significant:

One strand emphasizes that the US must maintain its position as a global center for technological innovation in order to ensure both the country's innovative strength and competitiveness. Stablecoins are referred to as 'native dollar instruments' for the digital world. Their integration into large platforms such as PayPal or Visa is seen as an indication that the dollar can dominate the next generation of payment transactions.

Regarding the issue of financial inclusion, proponents argue that stablecoins should be utilized to democratize access to dollar liquidity. People without bank accounts, especially in developing countries, could gain access to a stable means of payment through digital wallets. This narrative aligns with the agenda of international institutions, which define financial inclusion as a key development goal. Critics of this development, however, emphasize that this form of 'dollarization from below' increases dependence on the US.

In the context of geopolitical power projections, stablecoins are explicitly understood as a means of securing the dollar against emerging alternatives, such as the digital yuan or regional currencies within the BRICS+ framework. Stablecoins facilitate international payment flows and are simultaneously tied to U.S. financial markets. In doing so, they create a digital infrastructure that is difficult to circumvent globally. Washington has the opportunity to export its monetary sovereignty while establishing new forms of control.

These narratives suggest that the U.S. strategy is not aimed exclusively at economic aspects, but should be viewed as a comprehensive initiative to ensure the geopolitical relevance of the dollar in the digital age. Stablecoins serve as a tool for the digital expansion of the existing Bretton Woods order, whereby the associated opportunities and risks must be carefully considered.

POLICY AND REGULATORY FRAMEWORK OF THE US

Strategic Goals of the U.S. Government

The U.S. stablecoin strategy has the explicit goal of ensuring the digital security and expansion of its international currency, the dollar. While the People's Republic of China focuses on state-dominated models, such as the digital yuan, and the European Union pursues a regulation-oriented agenda, for example, with MiCAR and the digital euro, the U.S. government relies on a hybrid model that combines state regulation with the innovative power of private companies. Hong Kong has also recently passed a law on the licensing of stablecoins; the first applications are expected by the end of 2025. In the UK, the regulatory authority, the Financial Conduct Authority (FCA), has published proposals for the establishment of a British stablecoin regime.

The strategic guidelines can be summarized in three dimensions:

1. **Ensuring financial stability in the digital space**: Stablecoins should not grow as an uncontrolled parallel currency, but should be integrated into an orderly infrastructure. The government is pursuing a 'contain and leverage' approach, which consists of mitigating the risks associated with the uncontrolled growth of stablecoins and leveraging the benefits of digital currency, such as increased financial inclusion and efficiency.
2. **Strengthening demand for the dollar through digitalization**: The 1:1 dollar peg makes each stablecoin a digital extension of the dollar base. It stabilizes demand for government bonds and secures favorable financing conditions for the US. This is offset by the risk that stablecoins, as a substitute, could also reduce global demand for traditional reserve currencies. However, a multi-country model, which envisions a digital economy that encompasses the US, the rest of the world, and beyond, shows that the reserve demand effect prevails in the long term. This development results in a reduction in U.S. interest rates and an increase in foreign debt. At the same time, the expansion of the digital economy increases consumption volatility in the US, while it tends to decrease in the rest of the world (Azzimonti & Quadrini, 2025).
3. **Defending against geopolitical competition**: Stablecoins anchor the dollar in digital markets before alternatives (e.g., e-CNY, digital BRICS initiatives) gain traction. The strategy pursued by the US can therefore be viewed as preventive and is considered a form of hegemony. This strategy aims to build network effects that lead to the marginalization of other currencies.

Stablecoins are not seen as a threat, but as an instrument of U.S. geopolitical financial policy. This strategic thinking, unique to the U.S., is evident in both Treasury speeches and congressional hearings, making it clear to the public the U.S.'s distinct approach to regulating stablecoins.

The GENIUS Act Serves as a Regulatory Basis

The GENIUS Act (Guiding and Establishing National Innovation for U.S. Stablecoins Act), passed in 2024 and signed on July 18, 2025, serves as the central legal basis for the U.S. stablecoin strategy (The White House, 2025). For the first time, a coherent regulatory framework has been created that combines the issuance, reserve holding, and supervision of private stablecoin issuers.

The following points are of significant relevance to the law:

- Under the applicable provisions, issuers of fiat-backed stablecoins are required to obtain a federal license issued by the Federal Reserve.
- Stablecoins are subject to strict regulation, which requires full coverage by highly liquid assets. U.S. government bonds and deposits with the Federal Reserve serve as the primary components.
- There is an obligation to prepare quarterly audit reports, which independent auditors are required to prepare.
- Under current law, repurchase guarantees at par value are enshrined in law.
- Under the proposed law, open standards are required for interoperability to promote the integration of stablecoins into established payment networks (Visa, PayPal, SWIFT).

From a political perspective, the GENIUS Act is more than just a financial law: it focuses on the core instrument that directly strengthens the U.S. reserve currency. This strategic priority aims to raise public awareness of the U.S. focus on 'dollar digitalism.' The comprehensive nature of this legislation, with its wide-ranging implications, provides a strong foundation for the U.S. stablecoin strategy.

Role of the SEC, CFTC, Federal Reserve, and Treasury

Regulating stablecoins in the US is a complex undertaking involving multiple agencies with overlapping jurisdictions.

- The SEC (Securities and Exchange Commission) is tasked with reviewing the classification of certain stablecoins as securities. USDC and USDT are widely accepted as means of payment. In contrast, the SEC is investigating algorithmic and yield-generating stablecoins (e.g., with interest promises) as potential securities.

- The CFTC (Commodity Futures Trading Commission) acts as the competent authority for stablecoins when they are used as commodity equivalents in the context of derivatives trading. The CFTC claims a role in supervising stablecoin-based futures and swaps.
- The Federal Reserve plays a significant role in the context of the GENIUS Act. Its responsibilities include licensing and supervising issuers. At the same time, it acts as a 'safety net' by holding stablecoin reserves directly in its system (Fed accounts). According to the present study, stablecoin issuers have not yet had access to the Fed discount window.
- The Treasury Department plays a crucial role in the U.S. stablecoin strategy. It primarily tracks stablecoins from a macroeconomic and geopolitical perspective, ensuring that they do not pose a threat to the U.S. financial system. The Office of Terrorism and Financial Intelligence (TFI) within the Treasury Department emphasizes the relevance of stablecoins in the context of counterterrorism and sanctions enforcement, further underlining the department's key role in regulating stablecoins.

Table 2 in this study provides a clear overview of the institutional landscape's complexity. It shows that the Fed and the Treasury Department are using stablecoins strategically, while the SEC and the CFTC are competing for jurisdiction. This development could lead to regulatory fragmentation. The current institutional landscape illustrates that stablecoins serve a dual function as a financial market instrument and a geopolitical tool. Coordination between authorities remains a challenge, but the GENIUS Act is achieving increasing consolidation of this process.

Table 2. Roles and responsibilities of U.S. authorities regarding stablecoins

Authority	Primary responsibility	Focus on stablecoins	Potential conflicts/overlaps
SEC (Securities and Exchange Commission)	Investor protection, securities supervision	Classification of stablecoins with income or investment components as 'securities'; enforcement of registration requirements	Conflicts with the CFTC (commodity vs. security); criticism that payment stablecoins should not be considered securities
CFTC (Commodity Futures Trading Commission)	Supervision of derivatives and commodity markets	Regulation of stablecoin-based futures, swaps, and DeFi derivatives; classification of stablecoins as 'commodities'	Overlap with the SEC on stablecoin derivatives; limited resources for crypto oversight
Federal Reserve (Fed)	Monetary policy, financial stability, banking supervision	Licensing of stablecoin issuers under the GENIUS Act; custody of reserves (government bonds, deposits with the Fed)	Area of tension: control over the money supply vs. private issuers; risk of disintermediation of banks
US Department of the Treasury (including OFAC & TFI)	Fiscal policy, financial market supervision, enforcement of sanctions	Use of stablecoins to secure demand for U.S. government bonds; use in sanctions regimes and AML/CFT monitoring	Risk of political instrumentalization; international conflicts if stablecoins are used as a geopolitical instrument

Source: Own representation

As of July 2025, regulations for stablecoin issuers have been fully or partially in force in eleven of the 25 most significant countries. These countries account for approximately 38% of the total crypto value transferred in 2024. It is worth noting that the majority of countries implementing existing or planned regulations are predominantly advanced economies. In contrast, most emerging economies within this top 25 have not yet taken any regulatory initiatives—a remarkable finding considering that stablecoins often have the most significant appeal to users 'at the grassroots' in these markets (Chainalysis, 2025; CoinDesk Data, 2025).

Interaction with Private Actors

A significant feature of the U.S. strategy is the close connection between the state and the private sector. Government institutions do not primarily issue stablecoins, but rather by technologically innovative companies.

- Circle (USDC): Working closely with Coinbase, Circle is the institutional provider of the 'clean' stablecoin. USDC is particularly popular with banks and financial service providers that value regulatory compliance. Circle is seeking a banking license to ensure regulatory compliance and global scalability.

- Coinbase: As one of the largest cryptocurrency exchanges, Coinbase serves as both a distribution channel for USDC and an important advocate for stable regulatory conditions.
- PayPal (PYUSD): PYUSD marks the first entry of a global technology company into the stablecoin market. The combination of stablecoins with an established payment ecosystem could open up the mass market.
- Tether (USDT): Although Tether is not a strictly U.S.-based company, as it is based in El Salvador, it remains the stablecoin with the highest volume. The U.S. government has tolerated Tether so far, but sees USDC and PYUSD as the preferred instruments because they are more closely integrated into the U.S. regulatory framework.

This form of public-private partnership represents a strategic division of labor. Private companies focus on innovation and global reach, while the state provides regulatory support and integration into the global financial system.

Lobbying, Conflicts of Interest, and Systemic Risks

Despite its ambitious strategic orientation, U.S. stablecoin policy is subject to considerable criticism. A particularly controversial issue is the close influence of private sector players on the design of the regulatory framework. Companies such as Circle, Coinbase, and PayPal have invested considerable resources in lobbying in recent years to create a regulatory environment that benefits their business models. Critics argue that the GENIUS Act represents a form of regulatory capture. This is because the GENIUS Act reflects the interests of large market participants in key areas, thereby raising barriers to market entry for smaller providers. There is concern that this will lead to the formation of an oligopoly that secures the hegemony of the dollar, but at the same time restricts competition and innovation.

Furthermore, the close link between the issuance of stablecoins and the financing of the US government raises questions about conflicts of interest. When issuers hold the majority of their reserves in short-term U.S. Treasury bonds, there is a close link between private payment instruments and the financing of government debt. While this constellation results in increased demand for U.S. Treasury bonds and thus contributes to stabilizing the U.S. refinancing costs, it also carries the risk that stablecoins will become a politically motivated instrument of money creation that operates outside the direct control of the Federal Reserve. This could lead to a shadow sector of monetary policy that blurs the traditional distinction between public monetary sovereignty and private payment transactions.

The risk of confidence crises must also be taken into account. If doubts arise about the coverage of stablecoins, sudden waves of redemptions ('runs') could occur.

A sudden increase in the number of redemptions during a period of stress could force issuers to sell U.S. government bonds in a market environment where there are no intermediaries (broker-dealers) available to absorb the outflow. Given the dynamic development of this sector and the pending regulation by policymakers, a key question arises: Should issuers be given access to the Fed's discount window in the future, or are alternative protection mechanisms needed to ensure the stability of U.S. Treasury markets?

Finally, the international dimension is also problematic. The US considers stablecoins to be a tool for strengthening the dollar's hegemony. Other countries, on the other hand, could interpret this development as an attack on their own monetary sovereignty. Initial reactions, such as those in the EU with MiCAR or in China with the targeted promotion of the digital yuan, already indicate a fragmentation of regulation. The restriction or prohibition of U.S.-dominated stablecoins by so-called 'countries' has the potential to fragment global financial markets and escalate geopolitical tensions.

The present critique, therefore, extends beyond technical or regulatory aspects to include the democratic theory dimension of the stablecoin strategy. A profound change in the global monetary order is currently being driven by the interaction between the executive branch and large technology companies, without any broad parliamentary debate or international coordination having taken place. This constellation reinforces the impression of a democratic deficit and raises questions about the legitimacy of the new order. Stablecoins, therefore, represent a complex phenomenon that extends beyond the boundaries of technology. They are an expression of a political project that offers opportunities for innovation and stability, but also entails risks for competition, financial stability, and international cooperation.

ECONOMIC LOGIC OF THE DOLLAR STABLECOIN STRATEGY

A central mechanism of the U.S. strategy is the pegging of tokens to highly liquid U.S. assets (bond-based stablecoins). The majority of fiat-backed stablecoins, such as USDT, USDC, and PYUSD, are backed 1:1 by deposits and short-term government bonds. As a result, stablecoins can function as digital money market funds whose stability is directly linked to the demand for U.S. government bonds. Stablecoin providers currently hold USD 160 billion in dollar reserves. The available research shows that they support the market for short-term liabilities and channel liquidity into the dollar. With assets of $120 billion, Tether is one of the 20 largest creditors in the US (Chainalysis, 2025; CoinDesk Data, 2025). Demand, which is currently low, is expected to increase significantly in the future. This could lead to stablecoins becoming more important and the structure of government bonds shifting towards short-term securities. In the event of a significant devaluation of a stablecoin against the dollar and a massive flight from a primary cryptocurrency, the consequences for price development could be considerable. It is because, in such a scenario, issuers would be forced to sell large amounts of cryptocurrency. However, empirical analyses show that stablecoins differ significantly from traditional money market funds (MMFs). While MMFs respond to monetary tightening by increasing their holdings, stablecoins experience a decline in market capitalization. It has been found that both MMFs and traditional markets do not respond to crypto-specific shocks, whereas stablecoins themselves do respond to such shocks. This suggests that the stability of stablecoins depends less on a 'flight to quality' and more on the risk and interest rate environment determined by U.S. monetary policy (Aldasoro et al., 2025b). Prates (2025) points out that during the 2008 financial crisis, it was prime money market funds that collapsed due to their exposure to private and corporate securities. In contrast, government money market funds, which are based on cash and government bonds and are therefore structurally similar to today's regulated stablecoins, remained stable, recorded inflows, and did not require bailouts.

From a macroeconomic perspective, stablecoins play a crucial role in stabilizing demand for U.S. debt securities. The issuance of each new stablecoin unit requires investment in government bonds, effectively manifesting the 'Triffin dilemma' in a digital form. The high demand for dollar reserves leads to international demand for government bonds, while the large deficit in U.S. fiscal policy undermines the credibility of this policy. Stablecoins provide a solution to this structural tension by stabilizing demand for U.S. debt securities, thereby enhancing the credibility of U.S. fiscal policy (Lane, 2025).

Second, stablecoins contribute significantly to global liquidity circulation. The tokens circulate globally, while the underlying reserves remain in the U.S. financial system. This implies a global mobilization of capital, with no withdrawal from U.S. financial markets. This mechanism proves particularly advantageous for the US, as it expands the circle of 'dollar users' and increases the structural demand for U.S. government bonds. In periods of high debt and rising interest expenses, this acts as an invisible subsidy, reducing the U.S.'s refinancing costs. Critics argue that this is a form of 'planned dollarization' designed to channel global liquidity into U.S. securities.

Bond-backed stablecoins have significant macroeconomic implications, as they increase demand for U.S. Treasury bonds, thereby creating a form of digital government financing that secures favorable refinancing conditions for the U.S. Empirical analyses (2021–2025) show that inflows into dollar-based stablecoins reduce the yields on 3-month U.S. Treasury bonds by around 2–2.5 basis points in the short term, while outflows increase them by a multiple of this amount. The effect is therefore manifested in the very short term, without generating significant spillover effects on longer maturities. Tether and USDC are characterized by a significant market presence, which manifests itself in a high degree of influence. This leads to the conclusion that stablecoins are becoming increasingly relevant to the market for safe U.S. assets, thereby exerting an influence on monetary policy transmission, market stability, and the regulation of reserve practices (Ahmed et al., 2025a).

At the same time, bank-based stablecoins exhibit systemic vulnerability: since, like narrow banks, they cannot offer sufficient credit facilities, they are particularly susceptible to mutual run dynamics between banks and stablecoin issuers. One example of this is the 2023 case of Silicon Valley Bank. Furthermore, market volatility, rising interest rates, and the segmentation between crypto and traditional markets can be identified as factors that further jeopardize the stability of these constructs (Bofinger, 2025).

RISKS AND UNINTENDED CONSEQUENCES

Risks for Banks and Financial Intermediation

One of the most frequently discussed side effects of the stablecoin strategy is the risk of disintermediation of the banking sector (Awrey, 2024). Stablecoins undermine this model by offering digital deposit alternatives that circulate outside the banking system. The GENIUS Act primarily focuses on the primary market, resulting in a gap in the secondary market segment. For households and businesses, the allure of holding liquid assets in stablecoins is undeniable, given their ease of transfer, global usability, and integration into digital financial services. Critics see this as a threat to the banking system, as banks could lose deposits if stablecoins offering attractive interest rates enter the market (Chen & Phelan, 2025). Although this is legally prohibited for issuers, it can be legally circumvented via crypto platforms. This creates direct competition in the large deposit market with the banking sector. However, this trend could spell trouble for credit institutions, as it could lead to a potential erosion of their deposit base, thereby weakening their lending capabilities. This is particularly worrisome for regional banks in the US, which heavily rely on customer deposits.

The risk of stablecoins is further amplified during crises. If there are concerns about the stability of banks, depositors not only have the option to withdraw their deposits in cash but also to convert them into stablecoins. This process can be significantly faster and on a larger scale than traditional 'bank runs.' It raises the alarming possibility that stablecoins could worsen the role of classic banking crises.

Fragmentation of Global Regulation

Another risk is the increasing fragmentation of regulation. While the US has established a clear framework for stablecoins with the GENIUS Act, a comprehensive legislation that regulates stablecoins and their issuers, other countries are pursuing their own strategies. In the European Union, MiCAR, the Markets in Crypto-Assets Regulation, has created a comprehensive set of rules that impose strict requirements on issuers. Of particular relevance here is the restriction on so-called 'e-money tokens,' which are primarily linked to non-euro currencies. This provision indirectly aims to restrict USDC and USDT on the European market, underscoring the attempt to reduce dependence on the dollar. The counterpart to U.S. stablecoins, the leading euro stablecoin, Circle's EURC, has a modest market volume of just over €200 million. Overall, the Europe-wide market capitalization of euro stablecoins is currently estimated to be less than €500 million.

Moreover, European stablecoin laws could inadvertently create a vicious circle. Providers are mandated to hold 60% of their reserves at a bank, which could pose a potential threat to financial stability. This regulation could create a dangerous loop between stablecoins and banks, potentially leading to a financial crisis. In the event of a high number of redemptions by stablecoin users, the bank managing the stablecoin provider's reserves could face a liquidity crisis.

In contrast, private stablecoins are effectively banned in China. Instead, Beijing is focusing on expanding the digital yuan (e-CNY), as stablecoins pegged to the dollar are seen as a potential threat to monetary sovereignty. Other emerging markets, such as India and Nigeria, also have an ambivalent attitude. A large number of citizens use stablecoins to gain access to the dollar and hedge against the instability of the local currency. At the same time, governments are attempting to reduce their dependence on the reserve currency through capital controls. Coburger (2025) examines the impact of new forms of digital currencies on the perpetuation of deep-seated power asymmetries between economies in core and peripheral regions. Private households' strategies for monetary self-determination undermine national monetary sovereignty and reinforce external dependence on the dollar within a hierarchically structured international monetary system.

The current regulatory approaches are highly diverse, resulting in the fragmentation of the global financial architecture. As a result, cross-border transactions are becoming increasingly complex. The US is focusing on the global distribution of its stablecoins. However, the international environment could be characterized by protectionist countermeasures that have a lasting negative impact on the stability of the international monetary order.

Systemic Risks

Stablecoins also entail systemic risks. Their increasing relevance is leading to a shift in payment transactions that are no longer directly under the control of the Federal Reserve's balance sheet. This, in turn, weakens the central bank's ability to monitor and control cross-border transactions (Sachdeva & Saravelos, 2025).

A significant risk lies in the possibility of a stablecoin run. In this analysis, Saengchote and Samphantharak (2024) examine the collapse of Iron Finance's algorithmic stablecoin in June 2021 and draw parallels to the Terra Luna crash in May 2022. To this end, they reconstruct the events based on blockchain transaction data and highlight the structural weaknesses of algorithmic stablecoins. Small investors were particularly affected, whose loss of confidence triggered destabilizing 'bank runs'—a pattern that was repeated with UST. The study highlights the fragility of DeFi ecosystems and the risks associated with using algorithmic stablecoins and open blockchains as payment infrastructure.

Although issuers assure that tokens are redeemable at a 1:1 ratio at any time, this stability depends on the liquidity of their reserves. In the event of a demand for mass redemptions by users, issuers are required to liquidate government bonds or other large-scale assets. This could lead to the destabilization of bond markets during periods of stress. The analysis by Calandra et al. (2025) examines four stabilization strategies: two purely algorithmic approaches designed to prevent decoupling and mitigate hyperinflation of the token supply, and two hybrid models that introduce partial collateralization through USDT and BTC reserves. The simulation results show that these strategies significantly reduce the probability of system collapse under extreme market conditions, with the best approaches achieving improvements of between 60% and 96%. Such measures can help minimize systemic risks and increase stability.

The stability of stablecoins is highly dependent on the quality of information regarding their reserve holdings. The present study concludes that if the risks associated with these reserves are not clearly defined, parity remains stable in the event of minor shocks. However, negative market information with far-reaching implications can quickly lead to a collapse, even if the reserves initially appear solid. Regarding transparency, this has a mixed effect. It can reduce the risk of runs if market participants have high expectations of the quality of the reserves. Conversely, it can increase the risk if these expectations are low. This results in a fundamental conflict of objectives between the stability of the peg and the issuer's stability. Greater disclosure does not necessarily lead to increased robustness, but can even increase fragility (Ahmed et al., 2025b).

Stablecoin issuers face a structural trade-off: on the one hand, they must be able to service redemptions at any time, which requires liquid cash reserves; on the other hand, they strive for profitability by investing in interest-bearing government bonds. Simulations indicate that issuers primarily use cash for smaller redemptions to avoid incurring selling costs, whereas larger redemptions necessitate the sale of bonds. This could have destabilizing effects on the bond market. An adequate regulatory framework can reduce these risks. The advantage of liquidity requirements is that they limit market turbulence, while capital requirements help to reduce the probability of issuer default. Model calculations suggest that a combination of a 1% capital requirement and a 30% liquidity requirement could reduce the probability of default to nearly zero (0.05 basis points per year), while significantly mitigating the price impact on the government bond market (Goel et al., 2025).

Stablecoins have experienced significant growth, as well as notable slumps. A monetary policy analysis suggests that their weaknesses lie less in solvency than in on-chain liquidity mechanisms, which have so far only existed in a primitive form. The analogy with Eurodollars illustrates that the central promise of par settlement—repayment at face value at any time—is particularly vulnerable in times of crisis as long as there is a lack of robust liquidity buffers (Aldasoro et al., 2024).

A key risk of stablecoins stems from their dependence on centralized custodians, which makes them structurally vulnerable to devaluation—similar to traditional currencies under fixed exchange rate regimes. Empirical estimates based on spot and forward prices for Tether suggest that the risk of devaluation should not be considered purely theoretical. In the event of a complete default, the average annual probability of devaluation is approximately 60 basis points. However, it rose to over 200 basis points during the Terra Luna crash in 2022. The probability of a partial default is even more serious. The average probability of a partial default with a 5% devaluation (trading price 95 cents) is around 12 percentage points per year. The primary risk factors in this context are market volatility and transaction speed. It has been found that rising interest rates tend to increase the risk. Deviations from covered interest parity, therefore, indicate increasing segmentation between traditional financial markets and stablecoin markets. This segmentation reflects both the costs of arbitrage and the influence of leveraged trading, which increases the system's vulnerability in times of stress (Eichengreen et al., 2025).

In addition, there is a risk of liquidity crises. In the event of a high concentration of stablecoin reserves—for example, in short-term Treasury bills—shocks in the U.S. financial system could have a disproportionate impact on the stablecoin sector. The events surrounding Silicon Valley Bank in 2023 impressively demonstrated the rapid intensification of liquidity bottlenecks.

Cybersecurity also poses a significant risk. Stablecoins are based on digital infrastructures that are potentially vulnerable to hacker attacks, vulnerabilities in smart contracts, or state-sponsored cyberattacks. A successful attack on dollar-pegged stablecoins could not only lead to losses for users but also significantly undermine confidence in the architecture of these cryptocurrencies.

The systemic risks illustrate that stablecoins could trigger financial crises whose effects extend beyond the cryptocurrency sector. Stablecoins should not be considered risk-free digital dollar equivalents. Instead, they are associated with specific instabilities that could lead to significant contagion effects in the event of a crisis. To minimize these risks, a combination of increased transparency regarding reserve holdings and coherent regulatory oversight is necessary.

GEOPOLITICAL IMPACTS

Stablecoins as a Strategic Geopolitical Instrument of Power

Stablecoins are not only a technological or economic phenomenon, but also a deliberately deployed instrument of geopolitical power projection. The conversion of the dollar from a classic reserve currency into a digital infrastructure that enables global implementation is a process that is currently underway. Whereas dollar hegemony was previously based on institutions such as the Bretton Woods system or the dominance of the U.S. banking landscape, stablecoins enable a direct connection between U.S. capital markets and end-users worldwide, without the need for national banks or multilateral settlement mechanisms to act as intermediaries.

This change is relevant in terms of power politics, as it expands the US sphere of influence. Countries that do not deny their citizens access to stablecoins risk undermining their monetary policy autonomy. At the same time, it is worth noting that the US can exercise control through regulatory interventions and sanction mechanisms. Stablecoins are technically programmable, which means they can be configured to block specific addresses or freeze transactions. It could make geopolitical sanctions more effective and enforceable.

This represents a shift in geopolitical logic from the 'gunboat diplomacy' and financial sanctions of the 20th century to the 'code-based diplomacy' of the 21st century, where power is exercised over digital infrastructures. Stablecoins are therefore not just currencies, but part of a global digital ecosystem that is in American hands.

Impact on International Institutional Actors

The establishment of stablecoins presents new challenges for established institutions of the international financial order.

The International Monetary Fund (IMF) traditionally acts as a lender of last resort for countries affected by balance of payments crises. Stablecoins could undermine this function by giving households and businesses direct access to dollar liquidity. Instead of loans from the International Monetary Fund, countries in the Global South could increasingly resort to unofficial digital dollar resources. This would reduce the relevance of the IMF, but at the same time increase the risk of circumventing structural reform requirements.

The World Bank has a development agenda that could be redesigned, particularly in the area of financial inclusion. Stablecoins are being discussed as a possible influencing factor in this context. Although the World Bank has previously supported programs to promote local financial infrastructures, stablecoins represent an external, privately initiated solution. The present analysis shows that there could be a short-term acceleration of inclusion. In the long term, however, there is a risk that development programs will be undermined if national currencies are displaced.

The Bank for International Settlements (BIS) has been working extensively on the regulation of stablecoins and CBDCs in recent years. The aim is to develop global standards that serve to ensure financial stability. However, the rise of U.S. stablecoins is complicating this process as national interests diverge. While the US promotes global adoption, other countries seek to control and limit it. For the BIS, this raises the question of whether it can continue to function as a coordination platform or whether a fragmented 'monetary multipolarism' will emerge in which common standards are practically unenforceable.

International institutions are thus faced with a dilemma: either they accept stablecoins as a new reality and attempt to integrate them into multilateral frameworks, or they risk being marginalized if national strategies dominate the landscape, potentially leading to unforeseen risks.

Lines of Conflict with Alternative Currency Areas

Stablecoins are not entering a neutral environment, but a world in which alternative currency strategies already exist. The renminbi has been gradually used as a means of payment for oil and commodity transactions in China for years. The implementation of the digital yuan confirms this objective in the digital context. Saudi Arabia and Russia have signaled their willingness to conduct part of their energy trade in yuan. Stablecoins that strengthen the dollar are thus in direct competition with a commodity-backed renminbi network.

The EU, on the other hand, is pursuing a different logic. Its primary goal is not geopolitical expansion, but rather the protection of the internal market and limiting dependence on the dollar. The establishment of a digital euro could prove to be a long-term balancing tool by anchoring it in European value chains. According to the current draft concept for the digital euro, the CBDC is not an option for international payments. It should also be noted that only private individuals would be allowed to hold the digital euro. Companies, on the other hand, which are in a particularly advantageous position regarding the digital euro, should immediately convert their holdings into bank deposits. This study shows that the introduction of a CBDC has significant implications for the possible applications of stablecoins. In particular, the facilitation of international payments at lower cost and with greater speed, made possible by the elimination of intermediaries, is of significant relevance. Stablecoins also offer a higher level of security compared to bank deposits for large companies that need to hold large amounts of cash. The MiCAR regulation acts as a regulatory bulwark aimed at curbing U.S.-dominated stablecoins. The global expansion of dollar stablecoins poses a significant risk to European sovereignty. Bofinger (2025) emphasizes that the digital euro in its current conception—geared toward the internal market, retail, and limited by volume caps—is hardly a suitable counterweight to U.S. stablecoins. Instead, there is a risk that the EU will become dependent on private payment systems dominated by the US. Platforms such as VISA and PayPal are indicators of this. Bofinger cites both the creation of integrated European payment systems and, as a last resort, the issuance of a stablecoin by the ECB itself, based on tokenized central bank reserves, as alternatives. The current debate emphasizes the need to make the digital currency system more multilateral and strategic in order to establish a long-term counterweight to the U.S.-led infrastructure.

The BRICS+ countries (Brazil, Russia, India, China, South Africa, and new members such as Egypt and Saudi Arabia) are discussing the possibility of creating a multilateral digital reserve currency based on commodities or a basket of currencies. The joint payment system BRICS Pay, which has eleven members, is expected to undergo further expansion. It enables transactions in local currencies. However, the establishment of an independent BRICS reserve currency seems utopian as long as the yuan is not freely tradable and China shies away from the risk of capital flight. The gradual internationalization of the digital yuan, therefore, seems more realistic, as it could facilitate cross-border payments faster and more cost-effectively, thus representing a genuine alternative to the dollar's dominance in payment transactions. Although these projects are still in their early stages, they offer a narrative counterweight to U.S. stablecoins. Russia and China, in particular, view stablecoins as a geopolitical instrument of the US and are therefore committed to finding alternatives. Murakami and Viswanath-Natraj (2025) use a DSGE model to demonstrate that in emerging economies, ‘digital dollarization’ via stablecoins often leads to an increase in prosperity, as it enables consumption smoothing and hedging against macroeconomic fluctuations, while volatile cryptocurrencies such as Bitcoin (El Salvador) cause prosperity losses.

These lines of conflict illustrate that the global monetary order is transforming into a digital competitive arena. The forecast is that U.S. stablecoins will play a significant role in the real economy. This could have a counterproductive effect on projects such as the digital yuan or the BRICS basket. In its current form, however, the cryptosphere represents an extension of the global dollar standard (Olk & Miebs, 2025). This raises questions about the hypothesis that other countries could utilize cryptocurrencies to circumvent the constraints of the dollar system. Stablecoins are not only a technological advance, but also a geopolitical statement. Control over the digital infrastructure of the financial world is a decisive factor in determining the balance of power in the 21st century.

Projection of American Power Through Digital Financial Infrastructures

The projection of American power through stablecoins is primarily achieved through the digitization of the dollar infrastructure. Instead of traditional mechanisms, such as the presence of the U.S. military or the Bretton Woods institutions, it is now digital protocols, APIs, and platforms that generate hegemonic effects.

Stablecoins can be considered 'programmable dollars.' The US can write its monetary policy and regulatory powers directly into the code. The possibility is that sanctions will be automatically enforced, illegal transactions will be algorithmically blocked, and geopolitical preferences will be embedded in the architecture of payment flows. As a result, there is a shift in the exercise of power from a 'rule-based order' to a 'code-based order.'

At the same time, stablecoins have a significant presence in the American tech industry. Companies such as Circle, Coinbase, and PayPal not only act as financial service providers, but also function as geopolitical multipliers, contributing to the spread of the dollar across digital networks. This constellation represents a form of public-private partnership, where government interests and private sector innovations coexist in a symbiotic relationship.

The projection of American power via stablecoins has far-reaching consequences:

- Strengthening the sanctions regime: Stablecoins could be used as a more precise instrument to deny opponents access to global dollar flows.
- Dominance over data flows: Every stablecoin transaction generates data that is controlled by U.S.-regulated platforms. It also provides the US with valuable geopolitical information.
- Structural dependence: Countries that use stablecoins anchor their economies even more firmly in the dollar system—but this time in a digitalized form that is more difficult to reverse.

The geopolitical implication is therefore evident: stablecoins are more than just financial instruments. The US claims digital infrastructure hegemony for itself, which not only allows it to assert its role as a global leader but also to redefine this claim to leadership. The US essentially uses stablecoins to exercise its power in the 21st century primarily through digital financial infrastructures rather than military or diplomatic means.

FUTURE SCENARIOS AND POLICY OPTIONS

Scenario Analysis

Understanding the future of stablecoins and the global monetary order is not a straightforward task. It involves navigating through various paths and path dependencies. To gain a comprehensive view, we employ scenario analysis. This analytical tool allows us to capture a range of potential developments and their implications for stability, hegemony, and governance. Currently, three central scenarios stand out as plausible.

Scenario 1 – Strengthening the dollar's hegemony

In this scenario, the US succeeds in permanently establishing stablecoins as the dominant instrument for international payments. The GENIUS Act provides regulatory clarity, enabling large platforms like PayPal and Visa to integrate stablecoins into their infrastructures. The resulting network effects create digital lock-in dynamics that stabilize demand for U.S. dollars and government bonds. This scenario can be viewed as a digital reconfiguration of classic dollar hegemony, adding an infrastructural dimension. The strengthening of U.S. financial markets comes with the risk of solidifying structural dependencies.

Scenario 2 – Erosion through fragmentation

An alternative scenario is characterized by regulatory and geopolitical divergence. The European Union limits the use of U.S. stablecoins through MiCAR, the People's Republic of China intensifies the development of the e-CNY, and the BRICS alliance countries develop their own digital alternatives. This results in regional parallel architectures in which the dollar loses its universal reach. The global monetary order is characterized by an increase in multipolarity, with the dollar occupying a dominant position in the leading markets while losing relative importance at the international level. This scenario illustrates that technological innovations do not necessarily lead to hegemony, but rather become the subject of political debate.

Scenario 3 – Transformation to hybrid systems

A third scenario is based on a hybrid model in which stablecoins play a central role but are embedded in multilateral regulatory architectures. International organizations such as the BIS or the IMF develop coordination mechanisms that integrate stablecoins into a system of digital reserve currencies. The dollar continues to function as a reserve currency, but its influence is no longer unilateral; instead, it is based on cooperation and institutionalized governance. This scenario suggests the possibility of a 'digitized Bretton Woods order.'

Alternative Models

In addition to these scenarios, there are competing models that are actively promoted by different groups of actors:

One potential model for the future monetary order is a multi-currency structure. Economists argue that digital technologies could foster a multipolar system where the dollar, euro, yuan, and other currencies coexist. In this model, stablecoins pegged to different currencies could serve as bridge instruments, promoting balance and stability in the global monetary system.

Cooperation in the area of digital central bank currencies, as seen in projects such as mBridge (BIS, Hong Kong, Thailand, China, and the United Arab Emirates), demonstrates that CBDCs facilitate a multilateral architecture. In such an order, stablecoins could play a complementary role as an interoperability solution between national CBDCs (Lane, 2025).

These models suggest that the future monetary order does not necessarily have to be characterized by the hegemonic dominance of the dollar. However, they may instead exhibit a trend toward multipolar or cooperative arrangements.

Stablecoins are not just a temporary phenomenon, but a catalyst for a more comprehensive, profound digital transformation process in the financial market. The ongoing tokenization of assets and their embedding in DeFi architectures could contribute to the emergence of a global 'finternet' that organizes capital flows largely without traditional intermediaries. In such an order, the focus is less on the question of reserve quality and more on the privilege of integrity (Rey, 2025): the digital robustness that offers protection against cyberattacks, manipulation, and future threats from quantum computers. Achieving this privilege could mean playing a leading role in initiating the next wave of global currency dominance in the 21st century, comparable to the importance of military and institutional power in the 20th century.

Governance Issues

Regardless of the specific scenario, various dimensions of governance emerge that determine the system's stability. The security of stablecoins depends on the quality of their reserves and institutional anchoring. Central banks must design requirements in a way that minimizes liquidity crises and runs. Trust requires standardized disclosure requirements and audit processes. A lack of transparency can create instability, even when reserves are available. International cooperation is not just a desirable option, but a necessity in regulating a global, cross-border phenomenon such as stablecoins. National regulations are not sufficient to control this complex system. Multilateral minimum standards are necessary to ensure interoperability, prevent money laundering, and maintain security. It underscores the importance of global coordination in the financial market.

The central conflict lies in the fact that U.S. interests, namely the global enforcement of the dollar, clash with the sovereignty interests of other states. Governance thus manifests itself as a geopolitical field of negotiation. One promising approach is 'compliance by design,' in which regulatory requirements are integrated directly into the technical architecture. Zero-knowledge proofs (zkKYC) could enable identity checks without revealing sensitive data, while smart contracts would only execute transactions in compliance with relevant regulations. The implementation of such a regulatory layer would therefore contribute to stability, transparency, and data protection (Duffie et al., 2025).

Recommendations

1. Strengthening Financial Stability Through Targeted Regulation

This analysis concludes that stablecoins such as USDC and Tether invest significantly in short-term U.S. government bonds. This generates demand effects, which, however, can have a potentially destabilizing effect in the event of 'runs.' The analysis, therefore, recommends strengthening financial stability through targeted regulation. This analysis leads to the recommendation that regulatory requirements should focus not only on reserve quality but also on liquidity profiles (e.g., minimum cash reserves, stress tests for mass redemptions). This measure would help reduce the risk of a sudden sell-off of U.S. government bonds and reduce the systemic vulnerabilities described in Chapter 6.

2. International Coordination Against Fragmentation

The empirical results presented in Section 7 suggest a degree of regulatory fragmentation. The US (GENIUS Act), the EU (MiCAR), China (e-CNY), and the BRICS+ are pursuing divergent strategies. From a political perspective, therefore, it is not abstract 'coordination' that is recommended, but rather the establishment of a multilateral framework for interoperability, for example, through the IMF or the BIS. The goal is not to relinquish national sovereignty, but to create minimum standards for transparency, interoperability of reserve checks, and settlement interfaces. This directly addresses the risks of 'block formation' in the digital currency system identified in Chapter 7.

3. Mitigating Geopolitical Tensions Through Phased Areas of Application

Sections 5 and 7 explain that the US is using stablecoins as a tool to project international power. To avoid geopolitical escalations with China and the BRICS+ countries, it is advisable to limit their use functionally in sensitive areas. U.S. stablecoins could therefore be used primarily in areas where clear efficiency gains can be achieved, such as remittances or e-commerce. Their use in the commodity or energy trading sectors could be gradually regulated. This approach helps reduce the risk of stablecoins being perceived as a form of direct geopolitical influence. It also addresses the lines of conflict identified in section 7 in an evidence-based manner.

The resulting policy recommendations are therefore directly attributable to the identified mechanisms and risks. These recommendations aim to stabilize demand effects on the U.S. government bond market, curb regulatory divergences, and avoid geopolitical escalations. Evidence-based governance is therefore crucial for preventing such developments and ensuring the stability of the financial system.

CONCLUSION

Key Findings of the Analysis

The five research questions are summarized below.

RQ1: The role of stablecoins in U.S. strategy

Stablecoins should not be understood as a replacement for the dollar in U.S. strategy, but rather as a digital extension of the dollar. Monetary hegemony theory argues that traditional parameters—such as the size of the economy, the credibility of institutions, and military strength—must be supplemented by a new technological dimension. Hegemony in the digital age is no longer based solely on a central power's ability to provide liquidity, but also on its control over digital infrastructures and network effects. The pegging of stablecoins to the U.S. dollar stabilizes their global use in digital infrastructures. At the same time, their integration into platform economies (PayPal, Visa, Coinbase) creates a technological anchor for the dollar. Stablecoins are transforming the dollar from a reserve currency into a digital infrastructure hegemony, having a direct impact on the everyday economy of households and businesses. Stablecoins account for approximately three-quarters of trading volume. Stablecoins in other currencies are of secondary importance. The prices of all cryptocurrencies are always quoted in dollars, making it the central unit of account. The political projection of the existing reserve currency role into the digital space enables the US to strategically leverage its private innovation power to consolidate the structural dependence of other economies on the U.S. currency. In its current form, the cryptosphere represents an extension of the global dollar standard (Olk & Miebs, 2025). As a result, the US is increasingly shifting its power projection from traditional institutions to a 'code-based order.' These developments indicate an emerging transformation of 'world money' or 'money as an international value standard,' enabled by distributed ledger technology (Duque, 2025).

RQ2: Economic mechanisms

Stablecoins operate similarly to digital money market funds, with each unit of the issued securities backed by short-term U.S. government bonds or bank deposits. This setup leads to a systematic increase in demand for U.S. dollar liquidity and supports the U.S. refinancing costs. It also opens up new channels for international payment flows and trade finance by bypassing SWIFT and correspondent banks. The US benefits in two ways—first, by strengthening its capital markets, and second, by expanding the use of the dollar in emerging markets, where stablecoins often serve as the primary means of accessing foreign currencies.

RQ3: Political and regulatory measures

The regulatory framework provided by the GENIUS Act aims to integrate stablecoins into the U.S. financial architecture. It requires 1:1 coverage by liquid U.S. assets, imposes transparency requirements, and ties issuers to the Federal Reserve. In addition, the SEC and CFTC play a role in delineating responsibilities, while the Treasury Department uses stablecoins as a geopolitical tool, for instance, for sanctions enforcement. This architecture illustrates the 'contain and leverage' approach: risks are limited through regulation, while the hegemonic effect is exploited in a targeted manner.

RQ4: Risks and side effects

The strategy has significant side effects. First, disintermediation of the banking system can be observed. Deposits could migrate to stablecoins, which would weaken the lending market. Second, different regulatory approaches (MiCAR, e-

CNY, BRICS+) could lead to fragmentation of international financial markets into competing blocs. A third aspect is geopolitical tensions caused by the perception of U.S. stablecoins as an expression of economic power expansion. Finally, there is a systemic risk from potential 'runs' on stablecoins. In extreme cases, these could have repercussions on bond markets and exacerbate shocks in the U.S. financial system.

RQ5: Impact on the global monetary order

In the long term, the dollar stablecoin strategy raises the question of a new 'digital Bretton Woods order.' Stablecoins could create a digital lock-in dynamic that marginalizes alternative currency areas and technologically cements the hegemony of the dollar. At the same time, the likelihood of multipolar structures is increasing. The e-CNY is being pushed in China, the EU is developing the digital euro, and the BRICS+ are discussing commodity-linked alternatives. The development of stable dollar dominance or a fragmented, multipolar monetary order is significantly influenced by the global network effects of digital infrastructures.

Outlook: A Digital Bretton Woods System?

This study examines whether stablecoins mark the beginning of a digital Bretton Woods system. Following the historical Bretton Woods system, which institutionally anchored the dollar, stablecoins could create a digital order in which the dollar becomes structurally irreplaceable due to technological network effects. The two stablecoin providers, Tether and USDC, are natural monopolies that make it difficult for other providers to establish alternative stablecoins. An additional challenge for providers of stablecoins that do not peg their value to the dollar is ensuring the stability of their value.

However, the outcome is fraught with uncertainty. Three possible developments can be distinguished here: First, the hegemony of the dollar is strengthening as a result of the increasing acceptance and integration of stablecoins into global infrastructures. Second, the erosion of counterstrategies such as the digital yuan or the digital euro is gaining momentum. The third aspect is a hybrid transformation in which the dollar retains a dominant position but is increasingly integrated into multilateral coordination mechanisms.

The question of whether the US will maintain its dominance or establish a multipolar digital financial order depends mainly on two key factors: its ability to promote international cooperation and its resilience to systemic risks. Creating a new order that is not only hegemonic but also sustainable requires a balance of stability, transparency, and governance.

Stablecoins thus offer a historic opportunity to extend the dollar's role as a reserve currency into the digital age. At the same time, they have the potential to create new dependencies, instabilities, and conflicts. The development of the global financial order in the future will depend mainly on whether the world enters a digital Bretton Woods system or a fragmented era with multiple digital currency areas.

REFERENCES

Ahmed, R., & Aldasoro, I. (2025a). Stablecoins and safe asset prices. BIS Working Papers No 1270, May. https://www.bis.org/publ/work1270.pdf

Ahmed, R., Aldasoro, I., & Duley, C. (2025b). Public information and stablecoin runs. BIS Working Papers No 1164, January. https://www.bis.org/publ/work1164.pdf

Aldasoro, I., Aquilina, M., Lewrick, U., & Hyuk Lim, S. (2025a). Stablecoin growth – policy challenges and approaches. BIS Bulletin No 108. July 11, 2025. https://www.bis.org/publ/bisbull108.pdf

Aldasoro, I., Cornelli, G., Ferrari Minesso, M., Gambacorta, L., & Habib, M. (2025b). Stablecoins, money market funds and monetary policy. *Economics Letters*, *247*, 112203. DOI: 10.1016/j.econlet.2025.112203

Aldasoro, I., Mehrling, P., & Neilson, D. (2024). On par: A money view of stablecoins. *Journal of Financial Market Infrastructures*, *11*(4), 47–64.

Ante, L. (2025). From adoption to continuance: Stablecoins in cross-border remittances and the role of digital and financial literacy. *Telematics and Informatics*, *97*, 102230. DOI: 10.1016/j.tele.2024.102230

Aquilina, M., Frost, J., & Schrimpf, A. (2024). Decentralized finance (DeFi): A functional approach. *Journal of Financial Regulation*, *10*(1), 1–27. DOI: 10.1093/jfr/fjad013

Auer, R., Lewrick, U., & Paulick, J. (2025). DeFiying gravity? An empirical analysis of cross-border Bitcoin, Ether and stablecoin flows. BIS Working Papers No 1265. https://www.bis.org/publ/work1265.pdf

Awrey, D. (2024). *Beyond Banks: Technology, Regulation and the Future of Money*. Princeton University Press.

Azzimonti, M., & Quadrini, V. (2025). Digital economy, stablecoins, and the global financial system. NBER Working Paper No 34066. https://www.nber.org/papers/w34066

Baptista Palazzi, R., Schich, S., & de Genaro, A. (2025). Stablecoins as anchors? Unraveling information flow dynamics between pegged and unpegged crypto-assets and fiat currencies. *Journal of International Financial Markets, Institutions and Money*, *99*, 102108. DOI: 10.1016/j.intfin.2024.102108

Bertaut, C., von Beschwitz, B., & Curcuru, S. (2025). The international role of the U.S. Dollar – 2025 Edition. FEDS Notes. https://www.federalreserve.gov/econres/notes/feds-notes/the-international-role-of-the-u-s-dollar-2025-edition-20250718.html

Bofinger, P. (2025). Stablecoins and the Future of Money: Economic Principles and Policy Implications. IMK Study No 100. https://www.imk-boeckler.de/fpdf/HBS-009201/p_imk_study_100_2025.pdf

Calandra, F., Rossi, F. P., Fabris, F., & Bernardo, M. (2025). Learning from Terra-Luna: A simulation-based study on stabilizing algorithmic stablecoins. *Blockchain: Research and Applications, 100364*, 100364. Advance online publication. DOI: 10.1016/j.bcra.2025.100364

Catalini, C. (2025). How will stablecoins integrate with the financial system? Centre for International Governance Innovation. August 1, 2025. https://www.jstor.org/stable/resrep71787

Chainalysis (2025). The road to crypto regulation Part 2: Stablecoins at the crossroads of financial services and crypto. August 2025. https://www.chainalysis.com/blog/the-road-to-crypto-regulation-part-2-stablecoins/

Chatham House. (2025). US dollar dominance is both a cause and a consequence of US power. https://www.chathamhouse.org/2024/09/us-dollar-dominance-both-cause-and-consequence-us-power

Chen, W., & Phelan, G. (2025). Digital currency and banking-sector stability. *Journal of Financial Stability*, *78*, 101414. DOI: 10.1016/j.jfs.2025.101414

Coburger, C. (2025). *The digital dollarization dilemma: Stablecoins and monetary subordination. The.* Japanese Political Economy., DOI: 10.1080/2329194X.2025.2552378

CoinDesk Data. (2025). Stablecoins & CBDCs Report. August 2025. https://www.coindesk.com/research/stablecoins-and-cbdcs-report-august-2025

Duffie, D., Olowookere, O., & Veneris, A. (2025, September). Fighting financial crime doesn't have to come at the cost of privacy. *Finance & Development*, 32–36. https://www.imf.org/en/Publications/fandd/issues/2025/09/the-stablecoin-balancing-act-darrell-duffie

Duque, J. J. (2025). *Political economy of private cryptofinance. Technology and social relations. The.* Japanese Political Economy., DOI: 10.1080/2329194X.2025.2551630

Eichengreen, B. (2011). *Exorbitant Privilege: The Rise and Fall of the Dollar and the Future of the International Monetary System*. Oxford University Press.

Eichengreen, B., Nguyen, M. T., & Viswanath-Natraj, G. (2025). Stablecoin devaluation risk. *European Journal of Finance, 31*(11), 1469–1496. DOI: 10.1080/1351847X.2025.2505757

Fernandez-Mejia, J. (2024). Extremely stablecoins. *Finance Research Letters, 63*, 105268. DOI: 10.1016/j.frl.2024.105268

Goel, T., Lewrick, U., & Agarwal, I. (2025). Making stablecoins stable(r): Can regulation help? DOI: 10.2139/ssrn.5070116

Hui, C. H., Wong, A., & Lo, C. F. (2025). Stablecoin price dynamics under a peg-stabilising mechanism. *Journal of International Money and Finance, 152*, 103280. DOI: 10.1016/j.jimonfin.2025.103280

International Monetary Fund (IMF). (2025). IMF Data Brief: Currency composition of official foreign exchange reserves. https://data.imf.org/en/news/imf%20data%20brief%20jul%209

Kindleberger, C. P. (1973). *The World in Depression, 1929-1939*. University of California Press.

Kutler, J. (2025). The unsettled side of stablecoins. September 19, 2025. https://www.garp.org/risk-intelligence/technology/unsettled-side-stablecoins-250919

Lane, T. (2025). Opportunities for digital assets in a fractured world. CIGI Papers No. 326, July 2025. https://www.cigionline.org/static/documents/DADW-Lane_01.pdf

Martino, E. D., & Roos, Y. (2024). The law of algorithmic stablecoins in the EU. Amsterdam Center for Law & Economics Working Paper No. 2024-15. DOI: 10.2139/ssrn.5011467

Minsky, H. (1992). The financial instability hypothesis. The Jerome Levy Economics Institute Working Paper No. 74. https://www.levyinstitute.org/pubs/wp74.pdf

Murakami, D., & Viswanath-Natraj, G. (2025). Cryptocurrencies in emerging markets: A stablecoin solution? *Journal of International Money and Finance, 156*, 103344. DOI: 10.1016/j.jimonfin.2025.103344

Olk, C., & Miebs, L. (2025). A credit theory of anti-credit money: How the cryptocurrency sphere turned into a shadow banking system. *Review of International Political Economy, 32*(5), 1414–1441. Advance online publication. DOI: 10.1080/09692290.2025.2476738

Prates, M. (2025). What critics still get wrong about stablecoins. OMFIF, September 18, 2025. https://www.omfif.org/2025/09/what-critics-still-get-wrong-about-stablecoins

Rey, H. (2025, September). Stablecoins, tokens, and global dominance. *Finance & Development*, 24–27. https://www.imf.org/en/Publications/fandd/issues/2025/09/stablecoins-tokens-global-dominance-helene-rey

Rogoff, K. (2025). *Our Dollar, Your Problem: An Insider's View of Seven Turbulent Decades of Global Finance, and the Road Ahead.* Yale University Press.

Sachdeva, M., & Saravelos, G. (2025). What do stablecoins mean for dollar dominance? Deutsche Bank Research, September 10, 2025. https://www.dbresearch.com/PROD/RI-PROD/PDFVIEWER.calias?pdfViewerPdfUrl=PROD0000000000602780

Saengchote, K., & Samphantharak, K. (2024). Digital money creation and algorithmic stablecoin run. *Finance Research Letters, 64*, 105435. DOI: 10.1016/j.frl.2024.105435

The White House. (2025). Fact Sheet: President Donald J. Trump signs GENIUS Act into law. https://www.whitehouse.gov/fact-sheets/2025/07/fact-sheet-president-donald-j-trump-signs-genius-act-into-law/

Wang, C., Lu, D., Meihe, E., Mu, Y., & Peng, Y. (2025). Safe asset scarcity and multipolar international currency. *Economics Letters, 112621*, 112621. Advance online publication. DOI: 10.1016/j.econlet.2025.112621

Chapter 8
CBDCs in a High-Evasion Economy:
Seigniorage, Tax Collection, and Institutional Tensions

Harpreet Kaur
https://orcid.org/0000-0003-3043-9770
Christ University, India

Surbhi Srivastava
https://orcid.org/0000-0001-9572-1983
Christ University, India

Shanu Singh
https://orcid.org/0000-0002-1863-0364
Christ University, India

ABSTRACT

This chapter investigates the welfare implications of introducing Central Bank Digital Currency (CBDC) in an economy with tax evasion and varying degrees of central bank independence (CBI). The model considers scenarios with and without central bank independence, where the fiscal authority finances its expenditure through sales tax and/or seigniorage revenue from the central bank. The model analyses the equilibrium conditions for the coexistence of cash and CBDC, and it depends on the degree of CBI.

DOI: 10.4018/979-8-3373-3725-8.ch008

1. INTRODUCTION

Central Bank Digital Currencies (CBDCs) have recently emerged as a focal point of discussion among central banks and academic researchers. Unlike physical cash, CBDCs offer the unique potential to record all transaction information on a digital ledger maintained by the central bank (Adrian et al., 2018). This feature enables the potential sharing of transaction data with fiscal authorities for improved tax collection and allows CBDCs to bear interest due to verifiable ownership within the digital ledger. One of the key arguments in favor of CBDCs is their potential to reduce tax evasion, a phenomenon often associated with cash transactions. Proponents argue that governments should introduce CBDCs to enhance sales tax revenue (Bas et al., 2024; Camera et al., 2004). However, some contend that CBDCs may be unnecessary, as central banks can already levy inflation taxes on cash users. As Coulter (2023) suggested that in the past times central bank seigniorage has been utilized for government spending when tax revenues are insufficient, particularly during periods of severe tax evasion or wartime. In this respect, the effects of introducing CBDCs are closely tied to the concept of central bank independence (CBI) from fiscal authorities. Moreover, Coulter (2023) highlights, transferring seigniorage from the central bank to the fiscal authority can influence public expectations about inflation and, consequently, real economic allocations. However, the understanding of how CBDCs contribute to an economy where tax evasion exists and CBI matters is still limited (Akhtar et al., 2021).

The increasing interest in CBDCs for reducing tax evasion and improving government revenue has stimulated debate regarding their efficacy and extensive economic implications. Even though CBDCs offer the promise of intensified transparency and trackability in transactions, questions remain about their necessity and influence particularly in economies where cash is majorly used, and tax evasion is widespread (Camera et al., 2004). This is outlined rightly by Inder (2024) that the primary issue lies in determining whether these benefits of improved sales tax revenue collection and reduced tax evasion exceed the potential misrepresentations, such as effect on financial stability. Many studies have also stated that the potency of CBDCs has a strong association with CBI, as inadequate independence from fiscal authorities could form public belief about influencing actual allocations, inflation. Therefore, there is a need to survey how CBDCs can upgrade welfare while considering the role of CBI in forming economic outcomes (Akhtar et al., 2022; Kvedaravičiūtė & Šapkauskienė, 2024).

This study ia designed to examine how launching the CBDCs can influence welfare in an economy where tax evasion exists and cash is used as a medium of exchange (MOE). Based on the viewpoints of Sood and Singh (2024), CBDCs will never replace cash to reduce tax evasion, however, launching them with the practical interest rates can boost record-keeping trades and lower the incentive to evade sales tax (Inder, 2024). Building on monetary models proposed by Steele (2024) and Ozili (2023c), this research explores how CBDCs can refine welfare alongside CBI, aiming to provide deeper awareness into the impact of record-keeping MOEs on tax evasion. This paper will give a tribute to the existing literature by explicitly considering proportional sales taxes as a cost associated with CBDCs and shedding light on the crucial role of CBI in understanding the welfare effects of CBDCs (Van Roosebeke & Defina, 2023; Themistocleous et al., 2023).

By examining the equilibrium state for the coexistence of cash and CBDCs and addressing the efficient monetary and fiscal policy mix, the aim of this study is to contribute to the ongoing debate on the implications of CBDCs in the economies having tax evasion and diverse degrees of central bank independence. To answer the following questions, monetary model is situated in this study:

1. How does the introduction of a CBDCs affect social welfare in an economy where cash is used, tax evasion is possible, and what role does central bank independence (CBI) play in this relationship?
2. *Considering varying degrees of central bank independence and the need to address tax evasion, what is the prime mix of monetary and fiscal policies in an economy with both cash and CBDC?*
3. To what extent does the introduction of a CBDC, particularly one offering a positive interest rate, reduce the incentive for tax evasion compared to a cash-only economy, and what are the implications for government revenue?

The rest of the research paper is structured as follows: The Literature review section provides a brief overview of CBDCs, their role, and the global scenario. The Case Studies section explores the applicability of CBDCs with a focus on practical implications. In conclusion, the 'Discussion and Scope of Future Research' section offers essential insights into recent challenges and possible guidelines for future analysis.

2. BACKGROUND OF THE STUDY

2.1 CBDCs

This research is positioned within a growing body of literature. It examines the implications of CBDCs and their interactions with public finance, monetary policy, and central bank independence (CBI). Studies on CBDCsused to be primarily focused on their technological feasibility and how they could enhance the payment systems (Akhtar et al., 2023; Salampasis et al., 2023). But the latest research on this subject is now turning to the macroeconomic and welfare effects of these digital currencies. CBDC is a digital form of a country's national currency that is issued and regulated by the central bank. CBDCs are centralized and supported by the government, unlike cryptocurrencies, and are working as a legal tender that can be used for transactions, payments, and a store of value. CBDCs can be designed for retail use (available to the general public) or for wholesale use (limited to financial institutions), with the primary objectives being improved payment efficiency, widening financial inclusion, and strengthening monetary policy effectiveness while also reducing risks that are linked with cash transactions and financial crimes (Alam et al., 2024; Choi & Kim, 2024 ; Bas et al., 2024).

2.2 Global Scenario

As per the views of Moenjak (2024a) and Temperini et al (2024), CBDCs have been gathering widespread attention as a promising digital innovation for the financial systems. The growing number of facts and figures surrounding CBDCs, highlight their rapid exploration and projected impacts on various economies globally. CBDCs are showing transformative effectsin the financial spectrum. Their influence are from monetary policy, inflation control to potential competition with private cryptocurrencies.

Some media reports shows that over 80% of banks across the globe are analysing the potential of CBDCs through research, trials, and pilot programs.some of the examples of evaluations include China's digital yuan pilot, the Bahamas with its Sand Dollar (It is one of the first CBDCs to launch), and the European Central Bank, which is examining the feasibility of a digital euro (Akhtar et al., 2023). A recent survey shows that approximately 90% of central banks are either already working on their CBDCs or researching their benefits and limitations. This trend showcases a strong global push towards establishing secure, government-approved digital currencies not only to modernize payments but also to challenge the private digital assets (Central Bank of The Bahamas, 2019).

2.2.1 CBDCs, Monetary Policy, and Tax Evasion

A major area of investigation is that how the CBDCs might affect tax evasion, which is a occurrence that is often associated with the entry in the cash book . Many experts believe that CBDCs might help in reducing tax evasion and boost government revenue (Ogunmola & Das, 2024), but there are questions rising regarding the extent to which this is true, and the adverse effects that it could bring along with its espousal . This study builds on the work of Ozili (2023b) and Tercero-Lucas (2023), who develops a model of multiple means of settlement to verify the implications of introducing CBDCs. He works on subjects like theft, which are commonly associated with cash, and shows how CBDCs might help to reduce such issues. Apart from that, he also raises a potential issue and threat that paying interest on CBDC might threaten CBI. Adrian et al (2018) & Bas et al (2024) have provided conditions under which introducing CBDCs can implement a first-best allocation in a similar model with a fixed acquisition cost of CBDC. By openly embracing the concept of CBI and proposing a proportional sales tax for tax evasion incentives, this research paper complements both of their works and adds necessary recommendations and suggestions on the subject.

Another relevant piece of literature that explores the optimal design of monetary policy in the presence of tax evasion is the analysis presented by Board & Wehrli (2021). This provides a theory to guide the measurement of the economy's subterranean sector. Ghosh & Das (2024) performed a quantitative analysis of the public finance motive for inflation in order to explain the high rates of inflation in developing countries examining the connection between tax evasion and the ideal inflation tax, even showing that the ideal interest rate is positive when cash is used for shadow economy transactions.

2.2.1.1 Enhanced Monetary Policy Effectiveness

CBDCs offer new tools for central banks to manage the stability of an economy. They can be programmed, unlike cash, which allows for features like negative interest rates in order to encourage spending rather than saving. This facility could be useful when interest rates are already low, and where traditional monetary policy tools may lose their effectiveness. Since CBDCs offer direct ways to affect consumer behavior during recessions, a study released by BIS predicted that their use could increase the effectiveness of monetary policy by as much as 15% to 20% in such low-rate environments (Barnett, 1980).

Furthermore, CBDCs could enhance the ability of central banks' to monitor economic activity. Central banks could respond to inflation or deflation in an economy more quickly by using the transaction data generated by digital currency to gain better and faster insights into spending patterns and managing economic stability and growth using the real-time data (Azmi & Akhtar, 2022; Ladeira et al., 2024).

2.2.2 CBDCs and Institutional Design

2.2.2.1.Central Bank Independence (CBI)

Many studies states that there is a negative relationship between CBI and inflation (Themistocleous et al., 2023). The more independent a central bank is, the lower the inflation tends to be. Jagrič et al (2022) argued that outcomes could be improved by introducing a central bank which just had a stronger focus and a goal of keeping inflation towards the lower end. Umar et al (2024) raises concerns over redirecting the power to create money (seigniorage) from the central bank to the fiscal authority. On the other hand, Williamson (2019) is anxious about the case wherein the interest payment on CBDC might weaken the central bank's freedom .

The present research builds on these discussions by developing a model that combines CBDCs, tax evasion, and CBI, as well as offering a framework for understanding the complex interactions between these factors. This research also gives an idea on how CBDCs can affect welfare, tax revenue, and monetary policy effectiveness under different degrees of CBI, and seeks to provide important suggestions for policymakers who are considering the adoption and design of digital currencies. It complements the existing work by Ogunmola & Das (2024) and Adrian et al (2018) by directly considering proportional sales taxes and the importance of CBI's role.

2.2.2.2 Banking System and Financial Intermediation

The potential impact of CBDCs on commercial banks is the foremost topic in present research. Central banks face problems such as "disintermediation, " where consumers and businesses prefer to hold their money in CBDCs instead of traditional bank deposits. This shift eventually reduces the amount of commercial bank deposits, certainly affecting their capacity to lend and deranging their traditional role in financial Intermediation (IMF, 2023). As shown by the research on hypothetical deposit shifts even if only 10% of bank deposits shift to CBDCs, the reduction in bank deposits could reduce commercial banks' ability to provide loans and credit. This could lead to a decline in lending services in the economy. For example, in the U.K., in 2021, household deposits gathered roughly around £1.7 trillion, and a 10% migration to CBDCs could lessen the deposits by approximately £170 billion, impacting banks' ability to fund loans to a great extent. To prevent this, central banks implement a two-tier model that maintains the essential roles of commercial banking by handing out CBDCs through commercial banks rather than holding them directly (BIS, 2020).

2.2.2.3 CBDCs, Financial Inclusion and Accessibility

Financial inclusion is one of the most c convincing reasons for the adoption of CBDCs, especially in developing markets and underserved populations. Approximately 1.7 billion people in the world still don't have access to banking, with most of them residing in Africa, Latin America, and Southeast Asia. Digital currencies which are accessible through mobile devices offer a safe and a more simple way to send and receive payments without having to rely on traditional banks. According to Coulter (2023), financial access for these people could improve by up to 30% by using CBDCs that are offering low-cost, secure financial services to unbanked and underbanked groups. For instance, a study that was conducted in Africa emphasized on this point that even a minimal penetration of digital currency through mobile devices could potentially help millions, reducing transaction fees by over 50% in regions where handling cash is costly (Akhtar et al, 2024; Dong & Xiao, 2021; Singh et al., 2025).

2.2.2.4 CBDCs and Payment Efficiency

CBDCs also have the potential to make payments much smoother, both domestically and internationally. According to the current scenarios, traditional cross-border transactions can incur fees that are averaging between 5-7%, usually taking several days to process. Central banks with the help of CBDCs aim to reduce the reliance on intermediaries, which could result in faster and cheaper cross-border payments. CBDCs could cut cross-border transaction costs by up to 50%, as suggested by the projected data, thereby resulting in significant savings for both consumers and businesses engaged in international trade (Khan et al., 2024; Prodan et al., 2024).

Cross-border remittance markets, for example, are essential for economies that rely on foreign revenue. CBDCs could be very beneficial to them. Global remittance flows to low- and middle-income nations totaled over $540 billion in 2021, with an average transaction cost of 6.3%. Low-income households that rely on these funds could save billions of dollars a year if CBDCs were reduced to just 3%. Their disposable income and financial stability would then increase as a result (Salampasis et al., 2023).

2.3 CBDCs, Projected Adoption Rates and Future Implications

CBDCs are expected to become widely accessible over the next decade. BIS estimates that nearly 90% of the global population could have access to CBDCs by 2030 with several central banks moving from research to pilot stages. Although a few, like the People's Bank of China, are already conducting large-scale public trials. Projected CBDC adoption rates range from 40-60% by 2030 in advanced economies, while emerging markets may see even higher adoption because of the potential of CBDCs' in advancing financial inclusion (BIS, 2020).

The widespread adoption of CBDCs could primarily transform the global financial system, and could result in reduction in the role of cash. This results in changing the nature of central banking as well as introducing new dynamics in international trade. For instance, adopting digital yuan on a wider scale could influence the dominance of U. S. Dollar in the global trade to further impact the exchange rates and global finance. Such shifts may redefine economic and geopolitical relationships, with CBDCs serving as a tool for economic influence (Wong et al, 2024).

3 THEORETICAL BACKGROUND

3.1 Lagos and Wright Framework (2005)

A digital currency issued by the central bank might help solve the problem of tax evasion which hurts government budgets. We use a Lagos-Wright (2005) style model to study how CBDC affects tax compliance and economic welfare. The economy has two markets, one is the decentralized market (DM), where buyers and sellers trade one-on-one without formal rules, and the other is centralized market (CM), where trade is competitive and enforced. In the DM, there is a need for money, or a CBDC, because trust and contracts are missing. Unlike cash, a CBDC can be tracked and programmed, and thus the sellers who hide income face a higher chance of getting caught. Tax compliance has increased as a result. Our model employs a representative agent who plans their CBDC holdings according to costs and expectations for the future while alternating between buying and selling. While the government sets taxes and keeps an eye on CBDC use, the central bank, which is independent of the government's tax and spending decisions, controls CBDC issuance and interest rates. Tax evasion could be reduced with improved oversight and an independent central bank, which would facilitate DM trades and increase welfare through reduced expenses and increased tax revenue. In a competitive economy, this model demonstrates how CBDC can improve fiscal policy.

3.2 Williamson Framework (2019)

Central banks are considering using digital currencies, and Stephen Williamson's take on this is worth considering. His work builds on the Lagos-Wright model and sees CBDCs as digital money that is issued by governments and sitting alongside cash and bank deposits. This is an essential point of consideration because it changes the way money moves in the economy. Williamson digs into what would happen when CBDCs gain popularity and how they would shift the balance of banking and affect people's well-being. A major point he highlighted was is that if CBDCs pay interest or limit on who can use them,then they might pull money out of the regular banks, making it harder for those banks to lend which is a risk for economic security . On the other hand, he also advises that CBDCs can make transactions cheaper and help central banks to steer policy better if designed right. But it's not an all clear path as controlling money supply could get very difficult without careful planning. This model shows why getting CBDC design is the key for both efficiency and keeping the financial system operating smoothly.

3.3 Integrated Approach using Davoodalhosseini (2018) and Williamson (2019) Framework

This chapter builds upon and extends the foundational Lagos–Wright framework used by Davoodalhosseini (2018) and Williamson (2019), offering a more refined and policy-relevant analysis of Central Bank Digital Currencies (CBDCs). Although the former models used to focus on basic monetary trade-offs, such as removal of intermediaries, effects on well-being and efficiency, the present model introduces three key innovations. First, it particularly includes privacy as a usefulness-related feature, throwing light on growing concerns around observations and data autonomy in CBDC deployment. Secondly, the model includes organisational interaction by representing both the central bank and fiscal authority which allows for a deeper analysis of monetary–fiscal coordination under a CBDC regime. Finally, the model is empirically adjusted through relative case studies (China, Bahamas, Sweden), connecting theoretical insights with real-world policy experimentation. These improvements not only make the model more extensive in scope but also more applicable to the ongoing CBDC design debates taking place globally.

Table 1. Summary related to the key attributes across the three models

Parameters	Davoodalhosseini (2018)	Williamson (2019)	Author (s) Model
Model Type	Lagos–Wright framework	Lagos–Wright framework	Extended Lagos–Wright with institutional overlays
CBDC Focus	Interest-bearing CBDC vs. deposits	CBDC vs. bank money	Privacy-sensitive, programmable CBDC options
Main Variables	Utility, interest rate, consumption	Efficiency, liquidity, deposits	Privacy, utility, surveillance, institutional trust
Privacy Feature	Not modeled	Not modeled	Explicitly included in utility function
Agents	Households, banks, central bank	Households, central bank	Households, central bank, fiscal authority
Banking Sector	Explicit role of banks	Excluded	Implicit or optional, depending on design scenario
Institutional Dimension	Absent	Absent	Present (CB–fiscal coordination modeled)

continued on following page

Table 1. Continued

Parameters	Davoodalhosseini (2018)	Williamson (2019)	Author (s) Model
Empirical Use	No	No	Case studies from China, Sweden, Bahamas
Policy Contribution	Highlights risk of disintermediation	Suggests optimal CBDC design conditions	Emphasizes privacy–policy trade-offs, fiscal links, real-world feasibility

4. DATA AND ANALYSIS

4.1 Case Studies

In this study, we have taken international countries as prominent case studies and studied their impact on CBDCs. The cases are as given below:

4.1.1 Geographical Perspective: China

Attarde et al (2024) highlighted the significance of Central Bank Digital Currencies (CBDCs)in modernizing financial systems and reshaping global economic frameworks by exploring the developing landscape of CBDCs. His study examines China's Digital Yuan as a great action which is aimed at improving payment efficiency and financial inclusion. In contrast to the United States,which takes a cautious approach, as it prioritizes regulatory stability and the US dollar's dominance. Sweden's e-Krona shows a proactive model for digital currency adoption driven by decreasing cash usage. They highlighted that CBDCs have the potential to influence currency competition, which requires tight regulatory frameworks and technological advancements for successful coordination.

Certain projects have become notable case studies expressing both the potential and the challenges of executing digital currency systems as countries increasingly explore and pilot CBDCs. Case studies from China, India, Sweden, Bahamas, and the Eastern Caribbean provide information about how CBDCs can boost payment efficiency, improve financial inclusion, and serve as an option to private digital currencies. They also showcase operational challenges, such as balancing clarity with privacy and maintaining steadiness in the traditional banking systems (Akhtar et al., 2021; Central Bank of The Bahamas, 2019; Sood & Singh, 2024).

4.1.2 Geographical Perspective: India

As per the work of Alam et al (2024) The Reserve Bank of India (RBI) has issued the Digital Rupee ( ) which is a tokenized digital form of the Indian Rupee to act as a CBDC. It was proposed in January 2017 and was launched on December 1, 2022. The introduction of a CBDC in India necessitates legal and regulatory changes for phased implementation. The government officially announced the launch of the Digital Rupee in the 2022-23 Union Budget (Khan et al., 2024; Srivastava et al., 2025).

The RBI launched pilot programs for both wholesale (e -W) and retail (e -R) CBDCs. It began with the wholesale market on November 1, 2022, and the retail segment on December 1, 2022. The e -R is for consumer and business transactions while the e -W is intended for interbank settlements. The RBI aims to promote financial inclusion and non-anonymity through direct transfers, aligning with anti-money laundering and economic terrorism laws. The design of the CBDC must be in line with the objectives of monetary policy, financial stability, and efficient currency and payment systems (Azmi & Akhtar, 2022).

The exhibit highlights the continued preference of India for cash, especially for small-value transactions, posing a great challenge for the adoption of Digital Currencies (Li, 2011). Despite the increasing digital infrastructure, over 90% of payments below 100 are still made in cash, with digital modes gaining preference only for transactions above 2000. This suggests that while digital payment systems are expanding, cash remains deeply embedded in everyday financial behavior because of its ease of use, wide acceptability, and anonymity. For CBDCs to gain traction in such an environment, they must imitate the key features of cash, particularly for micro-payments, while also offering added benefits like convenience, security, and the potential for financial inclusion. This underscores the need for a carefully designed CBDC framework that addresses user behavior and trust, particularly among those who are reliant on physical currency (See Fig. 1).

Figure 1. India's attraction to cash.

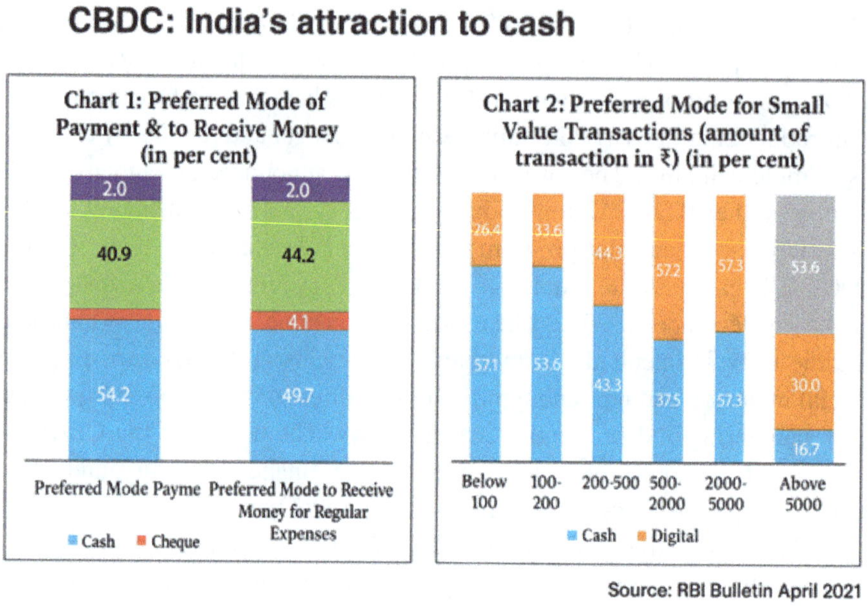

The Reserve Bank of India (RBI) has issued the Digital Rupee ( ) which is a tokenized digital form of the Indian Rupee to act as a digital currency. It was proposed in January 2017 and was launched on December 1, 2022. The introduction of a CBDC in India necessitates legal and regulatory changes for phased implementation. The government officially announced the launch of the Digital Rupee in the 2022-23 Union Budget (Themistocleous et al., 2023).

Bas et al. (2024) stated that the RBI launched pilot programs for both wholesale (e -W) and retail (e -R) CBDCs. It began with the wholesale market on November 1, 2022, and the retail segment on December 1, 2022. The e -R is for consumer and business transactions while the e -W is intended for interbank settlements. The RBI aims to promote financial inclusion and non-anonymity through direct transfers, aligning with anti-money laundering and economic terrorism laws. The design of the CBDC must be in line with the objectives of monetary policy, financial stability, and efficient currency and payment systems.

The charts, Figure 2, highlight the continued preference of India for cash, especially for small-value transactions, posing a great challenge for the adoption of CBDCs. Despite the increasing digital infrastructure, over 90% of payments below 100 are still made in cash, with digital modes gaining preference only for transactions above 2000. This suggests that while digital payment systems are expanding, cash remains deeply embedded in everyday financial behavior because of its ease of use, wide acceptability, and anonymity. For CBDCs to gain traction in such an environment, they must imitate the key features of cash, particularly for micro-payments, while also offering added benefits like convenience, security, and the potential for financial inclusion. This underscores the need for a carefully designed CBDC framework that addresses user behavior and trust, particularly among those who are reliant on physical currency (See Fig. 2; Temperini et al., 2024).

Figure 2. Preference of India for cash.

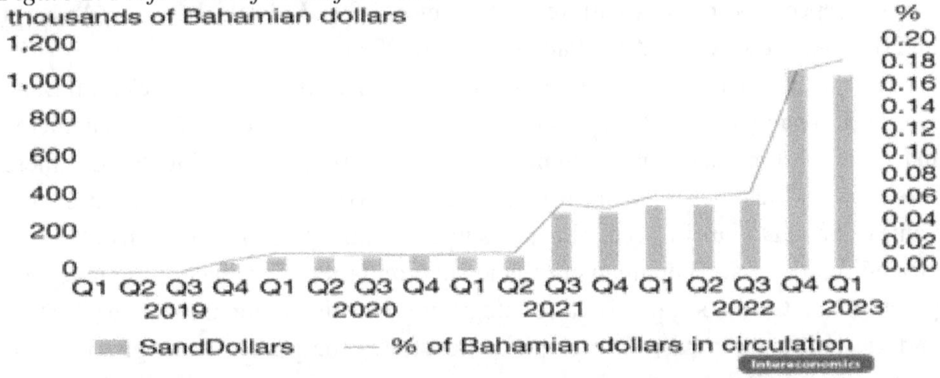

4.1.3 Geographical Perspective: Bahamas

The Sand Dollar in the Bahamas is among the first and most prominent examples of a CBDC. was created to meet financial demands in the Bahamas archipelago and was introduced in 2020. It is regarded as the first fully functional CBDC in the world. Remote villages have limited access to financial infrastructure because of the Bahamas' geographic arrangement, which consists of numerous islands with few inhabitants (Central Bank of The Bahamas, 2019).

The Sand Dollar was created as a mobile device-accessible digital currency with the goal of giving people in remote locations—where standard banking services are frequently unavailable—an effective and safe way to do business. It was hoped by the Bahamian government that digital currency would reduce the use of cash and lower transaction costs for people and businesses. Because it makes it possible for more people to receive financial services than would have been feasible with a traditional bank model, the Sand Dollar thus represents a substantial achievement in financial inclusion (Themistocleous et al., 2023).

Moenjak (2024b) states that the launch of Sand Dollar has resulted in the significant advantages including lower transaction costs and easier access to finance. However, the project Faced a number of difficulties, especially with regard to digital literacy and infrastructure modification. At first, it took a lot of resources and collaboration with local communities to guarantee mobile accessibility and teach the populace how to use the digital currency.

In order to make sure that the Sand Dollar wins over the public and could be smoothly included into the larger financial ecosystem, concerns related to the data security, privacy, and scalability are also required to be considered. Notwithstanding these barriers, such digital currency continues to be a significant case study that shows how CBDCs may deal with particular national problems. Such problems happen especially in areas with restricted financial and physical access (Ansar et al, 2022; Arora & Kaur, 2019; Fahad & Bulut, 2024).

The development of the Sand Dollar, also known as the Bahamian Central Bank Digital Currency (BCBDC), from its launch in late 2019 to early 2023 is depicted in figure 2. Adoption of such currencies were low at first, but starting in 2021, there was a rise, which increased dramatically in 2022. By the first quarter of 2023, the value of Sand Dollars in circulation had surpassed one million Bahamian dollars, or around 0.20% of all Bahamian currencies in circulation. This increasing tendency points to the CBDC's infrastructure integration into the national monetary system and growing public trust. The graph demonstrates the gradual yet significant integration of digital currency as a complement to traditional cash in the Bahamian economy (For Details, Refer Fig. 3; Fahad & Bulut, 2024; Kaur & Arora, 2019; Moenjak, 2024b)

Figure 3. Integration of digital currency.

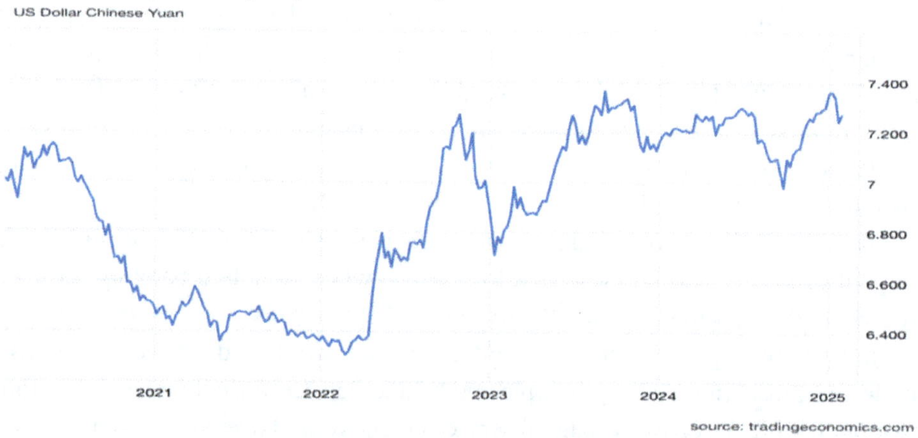

4.2 Other areas

Salampasis et al (2023) stated that because of its potential to change the way monetary policy is transmitted, manage inflation, promote financial inclusion, and alter the dynamic between central banks and the private cryptocurrency market, the introduction of CBDCs has generated a lot of interest. The potential impact of CBDCs on the transmission of monetary policy is one important concern. Bypassing conventional banking middlemen, central banks may be able to communicate with currency end users more directly thanks to CBDCs. By reaching consumers and companies more quickly, this direct conduit could increase the speed and reach of policy initiatives, such as adjustments in interest rates. The reduction of commercial banks' roles, however, may have complicated consequences, including a possible degradation in the banks' capacity to manage liquidity, lend, and support financial facilitation. Since CBDCs offer adaptability and interest-bearing capabilities that allow central banks to directly affect the rate of money and the behavior of savers and spenders, it is crucial to understand how they might affect the stability and adaptability of monetary policy across different economic situations. This makes them a unique tool for controlling inflation. In contrast to currency, CBDCs could be used to support policies that encourage or discourage economic behaviors, giving central banks greater precise control over inflationary or deflationary pressures. For instance, when economic activity needs to be encouraged, CBDCs could be made to have negative interest rates, which would discourage collecting and promote expenditure (Kim et al 2022, Li, 2021; TerceroLucas, 2023)

As per World Economic Forum (2019) report, although these skills improve instruments for managing inflation, they also carry hazards; if not properly controlled, an excessive dependence on digital systems could cause inflation instability or even disrupt the economy. Therefore, while central banks investigate CBDC implementations of interest in CBDC research as its role in increasing financial inclusion, it is crucial to comprehend the dual potential of CBDCs to stabilize or exacerbate inflation volatility. CBDCs may offer a convenient, safe online option for financial transactions in areas with restricted access to traditional banking services. High fees and minimum balance requirements, which frequently keep underprivileged communities out of traditional banking, could be removed by CBDCs by allowing people to have digital currency accounts directly with the central bank as exhibited in Figure 4.

Millions of people having businesses outside their official financial system may now benefit with access to financial services. However, with such amendments, public acceptance and accessibility— among underbanked groups — can make financial acceptance through digital currencies a huge success. This research also explores the potential benefits of digital currencies to bridge the gap in financial inclusion as well as to handle potential obstacles while creating a digital currency supporting the requirements of marginalized communities (Ozili, 2024, Wong et al., 2024).

Figure 4. CBCD cultivation.

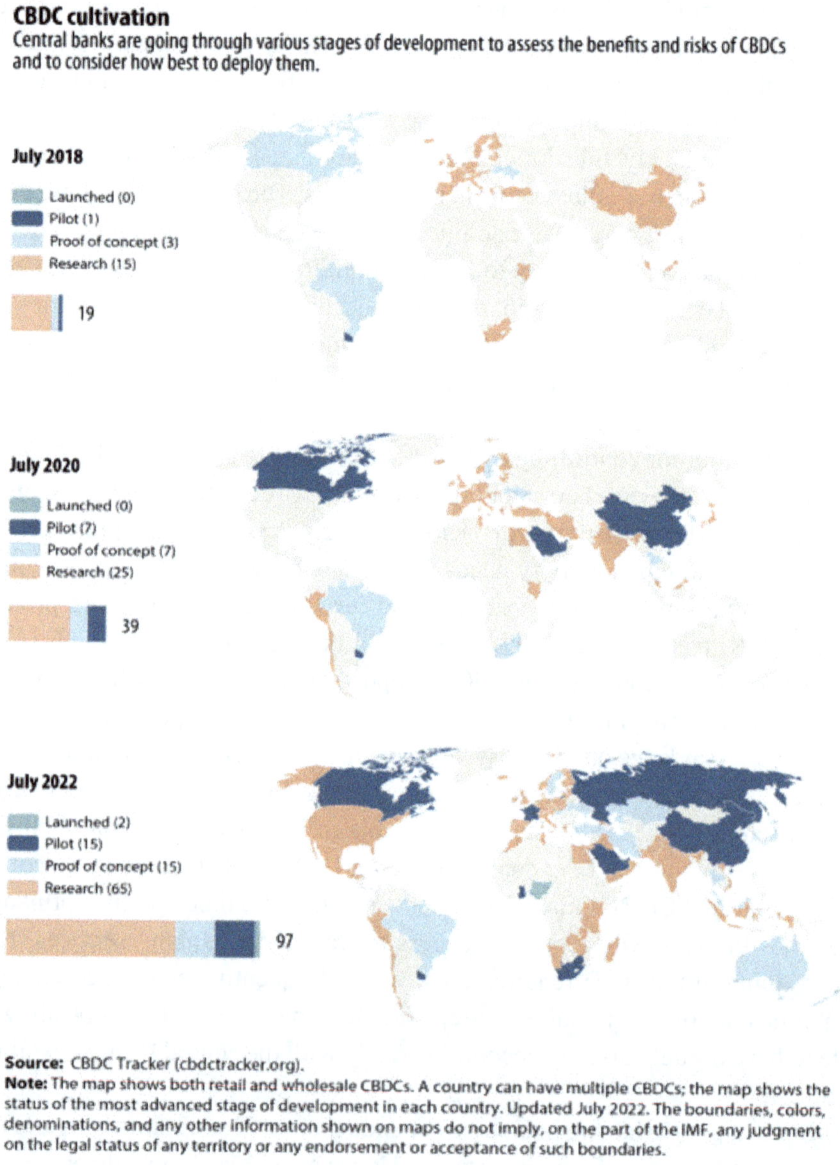

The increasing impact of private cryptocurrencies on CBDCs. CBDCs provide a stable, government-backed substitute that offers the stability and dependability of fiat currency in a digital format, in contrast to cryptocurrencies, which are decentralized and frequently prone to significant price volatility (Grima et al., 2023). Users may switch from erratic cryptocurrencies to more reliable CBDCs because of this stability. However, the autonomy and anonymity of cryptocurrencies—features that CBDCs might not be able to duplicate without jeopardizing central bank control—are frequently what make them so alluring. Policymakers face a challenging situation because of the interaction between cryptocurrencies and CBDCs; They must strike a balance between maintaining financial stability and regulatory control and providing a strong substitute for private digital assets. Important questions are also brought up by the possible effects of conventional financial systems (Choi & Kim, 2024).

The views corroborated by Hanafi & Rahman (2019) also strengthened that commercial banks may face a decline in deposits with consumers preferring to hold such currencies directly with the central bank. This might reduce their ability to lend and perform their functions as financial intermediaries. A substantial move toward CBDCs could upend established banking practices and have an impact on credit availability because commercial banks rely mostly on deposits for lending. Given banks' crucial role in managing economic risks and supplying liquidity, the effects on financial stability could be significant. This paper examines potential tactics to assist commercial banks in a financial environment that is integrated with CBDCs and evaluates how CBDCs might change the banking landscape (Van Roosebeke & Defina, 2023).

Nakashima & Saito, 2012 emphasized that another important aspect of CBDC is privacy. CBDCs give central banks unprecedented access to individual transactional data because they entail digitally recorded transactions, in contrast to cash, which is primarily anonymous. Such information often creates privacy issues even if it can support regulatory initiatives in fields like tax collection and anti-money laundering. A difficult task in CBDC design is striking a balance between the requirement to secure personal data and transparency for regulations. For instance, while a token-based CBDC might offer a certain level of privacy in transactions, it could also make it harder to tackle issues like money laundering and the financing of terrorism. This paper explores design frameworks that could guarantee enough privacy safeguards while upholding regulatory compliance, as well as how CBDCs might manage this trade-off (Choi & Kim, 2024).

At last, by reducing the tax evasion, specifically in economies with sizable underground sectors, CBDCs provide a chance to verify it. Governments may be able to have better notes on financial activity and improve tax compliance if all CBDC transactions are digitally recorded. Some economic processes may become more secretive because of this additional scrutiny, or the people who are worried about surveillance may oppose the initiation of CBDCs. This study assesses the feasibility of utilizing CBDCs to combat tax cheating without demoralizing economic participation and examining how they might change the dynamics of tax compliance (Coulter, 2023).

5. POLICY IMPLICATIONS

Global emerging economies are becoming progressively more digital, and one of the reasons why CBDCs have gained a lot of attention. As digital payment methods attract contraction and physical currency usage declines, such digital currencies offer a safe and state-backed alternative and maintains the universality and accessibility of cash. There is a big chance to improve financial inclusion using them. Access to official financial infrastructure is still restricted in many developing nations. Through the use of basic digital tools, like smartphones, CBDCs can help those who are underbanked or unbanked engage more completely in the economy. In this sense, CBDCs have the potential to significantly lessen the exclusion of underprivileged, isolated, or rural areas from formal financial institutions. Additionally, by lowering the operational and administrative expenses related to printing, shipping, and handling physical currency, CBDCs may help monetary systems better correspond with the objectives of digital modernity and sustainability (Inder, 2024; Ogunmola & Das, 2024).

From the perspective of Ozili (2023) - the payments infrastructure through CBDCs can increase the effectiveness of both domestic and international transactions. Conventional cross-border payment methods frequently depend on intricate interbank agreements and are costly and slow. Through real-time settlement processes, CBDCs could lessen these frictions and facilitate quicker and more affordable foreign transactions. CBDCs may promote deeper economic integration and increase participation in international trade by cutting out middlemen and transaction expenses, especially for small enterprises and households who depend on remittances.

CBDCs provide central banks with new instruments to carry out more accurate and successful monetary policy at the policy level. For example, central banks could more successfully apply negative interest rates during economic downturns to encourage consumption since digital currencies can be directly designed and delivered. In situations where traditional levers have declining returns, the granular control provided by CBDCs allows for more focused monetary interventions and improves the transmission of policy impacts. The issuance of CBDCs may help lower environmental expenses associated with currency production and shipping as well as fiscal costs associated with cash management (Barnett, 1980).

However, there are important policy trade-offs involved in the creation and application of CBDCs. The conflict between privacy and financial transparency is one of the most hotly debated. Digital currencies have the potential to improve traceability and reduce illegal financial flows, but they may also give rise to worries about data overflow and state surveillance. This questions the extent to which citizens are ready to support security and regulatory monitoring to forego financial privacy (Nakashima & Saito, 2012). Models such as the European Union's Digital Euro privacy pilot are common instances where the efforts to design systems striking an ignorance between providing transparency for higher-risk activities and allowing limited anonymity for small-value transactions. Such initiatives also highlighted the difficulties of creating them that uphold individual rights and satisfy compliance requirements (Kvedaravičiūtė & Šapkauskienė, 2024).

Ozili (2022) gave insights on another aspect with broad ramifications which is institutional trust. The public must have faith in the issuing authority to safeguard data, stop abuse, and guarantee operational dependability if CBDCs are to be widely adopted. The viability of the CBDC may be jeopardized if these guarantees are viewed as inadequate, as this could damage the central bank's reputation. Furthermore, disintermediation might reduce the lending capacity of the banking industry if people moved significant amounts of deposits from commercial banks to digital wallets run by the central bank. The availability of credit may be diminished, interest margins may be impacted, and systemic liquidity constraints may result. In order to solve this, a number of central banks are taking into account two-tier distribution models, in which commercial banks continue to act as middlemen, guaranteeing financial intermediation continuity while retaining central supervision (Prodan et al., 2024)

Central banks must assess if there is a strong case for adoption, particularly whether there is enough public and commercial demand, even though CBDCs may have a number of potential advantages. While some nations continue to weigh the risks and advantages, others have come to the conclusion that the benefits are not yet compelling. Along with market demand, financial stability issues also need to be properly taken into account. A liquidity crisis, for example, might be brought on by an abrupt and significant move away from commercial bank deposits and toward CBDCs, particularly during times of financial strain. In order to maintain systemic equilibrium, the possibility of such situations calls for protections and well specified restrictions on CBDC ownership (Wong et al., 2024).

Central banks for safeguarding the integrity of data security need to retain trust of customers which requires a faith in their capacity to handle risks including fraud, hacking, and infrastructure breakdown. Choi and Kim (2024) also supported the view that a degree of technical difficulty and institutional risk which was earlier outside the traditional lenses of central banks is now being considered while including the measures such as additional duty of protecting millions of digital wallets and real-time payment systems to successfully implement digital currencies usage with strong digital infrastructure, and broad cross-sector engagement as a primary requirement (Grima et al., 2023).

CBDCs can be concluded with a statement that is a significant turning point in the progression of contemporary monetary systems is that they provide central banks with effective new measures to improve policy responsiveness, and inclusivity. Its implementation is further required to be handled cautiously to stop unforeseen effects on institutional trust, privacy rights, and financial stability. Therefore, a thorough evaluation of systemic resilience and economic value must be the foundation for the choice to implement a CBDC (Hanafi & Rahman, 2019).

6. CONCLUSION, LIMITATIONS AND SCOPE FOR THE FUTURE RESEARCH

This study shows that tax evasion is present in welfare implications of introducing a CBDC in an economy where cash is used as a medium of exchange, and the degree of central bank independence (CBI) varies. The analysis reveals that the welfare effects of introducing a CBDC are contingent upon the level of CBI.

If there is no central bank, bringing in digital currency doesn't really make people better off, because the government can raise money through inflation just like it does with sales tax. On the contrary, with CBI, establishing CBDC can enhance welfare by correcting distortions related to matters such as tax evasion and the need to maintain sales tax revenue. The central bank can use monetary policy to incentivize CBDC use and discourage cash-based tax evasion. This study further complements existing studies conducted by Davoodalhosseini (2018) and Williamson (2019) and considered proportional sales taxes associated with CBDC and CBI. This adds to the discussion about how digital currencies might affect economies where people avoid paying taxes and where the central bank has different levels of independence These findings have important implications for policymakers considering the adoption of CBDCs. They suggest that the design of a CBDC and its integration with existing monetary and fiscal policies must consider the institutional framework, particularly the degree of CBI. Further research is needed to explore the robustness of these results in more complex models with features, such as financial intermediation and heterogeneous agents.

The present framework could be enhanced to include financial intermediaries, such as banks, to analyze the impact of CBDCs on the banking sector and financial stability. That would allow the banks to further examine the issues such as credit creation, disintermediation, and the role of CBDCs in interbank lending markets. The framework could be further developed including heterogeneous agents with different preferences, income levels, or access to technology. This would allow for a more nuanced analysis of the distributional effects of CBDCs and the potential for financial inclusion.

Another scope for further research is the exploration of different monetary policy rules including the examination of using the digital currencies to implement quantitative easing, negative interest rates, or unconventional policies. The future studies could investigate the privacy and data security implications of CBDCs, including the design of mechanisms to protect user data while maintaining the benefits of traceability and transparency. The present model could be improved by adding more real-life features, like prices that don't change quickly, the build-up of capital, and how people choose to work, to give a fuller view of how digital currencies affect the whole economy.

REFERENCES

Adrian, T., Muhleisen, M., & Obstfeld, M. (2018). Casting light on central bank digital currencies. *Staff Discussion Notes, 2018*(008), A001. DOI: 10.5089/9781484384572.006.A001

Akhtar, S., Alam, M., & Khan, M. M. (2021). YES bank fiasco: Arrogance or negligence. *Emerging Economies Cases Journal, 3*(2), 95–102. DOI: 10.1177/25166042211061003

Akhtar, S., Alam, M., & Khan, M. M. (2021a). Yes Bank fiasco: Arrogance or negligence. [ScienceGate]. *Emerging Economies Cases Journal, 3*(2), 95–102. DOI: 10.1177/25166042211061003

Akhtar, S., Alam, M., & Ansari, M. S. (2022). Measuring the performance of the Indian banking industry: Data envelopment window analysis approach. *Benchmarking, 29*(9), 2842–2857. DOI: 10.1108/BIJ-03-2021-0115

Akhtar, S., Alam, M., Khan, A., & Shamshad, M. (2023). Measuring technical efficiency of banks vis-à-vis demonetization: An empirical analysis of Indian banking sector using CAMELS framework. *Quality & Quantity, 57*(2), 1739–1761. DOI: 10.1007/s11135-022-01431-8

Akhtar, S., Azmi, S. N., Khan, P. A., Jan, A. A., & Ansari, Z. (2024). Unveiling the financial landscape: Analyzing profitability, productivity, and efficiency of banks in an emerging economy using the CAMELS framework and panel analysis. *Cogent Business & Management, 11*(1), 2399747. Advance online publication. DOI: 10.1080/23311975.2024.2399747

Alam, M., Akhtar, S., & Al-Faryan, M. A. S. (2024). Do Indian banks perform better in corporate governance than other SAARC nations? An empirical analysis. *Corporate Governance (Bradford), 24*(4), 799–830. Advance online publication. DOI: 10.1108/CG-02-2023-0059

Arora, S., & Kaur, H. (2019). Exploring the bank selection criteria in India: Scale development and validation. *International Journal of Bank Marketing, 37*(3), 666–690. DOI: 10.1108/IJBM-09-2017-0199

Attarde, K., Jaiswal, C., Khatwani, R., Pinto, G., & Kumar, V. (2024). A novel central bank digital currency framework design for offline and foreign transactions based on blockchain. Digital Policy. *Regulation & Governance*. Advance online publication. DOI: 10.1108/DPRG-08-2023-0139

Azmi, S. N., & Akhtar, S. (2022). Interactions of services export, financial development and growth: Evidence from India. *Quality & Quantity*, *57*(5), 4709–4724. DOI: 10.1007/s11135-022-01566-8

Bank for International Settlements (BIS). (2020). Central bank digital currencies: Foundational principles and core features. Retrieved from https://www.bis.org/publ/othp33.pdf

Barnett, W. A. (1980). Economic monetary aggregates an application of index number and aggregation theory. *Journal of Econometrics*, *14*(1), 11–48. DOI: 10.1016/0304-4076(80)90070-6

Bas, T., Malki, I., & Sivaprasad, S. (2024). Connectedness between Central Bank digital currency index, financial stability and digital assets. *Journal of International Financial Markets, Institutions and Money*, *92*, 101981. DOI: 10.1016/j.intfin.2024.101981

BIS. Central bank digital currencies: foundational principles and core features, https://www.bis.org/publ/othp33.pdf

Boar, C., & Wehrli, A. (2021). Ready, steady, go?-Results of the third BIS survey on central bank digital currency. BIS papers. https://www.bis.org/publ/bppdf/bispap114.pdf

Camera, G., Craig, B., & Waller, C. J. (2004). Currency competition in a fundamental model of money. *Journal of International Economics*, *64*(2), 521–544. DOI: 10.1016/j.jinteco.2003.09.002

Central Bank of The Bahamas. (2019). Sand Dollar: The Central Bank Identifies Preferred Technology Solutions Provider for Bahamas Digital Currency https://www.centralbankbahamas.com/news/press-releases/project-sand-dollar-the-central-bank-identifies-preferred-technology-solutions-provider-for-bahamas-digital-currency

Choi, J., & Kim, H. (2024). *Stablecoins and Central Bank digital currency: Challenges and opportunities*. Oxford Research Encyclopedia of Economics and Finance., DOI: 10.1093/acrefore/9780190625979.013.910

Coulter, K. A. (2023). A review of the proposed Bank of England's "retail" central bank digital currency (CBDC) as a cryptocurrency competitor. Fintech, Pandemic, and the Financial System: Challenges and Opportunities, 201-221. DOI: 10.1108/S1569-376720220000022010

Dong, M., & Xiao, S. X. (2021). Central Bank digital currency: A corporate finance perspective. SSRN Electronic Journal. DOI: 10.2139/ssrn.3911132

Fahad, S., & Bulut, M. (2024). Central bank digital currencies: A comprehensive systematic literature review on worldwide research emergence and methods used. *American Journal of Business, 39*(3), 137–157. Advance online publication. DOI: 10.1108/AJB-12-2023-0210

Ghosh, K., & Das, P. K. (2024). *Central bank digital currencies – A bibliometric analysis on research themes in pursuit of research trends*. International Journal of Law and Management., DOI: 10.1108/IJLMA-11-2023-0252

Hanafi, S. F., & Rahman, S. A. (2019), "Regulating Digital Currency: Taming the Unruly", Oseni, U.A., Hassan, M.K. and Hassan, R. (Ed.) Emerging Issues in Islamic Finance Law and Practice in Malaysia, Emerald Publishing Limited, Leeds, pp. 265-280. DOI: 10.1108/978-1-78973-545-120191021

Inder, S. (2024), "Empowering the Unbanked: The Intersection of Financial Inclusion and CBDC", Kumar, N., Sood, K., Özen, E. and Grima, S. (Ed.) The Framework for Resilient Industry: A Holistic Approach for Developing Economies (Emerald Studies in Finance, Insurance, and Risk Management), Emerald Publishing Limited, Leeds, pp. 65-74. DOI: 10.1108/978-1-83753-734-120241005

Jagrič, T., Fister, D., Amon, A., Jagrič, V., & Beloglavec, S. T. (2022). The Banking Industry in the Ecosystem of Digital Currencies and Digital Central Bank Currencies. In Grima, S., Özen, E., & Boz, H. (Eds.), *The New Digital Era: Digitalisation, Emerging Risks and Opportunities (Contemporary Studies in Economic and Financial Analysis, Vol. 109A)* (pp. 89–115). Emerald Publishing Limited., DOI: 10.1108/S1569-37592022000109A006

Kaur, H., & Arora, S. (2019). Demographic influences on consumer decisions in the banking sector: Evidence from India. *Journal of Financial Services Marketing, 24*(3), 81–93. DOI: 10.1057/s41264-019-00067-4

Khan, A. S., Akhtar, S., & Alam, M. (2024). How efficient are Indian banks? An application of stochastic frontier analysis. [IDEAS/RePEc, Emerald]. *Journal of Financial Economic Policy, 17*(1), 52–76. DOI: 10.1108/JFEP-11-2023-0338

Kim, Y. S., & Kwon, O.KIM. (2022). Central Bank digital currency, credit supply, and financial stability. *Journal of Money, Credit and Banking, 55*(1), 297–321. DOI: 10.1111/jmcb.12913

Kim, Y. S., Lee, H., & Lee, J. (2022). Central digital currency, credit supply, and financial stability. *Journal of Money, Credit and Banking, 54*(2-3), 621–649. DOI: 10.1111/jmcb.12826

Kvedaravičiūtė, E., & Šapkauskienė, A. (2024). Development of central bank digital currencies: A bibliometric analysis. *EuroMed Journal of Business*. Advance online publication. DOI: 10.1108/EMJB-12-2023-0140

Ladeira, W. J., Santini, F. D. O., Rasul, T., Cheah, I., Elhajjar, S., Yasin, N., & Akhtar, S. (2024). Big data analytics and the use of artificial intelligence in the services industry: A meta-analysis. *Service Industries Journal*, *44*(15-16), 1117–1144. DOI: 10.1080/02642069.2024.2374990

Li, Y. (2011). Currency and checking deposits as means of payment. *Review of Economic Dynamics*, *14*(2), 403–417. DOI: 10.1016/j.red.2009.11.002

Li, Y. (2021). Does institutional quality matter for central bank digital currency adoption? *Economic Analysis and Policy*, *72*, 265–277. DOI: 10.1016/j.eap.2021.05.002

Moenjak, T. (2024a). Central Bank Digital Currency (CBDC): Concepts, Wholesale and Cross-Border CBDC. In *Central Banking at the Frontier* (pp. 241–267). Emerald Publishing Limited., DOI: 10.1108/978-1-83797-130-520241014

Moenjak, T. (2024b), "Retail CBDC: Digital Banknotes and a Platform for Innovation", Central Banking at the Frontier, Emerald Publishing Limited, Leeds, pp. 269-289. DOI: 10.1108/978-1-83797-130-520241015

Nakashima, K., & Saito, M. (2012). On the comparison of alternative specifications for money demand: The case of extremely low interest rate regimes in Japan. *Journal of the Japanese and International Economies*, *26*(3), 454–471. DOI: 10.1016/j.jjie.2012.04.001

Nakashima, K., & Saito, M. (2012). On the comparison of alternative specifications for money demand: The case of extremely low interest rate regimes in Japan. *Journal of the Japanese and International Economies*, *26*(3), 454–471. DOI: 10.1016/j.jjie.2012.04.001

Ogunmola, G. A., & Das, U. (2024). Analyzing consumer perceptions and adoption intentions of central bank digital currency: A case of the digital rupee. Digital Policy. *Regulation & Governance*, *26*(4), 450–471. DOI: 10.1108/DPRG-09-2023-0136

Ozili, P. K. (2022). Central bank digital currency research around the world: A review of literature. *Journal of Money Laundering Control*, *26*(4), 450–471. DOI: 10.1108/JMLC-01-2022-0012

Ozili, P. K. (2023), "Redesigning the eNaira Central Bank Digital Currency (CBDC) for Payments and Macroeconomic Effectiveness", Tyagi, P., Grima, S., Sood, K., Balamurugan, B., Özen, E. and Eleftherios, T. (Ed.) Smart Analytics, Artificial Intelligence and Sustainable Performance Management in a Global Digitalised Economy (Contemporary Studies in Economic and Financial Analysis, Vol. 110B), Emerald Publishing Limited, Leeds, pp. 189-197. DOI: 10.1108/S1569-37592023000110B012

Ozili, P. K. (2023). CBDC, Fintech and cryptocurrency for financial inclusion and financial stability. Digital Policy. *Regulation & Governance*, *25*(1), 40–57. DOI: 10.1108/DPRG-04-2022-0033

Ozili, P. K. (2023). Central bank digital currency and bank earnings management using loan loss provisions. Digital Policy. *Regulation & Governance*. Advance online publication. DOI: 10.1108/DPRG-10-2022-0119

Ozili, P. K. (2023). Central bank digital currency can lead to the collapse of cryptocurrency. In Digital Transformation, Strategic Resilience, Cyber Security and Risk Management (pp. 191-198). Emerald Publishing Limited. DOI: 10.1108/S1569-37592023000111A013

Ozili, P. K. (2024). Determinants of global interest in central bank digital currency: The role of sustainable development and cryptocurrency. *Digital Transformation and Society*, *3*(2), 179–196. DOI: 10.1108/DTS-04-2023-0020

Prodan, S., Konhäusner, P., Dabija, D., Lazaroiu, G., & Marincean, L. (2024). The rise in popularity of central bank digital currencies: A systematic review. *Heliyon*, *10*(9), e30561. DOI: 10.1016/j.heliyon.2024.e30561 PMID: 38756603

Salampasis, D., Schueffel, P., Dominic, R., & Cameron, D. (2023). Central Bank Digital Currencies: Opening Pandora's Box or Paving the Future of Money? In Baker, H. K., Benedetti, H., Nikbakht, E., & Smith, S. S. (Eds.), *The Emerald Handbook on Cryptoassets: Investment Opportunities and Challenges* (pp. 283–306). Emerald Publishing Limited., DOI: 10.1108/978-1-80455-320-620221019

Singh, S., Srivastava, S., & Kaur, H. (2025). Greening the Portfolio: Investor Insights into Sustainable Development Opportunities in India. In *Green Horizons: Role of AI in Sustainable Finance* (pp. 237–253). Springer Nature Singapore. DOI: 10.1007/978-981-96-6495-5_13

Sood, K., & Singh, S. (2024). Multi-central bank digital currencies arrangements: A multivocal literature review. *China Finance Review International*, *14*(4), 813–841. Advance online publication. DOI: 10.1108/CFRI-09-2023-0221

Srivastava, S., Singh, S., & Kaur, H. (2025). Beyond the Bottom Line: An Impact of CO2 Emissions and R&D on Corporate Sustainability in India. In *Green Futures: Navigating the Path to Environmental Resilience* (pp. 311–326). Springer Nature Singapore. DOI: 10.1007/978-981-96-0843-0_16

Steele, G. S. (2024), "The Miner of Last Resort: Digital Currency, Shadow Money and the Role of the Central Bank", Levine, L. (Ed.) Technology vs. Government: The Irresistible Force Meets the Immovable Object (Studies in Media and Communications, Vol. 25), Emerald Publishing Limited, Leeds, pp. 197-221. DOI: 10.1108/S2050-206020240000025008

Temperini, J., D'Ippoliti, C., & Gobbi, L. (2024). Is the time ripe for helicopter money? Growth impact and financial stability risks of outright monetary transfers. *Structural Change and Economic Dynamics*, *69*, 24–36. DOI: 10.1016/j.strueco.2023.11.003

Tercero-Lucas, D. (2023). Central Bank digital currencies and financial stability in a modern monetary system. *Journal of Financial Stability*, *69*, 101188. DOI: 10.1016/j.jfs.2023.101188

Themistocleous, M., Rupino da Cunha, P., Tabakis, E., & Papadaki, M. (2023). Towards cross-border CBDC interoperability: Insights from a multivocal literature review. *Journal of Enterprise Information Management*, *36*(5), 1296–1318. DOI: 10.1108/JEIM-11-2022-0411

Umar, M., Shahzad, F., Iqbal, A., & Tong, F. (2024). Does institutional quality matter for Central Bank digital currency adoption? *Economic Analysis and Policy*, *83*, 378–389. DOI: 10.1016/j.eap.2024.06.022

Van Roosebeke, B., & Defina, R. (2023), "Central Bank Digital Currencies: The Motivation", in Kim, S.-J. (Ed.) Fintech, Pandemic, and the Financial System: Challenges and Opportunities (International Finance Review, Vol. 22), Emerald Publishing Limited, Leeds, pp. 185-200. DOI: 10.1108/S1569-376720220000022009

Wong, M.C.S., Chan, E.K.H., and Yousaf, I. (2024), "CBDCs, regulated stablecoins and tokenized traditional assets under the Basel Committee rules on cryptoassets", Journal of Financial Regulation and Compliance, Vol. ahead-of-print No. ahead-of-print. DOI: 10.1108/JFRC-03-2024-0050

World Economic Forum (WEF). (2019). Central Banks and Distributed Ledger Technology: How are Central Banks Exploring Blockchain Today? Retrieved from https://www3.weforum.org/docs/WEF_Central_Bank_Activity_in_Blockchain_DLT.pdf

Chapter 9
Artificial Intelligence Applications in Finance:
A Proposed Model

Vedantam Seetha Ram
https://orcid.org/0000-0002-6375-1501
Jain University, India

Sukirno Sukirno
https://orcid.org/0000-0002-1914-937X
Universitas Negeri Yogyakarta, Indonesia

Rama Rao Gangadhara Sakha
https://orcid.org/0000-0003-3578-8558
GITAM University, India

ABSTRACT

Artificial intelligence is being used across the domains irrespective of its pros and cons highlighted by various stakeholders across the globe. AI is having a decisive role in the finance field in bringing out innovative financial instruments that cater the economic growth. Current chapter is a literature survey driven one, for which research papers covering digital banking, technology applications in banking and finance industry, technology adoption, digital research study reports of governments, monitoring agencies and research organizations are considered. Finally, 43 variables are identified from dimensions as part of factors, like personal, psychological, technical, and policy maker's guidelines that have influence on the adoption of AI technology in finance field such that a model is proposed which helps prospective researchers as a tool. This chapter considers the pros and cons of AI technology in

DOI: 10.4018/979-8-3373-3725-8.ch009

finance field so that a corrective mechanism can be established in enhancing the quality of financial instruments to mitigate risk, such that a sustainable financial growth prevails.

1 INTRODUCTION

Increasing skilled labor force in the highly skilled job market paved way to the concept of age old subdued concept of artificial intelligence (AI) gaining momentum because of the advancements in computational, deep learning and data analytics technologies on one hand; industrial requirement for large and skilled labor force, demand-supply disparities in production and services segment, client requirements, changing tastes and preferences of end users on the other hand that allowed AI technology adopt generative mode for the benefit of the mankind. It has been in use in diversified fields of industry engagements including finance through the chatbots, virtual assistants, e-readers, social media platforms, information kiosk etc. as an interactive tool to understand the financial instruments effectively (Davenport et al., 2020; Haenlein & Kaplan, 2019; Hentzen et al., 2022; Pemer, 2021; Xu et al., 2020). As per the 2023 report of McKinsey & Company, the top trending technologies index shows a growth of 33 per cent in the AI applications from innovation to full level scaling by the firms in their adoption compared with other technologies with 86 billion US$ equity investment in applied AI in the year 2023 alone which is (-) 29 per cent over 2022 fiscal year. Investments in AI technology is primarily be done in the fields like aerospace and defense, agriculture, automotive and assembly, aviation, travel and logistics, legal and professional services, education, banking and financial services, healthcare and information technology services (Akhtar et al., 2022). The report further highlights that the industry investment on digital trust and cybersecurity is 34 billion US$ with (-) 34 per cent decline during the 2023 period compared with 2022. It is realized that the biggest gainer due to AI applications in the said period is electrification and renewables sector with 183 billion US$ equity investment in 2023 with one percent increment over 2022 (Lareina Yee et al., 2024). For the research and advancements in AI and its allied technologies' adoption and implementation process, private institutions are allocating funds of 20 to 30 billion US$ a year where US government itself has invested 2 billion US$ in the applications of AI in domains like defense sector during 2018 period to cater the requirements of learning and intelligence in advanced computing, AI's virtual reality and agents (Heller, 2019; Sheppard et al., 2018).

2 LITERATURE REVIEW

Modern day AI based designs contribute to the self-driven and emotion based viewer interface for direct interaction with the machines that reads emotions of individuals and suggests an appropriate financial instrument for investment decision made by them, which is an extension to the good old fashioned AI (GOFAI) that considers the behavioral processes and aspects of individuals (Mateas, 2001). Though GOFAI is used in media and digital content development, it helps the financial instrument development as well, as it reads the cultural processes while depicting a suggestion, which helps in understanding the conventional investment instruments' movement and mindset of investors as gizmos are used that simulates multiple times with various options of instruments such that a final financial advice can be made to an individual. Another option available for advisors is the use of interactionist AI instrument with client, or the client can directly use this instrument that measures an individual's investment orientation at different points in time in a given period of time to design portfolio. However, AI is one of the common mechanisms used in the present advisory services due to the technological advancement, where machines are trained rigorously with loads of data using machine learning and artificial neural network tools such that the data of various individuals that have failed or succeeded in their financial and investment decision making, paving way for the future investors, where one individuals' failed instrument could generate high returns to other and vice-versa as it uses multiple sets of data from internal as well as external sources in the form of an audio or a video or both and applies tools like data science, machine learning, natural language processes that captures data from open source ware which is driven by an internet protocol (IP) address that is unique in nature to identify the access point that helps in maintaining privacy and security. This whole process helps in faster access to data interpretations, customized user experience, quality data dissemination in wealth management practices which considers emotional quotient as well while offering the suggestions to the clients where cognitive computing technology helps the respective fields in addressing the computational errors and their estimation, which is highly prevailing in the fields such as financial accounting and advisory services (Gambhir & Bhattacharjee, 2021; Manyika, 2022; Mateas, 2001; Stephan De Spiegeleire, 2017).

Present day small businesses and start-up firms are emerging in the field of this new technology industry or based on the new technology like the AI, with emphasis on the manufacturing industry at the core. Business model innovation (BMI) has become an easy task because of AI applications, that solves difficulties prior to spending sums of money in real terms (Metzler et al., 2021). Tourism industry use AI and robotics to enhance the customer experience through chatbots, facial recognition, virtual reality, robotics, language translators and maps services in guiding as well as sharing tourist spot details with the prospective customers starting from visiting a right place to stay, eateries and people to meet for local guidance. Apart from guiding, AI helps in collecting and collating the client's experiences about their visit, stay, food, people, visiting places they recommend and on overall, their complete experience that helps prospective tourists, tourism planners and the tourism department of the government in improving quality of policies and guidelines to be set in future time period and on overall basis the tourism experience of the tourists which resembles the face of a place or country at the end in this globalized arena where competition is tough in convincing and satisfying a customer or client without the help of a support service (Samala et al., 2022).

Today, governments are developing killer robots based on the AI technology that uses lethal autonomous weapons system (LAWS) in defense segment for surveillance and other remote military operations, which could become future warfare system in defense of nations across the globe, as they use autonomous AI technology that is integrated with machine learning and deep learning technologies (Miller et al., 2021; Rodriguez, 2019) where the decision making guidance by the missiles is independent and it cannot be deviating not even by a weeny as it costs billions of US$ to governments apart from loss of lives. AI driven weapons design, development, testing, and deployment is based on reliability and availability analysis (Miller et al., 2021), which can be implemented in financial services as well to analyze the banking operations by adopting and applying dynamic continuous process improvement mechanism or situation awareness based agent transparency model (Chen et al., 2018; Mercado et al., 2016; Miller et al., 2021) that supports analyzing individual's decision choices such that client's privacy is upheld along with smooth operationalization. As financial services field is experiencing widespread change due to the implementation of machines and advanced technology. Technologies such as RegTech, AI and CharityTech are able to mitigate the accounting and audit frauds by helping countering the money laundering practices, terror financing and fraudulent reporting by firms including not for profit and non-government organizations that rely heavily on the donations or charity amount funded from various places and parties (Singh, 2024a; Singh & Lin, 2020). Other benefits include time saving, faster and easy analysis, risk mitigation analysis as investor's risk analysis plays crucial role while introducing a financial instrument into the market (Annu & Tripathi, 2024), accuracy in financial assessments and enriching the client audit service at their end with enhanced forecasting mechanism based on the historical data of self and of the industry at large (Ivy Munoko, 2020) that creates value to the firm coupled with firm performance analysis that uses self-learning algorithm like artificial neural network (ANN) which can deliver through virtual assistants (Khan et al., 2025; Wamba-Taguimdje et al., 2020) in the case of banking industry, where more than 70 per cent of the banks and 100 million people are using predictive analytics across the globe to reduce their repetitive job nature saving resources (African Center for Economic Transformation, 2023). With the help of financial technology intervention, terror attacks were spoiled in the past in US, where the homeland security could identify the money transfer happened from the UK to people in US and Canada, which was cross verified with travel data of such account holders then decoded the conversations along with large sums of money spending nature on unusual items that are not generally used for either personal or industrial consumption by the individuals. This mechanism of applying defense intelligence along with the use of FinTech technologies helped the governments in avoiding the terror attacks at multiple places at once during the 1999-2000-time period. The G-7 countries inter-governmental set-up body financial action task force (FATF) worked with other intelligence bodies has helped as an early warning for the terror financing activities that are undertaken against the member countries from time to time apart from helping others as well through their warning mechanism (Gowhor, 2022). Apart from using in the day to day business operational activities, AI helps predict the customer needs on the type of financial products they seek based on the historical satisfaction, emotions towards the product satisfaction levels, reaction to the existing products or service utilization with the help of predictive analytics, sentiment analysis technology of AI which also helps in understanding the importance of social support (Aysan et al., 2024; Chaturvedi et al., 2021; Lin & Lee, 2023) tools offered by the banks that leads to personal satisfaction motivating individuals in using the mobile banking continuously (Lin & Lee, 2023).

Another important field of AI application is in auditing, where clients seek digital auditing process be implemented in their organization, for which the firms are ready to invest on automation of their books of accounts (Pemer, 2021). Though audit function is a highly regulated mechanism, due to technological advancements, dilution is not possible here, however, it eases the financial burden on clients in recruiting junior staff. However, digitalization helps auditors in expanding their domain knowledge and offer allied professional services like bank advisory, business plan development, financial planning, operational analysis and legal advisory along with tax consultancy activities. Also, digitalization helps remote assessment of the client financial details, allows them to enter into new geographical and business domains due to diversity in every aspect (Pemer, 2021). In financial advisory services industry also, use of AI applications has increased more and it helps in identifying the appropriate tool of AI in offering a solution by the financial services firms for their clients based on client data. The economic and non-economic variables are equally dealt while simulating the historical data as its' availability is high. There are AI based data cleaning tools that filter the unrealistic, irregular pattern and unwanted data while analyzing it, considering only the relevant information for analysis purposes. This saves time for the advisors in explaining in detail about the portfolio of their clients. For this process, deep neural network technology is used by the firms which identifies the right data and images from the available pool of data (Landgrebe & Smith, 2021). AI research studies are primarily literature driven in the past that relied on the theory, context, characteristics and methodology (Hentzen et al., 2022; Paul & Rosado-Serrano, 2019) as their primary parameters, that helps in analyzing the current day requirements of the variables needed for the conduct of a research study. Library and information sciences researchers argue that women literacy and education play a crucial role in the development of a society that helps avoid the social conflicts if one adopts and uses AI tools in the form of open educational resources (OER) tools (Irvin & Bard, 2023), which can be adopted in financial services industry as well to improve the financial literacy. Researchers are highly concerned about the use of AI in education industry as well due to its adoption and application is restricted to content search, paraphrasing and content replacement tool for their academic requirements, rather using it for simulations, feasibility analysis learning which helps advance their skills, and this threatens the academic integrity at various levels, augmenting for a comprehensive mechanism to regulate the technology use based on industry needs (Volante et al., 2023).

3 METHODOLOGY

Introduction section covers the application of AI technology helped raising the following research questions during the study, that are listed below.

3.1 Research Questions

1. What technology applications in finance field research covers for diversified tools used for financial inclusion through AI technology?
2. How AI technology helps in understanding different theories that are applied in finance field?
3. Is there a scope for integrating dimensions like AI technology, monitoring and regulatory agencies role, ethics, theories and diversified functional domains that drive finance and its allied services effectively?

Present work is an insight into the applications of AI and its' allied technologies in the field of finance. Based on the overview of present applications, the following objectives have been set for the study.

3.2 Objectives

1. To assess literature available on the use of AI technology in financial inclusion, AI in finance field, role of monitoring and regulatory agencies in AI implementation, AI in various fields of study related to finance, ethical concerns in the use of AI technology.
2. To understand various theories of technology integration models to the finance field
3. To propose a model based on literature and technology integration theories for an effective implementation and use of AI technology in finance field leading to financial inclusion

3.3 Data Collection

The current thematic study aimed at reviewing the literature, based on which five dimensions are identified namely digital financial inclusion; digital financial applications with specific reference to AI technology; role of monitoring and regulatory agencies; the driving forces of AI technology in finance field and the ethical concerns in the adoption and implementation of AI technology. These dimensions along with variables quiet frequently repeatedly used for research are identified from literature collected from emeraldinsight and Jstor data bases for the time periods 2000 till 2024, covering for more than two decades of research literature on the integration of AI technology in finance field by the researchers. Each dimension is explained in detail in figure 1 through 5 with frequently and widely used variables by researchers in their works and the same have been highlighted to explain in detail in the present research work such that the prospective researchers can find frequently researched terms in the field and in the process, some of the dimensions are categorized under one factor, while others qualify for more than one, which helps in statistical tool selection while conducting research. These figures 1 to 5 helped the current research work to propose a model by the researchers as part of their qualitative research work and this helps the prospective researchers in working on effective implementation of AI technology that eases the BFSI industry's adoption mechanism, which further helps banking industry in high growth in business apart from greater financial inclusion based on client requirements (Akhtar et al., 2024).

4 DIGITAL FINANCIAL INCLUSION THROUGH AI

Generative AI is intervening much and taking over the banking, insurance and other financial services like the advisory through the use of FinTech, RegTech and

LawTech implementation which is in the process of adoption and implementation with a pace where the calculations, simulations and development happens independently in decision making compared to human expectations. Due to the voluminous free data available in market, the learning pace is high in solving the complex mathematical, engineering and medical problems apart from economic and financial markets in handling economic and fiscal frauds, crimes, credit risk calculations (Singh, 2024b).

Digital financial inclusion is the primary target in the implementation of advanced and new technologies like AI and ML such that individuals that are saving and investing in nominal amounts could make use of the benefit of these new mechanism (Kumari et al., 2024). Amongst banking, financial services and insurance (BFSI) segment, the core concern of the service providers is the privacy and security of their clients for which responsible AI technologies is one of the solutions that addresses digital fraud and money laundering complaints they receive from time to time (Uddin, S.M.M., Akhtar, 2025). Though AI is adopted in financial services segment, its full level usage is not done by the fields like credit risk assessment, customer eligibility analysis, non-performing assets assessment, credit management, working capital management among bank branches, industry and money market analysis such that a balance is strike between demand and supply inequalities of money, linking policy makers and client requirements, channelization of excess funds available with the financial institutions such that AI and ML utilization is done to the extent that satisfies the requirements of all the related stakeholders (Kumari et al., 2024; Meena et al., 2024; Mohsen et al., 2024). Personal banking is one of the fields where distributed ledger, AI, extended reality and quantum computing (DARQ) technologies can be implemented to understand, promote and recommend customized financial products of banks that mitigate risk and maximize returns to the bank customers (Gigante & Zago, 2023). Distributed ledger is advantageous as it doesn't store any data at any common place and often uses blockchain technology where the data fed is confirmed using a digitally encrypted cryptographic signature for security reasons, moreover, advanced computing techniques like quantum computing is also gaining momentum in finance field that adopts and uses an high-end machine learning phenomenon in data storage and its processing which can analyze complex algorithm as well that is need in accounting and audit functions apart from banking activities in preserving customer confidentiality (Naseema et al., 2025). AI, ML and Big Data applications enhance the asset management companies' functionality due to the customer's enhanced experience as it helps in a 360^0 view point in the customization of service opportunities offered by the banks in the form of internet or mobile banking process (Ladeira et al., 2024; Meola, 2020). As the present generation is highly reliant and comfortable in handling the digital banking process for their day-to-day transactions through mobile banking applications which at times is proven to be unsecure and require the attention of the tech developers towards the privacy and security issues using facial recognition, biometric authentication technology for a safer transacting experience which the banks are also preferring and incorporating in their bank applications proving their advancement in the use of new and advanced technologies (Bhatnagr & Rajesh, 2024). In meeting the new generation's personal and business requirements for an improved banking experience, the central bank of India that is reserve bank of India (RBI) has brought in electronic currency i.e. e , called 'e rupee' for trading purposes, which uses advanced data and text mining tools (Bhatnagr, 2024). Another advancement in modern technology adoption in the present times is about the belief and trustworthiness of its users. So companies started working on trustworthy AI which is the primary concern in the adoption and implementation of technology in a wider scale, as it is penetrating into an individual's personal, professional, financial and ethical issues directly through its use in medical, banking and financial, education and psychology fields that require trustworthiness in execution. So, robust policy decisions are needed for new technologies like this to rely on and implement (Braun et al., 2021; Buehler et al., 2024).

Figure 1 identifies the digital financial inclusion contributors that are multidimensional in nature. Some are personal factors, psychology driven, some are client or customer centric, some are monetary activities, some are quality oriented and some are monitoring and regulatory in nature.

Figure 1. Digital Financial Inclusion Contributors to AI

Figure 1 Digital Financial Inclusion Contributors to AI

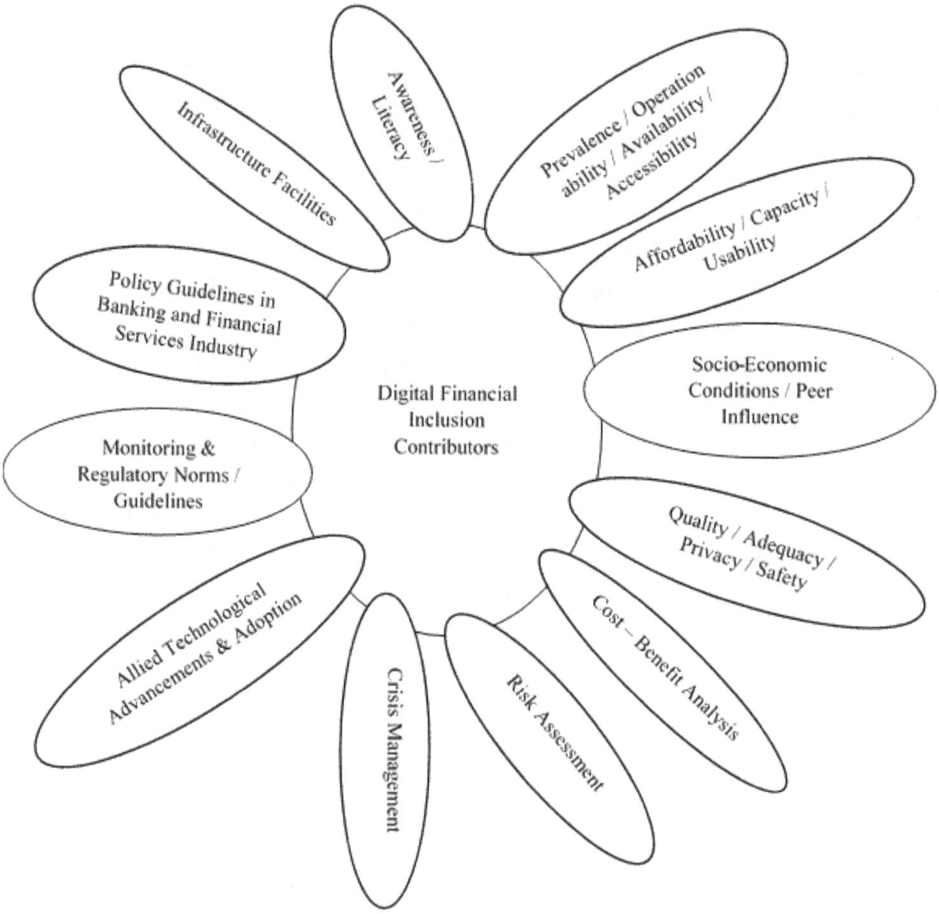

Source: Author Compilation based on Literature Review

Awareness, literacy, availability, affordability, accessibility, capacity to use, prevalence of technology, operation ability of technology and risk assessment skills of individuals are categorized under personal factors; while peer-influence, socio-economic factors, and crisis management are behavior related, so, are psychology driven factors. Client or customer centric factors include quality, adequacy, privacy and safety; while cost-benefit analysis is a monetary factor. Quality which plays major role in technology services section is driven by factors such as infrastructure facilities, quality, adequacy, privacy and safety, allied technological advancements and adoption, crisis management and risk assessment factors (Ansari et al., 2023).

The final process variables that needs testing are monitoring and regulatory norms and guidelines set by governments as well as the monitoring agencies to upgrade, update or replace the existing ones in place of the old wherever required.

5 AI IN FINANCE FIELD

Insolvency of banks in 2023 is an example of the need for the use of technology in predicting their operational efficiency and performance, which could have been analyzed applying predictive analytics tools; as bankruptcy of financial institutions has very high impact on the economies at global level. None can make the risk to be zero, but it can be mitigated to the possible extent by reducing the non-performing assets in the banks. AI finance is a new mechanism that is followed by firms in integrating AI with their financial process, which helps in integrating the finance function with that of others among the non-state owned enterprises in China (Shao et al., 2022). Technologies such as deep learning (DL), machine learning (ML), recurrent neural network (RNN) coupled with AI, helps in predicting bankruptcy (Fasano et al., 2024). Republic of Korea used support vector machine (SVM) and back-propagation neural network (BNN) languages to find out the bankruptcy and credit risk in banks in its' country (Shin et al., 2005) and found that SVM's performance in measuring bankruptcy is more robust than BPN. Strategic intelligence studies used algorithms to train technical indicators as input data and trained the machines to forecast the stock market movements. Clearer the financial input data provided for testing, effective are the results received during the process proving the efficient market hypothesis (EMH) theory to be prevailing. This procedure helps not only in proving theories, but also in identifying test variables that have higher influence on an investor's orientation of investment (Alex Avelar & Jordão, 2024).

Technology acceptance model (TAM) is one of the tools that explains the perseverance of individuals and corporates in the adoption and use of new technology (Oentoro, 2020). Perceived usefulness and perceived ease of use are the key factors that tests the inclination towards the modern technologies adoption by firms. Banking industry uses TAM to understand the client's behavior with the advancement of technology being adopted by them to cater the needs of customers (Lok, 2015). Stakeholder theory also studies the psychology dimensions of various stakeholders that are involved in the process of doing business from multidimensional process keeping in mind the ethical concerns making it as one of the forerunners in the present technology driven environment as well (Donaldson & Preston, 1995; Mahajan et al., 2023). Stakeholder theory covers wider spectrum of audience in research process that covers for almost all the segments involved in a business transaction (Akhtar, S., Alam, M., Khan, A., Shamshad, 2023).

Researchers observed during their studies that AI and ML are highly interconnected with research in finance field. It has its impact on investment decisions, financial markets, financial literacy, psychology of investors, economies and concepts of behavioral finance. Where, the theories of psychology connecting technology and advancements in technology are highly appreciated by researchers that helps in investment decision making choices of individuals (Annu & Tripathi, 2023). Big data analysis technology is a reliable tool in collating, filtering, cleaning and analyzing loads of data that is available in market across the globe. This tool not only makes available the data, but also provides an appropriate direction to the user in its proper use. Firms use this tool and enhance their customer satisfaction levels, client requirements and customization opportunities available to them. This tool further enhanced the organization's operational capacity, revenues and there by profits in the long term. It also reduces the processing cost of data, that helps firms reduce production cost there by the sales price of the product or service. Across the globe, financial services industry is highly relying on this AI support tool making one service provider different from the other, giving opportunity to choose for the prospective clients and customers while designing their portfolio of instruments for an effective investment (Mihet & Philippon, 2019). In the process of designing the AI tools, the corporates take into consideration various stakeholders' opinion about their requirements, usage, ease of use, accessibility and nature of similar instruments prevailing in the market place. AI doesn't recognize certain demographic variables like the gender, financial status of individuals and financial literacy exposure details, which also needs to be integrated in the present day financial services requirements (CCG Editors, 2023) and the same can be overcome with the help of same AI and ML tools using the big data analytics and deep learning technologies. Sustainability is the goal of any financial service for the corporates in analyzing the credit risk of clients, while risk mitigation and return maximization is the goal of every investor in markets across the globe that helps in financial inclusion of individuals which helps people and the country at large (Fazal et al., 2024). One of the sustainable development goals of United Nations is to offer financial stability that sustains for generations, which can be possible with the support of advanced technological intervention like the artificial intelligence (AI). Sustainable practices help accounting and finance field in avoiding the malpractices that are in place in reporting of financial details to the stakeholders apart from cost reduction, unbiased regulations implementation and increased productivity and financial efficiency of firms, encouraging the green investment practices, energy efficient spending by the institutions apart from increasing responsible banking practices in the industry (J. Nair et al., 2024; Quarshie, M. A., Djimatey, R., Akhtar, S., & Nawaah, 2025). Green finance, one of the sustainable practices in finance field is supported by digital processes makes it more effective in the implementation of FinTech practices in banks (Alam, M. & Akhtar, 2024), that help them compete in a healthy manner in the money market (Hidayat-ur-Rehman & Hossain, 2024; Jan, A. A., Lai, F. W., Asif, M., Akhtar, S., & Ullah, 2022). Behavioral tendencies of stakeholders can be measured with the help of AI technology, in marketing research, techniques like stimulus-organism-response model is popular in measuring the external stimuli influencing a customer's decision choice, which can be applied in finance field through AI technology to measure an instrument's quality and penetration into the market (Armutcu et al., 2024).

It is observed in fields like marketing that customers are sometimes technology averse which is called as algorithm aversion by the technology experts, which is due to the confidence they have on human intervention in financial advisory compared with technology use. This hinders the implementation of AI technology in the modern banking and investment advisory markets through user friendly tools and modern marketing techniques. Algorithm aversion is due to several internal as well as external factors, where an individual avoids taking the help of technology in their investment decision making when there are investment instruments that are highly volatile, when policy decisions, market conditions are rapidly changing, when political instability prevails in the country and like. Also, individuals rely on human advisors rather relying on algorithm based advisory under special circumstance like complex investment choices between instruments with similar risk and returns. A quiet contra condition prevails in markets with tech savvy and generation Z investors who prefer technological intervention in financial advisory being called as algorithm appreciation which is highly applied in numerical assessments based interventions. In long term investment choices, people prefer human intervention, while in swing-trading it is machine based; giving scope to the behavioral finance researchers to find out the reasons through the technical means (Koo, 2024).

Figure 2 is developed based on the AI applications in finance domain observed from the literature of over two decades, and the dimensions are captured such that prospective researchers can use for their research purposes. In the process, some of the dimensions are categorized under one factor based on the need while explaining such that statistical tool selection becomes easy while conducting research. There are eleven dimensions that are highlighted by researchers that contribute to the AI applications in finance field that can be segregated into product assessment, product marketing, customer profiling, client accounting and audit functions.

Product assessment covers bank / insurance product assessment (k) such that the characteristics of diversified products available in market can be segregated and offered to clients based on their need, which enhances the quality of investment advisory services (c) for a client. Product marketing assessment (a) is done to improve the sale ability of a financial instrument in an ethical manner with minimal regulatory constraints.

Figure 2. AI Applications in Finance

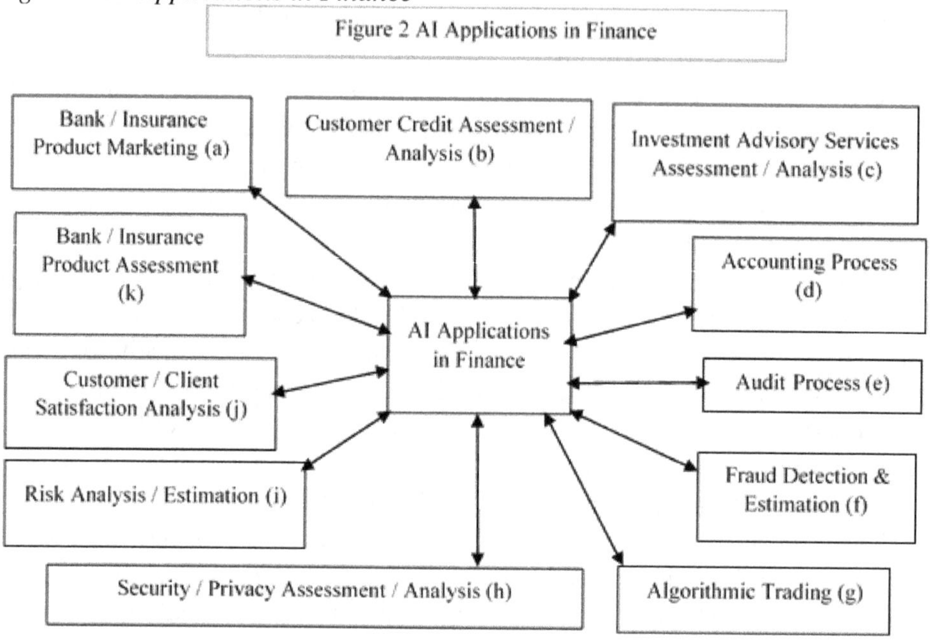

Source: Author's Compilation Based on AI Applications in Financial Services Industry

Customer credit assessment (b), security or privacy assessment (h), Client satisfaction analysis (j) help categorize customers into high, low or moderate risk takers, which further helps in customer credit profiling to the investment advisory firms such that an appropriate investment tool can be suggested to their clients. Client accounting (d) function covers for the accounting processes applied by the firms in analyzing the performance of investment options, apart from creating records for clients that helps them in their operational decisions as well. This accounting function leads to audit process (e) which helps in assessing and offering enough evidence about the performance of firms, investment options available in market such that a power packed suggestion can be made to the investors, as it covers fraud detection and estimation (f), which is estimated to grow to US$10.5 trillion by the end of 2025 from US$6 trillion in 2021 (Morgan, 2020); analyzing risks (i) associated with investment instruments or company selection which further helps in privacy and security (h) of investments, advisors and clients. So, figure 2 is an outline of various factors that use AI for their effective decision function which helps in conducting research in a right direction.

6 ROLE OF MONITORING AGENCIES AND REGULATORS IN AI IMPLEMENTATION

Policy makers play crucial role in the implementation of AI driven mechanism in investment market that helps in financial inclusion as well. Lot of regulations that are multidimensional in nature like the formulation and implementation of cyber laws, privacy laws, money market regulations, corporate laws and ethical guidelines needs to be drafted and implemented by the regulators in achieving success, apart from reaching out to all the stakeholders, the regulators need to keep in mind their interests. To prevent corporate entities misuse the AI technology, policy makers and governments need to bring-in more robust guidelines that mandates corporate entities in publishing their advancement and applications of AI technology in their business operations, such that monitoring and control are in place that helps government in implementing appropriate protocols for the proper use of technology for the good of humankind apart from preventing corporates from human rights violations, as advanced AI can recognize voice and facial expressions and reproduce an individual's voice; due to which activities like financial services, security and privacy concerns arise that leads to human rights violation (Buchanan, 2006; Rasser et al., 2019a; Sapignoli, 2021). China is one of the forerunners in implementing binding national regulations on AI use that generates, disseminates content with the help of algorithms, so, it put a regulation of disclosing how the AI algorithm is developed and used in implementation (Sheehan, 2023), where the initiatives taken by China are a wakeup call to all the countries to monitor and regulate the technology developers in their initiatives of user friendly, privacy driven and secured AI tools are offered by the firms. A global consensus needs to be arrived at in such policy implementations rather creating a trade war between the partner countries in the adoption and implementation of fair technology policies. Preliminary requirement for an effective AI adoption and implementation is digitalization of services, especially the banking activities, which in the present globalized world and free trade practices adoption era the need of the hour across nations (Marda, 2018). Increasing unemployment rate needs to be addressed by the governments and governments across the globe are concerned including the developed nations with a notion that AI is going to be the next big disruptor of economies that change the business theories and models prevailing apart from the ethical concerns they have (Erik Brattberg, 2020; Shaffer et al., 2020; Yang et al., 2024). The technological progress makes AI as one of the important skill that one should possess which not only helps industry in finding the best suited professional, but also mitigates the unemployment rates apart from enriching the quality of life with better wages (Masoud, 2024). If AI's involvement is not addressed by the governments, it may lead to power shifts in future times, as it affects the macroeconomic and non-economic factors in a widespread manner.

So far, 11 countries have formulated nonbinding principles, 11 have proposed for a legislative guidelines and finalized for generative AI adoption and use; while, other countries are using the AI technology without generic AI legislation (Kremer et al., 2023).

Figure 3. Role of Monitoring agencies and regulators in AI Implementation.

Figure 3 Role of Monitoring agencies and Regulators in AI Implementation

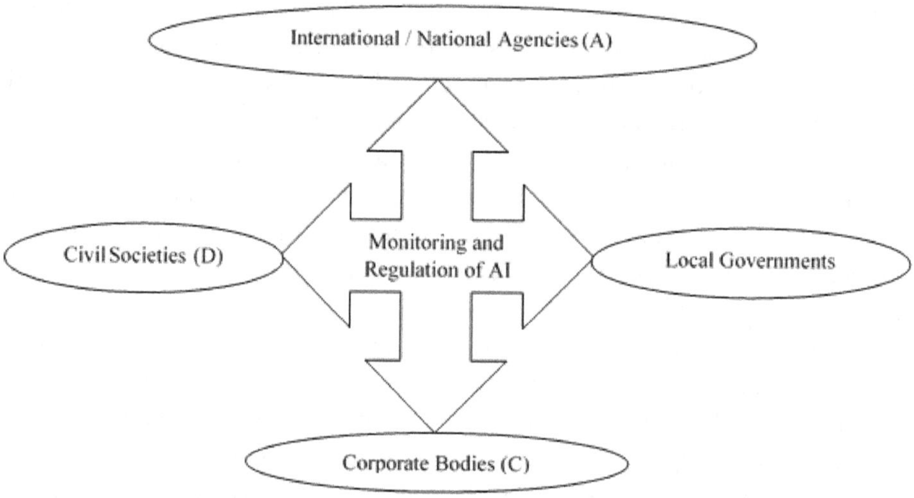

Source: Author Compilation based on Literature and Industry Observations

As explained earlier, monitoring and regulation play key role in the use and implementation of AI for an ethical purpose that yields right outcome. So, a comprehensive mechanism needs to function throughout the process that helps align diversified stakeholder's requirements. For this purpose, four key representatives are identified during the research (Figure 3), that is national and international government as well as non-governmental agencies (A) to offer the key essentials of monitoring and regulation at a broader scale based on the information collected by local governments (B), who are implementers of the policies decided at a broader level. These local governments collect and collate data from corporate bodies (C) and civil society (D) representatives at regular time intervals that serves as a feedback for the policy makers at broader level. Corporates (C) that are implementers of policy guidelines on AI, play crucial role due to their direct connect to the final customers or consumers. Hence, a regular feedback collection from the end user is possible to identify the pros and cons of adoption of AI. Another set that directly involves in the whole process is civic societies (D), who represent the whole society for the good and the bad that happens due to the advent and introduction of AI technology. So, a close connection and link needs to be maintained by government agencies and governments to collect feedback apart from corporates' feedback such that policy guidelines are implemented effectively. Hence, figure 3 network system is crucial for the success or failure of any new activity being introduced to large public such as AI technology.

7 AI IN DIVERSIFIED FIELDS

Another dimension of AI technology application is in the field of entrepreneurship starting from the pitch phase to the operationalization, which enhances the quality at all levels of decision making helping investors in gaining the right information. Diversified funding means are tested using AI technology with crowdfunding process and then to the other means like the private equity funding. This helps the field of entrepreneurial finance in a greater manner benefitting the incubators and accelerators in minimizing the pressure of searching for finances in alternative means. Accelerators are industry mentors and funding agencies that are different from the incubators which are managed by either government agencies or educational institutions. Hence, accelerators need to be communicated about the entrepreneurial financial aspect in an appropriate manner (Giuggioli et al., 2024) in the adoption of new technologies.

Figure 4. Driving Forces of AI from Diversified Fields

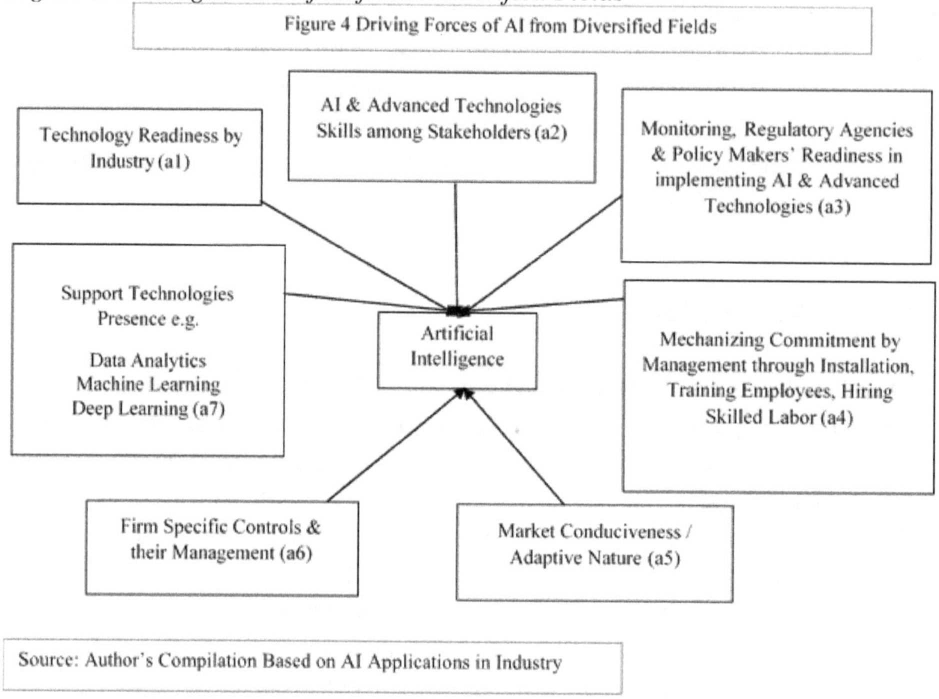

Diversified fields have to contribute to the AI technology, as all the products and services today are relying on adoption and use of technology. Figure 4 highlights various seven different dimensions that contribute to and drive the involvement, dependency and relying nature on this current day technology. Figure 4, Technology readiness (a1) by industry is vital in the implementation of AI technology. Unless the drivers of the technology i.e. industry, they are ready, it is an impossibility for any technology to be implemented or upgraded and hence, it is one of the dimensions that needs emphasis by the researchers. Support technologies (a7) like data analytics, machine learning and deep learning also needs to progress alongside, such that the core technology doesn't lose its' presence or otherwise reach to masses may not be possible. Not only this, advanced skills (a2) among stakeholders needs to be imparted, upgraded and sustained over a period of time such that the skills imparted can be utilized for better purposes based on the market conduciveness or adaptive nature (a5) of industry. It also helps in developing modern technologies to cater the needs of multiple stakeholders as managements often try fulfilling their mechanization commitments (a4) to outperform others in the market for which management control (a6) function needs to be effective (Wamba-Taguimdje et al., 2020). The different dimensions from a1 to a7, except a3 are multi-stakeholder functions, while policy maker's guidelines and control mechanism (a3) can be fulfilled only by the policy makers through their experiences, expertise and exposure to multi-dimensional, multi-national and self-centric socio-economic growth orientation by updating cyber security guidelines, countering privacy lapses at times as well as creating awareness among all the stakeholders across the nation and if possible across the globe.

8 ETHICAL CONCERNS IN THE ADOPTION AND USE OF AI TECHNOLOGY

Ethical considerations are more than financial considerations for a policy maker and governments to protect nation's interest apart from other stakeholders. Metaverse is becoming a buzz word today among financial institutions to simulate with the help of advanced technological adoption. Sectors like banking, insurance and other financial service segments use deep learning, machine learning technologies in analyzing the stakeholder participation, which require an ethical consideration while assessing the same is the pre-requisite of researchers (Singh, 2024a). AI misuse and the ethical aspects involvement is debated widely, since people use AI for both personal benefits in an unethical manner which cannot be undermined by the benefits of AI applications in the fields like medicine, space technology, defense surveillance, banking services, transportation, logistics and supply chain management, natural resource exploration and extraction industries. So, for a sustainable AI adoption, policy norms need to be drafted and worked upon keeping all the stakeholders concerned such that all the domains work hand-in-hand for an effective AI adoption and implementation (Rasser et al., 2019b).

Figure 5. Ethical concerns in the use of AI technology

Figure 5 Ethical Concerns in the use of AI Technology

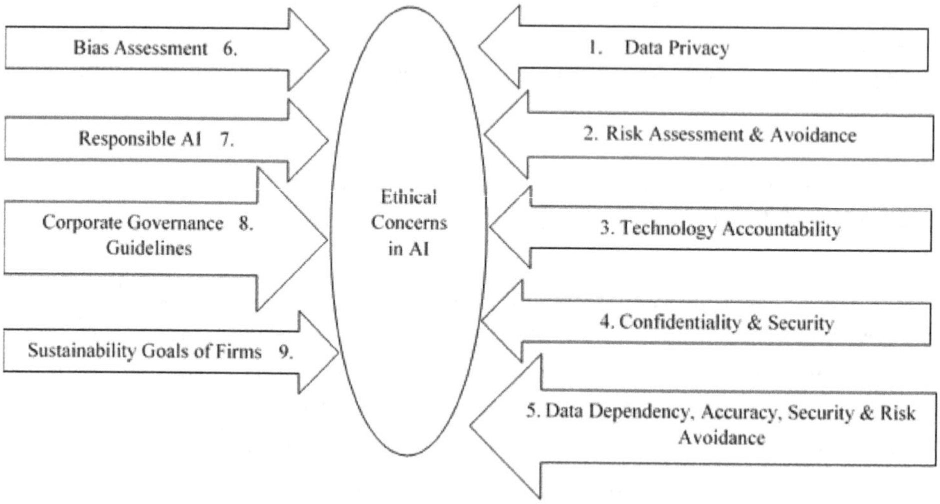

Source: Author's Compilation Based on AI Applications in Industry

One more factor that determines the success or failure of a technology in finance field is its' ethical concerns. From the literature, the researchers identified nine dimensions of ethical concerns to the AI technology drawn as figure 5. However, dimension 1 to 5 in figure 5 are privacy, security and risk assessment related only, that builds confidence in stakeholders in adoption and use of this technology, where policy makers, monitoring and regulatory agencies play a huge role; while technology service providers need to take utmost care in the implementation part and finally the end user also has to play a key role by opting an appropriate tool from an authenticated, licensed and reputed service provider such that post-sales support services are also important for a client. On the other hand, bias assessment (6) is like accounting function that postmortems after a transaction happens. Similarly, bias assessment takes place after the services are being either not to the standards or a security threat happens at organizational level. So, to counter this dimension, responsible AI (7) needs to be adopted as norm by firms that offer the service, and those who utilize the service in real terms, and hence has been made as a corporate governance guideline (8) by developed nations policy makers, while others are following the path such that the final dimension of the ethical concerns i.e. sustainable goals of firms (9), nation, and the United Nations are fulfilled, making technology reach to all the corners of the globe.

9 MODEL PROPOSED

After thoroughly reviewing the literature, five dimensions have been identified for which there are diversified contributory variables that are applicable in the finance field research. The first dimension is digital financial inclusion (figure 1) with twelve variables covering from financial literacy to policy guidelines governing the financial inclusion process. The second dimension is AI applications in finance field (figure 2) with eleven different variables that covers BFSI industries product marketing, strategies adopted in marketing, advisory services offered, accounting and audit procedures followed, fraud detection mechanism assessment, algorithmic trading practices with the help of AI technology, risk and privacy related issues analysis, BFSI product assessment post launch based on the customer's feedback. These variables are repeatedly being researched post 2015-time period by the researchers. The third dimension identified during the literature analysis is the role of monitoring and regulatory agencies (figure 3) in the form of guidelines in the implementation of AI technology. Researchers have identified four different stakeholders as variables that guide the role of monitoring and regulatory agencies, namely local governments, corporate bodies, civil societies and the national and international agencies working towards the guidelines framing mechanism. The prominence of these participant's research is found to be increasing since 2019-time period with emphasis on the ethical aspects as the key suggestion by the researchers paving way for another dimension that is ethical concerns in the use of AI technology (figure 5), on which the researchers have conducted their research work and have identified nine variables; namely, data dependency, data accuracy, data privacy, risk assessment, technology accountability, confidentiality linking to the sustainability goals of firms based on the corporate governance guidelines such that bias assessment can be done for the development and growth of responsible AI among corporate (Alam et al., 2024). Research was also conducted to understand the driving forces of AI technology into various fields (figure 4) of research that are linked with finance field among industry participants that helps in the adoption of AI technology by firms completely. Seven variables that act as contributory factors highly researched and found to be relevant in the literature during 2012 onwards are technology readiness, skill enhancement among employees, commitment by management towards AI technology adoption, market conduciveness, firm specific controls prevailing, and support technologies that drive AI technology adoption.

Based on the identified dimensions that contribute to overall growth and implementation of AI technology in finance industry, a model has been proposed that helps prospective researchers in the fields of financial instruments and financial inclusion research. For this purpose, the five dimension's variables are taken into consideration (figure 6) with all the dimensions having independent influence due to their variables, while monitoring and regulatory agencies dimension interlinking with other four dimensions apart from the market participants from industry like the banks, financial institutions, and financial instruments.

Figure 6. Proposed Model for the Artificial Intelligence Applications in Finance

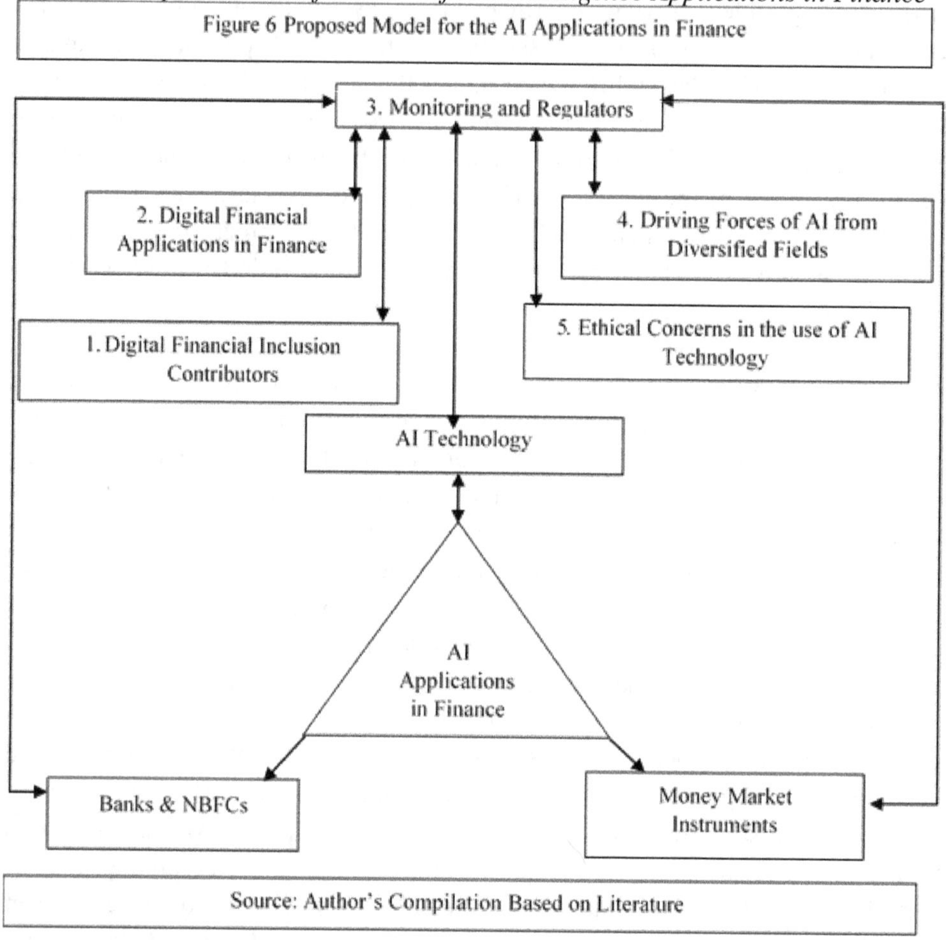

AI applications in finance has been proposed by the researchers through a model in Figure 6, that covers all the five factors that have been explained earlier from figure 1 through figure 5; which have multiple dimensions that drive each factor which has been shown in the figures depicted separately. The proposed model needs to be understood by researchers in consensus with dimensions and factors that are already discussed earlier. So, figure 6 is a rework of dimensions and factors that drive AI technology applicability in finance field for easy and effortless outcome. In the figure 6, 1, 2, 4 and 5 factors are two way connected, as the dimensions though independently formulate respective factors, they provide feedback to the monitoring and regulatory agencies from time to time for effective implementation and hence, item 3 i.e. monitoring and regulators act as controlling factor of AI technology that guide as well as take feedback and revert it to the respective contributory factors i.e. 1,2,4 and 5 for improvements in those respective processes. Monitoring and regulatory agencies through the AI technology approaches banks and financial institutions, money market for the study of factors' influence on the end users when new technology is adopted by them and collects feedback once again from the ground level such that the same can be passed on to the respective factor contributors for reassessment and modification if required. So, this whole recommendation works in a cyclical manner such that repetitive processes are observed again and again such that a robust mechanism is in place for a sustainable and ethically viable system is in place for the financial growth of an individual as well as of a nation (Azmi, S.N., Akhtar, 2023; J. Nair et al., 2024). AI applications in finance field model developed helps researchers, academia, industry and policy makers in analyzing various dimension's impact on the financial processes, such that a comprehensive mechanism can be developed for an effective advanced technology implementation. This doesn't restrict any of the stakeholders to a defined mechanism or factorial constraints, rather opens up new pathways to explore.

10 CONCLUSION

Present research work is a consolidation of various dimensions that finance field gets exposed to in real market conditions due to the adoption of technology, especially the AI technology which is helping as a support function in majority of business decisions in the field of finance. All the dimensions are categorized into factors and then a framework is developed such that it helps as a consolidated and condensed model that covers almost all the variables of various dimensions and factors that are researched by various authors. The various dimensions covered are personal, psychological, economic, monitoring, regulatory agencies and policy guidelines in the process of proposing the new model keeping in mind the AI technology integration. Also, each dimension is assessed separate for their understanding through literature available and then considered to represent respective factors.

REFERENCES

African Center for Economic Transformation. (2023). *Artificial Intelligence for Economic Policymaking: Context of AI Applications.* https://acetforafrica.org/

Akhtar, S., Alam, M., & Ansari, M. S. (2022). Measuring the performance of the Indian banking industry: Data envelopment window analysis approach. *Benchmarking, 29*(9), 2842–2857. DOI: 10.1108/BIJ-03-2021-0115

Akhtar, S., Alam, M., Khan, A., & Shamshad, M. (2023). Measuring technical efficiency of banks vis-à-vis demonetization: An empirical analysis of Indian banking sector using CAMELS framework. *Quality & Quantity, 57*(2), 1739–1761. https://doi.org/https://doi.org/10.1007/s11135-022-01431-8. DOI: 10.1007/s11135-022-01431-8

Akhtar, S., Azmi, S. N., Khan, P. A., Jan, A. A., & Ansari, Z. (2024). Unveiling the financial landscape: Analyzing profitability, productivity, and efficiency of banks in an emerging economy using the CAMELS framework and panel analysis. *Cogent Business & Management, 11*(1), 2399747. Advance online publication. DOI: 10.1080/23311975.2024.2399747

Alam, M., & Akhtar, S. (2024). Introduction to Green Finance and Technology Integration. In Syed Hasan Jafar, Raul Villamarin Rodrigue, Hemachandran Kannan, Shakeb Akhtar and Philipp Plugmann (1st Ed.), Harnessing Blockchain-Digital Twin Fusion for Sustainable Investments (Harnessing, pp. 1–19). IGI Global Scientific Publishing. https://doi.org/httpsdoi.org10.4018979-8-3693-1878-2.ch001

Alam, M., Akhtar, S., & Al-Faryan, M. A. S. (2024). Do Indian banks perform better in corporate governance than other SAARC nations? An empirical analysis. *Corporate Governance (Bradford), 24*(4), 799–830. DOI: 10.1108/CG-02-2023-0059

Alex Avelar, E., & Jordão, R. V. D. (2024). The role of artificial intelligence in the decision-making process: A study on the financial analysis and movement forecasting of the world's largest stock exchanges. *Management Decision*. Advance online publication. DOI: 10.1108/MD-09-2023-1625

Annu, , & Tripathi, R. (2024, December 18). Annu, & Tripathi, R. (2024). An insight of financial literacy and artificial intelligence to mitigate behavioral biases: A bibliometric and systematic review analysis using SPAR-4-SLR. *International Journal of Emerging Markets*. Advance online publication. DOI: 10.1108/IJOEM-07-2024-1110

Annu, & Tripathi, R. (2023). A bibliometric and systematic review analysis of adopting decision intelligence analytics for rational decision-making. *Qualitative Research in Financial Markets, 16*(5), 915–936. DOI: 10.1108/QRFM-01-2023-0005

Ansari, M. S., Akhtar, S., Khan, A., & Shamshad, M. (2023). Consequence of Financial Crisis on Liquidity and Profitability of Commercial Banks in India: An Empirical Study. *Studies in Economics and Business Relations, 3*(2), 36–50. DOI: 10.48185/sebr.v3i2.367

Armutcu, B., Tan, A., Ho, S. P. S., Chow, M. Y. C., & Gleason, K. C. (2024). The effect of bank artificial intelligence on consumer purchase intentions. *Kybernetes*. Advance online publication. DOI: 10.1108/K-01-2024-0145

Aysan, A., Dincer, H., Unal, I. M., & Yüksel, S. (2024). AI development in financial markets: A balanced scorecard analysis of its impact on sustainable development goals (February 2024). *Kybernetes*. Advance online publication. DOI: 10.1108/K-05-2024-1181

Azmi, S. N., & Akhtar, S. (2023). Interactions of services export, financial development and growth: Evidence from India. *Quality & Quantity, 57*(5), 4709–4724. https://doi.org/https://doi.org/10.1007/s11135-022-01566-8. DOI: 10.1007/s11135-022-01566-8

Bhatnagr, P. (2024). Enhancing digital currency adoption: Examining user experiences. *Management Decision*. Advance online publication. DOI: 10.1108/MD-05-2024-1111

Bhatnagr, P., & Rajesh, A. (2024). Artificial intelligence features and expectation confirmation theory in digital banking apps: Gen Y and Z perspective. *Management Decision*. Advance online publication. DOI: 10.1108/MD-07-2023-1145

Braun, M., Bleher, H., & Hummel, P. (2021). A Leap of Faith: Is There a Formula for "Trustworthy" AI? *The Hastings Center Report, 51*(3), 17–22. DOI: 10.1002/hast.1207 PMID: 33606288

Buchanan, B. G. (2006). A brief history of artificial intelligence. *AI Magazine, 26*(4), 53–60.

Buehler, K., Corsi, A., Jurisic, M., Lerner, L., Siani, A., & Weintraub, B. (2024). Scaling gen AI in banking: Choosing the best operating model. In *Financial Services Practice* (Issue March). https://www.mckinsey.com/industries/financial-services/our-insights/scaling-gen-ai-in-banking-choosing-the-best-operating-model

Chaturvedi, K., Akhtar, S., Azhar, N., & Shamshad, M. (2021). Impact Of Corporate Social Responsibility On Financial Performance Of Selected Banks In India: Based On Camel Model. *Studies in Economics and Business Relations*, *2*(2), 17–31. https://sebr.sabapub.com

Chen, J. Y. C., Lakhmani, S. G., Stowers, K., Selkowitz, A. R., Wright, J. L., & Barnes, M. (2018). Situation awareness-based agent transparency and human-autonomy teaming effectiveness. *Theoretical Issues in Ergonomics Science*, *19*(3), 259–282. DOI: 10.1080/1463922X.2017.1315750

Davenport, T., Guha, A., Grewal, D., & Bressgott, T. (2020). How artificial intelligence will change the future of marketing. *Journal of the Academy of Marketing Science*, *48*(1), 24–42. DOI: 10.1007/s11747-019-00696-0

Donaldson, T., & Preston, L. E. E. E. (1995). The Stakeholder Theory of the Corporation : Concepts, Evidence, and Implications Author (s): Thomas Donaldson and Lee E. Preston Source : The Academy of Management Review, Jan., 1995, Vol. 20, No. 1 (Jan., 1995), pp. Published by : Academy. *Academy of Management Journal*, *20*(1), 65–91. https://www.jstor.org/stable/258887

Editors, C. C. G. (2023). Equitable AI: It's a Matter of Urgency. *Hispanic Engineer & Information Technology, 38*(1), 36–40. https://search.ebscohost.com/login.aspx?direct=true&AuthType=ip&db=bth&AN=164771678&site=ehost-live

Erik Brattberg, R. C. and V. R. (2020). *National European Efforts on AI.* https://www.jstor.org/stable/resrep25784.6

Fasano, F., Adornetto, C., Zahid, I., La Rocca, M., Montaleone, L., Greco, G., & Cariola, A. (2024). The dilemma of accuracy in bankruptcy prediction: A new approach using explainable AI techniques to predict corporate crises. *European Journal of Innovation Management*, *28*(11), 1–22. DOI: 10.1108/EJIM-06-2024-0633

Fazal, A., Ahmed, A., & Abbas, S. (2024). *Importance of artificial intelligence in achieving sustainable development goals through financial inclusion.* Qualitative Research in Financial Markets., DOI: 10.1108/QRFM-04-2023-0098

Gambhir, B., & Bhattacharjee, A. (2021). Embracing the role of artificial intelligence in accounting and finance: Contemplating the changing skillset expectations. *Development and Learning in Organizations*, *36*(1), 17–20. DOI: 10.1108/DLO-01-2021-0016

Gigante, G., & Zago, A. (2023). DARQ technologies in the financial sector: Artificial intelligence applications in personalized banking. *Qualitative Research in Financial Markets*, *15*(1), 29–57. DOI: 10.1108/QRFM-02-2021-0025

Giuggioli, G., Pellegrini, M. M., & Giannone, G. (2024). Artificial intelligence as an enabler for entrepreneurial finance: A practical guide to AI-driven video pitch evaluation for entrepreneurs and investors. *Management Decision*. Advance online publication. DOI: 10.1108/MD-10-2023-1926

Gowhor, H. S. (2022). The existing financial intelligence tools and their limitations in early detection of terrorist financing activities. *Journal of Money Laundering Control, 25*(4), 843–863. DOI: 10.1108/JMLC-07-2021-0075

Haenlein, M., & Kaplan, A. (2019). A brief history of artificial intelligence: On the past, present, and future of artificial intelligence. *California Management Review, 61*(4), 5–14. DOI: 10.1177/0008125619864925

Heller, C. H. (2019). Implementation Opportunities from Modern Business Practices. *Naval War College Review, 72*(4), 73–100. https://www.jstor.org/stable/26775520

Hentzen, J. K., Hoffmann, A., Dolan, R., & Pala, E. (2022). Artificial intelligence in customer-facing financial services: A systematic literature review and agenda for future research. *International Journal of Bank Marketing, 40*(6), 1299–1336. DOI: 10.1108/IJBM-09-2021-0417

Hidayat-ur-Rehman, I., & Hossain, M. N. (2024). The impacts of Fintech adoption, green finance and competitiveness on banks' sustainable performance: Digital transformation as moderator. *Asia-Pacific Journal of Business Administration*. Advance online publication. DOI: 10.1108/APJBA-10-2023-0497

Irvin, V., & Bard. (2023). A Whole New Information World: AI, Bots, Metadata, and Discourse. In *International Journal of Information, Diversity and Inclusion* (Vol. 7, Issues 1–2, pp. 1–6). DOI: 10.33137/ijidi.v7i1/2.41079

Ivy Munoko, H. L. B.-L. and M. V. (2020). The Ethical Implications of Using Artificial Intelligence in Auditing. *Journal of Business Ethics, 167*(2), 209–234. https://www.jstor.org/stable/45386654

Jan, A. A., Lai, F. W., Asif, M., Akhtar, S., & Ullah, S. (2022). Embedding sustainability into bank strategy: Implications for sustainable development goals reporting. *International Journal of Sustainable Development and World Ecology, 30*(3), 229–243. https://doi.org/https://doi.org/10.1080/13504509.2022.2134230. DOI: 10.1080/13504509.2022.2134230

Naseema, N., Akhtar, S., & Jha, P. (2025). Blockchain Disrupting Supply Chain Finance: Transformative Solutions and Emerging Challenges. In Anamika Pandey and Fadi Al-Turjman, Transformation of Supply Chain Ecosystems, 33-47. https://doi.org/https://doi.org/10.1108/978-1-83549-246-820251003

Khan, A. S., Akhtar, S., & Alam, M. (2025). How efficient are Indian banks? An application of stochastic frontier analysis. *Journal of Financial Economic Policy, 17*(1), 52–76. DOI: 10.1108/JFEP-11-2023-0338

Koo, J. (2024). AI is not careful: Approach to the stock market and preference for AI advisor. *International Journal of Bank Marketing, 42*(7), 2117–2142. DOI: 10.1108/IJBM-10-2023-0568

Kremer, A., Luget, A., Mikkelsen, D., Soller, H., Strandell-Jansson, M., & Zingg, S. (2023). As GenAI advances, regulators—and risk functions—rush to keep pace. In *McKinsey* (Issue December). https://www.mckinsey.com/capabilities/risk-and-resilience/our-insights/as-gen-ai-advances-regulators-and-risk-functions-rush-to-keep-pace

Kumari, B., Kaur, J., & Swami, S. (2024). Adoption of artificial intelligence in financial services: A policy framework. *Journal of Science and Technology Policy Management, 15*(2), 396–417. DOI: 10.1108/JSTPM-03-2022-0062

Ladeira, W. J., Santini, F. de O., Rasul, T., Cheah, I., Elhajjar, S., Yasin, N., & Akhtar, S. (2024). Big data analytics and the use of artificial intelligence in the services industry: A meta-analysis. *Service Industries Journal, 44*(15–16), 1117–1144. DOI: 10.1080/02642069.2024.2374990

Landgrebe, J., & Smith, B. (2021). Making AI meaningful again. *Synthese, 198*(3), 2061–2081. DOI: 10.1007/s11229-019-02192-y

Lin, R. R., & Lee, J. C. (2023). The supports provided by artificial intelligence to continuous usage intention of mobile banking: Evidence from China. *Aslib Journal of Information Management, 76*(2), 293–310. DOI: 10.1108/AJIM-07-2022-0337

Lok, C. K. (2015). Adoption of smart cardbased E-payment system for retailing in Hong Kong using an extended technology acceptance model. *Advances in Business Marketing and Purchasing, 23B*, 255–466. DOI: 10.1108/S1069-09642015000023B003

Mahajan, R., Lim, W. M., Sareen, M., Kumar, S., & Panwar, R. (2023). Stakeholder theory. *Journal of Business Research, 166*(June), 114104. DOI: 10.1016/j.jbusres.2023.114104

Manyika, J. (2022). Getting AI Right. *The MIT Press, 151*(2), 5–27.

Marda, V. (2018). Artificial intelligence policy in India: A framework for engaging the limits of data-driven decision-making. *Philosophical Transactions. Series A, Mathematical, Physical, and Engineering Sciences, 376*(2133), 1–19. DOI: 10.1098/rsta.2018.0087 PMID: 30323001

Masoud, N. (2024). *Artificial intelligence and unemployment dynamics: an econometric analysis in high-income economies*. Technological Sustainability., DOI: 10.1108/TECHS-04-2024-0033

Mateas, M. (2001). Expressive AI: A Hybrid Art and Science Practice. *Leonardo*, *34*(2), 147–153. DOI: 10.1162/002409401750184717

Meena, R., Mishra, A. K., & Raut, R. K. (2024). Strategic insights: Mapping the terrain of artificial intelligence (AI) in banking through mixed method approach. *VINE Journal of Information and Knowledge Management Systems*. Advance online publication. DOI: 10.1108/VJIKMS-01-2024-0028

Meola, A. (2020, January). *Distributed ledger technology & the blockchain explained*. https://www.businessinsider.com/distributed-ledger-technology-blockchain

Mercado, J. E., Rupp, M. A., Chen, J. Y. C., Barnes, M. J., Barber, D., & Procci, K. (2016). Intelligent Agent Transparency in Human-Agent Teaming for Multi-UxV Management. *Human Factors*, *58*(3), 401–415. DOI: 10.1177/0018720815621206 PMID: 26867556

Metzler, D. R., Neuss, N., & Muntermann, J. (2021). Artificial Intelligence and Business Model Innovation in Incumbent Firms: A Cross-Industry Case Study. *Die Unternehmung*, *75*(3), 324–339. DOI: 10.5771/0042-059X-2021-3-324

Mihet, R., & Philippon, T. (2019). The economics of big data and artificial intelligence. *International Finance Review*, *20*, 29–43. DOI: 10.1108/S1569-376720190000020006

Miller, K. C., Bordetsky, A., Mun, J. C., Maule, R. W., & Pollman, A. G. (2021). Merging Future Knowledgebase System of Systems with Artificial Intelligence/Machine Learning Engines to Maximize Reliability and Availability for Decision Support. *Military Operations Research (Alexandria, Va.)*, *26*(4), 77–93. DOI: 10.5711/1082598326477

Mohsen, S. E., Hamdan, A., & Shoaib, H. M. (2024). Digital transformation and integration of artificial intelligence in financial institutions. *Journal of Financial Reporting and Accounting*. DOI: 10.1108/JFRA-09-2023-0544

Morgan, S. (2020). Cybercrime Magazine. *Cybersecurity Ventures*, 1:6. https://cybersecurityventures.com/cybercrime-damages-6-trillion-by-2021/

J. Nair, A., Manohar, S., & Mittal, A. (2024). AI-enabled FinTech for innovative sustainability: promoting organizational sustainability practices in digital accounting and finance. *International Journal of Accounting and Information Management*. DOI: 10.1108/IJAIM-05-2024-0172

Oentoro, W. (2020). *Mobile payment adoption process: a serial of multiple mediation and moderation analysis*. DOI: 10.1108/BL-09-2020-0059

Paul, J., & Rosado-Serrano, A. (2019). Gradual Internationalization vs Born-Global/ International new venture models: A review and research agenda. *International Marketing Review*, *36*(6), 830–858. DOI: 10.1108/IMR-10-2018-0280

Pemer, F. (2021). Enacting Professional Service Work in Times of Digitalization and Potential Disruption. *Journal of Service Research*, *24*(2), 249–268. DOI: 10.1177/1094670520916801

Quarshie, M. A., Djimatey, R., Akhtar, S., & Nawaah, D. (2025). Maximizing financial efficiency through technological synergy: Unleashing ICT for enhanced cash management in SMEs. *Journal of the International Council for Small Business*, 1–31. https://doi.org/https://doi.org/10.1080/26437015.2025.2461025

Rasser, M., Lamberth, M., Riikonen, A., & Guo, C. M. H. and P. S. (2019a). The American AI Century: IMPROVE GOVERNMENT READINESS. In *Center for a New American Security*.

Rasser, M., Lamberth, M., Riikonen, A., & Guo, C. M. H. and P. S. (2019b). *The American AI Century: SHAPE GLOBAL NORMS FOR AI USE.*

Rodriguez, T. N. and S. (2019). *A Candle in the Dark: A FRAMEWORK FOR UNDERSTANDING APPLIED AI.*

Samala, N., Katkam, B. S., Bellamkonda, R. S., & Rodriguez, R. V. (2022). Impact of AI and robotics in the tourism sector: A critical insight. *Journal of Tourism Futures*, *8*(1), 73–87. DOI: 10.1108/JTF-07-2019-0065

Sapignoli, M. (2021). Anthropology and the Ai-Turn in Global Governance. *AJIL Unbound*, *115*, 294–298. DOI: 10.1017/aju.2021.38

Shaffer, K. J., Gaumer, C. J., & Bradley, K. P. (2020). Artificial intelligence products reshape accounting: Time to re-train. *Development and Learning in Organizations*, *34*(6), 41–43. DOI: 10.1108/DLO-10-2019-0242

Shao, J., Lou, Z., Wang, C., Mao, J., & Ye, A. (2022). The impact of artificial intelligence (AI) finance on financing constraints of non-SOE firms in emerging markets. *International Journal of Emerging Markets*, *17*(4), 930–944. DOI: 10.1108/IJOEM-02-2021-0299

Sheehan, M. (2023)... *AI Regulations and How They Get Made.*, *24*(24), 108–125.

Sheppard, L. R., Karlén, R., Hunter, A. P., & Balieiro, L. (2018). Report Subtitle : THE IMPORTANCE OF THE AI ECOSYSTEM FRAMEWORK FOR. *Artificial Intelligence*, (May), 2020.

Shin, K. S., Lee, T. S., & Kim, H. J. (2005). An application of support vector machines in bankruptcy prediction model. *Expert Systems with Applications, 28*(1), 127–135. DOI: 10.1016/j.eswa.2004.08.009

Singh, C. (2024a). Artificial intelligence and deep learning: Considerations for financial institutions for compliance with the regulatory burden in the United Kingdom. *Journal of Financial Crime, 31*(2), 259–266. DOI: 10.1108/JFC-01-2023-0011

Singh, C. (2024b). *Is generative AI (arti fi cial intelligence) the next advent in the evolution offi nance and navigatingfi nancial crime and regulation ?* DOI: 10.1108/JFC-07-2024-0232

Singh, C., & Lin, W. (2020). Can artificial intelligence, RegTech and CharityTech provide effective solutions for anti-money laundering and counter-terror financing initiatives in charitable fundraising. *Journal of Money Laundering Control, 24*(3), 464–482. DOI: 10.1108/JMLC-09-2020-0100

Stephan De Spiegeleire, M. M. and T. S. (2017). *ARTIFICIAL INTELLIGENCE AND THE FUTURE OF DEFENSE: AI – TODAY AND TOMORROW* (Issue May 2024).

Uddin, S. M. M., & Akhtar, S. (2025). Convergence in efficiency and technology gap of Indian banks: implication of GFC and COVID-19. *Quality & Quantity, June*. https://doi.org/https://doi.org/10.1007/s11135-025-02195-7

Volante, L., DeLuca, C., & Klinger, D. A. (2023). Leveraging AI to enhance learning. *Phi Delta Kappan, 105*(1), 40–45. DOI: 10.1177/00317217231197475

Wamba-Taguimdje, S. L., Fosso Wamba, S., Kala Kamdjoug, J. R., & Tchatchouang Wanko, C. E. (2020). Influence of artificial intelligence (AI) on firm performance: The business value of AI-based transformation projects. *Business Process Management Journal, 26*(7), 1893–1924. DOI: 10.1108/BPMJ-10-2019-0411

Xu, Y., Shieh, C. H., van Esch, P., & Ling, I. L. (2020). AI customer service: Task complexity, problem-solving ability, and usage intention. [AMJ]. *Australasian Marketing Journal, 28*(4), 189–199. DOI: 10.1016/j.ausmj.2020.03.005

Yang, S., Hussain, M., Ammar Zahid, R. M., & Maqsood, U. S. (2024). The role of artificial intelligence in corporate digital strategies: Evidence from China. *Kybernetes*. Advance online publication. DOI: 10.1108/K-08-2023-1583

Yee, L., Chui, M., & Roberts, R. (2024). McKinsey Technology Trends Outlook 2024. In *McKinsey Digital* (Issue July). https://www.mckinsey.com/capabilities/mckinsey-digital/our-insights/the-top-trends-in-tech

Chapter 10

Combatting Bank Robbery and E-Banking Theft in North Central Nigeria With Advanced Artificial Intelligence (AI) Technology

Basil Osayin Daudu
https://orcid.org/0009-0000-9162-9426
Kogi State Univerisity, Nigeria

ABSTRACT

Banks are widely trusted as secure places for storing money and valuables, and provide essential services for physical and online transactions. However, despite their successes, the banking sector remains vulnerable to significant robbery and internet fraud losses. In North Central Nigeria, bank robberies occur seasonally despite security measures, while e-banking theft by internet fraudsters happens daily. Thus, this chapter is guided by the following objectives: (i) To investigate the techniques used by bank robbers and internet fraudsters in North Central Nigeria, (ii) To examine the impact of banking robbery and e-banking theft on the Nigerian economy, and (iii) To suggest artificial intelligence technology as a viable means of addressing bank robbery and e-banking theft in North Central Nigeria. With qualitative analysis, the chapter examines bank robbery and e-banking theft as unlawful and dishonest means of livelihood, and endorses advanced artificial intelligence (including robotics and others, for instance) as a potential solution to these problems in Nigeria.

DOI: 10.4018/979-8-3373-3725-8.ch010

1. INTRODUCTION

As a teenager, my father, a former banker, told me that robbing a bank in Nigeria, let alone accessing the vault where cash and valuables are stored, is a daunting prospect. I embraced my father's words for years. However, witnessing two bank robberies in Benue State and Kogi State as an adult, along with the recurring successful bank heists across Nigeria despite security measures, has convinced me that bank robbery in Nigeria is far from difficult. Unless a more sophisticated and practical strategy is implemented to tackle this issue, it will persist as a significant problem.

The financial industry comprises both banks and non-bank financial institutions, and plays a pivotal role in any economy. Nevertheless, banks are seen as the pillars of the financial industry. Little wonder Owolabi (2010) asserts that a functional banking industry contributes to the progress of any economy. In North-Central Nigeria, financial outlets facilitate economic transactions, ensuring the smooth operation of both online and physical financial transactions. Banking, including e-banking, provides platforms to meet the diverse financial needs of Nigerians, with various facilities put in place to facilitate this.

The banking industry in Nigeria has experienced significant growth, aided by the introduction of new regulatory controls in 2004, which have bolstered banks and enabled them to forge partnerships with foreign counterparts for managing the nation's foreign policies. Since 2004, Nigerian banks have made substantial investments in their technological infrastructure, aiming to establish e-banking services offering value-added products like internet banking and the deployment of ATMs (Chiemeke, Evwiekpaefe & Chete, 2006). Additionally, there was a growing demand for digital banking among consumers in Nigeria, driven as a result of the rising demand and usage of cyberspace. Internet access in Nigeria experienced significant growth, rising from 200,000 users in 2000 to 11 million users in 2009, making it the second-largest online user base in Africa (Internet World Stats, 2009).

Ololade, Salwu and Adekanmi (2020) assert that the rise of network and digital payment adoption as an easy payment method has also led to a rise in identity theft and data breaches within banks in Nigeria. The activities of bank robbers and cyber criminals pose a significant threat to the progress of banks in North Central Nigeria. These criminals have become increasingly sophisticated in their methods, taking great care to evade detection by security agencies. Consequently, the existing security measures appear ineffective, necessitating the adoption of more advanced security measures, such as artificial intelligence, to address the challenges of bank robbery and e-banking theft in Nigeria.

2. BACKGROUND

The roots of bank liquidation in Nigeria stretch back to the crises of the 1930s. The lack of trust in Nigeria's financial sector has been a persistent issue, resulting in the collapse of the majority of traditional banks, with only one, the National Bank, surviving. Similar crises took place during the banking growth and collapse of the late Forties, where only four local banks avoided liquidation. In the early 1950s, 16 out of 21 homegrown banks were liquidated, and during the late 90s, about 26 banks were affected while other banks had restructuring measures like acquisition, renaming, or new ownership (Nwankwo, 1992).

Fraud has consistently been a major factor contributing to significant bank failures during these reform periods. In an attempt to address fraudulent activities within the banking sector, legal regulatory policies were introduced such as the Special Tribunal (Miscellaneous Offences) Act 1990, CAMA (Companies and Allied Matters Act) 1990, the Nigeria Deposit Insurance Corporation Decree No. 22 of 1998, the National Drug Law Enforcement Agency Act 1990, the Banks Employees, Asset Declaration Act 1990, the Central Bank of Nigeria (CBN) Decree No, 24 of 1995, the Banks and Other Financial Institutions Decree (BOFID) of 1999, and the Economic and Financial Crimes Commission Act (EFCC) 2004.

According to Owolabi (2010), the Central Bank of Nigeria enacted a Mergers and Acquisitions (M&A) strategy to strengthen the financial sector in the country, which was concluded on December 31, 2005. Therefore, the central purpose of banking is to meet the financial demands of customers. Consequently, financial outlets like banks have adopted technology, digital payment platforms like POS, ATM, mobile phone USSD, and online transactions to ensure uninterrupted transactions irrespective of customer location. Bank robbers and cybercriminals also have access to both physical and online banking transactions, causing financial losses for banks, customers, and the economy at large. This often leads to business liquidation and the relocation of affected financial institutions by foreign investors, ultimately resulting in job losses.

The activities of bank robberies could lead to the shutdown of the affected banks for a while or forever, which may hurt customers as they would be forced to travel long distances to conduct transactions, especially in areas where digital banking is unavailable. Additionally, this may expose them to insecurity on the highway, like kidnapping, armed robbery, and accidents while on transit. Bank robbery and e-banking theft activities have virtually affected every part of Nigeria, and the impact on the nation is alarming that calling for an urgent intervention. Therefore, this chapter critically examines bank robbery and e-banking theft activities in North-Central Nigeria with emphasis placed on security issues such as fatalities, property damages, and financial loss.

3. THEMATIC REVIEW

3.1 Bank Robbery

Bank robbery involves robbery by threat against bank employees and customers. It is also considered a federal offence. On his part, Challinger (1989) outlines the operational aspects of armed robbery as follows: (i) the robber's need to declare their intent; (ii) the robber's necessity to gain and maintain control over individuals within the financial institution, often through intimidation; (iii) the robber's objective to obtain money; and (iv) the robber's imperative to successfully escape.

In the 1920s, American banks took proactive measures to address bank robbery by enhancing security features such as installing alarm systems and reinforcing vaults with concrete to make them blast-proof (Coyle, 2009). Present-day banks have further fortified their security protocols with modern advancements. These include motion-sensing and high-resolution color security cameras, time-locked heavy vault doors, silent alarms, exploding dye packs, bait money, and GPS tracking devices (*Inside GNSS*, 2012). Additionally, some banks employ armed or unarmed security guards to augment their security measures.

The advent of biometric technology has rendered non-violent methods of gaining access exceedingly difficult, even for seasoned safe hackers and code crackers. Modern vaults and safes are so heavily reinforced that attempting to breach them with explosives would likely draw unwanted attention and pose a risk of structural damage to the building. Despite these stringent security measures, bank robbers have devised tactics to circumvent vault and safe security features. For instance, they may resort to kidnapping the bank manager; however, this strategy is not always successful, as many banks have revoked the manager's ability to open the vault.

Bank robbery is just one facet of a broader spectrum of issues related to robbery and financial crimes involving banks. Weisel (2007) identified three key factors contributing to bank robbery: increased opportunity, enticing rewards, and employee compliance or acquiescence. He contends that the proliferation of bank outlets and extended operating hours heightens the likelihood of robberies. Banks remain highly attractive targets for robbery due to their lucrative nature, with approximately 80 percent of stolen money never being recovered. Bank robbers are categorized into two, viz., professional and amateurs, by tactics, preparations, and targets.

Professional bank robbers tend to employ violence and intimidation towards bank officials and customers, while amateurs execute their operations quietly to avoid drawing attention. Professionals use disguises and disable surveillance cameras and communication systems to weaken their victims. They also equipped themselves with sophisticated arms to execute prolonged operations, using high-performance vehicles or motorcycles as getaway transportation. In contrast, amateurs often rely on foot as their primary means of escape (Weisel, 2007).

The Niger-Delta region of Nigeria has records of bank robbery, coordinated armed assaults, and burglaries of commercial banks and bullion vans. The *Niger Delta Weekly* (2022) reported that between January 2018 and December 2021, more than 25 robbery incidents resulted in over 70 fatalities in the Niger Delta. Notably, robbery in Nigeria is of different categories addressed in different eras. The first is before 1900-1940s, which is the pre-colonial era, infested with deadly activities like raids, cattle rustling, and territorial wars. The second era is 1960s-1980s, which is the post-colonial era infested with armed robbery squads attacking bullion vans, banks, and the armed robbery special tribunal decree no. 47 of 1970 was introduced to curb the menace. The third era is 1980s-1999, which is a crime surge of highly trained robbery syndicates targeting banks, ATMs, military supply convoys, and oil bunkering. The fifth era is 1999-2010s, a democratic period infested with daylight heists, piracy, and kidnapping-for-ransom. Followed by the era 2010s-date, where cyber threats like identity theft, ATM card skimming, SIM swap fraud, and phishing attacks persist.

The implications of bank robbery could be social, economic, and political. Socially, bank robbery disrupts communities and instills fear in people, leading to the closure of banks and other physical financial institutions. Economically, bank robbery disrupts economic activities and discourages foreign investors from investing in their businesses, which may lead to job losses and a reduction in government revenue via taxation. Politically, the persistence of bank robbery undermines public trust in the government, which may lead to civil unrest.

3.2 E-banking Theft

E-banking has transformed the banking sector by providing 23/7 access to banking services, which has also transformed the way and manner people conduct their financial transactions (Nadagouder Chandrika, 2013). Internet or e-banking allows users with personal computers and internet access to connect to their bank's website and perform various banking functions virtually. Legally, e-banking is defined as banking activities accessed using computers, modems, and telephones (Ramnath, 2013). However, despite its convenience, electronic banking has also introduced new challenges, particularly in the realm of fraud.

Electronic banking fraud, as noted by Elumaro and Obamuyi (2018), poses significant risks and can result in substantial deficits for clients, corporations, and financial services providers. This form of fraud encompasses a wide range of activities, from small-scale schemes to sophisticated multi-million-dollar operations (Jolaiya, 2024). Techniques employed in electronic banking fraud include creating false accounts, using fake identities, manipulating account records, and unauthorized access to financial institution funds through stolen credit or ATM cards. The prevalence of bank fraud poses a serious threat to both financial institutions and their customers, potentially leading to financial losses and compromising the confidentiality of sensitive information (Elumaro & Obamuyi, 2018; Hoffman & Birnbrich, 2012).

The NDIC Annual (2022) reported that digital financial fraud cases have surged from 26,182 in 2017 to 37,817 in 2022, a noticeable spike of 44.4%. Similarly, the actual amount lost to fraud activities has risen in 2022 to 15.15 billion, compared to 2.37 billion and 2.4 billion in 2021 and 2020, respectively. The NDIC (2022) further reported that perpetrators of e-banking fraud are both external actors and bank staff. About 899 bank staff were reported to be involved in fraud and forgery in 2022, which is a significant increase from 320 staff in 2021.

The Federal Trade Commission (2024) submits that identity theft occurs when a person utilizes someone else's credentials to obtain smart cards, loans, or engage in other financial deals in the person's name. Therefore, internet banking fraud is a form of identity theft, facilitated via ways like phishing, hacking, card skimming, spyware, and lottery fraud scams, among others. Notably, Newman and McNally (2005) highlight three stages of identity fraud, viz. obtaining the victim's identity, perpetrating the fraud, and the consequences of the fraud.

4. BANKING POLICY ISSUES IN NIGERIA: REGULATORY COMPLIANCE, INSTITUTIONAL TRUST, PUBLIC SAFETY SPENDING, AND THE FISCAL BURDEN OF CYBERCRIME

For the past 20 years, Nigeria's banking sector has transformed as a result of economic liberalization, digital technology, and regulatory reforms. Nevertheless, the advent of cybercrime exposes banks to internal and systemic risks, which are addressed through four key policy areas, viz., regulatory compliance, institutional trust, public safety spending, and the fiscal impact of cybercrime.

Regulatory compliance implies banks adhering to guidelines formulated by financial authorities. In Nigeria, for instance, regulatory bodies like the Central Bank of Nigeria (CBN), Nigeria Deposit Insurance Corporation (NDIC), Securities and Exchange Commission (SEC), and Financial Reporting Council of Nigeria (FRCN) enforce legal rules. In an attempt to comply, banks invest in Know Your Customer (KYC), Anti-Money Laundering (AML), and Combating the Financing of Terrorism (CFT) frameworks. As such, the rise of open banking and digital finance also reshapes regulatory demands (Oni, 2012). Institutional trust is vital for a functional banking system, but in Nigeria, it is weakened by disturbing factors such as corruption, poor consumer protection, and cybercrime. Babaji (2024) reported that in

2023, banks lost over 14 billion to electronic fraud. In response, the CBN mandated banks to establish effective complaint resolution systems and promote transparency via its consumer protection blueprint. Therefore, the Nigerian government considers cybercrime as a serious national security concern, with particular reference to the financial sector, as reflected in the Nigeria Cybersecurity Strategy 2021-2024. Nevertheless, cybersecurity spending remains inadequate as limited funding was focused on surveillance instead of institutional defense, resulting in banks largely managing cyber threats independently, which causes inconsistent preparedness and higher costs. In other words, banks often rely on costly in-house or foreign cybersecurity services, with no national insurance fund to offset response and recovery costs (Ukhami & Abdulsalam, 2024).

Cybercrime places heavy financial pressure on Nigerian banks through direct costs like fraud losses and cybersecurity spending, and indirect costs such as reputational harm and customer attrition. The sector loses over $500 million annually, with top banks investing over 5 billion each in 2023 to combat threats. As cybercriminals adopt AI tools, costs are projected to rise further, impacting the wider economy by raising business costs, interest rates, and deepening financial exclusion, particularly in rural areas (Cybervergent Team, 2025).

5. CRIMINALITY AND MODES OF OPERATION IN NORTH CENTRAL NIGERIA

5.1 North Central Nigeria

Figure 1. Map of Nigeria showing North Central States

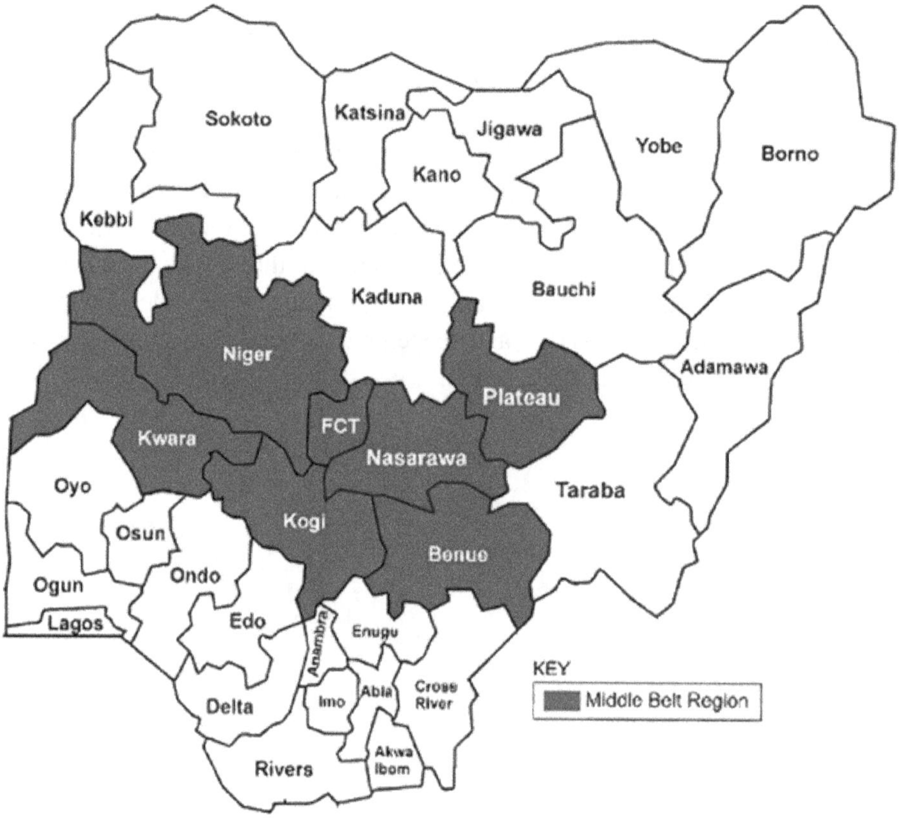

Figure 1 displays only the North Central States in Nigeria. Nigeria consists of 36 States and a Federal District in Abuja, the seat of the Federation. The North Central region, one of the six provinces, covers much of the Middle Belt and includes six States, namely, Benue, Kogi, Kwara, Nasarawa, Niger, and Plateau, along with the Federal Capital Territory (FCT), spanning from Cameroon to Benin. The zone features the Guinean forest-savanna mosaic and the Sudanian savanna. It houses a demographic of 20 million, around 11% of Nigeria's populace, with metropolitan centers like Abuja, Ilorin, and Jos ranking among the country's most populous.

5.2 Incidents and Causes of Bank Robbery

It was reported that some armed robbers launched surprise attacks on a police station and two banks in Offa, Kwara State, in April 2018, resulting in the deaths of 15 people, including nine police officers. On June 4, 2020, a group of 25 armed robbers killed a civilian and eight police officers during a coordinated assault in Isanlu, Kogi State (Sahara Reporters, 2020). Also, on June 13, 2024, in Abaji, robbers simultaneously attacked a First Bank branch and the Divisional Police Headquarters, engaging in a violent gun battle with security forces that led to fatalities (Channels TV, 2024).

It was reported that on October 20, 2023, a group of armed robbers attacked multiple banks in Otukpo, Benue State, resulting in many casualties and property damage (Vanguard News, 2023). A similar incident occurred in Lafia, Nasarawa State, in March 2024, where robbers looted the cash reserves of a commercial bank, and the culprits were apprehended afterward (Econs Intelligence, 2024). Vanguard News (2024) reported that in January 2024, a robbery occurred in Ilorin, Kwara State, where a bank suffered both structural and financial losses. Also, in May 2024, in Dadin Kowa Area of Jos, Plateau State, a young man attempted to rob a bank using fake explosives but was apprehended. In April 2025, in Minna, Niger State, a bank driver was murdered by suspected armed robbers. Earlier in March 2025, security personnel apprehended a group of armed robbers who were terrorizing in Wase and Bokkos Local Government Areas of Plateau State.

Table 1. Trends of Bank robbery incidents in North-Central Nigeria from 2020-2024

State	No. of Major Incidents	Key Cases	Trend
Benue	1	Otukpo (2023)	Multi-bank raid, lives lost, and cash taken
Kogi	4	Isanlu (2020), Kabba (2021), Ankpa (2023), Anyigba (2024)	High fatalities, cash taken
Kwara	1	Kaiama (2021)	High fatalities
Niger	2	Kagara (2020), Lapai (2022)	Lives lost, rural vulnerability
Plateau	2	Dadinkowa (2024), Bokkos (2024)	Foiled
Nasarawa	1	Lafia (2022)	Fatalities, cash taken
FCT Abuja	1	Mpape First Bank (2021)	Foiled

Source: Author's Compilation

Figure 2. Number of major incidents of Bank Robbery in North Central Nigeria

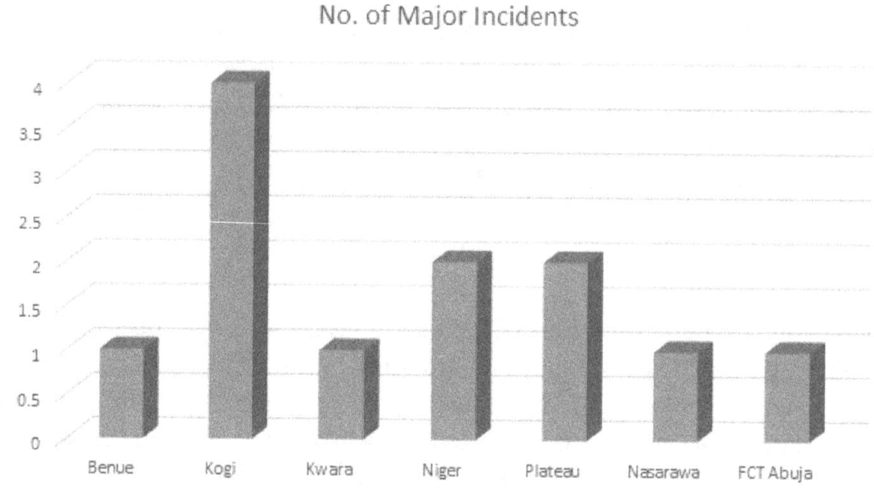

Source: Author's design using Excel

Table 1 illustrates the trends of Bank robbery incidents in North-Central Nigeria from 2020-2024, and Figure 2 displays the number of major incidents of bank robbery in North-Central Nigeria. Most bank robberies in North Central Nigeria occurred during daylight hours, and several factors contribute to this issue, including economic hardship such as poverty and unemployment, ongoing violence and conflict (World Bank Group, 2018), weak security systems marked by compromises, inadequate resources, and poor personnel training, the proliferation of illegal arms (Bulwark Intelligence, 2023), and the activities of organized crime groups (Thompson, 2025).

5.3 Bank Robbers' Techniques

Most successful bank robberies in North Central Nigeria employ a variety of effective techniques such as the use of informants, surveillance, thorough planning, police distraction, operational attire, weapons, and transportation systems.

5.3.1 Informants

Insider information is highly valuable, allowing bank robbers to plan effectively. With insights from informants, they acquire details about bank operations, staff numbers, security arrangements, transactions, and the contents of the vault. Akhagbemh (2021) reported that the Delta State Police Command apprehended Kingsley Gbeneku, an individual identified as the informant and an employee of a modern banking institution in Ughelli, Delta North. This arrest follows the successful intervention of the Eagle Net Special Squad of the Command, who thwarted a bank robbery attempt on April 7th.

5.3.2 Surveillance

Bank robbers do spend time surveying their target banks and surroundings. They might disguise themselves as customers to master the bank's layout, daily routine, and even staff. Omorogieva (2017) reported that in Lagos State, six elegantly attired individuals disembarked from two luxurious vehicles and proceeded directly to the banking hall, masquerading as customers.

5.3.3 Thorough Planning

Bank robbers meticulously prepare for months or even years before executing attacks. This meticulous planning contributes to the success of many bank robberies in Nigeria.

5.3.4 Police Distraction

Robbers often launch aggressive assaults on nearby police stations to divert attention and weaken security measures, sometimes targeting both police stations and banks simultaneously. Weakening law enforcement infrastructure provides them with ample time to carry out their operations, with some bank robberies lasting for hours, like the case of Otukpo, Benue State of Nigeria (Sanusi, 2023).

5.3.5 Use of Disguises and Protective Gear

Hood masks and gloves used by armed robbers help them evade detection by both people and CCTV cameras. They conceal their identities and avoid leaving fingerprints.

5.3.6 Explosives and Firearms

These facilitate swift and efficient bank robberies. With explosives and sophisticated guns, robbers breach security doors and gain access to both the banking hall and ATM vaults, obviously overpowering bank staff and security personnel.

5.3.7 Advanced Automobiles and Motorcycles

Bank robbers carefully use sophisticated cars and motorcycles, opting for those with untraceable license plate numbers. They may hijack cars and motorcycles before and after the operation or even switch vehicles during their getaway to avoid detection.

5.4 Internet Fraud Incidents in North Central Nigeria

It was reported that in 2024, the EFCC arrested several persons in Lokoja, Kogi State, for their alleged involvement in internet fraud. That same year, financial institutions across Nigeria, including those in Niger State, reportedly lost 52.26 billion to fraud stemming from a system error. On May 23, 2024, the EFCC apprehended 26 people in New Nyanya, Nasarawa State, acting on credible intelligence about their involvement in internet fraud; confiscated items included over 30 mobile phones and three laptops. In February 2025, it was reported that a Federal High Court in Makurdi sentenced 20 internet fraudsters to prison terms. Also, in March 2025, the EFCC arrested 14 suspected internet fraudsters in Jos, and later that same month, nine more suspects were apprehended in Abuja following credible intelligence on their involvement in online fraud (efcc.gov.ng).

Table 2. E-Banking and Identity Theft in North-Central Nigeria (2020-2025) and Technology-based Responses

<table>
<tr><th>Year</th><th>State</th><th>Method of Attack</th><th>Impact</th><th>Responses</th></tr>
<tr><td>2020</td><td>Abuja</td><td>Social engineering, SIM Swap</td><td>Financial losses</td><td rowspan="6">1. Banks should ensure real-time transaction alerts and enforce 2FA.
2. CBN/NIBSS should enhance the inter-bank fraud reporting system and enforce SIM revalidation policies.
3. Avoidance of public Wi-Fi for banking
4. States should launch fraud awareness via local radio, television channels, digital platforms, and youth centers.</td></tr>
<tr><td>2021</td><td>Benue</td><td>Phishing scam on mobile banking platform (FirstMonie)</td><td>Youth cooperative scammed</td></tr>
<tr><td>2022</td><td>Kwara and Niger</td><td>Fake investment app and ATM card cloning</td><td>Dozens scammed</td></tr>
<tr><td>2023</td><td>Nasarawa and Kogi</td><td>Phishing and SIM-swap on pensioner accounts; fake bank alert fraud via mobile apps</td><td>Retirees' bank accounts cleared.</td></tr>
<tr><td>2024</td><td>Abuja</td><td>BVN cloning</td><td>Cloned identities undetected for 3 years</td></tr>
<tr><td>2025</td><td>Plateau</td><td>Digital wallet hijack via spyware on Android phones</td><td>e-wallets cleared</td></tr>
</table>

Source: Author's Compilation

5.5 Cyber Criminals' Techniques

Cyber criminals employ various tactics, such as obtaining banking passwords like PINs, passwords, and certificates, or attempting to transfer funds into mule accounts to steal money. They may also seek to tarnish a bank's reputation by blocking its servers, preventing consumers from accessing their accounts (Claessens et al., 2002). Cyber-attacks manifest in different forms, including DoS attacks, social engineering, malicious software, junk mail, man-in-the-middle attacks, and Trojan horses (Daudu & Osimen, 2025).

Fraudulent activities conducted over the internet primarily target unsuspecting and less proficient users of e-banking, exploiting their trust in banks and their personnel. Other strategies employed by cyber criminals involve partnership with law enforcement personnel, bankers, and community-based or cross-border networks (Aransiola & Asindemade, 2011). Internet banking fraud often focuses on dormant accounts or those held by inactive account holders. Thus, cyber-criminal techniques are as follows:

5.5.1 Phishing

This is a deceptive tactic used by fraudsters to acquire personal information from unsuspecting individuals (Omodunbi, Odiase, Olaniyan & Esan, 2016). In this scheme, impostors posing as bank representatives create a fake website resembling the victim's bank. Besides targeting online banking users, phishing emails may also focus on online auction platforms or other internet payment services.

5.5.2 Spam

This involves unwanted digital messages like "junk mail" that are sent to email accounts or mobile phones. These messages are typically commercial and can be overwhelming due to their large quantity. They may aim to promote a product or service, direct you to a website for purchases, or deceive you into revealing classified records such as bank account details.

5.5.3 Spyware

Spyware, including Trojan horse, is typically software that covertly installs itself on a computer, extracting information without the user's consent or knowledge. This malicious software may gather personal or business data, utilize bandwidth, or utilize processing capacity, surreptitiously transferring it to an external party.

5.5.4 Card Skimming

This refers to an illicit duplication and capture of magnetic stripe and PIN data from smart cards. Skimming devices, known as card skimmers, are typically placed over card readers at ATM or point-of-sale (POS) devices to illicitly obtain information for fraudulent activities. Skimming incidents can occur at any bank ATM or through compromised EFTPOS machines. The stolen card and PIN details are then encoded onto counterfeit cards, enabling perpetrators to conduct fraudulent account withdrawals and transactions.

5.5.5 Electronic Fund Transfer at Point of Sale (EFTPOS) Skimming

This refers to the insertion of a foreign device into an EFTPOS machine, enabling the unauthorized copying and capturing of card and PIN details during transactions.

5.5.6 Hacking

This refers to unlawfully accessing a computer system. Hacking of IP addresses is a common practice, enabling hackers to create false online personal accounts and conduct illicit activities without revealing their true identity.

Identity theft, a common occurrence facilitated by the internet, involves criminals obtaining private data from your computer and subsequently creating dummy accounts or obtaining loans without your consent (Dubbey & Manna, 2015). Identity theft occurs when an individual gains unauthorized access to someone else's confidential details and exploits them for their advantage. Eseoghen (2020) asserts that fraud is established when there is evidence of dishonest intent to benefit oneself at the expense of others. In Nigeria, identity theft takes various forms and has negatively impacted the economy. As such, there is need for advanced data-driven security systems (Daudu, Osimen & Abubakar, 2025).

6. RECOMMENDING ADVANCED ARTIFICIAL INTELLIGENCE AS A PANACEA TO BANK ROBBERY AND E-BANKING THEFT

6.1 AI Application and Impact

The banking system plays a vital role in driving economic development (Akhtar, Alam & Khan, 2021), and artificial intelligence happens to be the tool for combatting financial fraud amid the rapid rise of financial technology (Adetunji & Chinonso, 2025). Research by Akhtar et al. (2024) and Khan, Akhtar and Alam (2025) suggests that bank consolidation can create strong synergies, enhancing profitability, efficiency, and financial stability, especially valuable for emerging economies like India during periods of crisis or instability.

AI-driven enterprise applications are used to enhance support, increase transactions, strengthen data protection, improve logistics, automate repetitive tasks, upgrade existing products, and explore new product possibilities. AI has the potential to impact almost every aspect of business operations by simulating human processes through computer systems. In the financial sector, AI applications include portfolio management, algorithmic trading, model validation, back testing, robo-advising, virtual customer assistants, regulatory compliance, and stress testing (Tucci, 2020; Citi, 2018; Eryk, 2020; Eno, 2022).

AI adoption is necessary to enhance economic development and combat cybersecurity challenges (Daudu, Osimen & Anaiye, 2024) and its impact is felt in the area of crime prevention (Sahay, 2024) like predictive policing (analyzing historical data to forecast regions with elevated crime likelihoods), video analytics (scrutinizes real-time footage from security cameras and public spaces to identify suspicious activities, individuals, and facilitate investigations), facial recognition (assists in identifying and apprehending offenders), and forensic analysis (examining extensive forensic data sets like fingerprints, DNA evidence, and ballistics). The adoption of these mechanisms in the banking system can curb the menace of bank robbery and e-banking theft.

6.2 A Conceptual Model

Figure 3. A Conceptual Model showing how AI reduces risk exposure across bank operations

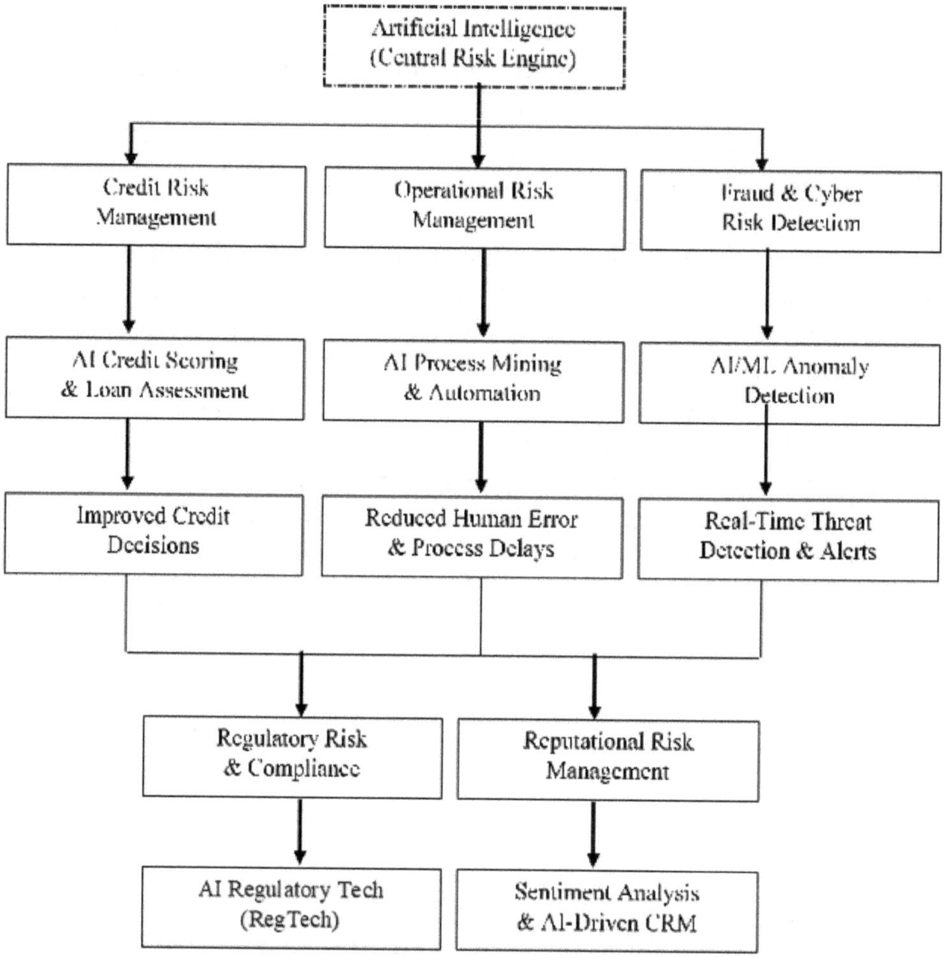

Source: Author's compilation of reports from CBN, Nigerian Fintechs, and Industrial banks

The conceptual model comprises several key elements: AI-driven credit scoring, process automation, fraud detection systems, RegTech solutions, and sentiment analysis. AI credit scoring reduces the likelihood of loan defaults by applying machine learning algorithms to evaluate applicants' risk profiles, an approach used by banks such as Kuda and FairMoney. Process automation addresses operational risks by streamlining routine tasks, thereby minimizing errors and boosting efficiency; Access Bank, for example, employs robotic process automation (RPA) in its internal operations. Fraud detection AI mitigates fraud risk by analyzing transactions in real time to identify suspicious behavior, as implemented by FirstBank. RegTech solutions manage regulatory and legal risks by using automated tools to ensure compliance with Central Bank of Nigeria (CBN) regulations. UBA collaborates with RegTech providers in this regard. Lastly, sentiment analysis helps manage reputational risk by monitoring customer sentiment through social media and feedback platforms, with institutions like Zenith Bank and GTBank leveraging customer relationship management (CRM) tools for this purpose.

Furthermore, AI supports law enforcement agencies like the Economic and Financial Crimes Commission (EFCC), the Nigeria Police Force, and the Central Bank of Nigeria's Financial Intelligence Unit in real-time detection, investigation, and prevention. For instance, machine learning algorithms can analyze millions of banking transactions to detect anomalies, map relationships between accounts, and uncover money laundering networks through advanced analytics (Obidimma & Ishiguzo, 2023).

AI enhances KYC/AML compliance, since regulatory compliance is one of the key pillars of financial integrity. AI enhances KYC procedures by employing facial recognition, biometric verification, and document scanning. These match customer information with national databases like the national identity number, bank verification number, and voter registration systems in real time (Humald, 2025).

AI is also a key driver of financial inclusion by simplifying access, reducing costs, and customizing financial services. It allows for the creation of alternative credit scoring systems that do not rely on formal credit bureau data (Li et al., 2024). This enables fintech platforms like Carbon, Fairmoney, and Renmoney to offer microloans to individuals and small businesses without collateral.

6.3 Policy Implications and Collaboration Strategies

Cybersecurity has become a concern for the global banking sector, with Nigerian banks facing distinct challenges due to rapid digitalization. As financial services increasingly rely on technologies like AI, machine learning, and blockchain, the threat space has grown more dense, requiring advanced cybersecurity measures (Oluwatosin, Johnson, Femi & Ogugua, 2024), which need the collective efforts of government agencies, cybersecurity firms, and international organizations (Odufisan, Abhulimen & Ogunti, 2025).

Table 3. Policy Implications and Collaborative Strategies for Combatting E-banking Theft and Bank Robbery in Nigeria

Stakeholder	Major Responsibilities	Policy Implications	Collaborative Actions
Banks	Secure customer funds and data; detect and prevent fraud	Enforce AI-driven monitoring; periodic cybersecurity audits	Coordinate with fintechs on real-time fraud detection
CBN (Central Bank of Nigeria)	Regulate financial institutions	Enforce cybersecurity frameworks and mandate fintech compliance	Launch a centralized fraud and threat intelligence
NDIC (Nigeria Deposit Insurance Corporation)	Insure depositor funds	Use risk-based insurance premiums tied to security readiness	Support the task force on bank security and fraud
Security Agencies (Police, DSS, EFCC)	Enforce criminal law	Expand digital forensics capacity	Real-time intel sharing with banks and fintechs
Fintech Firms	Deliver financial services digitally	Enforce strong KYC/AML practices	Share transaction data for fraud detection

Source: Author's Compilation

AI integration is a deeply policy-driven process, like the Central Bank of Nigeria, and Nigeria Deposit Insurance Corporation (NDIC), security forces, and fintech firms. As such, AI's utilization in Nigeria's banking sector is important to enhance compliance, boost operational efficiency, and expand financial inclusion.

6.4 Recommendations

The following suggestions, therefore, can serve as useful insights:

1. Banks should not be located across a town, but rather they should be in a centralized area with controlled access points. Security operatives should be stationed at these entrances, well-equipped to conduct thorough checks on individuals entering and leaving the vicinity.
2. Banks in Nigeria should strengthen their security architecture by implementing Biometric ATMs, which use biometric technologies like fingerprint, facial, iris, and voice recognition to verify users.
3. As bank robbers often disguise themselves with hood masks when targeting banks or entering towns, the Federal Government of Nigeria should empower its National Space Research and Development Agency with cutting-edge AI security tools. These tools would enable the identification of the culprits' true identities both before and after the attacks. Additionally, the use of portable AI-powered devices like Machine Learning-based Detection Algorithm Modules and Raman Spectroscopy-based Systems to detect explosive compounds is necessary in the fight against armed robbery.

4. The adoption of robotic technologies holds great potential in combating robbery and electronic fraud in Nigerian banks. These include security drones (cameras and sensors for identifying suspicious activities- Parrot Anafi USA), humanoid robots (Robotemi), mobile security robots (Rovotics R1), and drone swarms for real-time surveillance. In an era marked by rapid digitalization, robots may even facilitate maintaining personal connections with customers. Additionally, advancements in robotics are anticipated to result in smarter and more light-weight robots (GlobalData, 2022).

7. CONCLUSION

Combatting the menace of bank robbery and identity theft in North-Central Nigeria calls for a multifaceted approach that involves technological innovation and strategic planning. The utilization of security technologies like biometric ATMs, robotic surveillance systems, and data-driven monitoring devices can strengthen the protection of banks and their customers from cyber threats. As such, a strong collaboration involving government agencies, banking institutions, and law enforcement authorities guarantees shared intelligence, coordinated responses, and proactive measures to curb cybercriminal activities. Thereby, the banking sector in Nigeria would preserve its integrity in the digital age.

8. FUTURE DIRECTION

Combatting bank robbery and e-banking theft in Nigeria will likely see a significant integration of advanced technologies and skilled human resources. Based on this, future studies on bank robbery and e-fraud in Nigeria must work toward forward-thinking and interdisciplinary research. Adaptive and strategic responses will be needed as digital banking continues to reshape the financial domain.

REFERENCES

Adetunji, A. P., & Chinonso, O. (2025). The Role of AI in preventing financial fraud and enhancing compliance. *GSC Advanced Research and Reviews*, *22*(03), 269–282. DOI: 10.30574/gscarr.2025.22.3.0086

Akhagbemh, P. (2021). "Foiled Bank Robbery: Delta Police Arrest Staff Informant," AIT. https://ait.live/foiled-bank-robbery-delta-police-arrest-staff-informant/AN= 26521700& site=ehost-live

Akhtar, S., Alam, M., & Khan, M. M. (2021). YES Bank Fiasco: Arrogance or Negligence. *Emerging Economies Cases Journal*, *3*(2), 95–102. DOI: 10.1177/25166042211061003

Akhtar, S., Azmi, S. N., Khan, P. A., Jan, A. A., & Ansari, Z. (2024). Unveiling the financial landscape: Analyzing profitability, productivity, and efficiency of banks in an emerging economy using the CAMELS framework and panel analysis. *Cogent Business & Management*, *11*(1), 2399747. Advance online publication. DOI: 10.1080/23311975.2024.2399747

Annual Report, N. D. I. C. (2022). NDIC Publication. https://ndic.gov.ng/resources/publications/

Aransiola, J. O., & Asindemade, S. O. (2011). Understanding Cybercrime Perpetrators and the Strategies They Employ in Nigeria. *Cyberpsychology, Behavior, and Social Networking*, *14*(12), 759–763. http://search.ebscohost.com/login.aspx?direct=true&db=eoah&. DOI: 10.1089/cyber.2010.0307 PMID: 22007957

Babaji, U. (2024). Securing Financial Digital Inclusion: How Nigeria Can Protect Public from Cyber Fraud. https://wikkitimes.com/securing-digital-financial-inclusion-how-nigeria-can-protect-public-from-cyber-fraud/

Bank Robbery. (2017). https://www.fbi.gov/about us/investigate/vc_majorthefts/bankrobbery

Challinger, D. (1989). "Armed Robbery," AJC Seminar Proceedings 26, 22-24 March, Australian Institute of Criminology Caribeira, ACT.https://www.aic.gov.au/sites/default/files/2021-04/aic-seminar-proceedings-26.pdf

Channel, T. V. (2024, June 14). Military, police foil 15-man bank robbery operation in Abuja. https://www.channelstv.com/2024/06/14/military-police-foil-15-man-bank-robbery-operation-in-abuja

Chiemeke, S. C., Evwiekpaefe, A. E., & Chete, F. O. (2006). The Adoption of Internet Banking in Nigeria: An Empirical Investigation. *Journal of Internet Banking and Commerce, 11*(3). https://www.scirp.org/reference/referencespapers?referenceid=3780407

Citi. (2018). Bank of the future: The ABCs of digital disruption in finance. Citi Report.https://www.citigroup.com/global/insights/bank-future

Claessens, J., Dem, V., De Cock, D., Preneel, B., & Vandewalle, J. (2002). On the Security of Today's Online Electronic Banking Systems. *Computers & Security, 21*(3), 253–265. DOI: 10.1016/S0167-4048(02)00312-7

Coyle, D. (2009). "The Talent Code." https://archive.org/details/talentcodegreatn0000coyl

Cybervergent Team. (2025). Lessons for a secure financial future: What Nigerian Banks must learn from the 2024 cyber-attacks. https://www.cybervergent.com/articles/lessons-for-a-secure-financial-future- what-nigerian-banks-must-learn-from-the-2024-cyber-attacks

Daudu, B. O., & Osimen, G. U. (2025). Combatting Cyberthreats in African Digital Space with Artificial Intelligence. In Vajjhala, N. R., & Strange, K. D. (Eds.), *Cybersecurity in Knowledge Management: Cyberthreats and Solutions*. CRC Press., DOI: 10.1201/9781003498094-8

Daudu, B. O., Osimen, G. U., & Abubakar, A. T. (2025). Artificial Intelligence, Fintech, and Financial Inclusion in African Digital Space. Vikas Sharma, Munish Gupta, Nilesh Arora, Ajiaz A. Shaikh (eds). *Fintech and Financial Inclusion: Leveraging Digital Finance for Economic Empowerment and Sustainable Growth* (pp. 268-282). London: Routledge. DOI: 10.4324/9781003514114-19

Daudu, B. O., Osimen, G. U., & Anaiye, E. B. (2024). Sustainable Smart Cities in African Digital Space. In Whig, P., Sharma, P., Aneja, N., Elngar, A. A., & Silva, N. (Eds.), *Artificial Intelligence and Machine Learning for Sustainable Development: Innovations, Challenges, and Applications* (pp. 100–111). CRC Press., DOI: 10.1201/9781003497189-8

Elumaro, A. J., & Obamuyi, T. M. (2018). Cards frauds and customers' confidence in alternative banking channels in Nigeria. *European Scientific Journal, 14*(16), 40–60. DOI: 10.19044/esj.2018.v14n16p40

Eno, G. U. (2022). Integration of Artificial Intelligence Applications for Financial Process Innovation by Commercial Banks in Nigeria. *AKSU Journal of Administration and Corporate Governance*, 2(1), 125–137.

Eryk, L. (2020). Artificial intelligence in finance: Opportunities and challenges. https://towardsdatascience.com/artificial-intelligence-in-finance-opportunities-andchallenges-cee94f2f3858

GlobalData. (2022). Robotics in Banking–Thematic Intelligence. https://www.globaldata.com/store/report/robotic

Humald, M. (2025). The Difference between KYC and AML. https://binderr.com/resources/the-difference-between-kyc-and-aml

Inside GNSS. (2012). "Design of a GPS/GSM currency tracker device" https://www.insidegnss.com/auto/IGM1106_040_047.pdf

Intelligence, B. (2023, October 24). Unmasking the Complexities of Bank Robberies in Nigeria: Trends, Challenges and Security Measures. https://bulwarkintelligence.com/2023/10/24/unmasking-the-complexities-of-bank-robberies-in-nigeria-trends-challenges-and-security-measures

Intelligence, E. (2024, July 21). Nasarawa Police arrest armed robbery suspects, recover firearms, stolen items. https://eonsintelligence.com/details/crime-intelligence-10948010/nasarawa-police-arrest-armed-robbery-suspects-recover-firearms-stolen-items-523982752

Jolaiya, F. O. (2024). Effect of Electronic Fraud on the Financial Performance of Banks in Nigeria *Asian Journal of Economics. Business and Accounting*, *24*(4), 80–92. DOI: 10.9734/ajeba/2024/v24i41266

Khan, A. S., Akhtar, S., & Alam, M. (2025). How efficient are Indian banks? An application of stochastic frontier analysis. *Journal of Financial Economic Policy*, *17*(1), 52–76. DOI: 10.1108/JFEP-11-2023-0338

Li, C., Wang, H., Jiang, S., & Gu, Bin. (2024). The Effect of AI-Enabled Credit Scoring on Financial Inclusion: Evidence from One Million Underserved Population. *Forthcoming at MIS Quarterly*. https://ssrn.com/abstract=4812172

Nadagouder, S. V., & Chandrika, M. P. (2013). Law Relating to E-Banking in India – An Outreach Challenge. *International Journal of Current Research*, *5*(2), 3308–3512. http://www.journalcra.com

Newman, G. R., & McNally, M. (2005). Identity theft literature review. U.S. Department of Justice, National Institute of Justice. https://www.ncjrs.gov/pdffiles1/nij/grants/210459.pdf

Niger Delta Weekly. (2022). "Spotlighting the growing threat of bank robbery in the Niger Delta." https://p4p-nigerdelta.org/niger-delta-weekly-update-for-february-27-march-05-2022/

Nwankwo, G. O. (1992). Banking Fraud. Lecture delivered at the 5th Anniversary of Money Market Association of Nigeria.

Obidimma, E. O. C., & Ishiguzo, R. O. (2023). Artificial intelligence and cybercrime investigation in Nigeria: Addressing the legal and technical skills gaps. *African Journal of Criminal Law and Jurisprudence*, *8*, 30–36.

Odufisan, O. I., Abhulimen, O. V., & Ogunti, E. O. (2025). Harnessing artificial intelligence and machine learning for fraud detection and prevention in Nigeria. *Journal of Economic Criminology*, *7*, 100127. DOI: 10.1016/j.jeconc.2025.100127

Ololade, B. M., Salawu, M. K., & Adekanmi, A. D. (2020). E-Fraud in Nigerian Banks: Why and How? *Journal of Financial Risk Management*, *9*(3), 211–228. DOI: 10.4236/jfrm.2020.93012

Oluwatosin, R., Johnson, S. O., Femi, O., & Ogugua, C. O. (2024). Cybersecurity Dynamics in Nigerian Banking: Trends and Strategies Review. *Computer Science & IT Research Journal*, *5*(2), 336–364. DOI: 10.51594/csitrj.v5i2.761

Omodunbi, B. A., Odiase, P. O., Olaniyan, O. M., & Esan, A. O. (2016). Cybercrimes: Analysis, detection, and prevention. *Journal of Engineering Technology*, *1*(1), 37–42.

Omorogieva, M. (2017). *Nigeria: Bank Robbers on the Prowl*. Daily Champion., https://allafrica.com/stories/200706070741.html

Oni, S. A. (2012). Regulation and Supervision of Financial Institutions - the Nigerian Experience. *CBN Economic and Financial Review* 50(4), 107-129.https://dc.cbn.gov.ng/cgi/viewcontent.cgi?article=1094&context=efr

Owolabi, S. A. (2010). Fraud and Fraudulent Practices in Nigeria Banking Industry *African Research Review. An International Multi-Disciplinary Journal*, *4*(3b), 240–256.

Ramnath, A. P. (2013). *Advanced Law Lexicon*, 4th ed., Nagpur; Wadhwa and Co.
Ripples Nigeria. (20220. "Panic as armed robbers raid First Bank, Zenith Bank in Kogi, escape with cash." https://www.ripplesnigeria.com/panic-as-armed-robbers-raid-first-bank-zenith-bank-in-kogi-escape-with-cash/

Reporters, S. (2020, June 4). DPO, seven policemen killed in Kogi bank robbery. https://saharareporters.com/2020/06/04/update-dpo-seven-policemen-killed-kogi-bank-robbery

Sahay, N. (2024). *Robots vs. Robbers: How AI is Revolutionizing Crime Fighting: Is AI the Future of Crime Prevention? Examining the Pros and Cons.* https://nehasahay-5891.medium.com/robots-vs-robbers-how-ai-is-revolutionizing-crime-fighting-c6c93ef3f5a4

Sanusi, A. (2023). "Banks raid: Police confirm DPO, three cops killed, gun down fleeing robbers" *Punch.*https://punchng.com/benue-robbery-police-confirm-killing-of-two-suspects-condemn-officers-murder/

Television, C. (2014). "1 Police Officer, 2 Robbers Killed in Kogi Bank Robbery." https://www.channelstv.com/2014/01/11/1-police-officer-2-robbers-killed-in-kogi-bank-robbery/

The Federal Trade Commission. (2024). "Identity Theft". https://www.identitytheft.gov

Thompson, S. T. (2025). Exploring banditry in Nigeria. *Security Journal, 38*(1), 28. DOI: 10.1057/s41284-025-00477-1

Tucci, L. (2020). "A guide to artificial intelligence in the enterprise." https://www.techtarget.com/searchenterpriseai/Ultimate-guide-to-artificial-intelligence-inthe-enterprise

Ukhami, E. I., & Abdulsalam, D. (2024). Globalisation and National Security: Perspectives on Cybersecurity Threats in Nigeria. *Journal of Political Discourse, 2*(1/2), 273–286. https://www.jopd.com.ng

Vanguard. (2024). "Two killed as robbers raid banks in Kogi." https://www.vanguardngr.com/2024/03/two-killed-as-robbers-raid-banks-in-kogi/

Vanguard News. (2023, October 21). Benue bank robbery: Death toll rises as police confirm Otukpo DPO, 3 officers killed. https://www.vanguardngr.com/2023/10/benue-bank-robbery-death-toll-rises-as-police-confirm-otukpo-dpo-3-officers-killed

Vanguard News. (2024, May 20). Police parade suspect who stormed bank with fake bomb, demanded N100m. https://www.vanguardngr.com/2024/05/police-parade-suspect-who-stormed-bank-with-fake-bomb-demanded-n100m

Weisel, D. L. (2007). Bank Robbery. Problem-Oriented Guides for Police Problem-Specific Guides Series, Guide No. 48. U.S. Department of Justice, Office of Community Oriented Policing Services. www.cops.usdoj.gov

World Bank Group. (2018). Conflict and Violence in Nigeria: Results from the North East, North Central and South South Zones. https://documents1.worldbank.org/curated/en/111851538025875054/pdf/130198-WP-P160999-PUBLIC-26-9-2018-14-42-49-ConflictViolenceinNigeriaResultsfromNENCSSzonesFinal.pdf

ADDITIONAL READING

Adeyemo, F. (2024). *Banking Regulations in Africa: The case of Nigeria and Other Emerging Economies*. Routledge.

Doig, A. (2024). *Fraud: The Counter Fraud Practitioner's Handbook*. Routledge.

Jaishankar, K. (2011). *Cyber Criminology: Exploring Internet Crimes and Criminal Behavior*. CRC Press/Taylor & Francis Group.

Okoli, A. C., & Ngom, S. (2023). *Banditry and Security Crisis in Nigeria*. Routledge. DOI: 10.4324/9781003350149

Spicer, L. (2001). *Scams & Frauds: Financial Crime Exposed*. Trident Press.

KEY TERMS AND DEFINITIONS

Artificial Intelligence: Intelligent machines.

Bank Robbery: A forceful act of taking money or assets from a bank.

Biometric ATMs: Biometric Automated Teller Machines for secure authentication.

E-banking Theft: An illegal access to online banking accounts without permission.

Economy: resource management to guarantee people's well-being.

Fraud: Intentional deceit for personal gain.

North-Central Nigeria: A geographical area in Nigeria that includes Kwara, Kogi, Benue, Nasarawa, Plateau, and Niger, also referred to as the Middle Belt region.

Security: Safeguarding against potential threats.

Section 4
Financial Markets and Risks

Chapter 11
Navigating Uncertainty:
Global Stock Exchanges in the Age of Policy and Geopolitical Risk

Abhishek Sinha
https://orcid.org/0000-0001-6604-5461
Mahindra University, India

Vikas Maheshwari
Independent Researcher, UAE

ABSTRACT

The post-COVID era has brought extreme market volatility, fueled by policy divergence, retail trading frenzies, and disruptive technologies. Inflation in developed markets contrasts with China's deflation, while meme stocks, crypto, and algo trading amplify swings—even destabilizing traditionally safe Treasuries. Dark pools, zero-day options, and excessive leverage distort pricing, while geopolitical tensions trigger capital flight. Emerging markets face heightened risks due to weak oversight, but even advanced economies aren't immune. Solutions require coordinated regulation, transparency tools like blockchain, and stress-tested safeguards to prevent systemic crises in an increasingly fragmented financial landscape..

1. INTRODUCTION

Global financial markets are shaped by major events. The COVID-19 pandemic was one of the most disruptive major events in the recent past. It began as a health crisis in early 2020 (Baker et al., 2020). However, there was a cascading impact as markets witnessed unprecedented volatility. This led to swift response from regulators and exchanges globally. These changes make the pandemic a critical case

DOI: 10.4018/979-8-3373-3725-8.ch011

study for understanding market behaviour. The crisis was accompanied by economic uncertainty. Many of the working population were forced to work virtually from home. Subsequently, a large section of the employed class sought to use their additional time and savings to increase their income through financial markets. This new self-driven native digital class of retail investors disrupted the markets. They were not afraid of taking risks (Guest, 2021). They were awarded initially with high returns. This class of new investors had witnessed sharp recovery in global markets from the nadir of March 23, 2020. This led to positive reinforcement and hence saw more investors (mostly young) being directed by their "greed" instead of their "fear" as their emotions were led by 'Fear Of Missing Out- FOMO'. It will not be wrong to say that the markets were dictated by greed rather than fear. This led to an unanticipated increase in trading volume across the board. It was accompanied by sharp volatility among the retail-driven 'Meme Stocks' like Gamestop (GME US), AMC Entertainment Holdings (AMC US), and Tesla (TSLA US). This led to an average daily trading volume of 12 billion shares per day in US equities in 2022 compared to 8 billion shares per day in 2019 (Financial Industry Regulatory Authority, 2023); (Financial Industry Regulatory Authority., 2020)).)[1]. The sharp increase of 50% in trade volume dictated a shift in trading behaviour as new trading patterns and market dynamics continued to take the market into an uncharted area. This increase was not confined to the United States alone. Exchanges worldwide, including Tel Aviv and London reported significant upticks in daily turnover. For example, the Tel Aviv Stock Exchange saw a 35% rise in average daily volume during 2020 compared to the preceding five-year average (Hennessey, 2021). These shifts resulted in pandemic-era volatility which was accompanied by the entry of the retail investors. A new class of mostly young, fearless and digitally savvy retail investors emerged across the world, with 'Buy on Dips' mentality. These investors traded on Apps like Robinhood and eToro. This phenomenon aligns with prospect theory (Kahneman & Tversky, 1979). The theory explains how investors exhibited risk-seeking behaviour at every fall. Furthermore, uninitiated investors who are impacted by overconfidence generally resort to buying on every dip without deep diving into macro and fundamental factors that may have long term impact on the price. (Guest, 2021). On the other hand, social media create noise trader risk whose decision making was impacted by availability bias (Shiller, 1984; (De Long, Shleifer, Summers, & Waldmann, 1990)).

Consequently, there was a sharp rise in market valuations. Excess liquidity and heightened retail participation caused similar valuation spikes across major global indices. The sharp rise in market valuations can be explained by financial theory. Minsky's Financial Instability Hypothesis (Minsky, 1986) states that stable periods often lead to excessive risk-taking. During COVID-19, low rates and stimulus created a speculative boom. Investors increasingly used leverage, entering what Minsky called "Ponzi financing."

Tobin's q theory (Tobin, 1969) also applies. It suggests asset prices can detach from their true value when capital is cheap. This explains why P/E ratios reached unprecedented highs. Behavioural theories add further insight. Shiller's irrational exuberance (Shiller, 2000) describes how investors assume past gains will continue. Meanwhile, limits to arbitrage (Shleifer & Vishny, 1997) show why mispricing can persist. Together, these factors created a high risk high expected return system. The emergence and mass adoption of zero-commission trading platforms such as Robinhood and widespread lockdowns and fiscal stimulus payments led to a surge in retail participation. Eg: U.S. government provided approximately US 5.6 trillion in fiscal stimulus during the COVID-19 pandemic ((Tax Policy Center, 2023)). This included a combination of tax cuts, direct payments, enhanced unemployment benefits, business support programs, and healthcare funding.

The structure of trading itself has changed in fundamental ways. One major development has been the marked shift towards off-exchange venues. These alternative markets included alternative trading systems, dark pools, private rooms and retail wholeseller platforms such as Citadel Securities. According to Traders Magazine they accounted for approximately 45 percent of total stocks being traded in the US. This has led to lower control of the regulatory bodies on the overall system. Another enduring phenomenon is the intensification of the "intraday smile" trading pattern. These patterns in trading volumes exhibit even sharper spikes during the morning hours.

Institutional players like Citadel Securities have warned regulators about underappreciated risks in the transition to 24/7 trading ecosystems (Reuters, 2025). The firm's 2024 alert to the SEC highlighted critical gaps in settlement systems, liquidity fragmentation, and cybersecurity threats as markets extend beyond traditional hours. The risks exacerbated by the same retail trading boom that fuelled GameStop's volatility ((Massa, 2024)).

2. POST-PANDEMIC VOLATILITY – THE CHANGING PARADIGM

The financial and economic landscape in the aftermath of the COVID-19 pandemic evidenced a tectonic shift (He, Liu, Wang, & Yu, 2020). An increased volatility across markets and across geographies seems to be the "new normal". Market volatility today is no longer contingent only on economic cycles or isolated geopolitical events. The volatility seems to be a systemic feature of the financial markets. This shift was caused by factors such as the absence of coherent and unidirectional global economic policies, the continuous and unpredictable nature of technological disruption, and the growing influence of new types of market participants like retail traders and algorithmic investors and proliferation of new trading patterns like High Frequency Tradings (HFTs) and Zero Day Option Trading (0DTE). Volatility metrics reflect the changing trend. For instance, the CBOE Volatility Index (VIX), averaged around 15.1 in during 2015-2019 rising to 21.4 since 2020 till mid May 2025. It rose to 85 on 18th March 2020, 65 on 5th Aug 2024, and 60 on 7th April 2025 (levels not seen post 2008-09 GFC) and took the markets by surprise (CBOE,2024). Similar trends have been observed across geographies, both in equity and debt markets.

For example, the Nasdaq Composite experienced five corrections and three bear markets between 2020 and April 2025. Equivalently, European bond markets experienced yields fluctuating wildly in 2022–2023 during ECB policy changes. The CSI 300 index in China reached its highest level of quarterly volatility in more than a decade in late 2023 due to fears of deflation. The most recent example has been the effect of rising trade tensions. The U.S. Inflation Reduction Act tariffs rattled the markets. The countermeasures by China and the EU created an uncertain for manufacturing industries with a global supply chain run. Nifty 50 and Sensex in India experienced greater volatility after 2021. 30-day volatility of Nifty 50 averaged 13.2 for the period 2015-2019, while it increased to 16.1 since 2020 until mid-May 2025. Hence it could be concluded that high volatility was the new normal.

2.1 Rise of the Nationalist Governments and Economic Fragmentation

In the recent years it has been observed that countries across the globe have been impacted by policies favouring deglobalisation. According to Rodrik (2020) this can be attributed to increasing job losses resulting in inequality and job losses. This is because low skilled workers are impacted more than high skilled workers (Heckscher & Ohlin, 1991/1933). This led to policies like the U.S. CHIPS Act and the EU's Carbon Border Adjustment Mechanism. Governments across the globe seemed to show moderate to extreme traces of xenophobia. They include "America First" in the United States and "Atmanirbhar Bharat" in India. According to the IMF (2023), new trade restrictions have raised global trade costs by approximately 1.2% annually since the start of the pandemic. Concurrently, regional fiscal concerns have driven market volatility, as seen in 2022-2023 when Italian bond yields rose significantly due to investor fears over fiscal deviation under Prime Minister Meloni's government. These nationalist tendencies are evident in policy changes that gravitate towards trade restrictions, industrial subsidies, capital controls, and localization mandates. The global value chains are hence at risk of being disrupted. Thus, cross-border trades and investments are predicted to dwindle. Recently, post Trump Tariff announcement on 2nd April 2025, WTO in its 16th April report said that volume of world merchandise trade is expected to decline by 0.2% in 2025 under then conditions, which is nearly three percentage points lower than the baseline scenario.

2.1.1 Stagflation in the West vs. Deflation in China

Countries were wary of China flooding its goods and hence responded by trying to curb the inflow of Chinese goods. For instance, India implemented trade barriers on Chinese components. The focus was particularly on the electronics and telecommunications sector citing national security concerns. On the other hand, the United States imposed restrictions on technology transfers to Chinese firms. The decoupling of the US-China economic relationship threatens to impact the global economy adversely. On one hand, it raised costs and caused supply-side inflation in the consuming countries; and on the other hand, it impacted supply chain reliability. This led to higher risks and this risk had to be discounted in the valuations and hence had a direct impact on the financial markets.

Western economies especially EU faced stagflation post-pandemic. This was followed by increasing interest rates. China was facing the longest period of deflation since the 1990s, with a broad measure of economy-wide prices falling for five straight quarters through June.

Blanchard et al. (2022) attribute Western stagflation to supply-chain reconfiguration costs. On the other hand, China's deflation stems from a property crisis. The Fed's 2022–2023 rate hikes (from 0% to 5.5%) and Quantitative Tightening via Balance Sheet reduction (US Fed Assets reduced by 25% since April 2022 from US 8.9tn to US 6.7tn at April 2025 end), contrasted with the PBOC's easing via a mix of cuts in Interest Rate and Reserve Requirements, targeted sector support, financial markets stability etc. This divergence led carry-trade volatility (BIS Annual Report, 2023).

Hence it created conflicting macroeconomic environments. In the West, investors priced in aggressive tightening. However, in China, deflation risks led to an accommodative monetary policy (TOI Business Desk, 2025). This led to decoupling between larger economies and hence resulted in higher volatility.

2.1.2 Fiscal Extravagance and Its Monetary Fallout

The period post-COVID-19 saw divergent growth in GDP (International Monetary Fund [IMF], 2023). Governments around the world lay impetus on stimulus packages to bring the economy back on track. The U.S. fiscal stimulus ($8 trillion) between 2020 and 2022 elevated debt-to-GDP to 130% by 2023 from 100% at 2018 end and Fed Balance Sheet as % of GDP widening to 36.5% mid 2022 from 19.5% at 2018 end. Auerbach et.al. (2022) show that such a stimulus worsened inflation persistence. This had a negative impact on the Fed's inflation fight as the government became highly leveraged. High public debt levels raised long-term concerns about fiscal sustainability, US Dollar stability and its Reserve Currency status. Hence, the regulators were grappling with the old age conundrum how to control inflation without arresting growth.

The regulators in the USA resorted to higher interest rate regime. There was a marked departure from the regime where interest rates hovered around 0 percent. By July 2023, interest rate in US was almost touching 5.5 percent. This impacted the growth rate of the economy. On the other hand, the People's Bank of China (PBOC) maintained a dovish stance. This led to decoupling effect. Moreover, it stroked speculative carry trades. It led CNY to depreciate vis -a-vis USD during 2022 so as to ensure its export remained competitive. Hence, as a result the global debt market became highly unpredictable.

2.1.3 Role of the Inflation Reduction Act and Protectionist Measures

The U.S. Inflation Reduction Act (IRA) of 2022 was aimed at climate goals. However, it triggered a global race in industrial policy. It offered massive subsidies for clean energy and electric vehicles. This move is drawing investment away from Europe and Asia. Other economies responded with similar measures and created a subsidy war distorting capital allocation. It also reduced trade cooperation and hence resulted in fiscal deficits making economies more vulnerable.

Protectionist tariffs have been introduced on a few sectors such as steel, semiconductors, and green technologies. This has raised costs and hence caused higher inflation in countries relying on imports. These measures increased geopolitical risk premiums. Thus, they contribute to equity and commodity market volatility.

2.1.4 Divergent Central Bank Policies

Central banks pursued increasingly divergent strategies in response to their domestic macro environments. The Fed raised rates to 5.5% by mid-2023 (Federal Reserve, 2023). It was followed by the European Central Bank (ECB) Deposit Rate hike from Negative 50bps in 2022 to 4% by 2023 end, walking on a tightrope between inflation control and recession fears. Meanwhile, the PBOC (China) has since 2021 end, cut interest rates (1-year Prime Rate by 75bps to 3.1%), reduced reserve requirements for banks from 12.5% to 9% and injected liquidity US c650bn to counter its deflationary spiral.

These divergences distorted currency markets. It also caused capital flight from emerging economies Consequently, it altered risk-reward dynamics for global investors. The resulting reallocation of capital led to frequent market swings. The segments that were impacted more than the others included foreign exchange, commodities, and sovereign debt markets. The policy gap between central banks widened exchange-rate volatility. This led to emerging markets facing $65bn capital outflows in 2023.

2.1.5 Increase in Private Wealth and Rising Inequality

The period post-COVID-19 up to 2024 saw a northward movement in most pro-risk asset prices. Hence, between 2020 and 2024, global private wealth rose significantly. According to the Allianz Global Wealth Report 2024, private household financial assets grew by 7.6% in 2023. This exhibited a recovery from a previous decline. On the other hand, UBS reported a 4.2% increase in global wealth in 2023. Subsequently, real wealth grew by 8.4% due to easing inflation. The number of high-net-worth individuals (HNWIs) also rose. It peaked at 22.8 million globally. India alone added $590 billion in financial wealth in 2023. Hence, the asset market strengthened, and economic resilience was fuelled on the back of the global rise in private wealth. The wealth divide created a bifurcated market. Retail investors engaged in speculative trading without adequate risk buffers. This fuelled rallies, which were more volatile. Furthermore, specific asset classes such as cryptocurrencies and small-cap equities saw intermittent crashes in the market. This inequality translates into asymmetric market behaviour.

2.2. Supply-Side Complexities

Supply-side complexity was marked by the influx of loss-making high-visibility startups. This introduced asymmetry into market behaviour. There was a divorce between value and price. Hence, valuation signals became unreliable. This led to sharp corrections when expectations recalibrated, increased volatility and distorted capital allocation.

2.2.1 Listing of Loss-Making Startups with Brand Recall

The post-pandemic bull market facilitated the listing of numerous high-profile startups globally. In countries such as India, for the first time, loss-making companies were allowed to list through the QIB route. This restricted retail participation. The IPO of unprofitable firms (e.g., Zomato) reflected "narrative-driven valuations" (Gennaioli et al., 2023, JF). In Europe, similar trends were observed. Firms like Deliveroo in the UK and Auto1 in Germany got listed with a lot of fanfare. Deliveroo saw 60% post-IPO drops (LSEG, 2023). These companies lacked sustainable earnings despite huge brand recognition and witnessed sharp share prices decline post-listing, like their counterparts across the world. This led to global risk aversion and renewed importance of fundamental driven valuations. Subsequently heightened secondary market volatility was witnessed particularly in tech-heavy indices. This wave of underperformance highlighted the weakness in sentiment-driven valuations. It raised broader questions about the efficacy of listing frameworks during periods of speculative exuberance. Hence it eroded investor confidence in new listings and widened the gap between perceived innovation and actual profitability. The decoupling of valuations from fundamentals created bubbles prone to sudden corrections.

2.2.2 Zero-Commission Trading Platforms

Platforms like Robinhood, Zerodha, and Webull eliminated transaction costs. This led to democratizing access to financial markets. For instance, Robinhood's gamification increased retail trading by 300% (FINRA, 2023) on one hand. On the other hand, it amplified meme-stock volatility (Cong et al., 2022). This encouraged high-frequency speculative behaviour. One notable example was GameStop, whose stock skyrocketed from US 4.8 per share at Dec 2020 end to US 120 per share on 28th Jan 2021 as retail investors on Robinhood and other commission-free platforms fuelled a short squeeze (Cong et al., 2021; U.S. Securities and Exchange Commission (SEC), 2021). This class of retail investors often, without fully understanding the underlying fundamentals, put their money on meme stocks. This demonstrated pitfalls of viral, sentiment-driven trading in the digital age. Social Networks like Reddit and Wallstreetbets acted as a platform for the viral discussions and momentum thereafter. Retail investors engaged in momentum and herd-driven trades. Hence, they amplified volatility during earnings seasons, macro data releases or holiday inspired less volume days. Subsequently Zero-commission trading also changed institutional strategies. Market makers and hedge funds began exploiting retail flow data. This led to feedback loops that intensified price swings.

2.2.3 Rise of Riskier Products – 0DTE Options and Derivatives Mania

The proliferation of complex derivative instruments such as zero-day-to-expiry (0DTE) options introduced a new dimension of intraday volatility. By late 2024, 0DTE options accounted for nearly 40% of S&P 500 options volume. (CBOE, 2024). These tools were designed for hedging. However, this intensified intraday swings via gamma squeezes. Thus, market makers' hedging of call options created violent feedback loops in intraday trading (Avellaneda & Lipkin, 2023). However, later, these products became tools for speculative betting on short-term price movements. This rise in speculative derivatives distorted price discovery. Large intraday option volumes forced underlying asset prices to move in response to gamma hedging (i.e. other way round from the ideal investing scenario). Traditional valuation metrics became less reliable. As a result, blue-chip stocks experienced wild price swings unrelated to fundamentals.

2.2.4 Increased Linkages and Global Risk Transmission

Global financial markets became increasingly interconnected. Events in one geography immediately impact asset prices globally. ETFs, algorithmic trading, high-frequency strategies and technology evolution like blockchain ensured that risk transmission was near-instantaneous. Increased interdependence meant that risk events were no longer contained within regions. Contagion effects became more common. This led to synchronized drawdowns and greater volatility in diversified portfolios.

2.2.5 Elevated Valuations and Macroeconomic Uncertainty

Despite macro headwinds, equity valuations especially in U.S. tech remained elevated. The S&P 500's P/E ratio consistently hovered above historical averages. U.S. retail trading peaked at 25% of volume (FINRA, 2023). This was attributed to pandemic days savings and government led fiscal transfers (Baker et al., 2020). Investors betting on growth had to contend with rising interest rates at the back of declining earnings revisions coupled with global demand uncertainty.

This environment created an unstable equilibrium where any deviation from expectations (e.g., disappointing guidance, rate surprises) triggered sharp corrections. The narrow market leadership by a few mega-cap stocks added fragility. While, broader indices masked underlying weakness in smaller components.

2.3. Demand-Side Idiosyncrasies: Retail Frenzy and Democratized Speculation

The pandemic-induced lockdowns, combined with fiscal transfers and mobile-first brokerage platforms, resulted in a massive influx of retail traders. India saw a fourfold increase in Demat accounts. In the U.S. retail participation peaked at 25% of daily equity volume in 2021 and remained high through 2024. (FINRA, 2024).

Retail investors became key drivers of liquidity, especially in small-cap and thematic stocks. However, their lack of experience and short-term orientation made them susceptible to trends and social media hype.

2.3.1 Behavioural Biases and Misjudgement

Retail traders frequently exhibited cognitive biases which included overconfidence, confirmation bias, loss-aversion bias and recency effects. These led to irrational decision-making as the market was highly volatile. Many failed to understand the risk-return trade-offs of leveraged instruments, derivative exposure, or illiquid assets.

Behavioural missteps were further amplified by the echo chambers of social media. Influencers, YouTubers, and Reddit threads often displaced professional analysis. Hence, impetus shifted to price rather than value.

2.3.2 Meme Stocks, Cryptocurrencies, and the Valuation Dilemma

After 2020, the influence of social media on investment decision increased manifold. Influencers would predict the increase in prices of stocks such as GameStop and AMC Entertainment on social media platforms. This would lead to increase in the price of stocks as a result of frenzy buying from retail buyers through platforms such as Robinhood. These investors were famously called Robinhood investors and the stocks were termed meme stocks. As a result of the herd mentality and irrational exuberance markets moved away from intrinsic value. The same was observed in other classes of assets. Case in the point, was the cryptocurrencies. Even though it was very difficult to determine their value in the future as they did not have strong fundamentals, the prices remained high. In the case of bitcoins and Ethereum institutional investors spiked the demand. On the other had a few cryptocurrencies such as altcoins rode on the wave of unanticipated speculative demand. This led to markets witnessing all time high volatility. Hence, the task of balancing portfolios and aligning to their investment objectives became tougher. The period where investors panicked due to increased volatility was termed as crypto winters. The period recorded double digit losses. This was more evident during crypto winters in 2022-2023, a period that saw sustained double-digit losses across cryptocurrencies. It saw the collapse of Terra. This led to 60-billion-dollar value loss in market capitalisation due to Terra losing it USD peg (De Blasis et al., 2023). However, market experts believe that going forward institutionalisation of cryptocurrencies can help relatively stabilise the markets.

2.3.3 Leveraged Retail Investments and Risk Amplification

There are two reasons why investors end up taking unreasonably high risk. Firstly, the ease with which the margin loans are available. Secondly, complicated financial instruments and financial tools which allow investors to increase their exposure to loans. When markets fall, it has been observed that margin calls lead to a forced liquidation which steepens the fall. On the other hand, every rise leads to overconfidence of investors which in turn sees increased leveraged positions. Hence, as a result of leverage effect on the stocks it has been observed that the markets become highly volatile. The fragility of this ecosystem was most evident in events like the collapse of Terra-LUNA or FTX. These events led to millions of retail investors losing significant capital.

2.4 Outcome

To conclude, the increased volatility that has been observed off late can be attributed to nationalist induced macroeconomic policies leading to decisions which may not be economically sound. Moreover, increased direct retail participation along with herd mentality of the retail investors adds fuel to the fire. The market hence seems to have moved in uncharted area. Traditionally volatility in the market was attributed to primarily two factors - asset bubbles and policy missteps. However, the same is being blamed to factors mentioned above. Hence, as a result we have a market which is idiosyncratic and difficult to predict. Hence, a major rethinking is required both by regulators and financial exchanges on how to ensure stability going forward.

3. CRACKS IN THE MARKET INFRASTRUCTURE

Over the years the modern financial market infrastructure has become highly sophisticated and complex at the same time. Hence critical vulnerabilities such as regulatory gaps, technological complexity, and lack of transparency in trading mechanisms needs to be addressed urgently. Hence, the level of risk has increased exponentially.

This section examines four key areas where market infrastructure is faltering. It includes regulatory misalignment, opacity in modern trading, tech-driven turbulence, and leveraged innovation.

3.1. Regulatory Misalignment

Financial markets today have regulations which are inconsistent across jurisdictions. This leads to regulatory arbitrage. Hence, it helps market participants exploit differences in rules to gain an advantage. This may at times lead to systemic instability.

3.1.1 Lack of Coordinated Oversight Across Major Markets

The global nature of financial markets means that risks in one jurisdiction can quickly spill over into others. However, regulatory bodies such as the U.S. Securities and Exchange Commission (SEC), the European Securities and Markets Authority (ESMA), and the Financial Conduct Authority (FCA) in the UK often operate with divergent frameworks. For instance, while the U.S. imposes strict position limits on commodity derivatives, EU regulations were more lenient. They allowed traders to shift activities to less restrictive markets.

3.1.2 Fragmented Rules and Systemic Arbitrage

Fragmentation also enabled hedge funds and high-frequency trading (HFT) firms to engage in regulatory arbitrage. Basis trades exploited the pricing discrepancies between Treasury futures and cash bonds, leading to increased leverage in unseen ways. These transactions were often conducted in jurisdictions with the least regulatory oversight. This behaviour distorted market pricing and reportedly had serious implications. In April 2025 US Treasury rout led to spike in the yield post Trump's Liberation Day tariff announcement. The 2020 Treasury market turmoil is also an apt example. In this case, the hedge funds faced massive margin calls on basis trades. Thus, demonstrating how regulatory misalignment can amplify crises.

3.2. Opacity in Modern Trading

The rise of dark pools, internalization, and complex derivatives has eroded traditional price discovery mechanisms. Hence markets became more susceptible to sudden dislocations.

3.2.1 Dark Pools and Internalizers

Dark pools—private trading venues that do not publicly display orders—account for nearly 15% of U.S. equity volume. On one hand, they provide anonymity for large institutional trades. On the other hand, they also fragment liquidity and obscure true market prices. Retail brokers increasingly route orders to wholesalers like Citadel Securities (Ripple Labs Inc., 2025). This, in turn, internalizes trades rather than executing them on public exchanges. This practice, while cost-efficient, undermines transparency and can lead to worse execution prices for investors.

3.2.2 Basis Trades and Treasury Market Distortions

The U.S. Treasury market has seen growing distortions due to basis trades. Hedge funds borrow heavily in the repo market to exploit tiny pricing gaps between Treasury futures and the underlying bonds. However, these trades rely on stable funding conditions. Forced unwinds can trigger fire sales when repo rates spike. The September 2023 Treasury liquidity crunch underscored these vulnerabilities as yields swung violently despite no major macroeconomic news.

3.3. Tech-Driven Turbulence

The proliferation of algorithmic and AI-driven trading has introduced new forms of market instability, including flash crashes and self-reinforcing feedback loops.

3.3.1 AI-Based Quant and Algo Trading Models

Quantitative funds of late dominate trading. This can be attributed to machine learning models parsing vast datasets to execute strategies at microsecond speeds. Many AI models rely on similar data signals. This, in turn, leads to crowded trades. When these models simultaneously react to the same trigger, such as an unexpected Fed statement, they can exacerbate market moves and may cause deviation of asset prices away from their fundamental values.

3.3.2 Flash Crashes and Volatility Loops

Over the years High-frequency trading (HFT) has increased in financial markets. This proved beneficial for the market as it helped improve liquidity on one hand and tightened the bid ask spread when the markets were trading in charted area. However, there was an observation about the behaviour of high frequency traders that unnerved the regulator. In stressed markets, when the market needed liquidity the HFT traders would withdraw their money. This was by design and was directed at controlling the risk. This alleviated volatility and hence led to steeper downturns in the market. The 2022 "UK Gilts Crisis" serves as an apt case study. In this case, algorithmic trading strategies contributed to a self-reinforcing downward spiral in UK government bond prices. As pension funds faced margin calls on liability-driven investments (LDIs), HFT algorithms interpreted the selling pressure as a signal to reduce market-making activity. This created a liquidity vacuum that pushed yields higher in a destructive feedback loop. This forced the Bank of England to intervene with emergency bond purchases to stabilize the market (Bank for International Settlements, 2023).

Such episodes demonstrate how technology-driven markets can enter dangerous doom loops. Here, automated selling triggers more selling. Subsequently, human intervention became the only circuit breaker. The problem is compounded by the fact that many HFT algorithms are trained on historical data. It should be noted that historical data may not account for extreme stress scenarios. This may cause them to behave unpredictably during crises. Markets are becoming increasingly dominated by algorithmic trading. Hence, regulators must develop new tools to ensure liquidity provision during periods of stress. This potentially obliges market makers to maintain activity during volatility spikes or circuit breakers that temporarily halt algorithmic trading during disorderly markets. The very technologies designed to make markets more efficient may render them more fragile when tested by significant shocks.

3.4. Leveraged Innovation and Investor Exposure

Financial engineering has produced complex products that amplify risks for unsophisticated investors. These include leveraged ETFs and crypto derivatives.

3.4.1 Inverse and Leveraged ETFs

Leveraged and inverse exchange-traded funds (ETFs) represent one of the most misunderstood yet widely available financial products for retail investors. These complex instruments use derivatives and debt to amplify daily returns, which are either positively (leveraged) or negatively (inverse) relative to their underlying benchmarks. The critical feature that many investors fail to grasp is that these products reset their exposure daily. In other words, their long-term performance can diverge dramatically from the actual performance of the reference assets. It is especially true during the volatile market times. This is because the base effect works against the value of the leveraged ETF.

A white paper by the CFA Institute (2023) revealed alarming gaps in investor understanding. According to the paper, many retail participants mistakenly believe these products offer simple, long-term leveraged exposure. The daily reset mechanism, coupled with compounding effects, can lead to unexpected outcomes. This is true particularly in volatile markets. For instance, a triple-leveraged ETF tracking oil prices might lose value even if oil prices rise over an extended period. This can be attributed to the effects of volatility drag on the daily rebalancing. For example, since Feb 19th 2025 close until 14th May 2025, Nasdaq 100 ETF QQQ, declined by 3.72% (after intermittently declining by more than 20% and sharp recovery thereafter), its 3x Leveraged ETF TQQQ declined -21.9% during the same period.

The dangers became starkly apparent in 2023 when several triple-leveraged oil ETFs collapsed during a period of extreme commodity price swings. These products promised 3x the daily return of crude oil futures. However, in contrast, they suffered catastrophic losses that exceeded what many investors anticipated. The episode highlighted how embedded leverage can magnify losses just as easily as it can amplify gains, with the added risk of complete product liquidation during extreme market moves.

Regulators have grown increasingly concerned about these products being marketed to unsophisticated investors without adequate risk disclosures. Unlike traditional ETFs that track indices over time, leveraged products are designed strictly as short-term trading instruments. Their performance over weeks or months can bear little resemblance to the underlying assets' performance, creating potential for significant investor harm. Financial innovation continues to produce increasingly complex products. Hence, there is a need for better investor education. Moreover, prominent risk warnings so as to prevent similar disasters in the future is the need of the hour.

3.4.2 Perpetual Swaps and Crypto Volatility

The rise of perpetual swaps in cryptocurrency trading created a dangerous environment where retail investors can access unprecedented levels of leverage. It often amounted upto 100x their initial margin. These derivative instruments mimic traditional futures contracts but without expiration dates, have become particularly hazardous due to their combination of extreme leverage and the inherently volatile nature of crypto markets. Unlike regulated traditional financial markets, most crypto trading platforms operate without fundamental safeguards like circuit breakers or position limits. Thus, leaving traders exposed to sudden, catastrophic losses.

For example, the March 2024 Bitcoin flash crash is an apt example of how uncontrolled leverage can impact the market negatively. Bitcoins saw a fall of 30 percent in the prices in a few hours. This led to $5 billion in leveraged positions being automatically liquidated across exchanges (Young, 2024). Hence, this led to markets getting into a spiral. With every decline there was more margin calls, leading to unwinding of positions which led to further decline. The worst part was that the crypto currency exchanges did not halt transactions as is the case with traditional markets. Hence, crypto exchanges continued operating normally leading to higher losses.

Several structural issues make these events particularly dangerous:

- Many retail traders underestimate the risks of high leverage, lured by the potential for outsized gains

- Liquidation mechanisms often fail during extreme volatility, leaving traders unable to close positions or provide additional margins.
- The cross-exchange nature of crypto markets means liquidations on one platform can impact prices globally

These conditions create a perfect storm where novice investors can lose their entire position and potentially more, in cases of negative balance, within minutes. While some jurisdictions have begun implementing leverage limits, the global and decentralized nature of crypto trading means these protections remain inconsistent at best. Until comprehensive, internationally coordinated regulations are established, these periodic wipeouts will likely continue to be a routine feature of crypto derivatives markets.

3.5 Outcome

The cracks in today's market infrastructure represent growing fault lines that threaten global financial stability. These vulnerabilities are particularly concerning because they often operate beneath the surface of traditional oversight mechanisms. It allows risks to accumulate undetected until they erupt into full-blown crises. The 2023-2024 period alone has demonstrated how quickly localized stresses cascade into systemic disruptions. It has been evidenced in crypto markets, Treasury liquidity, or algorithmic trading.

The current fragmented regulatory landscape exacerbates these risks. Hence, it creates opportunities for arbitrage while leaving critical gaps in supervision. Dark pools and internalizers distort price discovery. On the other hand, AI-driven trading models and leveraged products amplify volatility and market momentum in unpredictable ways. In the meantime, the rapid growth of decentralized finance and cross-border digital assets has outpaced the development of corresponding safeguards. Without coordinated reforms, these structural weaknesses could trigger the next financial crisis. One that may originate in the shadows of modern finance rather than the traditional banking sectors.

Addressing these challenges requires more than incremental adjustments. It demands a fundamental rethinking of market oversight for the digital age. This includes harmonizing international regulations, enhancing transparency across all trading venues, and implementing dynamic risk controls for algorithmic systems. This would, in turn, result in establishing robust safeguards against excessive leverage. Critically, these reforms must be implemented through collaborative frameworks. The frameworks recognize the interconnected nature of modern finance.

The path forward is clear. The regulators should proactively strengthen the financial system's foundations. In case they feel compelled to do so, they will be forced to react to crises emerging from today's blind spots. The choice between prevention and damage control will determine whether the next decade is marked by financial stability or recurring disruptions. The time for coordinated action is now before market infrastructure cracks widen into chasms.

4. RESILIENCE FRAMEWORK FOR THE NEXT FINANCIAL DECADE

The resilience of global financial systems in the coming decade is contingent on real-time, anticipatory tools. These tools should adequately discount for the structural complexity of 21st-century finance. Traditional indicators and siloed institutional frameworks have proven insufficient to forecast or contain systemic shocks. This can be attributed to the lack of understanding of risks emanating from emerging technologies, geopolitical shifts, and decentralized financial structures (Caldara, 2022). The following pillars lay the foundation for a next-generation resilience architecture. The new gen architecture is not just reactive as predecessors. It is actively adaptive to evolving risks.

4.1. Real-Time, Risk-Adjusted Volatility Indexes

Volatility remains the most immediate signal of financial stress. However, conventional tools like the VIX are losing relevance. The VIX was originally designed to measure short-term volatility in U.S. equity markets (FRED Blog, 2025.). However, the VIX has repeatedly failed to reflect broader systemic pressures. The failure is more pronounced outside equities and the U.S. market. In 2024, during the U.S. regional banking tremors in the aftermath of the Silicon Valley Bank (SVB) failure, the VIX remained relatively muted. In contrast, the credit default swap (CDS) spreads on mid-tier banks surged (The Economist, 2024). This was coupled with crypto markets experiencing significant deleveraging. Such discrepancies underscore the urgent need for more granular, real-time. The answer to this can be risk-adjusted volatility measures (Hull & White, 2023). These would incorporate data from multiple asset classes. The metrics included bid-ask spreads, margin leverage in ETFs, and correlations under stress scenarios. Institutions like the Bank of England and the ECB have piloted composite indexes integrating liquidity strain, derivative leverage, and cross-asset contagion (Giles, 2025). MSCI has already launched dashboards to flag early warning signals. This is done by detecting co-movements between EM debt and global bond ETFs during the 2024 EM sell-off. Co-movements between EM debt and global bond ETFs during the 2024 EM sell-off have been detected. This approach calls for a paradigmatic shift from static, backward-looking indicators to dynamic risk mitigation tools. These seismograph-like tools detect financial pressure building beneath the surface before it erupts. The next generation of volatility indexes must reflect a multidimensional and multi-asset view of global risk. This would, in turn, help bridge gaps across fragmented markets and technological infrastructures.

4.2. Standardized Cross-Border Stress Tests

Stress testing has become a regulatory mainstay since the 2008 global financial crisis. However, its current implementation remains too narrow, old fashioned and bank-centric (Financial Stability Board, 2024). Basel III reforms improved banks' capital buffers. Nevertheless, modern financial crises often originate from beyond traditional banking institutions in asset managers, clearinghouses, ETFs, and even digital custodians. The interconnectedness of today's financial architecture requires a broader, standardized, cross-border stress testing regime. In 2023–24, events such as the liquidity freeze in U.S. Treasuries and the failure of a major Asian crypto custodian demonstrated how non-bank entities could trigger systemic tremors. In response, the Financial Stability Board (FSB) and IOSCO have advanced discussions on a Global Stress Testing Protocol (GSTP). This would simulate financial shocks, geopolitical tensions, cyberattacks, and climate-related events across jurisdictions. The ECB has already begun integrating climate risk into its supervisory models. On the other hand, IMF is pushing for resilience audits for emerging markets with high foreign debt exposure (IMF, 2023). Prominently, this new generation of stress tests must also examine transmission channels such as rehypothecation in shadow banking or collateral strains in repo markets to prevent the buildup of hidden systemic risks. Transparency of results, cross-jurisdictional data sharing, and regulatory harmonization are essential to ensuring these tests enhance market trust without compromising proprietary intelligence.

4.3. Blockchain-Powered Market Transparency Tools – The Way Ahead

Blockchain and Distributed Ledger Technology (DLT), initially associated with cryptocurrencies, are now central to discussions on modernizing financial market infrastructure (BIS Annual Report, 2023). Their potential lies not in price speculation but in delivering auditability, speed, and trust. DLT enables real-time settlement through smart contracts, reducing counterparty risk and significantly improving post-trade efficiency. In 2024, several initiatives demonstrated this potential. Project Guardian in Singapore, Project Helvetia in Switzerland, and JPMorgan's Onyx platform all showed that tokenized settlements can lower transaction costs and enhance real-time oversight (Bloomberg, 2024). Notably, the Hong Kong Monetary Authority conducted successful pilots issuing tokenized green bonds. This showed how DLT could expand fractional ownership and embed regulatory compliance directly into assets. The benefits are clearly translating into continuous auditability, fraud reduction, and improved collateral management. However, the path to full-scale adoption remains obstructed. Main causes include fragmented regulation, lack of legal clarity, and cyber risks Coordination across jurisdictions is essential. More so in the case of cross-chain interoperability and smart contract governance. The establishment of a global DLT standards board under the BIS or FSB could ensure security, resilience, and regulatory alignment as tokenized finance becomes mainstream. DLT risks would not be able to provide for the opacity of earlier financial innovations without structural changes advocated above (Swiss National Bank, 2024).

4.4. AI-Powered Monitoring Infrastructure – The Double-Edged Sword

Artificial Intelligence (AI) has already begun transforming financial surveillance. The same has been achieved by offering unprecedented precision in detecting manipulation and systemic build-up ((Guo & Tian, 2024), In 2024, Nasdaq's AI models pre-emptively flagged thousands of anomalous trades linked to meme-stock volatility. On the other hand, the UK's Financial Conduct Authority deployed machine learning tools to detect ESG greenwashing by analysing fund disclosures. AI's ability to process vast volumes of trading, sentiment, and disclosure data makes it an invaluable tool for regulators and exchanges. However, this utility comes with new and complex risks. Most notably, many AI models, particularly deep learning systems, operate as "black boxes," making their decisions hard to audit. Models trained on biased or outdated data may misclassify benign behaviour as malicious or miss novel manipulations such as flash loan exploits or coordinated digital pump-and-dump schemes. Worse still, bad actors can design trades specifically to exploit vulnerabilities in these models (Financial Stability Board, 2024). AI systems must meet stringent governance standards, including explainability, third-party audits, and ongoing retraining on emergent data so as to ensure trust and accountability. In 2024, the EU's AI Act began regulating high-risk financial algorithms. On the other hand, the SEC proposed new disclosure rules for AI systems used in surveillance and trading (European Commission, 2024). The future lies in hybrid supervision. This combines human judgment with machine precision. Hence, it would help in establishing a global compliance registry for AI models used in financial oversight. Such governance will be critical in ensuring that AI enhances, rather than undermines, systemic stability.

4.5 Outcome

The financial landscape of the 2020s demands fundamentally new approaches to systemic risk management. Traditional tools such as the VIX are not able to adequately provide for the risk arising out of interconnected and technology driven market. On the other hand, stress testing suffers from its limited use. Banking sector primarily resorts to conducting exhaustive stress tests. Going forward it is important to adopt an integrated and proactive approach to risk management. This would include creating a system which is equipped with advanced volatility measurement, comprehensive stress testing, using blockchain to increase transparency and AI equipped Surveillance (Bank for International Settlements., 2023))

Moreover, there exists a need for creating a risk management system that can weather the cross-market risks more effectively. There is a need for a two-pronged system which can handle the impact of multi-assets in one hand and can assess liquidity in the other. However, in order to deploy new technologies successfully, the regulators should be aware of the both the present and future impact of the change. Emerging technologies present both solutions and new challenges. For example, DLT offers transformative potential for market transparency and settlement efficiency. However, its benefits will remain constrained without international standards and regulatory coordination. AI surveillance tools, are powerful and have the ability to transform financial markets. However, the transformation cannot happen without governance checks and balances in order to prevent new forms of algorithmic risk and maintain market integrity.

The success at implementation level depends on two factors. Firstly, the risk management team should be able to work hand in hand with the financial and technological innovators to prevent systemic failures. Hence, there is a need for cooperation among all the three stakeholders- functional experts who introduce new products, technological experts who ensure digitalisation and the regulators who creates a fair playing ground for everyone. Secondly, the changes that are affected by regulators may have a cascading effect if made in silos as the markets are interconnected and any slippages may lead to the contagion effect.

The rate at which financial and technological innovation is taking place has left regulators with no choice but to adapt a proactive approach. Hence, tools and approaches suggested in this chapter would equip the regulator to create an efficient financial system.

5. IMPLEMENTATION ROADMAP: FROM SANDBOXES TO SOVEREIGN STANDARDS

The need of the hour is a robust financial system which is standardised globally. However, at the rate of innovation and digital automation increases creating a ubiquitous and robust system becomes a herculean task. We propose a carefully structured and multi-phased approach which neither comprises stability or growth. The focus of the whole process here should be to prevent systemic failures. Hence, a two-pronged approach could be adopted. Firstly, regulatory sandboxes could be used in order to test the innovative financial products and services in a controlled environment. Secondly. the roll out can be planned in a phased manner. The purpose of this strategy is to reduce systemic risk of innovation and hence balance innovation with stability. The success of this approach hinges on collaboration between the major stakeholders – financial institutions, technology enablement partners and regulators. Financial institutions and technology enablers should use stress test and scenario planning wherever applicable to reduce the contagion risk. The role of risk managers has to be that of a driver steering the process and imbibing the risk management tenets in all parties involved. This would enable a proactive approach and prevent any kind of snowballing effect from impacting the system at large. The regulators also have an important role to play. It has been observed that technological changes often outpace the rate at which regulators introduce regulations, thus planning roll out in phased manner will enable the watchdogs enough time to respond to the changes due to innovations.

Need of the hour is to use Artificial Intelligence based supervision system. Digital ledger system which supports real time recording of transactions using blockchain technology could also be deployed to improve the overall transparency in the markets. This would definitely make the markets more efficient. However, adoption of such technologies inherently may increase the overall risk in the system. Thus, it is advocated that such phased roll outs should be initiated by developed countries. They are better equipped to test these rollouts. Moreover, the investors in these countries are in a position to absorb the risk that arises in such situations. In the case of emerging market emphasis should be paid to increase the cybersecurity standards. The introduction of complicated products should be done in a phased manner. Moreover, the impact on volatility due to introduction of such product should be examined closely. Leveraged positions should be limited on complicated new products. It is also advised to limit retail participation wherever possible.

The success of feedback loops that enables monitoring and continuously strengthening the system is the need of the hour. Feedback systems should exhibit three characteristics. Firstly, real-time monitoring should lead to identifying anomalies and loopholes in the system. There is also a need for impact assessments. Finally, stakeholder engagement ensure that policies remain responsive to evolving market dynamics.

5.1. Global Regulatory Sandboxes

In financial markets, where there are numerous factors impacting the volatility and liquidity of the market there is a need for adopting new policies and technologies in a controlled environment. Off late there has been increase in cross border digital assets. These assets comprise of digital currencies such as bitcoins. Their ability to make cross border payments have increased the riskiness of the markets. The other challenge that exchange faces is to decide the leverage limits for complicated financial markets. These two factors have led to higher volatility in the markets. It has been observed that traditional regulation fails in the above condition. Hence regulatory sandboxes are widely acknowledged as a safe testing grounds when the Exchange and regulators want to proactively adopt new policies and technologies. This allows regulators and market participants to experiment in controlled environments. These sandboxes prove particularly valuable in such situations. Regulatory sandboxes were adopted by the Monetary Authority of Singapore (MAS) and the UK's Financial Conduct Authority (FCA) while testing the stablecoin transactions under the Project Guardian. Sandbox approach was adopted to test the stablecoin transactions. The project evaluated settlement efficiency and liquidity impacts. Similar initiatives have explored volatility caps in crypto derivatives. The European Securities and Markets Authority (ESMA) through sandbox approach affirmed that flash crashes could be prevented without using the traditional route which necessitated restricting liquidity. In commodity futures too, this approach has been used. It has been observed that determining margin requirement is fraught with risk for instruments such as perpetual swaps in commodity futures market. This could be attributed to increase in algo based trading in the segment. This led to The U.S. Commodity Futures Trading Commission (CFTC) has proposed sandbox trials for algorithmic trading firms to determine optimal margin requirements for perpetual swaps.

5.2. Phased Rollout and Feedback Loops

It should be noted that all the financial markets are not equally developed. Following successful sandbox testing, a carefully structured phased implementation became crucial to avoid market disruption. The regulators realise that the rate of implementation of reforms should be directly proportional to the maturity of the market and ability of the investors to absorb risk. Hence, it makes sense to roll out those implementations that are complicated first in countries such as US and UK. This should be followed by a strong feedback mechanism that helps make iterative changes. This tiered approach to adopting was propped by IMF (2023). In countries such as US and UK technological disruptions such as artificial intelligence may be introduced first. On the other hand, developing markets such as India and Brazil should test leverage and volatility control through stress testing. Moreover, countries such as Nigeria and Pakistan should aim at achieving higher level of digital competencies. Hence, the approach would help all countries and prevent systemic failures. Case in the point is the failure of Nigerian crypto exchange that suffered because of conspicuous absence of cybersecurity safeguards. ((Reuters, 2025)) Bank of England successfully evaluated new generation liquidity management tools. ran a pilot on how liquidity could be monitored hence helping the bank by preventing flash crashes.

5.3 Outcome

Globally the implementation roadmap follows a fragmented approach which may not be very useful to support interconnected global financial system. Hence, the two-pronged implementation roadmap that has been envisaged in this chapter can go a long way in improving the system as a whole. At present, the system is a fragmented and reactive system. The need of the hour is a more resilient, future-proof framework. By leveraging global regulatory sandboxes to test innovations in controlled environments and adopting phased rollouts tailored to market maturity levels, policymakers can balance financial stability with technological progress. The integration of robust feedback mechanisms includes real-time liquidity monitoring and dynamic impact assessments. This ensures that regulations remain adaptive to evolving market conditions. However, the success of these reforms ultimately hinges on international cooperation and the establishment of common standards to prevent regulatory arbitrage and systemic vulnerabilities. As financial markets continue to evolve at an unprecedented pace, proactive collaboration among regulators, institutions, and technology providers will be essential in building a financial ecosystem that is both innovative and resilient, one capable of withstanding future shocks while fostering sustainable economic growth. There are a few organizations that oversee financial markets internationally, such as International Organization of Securities Commissions (IOSCO), Financial Stability Board (FSB) but there is not a global financial market regulator or 'Interpol of global Financial/ Securities Market'

The time for decisive action is now, before the next crisis exposes the shortcomings of outdated regulatory paradigms.

6. FROM FRAGMENTATION TO RESILIENCE - BUILDING THE FINANCIAL SYSTEM OF THE FUTURE

The global financial system finds itself at a crossroads. The system faces challenges as a result of increasing innovations. These include continuous technological changes. It is further complicated by 24/7 markets. Off late geopolitical tensions and the mounting impact of climate change has added to the unpredictability of the markets. Markets has also witnessed decreasing liquidity during off-peak hours. This leads to abrupt price swings which in turn results in risk realignments. The cracks in the current system are becoming too big to ignore. For example, the financial architecture is fragmented and dominated by outdated structures. Moreover, the regulators work in silos which amplifies the problems. Regulatory blind spots caused due to inability to provide for changes such as leveraged position through crowd funding, trading environments which lack transparency, and crisis responses by regulators in silos needs to be checked. Hence, overhauling the global financial system is the need of the hour.

6.1 Reimagining the Architecture

This transformation must go beyond patchwork fixes. Hence, the ability to get the bigger picture is the need of the hour. It mandates decentralisation of financial infrastructure. This would in turn avoid single point of failure. However, it is important to ensure that the decentralised system is intricately connected. Traditional regulatory systems are reactive and rule based. However, the need of the hour is an AI based risk aware system.

6.2 Fixing Regulatory Misalignment

The starting point in order to build a robust system is to align the regulatory systems across the globe. Difference in regulations across countries allows for regulatory arbitrage. This may lead to higher levels of systemic risk. Different countries have different rules, which opens the door to regulatory arbitrage and lets systemic risks build up unnoticed. Regulatory bodies across the globe seems to have recognised this anomaly too. For instance, the Financial Stability Board's is recommending global standards for regulatory sandboxes and stress tests. Similarly, the formation of a task force on decentralized finance (DeFi) by the International Organization of Securities Commissions (IOSCO) is a welcome move.

6.3 Shedding Light on Dark Pools

The rise of dark pools and internalizers is a concern. On one had it distorts the price discovery process and on the other had it impacts the trust factor and subsequently the reputation of the company. Traditional transparency measures have struggled to address these points. However, distributed ledger technology (DLT) has a potential to disrupt the traditional system. It facilitates reporting in real-time while maintaining confidentiality. Countries are already piloting DLT-based trade reporting systems. However, the absence of shared data standards across regions limits their impact. but their success will hinge on establishing shared data standards and ensuring systems can communicate across borders and asset classes. The Bank for International Settlements' Unified Ledger Initiative is a promising step in this direction. However, global cooperation is still conspicuously absent.

6.4 Tackling AI and Algorithmic Risks

The risks posed by artificial intelligence and algorithmic trading demand an entirely new approach to market oversight. The "AI Flash Crash" in European markets in 2024 was a wake-up call. It was an example of how interacting algorithms can quickly spiral out of control. A promising solution lies in hybrid human-AI surveillance systems that blend machine learning's pattern recognition with human judgment and oversight. The European Union's AI Act has made explain ability a requirement for such systems, and the U.S. SEC's proposed rules for algorithmic transparency are also a step in the right direction. But here again, global standards will be crucial to avoid regulatory loopholes.

6.5 Rethinking Risk Controls

Complex financial products like perpetual swaps and derivatives with high embedded leverage pose another systemic threat. Static margin requirements often don't cut it during periods of market stress. Innovative approaches such as volatility-adjusted margins tighten automatically when markets get choppy. At present they are being tested in regulatory sandboxes. These dynamic tools can help prevent cascading failures. On the other hand, it still allowing markets to function efficiently in calmer times.

CONCLUSION

Creating a robust financial system cannot be based on a fragmented and static approach to control. It is about weaving together resilience, transparency, and adaptability. It involves adopting a three-pronged strategy. Firstly, be aware of how the markets operates. Secondly develop a system that monitors real time. Thirdly, one should ensure global coordination. The path forward is complex. However, the direction is clear. One needs to focus on standardisation of the processes. Hence, close collaboration between regulators, trading platforms, and clearinghouses needs to be emphasised.

The hidden danger of cybercrime in financial markets lies in penetrating the trading systems of big traditional investors and hedge funds to pass large orders and impact the market. This should also be proactively considered by the regulators across the world.

The envisioned future financial ecosystem should function like a "smart grid" for capital. It should be decentralized yet interconnected with real-time risk adjustments and automatic fail-safes. This analogy captures several key features of the transformed financial system we need to build. Like a modern electrical grid, the financial system of the future should be capable of routing around localized disruptions. It should be equipped to automatically isolate problems before they spread system-wide. It should incorporate distributed energy resources (in this case, distributed liquidity pools and risk-sharing mechanisms).

The choice facing the global financial community is stark. A proactive collaboration to build resilience or continued vulnerability to cascading crises. The roadmap for reform exists. We now have an opportunity to break this pattern by implementing preventative reforms before disaster strikes. The costs of inaction are measured through financial instability, negative wealth effect that can cause recession, constrained economic growth, and lost opportunities for innovation. It far outweighs the challenges of coordinated reform. The time to act is now, before the next crisis forces our hand.

REFERENCES

Auerbach, A., Gorodnichenko, Y., McCrory, P. B., & Murphy, D. (2022). Fiscal multipliers in the COVID-19 recession. *Journal of International Money and Finance, 126*, 102669. DOI: 10.1016/j.jimonfin.2022.102669 PMID: 35601810

Avellaneda, M., & Lipkin, M. (2023). Dynamic hedging and volatility in ETF markets. *Quantitative Finance, 23*(5), 789–805.

Baker, S. R., Bloom, N., Davis, S. J., & Terry, S. J. (2020). COVID-induced economic uncertainty. *NBER Working Paper No. 26983*. DOI: 10.3386/w26983

Bank for International Settlements. (2023). *Annual economic report 2023*. https://www.bis.org/publ/arpdf/ar2023e.htm

Bank for International Settlements (BIS). (2023). *The future of market infrastructure: 24/7 trading risks*. https://www.bis.org/publ/qtrpdf/r_qt2312a.htm

Blanchard, O., Amighini, A., & Giavazzi, F. (2022). *Macroeconomics: A European perspective* (5th ed.). Pearson.

Bloomberg. (2024, June 5). JPMorgan's Onyx platform cuts settlement times with blockchain.

Business Desk, T. O. I. (2025, March 10). Four flash sales in a day! China, world's second largest economy, hit by deflation—here's why economists are worried. *The Times of India*. https://timesofindia.indiatimes.com/business/international-business/four-flash-sales-in-a-day-china-worlds-second-largest-economy-hit-by-deflation-heres-why-economists-are-worried/articleshow/118840941.cms

Caldara, D., & Iacoviello, M. (2022). Measuring geopolitical risk. *The American Economic Review, 112*(4), 1194–1225. DOI: 10.1257/aer.20191823

CBOE Global Markets. (2024). VIX historical data. Retrieved August 6, 2024, from https://www.cboe.com/tradable_products/vix/vix_historical_data/

CFA Institute. (2023). *The hidden risks of leveraged ETFs*.

Cong, L. W., Li, X., Tang, K., & Yang, Y. (2021). Social media and retail trading: Evidence from Robinhood and GameStop. *Science, 373*(6561), 1084–1086.

De Blasis, R., Galati, L., Webb, A., & Webb, R. I. (2023). Intelligent design: Stablecoins (in)stability and collateral during market turbulence. *Financial Innovation, 9*(1), 85. Advance online publication. DOI: 10.1186/s40854-023-00492-4 PMID: 37192905

De Long, J. B., Shleifer, A., Summers, L. H., & Waldmann, R. J. (1990). Noise trader risk in financial markets. *Journal of Political Economy, 98*(4), 703–738. DOI: 10.1086/261703

European Securities and Markets Authority (ESMA). (2024, January 31). *ESMA report on trends, risks and vulnerabilities No. 1, 2024.* https://www.esma.europa.eu/sites/default/files/2024-01/ESMA50-524821-3107_TRV_1-24_risk_monitor.pdf

Financial Industry Regulatory Authority. (2020). *Market activity year-end 2019* [Fact sheet]. https://www.finra.org

Financial Industry Regulatory Authority (FINRA). (2023). *Market activity year-end 2022* [Fact sheet]. https://www.finra.org

Financial Stability Board. (2024). *Global Monitoring Report on Non-Bank Financial Intermediation 2024.* https://www.fsb.org/2024/12/global-monitoring-report-on-non-bank-financial-intermediation-2024/

Giles, M. (2025, July 29). ECB integrates climate risk into Eurozone financial framework. *The Financial Analyst.* https://thefinancialanalyst.net/2025/07/29/ecb-integrates-climate-risk-into-eurozone-financial-framework/

Guest, P. M. (2021). Risk management in financial institutions: A replication. *The Journal of Finance, 76*(5), 2689–2707. DOI: 10.1111/jofi.13063

Guo, R., & Tian, X. (2024). Regulatory transparency and regulators' effort: Evidence from public release of the SEC's review work. *Journal of Accounting Research, 62*(1), 229–273. DOI: 10.1111/1475-679X.12513

He, Q., Liu, J., Wang, S., & Yu, J. (2020). The impact of COVID-19 on stock markets. *Economic and Political Studies, 8*(3), 275–288. DOI: 10.1080/20954816.2020.1757570

Heckscher, E. F., & Ohlin, B. (1991). The Heckscher-Ohlin theory of trade. In H. S. Ellis & L. A. Metzler (Eds.), *International trade: Selected readings* (pp. 75–100). MIT Press. (Reprinted from E. F. Heckscher & B. Ohlin, 1933, *The MIT Press*)

Hennessey, Z. (2021, January 6). Tel Aviv Stock Exchange boasts peak year for 2020. *The Jerusalem Post.* https://www.jpost.com/jpost-tech/tel-aviv-stock-exchange-boasts-peak-year-for-2020-652889

Hull, J., & White, A. (2023). Beyond the VIX: A new approach to measuring financial stress. *Review of Financial Studies, 37*(2), 501–530. DOI: 10.1093/rfs/hhac123

International Monetary Fund (IMF). (2022). *Geoeconomic fragmentation and trade* (World Economic Outlook Report, October 2022). https://www.imf.org/en/Publications/WEO/Issues/2022/10/11/world-economic-outlook-october-2022

International Monetary Fund (IMF). (2023). *Global financial stability report: Geopolitics and financial stability.* https://www.imf.org/en/Publications/GFSR

International Monetary Fund (IMF). (2023). *World economic outlook, October 2023: Navigating global divergences.* https://www.imf.org/en/Publications/WEO/Issues/2023/10/10/world-economic-outlook-october-2023

Kahneman, D., & Tversky, A. (1979). Prospect theory: An analysis of decision under risk. *Econometrica, 47*(2), 263–292. DOI: 10.2307/1914185

Massa, A. (2024, February 12). Citadel Securities says round-the-clock stock trading carries risks. *Bloomberg.* https://www.bloomberg.com/news/articles/2024-02-12/citadel-securities-says-24-7-stock-trading-holds-hidden-risks

Minsky, H. P. (1986). *Stabilizing an unstable economy.* Yale University Press.

Reuters. (2025, April 30). Citadel Securities flags US regulator about 24-hour trading infrastructure risks. *Reuters.* https://www.reuters.com/sustainability/boards-policy-regulation/citadel-securities-flags-us-securities-regulator-about-24-hour-trading-risks-2025-04-30

Reuters. (2025, February 19). Nigeria seeks $81.5 bln in economic losses, back tax from Binance: court document. *Reuters.* https://www.reuters.com/world/africa/nigeria-seeks-815-bln-economic-losses-back-tax-against-binance-court-document-2025-02-19/

Ripple Labs Inc. (2025, May 28). Written input on regulatory sandboxes. U.S. Securities and Exchange Commission. https://www.sec.gov/files/ctf-written-input-ripple-letter-regulatory-sandboxes-052825.pdf

Rodrik, D. (2020). *Why does globalization fuel populism? Economics, culture, and the rise of right-wing populism* (NBER Working Paper No. 27526). National Bureau of Economic Research. DOI: 10.3386/w27526

U.S. Securities and Exchange Commission (SEC). (2021). *Staff report on equity and options market structure conditions in early

Shiller, R. J. (2000). *Irrational exuberance.* Princeton University Press.

Shiller, R. J., Fischer, S., & Friedman, B. M. (1984). Stock prices and social dynamics. *Brookings Papers on Economic Activity, 1984*(2), 457–498. DOI: 10.2307/2534436

Shleifer, A., & Vishny, R. W. (1997). The limits of arbitrage. *The Journal of Finance, 52*(1), 35–55. DOI: 10.1111/j.1540-6261.1997.tb03807.x

Swiss National Bank. (2023). Piloting monetary policy implementation on a DLT-based infrastructure – Issuance of digital SNB Bills (SNB Working Paper 2023-1). https://www.snb.ch

Tax Policy Center. (2023, May 11). *How did the fiscal response to the COVID-19 pandemic affect the federal budget outlook?* Urban Institute & Brookings Institution. https://taxpolicycenter.org/briefing-book/how-did-fiscal-response-covid-19-pandemic-affect-federal-budget-outlook

The Economist. (2024, November 14). Why financial markets are so oddly calm. https://www.economist.com/finance-and-economics/2024/11/14/why-financial-markets-are-so-oddly-calm

Tobin, J. (1969). A general equilibrium approach to monetary theory. *Journal of Money, Credit and Banking*, *1*(1), 15–29. DOI: 10.2307/1991374

Young, M. (2025, September 23). Crypto liquidations hit $1.8B in a day: Final flush or more to come? Cointelegraph. https://cointelegraph.com/news/1-8-billion-leveraged-positions-liquidated-final-flush-more-to-come\

ENDNOTE

1 The data has been accessed from FINRA website. However, as the link is not stable, hence not giving it.

Chapter 12

Analysing the Relationship Between Credit Default Swaps and the Financial Sector in G20 Countries:

Evidence From Asymmetric Causality Test

Niyaz Hasanov
Yelo Bank, Azerbaijan

Mehmet Levent Erdas
https://orcid.org/0000-0001-6594-4262
Akdeniz University, Turkey

ABSTRACT

Credit default swaps (CDS) have an important role in monitoring a country's credit risk. It is essentially accepted as a market-based benchmark for the country's credit risk. CDS spreads are mostly preferred by policy makers as an indicator in economic and financial markets. The purpose of this research is to determine whether there is a relationship between CDS spreads and the financial sector stock market in G20 countries. To this end, the research employs the asymmetric approach to evaluate daily data from 2019 to 2024 using Hatemi-J (2012) test. The findings mostly indicate that there are asymmetric relationships between CDS spreads and financial sector equity markets in G20 countries. Particularly, the findings mostly provide evidence that a positive shock in CDS spreads leads to a negative impact on financial sector

DOI: 10.4018/979-8-3373-3725-8.ch012

stocks markets in developed countries. By helping to understand the relationship between credit risk and equity markets, these findings provide policymakers with important insights for managing financial risks and developing economic strategies.

1. INTRODUCTION

Stock markets are commonly used as major indicators for monitoring economic, commercial and social activities. These indicators are used for measuring, explaining, monitoring and estimating inflation, production, consumer confidence, real exchange rate changes, labour structure and revenues (Bayramoğlu and Pekkaya, 2010). The indicators in financial markets are those that measure the proportional change in prices, costs and sales performance of investment instruments. Reducing complex processes to a single value, these indices are considered important indicators in capital markets. Indices that help rational investors in evaluating the returns of financial assets are mostly used as stock indices. These indicators aim to measure the collective performance of businesses operating in cities and serve as an effective performance indicator for investors (Bayrakdaroglu and Tepeli, 2018).

Stock indices are an important measure for evaluating the economic condition and are virtually the pulse of the economy. Serving as leading indicators of economic recession and recovery processes, these indices affect the general condition of the economy by reflecting expectations. In addition, they are often successful in evaluating structural changes in the economy, so they are an important source of information for investors and analysts (Bosworth et al., 1975). In stock exchanges, indices are calculated on a sectoral basis to meet various demands. Apart from the large economic indices created by companies operating in all areas of the economy, sectoral indices are also created to reflect the unity in the same industry and the same field of activity of a specific sector of the economy. Sectoral indices provide the opportunity to track current conditions and expectations in a particular sector from both an investment and regulatory perspective (Güzel, 2022).

A credit swap spreads (hereafter CDS) is a financial derivative tool that gives an investor to "swap" or offset credit risk with another investor. Specifically, the CDS buyer makes periodic payments to the seller in exchange for protection against the default or other credit events of a third party, known as the reference institution (Kantar, 2020). In the event of a credit event of the reference organisation, the seller pays compensation to the buyer, typically by paying the difference between the par value and the market value of the debt in default. This mechanism helps investors protect against potential losses originating from credit risk (Ergenç and Güneren, 2020).

A CDS is a financial instrument that transfers credit risk from one party to another. The CDS buyer makes ongoing payments to the seller, and the seller, in return, agrees to make payments to the buyer if the reference institution defaults on its debt obligations. This contractual arrangement allows the buyer to be protected against potential losses resulting from credit risk relating to the reference institution (Al-Own et al., 2018).

The purpose of this research is to explore the association between the country risk premium and the financial sector stock market. In this context, country risk premiums and financial sector stock market index data for G20 countries, excluding Russia, were utilised.

The results of this study provide important information in the processes of financial risk management, economic policy development and investment strategy formation. In addition, the study contributes to the understanding of the dynamics in global financial markets by revealing that the relations between CDS spreads and stock market index returns may differ from country to country.

The rest of the study continues as follows: Section 2 presents a brief research background between CDS and stock market. Section 3 provides sources of the data used as well as the methodology. The empirical findings and discussions are given in Section 4. In the last chapter, all results are interpreted and policy recommendations are offered.

2. LITERATURE REVIEW

A review of the literature reveals that there are many studies analysing the relationship between CDS and different economic variables. The most important of these are stock prices, stock market indices, GDP and exchange rates. In addition, the countries selected in the studies examined in the literature may include a single country or data sets that include groups of countries. In this context, the literature review of the studies on CDS premiums will be explained in order.

When the studies investigating the relation between CDS and stock market are examined, it is seen that Fung et al. (2008), Odum (2012), Avşarlıgil and Turgut (2021), Ballester and González (2004-2016), Boussada et al. (2023), Mateev and Marinova (2016), Vashkevich and Basazinew (2013), Gün (2018), Anton and Afloarei (2020), Chan-Lau and Kim (2004), Koy (2015), Zghal et al. (2018), Kiesel, et al. (2016), Forte and Pena (2009), Wang et al. (2023), Coronado et al. (2012) and Şahin and Özkan (2018) mostly found a significant, negative relation or a causal relation between the relevant variables.

When the studies investigating the relation between CDS premiums and stock prices are examined, it is seen that Fung et al. (2008), Norden and Weber (2009), Coronado et al. (2012), Jeanneret (2017), Yang et al. (2018), Mateev and Marinova (2016) and Kutuk and Okur (2020) revealed the existence of a negative and strong correlation between the relevant variables. Kırca et al. (2018) also included BIST in their study. These studies provide comprehensive analyses that investigate the existence of a relationship between CDS and stock market indices and stocks.

The studies summarised above provide important findings on the complex relationships between CDS and stock markets. Understanding these relations is of critical importance in terms of the efficiency of financial markets and risk management. This literature review constitutes the theoretical basis of the study to be conducted specifically for G20 countries. In this context, more detailed explanations of the studies examined are shown in Table 1 below.

Table 1. Research background

Author	Variables/Data	Model	Results
Chan-Lau and Kim (2004)	Daily data of CDS, bond, and stock for Brazil, Bulgaria, Colombia, Mexico, the Philippines, Russia, Türkiye, and Venezuela from March 19, 2001, to May 29, 2003	VAR Model	They asserted that the relation between the US equity market and CDS depends on the credit quality of the underlying reference institution.
Zhu (2006)	Examines the relationship between CDS, stock, and bond markets from 1999 to 2002	Cointegration Test, Granger Causality Test, VECM, and Panel Data Regression	It is shown that stocks lead CDSs and bonds, while CDS premiums also play a leading role for bonds.
Fung et al. (2008)	Spreads based on stock markets created from January 2001 to March 2004 and actual spreads in the CDX. NA.IG and CDX.NA.HY stock markets from April 2004 to December 2007	The Vector Autoregression (Var) Model	It shows that the link between the US stock market and the CDS depends on the credit quality of the underlying reference institution.
Forte and Pena (2009)	Data for CDSs and non-financial firms from North America and Europe with a minimum of 250 observations per company from September 12, 2001, to June 25, 2003	VECM	Empirical analysis indicates that stocks more frequently lead CDSs and bonds in North America and Europe, confirming the leading role of CDSs over bonds.
Coronado et al. (2012)	CDS premiums, bond, and stock prices for European countries	VAR Analysis, Granger Causality Test, and Panel Data Analysis	A negative association is determined between stock returns and CDS and changes in stock prices are found to lead to changes in CDS.
Vashkevich and Basazinew (2013)	Sovereign CDS and stock index markets in East Asia from 2007 to 2011	Merton Model	Shows a dynamic relationship between Asian sovereign CDSs and stock markets from 2007 to 2011.

continued on following page

Table 1. Continued

Author	Variables/Data	Model	Results
Koy (2015)	Daily prices of BIST 100, BIST 30 sector stock markets, and sub-sector stock markets, and Turkish CDS from January 2013 to April 2014	Vector Autoregression (VAR) Model	While stock indices and CDSs affect each other, the effect of stock indices on CDSs is greater than the effect of CDSs on stock indices.
Mateev and Marinova (2016)	Daily data of 5-year CDS and stock prices of firms quated in the Markit iTraxx Europe Index from 2008 to 2016	A Time-Varying Autoregressive Model (TVAR)	The long run relation observed between stock prices and CDSs of European investible companies indicates that there are important relationships between the two segments of the financial market
Kiesel et al. (2016)	CDS and stock markets from 2010 to 2013	Panel Regression	The results suggest that equity markets respond before CDS markets and predict credit events to some degree.
Gün (2018)	Weekly data of CDS spreads and major stock indices for Brazil, Chile, Colombia, the Czech Republic, Mexico, Peru, Poland, Russia, and Türkiye from January 2010 to December 2017	The Vector Autoregression (VAR) Model	They found that changes in stock returns lead to changes in CDS spreads, which suggests that former equity markets are able to predict CDS spreads.
Şahin and Özkan (2018)	CDS, exchange rates, and BIST 100 index from 2012 to 2017	Cointegration Test, Granger Causality Test	Found a bidirectional causality relationship between the BIST 100 index and CDS.
Zghal et al. (2018)	Daily and weekly data of European countries' CDS and sectoral stocks from 2007 to September 2017	Dynamic Conditional Correlation (DCC) Model, Asymmetric DCC-GARCH Model	Demonstrates the presence of a relationship between stock markets and CDSs and that CDSs provide strong protection against stock market fluctuations.
Anton and Afloarei (2020)	Daily data on stock markets and 5-year sovereign CDS spreads in USD	The Vector Autoregression (VAR) Model	The empirical results show that there is a mutual impact relationship between CDSs and stock markets in many countries.
Ballester and González-Urteaga (2020)	Stock markets and 5-year sovereign CDS returns for 14 European countries and the USA from 2004 to 2016	VAR Model	While stock market returns predict government CDS returns, government CDSs also predict volatility in stock returns, proving the connection between the markets.

continued on following page

Table 1. Continued

Author	Variables/Data	Model	Results
Avşarlıgil and Turgut (2021)	CDS and stock closing price data for Brazil, India, South Africa, Indonesia, and Türkiye from April 2015 to March 2019	Vector Error Correction Model (VECM	For India and Türkiye, a short-run causality relationship between stock markets and CDS and a long-run cointegration relationship between CDS and Turkish stock markets are also found.
Boussada et al. (2023)	Daily data of 5-year CDS contracts and stock markets for European countries from the beginning of 2010 to the end of 2017	The Vector Autoregression (VAR) Model	A significant association is found between changes in CDS and stock market returns.
Wang et al. (2023)	Information flow between equity and credit default swap (CDS) markets at the firm level before and after the global financial crisis	VAR	The findings suggest that the speed of adaptation of the CDS market to the changes in the stock market has enhanced since the crisis.

Source: Authors

This summary table provides an overview of the studies in the literature examining the relations between CDS premiums and economic variables. Most of the studies reveal a significant and generally negative relationship between CDS premiums and stock indices and stock prices. These findings provide important contributions to understanding the dynamics of financial markets and the factors that affect the determination of CDS premiums.

3. DATA AND RESEARCH METHODOLOGY

This paper empirically investigates between the CDS spreads and financial sector stock markets for G20 economies. In this study, five years of daily CDS and stock sector indices data for G20 countries (excluding Russia due to the unavailability of CDS data) were used. The data covers the daily closing prices from April 1, 2019, to March 31, 2024. The CDS data and stock index data were retrieved from investing.com database. The variables are calculated by taking the natural logarithm for consistency.

Before the econometric estimation of the model, it is significant to examine the statistical properties of the series used in this study. The descriptive statistics of the variables are shown as follows:

Table 2. Descriptive statistics of the series

Countries	Variables	Mean	Median	Max.	Min.	Std. Dev.	Jar-Bera
Turkiye	CDS	468.93	444.05	906	234.92	138.03	126.07
	BIST Financials	199.5	188.83	323.49	116.04	50.81	104.57
South Korea	CDS	31.95	30.23	76.77	17.94	10.42	239.02
	KOSDAQ Financials	0.85	0.78	2.3	0.3	0.37	541.39
Germany	CDS	13.52	12.02	27.5	8.83	4.25	341.25
	DAX Financial	2565.24	2573.21	3498.17	1604.5	505.62	87.24
USA	CDS	16.59	10.2	69.76	5.46	13.13	621.79
	NYSE Financials	8704.65	8703.75	10702.5	5036.4	1102.15	46.28
France	CDS	23.72	23.01	53.27	15.04	5.5	1165.53
	CAC Financials	885.4	914.05	1141.59	503.42	128.24	122.12
UK	CDS	23.17	23.33	50.21	9.41	8.91	43.71
	FTSE 350 Financial	14301.12	14085.81	18238.77	9087.09	2005.48	24.15
Italy	CDS	119.14	108.59	264.28	61.32	41.15	218.86
	FTSE All Share Financials	12810.45	12633.85	21874.9	7490.39	2588.9	89.81
Brazil	CDS	196.26	194.05	376.53	92.06	53.5	24.41
	Financials (IFNC)	1528.83	1693.5	2346.94	677.89	499.33	131.05
Argentina	CDS	1951.67	1401.51	15380.91	344.37	1685.27	7705.49
	S&P/BYMA Financials	18.93	17.14	49.2	9.04	6.65	535.41
Mexico	CDS	118.8	110.52	309.16	71.36	36.58	3112.58
	S&P/BMV Financials	5.12	4.83	8.86	2.22	1.41	35.84
Canada	CDS	38.28	38.6	42.09	36.26	1.07	85.82
	S&P/TSX Financial	259.62	262.26	341.53	137.26	39.21	28.55
India	CDS	79.19	78.3	95.08	73.37	4.87	1504.04
	S&P BSE Finance	99.37	102.74	127.47	50.57	16.54	178.57
China	CDS	55.08	50.85	134.52	29.09	18.43	176.91
	SZSE Financials	899.31	853.3	1233.08	648.37	156.96	120.44
Japan	CDS	21.73	20.82	47.85	15.42	4.92	1439.59
	Tokyo SE Financials	119.22	119.13	173.54	83.04	13.28	364.93
Saudi Arabia	CDS	69.66	64.13	232.39	46.17	24.27	7823.61
	Diversified Financials	1528.83	1693.5	2346.94	677.89	499.33	131.05
Indonesia	CDS	96.61	88.14	281.26	59.06	31.28	3544.76
	IDX Finance	2.72	0.1	74.83	0.08	4.57	174645.7

continued on following page

Table 2. Continued

Countries	Variables	Mean	Median	Max.	Min.	Std. Dev.	Jar-Bera
Australia	CDS	20.96	18.41	51.74	12.17	6.35	301.89
	S&P/ASX 200 Financials	4249.45	4290.22	5235.99	2131.92	544.02	352.05
South Africa	CDS	239.38	228.9	492.47	156.49	54.35	374.37
	FTSE/JSE Financial 15	896.04	906.5	1238.64	458.13	162.05	41.91

Source: Author calculated from research data

Table 2 presents the descriptive statistics for the series utilized in the empirical analysis. CDS values differ significantly among G20 countries. While developing countries such as Argentina and Türkiye have high CDS values, developed countries such as Germany, the US and Japan exhibit lower CDS values. For example, Argentina has an average CDS value of 1,951.67, while Germany has an average CDS value of 13.52. This indicates that Argentina has high credit risk, while Germany has a lower credit risk. The high standard deviations observed in CDS values reveal that in some countries, market volatility and uncertainty are high. The high variance in CDS values in countries such as Argentina, Brazil and Indonesia indicates that economic uncertainties and risks are higher in these countries. Developed countries generally have higher financial index values. For example, on average, while the US NYSE Financial index is 8,704.65, the UK FTSE 350 Financial Services Index is 14,301.12. These high values indicate the size and stability of the financial markets in these countries. Developing countries have lower financial index values. The financial indexes of countries such as Brazil, India and Türkiye have relatively low values, but with growth potential. This shows that the financial markets of these countries are developing and have potential growth areas. These statistics allow to make important inferences about countries' financial health and credit risk profiles. While the lower CDS values and higher financial indices of developed countries indicate that these countries have a more stable economic structure, the higher CDS values and variable financial indices of developing countries indicate that these countries have higher economic risks and growth potential.

The ZA test analyses the existence and effect of a single structural break in time series data. The test establishes the null hypothesis wherein the series contains a unit root and no break has occurred. The alternative hypothesis suggests that the series contains a unit root but a structural break has occurred at a certain point. In order for the test to be significant, the test statistic must exceed the critical value. The critical values were determined by ZA (1992) and if one's test statistic is greater than these values, it is accepted that there is a structural break in the series. After that, Hatemi-J

(2012) (hereafter HJ) test is employed to examine asymmetric relationships between series. The causality tests between series in VAR analysis can be performed in line with the cumulative sum's method (Hatemi-J, 2012: 449)[1].

Table 3. The results of ADF (1979) and PP (1988) test statistics

		ADF	ADF	PP	PP
Variables (Stock Markets)		**Intercept**	**Intercept and Trend**	**Intercept**	**Intercept and Trend**
BIST Financials	Level	-1.2685	-1.8596	-1.3348	-1.9208
	1st diff.	-36.0418*	-36.0484*	-36.0458*	-36.0519*
KOSDAQ Financials	Level	-0.9821	-1.7975	-1.0232	-1.8495
	1st diff.	-35.6236*	-35.6160*	-35.6338*	-35.6258*
DAX Financial Services	Level	-1.4060	-1.7099	-1.4060	-1.4060
	1st diff.	-33.6393*	-33.6272*	-33.6393*	-33.6272*
NYSE Financials	Level	-1.8948	-2.4086	-1.8801	-2.3958
	1st diff.	-12.3880*	-12.3895*	-40.1293*	-40.1197*
CAC Financials	Level	-2.3755	-2.7271	-2.2295	-2.5569
	1st diff.	-12.2895*	-12.2990*	-33.2533*	-33.2453*
FTSE 350 Financial Services	Level	-2.4113	-2.5406	-2.4033	-2.5471
	1st diff.	-13.2348*	-13.2297*	-33.7380*	-33.7248*
FTSE All Share Financials	Level	-1.0437	-2.5036	-0.8150	-2.2602
	1st diff.	-11.6579*	-11.7111*	-36.4430*	-36.4323*
Financials (IFNC)	Level	-2.3580	-2.2480	-2.5213	-2.4115
	1st diff.	-24.6296*	-24.6379*	-38.1903*	-38.1940*
S&P/BYMA General Financials	Level	-1.7718	-3.6492	-1.8037	-3.8453
	1st diff.	-34.9365*	-34.9265*	-34.9453*	-34.9352*
S&P/BMV Financials	Level	-0.8131	-2.8098	-0.6035	-2.2849
	1st diff.	-10.9074*	-10.9862*	-33.7125*	-33.6684*
S&P/TSX Capped Financial	Level	-2.0319	-2.4659	-1.8361	-2.2146
	1st diff.	-10.1143*	-10.1104*	-38.7165*	-38.7029*
S&P BSE Finance	Level	-1.7861	-2.7284	-1.4525	-1.4525
	1st diff.	-6.9059*	-6.9122*	-34.3178*	-34.3120*
SZSE Financials	Level	-1.4708	-1.5664	-1.4564	-1.5742
	1st diff.	-13.2506*	-13.2703*	-36.6424*	-36.6486*

continued on following page

Table 3. Continued

Variables (Stock Markets)		ADF Intercept	ADF Intercept and Trend	PP Intercept	PP Intercept and Trend
Tokyo SE Financials	Level	-1.1023	-2.0159	-1.1389	-2.0830
	1st diff.	-35.2970*	-35.3073*	-35.2932*	-35.3038*
Diversified Financials	Level	-0.9465	-1.7161	-0.8714	-1.6745
	1st diff.	-11.8662*	-11.8622*	-38.1307*	-38.1197*
IDX Finance	Level	-1.5951	-1.8129	-1.8142	-3.3495
	1st diff.	-23.3866*	-23.3902*	-67.7322*	-67.8754*
S&P/ASX 200 Financials	Level	-2.5999	-2.8201	-2.3668	-2.5566
	1st diff.	-9.3369*	-9.3422*	37.7954*	-37.7845*
FTSE/JSE Financial 15	Level	-2.6266	-2.6390	-2.4100	-2.4011
	1st diff.	-9.5642*	-9.5858*	-34.4719*	-34.4664*

Source: Author's computation.

Notes: For the spectral estimation method Bartlett Kernel was determined and for the Newey-West method Bandwidth options were used. *, ** and *** represent significance at the %1, %5, and %10, respectively.

Table 3 illustrates the results of the ADF and PP unit root tests with intercept and intercept and trend. According to the ADF and PP test results, most of the stock market indices are not stationary at the level, but become stationary at their first differences. For example, while the ADF and PP test values for Türkiye's BIST Financials index are -1.2685 and -1.3348 at the level, these values are -36.0418 and -36.0458 at their first differences, respectively. Similarly, Germany's DAX Financial Services Index has values of -1.4060 and -1.4060 at the level, and reaches values of -33.6393 and -33.6393 at their first differences, respectively. These results show that the first differences of the stock market indices should be taken to ensure stationarity, and indicate that these differences should be used to increase the reliability of the analyses.

Table 4. The results of ADF (1979) and PP (1988) test statistics

		ADF	ADF	PP	PP
Variables (CDS)		**Intercept**	**Intercept and Trend**	**Intercept**	**Intercept and Trend**
Turkiye	Level	-1.2685	-1.8596	-1.3348	-1.9208
	1st diff.	-15.2500*	-15.2625*	-32.5027*	-32.4978*
South Korea	Level	-1.9364	-2.2614	-2.0709	-2.3597
	1st diff.	-8.5271*	-8.5361*	-31.6982*	-31.6914*
Germany	Level	-2.8354	-3.0486	-2.3196	-2.4768
	1st diff.	-1.2784*	-2.4705*	-1.2252*	-2.4600*
USA	Level	-17.3320	-17.3346	-39.0357	-39.0295
	1st diff.	-12.3880	-12.3895	-40.1293	-40.1197
France	Level	-3.2389	-3.4309	-3.0742	-3.2734
	1st diff.	-11.4166*	-11.4177*	-37.4178*	-37.4072*
UK	Level	-1.7016	-1.7251	-1.7894	-1.8028
	1st diff.	-17.6602*	-17.6869*	-37.2493*	-37.2368*
Italy	Level	-1.8625	-2.1404	-1.8566	-2.1466
	1st diff.	-8.9591*	-8.9556*	-34.0946*	-34.0823*
Brazil	Level	-2.7721	-2.7548	-2.2934	-2.2195
	1st diff.	-8.3728*	-8.3934*	-33.0786*	-33.0712*
Argentina	Level	-3.1457	-5.0459	-13.3093	-22.8260
	1st diff.	-20.4529*	-20.4448*	-164.9557*	-164.8621*
Mexico	Level	-3.3067	-3.3125	-3.0004	-3.0064
	1st diff.	-13.0921*	-13.0889*	-33.6003*	-33.5878*
Canada	Level	-1.5686	-1.9925	-1.7707	-17.5668
	1st diff.	-15.7072*	-15.7534*	-18.4789*	-19.9537*
India	Level	-3.1643	-3.9116	-3.0253	-3.4823
	1st diff.	-9.8883*	-10.1615*	-38.2259*	-38.3561*
China	Level	-2.0488	-2.9129	-2.2445	-3.1671
	1st diff.	-9.4946*	-9.4917*	-32.6667*	-32.6548*
Japan	Level	-3.6034	-3.6234	-3.0926	-3.1101
	1st diff.	-8.4169*	-8.4136*	-36.6898*	-36.6804*
Saudi Arabia	Level	-2.5988	-3.3682	-2.5988	-3.3682
	1st diff.	-8.2860*	-8.2829*	-8.2860*	-8.2829*
Indonesia	Level	-3.5727	-3.5936	-2.9922	-3.0112
	1st diff.	-9.1891*	-9.1877*	-32.2122*	-32.2008*

continued on following page

Table 4. Continued

Variables (CDS)		ADF Intercept	ADF Intercept and Trend	PP Intercept	PP Intercept and Trend
Australia	Level	-2.3168	-2.4984	-2.2560	-2.2078
	1st diff.	-12.0193*	-12.0218*	-36.1403*	-36.1269*
South Africa	Level	-2.7766	-2.8766	-2.8056	-2.9253
	1st diff.	-33.5564*	-33.5446*	-33.5642*	-33.5524*

Source: Author's computation.

Notes: For the spectral estimation method Bartlett Kernel was determined and for the Newey-West method Bandwidth options were used. *, ** and *** represent significance at the %1, %5, and %10, respectively.

Table 4 presents the results of the ADF and PP unit root tests with intercept and intercept and trend. The ADF and PP test results for CDS data show that the CDS series of most countries are not stationary at the level, but become stationary when their first differences are taken. For example, Türkiye's CDS data were non-stationary at the level with values of -1.8509 (fixed) and -1.7474 (fixed-trend), but became stationary at their first differences with values of -15.2500 and -15.2625. Similarly, the US CDS data were non-stationary at the level (-1.2784 and -2.4705), but became stationary at their first differences (-17.3320 and -17.3346). This situation shows that financial data generally contain unit roots and that the first differences of the series should be taken for the reliability of the analysis.

Table 5. The results of one break unit root test

ZA (1992) Test				
Variables (Stock Markets)	**Model A**	**Breakpoint**	**Model C**	**Breakpoint**
BIST Financials (Turkiye)	-3.7515	29.07.2022	-4.0089	29.07.2022
KOSDAQ Financials (South Korea)	-2.9147	01.02.2023	-2.7288	01.02.2023
DAX Financial Services (Germany)	-4.3074	18.03.2022	-3.7825	18.03.2022
NYSE Financials (USA)	-3.4387	29.10.2020	-3.7937	29.10.2020
CAC Financials (France)	-3.3804	30.10.2020	-4.0195	30.10.2020
FTSE 350 Financial Services (UK)	-4.1711	10.02.2022	-4.0453	06.04.2022
FTSE All Share Financials (Italy)	-4.0773	20.02.2020	-4.1354	20.02.2020
Financials (IFNC) (Brazil)	-4.8970	26.02.2020	-4.8811	26.02.2020
S&P/BYMA Financials (Argentina)	-4.9900	21.12.2022	-4.9371	21.12.2022
S&P/BMV Financials (Mexico)	-5.2399	20.02.2020	-5.3564	20.02.2020

continued on following page

Table 5. Continued

ZA (1992) Test				
Variables (Stock Markets)	**Model A**	**Breakpoint**	**Model C**	**Breakpoint**
S&P/TSX Capped Financial (Canada)	-3.9259	02.11.2020	-4.1329	02.11.2020
S&P BSE Finance (India)	-3.3608	02.11.2020	-4.3171	25.09.2020
SZSE Financials (China)	-4.8879	19.06.2020	-5.2018	30.06.2020
Tokyo SE Financials (Japan)	-2.9735	18.02.2022	-3.7648	18.02.2022
Diversified Financials (Saudi Arabia)	-3.7563	02.11.2020	-4.1805	08.11.2020
IDX Finance (Indonesia)	-27.6871	12.10.2020	-28.3378	12.10.2020
S&P/ASX 200 Financials (Australia)	-3.7729	30.10.2020	-4.3207	30.10.2020
FTSE/JSE Financial 15 (South Africa)	-2.9735	18.02.2022	-3.7648	18.02.2022
	%1	**%5**	**%10**	
Model A	-5.34	-4.93	-4.58	
Model C	-5.57	-5.08	-4.82	

Source: Author's computation.

Notes: The values in the Model A and C indicate the t-statistic. The model A indicated the break on the fixed model and the model C indicates the break on the fixed and trend models. The critical values related to the statistics of the test were taken from the study of Zivot and Andrews (1992).

Table 5 reports the ZA tests with Model A and Model C for stock markets. According to the ZA test results, stock market sector indices of many country showed structural breaks on certain dates. For example, the breakpoint for Türkiye's BIST Financials index was determined as July 29, 2022 in Model A and Model C, and the test statistics were found as -3.7515 and -4.0089, respectively. Since these values are above the critical values, they show that the indices contain unit roots with structural breaks and are therefore not stationary. Similarly, a break was detected for Germany's DAX Financial Services index on March 18, 2022, and the test statistics were calculated as -4.3074 and -3.7825. These results show that the indices have structural breaks and are not stationary and that economic or financial events may cause these breaks. Similarly, structural breaks were detected for other countries on certain dates, and it was revealed that these breaks affected the stationarity properties of the indices.

Table 6. The results of one break unit root test

		ZA (1992) Test		
Variables (CDS)	**Model A**	**Breakpoint**	**Model C**	**Breakpoint**
Turkiye	-3.3667	24.05.2023	-3.3667	16.11.2021
South Korea	-4.3226	21.01.2022	-4.3226	21.01.2022
Germany	-3.6504	01.03.2022	-3.5370	22.06.2022
USA	-4.4984	18.03.2022	-5.2001	18.03.2022
France	-4.3542	27.05.2020	-4.4692	27.05.2020
UK	-4.0286	21.06.2022	-3.9174	21.06.2022
Italy	-3.9471	18.03.2022	-3.8867	18.03.2022
Brazil	-4.5531	24.02.2020	-4.8282	24.02.2020
Argentina	-7.4798	08.09.2021	-8.2219	11.02.2021
Meksika	-3.7203	30.03.2022	-4.1150	30.03.2022
Canada	-5.9738	19.05.2023	-6.6311	22.03.2021
India	-3.5662	17.09.2021	-3.5662	17.09.2021
China	-4.7600	06.01.2022	-4.7057	06.01.2022
Japan	-4.2180	15.05.2020	-4.3566	14.05.2020
Saudi Arabia	-4.1998	01.10.2020	-4.5597	02.06.2020
Indonesia	-3.6003	21.02.2020	-3.7930	21.02.2020
Australia	-3.8297	12.04.2022	-4.0581	20.04.2022
South Africa	-3.7360	20.02.2020	-4.0430	25.09.2020
		%1	**%5**	**%10**
Model A		-5.34	-4.93	-4.58
Model C		-5.57	-5.08	-4.82

Source: Author's computation.

Notes: The values in the Model A and C indicate the t-statistic. The model A indicated the break on the fixed model and the model C indicates the break on the fixed and trend models. The critical values related to the statistics of the test were taken from the study of Zivot and Andrews (1992).

Table 6 reports the ZA tests with Model A and Model C for CDS. According to the ZA test results, CDS data show structural breaks on certain dates in many countries. For example, for Türkiye's CDS data, the breakpoint was determined as May 24, 2023 in Model A and November 16, 2021 in Model C, and the test statistic for the break was found to be -3.3667 for both models. Since these values are above the critical values, they indicate that the series contain unit roots with structural breaks and are not stationary. These results show that the CDS data contain structural breaks depending on economic and financial events, and these breaks affect the stationarity properties of the series.

According to the ZA test results, the structural break dates determined in the stock market indices of many countries reflect the effects of the Covid-19 crisis. For example, a breakout was detected for Türkiye's BIST Financials index on July 29, 2022, for Germany's DAX Financial Services Index on March 18, 2022, and for the US's NYSE Financial Index on January 25, 2021. This provides important information to understand the long-term effects of the Covid-19 crisis on CDS spreads and how financial markets respond during crisis periods. These findings also reveal the wide-ranging effects of the pandemic on financial markets and how these effects may differ from country to country.

Before employing the HJ test, the consistency conditions (AR characteristic, autocorrelation, heteroscedasticity) in the empirical analysis are investigated. The consistency conditions necessary for the HJ test were provided in the analysis. The results of the HJ test between CDS and financial sector indexes are given in Table 7.

Table 7. The results of HJ (2012) asymmetric causality tests

Null Hypothesis	Test Value	Critical Bootstrap Value			Null Hypothesis	Test Value	Critical Bootstrap Value	
		1%	5%	10%			1%	5%
Germany								
$CDS^+ \neq> DAX^+$	2.188	9.033	3.488	2.269	$DAX^+ \neq> CDS^+$	1.377	13.421	3.016
$CDS^+ \neq> DAX^-$	3.566**	11.010	3.376	1.761	$DAX^+ \neq> CDS^-$	14.990*	7.907	3.836
$CDS^- \neq> DAX^-$	1.084	9.251	3.864	2.432	$DAX^- \neq>$CDS-	0.489	11.328	4.127
$CDS^- \neq> DAX^+$	28.956*	11.419	3.046	2.036	$DAX^- \neq> CDS^+$	5.226**	6.562	3.402
USA								
$CDS^+ \neq> NYSE^+$	0.740	18.725	3.71	1.603	$NYSE^+ \neq> CDS^+$	0.267	12.161	3.885
$CDS^+ \neq> NYSE^-$	4.204**	13.531	3.812	2.056	$NYSE^+ \neq> CDS^-$	9.106**	13.913	3.734
$CDS^- \neq> NYSE^-$	1.289	14.773	4.256	1.867	$NYSE^- \neq> CDS^-$	0.065	12.452	3.077
$CDS^- \neq> NYSE^+$	43.504*	26.740	7.845	4.384	$NYSE^- \neq> CDS^+$	10.040**	16.291	3.371
France								
$CDS^+ \neq>$ CAC+	2.369	13.809	4.532	2.474	$CAC^+ \neq> CDS^+$	1.300	16.534	6.280
$CDS^+ \neq> CAC^-$	24.818*	7.242	3.45	2.461	$CAC^+ \neq> CDS^-$	6.612**	7.550	2.618
$CDS^- \neq> CAC^-$	0.141	7.953	3.947	2.374	$CAC^- \neq> CDS^-$	0.129	11.541	4.529
$CDS^- \neq> CAC^+$	11.223*	8.406	3.795	2.734	$CAC^- \neq> CDS^+$	39.090*	17.045	2.986
UK								
$CDS^+ \neq> FTSEUK^+$	0.092	11.304	3.546	2.115	FTSEUK+$\neq> CDS^+$	1.393	7.509	3.382
$CDS^+ \neq> FTSEUK^-$	10.956*	7.581	4.054	2.651	$FTSEUK^+ \neq> CDS^-$	8.532**	8.586	2.915
$CDS^- \neq> FTSEUK^-$	0.541	8.102	3.624	2.524	$FTSEUK^- \neq> CDS^-$	0.361	9.763	4.105
$CDS^- \neq> FTSEUK^+$	15.595*	6.620	3.619	2.657	$FTSEUK^- \neq> CDS^+$	30.410*	10.941	3.371
Italy								

continued on following page

Table 7. Continued

Null Hypothesis	Test Value	Critical Bootstrap Value			Null Hypothesis	Test Value	Critical Bootstrap Value	
		1%	5%	10%			1%	5%
CDS$^+$≠>FTSEITA$^+$	0.010	13.310	5.990	3.395	FTSEITA$^+$≠>CDS$^+$	0.070	6.763	3.446
CDS$^+$≠>FTSEITA$^-$	26.668*	6.190	3.698	2.698	FTSEITA$^+$≠>CDS$^-$	3.225***	11.044	3.346
CDS$^-$≠> FTSEITA$^-$	2.855***	7.905	3.732	2.485	FTSEITA$^-$≠>CDS$^-$	0.058	7.869	2.664
CDS$^-$≠>FTSEITA$^+$	9.065*	8.771	3.843	2.79	FTSEITA$^-$≠>CDS$^+$	19.960*	10.444	3.771
Brazil								
CDS$^+$≠>IFNC$^+$	2.759	16.273	7.042	3.807	IFNC$^+$≠>CDS$^+$	3.342***	7.177	3.841
CDS$^+$≠>IFNC$^-$	27.399*	7.305	4.05	2.71	IFNC$^+$≠>CDS$^-$	21.120*	7.591	3.897
CDS$^-$≠>IFNC$^-$	1.796	7.326	3.819	2.542	IFNC$^-$≠>CDS$^-$	0.117	12.735	7.139
CDS$^-$≠>IFNC$^+$	10.798*	8.496	4.01	2.988	IFNC$^-$≠>CDS$^+$	8.435*	6.841	3.268
Argentina								
CDS$^+$≠>BYMA$^+$	0.092	7.419	3.871	2.468	BYMA$^+$≠>CDS$^+$	1.109	7.252	3.974
CDS$^+$≠>BYMA$^-$	0.062	6.977	3.893	2.806	BYMA$^+$≠>CDS$^-$	0.769	7.759	3.719
CDS$^-$≠>BYMA$^-$	0.103	7.884	3.818	2.732	BYMA$^-$≠>CDS$^-$	1.754	7.452	3.986
CDS$^-$≠>BYMA$^+$	0.000	6.736	3.731	2.562	BYMA$^-$≠>CDS$^+$	0.232	10.193	4.209
Mexico								
CDS$^+$≠>BMV$^+$	0.192	9.216	4.275	2.844	BMV$^+$≠>CDS$^+$	0.381	7.169	3.796
CDS$^+$≠>BMV$^-$	2.027	6.913	3.887	2.778	BMV$^+$≠>CDS$^-$	13.700*	8.149	3.846
CDS$^-$≠>BMV$^-$	0.000	7.056	3.85	2.638	BMV$^-$≠>CDS$^-$	0.523	17.738	6.219
CDS$^-$≠>BMV$^+$	21.989*	7.982	3.557	2.625	BMV$^-$≠>CDS$^+$	40.190*	8.251	3.457
Canada								
CDS$^+$≠>TSX$^+$	0.673	15.403	2.856	1.289	TSX$^+$≠>CDS$^+$	0.188	9.84	2.683
CDS$^+$≠>TSX$^-$	5.666**	8.414	3.721	2.515	TSX$^+$≠>CDS$^-$	12.340**	15.328	2.326
CDS$^-$≠>TSX$^-$	2.993***	8.133	3.914	2.388	TSX$^-$≠>CDS$^-$	0.028	20.697	6.612
CDS$^-$≠>TSX$^+$	3.256***	9.342	3.730	2.529	TSX$^-$≠>CDS$^+$	0.645	21.461	5.807
India								
CDS$^+$≠>BSE$^+$	2.383***	11.248	3.270	1.771	BSE$^+$≠>CDS$^+$	0.669	15.151	3.862
CDS$^+$≠>BSE$^-$	0.524	13.322	4.824	2.111	BSE$^+$≠>CDS$^-$	0.360	15.056	3.053
CDS$^-$≠>BSE$^-$	0.153	32.171	3.899	1.539	BSE$^-$≠>CDS$^-$	0.000	21.097	2.964
CDS$^-$≠>BSE$^+$	0.595	13.761	4.231	2.357	BSE$^-$≠>CDS$^+$	0.031	11.878	3.148
China								
CDS$^+$≠>SZSE$^+$	0.000	8.086	3.716	2.615	SZSE$^+$≠>CDS$^+$	0.440	5.719	3.205
CDS$^+$≠>SZSE$^-$	0.208	7.686	4.215	2.736	SZSE$^+$≠>CDS$^-$	0.067	7.502	3.905
CDS$^-$≠>SZSE-	0.095	7.201	3.849	2.644	SZSE$^-$≠>CDS$^-$	0.114	10.78	4.307
CDS$^-$≠>SZSE$^+$	0.002	7.479	3.748	2.497	SZSE$^-$≠>CDS$^+$	1.303	7.257	3.672
South Korea								
CDS$^+$≠>KOSDAQ$^+$	0.103	13.810	5.113	3.560	KOSDAQ$^+$≠>CDS$^+$	0.048	5.668	3.498

continued on following page

Table 7. Continued

Null Hypothesis	Test Value	Critical Bootstrap Value			Null Hypothesis	Test Value	Critical Bootstrap Value	
		1%	5%	10%			1%	5%
$CDS^{+}\neq>KOSDAQ^{-}$	16.733*	10.54	3.694	2.575	$KOSDAQ^{+}\neq>CDS^{-}$	10.870**	11.399	4.218
$CDS^{-}\neq>KOSDAQ^{-}$	0.468	10.739	3.909	2.52	$KOSDAQ^{-}\neq>CDS^{-}$	1.156	11.536	5.390
$CDS^{-}\neq>KOSDAQ^{+}$	11.140*	7.079	3.588	2.309	$KOSDAQ^{-}\neq>CDS^{+}$	5.670**	10.568	3.995
Japon								
$CDS^{+}\neq>TOPIX^{+}$	1.806	7.447	3.642	2.299	$TOPIX^{+}\neq>CDS^{+}$	0.373	10.046	4.185
$CDS^{+}\neq>TOPIX^{-}$	5.766**	7.187	3.585	2.631	$TOPIX^{+}\neq>CDS^{-}$	26.930*	13.018	3.862
$CDS^{-}\neq>TOPIX^{-}$	1.778	8.579	3.813	2.538	$TOPIX^{-}\neq>CDS^{-}$	0.456	8.586	4.177
$CDS^{-}\neq>TOPIX^{+}$	5.435**	7.621	3.939	2.661	$TOPIX^{-}\neq>CDS^{+}$	6.964**	8.840	3.625
Turkiye								
$CDS^{+}\neq>BIST^{+}$	1.319	13.685	5.985	3.823	$BIST^{+}\neq>CDS^{+}$	1.081	9.751	3.909
$CDS^{+}\neq>BIST^{-}$	1.538	6.589	3.684	2.705	$BIST^{+}\neq>CDS-$	0.043	10.178	4.065
$CDS^{-}\neq>BIST^{-}$	0.947	7.032	3.559	2.552	$BIST^{-}\neq>CDS^{-}$	0.823	7.218	4.099
$CDS^{-}\neq>BIST^{+}$	0.102	7.964	3.643	2.658	$BIST^{-}\neq>CDS^{+}$	77.270*	10.828	3.398
Saudi Arabia								
$CDS^{+}\neq>TDFI^{+}$	0.648	12.179	3.343	2.259	$TDFI^{+}\neq>CDS^{+}$	0.071	9.418	3.809
$CDS^{+}\neq>TDFI^{-}$	3.210***	6.444	3.487	2.527	$TDFI^{+}\neq>CDS^{-}$	37.870*	14.244	3.456
$CDS^{-}\neq>TDFI^{-}$	0.379	8.675	3.722	2.319	$TDFI^{-}\neq>CDS^{-}$	0.055	15.765	3.757
$CDS^{-}\neq>TDFI^{+}$	0.320	9.591	4.167	2.823	$TDFI^{-}\neq>CDS^{+}$	96.020*	12.446	4.185
Indonesia								
$CDS^{+}\neq>IDX^{+}$	0.038	25.341	2.387	0.894	$IDX^{+}\neq>CDS^{+}$	0.140	19.287	2.960
$CDS^{+}\neq>IDX^{-}$	0.008	17.371	3.276	1.502	$IDX^{+}\neq>CDS^{-}$	0.193	20.759	3.017
$CDS^{-}\neq>IDX^{-}$	0.304	13.273	3.38	1.606	$IDX^{-}\neq>CDS^{-}$	0.180	9.732	3.742
$CDS^{-}\neq>IDX^{+}$	0.599	12.182	2.891	1.617	$IDX^{-}\neq>CDS^{+}$	0.095	19.746	3.020
Australia								
$CDS^{+}\neq>ASX^{+}$	0.269	9.858	3.832	2.514	$ASX^{+}\neq>CDS^{+}$	0.687	9.425	4.068
$CDS^{+}\neq>ASX^{-}$	36.375*	11.178	3.254	2.283	$ASX^{+}\neq>CDS^{-}$	27.940*	15.085	3.880
$CDS^{-}\neq>ASX^{-}$	1.988	11.344	3.567	2.022	$ASX^{-}\neq>CDS^{-}$	0.015	11.907	3.319
$CDS^{-}\neq>ASX^{+}$	5.304**	9.410	3.817	2.413	$ASX^{-}\neq>CDS^{+}$	14.060*	9.173	3.423
South Africa								
$CDS^{+}\neq>JSA^{+}$	0.339	7.959	3.917	2.820	$JSA^{+}\neq>CDS^{+}$	2.307	7.521	3.688
$CDS^{+}\neq>JSA^{-}$	1.991	7.236	3.657	2.442	$JSA^{+}\neq>CDS^{-}$	7.381*	6.532	3.293
$CDS^{-}\neq>JSA^{-}$	2.413	8.219	3.801	2.685	$JSA^{-}\neq>CDS^{-}$	1.241	9.306	4.651
$CDS^{-}\neq>JSA^{+}$	0.336	6.678	3.598	2.470	$JSA^{-}\neq>CDS^{+}$	4.511**	6.640	3.747

Source: Own calculations.

Notes: *, ** and *** denote significance at the %1, %5, and %10, respectively. The denotation x ≠> y indicates the null hypothesis that variable x does not cause variable y. For example, CDS^{+} ≠> DAX^{-} means that a positive shock in CDS does not cause negative shocks in the DAX.

When the Hatemi J test results are analysed, in general, it is seen that there is a relationship between countries' CDS and financial sector indexes. The direction of this relationship is observed mainly from positive shocks of CDS to negative shocks of financial indexes. The results of the relationships between these variables are explained in detail below.

In developed countries, mostly a bidirectional causality relationship is observed between CDS and stock market indices. It has been observed that positive shocks in CDSs cause negative shocks in indices and that positive shocks in indices have a strong causal relationship with negative shocks in CDSs. This reveals that significant fluctuations are experienced in financial markets and that both markets mutually affect each other. This situation is not valid for the Republic of South Africa, which is among the developed countries.

In the Republic of South Africa, it was observed that positive or negative shocks in the financial sector index cause an opposite fluctuation in CDSs, while it was observed that shocks in CDSs did not have the same effect on the JSE Financials 15 Index. This shows that CDS can affect stock market indices in the Republic of South Africa market, but there is no reverse relationship. Among developing countries, Brazil, Mexico and Saudi Arabia show a bidirectional causality relationship. In these countries, it is found that CDS positive shocks have a strong causality relationship with negative shocks in the sector index and positive shocks in the sector index have a strong causality relationship with CDS negative shocks. It shows that CDS spreads and stock market indices mutually affect each other in these countries' markets. In Türkiye, China, India and Indonesia, which are among other developing countries that are members of the G20 group, no causality relationship is observed between CDS and stock market indices. It has been found that negative shocks in sectoral indices in these countries do not cause shocks in any direction on CDS, and similarly, CDSs do not have a significant effect on financial sector indices.

These evidence suggests that a rise in risk perception in financial stock markets will not have any impact on financial sector.

According to the results of the asymmetric causality test, no relationship was found between credit default swaps and stock market indices in Türkiye. This situation may be attributed to the structural conditions or risk perception of Türkiye's financial markets.

In addition, investor behaviour and risk management strategies in financial markets in Türkiye may limit the interaction between CDS and indices.

This situation shows that CDSs do not have a significant effect on stock market indices in the Turkish market and that index movements do not create a significant change on CDS premiums. In this context, the characteristics of Türkiye's financial markets and market structures may reveal a lower level of interaction compared to other countries.

The results of the asymmetric causality test show that the causal relations between credit default swaps and stock market differ between developed and developing countries. This demonstrates that the dynamics of financial markets can differ from each country to another and that each market has its own specific dynamics.

The results emphasise that investment and risk management strategies should be customised according to these dynamics. These results are extremely important in understanding the dynamics of financial markets. The bidirectional causality in developed countries reveals the complexity of the relationship between credit risk and stock performance in these markets. In particular, the fact that positive shocks in CDSs cause negative shocks in stock market indices shows that changes in investors' risk perception are quickly reflected in market prices.

In the Republic of South Africa, due to the structure of the financial system, shocks in stock market indices do not affect CDS spreads, but CDS spreads affect stock market indices. In developing countries, bidirectional causality in Brazil, Mexico and Saudi Arabia indicates that similar dynamics are valid in these markets. However, the absence of a significant causality relationship in Türkiye, China, India and Indonesia reveals that the financial systems in these countries have different dynamics.

4. CONCLUSION AND POLICY RECOMMENDATIONS

This study examines the relationship between CDS and financial sector stock market indices of 18 G20 countries. The data cover daily closing prices between April 1, 2019 and March 31, 2024. Our aim is to determine the causal relationships between CDS and stock market index daily closing prices and the direction of these relationships.

In these countries, it is found that CDS positive shocks have a strong causality relationship with negative shocks in the sector index and positive shocks in the sector index have a strong causality relationship with CDS negative shocks. On the other hand, no causal relationship was observed between CDS and stock market indices in developing countries such as Türkiye, China, India and Indonesia, which are members of the G20.

In general, this study provides important findings for the analysis of the relationships between CDS and stock market index closing prices. The results can provide valuable information for policy makers and investors, guiding them in the management of financial risks and the determination of investment strategies. It is recommended that future studies examine these relationships in more depth using longer data sets and different methodologies. There are several limitations to this study. First, the data set used in the analysis is limited to daily closing prices between

April 1, 2019 and March 31, 2024. Analyses using a longer time frame and higher frequency of data can provide more comprehensive and reliable results. Also, this study was limited to G20 countries only. In future studies, a wider range of countries from different economic groups and geographical regions can be examined to reach generally valid results. In addition, in this study, indices related to the financial sector were considered.

Investigating the relationship between country risk premiums and other stock market sector indices will provide stronger evidence for measuring the relationship between the two variables.

Methodologically, in addition to the ADF, PP and Zivot-Andrews tests used in this study, alternative stationarity tests and causality analysis methods can also be evaluated. Furthermore, models that analyse the impact of both structural breaks and financial crises in more detail can be used to better understand the dynamics of financial markets.

For example, more in-depth analyses can be made on the effects of major economic shocks such as the 2008 financial crisis and the Covid-19 pandemic.

As a result, the findings of this study have contributed to our better understanding of the dynamics of financial markets by revealing the complexity of the relationships between CDS and stock market index closing prices and the differences in these relationships across countries.

Future studies can make significant contributions to the literature by examining these relationships with wider data sets and methodologies and can provide stronger guidance in the management of financial risks and the development of investment strategies. For future research, the following ideas can also be considered examining the effects of different factors with different causality tests.

REFERENCES

Al-Own, B., Minhat, M., & Gao, S. (2018). Stock options and credit default swaps in risk management. *Journal of International Financial Markets, Institutions and Money*, *53*, 200–214. DOI: 10.1016/j.intfin.2017.09.021

Anton, S. G., & Afloarei Nucu, A. E. (2020). Sovereign credit default swap and stock markets in central and eastern European countries: Are feedback effects at work? *Entropy (Basel, Switzerland)*, *22*(3), 338. DOI: 10.3390/e22030338 PMID: 33286112

Avşarlıgil, N., & Turğut, E. (2021). A study on the relationship between CDS premiums and stock market indices: A case of the fragile five countries. *Istanbul Business Research*, *50*(2), 275–301. DOI: 10.26650/ibr.2021.50.808240

Ballester, L., & González-Urteaga, A. (2020). Is there a connection between sovereign CDS spreads and the stock market? Evidence for European and US returns and volatilities. *Mathematics*, *8*(10), 1667. DOI: 10.3390/math8101667

Bayrakdaroglu, A., & Tepeli, Y. (2018). An examination of the risk-return analysis of BIST city indices. *Journal of Accounting and Finance*, *147*, 2146–3042.

Bayramoğlu, M. F., & Pekkaya, M. (2010). *New developments in indices calculated by IMKB and IMKB city indices. Bahçeşehir University, Vocational School*. Zonguldak Karaelmas University, Faculty of Economics and Administrative Sciences.

Bosworth, B., Hymans, S., & Modigliani, F. (1975). The stock market and the economy. *Brookings Papers on Economic Activity*, *1975*(2), 257–300. DOI: 10.2307/2534104

Boussada, H., Prigent, J. L., & Soumare, I. (2023). On the sovereign debt crisis: Sovereign credit default swaps and their interaction with stock market indices. *Applied Economics*, *55*(1), 20–42. DOI: 10.1080/00036846.2021.1934392

. Chan-Lau, JA., Kim, YS. 2004. Equity prices, credit default swaps, and bond spreads in emerging markets. *International Monetary Fund*, 2004-027. DOI: 10.5089/9781451844559.001

Coronado, M., Corzo, M. T., & Lazcano, L. 2012. A case for Europe: The relationship between sovereign CDS and stock indices. *Frontiers In Finance And Economics*, 9(2), 32-63. https://ssrn.com/abstract=2190408

Ergenç, S., & Güneren, G. E. (2020). Examination of changes in credit default swap premiums in Turkey. *Istanbul Commerce University Journal of Social Sciences*, *19*(37), 449–461.

Forte, S., & Peña, J. I. (2009). Credit spreads: An empirical analysis on the informational content of stocks, bonds, and CDS. *Journal of Banking & Finance, 33*(11), 2013–2025. DOI: 10.1016/j.jbankfin.2009.04.015

Fung, H. G., Sierra, G. E., Yau, J., & Zhang, G. (2008). Are the U.S. stock market and credit default swap market related? Evidence from the CDX indices. *Journal of Alternative Investments, 11*(1), 43–61. DOI: 10.3905/jai.2008.708849

Gün, M. (2018). The co-movement of credit default swaps and stock markets in emerging economies. In *Recent Perspectives and Case Studies in Finance & Econometrics*. IJOPEC Publication.

Güzel, F. (2022). Volatility interaction of bist main sector indices: Findings regarding the covid-19 period. *Jour. of Social Economic Res., 22*(2), 128–138. DOI: 10.30976/susead.1123835

Hatemi-J, A. (2012). Asymmetric causality tests with an application. *Empirical Economics, 43*(1), 447–456. DOI: 10.1007/s00181-011-0484-x

Jeanneret, A. (2017). Sovereign default risk and the US equity market. *Journal of Financial and Quantitative Analysis, 52*(1), 305–339. DOI: 10.1017/S0022109016000776

Kantar, L. (2020). Credit default swaps premium with European debt crisis: Implementation on PIIGS countries. *Beykoz Akademi Dergisi, 8*(1), 20–35. DOI: 10.14514/BYK.m.26515393.2020.8/1.20-35

Kiesel, F., Kolaric, S., & Schiereck, D. (2016). Market integration and efficiency of CDS and equity markets. *The Quarterly Review of Economics and Finance, 61*, 210–223. DOI: 10.1016/j.qref.2016.02.010

Koy, A. 2015. The relationship between credit default swap spreads, equity indices and sector equity indices: An empirical study on Istanbul Stock Exchange. *Paper presented at the 17th International Academic Conference.*

Kutuk, T., & Okur, M. (2020). A comparative analysis of country ratings and credit default swap premiums in determining risk premium in BRICS-T countries. *Business and Economics Research Journal, 11*(2), 413–429. DOI: 10.20409/berj.2020.258

Mateev, M., & Marinova, E. (2016). Relation between credit default swap spreads and stock prices: A non-linear perspective. *In World Finance & Banking Symposium*, University of Dubai.

Odum, P. (2012). *An Assessment of the Relationship Between the Credit Default Swap Market and the Stock Market*. Lund University.

Şahin, E. E., & Özkan, O. (2018). The relationship between credit default swaps, exchange rate and BIST100 index. *Hitit University Jou. of Social Sci. Inst.*, *11*(3), 1939–1945. DOI: 10.17218/hititsosbil.450178

Vashkevich, A., & Basazinew, S. T. 2013. Relationship between sovereign credit default swap and stock markets: *The Case of East Asia. Umeå School of Business and Economics Master Thesis.*

Wang, R., Basu, A., & Clements, A. (2023). Are credit default swaps still a sideshow? How information flow between equity and CDS markets has changed since the financial crisis. *Global Finance Journal*, *57*, 100849. DOI: 10.1016/j.gfj.2023.100849

Zghal, R., Ghorbel, A., & Triki, M. (2018). Dynamic model for hedging of the european stock sector with credit default swaps and Euro STOXX 50 volatility index futures. *Borsa Istanbul Review*, *18*(4), 312–328. DOI: 10.1016/j.bir.2018.05.003

Zhu, H. (2006). An empirical comparison of credit spreads between the bond market and the credit default swap market. *Journal of Financial Services Research*, *29*(3), 211–235. DOI: 10.1007/s10693-006-7626-x

Zivot, E., & Andrews, K. (1992). Further evidence on the great crash, the oil price shock, and the unit root hypothesis. *Journal of Business & Economic Statistics*, *10*(3), 251–270. DOI: 10.1080/07350015.1992.10509904

ENDNOTES

* This paper is based on a master thesis titled "The Relationship of Credit Default Swaps and Stock Market Finance Sector Indices: A Research on the G20 Countries."

1 For a detailed explanation of equation in cumulative form, please see HJ (2012) asymmetric causality test.

Chapter 13
Climate Risk Assessment and Financial Modelling for Sustainable Enterprises

Ekta Saraswat
https://orcid.org/0009-0002-7488-282X
IILM University, Greater Noida, India

ABSTRACT

Climate change has emerged as one of the most pressing challenges of the 21st century, with significant economic, social, and environmental consequences. Financial modelling plays a crucial role in quantifying and mitigating these risks, enabling enterprises to make data-driven decisions that align with sustainability objectives. The rise of environmental, social, and governance (ESG) frameworks has further emphasized the need for sustainable financial planning, making it essential for businesses to adopt innovative tools and methodologies to assess climate-related risks. This chapter aims to explore the intersection of climate risk assessment and financial modelling, focusing on methodologies, tools, and strategies that support sustainable enterprises. By leveraging advancements in data analytics, artificial intelligence, and regulatory frameworks, organizations can integrate climate considerations into financial decision-making, ensuring resilience and long-term value creation.

INTRODUCTION

Climate change has become one of the most burning issues of the XXI century threatening the economy, social and environmental issues. Global warming, wors-

DOI: 10.4018/979-8-3373-3725-8.ch013

ening frequency of natural catastrophes, and changes in regulatory measures have resulted in significant threats to business and other financial institutions. Industrial enterprises in all sectors need to get used to this changing environment by completing the climate risk review process in their financial decision-making (Akhtar et al., 2021).

Climate change is not theoretically transforming the world economy, but actually doing it in real time. Logistics hub has been distorted by wildfires in Canada. In South Asia, agriculture has been devastated because of flooding. Heatwaves that stretched across Europe and North America presented energy systems and healthcare systems to the limit. These do not happen once. They are precursors of more systematic risks which are becoming more global in magnitude, more integrated and financial in impact.

Climate change is one of the many challenges facing enterprises, and it also acts as a test of fire to businesses that consider themselves sustainable that is, individuals or companies that are constructed based on the principles of environmental stewardship, social responsibility, and sustainable creation of value over time (Ansari et al., 2023). Such businesses by design purport to do things differently. They want to reduce harm, become innovative within their planetary boundaries, and be consistent with global agendas, such as the Sustainable Development Goals (SDGs) and the Paris Agreement. However, the heat is on: Given the worsening climate crisis, will sustainable firms actually resist and change with the times when it comes to climate shocks? Do they have strong financial models that would withstand their missions?

The premise that the author of this chapter is starting with is that sustainability needs to be quantifiable both in terms of finance and weather (Akhtar et al., 2021). Companies that fail to generate long-term value because their cash flows go bankrupt in a 3 to 4 degrees warmer world, cannot make this claim. Similarly, companies that are based on the assumption that the climate will act stably, i.e. with stationary prices of energy and resources, stationary accessibility of resources, stable functioning are not sustainable in any valuable sense.

Most businesses, including those in the sustainability arena, are still driven by financial projection models that are not fit to live in a climate peppered world. They are backward-looking, averaging based, and insensitive to a climate risk. Capital planning does not pay attention to adaptation costs. There is no scenario volatility in the rate of discounts. The preset insurance assumptions are obsolete. What comes out instead is the appearance of assuredness -an Excel-induced optimistic set-up that crumbles in the light of a storm, drought or a policy change.

New tools are required to get out of this. It is not more theory or hidden ESG scoring matrices but rather workable financial constructs that incorporate the facts of a warmer world. Model where the businesses can pose questions like: What will be our revenues in the event carbon taxes on the order of 100/ton become a reality?

How will a heatwave affect our cost of goods? Can we stay in business when our key supplier floods twice in five years? Do our current margins survive in a world where there is going to be no water?

One of those tools is presented in this chapter, namely, scenario-based cash flow modelling. It is not predictive as in predicting the year or the location that a disruption will take place. Instead, it is prospective: it assists business executives to plan a multiplicity of climate prospects and experiment on how their companies can manage under them (Akhtar et al., 2023). That lies at the very heart of the value of scenario thinking: this does change the nature of conversations about money - mostly, in fact, it changes the nature of money conversations, so that they stop being about, What do we think will happen? and turn into being about, Are we prepared to go through what might happen?

Scenario-based modelling implies construction of several financial forecasts using scientifically justified climate trajectories. They cover physical risks (floods, storms, rising sea-levels, extreme temperatures) and transition risks (carbon pricing, regulation, consumer preferences and technology changes) (Bolton et al., 2020). All scenarios alter the assumptions of the revenue growth, cost structure, the capital investment, the risk premiums and the liquidity planning. This pushes companies to come face to face with the uncomfortable and plan accordingly.

The chapter commences the review of the main financial modelling development starting off with the Free Cash Flow to Firm (FCFF) method. It also points to where climate risks would occur organically in the financial facts: in revenues (e.g., disrupted through supply or demand), in operating costs (e.g. energy, logistics, insurance), CapEx (e.g. climate adaptation, emissions compliance). It goes on to present a three-part scenario structure: a 2 o C managed transition scenario, a 3 o C delayed action scenario and a 4 o C+ failed transition scenario. Such scenarios are constructed on the basis of the IPCC projections, the NGFS pathways, and with locally modified variables including the local risks of floods or heat indexes.

In order to make the approach real, a full financial model of AgriTech Roots, a sustainable irrigation startup company running in climate-vulnerable regions is attached to the chapter. It demonstrates the impact of various climate futures on cash flow, CapEx timing, profitability and funding requirement; and the strategic response of the business in each scenario. The exposing model brings the notions of the fact that climate risk is not a single shock but rather a continuously changing pressure that redefines margin profiles, appetites of investments as well as enterprise viability.

The chapter also covers interpretation in addition to the numbers. Is there actually information on risk exposure and resilience in model outputs? In what way should they structure their pricing, growth planning, supplier strategy or communication to stakeholders? Where do internal carbon pricing, emergency reserves, or blended finance come in?

Lastly, the introduction deals with the availability of this approach. Scenario based modelling does not need enterprise level analytics teams. Excel spreadsheets can be used by small businesses on their way to big business. Lightweight models can be infused with open-source data provided by NASA, the IPCC, or the use of local meteorological services. The trick is not to postpone till things are perfect, the trick is to get started with what is imperfect.

The question in this century is not whether businesses can increase, but whether they will be able to grow within constraints, constraints in climate, constraints on resources, constraints in terms of social license (Carney, 2015). Those limits should be in financial modelling. In case of sustainable enterprises, it is not only about safeguarding the balance sheet. It is all about delivering on the promise of constructing sustainability, fair, and climate-resistant systems.

1. TYPES OF CLIMATE RISKS

The risks of climate can be classified into two broad categories that are highly interlinked; physical risks and transition risks. They both could have a tremendous impact on the financial position, operational capability, asset stocks, the supply chain and the long-term business strategy of a business and this is particularly so on the sustainability conscious companies. Being aware of these risks is the basic step toward incorporation of climate variables into financial models of an enterprise level. Climate change is not taking place therefore that should be accepted but how should it impact the sustainable enterprises and this should be put in place: geographically, economically, and operationally.

1.1 Physical Risks

Physical risks are the real-life impacts of a changing climate on Built and Natural Environment. These hazards can be in the form of acute situations, like hurricanes, wildfires or flash floods or chronic transitions, like rise in sea level, severe draught and degradation of the ecosystem. Such phenomena have quantifiable and in many cases increasing economic effects, such as not only direct destruction of assets but permanent loss of productivity.

1.2 Acute Physical Risk

Residual risks are adversely inclined as acute risks, which are usually extreme but swift disasters that are capable of demolishing the infrastructure, knocking logistics off course and placing personnel as well as their associates in grave danger, such as creating uncontrollable costs of repair and insurance (Network for Greening the Financial System [NGFS], 2022). They can easily be manifested in single capital expenses or insurance payments, but they also cause volatility and uncertainty in the business model.

Examples of acute risks are:

- Whether tropical cyclones or combination of a manufacturing hub or port.
- Wildfires which may break energy transmission or damage infrastructure in fields.
- Now the severe rainfall or flash floods which destroy crop, store or data centers.

One Category 4 hurricane making landfall at a logistic node could deprive companies of weeks of deliveries, ruin inventory, and soar insurance rates over the course of several years (Saba Publications, 2022). The occurrence and severity of such events are getting worse with major weather-related losses no longer exceptional tastes with the billion-dollar climate-related disasters happening at a significantly higher frequency level than in the past decades (Munich Re, 2023).

Example

Consider a solar energy company with installations in wildfire-prone regions of California or southern Europe. Increasing heat and dryness, driven by climate change, elevate the risk of wildfires that could destroy field infrastructure, reduce asset life, and dramatically raise insurance premiums—or render coverage unaffordable altogether (Task Force on Climate-related Financial Disclosures [TCFD], 2017). This isn't a speculative scenario: in 2020, several California solar farms were temporarily shut down due to wildfires, costing developers millions in downtime and repairs.

Or take an organic agriculture enterprise operating in central India. Declining rainfall and water table depletion may lead to lower crop yields, forcing the business to reconsider irrigation strategies, change crop varieties, or relocate altogether—each requiring significant capital outlay and affecting future cash flow projections.

1.2 Transition Risks

The transition risks are a result of the required changes in the economic, political, technological and social aspects in order to develop to a low-carbon, climate-resilient economy. These threats might not directly be due to the change of the environment but the actions on the same by the governments, investors and consumers. These changes create opportunities as well as threats in sustainable enterprises - depending on the timing, readiness, and flexibility.

Policy and regulatory risks

Following the strengthening of environmental regulations by governments, the costs of conducting business increase and the compliance requirements become increasingly complicated where the business comes in contact with greenhouse emissions, high-emitting materials, or operates in resource-employing industries (International Energy Agency [IEA], 2021). They may be:

- Emissions trading schemes and Carbon pricing.
- Mandatory climate reporting within systems such as TCFD, or ISSB.
- Prohibition (or tax reimbursement) of high-emission substances (e.g. single-use plastics, fossil-based inputs).

Some of the green procurement regulations that disregard the suppliers who are not green.

Regulatory risk can be abrupt and front-loaded, so it is hard to forecast financially. The increase of carbon tax to $100 per metric ton, which is considered realistic in many G20 economies today, could completely change the business cost profile in companies that use substantial amount of energy or have exposure to freight.

Market and Consumer Shifts

The expectations of investors and awareness levels of consumers are also changing at a fast rate. Companies whose packaging, sourcing or energy sources are not sustainable can lose their sales, brand strength, or be divested by investors (KPMG, 2020). Even those businesses that are sustainable may become overtaken, in the event they are unable to go along with newer more rigorous requirements.

Rising net-zero procurement models, B Corp designations and the growth of ESG funds are raising the scrutiny of the market (McKinsey & Company, 2020). Reputational risk in this area tends to be reputational in character but reputational damage soon gets turned into financial damages through a lack of customer loyalty, a loss of partnerships, or screening out of impact investment portfolios.

Technological Disruption

The use of low-carbon technologies would also make conventional business models obsolete as they get more affordable. Just think about the replacement of diesel generators with solar and battery, or the change in input requirements and water management due to precision agriculture. The collapse of the changing of new technologies in sustainable enterprises has a possibility of turning inefficient or irrelevant even in the presence of the mission.

Reputational and Social License Risks

There is growing shareholder activism, civil society campaigns and public scrutiny. Firms with opaque emissions reporting, diversity policy and climate resiliency plans are increasingly vulnerable to backlash. This may result in boycotts, hemorrhaging staff or missing out on important business partnerships- particularly in areas where brand has a direct relationship with moral authority.

Example

Companies that deal in virgin plastic can easily lose customers as new regulations to be implemented by the government push towards compostable or completely recyclable packages into the markets. In the meantime, a fashion brand that does not have verified climate disclosures might become the object of investor backlash or reputational damage through social media channels, even though it performs well financially.

1.3 Interactions and Overlaps

In practice, physical and transition risks rarely act in isolation. Often, one triggers or amplifies the other. For example, a coastal warehouse (physical risk) might be severely damaged by a storm. When the company rebuilds, it may face stricter building codes, ESG-aligned supplier mandates, and higher insurance premiums (transition risks). Conversely, a company investing in carbon-neutral production might face initial capital costs (transition risk), only to gain long-term resilience to carbon market volatility (physical + policy synergy).

This risk convergence makes financial modelling more complex—but also more necessary. Sustainable enterprises must evaluate:

- How a physical risk event changes their regulatory exposure.
- How transition policies affect their ability to adapt to climate events.
- How both impact long-term profitability and investor perception.

Figure 1. Types of Climate Risk and Their Primary Financial Impact Zones

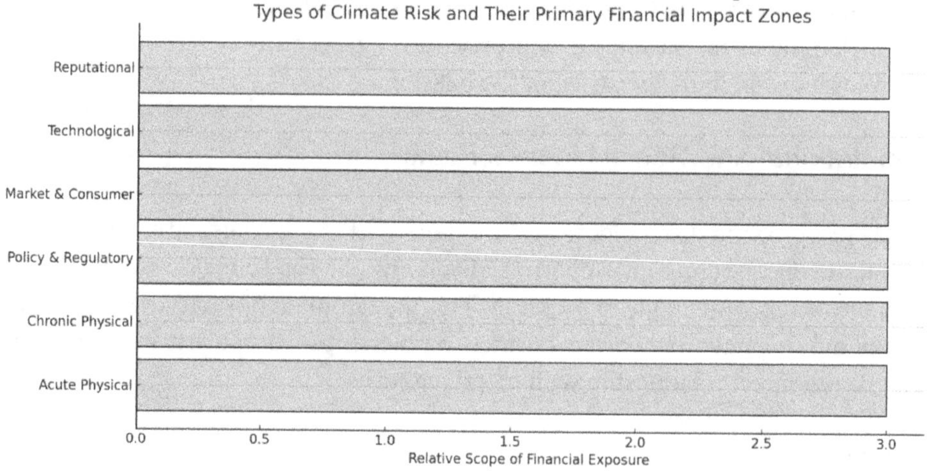

Table 1. Risk types and descriptions and their financial impact areas.

Risk Type	Description	Financial Impact Areas
Acute Physical	Sudden events like floods, hurricanes, wildfires disrupting operations.	CapEx for repairs, increased insurance, downtime loss.
Chronic Physical	Long-term shifts like sea-level rise, drought, and heat stress.	Productivity decline, asset depreciation, adaptation costs.
Policy & Regulatory	New laws: carbon pricing, reporting mandates, material bans.	Increased compliance cost, taxes, operational constraints.
Market & Consumer	Shifting demand toward sustainable products, green procurement.	Revenue volatility, branding risk, loss of market access.
Technological	Disruption from cleaner tech displacing traditional systems.	Asset write-offs, increased CapEx, retraining needs.
Reputational	Loss of public trust, stakeholder pressure, or activist scrutiny.	Sales impact, investor exit, HR & legal cost escalation.

Financial models that treat climate risk as a siloed variable fail to capture this interdependence. A comprehensive approach—rooted in scenario analysis and integrated forecasting—enables enterprises to prepare for cascading risk, allocate capital more wisely, and avoid being blindsided by compounding climate stressors.

These risk categories directly inform scenario-based financial models:

- **Acute and chronic physical risks** affect capital expenditure (e.g., rebuilding, infrastructure upgrades) and operating costs (e.g., insurance, maintenance), and should be reflected in annual CapEx forecasts and scenario-adjusted OPEX.

- **Policy and regulatory risks** impact tax rates, compliance costs, and discount rates—requiring adjustment in long-term financial projections.
- **Market and consumer shifts** alter revenue growth rates and pricing assumptions, requiring revenue modelling to include climate scenario multipliers.
- **Technological risks** may trigger premature asset depreciation or demand new CapEx, directly altering balance sheet projections.
- **Reputational risks** influence investor perception, access to capital, and customer churn, and may be represented by changes in discount rate or revenue volatility in models.

Each risk type becomes a **variable input** in climate scenario modelling, helping sustainable enterprises map financial exposure and resilience over time.

2. CLIMATE RISK ASSESSMENT FRAMEWORK

There is more to climate awareness than sustainable enterprises require. They require a mechanism that determines, examines and plans the risks that relate to climate. A formal framework of appraisals enables organizations to evaluate the possible effects and incorporate them into their planning (both business and financial) (UNEP Finance Initiative, 2021).

2.1 Diagnosis of Exposure

The initial step involves the mapping of the exposure of the business to climate-related threats where and how. This includes:

- Assets: buildings, infrastructure, equipments.
- Operations: energy, water dependence, transportation, logistics.
- Supply chains: dependence on upstream and downstream, geographic dependency.
- Markets and customers: climate awareness, regulatory environments and consumer behavior sensitivity.

Tool Example: Geographic Information Systems (GIS) may be used to document facilities and suppliers in areas that are prone to disasters such as flood plains, or wild-fire areas.

2.2 Vulnerability Analysis

As soon as exposures have been identified, then comes the question of analyzing vulnerability; that is, how bad these exposures could become.

- Considerations on physical vulnerability age, Physical resilience of infrastructure, backup systems.
- Financial exposure: reliance on cash flow, insurance cover, asset concentration.
- Vulnerability of the organization: the preparedness of the workforce, emergency operations, the ability to adapt.

This can involve conducting interviews with the stake holders, internal audits as well as third party evaluation.

2.3 Situation Analysis

Businesses are supposed to model the way that various climatic futures would affect them to be able to take into consideration uncertainty. That is where scenario analysis comes to play.

- Apply universally known such scenario as:
- Shared Socioeconomic Pathways (SSPs) of IPCC, or Representative Concentration Pathways (RCPs) of the IPCC.
- Climate scenarios of NGFS (Network for Greening the Financial System) for macro-financial modeling.
- Set timelines (2030, 2050, 2100), as well as variables: temperature increase, quantity of emissions, the level of policies.

2.4 Tools and Data Sources

Reliable risk assessment requires good data and the right tools. Common sources include:

- **Climate Data**: NASA Earth Exchange, CMIP6, Copernicus Climate Data Store.
- **Risk Tools**: ClimateIQ, Four Twenty Seven, Acclimatise, S&P's Trucost.
- **Disclosure Frameworks**: TCFD (Task Force on Climate-related Financial Disclosures), CDP.

Using credible sources not only improves internal accuracy but also strengthens external reporting and investor confidence.

In the next section we will be looking at the fundamentals of cash flow modelling and then in later stages a scenario analysis will be done in detail.

3. FUNDAMENTALS OF CASH FLOW MODELLING

Before climate risk enters the picture, it's important to understand the backbone of any financial forecast: the cash flow model. This section breaks down the key components of a typical enterprise-level cash flow model and shows where climate variables can be inserted.

The following schematic illustrates the methodological flow of integrating climate variables into FCFF modelling for sustainable enterprises:

Figure 2. Integrating Climate Variable into FCFF Modelling: Methodology Flow.

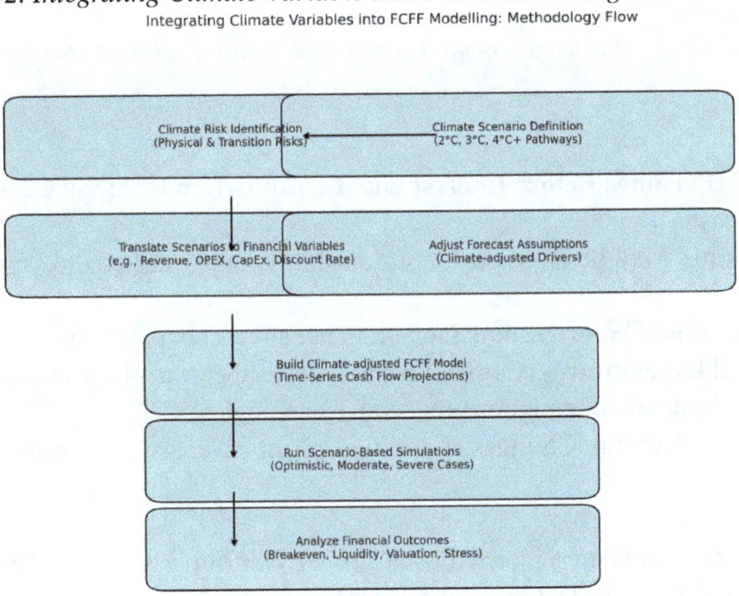

3.1 Purpose of a Cash Flow Model

A cash flow model provides the answer to one basic question:

Does this enterprise predict to produce over a period of time, more than it consumes with realistic assumptions?

To sustainable enterprises as well, it discloses:

- The amount of available runway in various stresses conditions.
- Primary investments, when they work (or not).
- Whether environmental programs entrench the bottom line or undermine the bottom line.

3.2 Core Structure: Free Cash Flow to Firm (FCFF)

One common approach is **Free Cash Flow to the Firm**, which represents the cash available to all capital providers after operating expenses and capital investments.

Core formula:

$$FCFF = EBIT \times (1 - Tax\ Rate) + Depreciation/Amortization - CapEx - \Delta WorkingCapital$$

Components:

- **EBIT (Earnings Before Interest and Taxes)**: Driven by revenue and operating costs.
- **Tax Rate**: May be adjusted for sustainability-linked tax credits or carbon levies.
- **Depreciation/Amortization**: Non-cash, but affects tax payments.
- **Capital Expenditures (CapEx)**: Includes investments in physical assets, climate adaptation, or emissions-reducing technologies.
- **Working Capital Changes**: Cash tied up in inventory, receivables, and payables.

These components are projected over a 5–10 year horizon, then a **Terminal Value** is calculated to reflect long-term business value.

3.3 Where Climate Risk Fits In

Table 2. Here's where we start to align the financial mechanics with climate scenarios:

Model Component	Climate Risk Impact
Revenue	Demand shifts due to regulation, climate shocks, or consumer behavior
Operating Costs (OPEX)	Increased costs from energy, insurance, logistics, or raw materials
CapEx	New spending for resilience or decarbonization
Working Capital	Disruptions in supply chain affecting inventory and payables
Discount Rate	Adjusted for scenario volatility or transition risk
Terminal Value	Re-evaluated under long-term climate scenarios (e.g., 2°C vs. 4°C futures)

3.4 Example: Basic Model Before Climate Adjustments

Table 3. Let's say a sustainable packaging startup has this base model:

Year	Revenue	EBIT Margin	CapEx	Net Working Capital Change	FCFF
Year 1	$2M	15%	$250K	$50K	$200K
Year 2	$2.5M	18%	$300K	$70K	$320K
...	...	...	...	...	...

This forecast assumes stable conditions. In reality, rising resin prices (transition risk), energy inflation (physical risk), or new packaging laws could all change these numbers.

3.5 Why It Matters

Not having adjusted the model to climate risk:

- There can be an over-ambitious revenue forecast.

Cost assumptions may prove to be lower than volatility.
Investors and lenders can consider that the model is outdated or superficial.
A cash flow model that incorporates climate change perception forecasts such uncertainties and indicates that the business is not only viable in theory- but it is financially sturdy in reality.

4. CLIMATE SCENARIO DESIGNS

Climate scenario planning is the development of a series of what would happen futures by making differing assumptions about what might happen physically, what might happen with regulations, and what might happen with markets (World Economic Forum, 2023). Your climate-adjusted financial model will rely on these scenarios.

4.1 What is a Climate Scenario?

Climate scenario is a kind of future construction which is constructed through specific variables like:

- Increase in the temperature of the world (e.g. 1.5 C, 2 C, 4 C).
- Prices of carbon.
- Intensity and occurrence of extraordinary weather Conditions.
- Availability of resources (e.g. water stress, energy prices).
- Policy and regulatory measures (e.g. emissions limits, required reporting).

The two set of scenarios present a range of issues and opportunities to your business- and generate different financial results.

4.2 Sources of Climate Scenarios

The sources to rely on:

- Intergovernmental Panel on climate change (IPCC): SSPs (Shared Socioeconomic Pathways); RCPs (Representative Concentration Pathways).
- NGFS (Network for Greening the Financial System): Direction of solvability pathways to climate macro-financial stress tests (International Organization for Standardization [ISO], 2019).
- IEA (International Energy Agency): Scenarios on the transition on energy.
- Regional climate modeling: Regional climate predictions, regional impact assessments.

These give scenarios templates of various climatic futures. The following is a three-scenario model that can be implemented on a sustainable business:

Scenario 1: Managed Transition (Best Case – 1.5°C–2°C World)

- Carbon tax by Year 5 = 50/ ton

- The level of supply chain is largely steady; low risk of disruption.
- Sustainable products are demanded by the consumers; Increase in revenue.
- The costs of renewable energies go down; energy prices decrease.

The events of climate are restricted; insurance expenses consistent.
Implication: Favourable for sustainable businesses. Model moderate upside.

Scenario 2: Delayed Transition (Base Case – 2.5°C–3°C World)

- Carbon tax gradually increases to an amount of 80/ton in Year 10.
- Increase in energy and logistics cost, up to a moderate degree.
- An operation is disrupted by a big climate event (e.g. flood, wildfire).
- Companies that do not disclose emissions have an increased reputational risk.

Implication: Mixed impacts. Model increased OPEX and one-time disruptions.

Scenario 3: Failed Transition (High Risk – 4°C+ World)

- Non consistent or extreme carbon pricing ($100+/ton).
- The number of physical climate shocks rises (floods, heatwaves).
- Water scarcity has an impact on production and input supply.
- It gets expensive to insure or even it is not insurable.
- CapEx on climate adaptation is acute and massive.

Implication: Stress test survival. Model revenue contraction, cost spikes, asset write-downs.

Table 4. Now, apply each scenario's logic to the financial model:

Variable	Managed Transition	Delayed Transition	Failed Transition
Revenue Growth	+10%/year	+5%/year	-5%/year
Energy Cost Increase	-2%/year	+5%/year	+12%/year
Carbon Tax	$50/ton (Yr 5)	$80/ton (Yr 10)	$120/ton (Yr 5)
Insurance Premiums	Stable	+15% (once)	+30%/year
CapEx for Resilience	Low ($50K)	Medium ($150K)	High ($500K+)
Discount Rate	8%	10%	12–14%

These inputs will feed directly into the next section: modifying the base financial model to reflect climate risk.

5. FINANCIAL MODEL FORMATION

In this section, the process of converting climate scenarios into a financial representation of the real-world risk is walked through. Our working example will be a hypothetical sustainable enterprise EcoPack that is a packaging firm that switches plastic materials with biodegradable ones.

5.1 Step 1: Build the Base Model (No Climate Adjustment)

Table 5. EcoPack's simplified 5-year forecast, using a traditional Free Cash Flow to Firm (FCFF) model:

Year	Revenue	EBIT Margin	EBIT	CapEx	Working Capital Δ	FCFF
1	$2.0M	15%	$300K	$250K	$50K	$0
2	$2.5M	18%	$450K	$300K	$70K	$80K
3	$3.1M	20%	$620K	$350K	$90K	$180K
4	$3.8M	22%	$836K	$375K	$100K	$361K
5	$4.5M	22%	$990K	$400K	$110K	$480K

Assumptions are stable operations, modest growth, and no major climate disruptions. Now let's add climate dimensions in the next step:

5.2 Step 2: Adjust Inputs for Climate Scenarios

We apply assumptions from Section 4 to generate three financial paths:

Scenario A: Managed Transition (Low Risk)

- Demand of sustainable packaging is on the rise.
- The price of energy is reduced a little.
- Carbon tax of 50/ton impacts on the goods price.

Outcome: Marginal decrease in EBITS margins (1-2 percent), CapEx after automation (~$50K one time), good cash flow.

Scenario B: Delayed Transition (Moderate Risk)

- Year 3 moderate carbon tax ($80/ton).

- The prices of energy and logistics grow with 5-7 percent per year.
- Yr 3 disruption of the supply chain (one-time hit).

Adjustments:

- In Year 3 revenue decreases a bit, and growth is slowing to 5-6%.
- There is an increase in operating costs: the EBIT margin becomes 16-18%.
- The impact is an increase of CapEx because of adaptation needs (~$150K).
- The insurance premiums are high after the disruption.

Result: FCFF compressed in mid-term, with slower recovery.

Scenario C: Failed Transition (High Risk)

- An early boom in carbon pricing occurs to $120/ton.
- Two weather incidences occur in Year 2 and in Year 4.
- CapEx of half a million on relocation/floodproofing of factory.
- At Year 4 no insurance available.

Adjustments:

- Revenue declines or attains stagnation (-5% YoY past Year 2).
- EBIT margin declines to 10-12%.
- Year 2-4, negative FCFF.
- The rate of discount goes up to 14 due to uncertainty.

Result: Company may run out of cash without external funding or aggressive restructuring.

5.3 Step 3: Compare Outcomes

Table 6. Compare Outcomes

Metric	Scenario A	Scenario B	Scenario C
Year 5 Revenue	$4.6M	$4.0M	$3.1M
Year 5 FCFF	$500K	$260K	-$120K
Total 5-Year FCFF	$1.1M	$710K	-$340K
NPV (8–14% Discount)	High	Moderate	Negative
Risk Level	Low	Medium	High

This allows EcoPack's leadership to see:

- Which climate outcomes break their model.
- What level of CapEx or pricing flexibility they need to remain viable.
- Whether current reserves or funding are enough to survive high-risk scenarios.

5.4 Step 4: Strategic Use of the Model

From these outputs, EcoPack can:

- Adjust product pricing to absorb carbon taxes.
- Seek green bonds or adaptation grants to fund CapEx.
- Pivot sourcing to more resilient suppliers.
- Use Scenario A as a base case, but plan cash reserves as if Scenario B hits.

6. CASE EXAMPLE: CLIMATE ADJUSTED FINANCIAL MODEL AGRITECH ROOTS

AgriTech roots is a sustainable business in India, which offers an artificial intelligence-powered irrigation system to smallholder farms. It derives its revenue based on crop yield and uptake farmer-based which is highly susceptible to climatic conditions.

6.1 Business Model Snapshot

- **Revenue**: Subscription model ($50–100/month/system), plus sensor hardware sales.
- **Operating Costs**: Manufacturing, field support, energy, and data infrastructure.
- **CapEx**: Includes R&D, factory upgrades, and regional expansion.
- **Climate Exposure**:
  - o Drought reduces crop yields → lower adoption/retention.
  - o Heatwaves damage field equipment → increased maintenance costs.
  - o Transition risk: water pricing policy, irrigation subsidies, green financing.

6.2 Scenarios Applied

Scenario A: Pro-Growth, 2°C World

- Government priorities to climate-smart agriculture.
- Subsidies of adopting@ water policy also apply.
- Low damage of equipment; moderate temperature rise.

Scenario B: Volatile, 3°C World

- The farmers are prone to serious droughts.
- Policy is irregular; there is a delay of subsidies.
- The input costs increase to a moderate level; a single significant climate shock in Year 3.

Scenario C: Disrupted, 4°C+ World

- Failure of crops in the main areas.
- A political aspect is added to water and subsidies are withdrawn.
- Recurring loss of field equipment; increasing delivery and maintenance cost.
- Trust in the investors is lost; shortfall in funding at Year 4.

6.3 Financial Outputs

Table 7. Financial Outputs (5-Year Summary)

Metric	Scenario A	Scenario B	Scenario C
Year 5 Revenue	12 Cr	9.5 Cr	6 Cr
EBIT Margin (Year 5)	20%	15%	8%
Cumulative CapEx (5 years)	4 Cr	6 Cr	9 Cr
FCFF (Year 5)	1.5 Cr	0.85 Cr	- 0.5 Cr
Total FCFF (5 Years)	4.8 Cr	2.6 Cr	- 0.9 Cr
Implied NPV (10–14% disc.)	2.5 Cr	1.1 Cr	Negative
Required Emergency Funding	0	0	2.5 Cr
Break-even Year	Year 3	Year 4	Never

6.4 Insights & Strategic Adjustments

Under Scenario A:

- Great rationale of expanding to additional 3 states by the Year 4.
- Government liaisons are important drivers of growth.
- Carbon reporting and water efficiency are the keys to releasing green finance.

Under Scenario B:

- One year extension of expansion to save working capital.
- Employees need to develop local repair centers to minimize downtimes on service during climate shocks.
- Submit applications (commercial/climate adaptation grants).

Under Scenario C:

- Delay projects that have CapEx; focus on cash conservation.
- Aim to have off-grid solar-powered system redesign as a way of cutting down the risk of energy.
- Adjust unit economics and subscription business to endure lower adoption.

Table 8. From the below table we can see the summarised version of the different scenarios in the financial Model:

Metric	Scenario A (2Â°C)	Scenario B (3Â°C)	Scenario C (4Â°C+)
Year 5 Revenue (â,¹ Cr)	12	9.5	6
EBIT Margin (Year 5)	20%	15%	8%
Cumulative CapEx (5 years) (â,¹ Cr)	4	6	9
FCFF (Year 5) (â,¹ Cr)	1.5	0.85	-0.5
Total FCFF (5 Years) (â,¹ Cr)	4.8	2.6	-0.9
Implied NPV (10â€"14% Discount Rate) (â,¹ Cr)	2.5	1.1	Negative
Required Emergency Funding (â,¹ Cr)	0	0	2.5
Break-even Year	Year 3	Year 4	Never

Figure 3. Revenue vs Total FCFF Across Climate Scenarios.

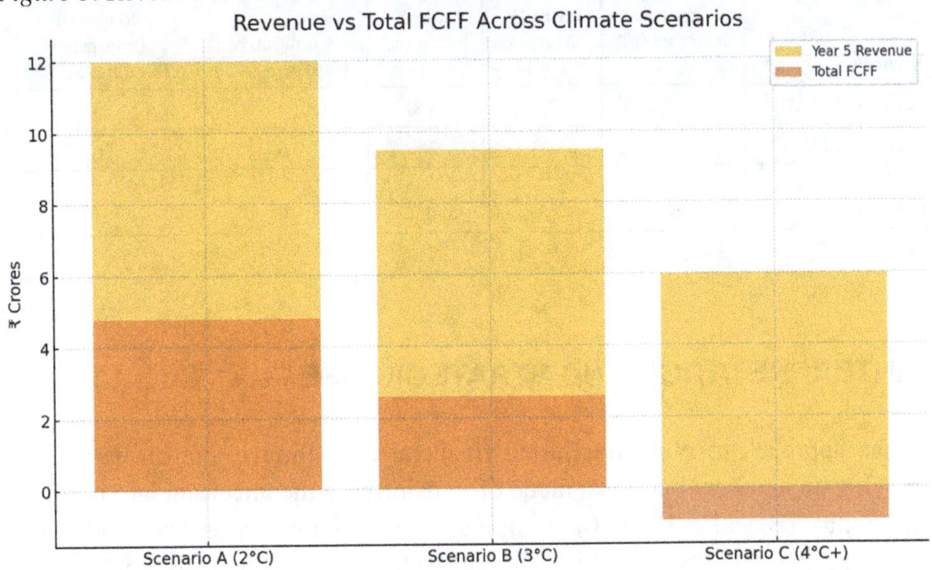

Figure 4. Capital Expenditure and Emergency Funding Needs.

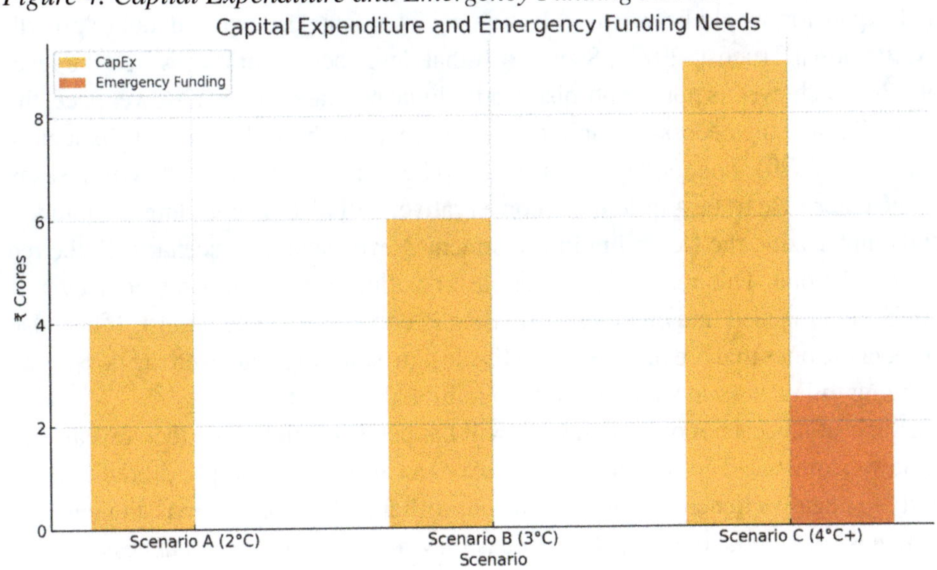

Table 9. Scenario review.

Scenario	Year 5 Revenue (â‚¹ Cr)	EBIT Margin (%)	Total FCFF (â‚¹ Cr)	Cumulative CapEx (â‚¹ Cr)	Required Emergency Funding (â‚¹ Cr)
Scenario A (2Â°C)	12	20	4.8	4	0
Scenario B (3Â°C)	9.5	15	2.6	6	0
Scenario C (4Â°C+)	6	8	-0.9	9	2.5

7. INTERPRETATION AND STRATEGIC USE

The approach to climate-adjusted financial modelling is not an exercise in worrying up numbers but it is a mode of transforming the uncertain into informed opportunity (BlackRock, 2020). Building scenario-based cash flow models and examining them will be useful to enhance the knowledge of the sustainable enterprise about how the effects of climate risk can define its future, and what must be done to become resilient.

Take a situation of AgriTech Roots. The Scenario A is a world of less than 2 C of warming and in such case the operations will be viable, the cash flow will be good and expansion would be worth it. It is an environmental friendly model to growth (S&P Global Trucost, 2021). Scenario B that describes a world in which the level of a 3C is achieved is not as optimistic: additional revenues rise at a slower pace, the costs rise, and the necessary capital expenditure has to be well-timed (Tuhkanen & Vulturius, 2020). The model in this case will be just like a guard rail it will just say to the enterprise to be a little more conservative, will also be guarding its liquidity and emphasizing the flexibility in investment. Nevertheless, in scenario C, the red alert is the one. This results in poorer cash position of the company, breakeven is not being breached and emergency funding is considered to be a must. It can also compel the ones that are involved with the design, sourcing, and even the possibility of being in business in some markets to rethink their strategies.

Such situations not only state what will happen financially, but they reveal strategic weaknesses. The rise in carbon price can cause a low margin product line to unity to negative hence making the line unprofitable. Because there is an increased grossness of floods, the supply chain has may be stripped of its weaknesses (Golnaraghi, 2021). High CapEx requirements to correct climatic situation High CapEx requirements may prove an extreme climate, which even profitable businesses could be incapable of managing. Each lesson of the model would become a lever: to reform the prices, delay the expansion, alter the product strategy or anticipatory funding.

Notably, the models will be in a position to improve external interaction. Data is power, and investors no longer content with blanket, token-like, ESG statements, require data. The risks related to climate are also more effectively presented in the form of the scenario-based, measurable Finnancial projections, which means the readiness and transparency (United Nations Environment Programme [UNEP], 2021). By auditing the green bonds or sustainability-linked loans made by lenders, they stand at a better position to make an evaluation on the risk adjusted returns. Even the policy partners would have a better disposition to support businesses capable of presenting a sober image of climate economics.

To facilitate this approach becoming a habit and affordable, the sustainable businesses are being recommended to incorporate modelling into the yearly business planning exercise - update assumptions, year in, year out, and compare them to what is occurring in the real world, whether it is IPCC reports, carbon prices or weather changes of local nature (G20 Sustainable Finance Working Group, 2021). Though this may be seeming as technical the entry point will be reduced drastically. Simple climate scenarios can be programmed in Excel or in Google Sheet. Examples of open-source platforms that contain risk datasets and templates include Climada, ClimateIQ or Carbon Delta.

In case they are in search of a ready-made guidance, there are frameworks that can offer common ground; such as the Task Force on Climate-related Financial Disclosures (TCFD) framework, the NGFS Climate Scenarios, and the International Sustainability Standards Board (ISSB).

Finally, Climate-informed financial modelling allows businesses not only the means of adapting, but also leading (Eccles & Klimenko, 2019). It incorporates climatological intelligence into the genes of organizational strategy - so that we don't not make decisions out of fear of the future but out of mastery of the future.

Policy Integration and Strategic Application

Governments and their public institutions may not only use it to determine the vulnerability of enterprises but also take proactive and specific climate-policy making. Taking an example, there could be a possibility of proving how the firm-level cash flows are affected by the different possible climate regime outcomes and thus which sectors have the greatest insolvency risk in both extreme weather scenarios and a pricing regime of carbon emissions (World Bank, 2021). Based on this knowledge, it is possible to set adaptation lower in priority to vulnerable sectors (ex. agriculture, logistics, or energy-intensive small and medium businesses) or develop tax credits on the basis of incentives to implement the resilience technology as soon as possible. And the governments can use industry-wide FCFF estimates to facilitate the implementation of green infrastructure funds or structure whatever they will to de-risk their blending finance mechanisms the private investment in climate-exposed locations. The incorporation of climatic modeling in financial models has also come up with evidence-based business input as to the calibration nature of carbon price which has helped policy makers evaluate the level of impact on profitability and the time frame within which the investment and reduction in the level of emission of respective sectors take place (Whelan & Fink, 2016). Second, the financial modelling in its turn can become both an instrument of business resilience, and of wiser investments of the citizens or even of a public authorities and comes up with a regulatory design, and even planning towards just transition.

CONCLUSION: REFRAMING FINANCIAL RESILIENCE IN A CLIMATE-RISK ERA

Representing a financial ordeal and no longer being merely an environmental issue, climate crisis is a financial affair. It alters the assumptions which have so far served to support conventional business planning to sustainable businesses. Pre-determined costs cease to be so. Historical aspects of stability are misleading. Value does not relate linearly. It is not advantageous anymore to be nice to have, and being resilient is a competitive need now. The chapter has expressed in realistic financial terms, that climate risk must be central in terms of decision making by enterprises (Ansari et al., 2023). And one of its successes has been to lay on the table a single said practical flexible approach to just that scenario-based cash flow modelling under climate risk.

Through this way businesses will be in a position to respond to stop guessing and start quantifying. They can correct the vaguely relaxed attitude they have to climate policies and policies with specific and falsifiable statements. They can transform themselves to proactive. Most importantly, they will also be able to thrive, even flourish in an environment that is volatile, disruptive and one that is transforming so far and so rapidly.

A Shift in Financial Mindset

The exercise is launched by criticizing the assumptions embedded in conventional financial models. Conventional cash flow estimates are based on predictable operating conditions and steady state. They are retro-fitting in nature. It is a policy in a world where tomorrow resembles today. That assumption is hazardous with the change of climate.

Distribution centers are erased by floods. Agricultural outputs are eradicated by droughts. Heatwaves are the halting of manufacturing lines. Profit margins can be turned upside in a single night through carbon pricing. The regulatory friction and scarcity of resources break global supply chains into smaller ones. They are not just hypothetical, consequential events currently taking shape in all spheres, be it food and fashion, energy and electronics, etc.

However, quite a few companies keep planning and investing as though these risks do not exist. The blind spot is no more tenable.

Cash flow modelling with scenario is practical and strategic. It does not plan to foresee the future, but to plan against a diversity of futures that are possible (Akhtar et al., 2022). It unites scientific vignettes (such as those produced by the IPCC or NGFS) with working reality: it makes them quantitative economic metrics that count: revenue, cost, capital spending, cash flow, value.

From Abstraction to Application

This involves businesses building climate scenarios which act as lenses through which the businesses can consider their operations: a 2 degree Celsius-managed transition, a 3 degree Celsius- delayed transition and a 4 degree Celsius+failed transition. Each scenario shows variants of the future, which is impacted by physical and transition risks (e.g., extreme weather, water stress, regulation, market changes, disruption of technology).

These situations subsequently signal changes to fundamental financial forces:

The revenue forecasts become flexible to ensure that sudden changes in demand, supply interruption, or market access interruption occur.

Operating cost is balanced on energy cost fluctuations, transportation difficulties and regulatory expenditures.

- Adaptation needs, can be read out of capital expenditures, flood protection or resilient infrastructure.
- There will be larger discount rates because of the volatility and uncertainty of the climate.

As the example of AgriTech Roots, a startup using AI to power irrigation showed, that is how such scenarios are unfolding in terms of financial life of real companies (Akhtar et al., 2021). In a stable scenario of 2deg, the company is growing in good health, breaks even in the third year and generates cash. It opts to weather disruption by growing more slowly and keeping spending conservative under a moderate 3 o C scenario. Under a 4C+ world, earning drops by a third, expenses increase, and cash flow turns adverse, provoking emergency financing and acute prioritizing.

This is not modelling in theory- this is financial planning in the climate reality. It helps entrepreneurs and CFOs have the foresight to understand that they should either grow now or wait, seek aggressive funding or save the cash, focus on innovation or on risk management. It also provides help to the board and investors in how to go about with the downside that is not a reason to pull back, but steps in going back to being stronger.

Strategy, Capital, and Survival

The applications of this technique of modelling to high stakes decision making, or capital allocation, market entry, pricing strategy, infrastructure investment, are the most powerful. There are situations that weaken and boost the viability of sustainable enterprises and as soon as the sustainable enterprises acknowledge that, they are capable of aligning their strategic plans.

As an example, a business experiencing a significant worsening of cash flow in a situation of a high-carbon price would consider quickening the transition to renewables, or repurposing the product to achieve reduced emissions. When a company anticipates a loss of insurance arising because of the recurrent climatic shocks, it can construct a reserve or explore parametric insurance. Other industries might switch towards shorter supply chain, local supply and distribution or digital distribution to minimize physical perils.

Communication between a business organization and the outside world may also be driven using scenario outputs (Ansari et al., 2022). There is growing pressure by investors on TCFD-aligned risk disclosures. Government is designing subsidy and procurement based on the sustainability levels. Issuers of green bonds and ESG-friendly funds need a demonstration of sustainability in a hotter planet. The signal that one business is ready and credible is in the ability to demonstrate that models of financial results have undergone climate testing.

This is not only because of risk management but it is about positioning. Climate opportunity is usually served best by enterprises willing to model climate risk. They will get their climate-aligned products to the market faster, they will be more responsive in changing regulations, and they will be more appealing to low-carbon, high-resilience portfolio providers of capital.

Tools and Accessibility

The positive aspect of it is that no esoteric software and high profile skills are needed to follow this model of modelling. It may be applied on tools known to many businesses, such as Excel, Google Sheets, Python, or dashboards on the cloud. NASA open-source data, IPCC data, World Bank or local climate centers provide plausible inputs. Innovations such as Climada, ClimateIQ and Carbon Delta are becoming easier to use.

Not being perfect is not the key, consistency is the key to the beginners. Models, even the simplest without too many assumptions, clearly stated, and revised each year, are preferable to complete disregard of climate variables. Through time, as internal capacity is developed, these models may become more complex- Monte Carlo simulations, sensitivity analysis, or machine learning layers can be added.

Notably the modelling process in itself creates awareness in departments. Development of sustainable language at the finance level starts. Product managers will observe the impact of materials or design decision over viability in the long-term scope. CEOs get a better plan of risk-reward dynamics in unpredictable times.

The Broader Value

The emergence of ripple effects occurs at the level of the systems due to the financial modelling based on scenarios. The further business people use it, the more transparent the supply chain can be, the greater will be the right pricing of the capital and the entire industry will be climate-literate. The banking institutions are able to lend in a more suitable way. Regulators are able to produce smart disclosures. Investors can distinguish a difference between climate talk and climate proof.

This has colossal implications on the sustainable enterprises. A strategy of this kind would help prove the fact that there is no incompatibility between good and well. It converts the so-called trade-off between sustainability and corporate profitability into an even sounder one: how do we generate income in a climate-change world?

It is possibly the largest value of it all though to re-translate this framing, in which climate risk is no longer to be considered as a burden of compliance, but rather, as a strategy driver. Firms which will embrace it will even outlive their rivals. The future markets will be determined by them.

Last Note: Preparation based on the world we Live in

The climate no longer has an ideal future that is far away in the imagination. Here it is--worse, more dangerous, proceeding more rapidly, said Canada, than the majority of models had pre-ditcted. To the sustainable businesses, the choice is easy: think about how to cope with that reality, or plow over the top of it.

The feasible, flexible and executable plan of action comes with the financial modelling of scenarios. It does not presume the extend to eliminate risk. Nonetheless, it gives decision- makers the expertise to understand it, respond to it as well as wind up having business which can be defined as being not only climate-minded- but also climate-resistant. The enterprises that fit the mold of risk will be on the forefront in a world that rewards foresight. And those that model most, often, truthfully (that is, sincerely), and strategically, will endure.

REFERENCES

G20 Sustainable Finance Working Group. (2021). *G20 Sustainable Finance Roadmap*. https://www.g20.org/

Akhtar, S., Alam, M., & Ansari, M. S. (2022). Measuring the performance of the Indian banking industry: Data envelopment window analysis approach. *Benchmarking*, *29*(9), 2842–2857.

Akhtar, S., Alam, M., Khan, A., & Shamshad, M. (2023). Measuring technical efficiency of banks vis-à-vis demonetization: An empirical analysis of Indian banking sector using CAMELS framework. *Quality & Quantity*, *57*(2), 1739–1761. DOI: 10.1007/s11135-022-01431-8

Akhtar, S., Alam, M., & Khan, M. M. (2021). YES Bank fiasco: Arrogance or negligence. *Emerging Economies Cases Journal*, *3*(2), 95–102. DOI: 10.1177/25166042211061003

Ansari, M. S., Akhtar, S., Khan, A., & Shamshad, M. (2023). Consequence of financial crisis on liquidity and profitability of commercial banks in India: An empirical study. *Studies in Economics and Business Relations*, *3*(2), 36–50. DOI: 10.48185/sebr.v3i2.367

Ansari, M. S., Akhtar, S., Khan, A., & Shamshad, M. (2022). Consequence of financial crisis on liquidity and profitability of commercial banks in India: An empirical study. *Studies in Economics and Business Relations*, *3*(2), 36–50. https://www.sabapub.com/index.php/sebr/article/view/366

BlackRock. (2020). *Sustainability: The future of investing*. https://www.blackrock.com/corporate/about-us/sustainability-resilience

Bolton, P., Després, M., Pereira da Silva, L. A., Samama, F., & Svartzman, R. (2020). *The green swan: Central banking and financial stability in the age of climate change*. Bank for International Settlements. https://www.bis.org/publ/othp31.pdf

Carney, M. (2015). *Breaking the tragedy of the horizon–climate change and financial stability*. Bank of England. https://www.bankofengland.co.uk/speech/2015/breaking-the-tragedy-of-the-horizon-climate-change-and-financial-stability

Eccles, R. G., & Klimenko, S. (2019). The investor revolution: Shareholders are getting serious about sustainability. *Harvard Business Review*, *97*(3), 106–116.

Golnaraghi, M. (2021). *Climate Change and the Insurance Sector: Risk, Regulation, and Resilience*. The Geneva Association. https://www.genevaassociation.org/

Intergovernmental Panel on Climate Change (IPCC). (2021). *Climate Change 2021: The Physical Science Basis*. https://www.ipcc.ch/report/ar6/wg1/

International Energy Agency (IEA). (2021). *Net Zero by 2050: A Roadmap for the Global Energy Sector*. https://www.iea.org/reports/net-zero-by-2050

ISO. (2019). *ISO 14091: Adaptation to climate change — Guidelines on vulnerability, impacts, and risk assessment*. International Organization for Standardization.

KPMG. (2020). *A guide to scenario analysis for climate change risk assessment*. https://home.kpmg/xx/en/home/insights/2020/06/scenario-analysis-guide.html

McKinsey & Company. (2020). *Climate risk and response: Physical hazards and socioeconomic impacts*. https://www.mckinsey.com/business-functions/sustainability/our-insights

Network for Greening the Financial System (NGFS). (2022). *NGFS climate scenarios for central banks and supervisors*. https://www.ngfs.net/en/ngfs-climate-scenarios-central-banks-and-supervisors

S&P Global Trucost. (2021). *Physical risk data for financial institutions*. https://www.spglobal.com/esg/

Task Force on Climate-related Financial Disclosures (TCFD). (2017). *Final report: Recommendations of the Task Force on Climate-related Financial Disclosures*. https://www.fsb-tcfd.org/publications/

Tuhkanen, H., & Vulturius, G. (2020). *Climate risk information for adaptation: Assessing the needs of financial institutions*. Stockholm Environment Institute. https://www.sei.org/publications/climate-risk-finance/

UNEP. (2021). *Adaptation Gap Report 2021: The Gathering Storm*. https://www.unep.org/resources/adaptation-gap-report-2021

UNEP Finance Initiative. (2021). *The Climate Risk Landscape: A Synthesis of Tools and Approaches*. https://www.unepfi.org/publications/the-climate-risk-landscape/

Whelan, T., & Fink, C. (2016). *The comprehensive business case for sustainability*. Harvard Business Review. https://hbr.org/2016/10/the-comprehensive-business-case-for-sustainability

World Bank. (2021). *Climate Risk Country Profiles*. https://climateknowledgeportal.worldbank.org/

World Economic Forum. (2023). *Global Risks Report 2023*. https://www.weforum.org/reports/global-risks-report-2023

KEY TERMS AND DEFINITIONS

Capital Expenditures (CapEx): funds used by a company to acquire or upgrade physical assets such as property, buildings, or equipment.

Free Cash Flow to Firm (FCFF): a method to calculate the amount of cash a company generates after accounting for capital expenditures, used in enterprise valuation.

Net Present Value (NPV): the value of all future cash flows (positive and negative) over the entire life of an investment discounted to the present.

Representative Concentration Pathways (RCPs): greenhouse gas concentration trajectories adopted by the IPCC, representing different climate futures.

Task Force on Climate-related Financial Disclosures (TCFD): an international initiative that develops consistent climate-related financial risk disclosures for use by companies.

Section 5

Inclusive Finance and Innovations

Chapter 14
Mapping the Landscape:
A Bibliometric Analysis of FinTech Innovations in the Banking Industry

Mohammad Ammar Ahsan
Aligarh Muslim University, India

Mohd Salim
https://orcid.org/0000-0003-0162-8433
Woxsen University, India

Parvez Alam Khan
https://orcid.org/0000-0001-8200-2461
University Technology Petronas, Malaysia

Shakeb Akhtar
https://orcid.org/0000-0003-2069-6669
University of Technology and Applied Science, Ibra, Oman & INTI International University, Nilai, Malaysia

ABSTRACT

In the wake of the 2008 financial crisis, Financial Technology (FinTech) innovations emerged as transformative forces in the banking industry. This bibliometric analysis investigates the integration of FinTech in banking by examining growth in Scopus-indexed publications post-crisis, identifying top contributing journals, authors, countries, and institutions, and exploring emerging research themes. The chapter aims to build a theoretical structure of FinTech adoption in banking and assess how it evolved in response to post-crisis challenges and opportunities. Using scientific mapping and performance analysis through Biblioshiny, this research

DOI: 10.4018/979-8-3373-3725-8.ch014

analyses highly cited documents sourced from Scopus. It provides key publication metrics, visualizes research development, identifies trending topics, and proposes a structured research agenda.

INTRODUCTION

Over the last few decades, the world has witnessed remarkable technological advancements. It has impacted anything and everything that people can comprehend, leaving an enduring mark. Numerous examples exist of technology producing and breaking lives and enterprises, the banking industry being one of them (Sardana & Singhania, 2018). An important factor in a country's economic growth is the banking industry. An effective financial system strengthens the country's financial infrastructure by enabling the effective distribution, oversight, and deployment of cash (Isayas, 2022). Technology has changed the financial services sector, and financial institutions rely more on non-branch banking to add customer value (Akhtar et al., 2021). IT is now a vital tool that banks need to stay competitive and offer additional advantages to their consumers (Shukla & Singh, 2014). While pinpointing the exact beginnings of this movement might be difficult, the 2008 Global Financial Crisis (GFC) is frequently cited as a pivotal event that ignited the Fintech movement (Giglio, 2022). This crisis revealed flaws and inefficiencies in existing financial systems, resulting in a loss of confidence in conventional organizations (Uddin & Akhtar, 2025). As a result, there was an increase in demand for more translucent, effective, and innovative financial solutions (Hasan et al., 2024).

In the realm of evolving technologies that facilitate the expansion of financial systems, the concept of customer experience is acquiring new interpretations. The adoption of financial digitization by customers is positively impacted by banks' technological investments (Carbó-Valverde et al., 2020). However, this integration has a long history during which finance and technology have evolved together (Puschmann & Leifer, 2020). The Financial Services business is undergoing a transformation, with startups in financial technologies and financial innovation reshaping the competitive environment (Ansari et al., 2022). The core framework of the banking and capital markets sector is experiencing substantial transformation due to several disruptive forces. The banking industry has significantly transformed due to the rapid acceleration of financial innovation and new financial services (Barroso et al., 2022). FinTech refers to a range of new services enabled by advancements in information and communication technologies including InsurTech, robo-advisors, peer-to-peer financing, crowdlending, crowdfunding, mobile banking, electronic money, and cryptocurrencies (Utami et al., 2021).

Between 2015 and 2019, the global consumer acceptance of FinTech products and businesses increased significantly. Over 75 percent of users worldwide have used a payment service or a money transfer as of 2019. The usage of InsurTech has increased significantly, from 8% in 2015 to over 50% in 2019. Around the world, there are already a significant number of FinTech businesses operating in EMEA and APAC in addition to North America (Statista, 2024). A McKinsey survey from 2021 revealed that 41% of retail consumers expressed a desire to become more acquainted with FinTech solutions (Tabassum et al., 2025). In emerging economies, there is a greater need and demand for FinTech products (Anan et al., 2023).

Bibliometric analysis has been extensively employed across diverse disciplines, including but not limited to social science, artificial intelligence, finance and economics, bitcoin, and blockchain, as evidenced by the various research (Nasir et al., 2020); (Li & Xu, 2022); (Merigó et al., 2016); (Miau & Yang, 2018); (Tabassum, Haque, Ahsan, Salim, & Khan, 2025). The bibliometric evaluation method employs quantitative instruments for the examination of bibliometric data, including article or document references (Donthu et al., 2021). Bibliometrics, as a quantitative and statistical examination of scientific literature, can render the study in a more comprehensible manner by employing tools from scientific visualisation analysis, such as CiteSpace or Vosviewer (Stopar & Bartol, 2019). The freely accessible bibliometrics R program facilitates statistical analysis and visualisation, particularly through diverse mapping approaches (Akhtar et al., 2022). Bibliometric evaluation is a contemporary research instrument that has become increasingly popular across various academic fields, including finance (Akhtar et al., 2023). Biblioshiny has been used in this study as it facilitated a systematic and comprehensive evaluation, providing metrics and figures that enriched the comprehension of the research landscape (Hasan et al., 2025).

The potential and risks that FinTech presents to banks, as well as the impact on the primary duties of financial institutions and their position in contemporary banking ecosystems, are of the utmost importance, given the significance of financial institutions in the banking industry (Naseema et al., 2025). Several bibliometric analyses have been produced by the increasing quantity of academic publications regarding FinTech. While some research has explored the research on FinTech in general (Chen & Peng, 2020); (Aysan & Nanaeva, 2022). Increasingly, bibliometric evaluations focus on particular sectors of FinTech, such as FinTech legislation (Lakhe & Kulkarni, 2020), blockchain, and Cryptocurrencies (Firdaus et al., 2019). However, as far as the authors are aware, no bibliometric assessment has been done on the influence of FinTech services on the banking sector following the GFC (2008) (Salim et. al., 2025). Contributing to the work's uniqueness is the fact that this is the earliest effort to offer a bibliometric analysis on the subject (Quarshie et al., 2025).

This study looks at the existing research on FinTech as a radical transformation of the established financial system following the 2008 financial crisis to close this gap.

To investigate, the frontiers and research perspectives of the financial areas that have been disrupted and rebuilt, this work examined the following research questions:

RQ1: How much have we seen an increase in publications indexed in the Scopus (SCO) database post 2008 financial crisis on integrating FinTech and banking?

RQ2: Which authors, countries, and journals have contributed the most to the surge of the prospect of FinTech implementation in the banking industry?

RQ3: What are the main emerging research topics and subtopics on FinTech adoption in the banking industry?

These research questions can be addressed using bibliometric analysis, which maps the research landscape rigorously and identifies trends in authorship, cited activity, journal output, and study themes. In view of these questions, the main aim of this study is to provide a theoretical structure of FinTech adoption in the banking industry. Specifically, how FinTech has responded to and been shaped by the opportunities and challenges that emerged during and after the 2008 financial crisis.

RESEARCH METHODOLOGY

In this paper, we conducted a systematic literature review using a bibliometric analysis that focused on a comprehensive understanding of the current state of FinTech innovation and the banking sector as a research field. Additionally, we aimed to collect and connect as many relevant existing studies as possible. The primary advantage of bibliometrics is that the large number of data generated is usually concise, straightforward, impartial (Jokić & Ball, 2006; Salim et al., 2023), and as visually simplified as possible (Xue et al., 2022). Because of its focus on the literature's internal relationships, bibliometric analysis is considerably more suited to academic research (Zhao, Zhang, & Kwon, 2018). By analysing bibliometric data, researchers can acquire a sense of the history of the field's development over time, gain insight into its current status, and get direction for future studies (Bilal et al., 2022; Durieux & Gevenois, 2010). The detailed method of article collection, screening, analysis, and visualisation of data is highlighted in Figure 1 Prisma Framework.

Figure 1. Prisma Framework

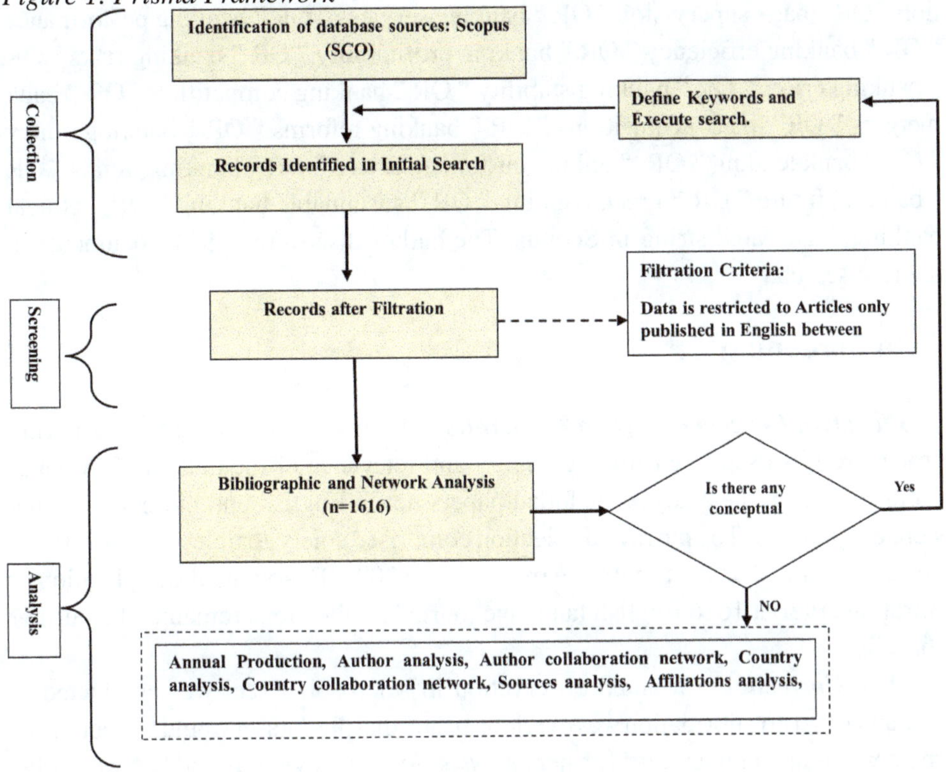

Data Collection

Database: Picking the correct database(s) is the first step in conducting the bibliometric study (Ayan, Güner, & Son-Turan, 2022). This analysis considers the most popular bibliometric database, Scopus by Elsevier (Zhu & Liu, 2020).

Search Criteria: This study used ("Fintech" OR "Financial Technology" OR "Digital Finance" OR "Robo-Advisors" OR "Cryptocurrency" OR "Blockchain Technology" OR "Peer-to-Peer Lending" OR "Mobile Payments" OR "Open Banking" OR "Neobanks" OR "RegTech" OR "Regulatory Technology" OR "Insurtech" OR "Insurance Technology" OR "AI in Finance" OR "Machine Learning in Finance" OR "Big Data in Finance" OR "Financial Inclusion" OR "Payment Innovation" OR "Financial Disruption" OR "Cybersecurity in Finance" OR "Tokenization in Finance" OR "Digital Identity in Finance" OR "Blockchain-based Smart Contracts" OR "Financial APIs" OR "Crowdfunding in Finance" OR "Alternative Lending") AND ("banking industry " OR " banking sector " OR " banking system " OR " commercial banking " OR " retail banking " OR " investment banking " OR " central banking " OR " bank management " OR " financial institutions " OR " bank regulation " OR " bank supervision " OR " banking services " OR " banking performance " OR " banking efficiency " OR " banking profitability " OR " banking risks " OR " banking crises " OR " banking stability " OR " banking competition " OR " bank mergers " OR " bank acquisitions " OR " banking reforms " OR " banking policy " OR " bank lending " OR "banking customer service " OR " banking trends " OR " banking future " OR " green banking " OR " sustainable banking " OR " ethical banking)" as search string in Scopus. The author discovered 1911 documents in the first search.

Data Screening

Filtration Criteria and Data Preparation: In this research a rigorous filtering procedure was used to ensure the quality and relevance of the dataset. The initial exclusions from the analysis included papers not in English and publications that were not journals. The narrowed selection comprised solely Articles. The investigation concentrated on the timeframe from 2009 to 2024. Following the application of filtration criteria, 1616 English language journal publications remained for further analysis.

Data Corrections: Manual observation in Microsoft Excel was conducted to guarantee that no information was overlooked and that the dataset would be accurately and consistently prepared for further analysis. Author Keywords and Keyword Plus submissions were manually standardised. Normalisation refers to the standardisation of various concepts into cohesive keywords. For example, versions of "blockchain" include "block-chain" and "blockchain technology," which needed to be standardised to "blockchain." Similarly, "covid-19", "covid19", "pandemic", "19-pandemic", and "covid-19-pandemic" were all standardised to "covid-19". Similarly, "financial technology" and "financial tech" were both consolidated into "fintech". The cleaning was conducted using the Replace function in Microsoft Excel, facilitating an accurate keyword count and ensuring the integrity of the subsequent bibliometric study.

ANALYSIS

The current study used the Biblioshiny program, a robust tool for analysis and visualisation, to establish the present and future of the hybrid work model. Biblioshiny was developed by Massimo Aria and offers a full-featured and highly user-friendly interface that accommodates users with extensive experience programming R, built on top of the Shiny package for R programming language (Aria & Cuccurullo, 2017; Salim, Khan, et al., 2025).

To install it, we used the following commands for installation package install. packages "bibliometrix", then the library bibliometrix, and the command "biblioshiny" in the RStudio command workspace. Our Biblioshiny analyses included extensive topics within the Performance Analysis and Network Mapping area, which included Positive and Negative Performance Analysis, Performance Comparison, and Network Mapping (Moral-Muñoz et al., 2020). In Performance Analysis, we have analyzed the most recent trend publications, citing the most relevant articles and countries, countries of the Most Relevant Sources, and the Most Productive Institutions, in this area. In addition to Positive and Negative Performance Analysis, combined with Comparative Performance Analysis, we have carried out Science Mapping, Keyword Co-occurrence this provided us with valuable information within the hybrid work framework.

With Biblioshiny's Performance Analysis, we had a comprehensive overview of the research that has been done, and we also have got insights into potential future research in this dynamic area. We believe that, by using this programme, we have gained valuable understanding and conclusion-making from the bibliometric data, which was possible to interpret and combine performance and network data in a multidimensional form.

RESULTS

Descriptive Statistics

Descriptive Analysis in bibliometric studies provides a comprehensive overview of the research landscape, highlighting the volume, growth, and key characteristics of scholarly outputs (Ramakreshnan et al., 2021; Salim, Ahsan, & Khan, 2025). In the context of the FinTech and banking industry, this study focuses on articles published since the global financial crisis of 2008, a pivotal period that has significantly shaped financial innovations and regulatory landscapes.

Figure 2. Predominantly collaborative research output.

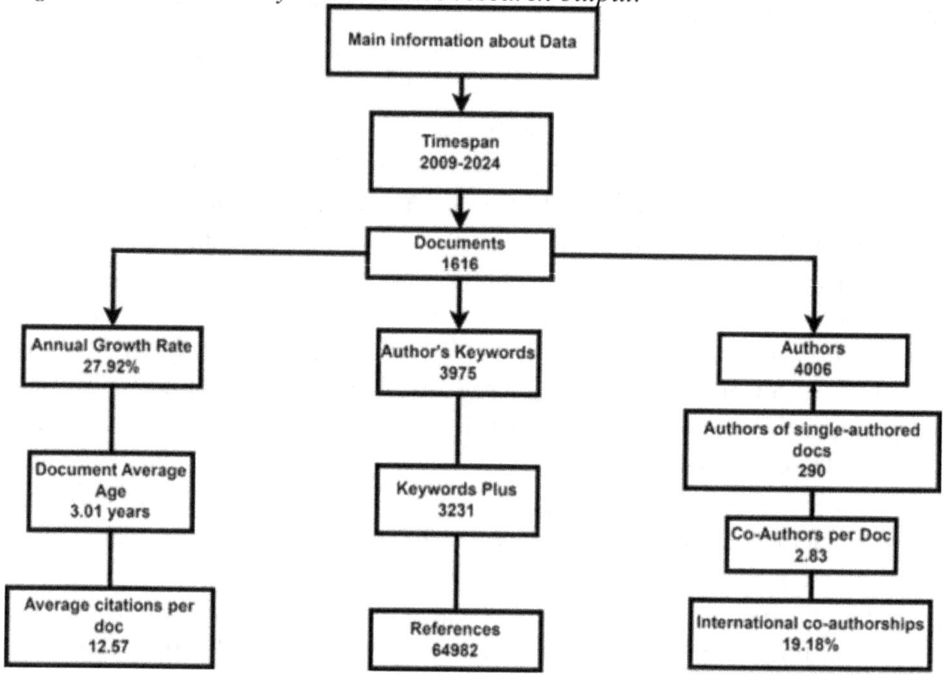

From 2009 to 2024, the study encompasses 1,616 documents sourced from 882 different journals, books, and other publications. This is a remarkable annual growth rate of 27.92%. This circumstance has consequently demonstrated considerable expansion in the field. The average document age is 3.01 years, indicating a recent surge in research output, while the average of 12.57 citations per document reflects the significant impact of these works.

This analysis utilises 3,231 Keywords Plus and 3,975 Author's Keywords, reflecting the broad and developing research subjects in FinTech and banking. The chosen literature include contributions from 4,006 authors, with 271 single-authored publications indicating that research output is predominantly collaborative (As shown in figure 2).

Comprehending the essence of Descriptive Analysis in this context is crucial for grasping the dynamics and growth patterns within FinTech and banking research. Identifying the volume of papers and their citation impact significantly enhances the comprehension of the field's maturity and contributions (De Bellis, 2009). The rapid development rate and recent publication timeline of the evidence signify the dynamism of a burgeoning study domain driven by the necessity to confront issues arising from ongoing innovation after the 2008 financial crisis (Chaturvedi et al., 2021).

ANNUAL SCIENTIFIC PRODUCTION

In bibliometric investigations, annual production analysis organises research output chronologically to illustrate patterns across time (Abdeljaoued et al., 2020). this study on FinTech and the banking sector following the Global Financial Crisis of 2008. This work seeks to elucidate the evolution of scholarly attention in this topic.

The annual growth of FinTech and banking articles from 2009 to 2024 is notably significant. Initially including 5 papers in 2009, the field had consistent growth, culminating in 38 articles by 2016. The increasing trend intensified markedly, reaching 51 the subsequent year and escalating further to 126 in 2019 (See figure 3).

The impact of global events, notably the COVID-19 pandemic, is apparent, as seen by a significant increase to 187 articles in 2020, followed by 215 articles in 2021. The expansion persisted, culminating in 377 articles in 2023. Despite a minor decline, production in 2024 remains elevated, with 201 items.

Figure 3. Annual Scientific Puroduction

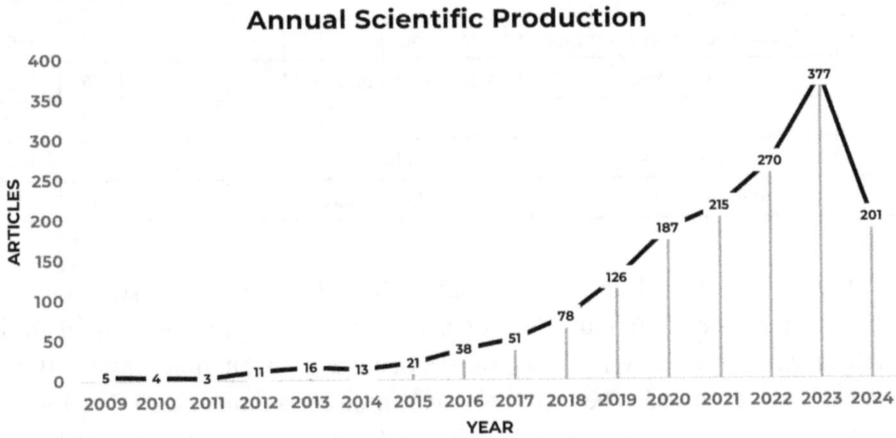

The Annual Production Analysis indicates rapid expansion in this sector and an increasing research focus, particularly aligned with global economic and technical transformations. The ongoing increase of publications highlights the essential significance of FinTech and banking technologies in addressing contemporary financial issues (Cai et al., 2022).

Author Analysis

Author Analysis offers essential insights into the contributions and impacts of various scholars within the FinTech and Banking sectors. The study evaluates prominent authors based on critical criteria including TP, h-index, total citations, and average citations per work. This measure identifies notable researchers and their contributions, facilitating discussions on future research directions and collaborations (Mahapatra et al., 2023).

Table 1. Most Relevant Author

Rank	Authors	Country	TP	h_index	TC	AC
1	Allam Hamdan	Bahrain	7	6	104	14.86
2	Sulaiman Khan	Qatar	7	6	145	20.71
3	Hasanul Banna	United Kingdom	7	5	130	18.57
4	Bhuvana Manoharan	India	7	5	62	8.86
5	Vasantha Shanmugam	India	7	5	62	8.86
6	Ayman Abdalmajeed Alsmadi	Jordan	7	4	74	10.57
7	Pranav Kumar	United Arab Emirates	7	2	17	2.43
8	Arti Singh	India	7	1	24	3.43
9	Manaf Al-Okaily	Jordan	6	3	61	10.17
10	Anil Kumar Bandrana	United Kingdom	6	3	33	5.50

Allam Hamdan from Bahrain and Sulaiman Khan from Qatar are in the forefront, each with an h-index of 6, indicating significant effect and consistency in their research endeavours. However, Khan possesses a higher total citation. Hasanul Banna from the UK is expected to be extremely influential according to his TC of 130 and AC of 18.57, indicating well-cited and impactful works. Indian authors Bhuvana Manoharan and Vasantha Shanmugam possess an h-index of 5, with a total of 62 citations, as illustrated in Table 1, highlighting India's increasing prominence in FinTech research.

Ayman Abdalmajeed Alsmadi from Jordan possesses an h-index of 4, indicating a relatively modest scholarly effect, however he has garnered 74 citations and an average citation count of 10.57. Likewise, the representative from the United Arab Emirates, Pranav Kumar, possessing an h-index of 2 and a total of 17 citations, falls within the category of emerging yet modest contributions.

These author metrics, once analysed, facilitate the identification of prominent academics, emerging trends, and potential gaps within the FinTech and Banking sectors. These, together with prior studies, have illuminated the principal contributors involved in shaping this field, so facilitating informed decisions for future research and innovation plans (Afjal, 2023).

Author Collaboration Network Analysis

Author Collaboration Network Analysis has been employed to illustrate the interconnections among researchers in the FinTech and Banking sectors, which is crucial for comprehending the collaborative dynamics that propel innovation and research effect. This illustrates the links among authors, with nodes symbolising individual researchers and the thickness of the connections between nodes reflecting the intensity of their collaboration, as demonstrated by (Uddin et al., 2013).

Figure 4. The varying degrees of collaboration.

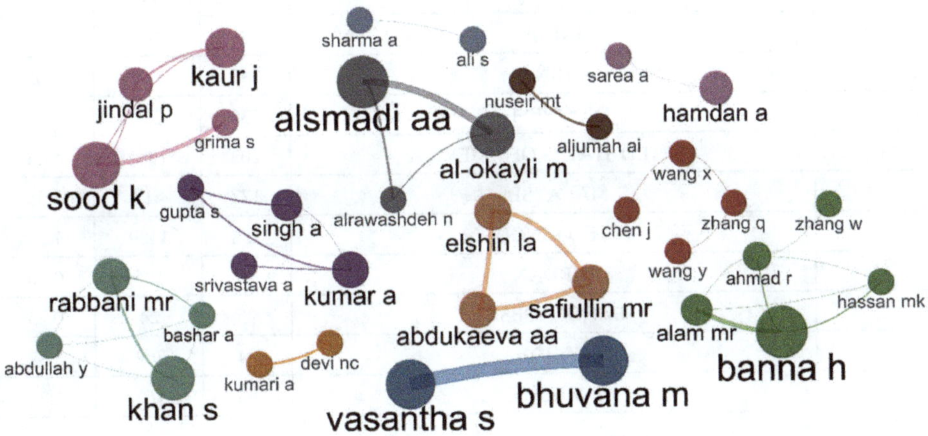

Cluster 1 include writers such as Wang X and Wang Y, demonstrating a robust cooperation network. A distinct group of authors with significant interconnections in Cluster 2 is Bhuvana M and Vasantha S. Cluster 3 include Hasanul Banna and Ahmad R, indicating a robust collaboration, while Cluster 4 includes Singh A and Kumar A, representing another significant collaborative cluster. Cluster 5 - Kumari A and Devi NC; Cluster 6 - Aljumah AI and Nuseir MT; Cluster 7 - Kaur J and Sood K; Cluster 8 - Alsmadi AA and Al-Okaily M; Cluster 9 - Khan S and Rabbani MR; Cluster 10 - Abdukaeva AA and Elshin LA. Figure 4 distinctly indicates that all clusters exhibit varying degrees of collaboration and influence upon one another.

Comprehending these clusters and the robustness of their connectivity offers insights into significant collaborative networks and possible deficiencies within the FinTech research domain. This approach directly connects to prior findings by emphasising significant relationships that shape the field, thereby guiding tactics aimed at improving research impact and cultivating new partnerships (Rybnicek & Königsgruber, 2019).

Country Analysis

Country analysis in bibliometric studies illustrates the global distribution and influence of research output in FinTech and the banking sector. Countries are rated based on metrics like total citations (TC), total publications (TP), and average citations per paper (AC) for each nation. The indicators below illustrate the research output and impact of countries in this domain (Yuh-Shan et al., 2023).

Table 2. Most Productive Country

Rank	Country	TP	TC	AC
1	INDIA	931	2435	2.62
2	CHINA	332	2339	7.05
3	INDONESIA	236	229	0.97
4	UNITED STATES OF AMERICA	203	1061	5.23
5	MALAYSIA	177	413	2.33
6	UNITED KINGDOM	158	1189	7.53
7	JORDAN	145	125	0.86
8	BANGLADESH	95	24	0.25
9	ITALY	94	364	3.87
10	BAHRAIN	93	162	1.74

India ranks first with 931 articles and a total of 2,435 citations, reflecting significant output with moderate impact, evidenced by an AC of 2.62. China follows closely with 332 articles and 2,339 total citations, indicating a significant effect per paper; its AC is 7.05. Indonesia has published 236 papers and received 229 citations, resulting in a lower impact with an AC of 0.97. The United States, while having fewer publications—203—exhibits a remarkably high overall citation count of 1,061, resulting in a commendable impact per piece, with an average citation (AC) of 5.23.

Figure 5. No. of papers across countries

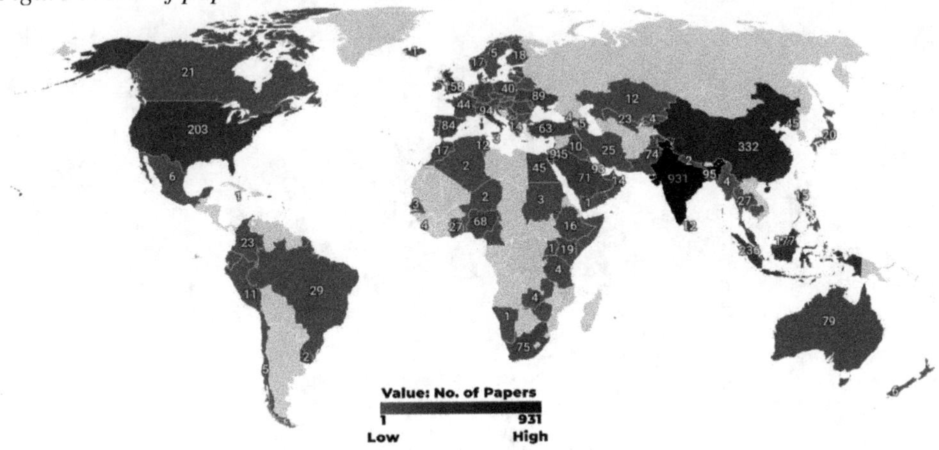

The United Kingdom is the most prominent, with 158 articles and an AC of 7.53, indicating good research quality. Jordan's 145 publications reflect emerging research activity, though with a lower impact (AC of 0.86). Bangladesh, despite 95 publications, has a minimal impact with an AC of 0.25. Italy, with 94 publications and an AC of 3.87, and Bahrain, with 93 publications and an AC of 1.74, also contribute to the global research landscape (See table 2 & figure 5).

Understanding Country Analysis helps identify key contributors and potential gaps in the FinTech research arena (Wojcik, 2021). This analysis highlights influential countries shaping the field, connecting to earlier findings by emphasizing the global distribution and impact of collaborative research efforts.

Country Collaboration Network Analysis

Country Collaboration Network Analysis examines how countries collaborate on research within the FinTech and Banking Industry. This study maps these collaborations, where nodes represent countries, and the thickness of connections between nodes indicates the strength of their collaborative efforts (Thavorn et al., 2021). Understanding these networks is crucial for identifying key players and potential gaps in global research cooperation.

Figure 6. Web of contributors and their countries of origin

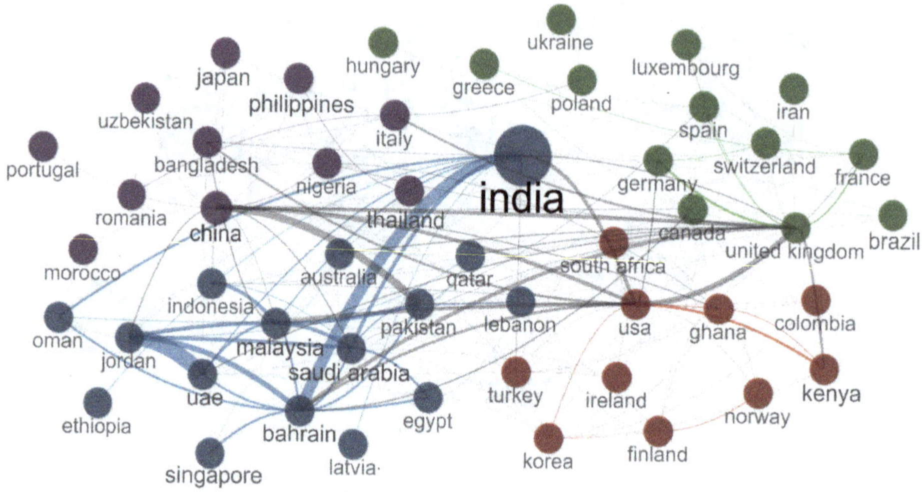

Cluster 1 (red) includes the USA, South Africa, Turkey, Korea, Ghana, Colombia, Ireland, Kenya, Finland, and Norway, highlighting strong intercontinental collaborations. Cluster 2 (blue) consists of India, Indonesia, Malaysia, Jordan, Bahrain, UAE, Australia, Pakistan, Saudi Arabia, Egypt, Singapore, Ethiopia, Lebanon, Latvia, Oman, Qatar, emphasizing significant regional and cross-regional collaborations.

Cluster 3 (green) features the UK, Ukraine, Spain, Germany, France, Poland, Brazil, Iran, Canada, Hungary, Switzerland, Greece, Luxembourg, showcasing robust connections within Europe and extending to South America and Asia. Cluster 4 (purple) includes China, Bangladesh, Italy, Nigeria, Romania, Thailand, Uzbekistan, Japan, Morocco, Portugal, Philippines, highlighting extensive collaborations across Asia, Europe, and Africa (As shown in figure 6).

The nodes denote individual countries, with the thickness of connections between nodes indicating the strength of their collaborative relationships. Stronger connections suggest more frequent or impactful collaborations, while thinner connections indicate less frequent interactions (Abbasi et al., 2011).

Understanding Country Collaboration Network Analysis is vital for recognizing the global distribution of research efforts and identifying leading countries and collaborations in FinTech. This analysis connects with earlier findings by pinpointing influential countries and their partnerships, further enriching the understanding of the FinTech research landscape and guiding future collaborative efforts (Kwong et al., 2023); (Ololade, 2024); (Alka et al., 2024).

Affiliation Analysis

Affiliation Analysis examines the contributions of various institutions in the FinTech and Banking Industry, shedding light on research productivity and collaboration (Bhatt et al., 2022). This study highlights the top institutions based on their total publications (TP) since 2019, offering insights into the emerging trends and influential players in the field. Notably, no publications were recorded before 2019, indicating the recent surge in research interest in FinTech and Banking.

Table 3. Most productive Institution

Rank	Affiliation	Country	TP	University Production each Year					
				2019	2020	2021	2022	2023	2024
1	AHLIA UNIVERSITY	Bahrain	19	2	4	5	3	2	3
2	CHITKARA BUSINESS SCHOOL CHITKARA UNIVERSITY	India	17	0	0	3	12	2	0
3	SPIRU HARET UNIVERSITY	Romania	10	0	0	0	0	10	0
4	FINANCIAL UNIVERSITY UNDER THE GOVERNMENT OF THE RUSSIAN FEDERATION	Russia	9	1	4	3	0	1	0
5	DEPARTMENT OF ACCOUNTING AND FINANCE UCSI UNIVERSITY	Malaysia	8	0	1	2	1	1	3
6	FACULTY OF ECONOMICS RANGSIT UNIVERSITY	Thailand	8	1	0	1	2	2	2
7	FACULTY OF ECONOMICS AND BUSINESS UNIVERSITAS AIRLANGGA	Indonesia	8	0	2	1	0	2	3
8	INSTITUTE OF ISLAMIC BANKING AND FINANCE INTERNATIONAL ISLAMIC UNIVERSITY	Malaysia	8	0	1	1	2	2	2
9	FACULTY OF ECONOMICS AND BUSINESS UNIVERSITAS BRAWIJAYA MALANG	Indonesia	7	1	0	1	1	2	2
10	FACULTY OF ECONOMICS AND BUSINESS UNIVERSITAS BRAWIJAYA MALANG	Indonesia	7	0	2	0	1	2	2

Ahlia University in Bahrain leads with 19 publications, consistently contributing 2-5 papers annually. Chitkara Business School at Chitkara University, India, follows with 17 publications, primarily emerging in 2021 with 3 papers and peaking in 2022 with 12 papers. Spiru Haret University in Romania, with 10 publications all in 2023, reflects a sudden, significant entry into the field.

The Financial University under the Government of the Russian Federation has 9 publications, showing consistent output, particularly in 2019 and 2020. UCSI University's Department of Accounting and Finance in Malaysia has 8 publications, demonstrating a steady increase in contributions, especially in 2024. Similarly, Rangsit University in Thailand and Universitas Airlangga in Indonesia each have 8 publications, reflecting steady research activity (See table 3).

Understanding Affiliation Analysis is crucial as it identifies leading institutions and trends, guiding future research collaborations and funding. This analysis complements earlier findings by highlighting key contributors and their research impact, further enriching the understanding of the FinTech research landscape (Asif et al., 2023; Zou et al., 2023).

Affiliation Collaboration Network Analysis

Analysing the Affiliation Collaboration Network is crucial for comprehending the interconnectedness of institutions contributing to research in FinTech and the Banking Industry. The subsequent map depicting university collaboration employs nodes to represent institutions, with the thickness of links signifying the strength of their collaboration (Chen et al., 2020; Toha, Khan, Irfan, Salim, & Khan, 2024).

Figure 7. Web of contributors' affiliations and institutions

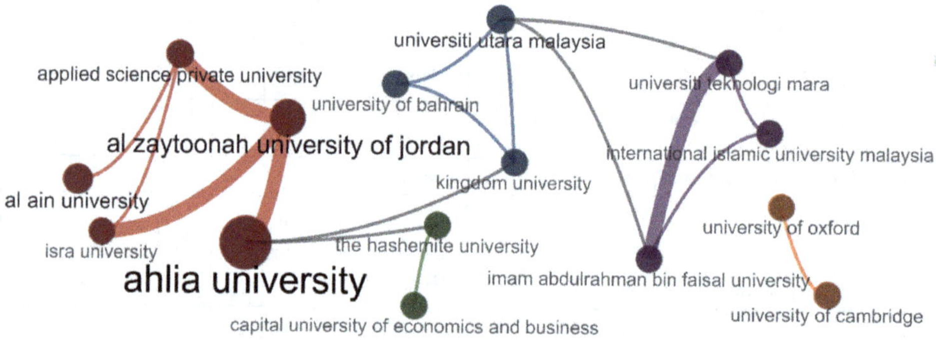

Cluster 1 comprises Ahlia University, Al Ain University, Isra University, Al Zaytoonah University of Jordan, and Applied Science Private University; hence, the regional collaborative network is highly effective. Cluster 2, depicted in blue, comprises the University of Bahrain, Universiti Utara Malaysia, and Kingdom University, whose contacts have significant importance at a cross-border level. Finally, Cluster 3, represented in green, encompasses The Hashemite University and Capital University of Economics and Business, where international collaborative networks seem to emerge. The clusters are depicted in purple and comprise the International Islamic University Malaysia, Universiti Teknologi MARA, and Imam Abdulrahman Bin Faisal University, suggesting they may engage in vigorous regional collaboration. Cluster 5, in orange, comprising University of Cambridge and University of Oxford, indicates high-impact global research collaborations (As shown in figure 7).

Understanding these clusters helps identify key institutional collaborations driving innovation in FinTech. This analysis connects with earlier findings by emphasizing the importance of collaborative networks and highlighting influential institutions shaping the field (Liang & Liu, 2018; Salim, Khan, Shamim, & Management, 2022).

Source Analysis

Source Analysis in bibliometric studies assesses the influence and reach of various journals and publications within the FinTech and Banking Industry. This study examines key sources based on total publications (TP), h-index, total citations (TC), and average citations per paper (AC), providing insights into their impact and prominence (Li et al., 2020; Toha, Johl, Khan, Salim, & Quantity, 2025).

Table 4. Most Prominent Sources

Rank	Source	TP	h_index	TC	AC
1	LECTURE NOTES IN NETWORKS AND SYSTEMS	41	5	65	1.59
2	ACM INTERNATIONAL CONFERENCE PROCEEDING SERIES	24	5	58	2.42
3	SUSTAINABILITY (SWITZERLAND)	22	13	491	22.32
4	BANKS AND BANK SYSTEMS	17	5	68	4.00
5	JOURNAL OF RISK AND FINANCIAL MANAGEMENT	17	3	39	2.29
6	STUDIES IN SYSTEMS, DECISION AND CONTROL	15	1	1	0.07
7	INTERNATIONAL JOURNAL OF BANK MARKETING	14	9	573	40.93
8	LECTURE NOTES IN COMPUTER SCIENCE	14	5	161	11.50
9	RESEARCH IN INTERNATIONAL BUSINESS AND FINANCE	14	5	328	23.43
10	FINANCE RESEARCH LETTERS	13	8	647	49.77

"Lecture Notes in Networks and Systems" leads with 41 publications, an h-index of 5, and 65 total citations, though its impact per paper (AC) is relatively low at 1.59. The "ACM International Conference Proceeding Series" follows with 24 publications and an AC of 2.42, indicating moderate influence. "Sustainability (Switzerland)" stands out with 22 publications, a high h-index of 13, and 491 total citations, showcasing a substantial impact with an AC of 22.32.

"Banks and Bank Systems" and the "Journal of Risk and Financial Management" both have 17 publications, but the former has a higher AC of 4.00 compared to 2.29. "Studies in Systems, Decision and Control" has 15 publications but minimal impact (AC of 0.07). The "International Journal of Bank Marketing," with an h-index of 9 and an impressive AC of 40.93, indicates high research quality.

"Lecture Notes in Computer Science" and "Research in International Business and Finance" both have 14 publications, with ACs of 11.50 and 23.43, respectively, highlighting significant contributions. "Finance Research Letters," with 13 publications, excels with an h-index of 8 and the highest AC of 49.77, emphasizing its high influence (See table 4).

Understanding Source Analysis identifies key publications driving research in FinTech, guiding researchers towards influential journals and enhancing the field's knowledge base. This analysis connects to earlier findings by pinpointing pivotal sources and their contributions to collaborative research efforts (Palupiningtyas et al., 2023).

Co-Word Network Analysis

Co-Word Network Analysis examines the relationships and frequency of terms appearing together in the literature, providing insights into key research themes and their interconnectedness (Kumar et al., 2023). In the context of the FinTech and Banking Industry, this analysis identifies major research clusters and their focus areas, guiding future research directions.

Figure 8. Web of key terms

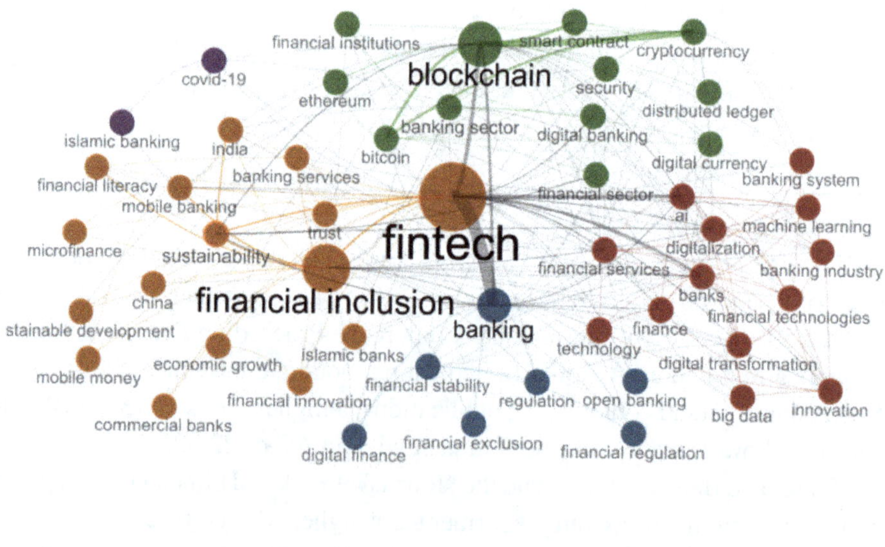

Cluster 1, "FinTech and Digital Banking" (red), includes terms like banks, AI, financial services, digitalization, and machine learning, indicating a strong emphasis on technological advancements and their integration into banking. Cluster 2, "Regulatory Frameworks in Digital Banking" (blue), comprises terms such as banking, open banking, financial stability, and regulation, highlighting the importance of regulatory measures in digital banking environments.

Cluster 3, "Blockchain and Digital Currency in Banking" (green), includes blockchain, cryptocurrency, bitcoin, and smart contracts. This cluster focusses on the increasing significance of blockchain technology and digital currencies in banking. Cluster 4, "Covid-19 & Islamic Banking" (purple), encompasses the terms Covid-19 and Islamic banking, thereby pertaining to studies on the pandemic's impact and the distinct characteristics of Islamic finance.

Cluster 5 "Financial Inclusion and Innovation in Emerging Markets" encompasses issues such as FinTech, financial inclusion, mobile banking, and microfinance. It emphasises the significance of FinTech in promoting financial inclusion and innovation, especially in developing nations. Figure 8 demonstrates this.

In this network, nodes signify specific terms, while the thickness of the links between them indicates the strength of their co-occurrence (Lozano et al., 2019). robust links between phrases indicate closely related study domains, while the thickness between the clusters can also influence the extent of inter-cluster interactions (Franco & Esteves, 2020).

Comprehending Co-Word Network Analysis is essential, as it elucidates the principal issues and subjects of research and their interrelations within the FinTech and Banking Sector. This study enables the identification of key research clusters and their interrelations, previously recognised as significant sources and outcomes of collaboration, so providing a comprehensive overview of the research area's structure inside the paper (Guzmán et al., 2024).

DISCUSSION

The bibliometric examination of FinTech and banking studies spans from 2009 to 2024. Compared to the magnitude of scientific output associated with the 2008 global financial crisis, which expedited inventions and intensified regulatory reforms, the yearly growth rate of scientific output in the research area was remarkable, reaching 27.92% per year. The sample comprises 1,616 papers sourced from 882 distinct objects, encompassing journals, books, and other publication types. This signifies advancement in a rapidly evolving research domain (Jan et al., 2023). Given the document's age of 3.01 years and an average of 12.57 citations per document, these research are inherently impactful. There is significant interest in the dynamic evolution of FinTech and banking studies, evidenced by their quick expansion and recent increase in publications, highlighting the necessity for ongoing study and innovation in light of financial crises and regulatory frameworks.

Annual scientific output has escalated, demonstrating a significant surge in research articles over time, particularly in reaction to global occurrences like the COVID-19 pandemic. The 2023 peak of 377 publications indicates significant interest and effort in this topic (Alam & Akhtar, 2024). These examples demonstrate how worldwide events can impact research activity, and conversely, economic crises, pandemics, and other global occurrences may require academic engagement and productivity. It demonstrates the research community's responsiveness to pressing global challenges.

The author analysis identifies the primary contributors based on their elevated h-indices and total citations, indicating that Allam Hamdan and Sulaiman Khan have significantly influenced and sustained research contributions. FinTech research is collaborative, with 4,006 distinct authors in this dataset, of whom 271 authored single-authored documents. This study is crucial for comprehending prominent scholars and the collaborative environment in the area, with the objective of finding influential leaders and establishing new research partnerships to advance the discipline.

Country analysis highlights India's leading position with 931 publications, while China, the United States, and the United Kingdom also show significant contributions. The collaborative network analysis of countries and affiliations reveals strong intercontinental and regional partnerships, essential for driving innovation and research impact in FinTech. Recognizing the geographic distribution and collaborative networks of research efforts helps pinpoint key regions driving innovation and provides opportunities for strengthening international cooperation and knowledge exchange.

Institutions like Ahlia University and Chitkara Business School emerge as key players, contributing significantly to the research output. Highlighting the contributions of specific institutions can guide potential collaborations and funding opportunities, enabling other institutions to benchmark their research efforts and strategies to enhance their impact in the FinTech domain.

Source analysis identifies influential journals such as "Sustainability (Switzerland)" and "Finance Research Letters," which have high h-indices and average citations per paper, indicating their prominence in the field. Recognizing high-impact journals helps researchers target their publications to maximize visibility and influence, contributing to the broader dissemination and impact of their work within the FinTech and banking research community.

The co-word network analysis highlights major research clusters, including "FinTech and Digital Banking," "Regulatory Frameworks in Digital Banking," and "Blockchain and Digital Currency in Banking," reflecting the diverse and interconnected nature of research themes. Understanding the key research clusters and their interconnections provides a roadmap for future research directions, helping scholars identify emerging trends and critical areas needing further exploration, thereby enhancing the strategic development of FinTech research.

Comprehending these patterns and trends is crucial for guiding future research, fostering collaboration, and amplifying the effects of innovations in the financial industry. Insights derived from the analysis would enable researchers, policymakers, and industry stakeholders to engage in strategic decision-making to address current issues and opportunities related to financial innovation.

Limitation

Despite the thoroughness of the current bibliometric investigation, the subsequent limitations regarding the scope and context of the findings must be acknowledged:

Database Dependency: It relies on a single database, Scopus, which, despite its comprehensiveness, cannot encompass all theses and dissertations produced, particularly those in non-English languages or those disseminated in non-mainstream magazines. This inherent constraint of the database may result in an imperfect representation of the global research landscape on FinTech developments in banking.

Temporal Scope: The study will encompass papers from 2009 to 2024. Although this time signifies significant advancements during the 2008 financial crisis, it may overlook earlier foundational efforts that established the groundwork for subsequent study. This temporal constraint obstructs a comprehensive understanding of the evolution of FinTech breakthroughs and their historical context.

Publication Bias: It is susceptible to publication bias, wherein a limited number of frequently referenced journals may overshadow the literature, marginalising contributions from less-cited sources. This distortion may occur in the impression of the research landscape and the significance of a particular study.

Cultural and Regional Differences: This research may not encompass the diverse cultural and regional disparities in FinTech spread and innovation. The orientation and emphasis of research vary considerably among locations, mirroring local economic circumstances, regulatory frameworks, and cultural factors. This may impose a constraint on the overall applicability of the findings.

Accelerated Technological Advancement: Due to the swift progression of technology in FinTech, the research landscape is expected to evolve rapidly. This implies that the conclusions of this study will soon become irrelevant, necessitating continuous follow-up and updates to keep abreast of advancements.

Methodological Constraints: Despite their potency, bibliometric methods possess inherent limits. These methodologies mostly provide quantitative summaries and lack the complex qualitative dimensions of depth in innovation, practical application, and industry effect.

Directions for Future Research

This paper presents several intriguing directions for future investigation:

Expanded Databases: Encompassing Web of Science, Google Scholar, and regional databases. This would offer a comprehensive overview of the entire research scene.

Longitudinal Studies: The temporal scope may be broadened to encompass prior research to delineate FinTech advances and their basic theories throughout historical progression. Longitudinal studies can be utilised to assess the enduring effects of early inventions on contemporary practices.

Thematic Deep Dives: Future research may concentrate on particular subfields of FinTech, like InsurTech, RegTech, and robo-advisors. This thematic analysis could provide profound insights into specialised sectors and their unique challenges and opportunities.

Qualitative Analysis: This involves augmenting the quantitative bibliometric research with comprehensive case studies, expert interviews, and thorough content analysis, which may provide deeper insights into the contextual and practical ramifications of FinTech advances.

Impact on Financial Inclusion: Analysing the role of FinTech in advancing financial inclusion, particularly in emerging nations, may elucidate its potential for generating social impact. Researching how FinTech solutions are addressing or can address the financial requirements of under-represented people would be beneficial.

Regulatory and Ethical Considerations: Additional research is necessary to elucidate the complexities of the regulatory framework and the ethical ramifications of FinTech innovation. It is essential to comprehend the balance between innovation and regulation for sustainable development in this domain.

CONCLUSION

This bibliometric analysis offers valuable insights into the growing interconnection between FinTech and the banking sector after the 2008 financial crisis. This post-crisis period has witnessed an increase in academic focus, with publications steadily rising over the past decade as the world sought novel financial solutions. It identifies the journals, institutions, and countries leading this revolution, demonstrating a concerted effort to advance financial innovation.

It shows numerous emerging topics in blockchain, digital banking, and AI-driven financial services that will define the future. These domains exemplify the forefront of FinTech adoption, as scholars and industry experts engage with these trends to confront emerging challenges and opportunities directly. This report delineates the current research environment while also highlighting the most potential avenues for future development. The incorporation of FinTech into conventional banking has evidently progressed beyond mere experimentation and is transforming the entire industry, as seen by the growing research trends discussed herein.

STATEMENTS OF ETHICAL APPROVAL

Manuscripts reporting studies does not involving human participants, human data or human tissue or even animal.

CONFLICT OF INTEREST

The authors declare that they have no competing interests.

FUNDING INFORMATION

This research did not receive any grant from funding agencies in the public, commercial, or nonprofit sectors.

DECLARATION OF AI TECHNOLOGY USAGE

Manuscripts reporting studies does not involving any sort of AI Technology usage.

REFERENCES

Abbasi et al. (2011). Evolutionary dynamics of scientific collaboration networks: multi-levels and cross-time analysis. *89*(2), 687-710.

Abdeljaoued et al. (2020). Bibliometric analysis of the evolution of biochar research trends and scientific production. *22*, 1967-1997.

Afjal, M. (2023). Bridging the financial divide: a bibliometric analysis on the role of digital financial services within FinTech in enhancing financial inclusion and economic development. *10*(1), 1-27.

Akhtar, S., Alam, M., & Khan, M. M. (2021). YES bank fiasco: Arrogance or negligence. *Emerging Economies Cases Journal*, *3*(2), 95–102.

Akhtar, S., Alam, M., & Ansari, M. S. (2022). Measuring the performance of the Indian banking industry: Data envelopment window analysis approach. *Benchmarking*, *29*(9), 2842–2857.

Akhtar, S., Alam, M., Khan, A., & Shamshad, M. (2023). Measuring technical efficiency of banks vis-à-vis demonetization: An empirical analysis of Indian banking sector using CAMELS framework. *Quality & Quantity*, *57*(2), 1739–1761.

Alam, M., & Akhtar, S. (2024). Introduction to green finance and technology integration. In *Syed Hasan Jafar, Raul Villamarin Rodriguez, Hemachandran Kannan, Shakeb Akhtar and Philipp Plugmann, Harnessing blockchain-digital twin fusion for sustainable investments* (pp. 1–19). IGI Global., DOI: 10.4018/979-8-3693-1878-2.ch001

Alka et al. (2024). Tracking the footprints of global entrepreneurship research: A theoretical exploration of landscape of global entrepreneurship through a bibliometric perspective. *14*(1), 21.

Anan et al. (2023). FINTECHS: a new paradigm of growth. McKinsey & Company. In.

Ansari, M. S., Akhtar, S., Khan, A., & Shamshad, M. (2022). Consequence of financial crisis on liquidity and profitability of commercial banks in India: An empirical study. *Studies in Economics and Business Relations*, *3*(2), 36–50.

Aria, M., & Cuccurullo, C. J. J. o. i. (2017). bibliometrix: An R-tool for comprehensive science mapping analysis. *11*(4), 959-975.

Asif, M., Khan, P. A., Irfan, F., Salim, M., Jan, A., Khan, M. J. E. S., & Research, P. (2023). Is gender diversity is diversity washing or good governance for firm sustainable development goal performance: A scoping review. *30*(53), 114690-114705.

Ayan, B., Güner, E., & Son-Turan, S. J. L. (2022). Blockchain Technology and Sustainability in Supply Chains and a Closer Look at Different Industries: A Mixed Method Approach. *6*(4), 85.

Aysan, A. F., & Nanaeva, Z. (2022). Fintech as a financial disruptor: A bibliometric analysis. *1*(4), 412-433.

Bhatt et al. (2022). Decoding the trinity of Fintech, digitalization and financial services: An integrated bibliometric analysis and thematic literature review approach. *10*(1), 2114160.

Bilal, Hysa, E., Akbar, A., Yasmin, F., Rahman, A. u., Li, S. J. R. M., & Policy, H. (2022). Virtual Learning During the COVID-19 Pandemic: A Bibliometric Review and Future Research Agenda. 1353-1368.

Cai et al. (2022). Trends in fintech research and practice: Examining the intersection with the information systems field. *50*(1), 40.

Carbó-Valverde et al. (2020). The effect of banks' IT investments on the digitalization of their customers. *11*, 9-17.

Chaturvedi, K., Akhtar, S., Azhar, N., & Shamshad, M. (2021). Impact of corporate social responsibility on financial performance of selected banks in india: Based on camel model. *Studies in Economics and Business Relations*, *2*(2).

Chen et al. (2020). Do research institutes benefit from their network positions in research collaboration networks with industries or/and universities?, *94*, 102002.

Chen, T.-H., & Peng, J.-L. (2020). Statistical and bibliometric analysis of financial innovation. *38*(2), 308-319.

C, M. A., Djimatey, R., Akhtar, S., & Nawaah, D. (2025). Maximizing financial efficiency through technological synergy: Unleashing ICT for enhanced cash management in SMEs. Journal of the International Council for Small Business, 1-31.

De Bellis, N. (2009). *Bibliometrics and citation analysis: from the science citation index to cybermetrics*: scarecrow press.

Donthu et al. (2021). How to conduct a bibliometric analysis: An overview and guidelines. *133*, 285-296.

Durieux, V., & Gevenois, P. A. J. R. (2010). Bibliometric indicators: quality measurements of scientific publication. *255*(2), 342-351.

Firdaus et al. (2019). The rise of "blockchain": bibliometric analysis of blockchain study. *120*, 1289-1331.

Franco, M., & Esteves, L. (2020). Inter-clustering as a network of knowledge and learning: Multiple case studies. *5*(1), 39-49.

Giglio, F. (2022). Fintech: A literature review. *15*(1), 80-85.

Guzmán et al. (2024). Scientific Production on Leadership in Social Entrepreneurship: Co-Word Analysis and Network Mapping. *6*(2).

Hasan et al. (2024). Exploring small and medium enterprises access to finance: a bibliometric analysis. *5*(1), 15-46.

Hasan, . (2025). AI-Driven Optimization of Renewable Energy Investments. In *Green Horizons: Role of AI in Sustainable Finance* (pp. 305–331). Springer. DOI: 10.1007/978-981-96-6495-5_17

Isayas, Y. N. (2022). Determinants of banks' profitability: Empirical evidence from banks in Ethiopia. *10*(1), 2031433.

Jan, A. A., Lai, F. W., Asif, M., Akhtar, S., & Ullah, S. (2023). Embedding sustainability into bank strategy: Implications for sustainable development goals reporting. *International Journal of Sustainable Development and World Ecology, 30*(3), 229–243.

Jokić, M., & Ball, R. (2006). *Qualität und Quantität wissenschaftlicher Veröffentlichungen: Bibliometrische Aspekte der Wissenschaftskommunikation* (Vol. 15): Forschungszentrum Jülich.

Kumar et al. (2023). Mapping the evolution of research themes in business ethics: a co-word network analysis. *53*(3), 491-522.

Kwong et al. (2023). Green FinTech innovation as a future research direction: a bibliometric analysis on green finance and FinTech. *15*(20), 14683.

Lakhe, P., & Kulkarni, M. (2020). FinTech regulations: Need, superpowers and bibliometric analysis. 1-11.

Li et al. (2020). A bibliometric analysis of symmetry (2009–2019). *12*(8), 1304.

Li, B., & Xu, Z. (2022). A comprehensive bibliometric analysis of financial innovation. *35*(1), 367-390.

Liang, X., & Liu, A. M. (2018). The evolution of government sponsored collaboration network and its impact on innovation: A bibliometric analysis in the Chinese solar PV sector. *47*(7), 1295-1308.

Lozano et al. (2019). Complex network analysis of keywords co-occurrence in the recent efficiency analysis literature. *120*, 609-629.

Mahapatra et al. (2023). Metrics employed in the evaluation of research productivity: A systematic literature review. *55*(3), 868-885.

Merigó et al. (2016). Bibliometric overview of business & economics research.

Miau, S., & Yang, J.-M. (2018). Bibliometrics-based evaluation of the Blockchain research trend: 2008–March 2017. *30*(9), 1029-1045.

Moral-Muñoz et al. (2020). Software tools for conducting bibliometric analysis in science: An up-to-date review. *29*(1).

Naseema, N., Akhtar, S., & Jha, P. (2025). Blockchain Disrupting Supply Chain Finance: Transformative Solutions and Emerging Challenges. In Anamika Pandey and Fadi Al-Turjman, Transformation of Supply Chain Ecosystems, 33-47.

Nasir et al. (2020). A bibliometric analysis of corona pandemic in social sciences: a review of influential aspects and conceptual structure. *8*, 133377-133402.

Ololade, Y. J. (2024). SME financing through fintech: an analytical study of trends in Nigeria and the USA. *6*(4), 1078-1102.

Palupiningtyas, ., (2023). *Bibliometric Analysis of Social and Environmental Innovation Research Developments: Trend Identification, Key Concepts, and Collaboration in the Scientific Literature.*, *1*(04), 245–254.

Puschmann, T., & Leifer, L. (2020). Sustainable Digital Finance: The Role of FinTech, InsurTech & Blockchain for Shaping the World for the Better. In: University of Zurich: Zurich, Switzerland, Stanford University: Standford....

Ramakreshnan et al. (2021). A comprehensive bibliometrics of 'walkability' research landscape: visualization of the scientific progress and future prospects. *28*, 1357-1369.

Rybnicek, R., & Königsgruber, R. (2019). What makes industry–university collaboration succeed? A systematic review of the literature. *89*(2), 221-250.

Salim, M., Ahsan, M. A., & Khan, P. A. J. B. A. I. J. (2025). Decoding sustainability: a tempting bibliometric review of blockchain in climate action for emerging trends and future directions.

Salim, M., Khan, M., Shamim, M. J. A.-B. J. o. F., & Management. (2022). A critical appraisal of ASPIRE scheme of India. *10*(2), 63-73.

Salim, M., Khan, P. A., Jalil, N. A., Johl, S. K., Jafar, S. H., Irfan, F., & Khan, M. J. K. S. S. (2023). Fusion of blockchain and sustainable development goals: a bibliometric analysis for future trends. 633–654-633–654.

Salim, M., Khan, P. A., Rahman, H., Asif, M., Jan, A., & Khan, M. N. (2025). Trends and Future Directions on Adoption of Blockchain Technology for SDGs in VUCA World: A Bibliometric Analysis. *Business Strategy & Development*, *8*(3), e70149. DOI: 10.1002/bsd2.70149

Sardana, V., & Singhania, S. (2018). Digital technology in the realm of banking: A review of literature. *1*(2), 28-32.

Shukla, M. S., & Singh, M. P. (2014). E-Commerce: A Virtual Assistance Making Life Challenging Or Simpler. 281.

Statista. (2024). https://www.statista.com/statistics/893954/number-fintech-startups-by-region/

Stopar, K., & Bartol, T. (2019). Digital competences, computer skills and information literacy in secondary education: mapping and visualization of trends and concepts. *118*(2), 479-498.

Tabassum, S., Haque, S. I., Ahsan, M. A., Salim, M., & Khan, P. A. (2025). *Assessing Employees' Engagement in Hybrid Work Arrangement: Mediating role of Employee Voice for Achieving SDG 8 and SDG 10.* Paper presented at the International Conference on Environmental, Social, and Governance (ICESG 2024). DOI: 10.2991/978-2-38476-358-0_24

Thavorn et al. (2021). Collaboration network and trends of global coronavirus disease research: a scientometric analysis. *9*, 45001-45016.

Toha, M. A., Johl, S. K., Khan, P. A., Salim, M. J. Q., & Quantity. (2025). Why diverse boards are market game-changers: driving the sustainable future from the lens of proactive eco-innovation for firm market performance. 1-30.

Toha, M. A., Khan, P. A., Irfan, F., Salim, M., & Khan, M. (2024). Unboxing eco-innovation and ESG for circular economy. In *Climate Governance and Corporate Eco-innovation: A Framework for Sustainable Companies* (pp. 353–366). Springer. DOI: 10.1007/978-3-031-56423-9_13

Uddin et al. (2013). Network effects on scientific collaborations. *8*(2), e57546.

Uddin, S. M. M., & Akhtar, S. (2025). Convergence in efficiency and technology gap of Indian banks: Implication of GFC and COVID-19. *Quality & Quantity*, •••, 1–20.

Utami et al. (2021). Adoption of FinTech products: a systematic literature review. *16*(3), 233-248.

Wojcik, D. (2021). Financial geography I: Exploring FinTech–maps and concepts. *45*(3), 566-576.

Xue, X., Yang, X., Deng, Z., Tu, H., Kong, D., Li, N., & Xu, F. J. F. i. P. H. (2022). Global trends and hotspots in research on rehabilitation robots: a bibliometric analysis from 2010 to 2020. *9*, 806723.

Yuh-Shan et al. (2023). Publication performance and trends in Total Quality Management research: a bibliometric analysis. *34*(1-2), 97-130.

Zhao, H., Zhang, F., & Kwon, J. J. I. B. R. (2018). Corporate social responsibility research in international business journals: An author co-citation analysis. *27*(2), 389-400.

Zhu, J., & Liu, W. J. S. (2020). A tale of two databases: The use of Web of Science and Scopus in academic papers. *123*(1), 321-335.

Zou et al. (2023). Insight into digital finance and fintech: A bibliometric and content analysis. *73*, 102221.

Chapter 15
Implications of Financial Literacy on Pawnshop Usage

José G. Vargas-Hernandez
https://orcid.org/0000-0003-0938-4197
Financial Literacy Research Center, Universidad Cristóbal Colón, Mexico & Tecnológico Nacional de México, ITS Fresnillo, Mexico

Csongor Czipf
https://orcid.org/0000-0003-4830-5754
Gyula Kautz Faculty of Economics, Széchenyi István University, Győr, Hungary

Absalón J. Salmerón-Zapata
https://orcid.org/0009-0002-2621-2426
Financial Literacy Research Center, Universidad Cristòbal Colòn, Mexico

Selene Castañeda-Burciaga
https://orcid.org/0000-0002-2436-308X
Universidad Politécnica de Zacatecas, Mexico

Omar A. Guirette-Barbosa
https://orcid.org/0000-0003-1336-9475
Universidad Politécnica de Zacatecas, Mexico

ABSTRACT

This chapter aims to analyze financial literacy implications on pawnshop usage. The analysis departs from the assumption that individuals and micro-organizations lacking financial literacy and lower opportunities to have access to short-term credit provided by formal financing and banking institutions, are more likely to use

DOI: 10.4018/979-8-3373-3725-8.ch015

pawnshops to get easily and fastest financial resources urgently needed for survival, living expenses and other required matters. The method used is the semi-structured interviews to borrowers followed by meta-analysis and meta-cognitive approaches based on conceptual, theoretical and empirical literature review. The chapter concludes that the financial literacy of undeserved individuals and micro-organizations, tend to reduce their access to formal financial and banking institutions to get credit, driving them to use pawnshops.

INTRODUCTION

To evaluate the effect of financial literacy on the use of pawnshop and other financial product services. The majority of professionals during professional operations encounter some financially excluded individuals who cannot repay the services used. Belief in the financial institution's pawnshop services affects financial service product usage decisions. There is a positive correlation between the financial management skills affecting decision-making to become a pawnshop customer and customer. Financial management skills affect decision-making to become pawnshop customer (Mukti, Tulasmi, Shohiha, Garbo, & Mubasiroh, 2022).

The ability of people in finance management affects user services of pawnshop product to become more selective. People who are better in finance management are more eager to use service products of pawnshop to sponsor investment and less eager to mortgage their possessions (Fraczek & Klimontowicz, 2015; Setiawati, 2018; Pokrikyan, 2016).

The innovation in financial services is in need of being balanced against the development of the financial management and financial literacy skills that lead individuals who can cope with family economy income. The level of financial knowledge influences the individual choices concerning financial conduct (Hung, 2009). Financial product, service and activity knowledge led to having accounts open at financial institutions. Data about bank loans and savings, instalments, and security money does not affect the financial access. Individuals who have data about the instalment procedure does not affect microfinance access.

Semi-structured interviews provide information on issues of concern to facilitate profound understanding on the topic of pawnshops. The evidence shows that finance influences decision making regarding the use of pawn service products on the basis of variables knowledge of finance management, finance management skills and experience, and pawner beliefs (Mukti et al., 2022).

FINANCIAL LITERACY

The study of the concept of financial literacy addressed the excluded group on the core topic of finance-related knowledge of specific financial services and products in formal financial systems to promote financial inclusion in theoretical and applied terms. Regarding the conceptual definitions of financial literacy, it is taken as knowledge, skills, and self-confidence in making sound money management decisions. Financial knowledge increases the level of financial literacy of a person in making better decisions by incorporating knowledge regarding money concepts, products, and services together with self-assurance and abilities in taking advantages and managing financial opportunities' risks and other activities to improve the financial well-being (Setyowati, 2003).

Personal status is determinant variable in determining pawnshop type, with the conclusion that single users-customers lack any prominent preference, though married user-customers prefer to transact business with Islamic pawnshops in order to access instant cash while widow and widower users-customers favor traditional pawnshops. With regards to the personal characteristics, pawnsbroking customers are generally females with a family at their mid-life when the financial pressures to sustain the family and setting up home, they resided in homes of low incomes (Kemspon, 2002). The level of money knowledge influences the personal decisions on the money behavior (Hung, 2009). Levels of financial literacy and inclusion can be enhanced by bringing policymaking and regulatory issues to the fore with the understanding that changes can have an impact on financial service and product providers as well as consumers (Babych et al., 2018). Financial inclusion and literacy rise lead to rising account ownership.

Detailed recording of expenditures is a cautious financial behavior and attitude used as a tool to control finances, which is likely to be observed at low levels of income rather that at high levels of financial literacy leading to individuals and families that have problems to meet the ends, deeply debt fearful (Babych et al., 2018). The majority of people possess poor basic financial literacy that prevents them from knowing and utilizing financial services. Financial literacy as a driver increases financial inclusion (Morgan & Trinh 2019; Kodongo, 2018). Financial literacy is associated with financial inclusion, both hampered by the poor understanding of financial products and financial services.

Financial literacy is an enabler of financial inclusion. Financial literacy initiatives address the question of knowledge and confidence in the application of financial products that are communicated through multiple channels. Financial service investors, providers, and members of supporting organizations confirm that restricted financial literacy is a barrier to financial inclusion (Gardeva & Rhyne, 2011). Financial instruments to improve financial literacy and inclusion are steered by best practices. Low literacy and financial inclusion are associated due to several reasons that may be responsible for this association from both the demand side and the supply side. Low confidence, attitudes, behaviors, and awareness creating access barriers to utilize different financial products and services in meeting some needs are all constraints to their use. Demand-side barriers include low levels of financial literacy, language barriers, etc. and among the supply-side barriers are geographical and regulatory constraints.

Access to financial products and services requires an enhanced level of public financial literacy (Li & Qian, 2020). Financial literacy and finance knowledge deprivation is also assumed to be a barrier to financial access. Financial literacy involves training activities, sensitization raising communication campaigns, pilot schemes like school bank, inclusion in school academic curriculums, etc. Financial literacy training has an impact on financial inclusion.

People who undergo financial literacy training can be expected to have higher prospects of having a bank account and more advantages to avail financial assistance. Female-household are a beneficiary of ownership of an account while male household beneficiary only influenced savings behavior and financial support (Koomson, Villano, & Hadley, 2019). Beneficiaries of financial literacy training have higher opportunities of deepening financial inclusion, more among young men's households. Financial inclusion deepens through the giving of financial literacy. Financial literacy training bridges the financial gap with significant influence of demographic factors on microfinance, banking and fin tech access. Income has implications for financial literacy and thus people with higher income level are more likely to have a bank account and fintech user (Grohmann et al., 2018).

Financial literacy training affects the depth of financial inclusion on the basis of randomized data. The CALD project addresses humanitarian entrants' financial literacy and financial inclusion needs through resources used by agencies and direct channels such as radio. Financial literacy encompasses awareness, knowledge, skills, attitudes and behavior necessary to make informed financial decisions and achieve personal financial well-being (Atkinson & Messy, 2012). Financial literacy, awareness and advice are necessary to establish an inclusive financial sector through initiatives and provisions. Financial inclusion and financial literacy are two factors that are complementary and correlated with a causation relationship. Low incomes may be the cause of low levels of financial inclusion leading to low financial literacy. The vulnerable household population contains lower financial literacy and inclusion are engaged in low-income subsistence with no savings and credit characterized as financially fearful (Babych, Grigolia, & Keshelava, 2018). Poor parts of the population are financially included due to low literacy rates and incomes

High levels of knowledge of financial literacy enable a person to make rational financial decisions (Frączek & Klimontowicz, 2015). Lower financial literacy is less likely to use reward credit cards compared to financially literate and sophisticated consumers, something that offers proof that financial products can exploit financial literacy limitations (Ricaldi, Finke & Huston, 2013). Financial literacy facilitates one to better understand the intricacies that are involved in financial products and services leading to individuals making decisions to hunt around for the best bargain instead of taking the most convenient bargain offered.

The relationship between reward cards used to segment consumers sensitive to rebates and financial literacy as an instrument and furnishing evidence for credit card rebates is akin to market characteristics that cause welfare transfers between sophisticated and naive consumers. Providing financial literacy knowledge and skills management to households to run their economies motivates them to believe in financial institutions strengthening and improvement of the work of financial literacy by developing and enacting organizational strategies increases the financial status of populations. Financial institutions develop financial products for sustainability business and enabling capital growth for financial security in financial management (Jayanti & Karnowati, 2023).

Financial literacy covers the operations of fringe economy enterprises and business models, regulation cost and non-predatory economic, financial and credit services such as pawnshops, payday lenders, rent to own business, car title pawns, buy here and pay here, etc. (Karger, 2015). Policymaking towards long-term viability is developed by the government and regulators for the improvement of the financial access and consumer protection of pawnshop customers with good information to improve the empowerment of society. Alternative monetary policy options need to comprehensively deal with increasing the nexus between financial literacy and inclusion. World and national data are used in analyzing and monitoring financial exclusion, financial literacy and financial education. World Bank (WB) has engaged in Microfinance Networks developing a project of financial literacy and financial inclusion focused on cash transfer to recipients ultra-poor.

National and local economies need financial consumer protection strategies, financial literacy, and financial inclusion strategies with a focus on specific process areas like improving access through financial literacy and financial inclusion through financial services and products such as cash transfer in remote communities. The National Financial Literacy Strategy targets as the unbanked segment who are campaigning for strengthening the ties between financial access strategies, financial education and asset building. The financial literacy strategy decides the role of improved financial literacy to prevent financial exclusion. The action steps in order to improve financial literacy and inclusion are to facilitate financial advice, announcements by public radio and television and access by means. The ultra-poor segment hasn't been targeted through financial education programs despite the fact that they provide counsel.

Literacy and financial education reduce the barriers of vulnerable populations in order to increase the confidence level in approaching more suitable financial products, services and means. The population groups target of financial education for financial training and literacy are unaware which might have a positive effect on financial inclusion and literacy on account ownership and might be more prone to increase inclusive finance (Koomson et al., 2019). Financial education for national policymaking for financial inclusion led to governments reacting to financial inclusion and the needs of financial education through collective policies that were designed to solve supply and demand problems. Individual-level examination of financial literacy and inclusion with appreciation for the distinctive character of skills like self-reported limitations of individuals seeking access to financial services and products, where it is appreciated the relevance of money management practices of households.

For examining the financial inclusion, literacy and understanding the intra-household decision it is necessary to combine quantitative with qualitative findings. The development of financial education and literacy programs has a few challenges to be addressed such as the language barrier for the financially excluded (GAO, 2010; Barcellos et al., 2012). Financial literacy by increased financial education bridging financial vulnerability because of individual circumstances and mental constraints and increasing financial inclusion levels. At the national level, each country possesses its database synthesizing macro-level-data and supply-side data.

National framework for development policies is developed and implemented towards improving financial literacy and inclusion with focus on the financial consumer protection for the financially excluded. Poor financially excluded individuals and groups are prevented from achieving financial inclusion, among other factors, lack of institutional branches in poor area lands, low incomes, lack of formal identification documents, lack of confidence on financial product and service providers. Complementary policy on financial consumer protection and education to increase the level of financial inclusion is required. Enhancing efforts on financial literacy, financial inclusion and consumer protection policy enhances the degree of financial consumer awareness.

The interest of international policy in financial literacy and associated inclusion is reflected by strategic actions as expressed in financial education and consumer protection. Pawnshops are enjoined to be yielding to regulatory compliance to International Financial Report Standards (IFRS) and other rules (Bondarenko & Sitenko, 2020). Consumer and user perspective of the offer process influences consumption and usage of a good and services and financial literacy (Trinh, Morgan, Sonobe, 2020).

There is empirical data of financial literacy which is concerned with financial inclusion but not many attempts to quantify these two variables. Among the international financial literacy and financial inclusion measures are the CGAP, IFC, OECD and World Bank, which focus on financial literacy, quality of product and consumer protection. Financial Literacy Measurement Survey has been developed in order to identify and describe policy guidance of best practice. Evidence is connected with financial literacy regarding knowledge on financial exclusion. Evidence of the success of methods are some described studies such as the OECD/INFE. The OECD/INFE measure of financial literacy survey is an international survey of product awareness, use, selection and utilization of product and services made available at the national level, combining individual measures of financial literacy and financial inclusion.

It is uncovered by the OECD/INFE Financial Literacy Measurement Survey and national surveys that few people make informed financial product and service choices, requiring to fulfill a need for financial education and knowledge activities to improve financial inclusion activities (Atkinson & Messy, 2012). The OECD/INFE Survey on Financial Literacy Measurement explores financial exclusion of individuals and if the empirical financial inclusion is correlated to financial literacy. The OECD/INFE Survey of financial inclusion and financial literacy from the demand side is demand and use of database for financial services and literacy by households and groups at risk of financial exclusion. Demand side: Information enable policy-making to quantify excluded groups of people vulnerable to financial literacy and inclusion in case they require financial education.

Financial literacy of the community is influenced by several factors like social group, family size, age, gender, marital status, occupation, religion, education level, and income, etc. (Babajide et al. 2021; P A. A. N. & Akhtar, 2021). Analysis of financial literacy and inclusion indicators by gender shows that women are less informed about financial literacy and inclusion and less active compared to men in financial consumption (Atkinson & Messy, 2012: OECD, 2013). Social determinants of a community include the level of financial literacy brought about by establishing microfinance units and digital services in partnership with other stakeholders such as private investments, banking and non-banking financial institutions, pawnshops, local government, etc.

Microfinance Fin Tech access is associated with financial literacy based on regression result in a logit model (Hasan, Le, & Hoque, 2021). Financial digital applications encourage financial inclusion and quality of life and community well-being improvement (Meilani et al., 2022). The ultra-poor with very low, fluctuating and volatile incomes is a high-priority group for financial literacy and inclusion because they have no or little ability to use digital technology to extend financial services and electronic payments.

Financial literacy is influenced by different determinants such as digital economy, capital quality demands, communal governance and discussion, leadership, legality, etc. Financial education influences financial literacy affecting the financial planning and investment choice-making leading to the community well-being (Kaiser, Lusardi, Menkhoff & Urban, 2022; Wagner, 2015; Panos & Wilson, 2020). The digital financial awareness involves both financial awareness and digital awareness (Normawati et al., 2021) that allows to understand issues about access to the financial industry for effective financial planning (Safitri et al., 2022).

The AI solutions by financial institutions must take the initiative in their role towards developing financial awareness so that the users can effectively adapt to these changes. Digital financial awareness influences sustainable MSMEs. The diversity of educational levels, genders, ages, and professions of individuals who require financial literacy guidance to make decisions in choosing the quality pawnshop goods suited to their financial needs (Mukti, Tulasmi, Shohiha, Garbo, & Mubasiroh, 2022). It is assumed that there are variations in financial literacy by region and differences in access to finance.

MSME entrepreneurs must learn and understand some important financial principles, improving capability to operate their finance becoming more competent decision-makers, better financial planning, budgeting and control (Judijanto & Asfahani, 2022; Rohman et al., 2023). Financial literacy and inclusion analysis based on regulatory guidelines, policy and strategic reports aim to increase household and SMEs' access to financial institutions like pawnshops and online credit and loan institutions. Causes analysis of low rates among vulnerable groups to formulate policy recommendations to address the phenomenon of financial inclusion (Grigolia, & Keshelava, 2018).

Enhanced financial literacy has the potential to enhance MSME owners with the knowledge guiding them to react proactively with actions towards finding and managing their finances more effectively, resulting in organizational resilience and enterprise development. Inclusive development is a prerequisite for economic, social and political as well as financial stability. Informal economic activities are prone to uncertainty based on unbanked cash transactions isolated from financial systems.

Enhancement of financial literacy and access to micro-finance for MSME owners, to drive local socio-economic development, through the Participatory Action Research method involving mutual needs determinations and feedback systems (Nugrahanti, Lanjarsih & Mutumanikam, 2024).

Such a new generation of financial literacy establishes a lasting legacy on owners to become more professional in their finances overcome financial challenges through budgeting and making well-informed finance decisions and promote socio-economic development and stability.

Financial literacy, financial inclusion, and consumer protection are intertwined strands pursuing financial stability. Micro, Small, and Medium Enterprises (MSMEs) need the support of financial management with the enhancement of financial literacy with micro-financing access to pursue increasing local socio-economic growth.

Payment cards utilized in mobile banking is a tool that is capable of spanning the financial inclusion deficiencies on regions with poor monetary infrastructure turning into a safe replacement for monetary transactions in domestic payment mechanisms enabling disadvantaged segments to make a fair price for merchandise escalating monetary literacy and inclusion and entrenching trust and digital safety (Babai, 2024).

Financial literacy forms an integral part of financial inclusion. For example, rural societies that are acquainted with financial services have more opportunities of being integrated into the finance systems. The Kiva, micro-lending website has not-for-profit partners that are varied and incorporate financial and micro enterprise education with loan delivery, for example, organizations that collects on a monthly basis offering interactive education. Designing and executing MSMEs community service project on financial literacy and management can offer greater financial knowledge and practices, enhanced financial literacy and comprehension of financial concepts and towards the economic stability of the MSMEs. Financial inclusion and literacy are critical in the promotion of the financial well-being of households and SMEs.

Financial literacy and inclusion association is reflected in research, necessary for understanding household financial decision making and access with regard to financial services and products. Large-scale data enable comparisons of initiatives and efforts in financial literacy education and inclusion. Financial literacy information and in the context of financial product and service needs among the targeted vulnerable groups must be gathered in order to determine that financial products and financial processes can be utilized in compensating and coping with financial risks (OECD, 2013b). The findings of the research indicate that subjects who socialized pawnshops had low-level financial literacy pawnshops but increasing familiarity with products in pawnshops as a result of the pandemic crisis as a result of the pandemic crisis (Sukardi, Wijayanti & Fachrurazi, 2023).

Empirical data supporting that marketing activity affects financial literacy of citizens making use of pawnshop facilities during the pandemic crisis because of need pressures and hardship on capitals and money. Appointment and establishment of a supreme national policy for financial literacy and inclusion should include associated socio-economic issues like education, consumer protection, employment prospects, etc. in the direction of sound financial behavior towards further financial integration (Babych, Grigolia, & Keshelava, 2018).

PAWNSHOP

Pawnshop is a re-investing capital institution that has been obtained from other economic activities. People pawn their gold, movable properties and valuable items in order to have easy, fast and simple ways of obtaining cash driven by the need of funds to start or boost a micro social enterprise, small business or personal financing. Pawnshop is an instant solution towards meeting urgent financial needs by utilizing useful properties as securities (Wati, 2023). Financial education indicators and low incomes may prove to be inadequate for the development of the financial sector, which means the majority of citizens do not have an adequate level of financial skills and cannot understand over and beyond the basic financial principles, making decisions without having full knowledge about all the financial services and products available (Babych, Grigolia, & Keshelava, 2018).

Pawnshop is a non-banking financial institution providing credit services comprising collateral-backed loans, movables, appraisal services, and other services (Hasyim et al., 2023). Pawnshop is a non-banking financial institution that contributes to socio-economic advancement by providing loans to prospective lenders against precious assets such as diamonds, jewelry, laptop computers, motorbikes, electronic devices, etc. (Hidayati & Fainani, 2023).

Financial and credit arrangements predominantly offered by civil society organizations, who have become the leading player in fueling financialization via the interaction of various financial instruments, drawn from general strategies such as the cash transfers, pawnshops, microcredit, schemes building assets, among others, are all linked to financial literacy and financial empowerment schemes (Buckland, 2018).

Pawnbrokers are used primarily for the purpose of obtaining cash loans but diversified their operations and products to other financial services such as payday loans and cheque cashing, new and second-hand jewellery retailing, gold buying, etc. (Collard & Hayes, 2010). Pawnshop operations are increasing due to changes in consumer behavior and economic development to manage their finances, community empowerment and education capital requirements. Pawnshop customers are relevant to quantitative impact in financial inclusion terms. Customers frequent pawnshops that process varying collateral pledged, loan approval speed, distance to workplace and home, staff competent and well-versed, loyalty factor, etc.

Pawnshop financial institution is chosen to study due to interest in the pawnshop financial sector. Loan disbursement of pawnshop systems disbursements of loan money benefit the community to meet their financial and economic requirements in an easy, quick and convenient way, thus leading to a type of financial solutions by availing finance to support micro, small and medium-scale enterprises. Financing in terms of offering loans for individuals who are not looked upon as creditworthy is being provided by shop keeping, pawn broking, mutual assistance rendered by religious bodies and lottery (Avallone & Strangio, 2024). With pawnshop products, it is a choice to do usury-free financial transactions (Yulianto, 2018).

Traditional pawnshops charge higher interest and fees, which could be disallowed by the Islam pawnshops on grounds of an element of interest-free loans by definition and must have a minimum charge as a fee to keep the items of pawning based on value for collateral. The pawnshop company provides a pawn proof letter that is signed by the borrower who is looking for collateralized financing and the pawn official (Abdul-Razak, 2011). The customers of the pawnshop have diversified and unique education levels, ages, genders, occupations leading to decision-making influenced indicators like financial knowledge, management ability, trust, and belief in pawnshop institutions (Mukti, Tulasmi, Shohiha, Garbo, & Mubasiroh, 2022).

Pawnshop knowledge is not the decisive factor of whether to be a pawnshop user and a customer. Mukti, Tulasmi, Shohiha, Garbo, & Mubasiroh, (2022) learned that there is a positive relationship on the variable of pawnshop knowledge and awareness to becoming a pawnshop customer. Traditional and conventional financing includes sources from the private sector, banks, and credit unions.

Financial literacy for literacy providing information to distinguish between the variances available among the diverse traditional pawnshop services and products and other pawnshops. Conventional or traditional pawnshop is a financial organization which operates with an interest system to be obtained that is a bane to society and with a limited function in community empowerment since it failed to take note of honesty and safety of transaction and conditions of the contract (Ulidaman, 2019). Traditional pawnshops is a popular monetary alternative to obtain instant capital and loans on the basis of collateral offering useful goods as a good option for people who are deprived of financial loans and bank credit from other financial organizations.

Traditional pawnshops charges the user a high rate of interest using conventional monetary doctrines and availing huge loans. Conventional or traditional pawnshop is an appropriate solution to resolve quickly the financial problems. Pawnshops have a relevant function in developing financial literacy awareness, education and outreach activities. Sharia and conventional pawnshops are two lending institutions that utilize principles and strategies other to extend credit facilities that empower society and the community and improve the Indonesian people's financial status.

The operational financial concept and practice are the distinctions of Sharia pawnshops and common pawnshops. Common pawnshop operates under conventional economic principles using interest to stimulate borrowing. The Sharia pawnshop operates under Islamic law practiced under financial principles to provide non-clashing transactions and prohibiting the interest system (Firdaus et al., 2023; Hariss, 2020; Hidayati & Fainani, 2023). Islamic pawn broking aims to provide an alternative financing in permissible principles in a bid to reverse financial exclusion of poor and low-income social groups towards improving the well-being of society. Islamic pawn broking aims to create alternative financing in an attempt to put an end to the interest rates and auctioning with the aim of improving the well-being of poor and low-income social groups (Aziz, 2001).

Values of Sharia pawnshops prioritize justice and equity in financial services through financial accessibility to all segments of society that encourage equality in financial engagement. The ethical bases of Sharia pawnshops on equality and justice provide equal access to finances, offer financial products based on moral values, enable loans that help individuals, families and micro business to meet economic needs without interest resulting in opening job opportunities, build economic potential and empower communities Sharia Pawnshop is a financial institution providing credit to the public among those who have trouble obtaining bank and loans and other funding sources while complying with pawnshop rules and regulations.

Sharia is an Islamic pawnshop which provides easy, quick, and compliant access to instant money, recommended in order to take care of immediately MSMEs' micro-financial needs to complement the socio-economic framework (Hilaluddin & Abdullah, 2024). Sharia pawnshops business and operations are regulated by sharia law and contract conditions of faithfulness and security of transactions in accordance with Islamic law (Hidayati & Fainani, 2023). Sharia pawnshops are sales and purchases based on Islamic law and meeting some terms and conditions of contractual requirements, such as honesty and security requirements (Firdausi & Ardyansyah, 2023; Hafizh & Yanti, 2023; Hanifah et al., 2018; Lesmono, 2022; Rolanda et al., 2023).

Sharia pawnshops are financed by channels such as Sharia bank loans to build and establish businesses that are beneficial to stakeholders, investments to settle gold installment payments, capital funding from Arum financing (Putri et al., 2023). Contracts are on rental fees guided by the fatwa to guarantee standards and moral practice (Yanthiani, 2020). Sharia pawnshops also have a higher level of empowering the community by providing Islamic principles' financial products prohibiting all types of interest and highlighting honesty and security of the transaction based on terms regulated through an Islamic law (Rahmadanti & Sugiarti, 2024).

Pawnshops as financial institutions are socially responsible to increase high awareness to the society, upholding social justice to the borrowers of loans in regard to other alternative sources of pawning. Financial institutions of pawnshops are socially responsible to improve awareness of products and services and to inform the society according to ethical principles and practices of justice, fairness, transparency, honesty, etc.

FINANCIAL LITERACY IMPLICATIONS ON PAWNSHOP USAGE

There is empirical evidence that establishes a significant relationship between financial literacy and the practices of personal financial management, including financial planning and prudent use of credit. Financial literacy studies are essential when considering consumer behavior. Financial illiteracy has been linked to negative implications like financial insecurity, bad credit record, and over-debt (Lusardi & Mitchell, 2014; Pérez-Lopez, 2020). Empirical literature review identifies some segments of population with lower levels of financial literacy, income, and education such as excluded individuals, minorities, and women. This finding suggests policing financial literacy programs need to be tailored and specifically designed to address the exact requirements of different demographic segments of population.

A combination of some of the major findings on organizational economics, financial literacy, and pawnshops considers financial literacy as the major determinant of organizational and individual financial success. Organizational economics investigates how firms prepare, structure, and implement. Financial literacy is linked to organizational economics in order to support decision-making. Financial literacy is a key component that involves knowledge, attitudes, behavior and skills needed to make sound financial decisions with far-reaching effects on influencing one's economic behavior on saving, investing, lending, and managing debt money habits, and by extension, to individuals' and organizations' well-being, and communities (Lusardi & Mitchell, 2014; Lusardi, 2019; Hermawan et al., 2022).

Financial literacy can be defined as the ability to use finance skills and knowledge. Finance knowledge is investment in human capital needed to reduce finance literacy Organizational economics can be applied to financial literacy, financial well-being, in the sense that it provides a framework for analyzing the structure, decision and strategic alternatives on the interacting between firms and markets taking into consideration such issues as organizational design, incentives, financial decisions on investments and credits, information flows, etc. Financial literacy is relevant for organizational decision-making with significant implications on investment and credit decisions and organizational performance.

Pawnshops bridges organizational economics at the micro-level analysis of financial behavior of organizational response to finance needs. Pawnshops are pivotal in offering a way of promoting financial literacy and inclusion by lending money short-term to financially excluded groups of society with no access to conventional and formal financial institutions and banking facilities, offering a viable alternative to financially in need persons with no credit history, low income, and with no access to the mainstream traditional financial institutions.

Financial literacy, in this context, is an individual attribute and an essential organizational competency. Organizations with higher financial literacy levels become more capable of making wise investment and credit decisions, managing financial risks, and making optimal financial resource allocations. The ability to analyze financial statements, market trends, and predict financial implications of strategic decisions are all essential aspects of organizational financial literacy. Pawnshops play a critical role in providing financial literacy and complement financial inclusion by providing credit to the poor. The meeting point of organizational economics and financial literacy is particularly significant in the situations of change and competitiveness where financial and credit institutions must respond aggressively to changing financial market situations and opportunities.

Pawnshops is a unique meeting point of organizational economics and micro-scale financial credit conduct. Pawnshop institutions offer micro, small and medium enterprises and individuals the opportunity to respond aggressively to financial needs outside the ambit of traditional banking systems. From organizational economics perspective, pawnshops are a business model that provides an interesting case to analyze the degree of financial literacy of particular segment of population in short-term collateral-secured loans need.

Organizational responses of pawnshops to the urgent demands of money among individuals and micro-organizations are operational strategies on risk management practices, pricing models, customer relationship management, etc. Pawnshop business strategies' dynamics enlivens financial issues of economic behavior of individual and micro-firms facing financial trouble, financial literacy and education, financial inclusion, easy and fast access to credit, etc. Pawnshops operate under domestic and federal policy and regulatory environments moving toward engagement with other formal financial institutions enlivening financial well-being as well as consumer protection.

Policies aimed at improving financial literacy and promoting financial inclusion that make a positive contribution towards improving economic well-being of individuals, organizations, and communities. Policy and regulatory aspects of pawnshops play an important role in consumer protection and promoting fair lending practices. Pawnshops are controlled by numerous types of legislation at the local, state, and federal level, which are designed to prevent predatory lending, promote transparency, and safeguard the interests of borrowers. These legislations would traditionally address topics of interest rate limits, disclosure of charges, loan terms, and collateral redemption process. The regulating environment governing pawnshops is designed to balance providing credit access to low-income groups with protecting the borrowers from exploitative or abusive lending practices.

A good regulatory program and inspection are critical in ensuring that pawnshops behave reasonably and contribute positively to the financial well-being of their communities. Pawnshops too fall within the jurisdiction of policymaking, regulations aimed at consumer protection; against unfair lending and borrowing. Additionally, pawnshops are typically required to maintain detailed records of transactions and report suspicious activity to law enforcement agencies to preclude money laundering and other illicit activities. Financial literacy is central to guiding organizational decision-making, risk management, investment and personal finance of individuals and micro-organizations.

Strong financial literacy building blocks of individuals and organizations force to make sound financial decisions in line with their strategic goals and leading to achieving higher shareholder value. Individuals and micro-organizations considering their capital investment needs, require financial behavior and attitudes and understanding to analyze the finance viability, risk capital management of the project, etc. to decide on risk-adjusted returns on investment, cash flows, internal rate of return, etc. These parameters' analysis requires the use of financial concepts and analytical tools.

There is a requirement of financial literacy for budgeting, forecasting, financial control of resource allocation making the financial sustainability of the organization. Building financial literacy within the organizational members and stakeholders, enhance the ability to achieve strategic objectives and manage complexity in financial crises. Pawnshops are financial intermediaries with a specific role in financial inclusion through providing excluded individuals by formal and conventional financial and banking institutions for easy and quick access to credit. Organizational economics defines pawnshops as having a specific role within the financial system through providing collateral-backed short-term loans. Understanding organizational economics of pawnshop business provides one with an appreciation for their role in meeting the financial needs of some sections of society.

The pawnshops are institutions which serve as the economic lifeline of social sections of society with no access to the formal financial and banking products and services such as credit cards and bank loans. Pawnshops provide collateral-based short-term loans in which individuals and micro-organizations can borrow funds against the value of goods, such as jewelry, gold, silver, electronics, tools, etc. The service and product offerings of pawnshops are advantageous to poor and low-income individuals, small and micro-enterprise operators, who are limited in their credit history to obtain conventional loans. Ease and accessibility of the pawnshops make them capable of plugging the financial void as well as extending financial coverage to such marginalized people. The simplicity and convenience of pawnshops make them prone to becoming lucid parts of the financial system of credit and investment in communities with limited coverage of formal finances and banks.

Pawnshops provide short-term collateralized loans, which allow individuals to secure a loan based on the value of their items, such as jewelry, appliances, or equipment. The facility is particularly important for individuals in need of immediate access to money in case of emergencies or unexpected expenditures. By offering a readily accessible source of credit, pawnshops enable the bridging of the financial gap and financial inclusion for under-served populations to achieve a more equitable and inclusive financial system. Organizational economics of pawnshop business is characterized by offering short-term loans to financially needed individual and micro-organizations secured by collateral, performing differently within the financial system. Pawnshops offer a distinct products and services through receiving personal belongings as collateral for a loan, allowing customers to access cash without undergoing extensive credit checks or sharing financial information.

The loaned money is typically based on the value of the collateral when it is appraised, and the borrower has a given time limit to pay back the loan with fees and interest. The interest rates and service charges offered by pawnshops are higher compared to other lenders, which reflects the higher risk and transaction and management costs associated with this kind of lending. In case of default on repayment within the stipulated time, the pawnshop will sell the collateral to recover the outstanding loan. This model allows pawnshops to efficiently balance risk as well as provide borrowers immediate access to credit. Finally, financial literacy is a key driver of organizational and individual financial performance.

Organizational economics-wise, financial literacy allows firms to make informed decisions, efficiently handle risks, and support sustainable growth. Individuals, at their level, are able to make smart financial decisions, accumulate wealth, and buffer their financial lives with financial literacy. Pawnshops, as unique financial institutions, help facilitate access to credit by marginalized groups, pointing toward the importance of financial inclusion. The convergence of organizational economics, financial literacy, and pawnshops teaches us the importance of holistic methods of financial well-being for all walks of society.

CONCLUSION

Where loans are accessed by individuals, or where pawnshops are negotiated, there is a requirement to deliver financial literacy and savings programs. Financial management skills decide the personal decisions of becoming a pawnshop consumer of service and pawnshop customer.

Business models are identified by digital economy and facilitating financial literacy. An organizational model to enhance financial literacy facilitated by digital economy building digital markets can be stated based on online and e-ticketing services, cashless payment systems and integrating waste management and savings and creating microfinance institutions. Research also needs to examine the performance of diverse financial literacy program designs, delivery and assessment practices.

Additional studies are required to examine the long-term consequences of financial literacy interventions and the evolving role of pawnshops in the financial industry.

Longitudinal studies are necessary to establish the long-term consequences of financial literacy interventions on organizational and individual financial behavior and outcomes. There is a need to increase financial literacy to fill the gap that is rampant in gender financial inclusion. A National Index of financial literacy and inclusion must be undertaken by the economies of underdeveloped and developing nations.

Future research needs to consider looking at investigating and examining the long-term impact of financial literacy programs and the evolving role of pawnshops in the financial marketplace.

Research further needs to investigate the evolving role of pawnshops in the financial system, particularly in the context of technological advances and non-traditional lending platforms.

By bridging these research gaps, policymaking and practice can develop effective policies for promoting financial literacy, financial inclusion, and financial well-being for all levels of society

REFERENCES

Abdul-Razak, A. (2011). *Economic and religious significance of the Islamic and conventional pawnbroking in Malaysia: behavioural and perception analysis* (Doctoral dissertation, Durham university).

Atkinson, A., & Messy, F.-A. (2012), Measuring Financial Literacy: Results of the OECD / International Network on Financial Education (INFE) Pilot Study, *OECD Working Papers on Finance, Insurance and Private Pensions, No. 15*, OECD Publishing. DOI: 10.1787/20797117

Avallone, P., & Strangio, D. (2024). Different Forms of Microcredit and Social Business—Microfinance in Global History from the Late Medieval to the Modern. In: Avallone, & Strangio, (2024). In *Different Forms of Microcredit and Social Business: Microfinance in Global History from the Late Medieval to the Modern* (pp. 1-15). Cham: Springer Nature Switzerland. DOI: 10.1007/978-3-031-60942-8_1

Aziz, Z. A. (2001). *Ar-rahnu, an Alternative Financing Mode for Microcredit.* Paper presented at the Seminar on Understanding the Concept and Application of Ar- rahnu on 12th November 2002, Kuala Lumpur. Available at <URL: https://www.mifc.com/publication/p.9.5.pdf> Access Date 21st Mar 2008.

Babai, M. (2024), *Strategies for Financial Inclusion and the Unbanked Population in India, and how this effect businesses and entrepreneurs in Financial Sectors of India.* Senior Projects Fall 2024. 37. https://digitalcommons.bard.edu/senproj_f2024/37

Babajide, A. *et al.* (2021). Financial literacy, financial capabilities, and sustainable business model practice among small business owners in Nigeria, *J. Sustain. Financ. Invest.*, pp. 1–23, 2021, .DOI: 10.1080/20430795.2021.1962663

Babych, Y., Grigolia, M., & Keshelava, D. (2018). *Financial inclusion, financial literacy, and financial education in Georgia* (No. 849). ADBI Working Paper.

Barcellos, S. H., Smith, J. P., Yoong, J. K., & Carvalho, L. (2012), *Barriers to Immigrant Use of Financial Services The Role of Language Skills, U.S. Experience, and Return Migration Expectations Report to the Social Security Administration* https://www.rand.org/content/dam/rand/pubs/working_papers/2012/RAND_WR923.sum.pdFinancial

Bondarenko, N., & Sitenko, V. (2020). Improving The Accounting For Credit Transactions In Pawnshops. *Oblìk Ì Finance*, 2(88), 5–11. https://Doi.Org/10.33146/2307-9878-2020-2(88)-5-11

Buckland, J. (2018). Credit, Cash, Savings, and Financial Literacy Delivered Through Civil Society. In: *Building Financial Resilience*. Palgrave Macmillan, Cham. DOI: 10.1007/978-3-319-72419-5_5

Collard, S., & Hayes, D. (2010). *Pawnbroking Customers in 2010: A Survey – A Report to the National Pawnbrokers Association*. Personal Finance Research Centre., URL https://www.bristol.ac.uk/geography/research/pfrc/t

Firdausi, F. N., & Ardyansyah, F. (2023). Implementation of Sharia Marketing Strategy As A Solution To Increase Linkaja Syariah Consumer Loyalty. *JESI (Indonesian Sharia Economic Journal),* 13(1), 74–81. https://Doi.Org/10.21927/Jesi .2023.13(1).74-81

Frączek, B., & Klimontowicz, M. (2015). Financial literacy and its influence on young customers' decision factors. *J Innov Manag*, *3*(1), 62–84. DOI: 10.24840/2183-0606_003.001_0007

GAO. (2010), *Factors Affecting the Financial Literacy of Individuals with Limited English Proficiency Consumer Finance Report to Congressional Committees* http://www.gao.gov/assets/310/304561.pdf

Gardeva, A., & Rhyne, E. (2011). *Opportunities and Obstacles to Financial Inclusion. Survey Report.* Center for Financial Inclusion at ACCION International https://centerforfinancialinclusionblog.files.wordpress.com/2011/07/opportunities -and-obstacles-to-financial-inclusion_110708_final.pdf

Grohmann, A., Klühs, T., Menkhoff, L. (2018). Does financial literacy improve financial inclusion? Cross country evidence. *World Dev* 111:84–96. https://doi.org/ . world dev. 2018. 06. 020.DOI: 10. 1016/j

Hafizh, N. A., & Yanti, N. N. (2023). Restructuring Mechanism in Resolving Problematic Murabahah Financing at Bank Sumut Syariah KC Medan Katamso. *Brilliance,* 3(2), 260–277. https://Doi.Org/10.55606/Cemerlang.V3i2.1207

Hanifah, A., Santoso, B., & Navianto, I. (2018). The Urgency of Setting Up a Private Pawn Company Using an Online System. *Al-Mustashfa: Research Journal of Sharia Economic Law*, 3(1), 30. Https://Doi.Org/10.24235/Jm.V3i1.2935

Hariss, A. (2020). Settlement of Defaults in Gold Pawn Agreements Between Customers and the Limited Liability Company PawnshopsJambi Branch. Legalitas: *A Law Journal,* 12(1), 94. Https://Doi.Org/10.33087/Legalitas.V12i1.196

Hasan, M., Le, T., & Hoque, A. (2021). How does financial literacy impact on inclusive finance? *Financial Innovation*, *7*(1), 40. DOI: 10.1186/s40854-021-00259-9

Hasyim, S. DM, Sipahutar, IM, & Rogantina, V. (2023). Analysis of The Role Of Pawnshops In UMKM Business Development (Case Study At PT. Pawnshops Kanwil Medan). *Indonesian Journal Of Accounting And Financial Technology*, 1(2), 71–82. https://Doi.Org/10.55927/Crypto.V1i2.4268

Hermawan, A., & Susanti, E. (2022). Optimization of Improving Organizational Citizenship Behaviour (OCB) through Personality Strengthening, Interpersonal Communication, and Organizational Justice. *Indonesian Journal of Education and Mathematical Science*, *3*(3), 118–125.

Hilaluddin, N., & Abdullah, A. (2024). The Relevance of Ar-Rahnu for MSME (Micro, Small, and Medium-Sized Enterprises) Community in Assuring Financial Well-Being. In *Artificial Intelligence (AI) and Customer Social Responsibility (CSR)* (pp. 797–813). Springer Nature Switzerland. DOI: 10.1007/978-3-031-50939-1_64

Hung, A. A., Parker, A. M., & Yoong, J. K. (2009). Defining and Measuring Financial Literacy. *RAND Labor and Population*, *2009*, 4.

Jayanti, E., & Karnowati, N. B. (2023). *Digitalisasi Umkm Dan Literasi Keuangan Untuk Keberlanjutan Umkm Di Kabupaten Cilacap*. Kajian Bisnis Sekolah Tinggi Ilmu Ekonomi Widya Wiwaha, 31(1), 51–64. Https://Doi.Org/10.32477/Jkb.V31i1.504

Judijanto, L., & Asfahani, A. (2022). 21st Century Economic Transformation: The Impact of Artificial Intelligence on Markets and Employment. *Journal of Artificial Intelligence and Development*, *1*(1).

Kaiser, T., Lusardi, A., Menkhoff, L., & Urban, C. (2022). Financial education affects financial knowlegde and downstream behaviors. *Journal of Financial Economics*, *145*(2), 255–272. DOI: 10.1016/j.jfineco.2021.09.022

Karger, H. (2015). Curbing the financial exploitation of the poor: Financial literacy and social work education. *Journal of Social Work Education*, *51*(3), 425–438. DOI: 10.1080/10437797.2015.1043194

Kemspon, E. (2002). *Over-indebtedness in Britain*. Department of Trade and Industry.

Kodongo, O. (2018) Financial regulations, financial literacy, and financial inclusion: insights from Kenya. *Emerg Mark Financ Trade* 54(12):2851–2873. https://doi.org/ . 2017. 14183DOI: 10. 1080/ 15404 96X

Koomson I, Villano RA, Hadley D (2019) Intensifying financial inclusion through the provision of financial literacy training: a gendered perspective. *Appl Econ* 52(4):1–13. https://doi.org/ . 2019. 16459 43DOI: 10. 1080/ 00036 846

Lesmono, B. (2022). Literature Study of Sharia Pawnshops in Indonesia. *Scientific Journal of Islamic Economics*, 8(1), 599. Https://Doi.Org/10.29040/Jiei.V8i1.4368

Li, R., & Qian, Y. (2020) Entrepreneurial participation and performance: the role of financial literacy, *Manag. Decis.*, 58, (39, pp. 583–599, 2020, DOI: 10.1108/MD-11-2018-1283

Lusardi, A. (2019). Financial Literacy and the Need for Financial Education*: Evidence and Implications. Swiss Journal of Economics and Statistics*, *155*(1), 1. Advance online publication. DOI: 10.1186/s41937-019-0027-5

Lusardi, A., & Mitchell, O. (2014). The Economic Importance of Financial Literacy: Theory and Evidence. *Journal of Economic Literature*, *52*(1), 5–44. DOI: 10.1257/jel.52.1.5 PMID: 28579637

Meilani, A. R., Hasibuan, N. M., & Nasution, M. L. I. (2022). Service Strategy And Implementation Of Digital Sharia Pawnshops In Increasing The Number Of Customers In Rantau Prapat. *Journal of Economics, Management. Accounting and Finance*, *3*(3). https://Doi.Org/10.53697/Emak.V3i3.579

Morgan P, Trinh L (2019) Determinants and impacts of financial literacy in Cambodia and Viet Nam. *J Risk Financ Manag* 12(1):19. Page 23 of 23DOI: 10.3390/jrfm12010019

Mukti, T., Tulasmi, T., Shohiha, A., Garbo, A., & Mubasiroh, S. L. (2022). The effect of sharia financial literacy on the decision of the use of service products in the sharia pawn in Yogyakarta. *KnE Social Sciences*, 273-284.

Normawati, R., Rahayu, S., & Worokinasih, S. (2021). *Financial Knowledge, Digital Financial Knowledge, Financial Attitude, Financial Behaviour And Financial Satisfaction On Millennials*. Https://Doi.Org/10.4108/Eai.6-3-2021.2305967

Nugrahanti, T. P., Lanjarsih, L., & Mutumanikam, P. R. (2024). Financial management and accounting education in improving the village local economy for MSMES in Godobangkong Vilage. *Community Development Journal: Jurnal Pengabdian Masyarakat*, *5*(4), 5891–5898. DOI: 10.31004/cdj.v5i4.30358

OECD (2013), *Financial literacy and inclusion*: Results of OECD/INFE survey across countries and by gender.

OECD (2013b). *Financial Literacy Framework, in OECD, PISA 2012 Assessment and Analytical Framework: Mathematics, Reading, Science, Problem Solving and Financial Literacy*, OECD Publishing. doi: DOI: 10.1787/9789264190511-7-en

P A. A. N. & Akhtar, S. M. J. (2021). Determinants of financial literacy in rural India: A study of Aligarh district. *Int. J. Financ. Eng*, *8*(2).

Panos, G., & Wilson, J. (2020). Financial literacy and responsible finance in the FinTech era: Capabilities and challenges. *European Journal of Finance*, *26*(4–5), 297–301. DOI: 10.1080/1351847X.2020.1717569

Pérez-López, I. J. (2020). *De las 7 Bolas de Dragón a los 7 Reinos de Poniente: viajando por la ficción para transformar la realidad.* CopiDeporte S.L.

Putri, J. K. Sugianto, & Nasution, J. (2023). The Influence of Capital, Production Costs, and Sharia Pawnshop Financing on Micro Business Income Levels in Langsa City. *Jemsi (Journal of Economics, Management and Accounting)*, 9(5), 1813–1822. https://Doi.Org/10.35870/Jemsi.V9i5.1470

r, N., & Fainani, F. (2023). Analysis of the Position of Collateral in Financing at Sharia Pawnshops(Case Study of Sharia Pawnshop Prenduan Branch). Muqaddimah: *Journal of Economics, Management, Accounting and Business*, 1(2), 105–118. https://Doi.Org/10.59246/Muqaddimah.V1i2.189

Rahmadanti, N. I., & Sugiarti, D. (2024). Comparative Analysis Between Sharia Pawnshops and Conventional Pawnshops in *The Economic Empowerment of Indonesian Communities* 4 1 (2024): *Proceeding of The 7th International Seminar on Business, Economics, Social Science, and Technology (ISBEST)* / DOI: 10.33830/isbest.v4i1.3394

Ricaldi, L., Finke, M., & Huston, S. (2013). Financial literacy and shrouded credit card rewards. *Journal of Financial Services Marketing*, *18*(3), 177–187. DOI: 10.1057/fsm.2013.11

Rohman, A., Asfahani, A., & Iqbal, K. (2023). Comprehensive Analysis of AI's Contribution to Communnity *Development Journal,* 5(4).Tahun 2024, Hal. 5891-5898P-ISSN 2721-4990|

Rolanda, I., Mulia, A. A., & Laksmiwati, M. (2023). Increasing Financial Literacy for Students at the Literacy Smart House (Rpa) Kandang Gede, Kresek, Tangerang, Banten. *Krishna,* 3(1), 126–135. Https://Doi.Org/10.36080/Kresna.V3i1.70

Safitri, N., Permadi, I., Fathussyaadah, E., Tinggi Ilmu Ekonomi, P. G. R. I., & Sukabumi, S. (2022). Literasi Keuangan Digital, Keberlanjutan Usaha Industri Kecil Dan Menengah Serta Dampaknya Terhadap Kesejahteraan Keuangan. *Jurnal Ilmiah MEA (Manajemen, Ekonomi, & Akuntansi),* 6(3), 1203–1214. Http://Www.Journal .Stiemb.Ac.Id/Index.Php/Mea/Article/View/2478

Setyowati, A. (2003). Harmadi H, Sunarjanto S. Islamic Financial Literacy and Personal Financial Planning: A Socio-Demographic Study. *J Keuang dan Perbank.* 2018;22(1):63–72.

Sukardi, B., Wijayanti, N. R., & Fachrurazi, F. (2023). *Literacy and strategic marketing to raise public awareness using Sharia pawnshops during the COVID-19 pandemic*. Qualitative Research in Financial Markets.

Trinh, Q. L., Morgan, P. J., & Sonobe, T. (2020). Investment behavior of MSMEs during the downturn periods: Empirical evidence from Vietnam. *Emerging Markets Review*, 45, Elsevier BV; 2020. p. 100739.

Ulidaman, N. (2019). Rationalization of Sharia Pawnshopsat the Ternate Sharia Pawnshop Bastiong Unit as a Non-Bank Financial Institution. *Foramadiahi: Journal of Educational and Islamic Studies,* 10(1), 90. Https://Doi.Org/10.46339/Foramadiahi.V10i1.115

Wagner, W. (2015). Representation in action. In Sammut, G., Andreouli, E., Gaskell, G., & Vasiner, J. (Eds.), *The Cambridge Handbook of Social Representation* (pp. 12–28). Cambridge University Press. DOI: 10.1017/CBO9781107323650.004

Wati, K. (2023). The Influence of Ar-Rahn Financing for Motor Vehicle Owner Book Micro Businesses on the Development of Customers' Micro, Small and Medium Enterprises at the Ahmad Yani Sharia Pawnshop, Pontianak. *Indonesian Muamalat Journal*, 3(2). https://Doi.Org/10.26418/Jmi.V3i2.68243

Yanthiani, L. (2020). Moral Value Of Ijarah And Ujrah: Review Of Rahn Concept In Islam. International. *Journal of Islamic Archipelago*, *8*(1), 1–9. https://Doi.Org/10.15575/Ijni.V8i1.84. DOI: 10.15575/ijni.v8i1.8490

Yulianto, A. (2018). *Pengaruh Literasi Keuangan Syariah Terhadap Keputusan* Penggunaan Produk atau Layanan Lembaga Keuangan Syariah. dspace.uii.ac.id; 2018. DOI Page 283DOI: 10.18502/kss.v7i10.11365

Compilation of References

Abad, J., Nuño, G., & Thomas, C. (2025). CBDC and the operational framework of monetary policy. *Journal of Monetary Economics*, *151*, 103762. DOI: 10.1016/j.jmoneco.2025.103762

Abbasi et al. (2011). Evolutionary dynamics of scientific collaboration networks: multi-levels and cross-time analysis. *89*(2), 687-710.

Abdeljaoued et al. (2020). Bibliometric analysis of the evolution of biochar research trends and scientific production. *22*, 1967-1997.

Abdul-Razak, A. (2011). *Economic and religious significance of the Islamic and conventional pawnbroking in Malaysia: behavioural and perception analysis* (Doctoral dissertation, Durham university).

Acemoglu, D., Ozdaglar, A., & Tahbaz-Salehi, A. (2015). Systemic risk and stability in financial networks. *The American Economic Review*, *105*(2), 564–608. DOI: 10.1257/aer.20130456

Adebambo, S., Olayemi, A., & Adeyemi, O. (2025). Sustainable banking and bank stability in Nigeria: Empirical evidence from deposit money banks. *Journal of Sustainable Finance & Investment*, *15*(2), 123–140.

Adekunle, W., & Ndukwe, I. (2018, June 2). *The Impact of Exchange Rate Dynamics on Agricultural Output Performance in Nigeria* [MPRA Paper]. https://mpra.ub.uni-muenchen.de/87750/

Adetunji, A. P., & Chinonso, O. (2025). The Role of AI in preventing financial fraud and enhancing compliance. *GSC Advanced Research and Reviews*, *22*(03), 269–282. DOI: 10.30574/gscarr.2025.22.3.0086

Adrian, T., & Ashcraft, A. B. (2012). Shadow banking: A review of the literature. *Federal Reserve Bank of New York Staff Reports*, No. 580. https://www.newyorkfed.org/research/staff_reports/sr580.html

Adrian, T., Muhleisen, M., & Obstfeld, M. (2018). Casting light on central bank digital currencies. *Staff Discussion Notes, 2018*(008), A001. DOI: 10.5089/9781484384572.006.A001

Afjal, M. (2023). Bridging the financial divide: a bibliometric analysis on the role of digital financial services within FinTech in enhancing financial inclusion and economic development. *10*(1), 1-27.

African Center for Economic Transformation. (2023). *Artificial Intelligence for Economic Policymaking: Context of AI Applications*. https://acetforafrica.org/

Aggarwal, P., & Bajaj, R. J. P. J. B. L. (2016). The Strategic Debt Restructuring Regime in India. *Does It Need Strategic Restructuring., 12*, 45.

Agoraki, M. E. K., Delis, M. D., & Pasiouras, F. (2011). Regulations, competition and bank risk-taking in transition countries. *Journal of Financial Stability*, *7*(1), 38–48. https://mpra.ub.uni-muenchen.de/121587/1/MPRA_paper_121587.pdf. DOI: 10.1016/j.jfs.2009.08.002

Agosin, M. R., & Huaita, F. (2011). Capital flows to emerging economies: Minsky in the tropics. *Cambridge Journal of Economics*, *35*(4), 663–683. DOI: 10.1093/cje/beq047

Ahmad, A., Khan, A., Akhtar, S., & Akram, H. W. (2021). Examining the Development of Banking Sector Regulations and Supervision Practices across BRICS and G7 Countries. *Complexity, 2021*(1). DOI: 10.1155/2021/1192829

Ahmed, R., & Aldasoro, I. (2025a). Stablecoins and safe asset prices. BIS Working Papers No 1270, May. https://www.bis.org/publ/work1270.pdf

Ahmed, R., Aldasoro, I., & Duley, C. (2025b). Public information and stablecoin runs. BIS Working Papers No 1164, January. https://www.bis.org/publ/work1164.pdf

Akerlof, G. A., & Shiller, R. J. (2009). *Animal spirits: How human psychology drives the economy, and why it matters for global capitalism.*

Akhagbemh, P. (2021). "Foiled Bank Robbery: Delta Police Arrest Staff Informant," AIT. https://ait.live/foiled-bank-robbery-delta-police-arrest-staff-informant/AN=26521700& site=ehost-live

Akhtar, S., Alam, M., & Khan, M. M. (2021). YES Bank Fiasco: Arrogance or Negligence. Emerging Economies Cases Journal, 3(2), 95-102. (Original work published 2021)DOI: DOI: 10.1177/25166042211061003

Akhtar, S., Alam, M., & Ansari, M. S. (2022, November 24). Measuring the performance of the Indian banking industry: Data envelopment window analysis approach. *Benchmarking*, *29*(9), 2842–2857. DOI: 10.1108/BIJ-03-2021-0115

Akhtar, S., Alam, M., Khan, A., & Shamshad, M. (2023). Measuring technical efficiency of banks vis-à-vis demonetization: An empirical analysis of Indian banking sector using CAMELS framework. *Quality & Quantity*, *57*(2), 1739–1761. DOI: 10.1007/s11135-022-01431-8

Akhtar, S., Alam, M., & Khan, M. M. (2021). YES bank fiasco: Arrogance or negligence. *Emerging Economies Cases Journal*, *3*(2), 95–102.

Akhtar, S., Azmi, S. N., Khan, P. A., Jan, A. A., & Ansari, Z. (2024). Unveiling the financial landscape: Analyzing profitability, productivity, and efficiency of banks in an emerging economy using the CAMELS framework and panel analysis. *Cogent Business & Management*, *11*(1), 2399747. Advance online publication. DOI: 10.1080/23311975.2024.2399747

Akinbami, F. (2011). Financial services and consumer protection after the crisis. *International Journal of Bank Marketing*, *29*(2), 134–147. DOI: 10.1108/02652321111107620

al, H. e. (2009). Systemic risk in the financial sector: An analysis of the subprime-mortgage financial crisis. *157*(2), 129-207.

Alam, M., & Akhtar, S. (2024). Introduction to Green Finance and Technology Integration. In Syed Hasan Jafar, Raul Villamarin Rodrigue, Hemachandran Kannan, Shakeb Akhtar and Philipp Plugmann (1st Ed.), Harnessing Blockchain-Digital Twin Fusion for Sustainable Investments (Harnessing, pp. 1–19). IGI Global Scientific Publishing. https://doi.org/httpsdoi.org10.4018979-8-3693-1878-2.ch001

Alami, I. (2018). On the terrorism of money and national policy-making in emerging capitalist economies. *Geoforum*, *96*, 21–31. DOI: 10.1016/j.geoforum.2018.07.012

Alami, I., Alves, C., Bonizzi, B., Kaltenbrunner, A., Koddenbrock, K., Kvangraven, I., & Powell, J. (2023). International financial subordination: A critical research agenda. *Review of International Political Economy*, *30*(4), 1360–1386. DOI: 10.1080/09692290.2022.2098359

Alam, M., & Akhtar, S. (2024). Introduction to green finance and technology integration. In *Syed Hasan Jafar, Raul Villamarin Rodriguez, Hemachandran Kannan, Shakeb Akhtar and Philipp Plugmann, Harnessing blockchain-digital twin fusion for sustainable investments* (pp. 1–19). IGI Global., DOI: 10.4018/979-8-3693-1878-2.ch001

Alam, M., Akhtar, S., & Al-Faryan, M. S. (2023). Do Indian banks perform better in corporate governance than other SAARC nations? An empirical analysis. *Corporate Governance (Bradford)*, *24*(4), 799–830. DOI: 10.1108/CG-02-2023-0059

Aldasoro, I., Aquilina, M., Lewrick, U., & Hyuk Lim, S. (2025a). Stablecoin growth – policy challenges and approaches. BIS Bulletin No 108. July 11, 2025. https://www.bis.org/publ/bisbull108.pdf

Aldasoro, I., Cornelli, G., Ferrari Minesso, M., Gambacorta, L., & Habib, M. (2025b). Stablecoins, money market funds and monetary policy. *Economics Letters*, *247*, 112203. DOI: 10.1016/j.econlet.2025.112203

Aldasoro, I., Mehrling, P., & Neilson, D. (2024). On par: A money view of stablecoins. *Journal of Financial Market Infrastructures*, *11*(4), 47–64.

Alex Avelar, E., & Jordão, R. V. D. (2024). The role of artificial intelligence in the decision-making process: A study on the financial analysis and movement forecasting of the world's largest stock exchanges. *Management Decision*. Advance online publication. DOI: 10.1108/MD-09-2023-1625

Alka et al. (2024). Tracking the footprints of global entrepreneurship research: A theoretical exploration of landscape of global entrepreneurship through a bibliometric perspective. *14*(1), 21.

Al-Own, B., Minhat, M., & Gao, S. (2018). Stock options and credit default swaps in risk management. *Journal of International Financial Markets, Institutions and Money*, *53*, 200–214. DOI: 10.1016/j.intfin.2017.09.021

Aluko, A., & Bagheri, M. (2012). The impact of money laundering on economic and financial stability and on political development in developing countries. *Journal of Money Laundering Control*, *15*(4), 442–457. DOI: 10.1108/13685201211266024

Ams, J., Asonuma, T., Bergthaler, W., DeLong, C., Mehdi, N. E., Flanagan, M., Hagan, S., Liu, Y., Lundgren, C., Mühleisen, M., Pienkowski, A., Pinto, G., & Robert, E. (2018). *Prevention and resolution of sovereign debt crises*. Selected Legal and Institutional Papers Series., DOI: 10.5089/9781484371329.009

Anan et al. (2023). FINTECHS: a new paradigm of growth. McKinsey & Company. In.

Annu, & Tripathi, R. (2023). A bibliometric and systematic review analysis of adopting decision intelligence analytics for rational decision-making. *Qualitative Research in Financial Markets*, *16*(5), 915–936. DOI: 10.1108/QRFM-01-2023-0005

Annual Report, N. D. I. C. (2022). NDIC Publication. https://ndic.gov.ng/resources/publications/

Annu, , & Tripathi, R. (2024, December 18). Annu, & Tripathi, R. (2024). An insight of financial literacy and artificial intelligence to mitigate behavioral biases: A bibliometric and systematic review analysis using SPAR-4-SLR. *International Journal of Emerging Markets*. Advance online publication. DOI: 10.1108/IJOEM-07-2024-1110

Ansari, M. S., Akhtar, S., Khan, A., & Shamshad, M. (2022). Consequence of financial crisis on liquidity and profitability of commercial banks in India: An empirical study. *Studies in Economics and Business Relations*, *3*(2), 36–50. https://www.sabapub.com/index.php/sebr/article/view/366

Ansari, M. S., Akhtar, S., Khan, A., & Shamshad, M. (2023). Consequence of Financial Crisis on liquidity and profitability of commercial banks in India: An empirical study. *Studies in Economics and Business Relations*, *3*(2), 36–50. DOI: 10.48185/sebr.v3i2.367

Ante, L. (2025). From adoption to continuance: Stablecoins in cross-border remittances and the role of digital and financial literacy. *Telematics and Informatics*, *97*, 102230. DOI: 10.1016/j.tele.2024.102230

Anton, S. G., & Afloarei Nucu, A. E. (2020). Sovereign credit default swap and stock markets in central and eastern European countries: Are feedback effects at work? *Entropy (Basel, Switzerland)*, *22*(3), 338. DOI: 10.3390/e22030338 PMID: 33286112

Aquilina, M., Frost, J., & Schrimpf, A. (2024). Decentralized finance (DeFi): A functional approach. *Journal of Financial Regulation*, *10*(1), 1–27. DOI: 10.1093/jfr/fjad013

Aransiola, J. O., & Asindemade, S. O. (2011). Understanding Cybercrime Perpetrators and the Strategies They Employ in Nigeria. *Cyberpsychology, Behavior, and Social Networking*, *14*(12), 759–763. http://search.ebscohost.com/login.aspx?direct=true&db=eoah&. DOI: 10.1089/cyber.2010.0307 PMID: 22007957

Aria, M., & Cuccurullo, C. J. J. o. i. (2017). bibliometrix: An R-tool for comprehensive science mapping analysis. *11*(4), 959-975.

Armutcu, B., Tan, A., Ho, S. P. S., Chow, M. Y. C., & Gleason, K. C. (2024). The effect of bank artificial intelligence on consumer purchase intentions. *Kybernetes*. Advance online publication. DOI: 10.1108/K-01-2024-0145

Arora, S., & Kaur, H. (2019). Exploring the bank selection criteria in India: Scale development and validation. *International Journal of Bank Marketing*, *37*(3), 666–690. DOI: 10.1108/IJBM-09-2017-0199

Asif, M., Khan, P. A., Irfan, F., Salim, M., Jan, A., Khan, M. J. E. S., & Research, P. (2023). Is gender diversity is diversity washing or good governance for firm sustainable development goal performance: A scoping review. *30*(53), 114690-114705.

Atkinson, A., & Messy, F.-A. (2012), Measuring Financial Literacy: Results of the OECD / International Network on Financial Education (INFE) Pilot Study, *OECD Working Papers on Finance, Insurance and Private Pensions, No. 15*, OECD Publishing. DOI: 10.1787/20797117

Attarde, K., Jaiswal, C., Khatwani, R., Pinto, G., & Kumar, V. (2024). A novel central bank digital currency framework design for offline and foreign transactions based on blockchain. Digital Policy. *Regulation & Governance*. Advance online publication. DOI: 10.1108/DPRG-08-2023-0139

Auer, R., Lewrick, U., & Paulick, J. (2025). DeFiying gravity? An empirical analysis of cross-border Bitcoin, Ether and stablecoin flows. BIS Working Papers No 1265. https://www.bis.org/publ/work1265.pdf

Auerbach, A., Gorodnichenko, Y., McCrory, P. B., & Murphy, D. (2022). Fiscal multipliers in the COVID-19 recession. *Journal of International Money and Finance*, *126*, 102669. DOI: 10.1016/j.jimonfin.2022.102669 PMID: 35601810

Avallone, P., & Strangio, D. (2024). Different Forms of Microcredit and Social Business—Microfinance in Global History from the Late Medieval to the Modern. In: Avallone, & Strangio, (2024). In *Different Forms of Microcredit and Social Business: Microfinance in Global History from the Late Medieval to the Modern* (pp. 1-15). Cham: Springer Nature Switzerland. DOI: 10.1007/978-3-031-60942-8_1

Avellaneda, M., & Lipkin, M. (2023). Dynamic hedging and volatility in ETF markets. *Quantitative Finance*, *23*(5), 789–805.

Avşarlıgil, N., & Turğut, E. (2021). A study on the relationship between CDS premiums and stock market indices: A case of the fragile five countries. *Istanbul Business Research*, *50*(2), 275–301. DOI: 10.26650/ibr.2021.50.808240

Awrey, D. (2024). *Beyond Banks: Technology, Regulation and the Future of Money*. Princeton University Press.

Ayan, B., Güner, E., & Son-Turan, S. J. L. (2022). Blockchain Technology and Sustainability in Supply Chains and a Closer Look at Different Industries: A Mixed Method Approach. *6*(4), 85.

Aysan, A. F., & Nanaeva, Z. (2022). Fintech as a financial disruptor: A bibliometric analysis. *1*(4), 412-433.

Aysan, A., Dincer, H., Unal, I. M., & Yüksel, S. (2024). AI development in financial markets: A balanced scorecard analysis of its impact on sustainable development goals (February 2024). *Kybernetes*. Advance online publication. DOI: 10.1108/K-05-2024-1181

Aziz, Z. A. (2001). *Ar-rahnu, an Alternative Financing Mode for Microcredit.* Paper presented at the Seminar on Understanding the Concept and Application of Ar- rahnu on 12th November 2002, Kuala Lumpur. Available at <URL: https://www .mifc.com/publication/p.9.5.pdf> Access Date 21st Mar 2008.

Azmi, S. N., & Akhtar, S. (2023). Interactions of services export, financial development and growth: Evidence from India. *Quality & Quantity*, *57*(5), 4709–4724. Advance online publication. DOI: 10.1007/s11135-022-01566-8

Azubuike, V. osai, Nwogwugwu, U., & Nwokoye, E. (2023). The Role of Agriculture in Economic Development. *Journal of International Economic Relations and Development Economics, 3*(2), 103–111. https://www.theinterscholar.org/journals/index.php/jierade/article/view/208

Azzimonti, M., & Quadrini, V. (2025). Digital economy, stablecoins, and the global financial system. NBER Working Paper No 34066. https://www.nber.org/papers/w34066

Babai, M. (2024), *Strategies for Financial Inclusion and the Unbanked Population in India, and how this effect businesses and entrepreneurs in Financial Sectors of India.* Senior Projects Fall 2024. 37. https://digitalcommons.bard.edu/senproj_f2024/37

Babaji, U. (2024). Securing Financial Digital Inclusion: How Nigeria Can Protect Public from Cyber Fraud. https://wikkitimes.com/securing-digital-financial-inclusion -how-nigeria-can-protect-public-from-cyber-fraud/

Babajide, A. *et al.* (2021). Financial literacy, financial capabilities, and sustainable business model practice among small business owners in Nigeria, *J. Sustain. Financ. Invest.*, pp. 1–23, 2021, .DOI: 10.1080/20430795.2021.1962663

Babych, Y., Grigolia, M., & Keshelava, D. (2018). *Financial inclusion, financial literacy, and financial education in Georgia* (No. 849). ADBI Working Paper.

Badarinza, C., & Ramadorai, T. (2018). Home away from home? Foreign demand and London house prices. *Journal of Financial Economics*, *130*(3), 532–555. DOI: 10.1016/j.jfineco.2018.07.010

Baker, S. R., Bloom, N., Davis, S. J., & Terry, S. J. (2020). COVID-induced economic uncertainty. *NBER Working Paper No. 26983*. DOI: 10.3386/w26983

Balaji, K. (2024). Exchange-Traded Funds (ETFs): Redefining Financial Instruments in the 21st Century. In Faxing, L., & Kok Loang, O. (Eds.), (pp. 283–310). Advances in Finance, Accounting, and Economics. IGI Global., DOI: 10.4018/979-8-3693-8583-8.ch011

Balaji, K. (2024). Neuromarketing and Sustainable Finance: Real-World Case Studies of Green Investment Promotions. In Taneja, S., Chahal, B. P. S., Johri, A., Ozen, E., & Kumar, P. (Eds.), (pp. 169–204). Advances in Business Strategy and Competitive Advantage. IGI Global., DOI: 10.4018/979-8-3693-9117-4.ch010

Balaji, K. (2025). Revolutionizing High-Frequency Trading: The Impacts of Financial Technology and Data Science Innovations. In Chen, H. (Ed.), (pp. 103–124). Advances in Finance, Accounting, and Economics. IGI Global., DOI: 10.4018/979-8-3693-8186-1.ch004

Baldwin, R., & Tomiura, E. (2020). Thinking ahead about the trade impact of COVID-19. In Baldwin, R. E., & Evenett, S. J. (Eds.), *COVID-19 and trade policy: Why turning inward won't work* (pp. 59–71). CEPR Press.

Ballester, L., & González-Urteaga, A. (2020). Is there a connection between sovereign CDS spreads and the stock market? Evidence for European and US returns and volatilities. *Mathematics*, *8*(10), 1667. DOI: 10.3390/math8101667

Bank for International Settlements (BIS). (2020). Central bank digital currencies: Foundational principles and core features. Retrieved from https://www.bis.org/publ/othp33.pdf

Bank for International Settlements (BIS). (2023). *The future of market infrastructure: 24/7 trading risks.* https://www.bis.org/publ/qtrpdf/r_qt2312a.htm

Bank for International Settlements. (2019). Proportionality in bank regulation and supervision – a joint global survey. https://www.bis.org/bcbs/publ/d523.pdf

Bank for International Settlements. (2023). *Annual economic report 2023.* https://www.bis.org/publ/arpdf/ar2023e.htm

Bank regulation definition, importance & examples – IDnow. (n.d.). IDnow. Retrieved June 2, 2025, from https://www.idnow.io/glossary/bank-regulation/

Bank Robbery. (2017). https://www.fbi.gov/about us/investigate/vc_majorthefts/bankrobbery

Baptista Palazzi, R., Schich, S., & de Genaro, A. (2025). Stablecoins as anchors? Unraveling information flow dynamics between pegged and unpegged crypto-assets and fiat currencies. *Journal of International Financial Markets, Institutions and Money*, *99*, 102108. DOI: 10.1016/j.intfin.2024.102108

Barcellos, S. H., Smith, J. P., Yoong, J. K., & Carvalho, L. (2012), *Barriers to Immigrant Use of Financial Services The Role of Language Skills, U.S. Experience, and Return Migration Expectations Report to the Social Security Administration* https://www.rand.org/content/dam/rand/pubs/working_papers/2012/RAND_WR923.sum.pdFinancial

Barnett, W. A. (1980). Economic monetary aggregates an application of index number and aggregation theory. *Journal of Econometrics*, *14*(1), 11–48. DOI: 10.1016/0304-4076(80)90070-6

Basel Committee on Banking Supervision. (1999). Supervisory lessons to be drawn from the Asian crisis (Working Paper No. 2). https://www.bis.org/publ/bcbs_wp02.pdf

Basel Committee on Banking Supervision. (2006). Core principles methodology. https://www.bis.org/publ/bcbs130.pdf

Basel Committee on Banking Supervision. (2017). Basel III: Finalising post-crisis reforms. https://www.bis.org/bcbs/publ/d424.htm

Basel Committee on Banking Supervision. (2017, December 7). Basel III: International regulatory framework for banks. https://www.bis.org/bcbs/basel3.htm

Basel Committee on Banking Supervision. (2019). Core principles for effective banking supervision.

Basel Committee on Banking Supervision. (2021). Assessing the impact of Basel III: Evidence from macroeconomic models: literature review and simulations. In *Working Paper 38*. https://www.bis.org/bcbs/publ/wp38.pdf

Basel Committee on Banking Supervision. (2021). Basel III monitoring report September 2021 (by Birn, M., Martiarena, G. A., Yen, G., et al.). https://www.bis.org/bcbs/publ/d524.pdf

Bas, T., Malki, I., & Sivaprasad, S. (2024). Connectedness between Central Bank digital currency index, financial stability and digital assets. *Journal of International Financial Markets, Institutions and Money*, *92*, 101981. DOI: 10.1016/j.intfin.2024.101981

Battiston, S., Mandel, A., Monasterolo, I., Schütze, F., & Visentin, G. (2017). A climate stress-test of the financial system. *Nature Climate Change, 7*(4), 283–288. DOI: 10.1038/nclimate3255

Bayrakdaroglu, A., & Tepeli, Y. (2018). An examination of the risk-return analysis of BIST city indices. *Journal of Accounting and Finance, 147*, 2146–3042.

Bayramoğlu, M. F., & Pekkaya, M. (2010). *New developments in indices calculated by IMKB and IMKB city indices. Bahçeşehir University, Vocational School.* Zonguldak Karaelmas University, Faculty of Economics and Administrative Sciences.

Bernanke, B. S. (2015). *The courage to act: A memoir of a crisis and its aftermath.* W. W. Norton & Company.

Bertaut, C., von Beschwitz, B., & Curcuru, S. (2025). The international role of the U.S. Dollar – 2025 Edition. FEDS Notes. https://www.federalreserve.gov/econres/notes/feds-notes/the-international-role-of-the-u-s-dollar-2025-edition-20250718.html

Bharath, A. (2024). Cyber Resilience of the Central Bank Digital Currency Ecosystem. *Fintech Notes, 2024*(003), 1. DOI: 10.5089/9798400286995.063

Bhatnagr, P. (2024). Enhancing digital currency adoption: Examining user experiences. *Management Decision*. Advance online publication. DOI: 10.1108/MD-05-2024-1111

Bhatnagr, P., & Rajesh, A. (2024). Artificial intelligence features and expectation confirmation theory in digital banking apps: Gen Y and Z perspective. *Management Decision*. Advance online publication. DOI: 10.1108/MD-07-2023-1145

Bhatt et al. (2022). Decoding the trinity of Fintech, digitalization and financial services: An integrated bibliometric analysis and thematic literature review approach. *10*(1), 2114160.

Bilal, Hysa, E., Akbar, A., Yasmin, F., Rahman, A. u., Li, S. J. R. M., & Policy, H. (2022). Virtual Learning During the COVID-19 Pandemic: A Bibliometric Review and Future Research Agenda. 1353-1368.

BIS. Central bank digital currencies: foundational principles and core features, https://www.bis.org/publ/othp33.pdf

BlackRock. (2020). *Sustainability: The future of investing*. https://www.blackrock.com/corporate/about-us/sustainability-resilience

Blanchard, O., & Summers, L. H. (2017). Rethinking stabilization policy: Evolution or revolution? *NBER Working Paper No. 24179*. National Bureau of Economic Research. https://www.nber.org/papers/w24179

Blanchard, O., Amighini, A., & Giavazzi, F. (2022). *Macroeconomics: A European perspective* (5th ed.). Pearson.

Bloomberg. (2020). S&P 500 index data. Retrieved from https://www.bloomberg.com/quote/SPX:IND

Bloomberg. (2024, June 5). JPMorgan's Onyx platform cuts settlement times with blockchain.

Boar, C., & Wehrli, A. (2021). Ready, steady, go?-Results of the third BIS survey on central bank digital currency. BIS papers. https://www.bis.org/publ/bppdf/bispap114.pdf

Bofinger, P. (2025). Stablecoins and the Future of Money: Economic Principles and Policy Implications. IMK Study No 100. https://www.imk-boeckler.de/fpdf/HBS-009201/p_imk_study_100_2025.pdf

Bolton, P., Després, M., Pereira da Silva, L. A., Samama, F., & Svartzman, R. (2020). *The green swan: Central banking and financial stability in the age of climate change*. Bank for International Settlements. https://www.bis.org/publ/othp31.pdf

Bondarenko, N., & Sitenko, V. (2020). Improving The Accounting For Credit Transactions In Pawnshops. *Oblìk Ì Finance*, 2(88), 5–11. https://Doi.Org/10.33146/2307-9878-2020-2(88)-5-11

Bonizzi, B., & Kaltenbrunner, A. (2019). Liability-driven investment and pension fund exposure to emerging markets: A Minskyan analysis. *Environment and Planning A. Environment & Planning A*, *51*(2), 420–439. DOI: 10.1177/0308518X18794676

Borio, C. (2014). The financial cycle and macroeconomics: What have we learnt? *Journal of Banking & Finance*, *45*, 182–198. DOI: 10.1016/j.jbankfin.2013.07.031

Bosiu, T. The impact of competition on bank risk-taking in sub-Saharan Africa.

Bosworth, B., Hymans, S., & Modigliani, F. (1975). The stock market and the economy. *Brookings Papers on Economic Activity*, *1975*(2), 257–300. DOI: 10.2307/2534104

Boussada, H., Prigent, J. L., & Soumare, I. (2023). On the sovereign debt crisis: Sovereign credit default swaps and their interaction with stock market indices. *Applied Economics*, *55*(1), 20–42. DOI: 10.1080/00036846.2021.1934392

Braun, M., Bleher, H., & Hummel, P. (2021). A Leap of Faith: Is There a Formula for "Trustworthy" AI? *The Hastings Center Report, 51*(3), 17–22. DOI: 10.1002/hast.1207 PMID: 33606288

Brownbridge, M., & Kirkpatrick, C. (2000). Financial regulation in developing countries. *The Journal of Development Studies, 37*(1), 1–24. DOI: 10.1080/713600056

Brummer, C. (2012). Financial Stability Board Charter. *International Legal Materials, 51*(4), 828–839. DOI: 10.5305/intelegamate.51.4.0828

Buchanan, B. G. (2006). A brief history of artificial intelligence. *AI Magazine, 26*(4), 53–60.

Buckland, J. (2018). Credit, Cash, Savings, and Financial Literacy Delivered Through Civil Society. In: *Building Financial Resilience*. Palgrave Macmillan, Cham. DOI: 10.1007/978-3-319-72419-5_5

Buehler, K., Corsi, A., Jurisic, M., Lerner, L., Siani, A., & Weintraub, B. (2024). Scaling gen AI in banking: Choosing the best operating model. In *Financial Services Practice* (Issue March). https://www.mckinsey.com/industries/financial-services/our-insights/scaling-gen-ai-in-banking-choosing-the-best-operating-model

Business Desk, T. O. I. (2025, March 10). Four flash sales in a day! China, world's second largest economy, hit by deflation—here's why economists are worried. *The Times of India.* https://timesofindia.indiatimes.com/business/international-business/four-flash-sales-in-a-day-china-worlds-second-largest-economy-hit-by-deflation-heres-why-economists-are-worried/articleshow/118840941.cms

C, M. A., Djimatey, R., Akhtar, S., & Nawaah, D. (2025). Maximizing financial efficiency through technological synergy: Unleashing ICT for enhanced cash management in SMEs. Journal of the International Council for Small Business, 1-31.

Cai et al. (2022). Trends in fintech research and practice: Examining the intersection with the information systems field. *50*(1), 40.

Calandra, F., Rossi, F. P., Fabris, F., & Bernardo, M. (2025). Learning from Terra-Luna: A simulation-based study on stabilizing algorithmic stablecoins. *Blockchain: Research and Applications, 100364*, 100364. Advance online publication. DOI: 10.1016/j.bcra.2025.100364

Caldara, D., & Iacoviello, M. (2022). Measuring geopolitical risk. *The American Economic Review, 112*(4), 1194–1225. DOI: 10.1257/aer.20191823

Camera, G., Craig, B., & Waller, C. J. (2004). Currency competition in a fundamental model of money. *Journal of International Economics, 64*(2), 521–544. DOI: 10.1016/j.jinteco.2003.09.002

Cao, H., Huang, Y., Huang, Y., Yeung, B., & Zhang, X. (2023). Fintech, financial inclusion, digital currency, and CBDC. *The Journal of Financial Data Science, 9*, 100115. DOI: 10.1016/j.jfds.2024.100115

Caprio, G., & Honohan, P. (1999). Restoring banking stability: Beyond supervised capital requirements. *The Journal of Economic Perspectives, 13*(4), 43–64. DOI: 10.1257/jep.13.4.43

Carbó-Valverde et al. (2020). The effect of banks' IT investments on the digitalization of their customers. *11*, 9-17.

Carney, M. (2015). *Breaking the tragedy of the horizon–climate change and financial stability*. Bank of England. https://www.bankofengland.co.uk/speech/2015/breaking-the-tragedy-of-the-horizon-climate-change-and-financial-stability

Carpenter, S. B., & Demiralp, S. (2010). Money, Reserves, and the Transmission of Monetary Policy: Does the Money Multiplier Exist? *Finance and Economics Discussion Series, 2010.0*(41), 1–55. DOI: 10.17016/feds.2010.41

Caruana, J. (2010, February 12). Systemic risk: How to deal with it? https://www.bis.org/publ/othp08.htm

Case-Shiller. (2022). S&P CoreLogic Case-Shiller U.S. National Home Price Index. Retrieved from https://www.spglobal.com/spdji/en/indices/indicators/sp-corelogic-case-shiller-us-national-home-price-nsa-index/

Catalini, C. (2025). How will stablecoins integrate with the financial system? Centre for International Governance Innovation. August 1, 2025. https://www.jstor.org/stable/resrep71787

CBOE Global Markets. (2024). VIX historical data. Retrieved August 6, 2024, from https://www.cboe.com/tradable_products/vix/vix_historical_data/

Census Bureau. (2021). Income and poverty in the United States: 2020. U.S. Census Bureau. https://www.census.gov/library/publications/2021/demo/p60-273.html

Central Bank of The Bahamas. (2019). Sand Dollar: The Central Bank Identifies Preferred Technology Solutions Provider for Bahamas Digital Currency https://www.centralbankbahamas.com/news/press-releases/project-sand-dollar-the-central-bank-identifies-preferred-technology-solutions-provider-for-bahamas-digital-currency

CFA Institute. (2023). *The hidden risks of leveraged ETFs.*

Chainalysis (2025). The road to crypto regulation Part 2: Stablecoins at the crossroads of financial services and crypto. August 2025. https://www.chainalysis.com/blog/the-road-to-crypto-regulation-part-2-stablecoins/

Challinger, D. (1989). "Armed Robbery," AJC Seminar Proceedings 26, 22-24 March, Australian Institute of Criminology Caribeira, ACT.https://www.aic.gov.au/sites/default/files/2021-04/aic-seminar-proceedings-26.pdf

Channel, T. V. (2024, June 14). Military, police foil 15-man bank robbery operation in Abuja. https://www.channelstv.com/2024/06/14/military-police-foil-15-man-bank-robbery-operation-in-abuja

Chatham House. (2025). US dollar dominance is both a cause and a consequence of US power. https://www.chathamhouse.org/2024/09/us-dollar-dominance-both-cause-and-consequence-us-power

Chaturvedi, K., Akhtar, S., Azhar, N., & Shamshad, M. (2021). Impact Of Corporate Social Responsibility On Financial Performance Of Selected Banks In India: Based On Camel Model. *Studies in Economics and Business Relations*, *2*(2), 17–31. https://sebr.sabapub.com

Chaturvedi, K., Akhtar, S., Azhar, N., & Shamshad, M. (2021). Impact of corporate social responsibility on financial performance of selected banks in india: Based on camel model. *Studies in Economics and Business Relations*, *2*(2).

Chen et al. (2020). Do research institutes benefit from their network positions in research collaboration networks with industries or/and universities?, *94*, 102002.

Chen, T.-H., & Peng, J.-L. (2020). Statistical and bibliometric analysis of financial innovation. *38*(2), 308-319.

Chen, H., & Siklos, P. L. (2022). Central bank digital currency: A review and some macro-financial implications. *Journal of Financial Stability*, *60*, 100985. DOI: 10.1016/j.jfs.2022.100985

Chen, J. Y. C., Lakhmani, S. G., Stowers, K., Selkowitz, A. R., Wright, J. L., & Barnes, M. (2018). Situation awareness-based agent transparency and human-autonomy teaming effectiveness. *Theoretical Issues in Ergonomics Science*, *19*(3), 259–282. DOI: 10.1080/1463922X.2017.1315750

Chen, W., & Phelan, G. (2025). Digital currency and banking-sector stability. *Journal of Financial Stability*, *78*, 101414. DOI: 10.1016/j.jfs.2025.101414

Chetty, R., Friedman, J. N., Hendren, N., Stepner, M., & the Opportunity Insights Team. (2020). The economic impacts of COVID-19: Evidence from a new public database built using private sector data. *NBER Working Paper No. 27431*. National Bureau of Economic Research. https://www.nber.org/papers/w27431

Chiemeke, S. C., Evwiekpaefe, A. E., & Chete, F. O. (2006). The Adoption of Internet Banking in Nigeria: An Empirical Investigation. *Journal of Internet Banking and Commerce, 11*(3). https://www.scirp.org/reference/referencespapers?referenceid=3780407

Choi, J., & Kim, H. (2024). *Stablecoins and Central Bank digital currency: Challenges and opportunities*. Oxford Research Encyclopedia of Economics and Finance., DOI: 10.1093/acrefore/9780190625979.013.910

CIGI. (2013). Financial inclusion and global regulatory standards (CIGI Papers No. 7). https://www.cigionline.org/static/documents/new_thinking_g20_no7.pdf

Citi. (2018). Bank of the future: The ABCs of digital disruption in finance. Citi Report.https://www.citigroup.com/global/insights/bank-future

Claessens, J., Dem, V., De Cock, D., Preneel, B., & Vandewalle, J. (2002). On the Security of Today's Online Electronic Banking Systems. *Computers & Security, 21*(3), 253–265. DOI: 10.1016/S0167-4048(02)00312-7

Coburger, C. (2025). *The digital dollarization dilemma: Stablecoins and monetary subordination. The*. Japanese Political Economy., DOI: 10.1080/2329194X.2025.2552378

CoinDesk Data. (2025). Stablecoins & CBDCs Report. August 2025. https://www.coindesk.com/research/stablecoins-and-cbdcs-report-august-2025

Collard, S., & Hayes, D. (2010). *Pawnbroking Customers in 2010: A Survey – A Report to the National Pawnbrokers Association*. Personal Finance Research Centre., URL https://www.bristol.ac.uk/geography/research/pfrc/t

Cong, L. W., Li, X., Tang, K., & Yang, Y. (2021). Social media and retail trading: Evidence from Robinhood and GameStop. *Science, 373*(6561), 1084–1086.

Congressional Budget Office (CBO). (2014). The effects of the American Recovery and Reinvestment Act of 2009. https://www.cbo.gov/publication/49958

Congressional Budget Office (CBO). (2021). The budget and economic outlook: 2021 to 2031. https://www.cbo.gov/publication/56970

Consumer Financial Protection Bureau. (2024). About us. https://www.consumerfinance.gov/about-us/the-bureau/

Coronado, M., Corzo, M. T., & Lazcano, L. 2012. A case for Europe: The relationship between sovereign CDS and stock indices. *Frontiers In Finance And Economics*, 9(2), 32-63. https://ssrn.com/abstract=2190408

Coulter, K. A. (2023). A review of the proposed Bank of England's "retail" central bank digital currency (CBDC) as a cryptocurrency competitor. Fintech, Pandemic, and the Financial System: Challenges and Opportunities, 201-221. DOI: 10.1108/S1569-376720220000022010

Council on Foreign Relations. (2023). What is the Dodd-Frank Act? https://www.cfr.org/backgrounder/what-dodd-frank-act

Coyle, D. (2009). "The Talent Code." https://archive.org/details/talentcodegreatn0000coyl

Cybervergent Team. (2025). Lessons for a secure financial future: What Nigerian Banks must learn from the 2024 cyber-attacks. https://www.cybervergent.com/articles/lessons-for-a-secure-financial-future- what-nigerian-banks-must-learn-from-the-2024-cyber-attacks

Das, M. (2023). Implications of Central Bank Digital Currencies for Monetary Policy Transmission. *Fintech Notes, 2023*(010), 1. DOI: 10.5089/9798400252792.063

Daudu, B. O., Osimen, G. U., & Abubakar, A. T. (2025). Artificial Intelligence, Fintech, and Financial Inclusion in African Digital Space. Vikas Sharma, Munish Gupta, Nilesh Arora, Ajiaz A. Shaikh (eds). *Fintech and Financial Inclusion: Leveraging Digital Finance for Economic Empowerment and Sustainable Growth* (pp. 268-282). London: Routledge. DOI: 10.4324/9781003514114-19

Daudu, B. O., & Osimen, G. U. (2025). Combatting Cyberthreats in African Digital Space with Artificial Intelligence. In Vajjhala, N. R., & Strange, K. D. (Eds.), *Cybersecurity in Knowledge Management: Cyberthreats and Solutions*. CRC Press., DOI: 10.1201/9781003498094-8

Daudu, B. O., Osimen, G. U., & Anaiye, E. B. (2024). Sustainable Smart Cities in African Digital Space. In Whig, P., Sharma, P., Aneja, N., Elngar, A. A., & Silva, N. (Eds.), *Artificial Intelligence and Machine Learning for Sustainable Development: Innovations, Challenges, and Applications* (pp. 100–111). CRC Press., DOI: 10.1201/9781003497189-8

Davenport, T., Guha, A., Grewal, D., & Bressgott, T. (2020). How artificial intelligence will change the future of marketing. *Journal of the Academy of Marketing Science, 48*(1), 24–42. DOI: 10.1007/s11747-019-00696-0

De Bellis, N. (2009). *Bibliometrics and citation analysis: from the science citation index to cybermetrics*: scarecrow press.

De Blasis, R., Galati, L., Webb, A., & Webb, R. I. (2023). Intelligent design: Stablecoins (in)stability and collateral during market turbulence. *Financial Innovation*, *9*(1), 85. Advance online publication. DOI: 10.1186/s40854-023-00492-4 PMID: 37192905

De Haan, J., Eijffinger, S. C., & Waller, S. (2005). *The European Central Bank: credibility, transparency, and centralization*. MIT press. DOI: 10.7551/mitpress/2847.001.0001

De Long, J. B., Shleifer, A., Summers, L. H., & Waldmann, R. J. (1990). Noise trader risk in financial markets. *Journal of Political Economy*, *98*(4), 703–738. DOI: 10.1086/261703

De Mendonça, H. F., Galvão, D. J. C., & Loures, R. F. V. (2012). Financial regulation and transparency of information: Evidence from banking industry. *Journal of Economic Studies (Glasgow, Scotland)*, *39*(4), 380–397. DOI: 10.1108/01443581211255602

Demirguc-Kunt, A. (1989). Deposit-institution failures: a review of empirical literat. Economic review-federal reserve bank of cleveland, 25(4), 2.

Donaldson, T., & Preston, L. E. E. E. (1995). The Stakeholder Theory of the Corporation : Concepts, Evidence, and Implications Author (s): Thomas Donaldson and Lee E. Preston Source : The Academy of Management Review, Jan., 1995, Vol. 20, No. 1 (Jan., 1995), pp. Published by : Academy. *Academy of Management Journal*, *20*(1), 65–91. https://www.jstor.org/stable/258887

Dong, M., & Xiao, S. X. (2021). Central Bank digital currency: A corporate finance perspective. SSRN Electronic Journal. DOI: 10.2139/ssrn.3911132

Donthu et al. (2021). How to conduct a bibliometric analysis: An overview and guidelines. *133*, 285-296.

Duffie, D., Olowookere, O., & Veneris, A. (2025, September). Fighting financial crime doesn't have to come at the cost of privacy. *Finance & Development*, 32–36. https://www.imf.org/en/Publications/fandd/issues/2025/09/the-stablecoin-balancing-act-darrell-duffie

Duque, J. J. (2025). *Political economy of private cryptofinance. Technology and social relations. The*. Japanese Political Economy., DOI: 10.1080/2329194X.2025.2551630

Durieux, V., & Gevenois, P. A. J. R. (2010). Bibliometric indicators: quality measurements of scientific publication. *255*(2), 342-351.

Eccles, R. G., & Klimenko, S. (2019). The investor revolution: Shareholders are getting serious about sustainability. *Harvard Business Review*, *97*(3), 106–116.

Editors, C. C. G. (2023). Equitable AI: It's a Matter of Urgency. *Hispanic Engineer & Information Technology, 38*(1), 36–40. https://search.ebscohost.com/login.aspx?direct=true&AuthType=ip&db=bth&AN=164771678&site=ehost-live

Eichengreen, B. (2011). *Exorbitant Privilege: The Rise and Fall of the Dollar and the Future of the International Monetary System.* Oxford University Press.

Eichengreen, B. (2015). *Hall of mirrors: The Great Depression, the Great Recession, and the uses—and misuses—of history.* Oxford University Press.

Eichengreen, B., Nguyen, M. T., & Viswanath-Natraj, G. (2025). Stablecoin devaluation risk. *European Journal of Finance*, *31*(11), 1469–1496. DOI: 10.1080/1351847X.2025.2505757

Eichengreen, B., & Sachs, J. (1985). Exchange rates and economic recovery in the 1930s. *The Journal of Economic History*, *45*(4), 925–946. DOI: 10.1017/S0022050700035178

el Armali, J. (2023). Central bank digital currency and fiscal policy in a Diamond-Dybvig Model. *Journal of Government and Economics*, *12*, 100089. DOI: 10.1016/j.jge.2023.100089

Elumaro, A. J., & Obamuyi, T. M. (2018). Cards frauds and customers' confidence in alternative banking channels in Nigeria. *European Scientific Journal*, *14*(16), 40–60. DOI: 10.19044/esj.2018.v14n16p40

Eno, G. U. (2022). Integration of Artificial Intelligence Applications for Financial Process Innovation by Commercial Banks in Nigeria. *AKSU Journal of Administration and Corporate Governance*, *2*(1), 125–137.

Ergenç, S., & Güneren, G. E. (2020). Examination of changes in credit default swap premiums in Turkey. *Istanbul Commerce University Journal of Social Sciences*, *19*(37), 449–461.

Ergüven, E. (2020). The Political Economy of Housing Financialization in Turkey: Links With and Contradictions to the Accumulation Model. *Housing Policy Debate*, *30*(4), 559–584. DOI: 10.1080/10511482.2019.1681017

Erik Brattberg, R. C. and V. R. (2020). *National European Efforts on AI.* https://www.jstor.org/stable/resrep25784.6

Eryk, L. (2020). Artificial intelligence in finance: Opportunities and challenges. https://towardsdatascience.com/artificial-intelligence-in-finance-opportunities-andchallenges-cee94f2f3858

Espinoza, M. R. A., & Prasad, A. (2010). Nonperforming loans in the GCC banking system and their macroeconomic effects. International Monetary Fund.

Eurofi. (2024). Banking union challenges [PDF]. https://www.eurofi.net/wp-content/uploads/2024/12/the-eurofi-financial-forum_budapest_banking-union-challenges_summary_september-2024.pdf

European Banking Authority (EBA). (2022). Risk dashboard: Q2 2022. https://www.eba.europa.eu/risk-analysis-and-data/risk-dashboard

European Banking Authority. (2024). Deposit guarantee schemes data. https://www.eba.europa.eu/activities/single-rulebook/regulatory-activities/depositor-protection/deposit-guarantee-schemes-data

European Central Bank (ECB). (2021). Pandemic Emergency Purchase Programme (PEPP). https://www.ecb.europa.eu/mopo/implement/pepp/html/index.en.html

European Central Bank. (2024). Understanding the banking union and ESFS. https://www.bankingsupervision.europa.eu/about/thessm/bankingunion/html/index.en.html

European Central Bank. (2024, September 18). Milestones. https://www.bankingsupervision.europa.eu/about/thessm/milestones/html/index.en.html

European Commission. (2021). NextGenerationEU: Recovery plan for Europe. https://ec.europa.eu/info/strategy/recovery-plan-europe_en

European Securities and Markets Authority (ESMA). (2024, January 31). *ESMA report on trends, risks and vulnerabilities No. 1, 2024.* https://www.esma.europa.eu/sites/default/files/2024-01/ESMA50-524821-3107_TRV_1-24_risk_monitor.pdf

Fahad, S., & Bulut, M. (2024). Central bank digital currencies: A comprehensive systematic literature review on worldwide research emergence and methods used. *American Journal of Business*, *39*(3), 137–157. Advance online publication. DOI: 10.1108/AJB-12-2023-0210

Faruq, A. T. M. O., & Huq, M. T. (2024). The role of central banks in advancing sustainable finance. *arXiv*. https://arxiv.org/abs/2411.13576

Fasano, F., Adornetto, C., Zahid, I., La Rocca, M., Montaleone, L., Greco, G., & Cariola, A. (2024). The dilemma of accuracy in bankruptcy prediction: A new approach using explainable AI techniques to predict corporate crises. *European Journal of Innovation Management*, *28*(11), 1–22. DOI: 10.1108/EJIM-06-2024-0633

Fazal, A., Ahmed, A., & Abbas, S. (2024). *Importance of artificial intelligence in achieving sustainable development goals through financial inclusion*. Qualitative Research in Financial Markets., DOI: 10.1108/QRFM-04-2023-0098

Federal Emergency Management Agency (FEMA). (2020). Defense Production Act. https://www.fema.gov/disasters/defense-production-act

Federal Reserve. (2022). Balance sheet trends. https://www.federalreserve.gov/monetarypolicy/bst_recenttrends.htm

Federal Reserve. (2023). Monetary policy reports. https://www.federalreserve.gov/monetarypolicy/2023-03-mpr-summary.htm

Federal Reserve. (2023). Volcker Rule: Final amendments. https://www.federalreserve.gov/newsevents/pressreleases/bcreg20230728a.htm

Fernandez-Mejia, J. (2024). Extremely stablecoins. *Finance Research Letters*, *63*, 105268. DOI: 10.1016/j.frl.2024.105268

Fernando de Oliveira, S., Lugo, D. B., Ladeira, W. J., Akhtar, S., Luciana da Silva, R., & Sott, M. K. (2024, November 20). Corporate social responsibility as a moderator of loyalty antecedents in the Brazilian banking context. *International Journal of Bank Marketing*, *42*(7), 2075–2098. DOI: 10.1108/IJBM-12-2023-0667

Ferrer, R., Benitez, R., & Bolos, V. J. (2024). Interdependence between green financial instruments and major conventional assets: A wavelet-based network analysis. *arXiv*. https://arxiv.org/abs/2410.15751

Financial Industry Regulatory Authority (FINRA). (2023). *Market activity year-end 2022* [Fact sheet]. https://www.finra.org

Financial Industry Regulatory Authority. (2020). *Market activity year-end 2019* [Fact sheet]. https://www.finra.org

Financial regulation after the "Subprime" crisis: What lessons can be learned and what reforms undertaken? (n.d.). Retrieved June 2, 2025, from https://www.robert-schuman.eu/en/european-issues/246-financial-regulation-after-the-subprime-crisis-what-lessons-can-be-learned-and-what-reforms

Financial Stability Board (FSB). (2020). Holistic review of the March market turmoil. https://www.fsb.org/2020/11/holistic-review-of-the-march-market-turmoil/

Financial Stability Board (FSB). (2021). Global monitoring report on non-bank financial intermediation 2021. https://www.fsb.org/2021/12/global-monitoring-report-on-non-bank-financial-intermediation-2021/

Financial Stability Board. (2024). *Global Monitoring Report on Non-Bank Financial Intermediation 2024*. https://www.fsb.org/2024/12/global-monitoring-report-on-non-bank-financial-intermediation-2024/

Financial Times. (2024, December 10). Can banks really fix the climate crisis? Financial Times. https://www.ft.com/content/af604f2f-aa1d-486d-85c1-c5cdfc73999e

Firdaus et al. (2019). The rise of "blockchain": bibliometric analysis of blockchain study. *120*, 1289-1331.

Firdausi, F. N., & Ardyansyah, F. (2023). Implementation of Sharia Marketing Strategy As A Solution To Increase Linkaja Syariah Consumer Loyalty. *JESI (Indonesian Sharia Economic Journal),* 13(1), 74–81. https://Doi.Org/10.21927/Jesi.2023.13(1).74-81

Forte, S., & Peña, J. I. (2009). Credit spreads: An empirical analysis on the informational content of stocks, bonds, and CDS. *Journal of Banking & Finance*, *33*(11), 2013–2025. DOI: 10.1016/j.jbankfin.2009.04.015

Frączek, B., & Klimontowicz, M. (2015). Financial literacy and its influence on young customers' decision factors. *J Innov Manag*, *3*(1), 62–84. DOI: 10.24840/2183-0606_003.001_0007

Franco, M., & Esteves, L. (2020). Inter-clustering as a network of knowledge and learning: Multiple case studies. *5*(1), 39-49.

Friedman, M., & Schwartz, A. J. (1963). *A monetary history of the United States, 1867–1960*. Princeton University Press.

Fung, H. G., Sierra, G. E., Yau, J., & Zhang, G. (2008). Are the U.S. stock market and credit default swap market related? Evidence from the CDX indices. *Journal of Alternative Investments*, *11*(1), 43–61. DOI: 10.3905/jai.2008.708849

G20 Sustainable Finance Working Group. (2021). *G20 Sustainable Finance Roadmap*. https://www.g20.org/

Gambhir, B., & Bhattacharjee, A. (2021). Embracing the role of artificial intelligence in accounting and finance: Contemplating the changing skillset expectations. *Development and Learning in Organizations*, *36*(1), 17–20. DOI: 10.1108/DLO-01-2021-0016

GAO. (2010), *Factors Affecting the Financial Literacy of Individuals with Limited English Proficiency Consumer Finance Report to Congressional Committees* http://www.gao.gov/assets/310/304561.pdf

Gardeva, A., & Rhyne, E. (2011). *Opportunities and Obstacles to Financial Inclusion. Survey Report.* Center for Financial Inclusion at ACCION International https://centerforfinancialinclusionblog.files.wordpress.com/2011/07/opportunities-and-obstacles-to-financial-inclusion_110708_final.pdf

Ghansham, A. S., & Sriwastaw, S. K. Trust in Turbulent Times: Effects of NPAs on SBI Depositors During the Pandemic Years.

Ghosh, S., Sugawara, N., & Zalduendo, J. (2011). Bank Flows and Basel III—Determinants and regional differences in emerging markets. In *World Bank, Washington, DC eBooks*. DOI: 10.1596/10099

Ghosh, K., & Das, P. K. (2024). *Central bank digital currencies – A bibliometric analysis on research themes in pursuit of research trends*. International Journal of Law and Management., DOI: 10.1108/IJLMA-11-2023-0252

Gigante, G., & Zago, A. (2023). DARQ technologies in the financial sector: Artificial intelligence applications in personalized banking. *Qualitative Research in Financial Markets*, *15*(1), 29–57. DOI: 10.1108/QRFM-02-2021-0025

Giglio, F. (2022). Fintech: A literature review. *15*(1), 80-85.

Giles, M. (2025, July 29). ECB integrates climate risk into Eurozone financial framework. *The Financial Analyst.* https://thefinancialanalyst.net/2025/07/29/ecb-integrates-climate-risk-into-eurozone-financial-framework/

Giuggioli, G., Pellegrini, M. M., & Giannone, G. (2024). Artificial intelligence as an enabler for entrepreneurial finance: A practical guide to AI-driven video pitch evaluation for entrepreneurs and investors. *Management Decision.* Advance online publication. DOI: 10.1108/MD-10-2023-1926

Global Financial Stability Report. (2018, October). A decade after the global financial crisis: Are we safer? DOI: 10.5089/9781484375594.082

GlobalData. (2022). Robotics in Banking–Thematic Intelligence. https://www.globaldata.com/store/report/robotic

Goel, T., Lewrick, U., & Agarwal, I. (2025). Making stablecoins stable(r): Can regulation help? DOI: 10.2139/ssrn.5070116

Golnaraghi, M. (2021). *Climate Change and the Insurance Sector: Risk, Regulation, and Resilience*. The Geneva Association. https://www.genevaassociation.org/

Gowhor, H. S. (2022). The existing financial intelligence tools and their limitations in early detection of terrorist financing activities. *Journal of Money Laundering Control*, *25*(4), 843–863. DOI: 10.1108/JMLC-07-2021-0075

Grohmann, A., Klühs, T., Menkhoff, L. (2018). Does financial literacy improve financial inclusion? Cross country evidence. *World Dev* 111:84–96. https://doi.org/ . world dev. 2018. 06. 020.DOI: 10. 1016/j

Guest, P. M. (2021). Risk management in financial institutions: A replication. *The Journal of Finance*, *76*(5), 2689–2707. DOI: 10.1111/jofi.13063

Gulati, R. (2020). Demystifying gaps and testing for convergence in bank regulations impacting the competitive environment: A case of India and its peers in BRICS. *Journal of Financial Regulation and Compliance*, *29*(1), 15–43. DOI: 10.1108/ JFRC-01-2020-0005

Gün, M. (2018). The co-movement of credit default swaps and stock markets in emerging economies. In *Recent Perspectives and Case Studies in Finance & Econometrics*. IJOPEC Publication.

Guo, R., & Tian, X. (2024). Regulatory transparency and regulators' effort: Evidence from public release of the SEC's review work. *Journal of Accounting Research*, *62*(1), 229–273. DOI: 10.1111/1475-679X.12513

Güzel, F. (2022). Volatility interaction of bist main sector indices: Findings regarding the covid-19 period. *Jour. of Social Economic Res.*, *22*(2), 128–138. DOI: 10.30976/susead.1123835

Guzmán et al. (2024). Scientific Production on Leadership in Social Entrepreneurship: Co-Word Analysis and Network Mapping. *6*(2).

Haenlein, M., & Kaplan, A. (2019). A brief history of artificial intelligence: On the past, present, and future of artificial intelligence. *California Management Review*, *61*(4), 5–14. DOI: 10.1177/0008125619864925

Hafizh, N. A., & Yanti, N. N. (2023). Restructuring Mechanism in Resolving Problematic Murabahah Financing at Bank Sumut Syariah KC Medan Katamso. *Brilliance,* 3(2), 260–277. https://Doi.Org/10.55606/Cemerlang.V3i2.1207

Hale, T., Angrist, N., Goldszmidt, R., Kira, B., Petherick, A., Phillips, T., Webster, S., Cameron-Blake, E., Hallas, L., Majumdar, S., & Tatlow, H. (2021). A global panel database of pandemic policies (Oxford COVID-19 Government Response Tracker). *Nature Human Behaviour*, *5*(4), 529–538. DOI: 10.1038/s41562-021-01079-8

Hanafi, S. F., & Rahman, S. A. (2019), "Regulating Digital Currency: Taming the Unruly", Oseni, U.A., Hassan, M.K. and Hassan, R. (Ed.) Emerging Issues in Islamic Finance Law and Practice in Malaysia, Emerald Publishing Limited, Leeds, pp. 265-280. DOI: 10.1108/978-1-78973-545-120191021

Hanifah, A., Santoso, B., & Navianto, I. (2018). The Urgency of Setting Up a Private Pawn Company Using an Online System. *Al-Mustashfa: Research Journal of Sharia Economic Law*, 3(1), 30. Https://Doi.Org/10.24235/Jm.V3i1.2935

Hariss, A. (2020). Settlement of Defaults in Gold Pawn Agreements Between Customers and the Limited Liability Company PawnshopsJambi Branch. Legalitas: *A Law Journal,* 12(1), 94. Https://Doi.Org/10.33087/Legalitas.V12i1.196

Hasan et al. (2024). Exploring small and medium enterprises access to finance: a bibliometric analysis. *5*(1), 15-46.

Hasan, M., Le, T., & Hoque, A. (2021). How does financial literacy impact on inclusive finance? *Financial Innovation*, *7*(1), 40. DOI: 10.1186/s40854-021-00259-9

Hasyim, S. DM, Sipahutar, IM, & Rogantina, V. (2023). Analysis of The Role Of Pawnshops In UMKM Business Development (Case Study At PT. Pawnshops Kanwil Medan). *Indonesian Journal Of Accounting And Financial Technology*, 1(2), 71–82. https://Doi.Org/10.55927/Crypto.V1i2.4268

Hatemi-J, A. (2012). Asymmetric causality tests with an application. *Empirical Economics*, *43*(1), 447–456. DOI: 10.1007/s00181-011-0484-x

Heckscher, E. F., & Ohlin, B. (1991). The Heckscher-Ohlin theory of trade. In H. S. Ellis & L. A. Metzler (Eds.), *International trade: Selected readings* (pp. 75–100). MIT Press. (Reprinted from E. F. Heckscher & B. Ohlin, 1933, *The MIT Press*)

Heller, C. H. (2019). Implementation Opportunities from Modern Business Practices. *Naval War College Review*, *72*(4), 73–100. https://www.jstor.org/stable/26775520

Hellmann, T. F., Murdock, K. C., & Stiglitz, J. E. (2000). Liberalization, moral hazard in banking, and prudential regulation: Are capital requirements enough? *The American Economic Review*, *90*(1), 147–165. DOI: 10.1257/aer.90.1.147

Hennessey, Z. (2021, January 6). Tel Aviv Stock Exchange boasts peak year for 2020. *The Jerusalem Post*. https://www.jpost.com/jpost-tech/tel-aviv-stock-exchange-boasts-peak-year-for-2020-652889

Hentzen, J. K., Hoffmann, A., Dolan, R., & Pala, E. (2022). Artificial intelligence in customer-facing financial services: A systematic literature review and agenda for future research. *International Journal of Bank Marketing*, *40*(6), 1299–1336. DOI: 10.1108/IJBM-09-2021-0417

He, Q., Liu, J., Wang, S., & Yu, J. (2020). The impact of COVID-19 on stock markets. *Economic and Political Studies*, *8*(3), 275–288. DOI: 10.1080/20954816.2020.1757570

Hermawan, A., & Susanti, E. (2022). Optimization of Improving Organizational Citizenship Behaviour (OCB) through Personality Strengthening, Interpersonal Communication, and Organizational Justice. *Indonesian Journal of Education and Mathematical Science*, *3*(3), 118–125.

Hidayat-ur-Rehman, I., & Hossain, M. N. (2024). The impacts of Fintech adoption, green finance and competitiveness on banks' sustainable performance: Digital transformation as moderator. *Asia-Pacific Journal of Business Administration*. Advance online publication. DOI: 10.1108/APJBA-10-2023-0497

Hilaluddin, N., & Abdullah, A. (2024). The Relevance of Ar-Rahnu for MSME (Micro, Small, and Medium-Sized Enterprises) Community in Assuring Financial Well-Being. In *Artificial Intelligence (AI) and Customer Social Responsibility (CSR)* (pp. 797–813). Springer Nature Switzerland. DOI: 10.1007/978-3-031-50939-1_64

History of the Basel Committee. (2014, October 9). Retrieved June 2, 2025, from https://www.bis.org/bcbs/history.htm

Houston, J. F., Lin, C., & Ma, Y. (2012). Regulatory arbitrage and international bank flows. *The Journal of Finance*, *67*(5), 1845–1895. DOI: 10.1111/j.1540-6261.2012.01774.x

Hui, C. H., Wong, A., & Lo, C. F. (2025). Stablecoin price dynamics under a peg-stabilising mechanism. *Journal of International Money and Finance*, *152*, 103280. DOI: 10.1016/j.jimonfin.2025.103280

Hull, J., & White, A. (2023). Beyond the VIX: A new approach to measuring financial stress. *Review of Financial Studies*, *37*(2), 501–530. DOI: 10.1093/rfs/hhac123

Humald, M. (2025). The Difference between KYC and AML. https://binderr.com/resources/the-difference-between-kyc-and-aml

Hung, A. A., Parker, A. M., & Yoong, J. K. (2009). Defining and Measuring Financial Literacy. *RAND Labor and Population*, *2009*, 4.

IMF. (2024). Fintech applications for boosting climate finance in emerging markets. https://www.elibrary.imf.org/view/journals/066/2024/008/article-A001-en.xml

Inder, S. (2024), "Empowering the Unbanked: The Intersection of Financial Inclusion and CBDC", Kumar, N., Sood, K., Özen, E. and Grima, S. (Ed.) The Framework for Resilient Industry: A Holistic Approach for Developing Economies (Emerald Studies in Finance, Insurance, and Risk Management), Emerald Publishing Limited, Leeds, pp. 65-74. DOI: 10.1108/978-1-83753-734-120241005

Inside GNSS. (2012). "Design of a GPS/GSM currency tracker device" https://www.insidegnss.com/auto/IGM1106_040_047.pdf

Intelligence, B. (2023, October 24). Unmasking the Complexities of Bank Robberies in Nigeria: Trends, Challenges and Security Measures. https://bulwarkintelligence.com/2023/10/24/unmasking-the-complexities-of-bank-robberies-in-nigeria-trends-challenges-and-security-measures

Intelligence, E. (2024, July 21). Nasarawa Police arrest armed robbery suspects, recover firearms, stolen items. https://eonsintelligence.com/details/crime-intelligence-10948010/nasarawa-police-arrest-armed-robbery-suspects-recover-firearms-stolen-items-523982752

Intergovernmental Panel on Climate Change (IPCC). (2021). *Climate Change 2021: The Physical Science Basis.* https://www.ipcc.ch/report/ar6/wg1/

International Air Transport Association (IATA). (2020). Air passenger market analysis. https://www.iata.org/en/publications/economics/

International and national regulatory frameworks – Oesterreichische Nationalbank (OeNB). (n.d.). Retrieved June 2, 2025, from https://www.oenb.at/en/financial-market/banking-supervision/regulatory-frameworks.html

International Energy Agency (IEA). (2021). *Net Zero by 2050: A Roadmap for the Global Energy Sector.* https://www.iea.org/reports/net-zero-by-2050

International Energy Agency (IEA). (2022). Gas market report, Q1 2022. https://www.iea.org/reports/gas-market-report-q1-2022

International Monetary Fund (IMF). (2021). World Economic Outlook: Recovery during a pandemic. https://www.imf.org/en/Publications/WEO/Issues/2021/10/12/world-economic-outlook-october-2021

International Monetary Fund (IMF). (2022). *Geoeconomic fragmentation and trade* (World Economic Outlook Report, October 2022). https://www.imf.org/en/Publications/WEO/Issues/2022/10/11/world-economic-outlook-october-2022

International Monetary Fund (IMF). (2022). World Economic Outlook: War sets back the global recovery. https://www.imf.org/en/Publications/WEO/Issues/2022/04/19/world-economic-outlook-april-2022

International Monetary Fund (IMF). (2023). *Global financial stability report: Geopolitics and financial stability.* https://www.imf.org/en/Publications/GFSR

International Monetary Fund (IMF). (2023). *World economic outlook, October 2023: Navigating global divergences.* https://www.imf.org/en/Publications/WEO/Issues/2023/10/10/world-economic-outlook-october-2023

International Monetary Fund (IMF). (2025). IMF Data Brief: Currency composition of official foreign exchange reserves. https://data.imf.org/en/news/imf%20data%20brief%20jul%209

International Monetary Fund. (2010). Impact of regulatory reforms on large and complex financial institutions. https://www.imf.org/external/pubs/ft/spn/2010/spn1016.pdf

Irvin, V., & Bard. (2023). A Whole New Information World: AI, Bots, Metadata, and Discourse. In *International Journal of Information, Diversity and Inclusion* (Vol. 7, Issues 1–2, pp. 1–6). DOI: 10.33137/ijidi.v7i1/2.41079

Irwin, D. A. (2011). *Peddling protectionism: Smoot-Hawley and the Great Depression.* Princeton University Press.

Isayas, Y. N. (2022). Determinants of banks' profitability: Empirical evidence from banks in Ethiopia. *10*(1), 2031433.

ISO. (2019). *ISO 14091: Adaptation to climate change — Guidelines on vulnerability, impacts, and risk assessment.* International Organization for Standardization.

Ivy Munoko, H. L. B.-L. and M. V. (2020). The Ethical Implications of Using Artificial Intelligence in Auditing. *Journal of Business Ethics, 167*(2), 209–234. https://www.jstor.org/stable/45386654

J. Nair, A., Manohar, S., & Mittal, A. (2024). AI-enabled FinTech for innovative sustainability: promoting organizational sustainability practices in digital accounting and finance. *International Journal of Accounting and Information Management.* DOI: 10.1108/IJAIM-05-2024-0172

Jacob, J. M., & Rosemary, E. A. (2019). Effects of Exchange Rate Fluctuation on Economic Growth in Nigeria 1981-2018. *International Journal of Intellectual Discourse, 2*(2), 1–11. https://ijidjournal.org/index.php/ijid/article/view/105

Jagrič, T., Fister, D., Amon, A., Jagrič, V., & Beloglavec, S. T. (2022). The Banking Industry in the Ecosystem of Digital Currencies and Digital Central Bank Currencies. In Grima, S., Özen, E., & Boz, H. (Eds.), *The New Digital Era: Digitalisation, Emerging Risks and Opportunities (Contemporary Studies in Economic and Financial Analysis, Vol. 109A)* (pp. 89–115). Emerald Publishing Limited., DOI: 10.1108/S1569-37592022000109A006

Jan, A. A., Lai, F. W., Asif, M., Akhtar, S., & Ullah, S. (2022). Embedding sustainability into bank strategy: Implications for sustainable development goals reporting. *International Journal of Sustainable Development and World Ecology, 30*(3), 229–243. DOI: 10.1080/13504509.2022.2134230

Jayanti, E., & Karnowati, N. B. (2023). *Digitalisasi Umkm Dan Literasi Keuangan Untuk Keberlanjutan Umkm Di Kabupaten Cilacap.* Kajian Bisnis Sekolah Tinggi Ilmu Ekonomi Widya Wiwaha, 31(1), 51–64. Https://Doi.Org/10.32477/Jkb.V31i1.504

Jeanneret, A. (2017). Sovereign default risk and the US equity market. *Journal of Financial and Quantitative Analysis, 52*(1), 305–339. DOI: 10.1017/S0022109016000776

Jeucken, M. (2001). *Sustainable finance and banking: The financial sector and the future of the planet.* Earthscan Publications.

Jha, P., Akhtar, S., & Rana, P. (2025). The Swift Rise and Sudden Fall: Examining the Collapse of Silicon Valley Bank. *Emerging Economies Cases Journal, 0*(0), 25166042251319596. Advance online publication. DOI: 10.1177/25166042251319596

Jokić, M., & Ball, R. (2006). *Qualität und Quantität wissenschaftlicher Veröffentlichungen: Bibliometrische Aspekte der Wissenschaftskommunikation* (Vol. 15): Forschungszentrum Jülich.

Jokipii, T., & Monnin, P. (2012). The impact of banking sector stability on the real economy. *Journal of International Money and Finance, 32*, 1–16. DOI: 10.1016/j.jimonfin.2012.02.008

Jolaiya, F. O. (2024). Effect of Electronic Fraud on the Financial Performance of Banks in Nigeria *Asian Journal of Economics. Business and Accounting, 24*(4), 80–92. DOI: 10.9734/ajeba/2024/v24i41266

Judijanto, L., & Asfahani, A. (2022). 21st Century Economic Transformation: The Impact of Artificial Intelligence on Markets and Employment. *Journal of Artificial Intelligence and Development, 1*(1).

Kadanda, D., Raj, K. J. J. o. S., & Development, E. (2018). Non-performing assets (NPAs) and its determinants: a study of Indian public sector banks. *20*(2), 193-212.

Kahneman, D., & Tversky, A. (1979). Prospect theory: An analysis of decision under risk. *Econometrica, 47*(2), 263–291. DOI: 10.2307/1914185

Kaiser, T., Lusardi, A., Menkhoff, L., & Urban, C. (2022). Financial education affects financial knowlegde and downstream behaviors. *Journal of Financial Economics, 145*(2), 255–272. DOI: 10.1016/j.jfineco.2021.09.022

Kalu, E. U., Ugwu, O. E., Ndubuaku, V. C., & Ifeanyi, O. P. (2019). Exchange Rate and Foreign Reserves Interface: Empirical Evidence from Nigeria. *The Economics and Finance Letters, 6*(1), 1–8. https://ideas.repec.org//a/pkp/teafle/v6y2019i1p1-8id1615.html

Kantar, L. (2020). Credit default swaps premium with European debt crisis: Implementation on PIIGS countries. *Beykoz Akademi Dergisi, 8*(1), 20–35. DOI: 10.14514/BYK.m.26515393.2020.8/1.20-35

Karger, H. (2015). Curbing the financial exploitation of the poor: Financial literacy and social work education. *Journal of Social Work Education, 51*(3), 425–438. DOI: 10.1080/10437797.2015.1043194

Kaur, H., & Arora, S. (2019). Demographic influences on consumer decisions in the banking sector: Evidence from India. *Journal of Financial Services Marketing, 24*(3), 81–93. DOI: 10.1057/s41264-019-00067-4

Kemspon, E. (2002). *Over-indebtedness in Britain*. Department of Trade and Industry.

Kenyon, C., Berrahoui, M., & Macrina, A. (2022). Transparency principle for carbon emissions drives sustainable finance. *arXiv*. https://arxiv.org/abs/2202.07689

Keohane, R. O., & Nye, J. S.Jr. (1973). Power and interdependence. *Survival, 15*(4), 158–165. DOI: 10.1080/00396337308441409

Khan, A., Akhtar, S., & Alam, M. (2024). How efficient are Indian banks? An application of stochastic frontier analysis. Journal of Financial Economic Policy. DOI: DOI: 10.1108/JFEP-11-2023-0338

Khiaonarong, T., Das, B., Zhang, C., Gersl, A., Goh, T., Lohmus, P., & Wilson, C. (2023). *Financial sector stability review*. Retrieved from.

Kiesel, F., Kolaric, S., & Schiereck, D. (2016). Market integration and efficiency of CDS and equity markets. *The Quarterly Review of Economics and Finance, 61*, 210–223. DOI: 10.1016/j.qref.2016.02.010

Kim, J. D. (2020). Transition towards green banking: Role of financial regulators and financial institutions. *Asian Journal of Sustainability and Social Responsibility, 5*(5), 5. Advance online publication. DOI: 10.1186/s41180-020-00034-3

Kim, Y. S., & Kwon, O.KIM. (2022). Central Bank digital currency, credit supply, and financial stability. *Journal of Money, Credit and Banking, 55*(1), 297–321. DOI: 10.1111/jmcb.12913

Kim, Y. S., Lee, H., & Lee, J. (2022). Central digital currency, credit supply, and financial stability. *Journal of Money, Credit and Banking*, *54*(2-3), 621–649. DOI: 10.1111/jmcb.12826

Kindleberger, C. P. (1973). *The World in Depression, 1929-1939*. University of California Press.

King, M. R. (2013). The Basel III Net Stable Funding Ratio and bank net interest margins. *Journal of Banking & Finance*, *37*(11), 4144–4156. DOI: 10.1016/j.jbankfin.2013.07.017

Kodongo, O. (2018) Financial regulations, financial literacy, and financial inclusion: insights from Kenya. *Emerg Mark Financ Trade* 54(12):2851–2873. https://doi.org/ . 2017. 14183DOI: 10. 1080/ 15404 96X

Kolte, A., Patil, A., & Mal, H. (2021). Monetary policy in tough times-case study approach. *International Journal of Intelligent Enterprise*, *8*(1), 105–122. DOI: 10.1504/IJIE.2021.112323

Koo, J. (2024). AI is not careful: Approach to the stock market and preference for AI advisor. *International Journal of Bank Marketing*, *42*(7), 2117–2142. DOI: 10.1108/IJBM-10-2023-0568

Koomson I, Villano RA, Hadley D (2019) Intensifying financial inclusion through the provision of financial literacy training: a gendered perspective. *Appl Econ* 52(4):1–13. https://doi.org/ . 2019. 16459 43DOI: 10. 1080/ 00036 846

Koy, A. 2015. The relationship between credit default swap spreads, equity indices and sector equity indices: An empirical study on Istanbul Stock Exchange. *Paper presented at the 17th International Academic Conference*.

KPMG. (2020). *A guide to scenario analysis for climate change risk assessment*. https://home.kpmg/xx/en/home/insights/2020/06/scenario-analysis-guide.html

Kremer, A., Luget, A., Mikkelsen, D., Soller, H., Strandell-Jansson, M., & Zingg, S. (2023). As GenAI advances, regulators—and risk functions—rush to keep pace. In *McKinsey* (Issue December). https://www.mckinsey.com/capabilities/risk-and-resilience/our-insights/as-gen-ai-advances-regulators-and-risk-functions-rush-to-keep-pace

Kumar et al. (2023). Mapping the evolution of research themes in business ethics: a co-word network analysis. *53*(3), 491-522.

Kumari, B., Kaur, J., & Swami, S. (2024). Adoption of artificial intelligence in financial services: A policy framework. *Journal of Science and Technology Policy Management, 15*(2), 396–417. DOI: 10.1108/JSTPM-03-2022-0062

Kumhof, M., Rancière, R., & Winant, P. (2015). Inequality, leverage, and crises. *The American Economic Review, 105*(3), 1217–1245. DOI: 10.1257/aer.20110683

Kupiec, P. (2005). The IMF–World Bank financial sector assessment program: A view from the inside. In *Systemic Financial Crises: Resolving Large Bank Insolvencies* (pp. 69-81): World Scientific. DOI: 10.1142/9789812569479_0006

Kutler, J. (2025). The unsettled side of stablecoins. September 19, 2025. https://www.garp.org/risk-intelligence/technology/unsettled-side-stablecoins-250919

Kutuk, T., & Okur, M. (2020). A comparative analysis of country ratings and credit default swap premiums in determining risk premium in BRICS-T countries. *Business and Economics Research Journal, 11*(2), 413–429. DOI: 10.20409/berj.2020.258

Kvedaravičiūtė, E., & Šapkauskienė, A. (2024). Development of central bank digital currencies: A bibliometric analysis. *EuroMed Journal of Business*. Advance online publication. DOI: 10.1108/EMJB-12-2023-0140

Kwong et al. (2023). Green FinTech innovation as a future research direction: a bibliometric analysis on green finance and FinTech. *15*(20), 14683.

Ladeira, W. J., Santini, F. O., Rasul, T., Cheah, I., Elhajjar, S., Yasin, N., & Akhtar, S. (2024). Big data analytics and the use of artificial intelligence in the services industry: A meta-analysis. *Service Industries Journal, 44*(15-16), 1117–1144. Advance online publication. DOI: 10.1080/02642069.2024.2374990

Lakhe, P., & Kulkarni, M. (2020). FinTech regulations: Need, superpowers and bibliometric analysis. 1-11.

Lakštutienė, A. J. E. e. (2008). Correlation of the indicators of the financial system and gross domestic product in European Union countries. (3 (58)), 7-18.

Landgrebe, J., & Smith, B. (2021). Making AI meaningful again. *Synthese, 198*(3), 2061–2081. DOI: 10.1007/s11229-019-02192-y

Lane, T. (2025). Opportunities for digital assets in a fractured world. CIGI Papers No. 326, July 2025. https://www.cigionline.org/static/documents/DADW-Lane_01.pdf

Lannquist, A. (2023). Central Bank Digital Currency's Role in Promoting Financial Inclusion. *Fintech Notes, 2023*(011), 1. DOI: 10.5089/9798400253331.063

Lastra, R. M. J. W. I. L. (2025). Central Banking in a Time of Crisis. *The Bank of England.*, *42*, 143.

Lesmono, B. (2022). Literature Study of Sharia Pawnshops in Indonesia. *Scientific Journal of Islamic Economics*, 8(1), 599. Https://Doi.Org/10.29040/Jiei.V8i1.4368

Li et al. (2020). A bibliometric analysis of symmetry (2009–2019). *12*(8), 1304.

Li, B., & Xu, Z. (2022). A comprehensive bibliometric analysis of financial innovation. *35*(1), 367-390.

Li, C., Wang, H., Jiang, S., & Gu, Bin. (2024). The Effect of AI-Enabled Credit Scoring on Financial Inclusion: Evidence from One Million Underserved Population. *Forthcoming at MIS Quarterly*. https://ssrn.com/abstract=4812172

Li, R., & Qian, Y. (2020) Entrepreneurial participation and performance: the role of financial literacy, *Manag. Decis.*, 58, (39, pp. 583–599, 2020, DOI: 10.1108/MD-11-2018-1283

Li, S. (2021). Bank Competition, Regulation, and efficiency. In *Contributions to finance and accounting* (pp. 133–178). DOI: 10.1007/978-981-16-3509-0_5

Liang, X., & Liu, A. M. (2018). The evolution of government sponsored collaboration network and its impact on innovation: A bibliometric analysis in the Chinese solar PV sector. *47*(7), 1295-1308.

Lin, R. R., & Lee, J. C. (2023). The supports provided by artificial intelligence to continuous usage intention of mobile banking: Evidence from China. *Aslib Journal of Information Management*, *76*(2), 293–310. DOI: 10.1108/AJIM-07-2022-0337

Li, Y. (2011). Currency and checking deposits as means of payment. *Review of Economic Dynamics*, *14*(2), 403–417. DOI: 10.1016/j.red.2009.11.002

Li, Y. (2021). Does institutional quality matter for central bank digital currency adoption? *Economic Analysis and Policy*, *72*, 265–277. DOI: 10.1016/j.eap.2021.05.002

Llewellyn, D. T., & Yan, M. (2025, May 14). It is wrong to downgrade Basel's role in climate risk. Financial Times. https://www.ft.com/content/f5d55610-7798-48bb-ab34-2f92f85de15d

Lok, C. K. (2015). Adoption of smart cardbased E-payment system for retailing in Hong Kong using an extended technology acceptance model. *Advances in Business Marketing and Purchasing*, *23B*, 255–466. DOI: 10.1108/S1069-09642015000023B003

Lozano et al. (2019). Complex network analysis of keywords co-occurrence in the recent efficiency analysis literature. *120*, 609-629.

Lusardi, A. (2019). Financial Literacy and the Need for Financial Education: *Evidence and Implications. Swiss Journal of Economics and Statistics, 155*(1), 1. Advance online publication. DOI: 10.1186/s41937-019-0027-5

Lusardi, A., & Mitchell, O. (2014). The Economic Importance of Financial Literacy: Theory and Evidence. *Journal of Economic Literature, 52*(1), 5–44. DOI: 10.1257/jel.52.1.5 PMID: 28579637

Mahajan, R., Lim, W. M., Sareen, M., Kumar, S., & Panwar, R. (2023). Stakeholder theory. *Journal of Business Research, 166*(June), 114104. DOI: 10.1016/j.jbusres.2023.114104

Mahapatra et al. (2023). Metrics employed in the evaluation of research productivity: A systematic literature review. *55*(3), 868-885.

Malik, M. S., Irfan, M., & Munir, S. (2024). Developing a sustainable finance index and its implications on inter-intra banking sector. *SAGE Open, 14*(1), 21582440241271232. Advance online publication. DOI: 10.1177/21582440241271232

Manyika, J. (2022). Getting AI Right. *The MIT Press, 151*(2), 5–27.

Marda, V. (2018). Artificial intelligence policy in India: A framework for engaging the limits of data-driven decision-making. *Philosophical Transactions. Series A, Mathematical, Physical, and Engineering Sciences, 376*(2133), 1–19. DOI: 10.1098/rsta.2018.0087 PMID: 30323001

Martino, E. D., & Roos, Y. (2024). The law of algorithmic stablecoins in the EU. Amsterdam Center for Law & Economics Working Paper No. 2024-15. DOI: 10.2139/ssrn.5011467

Masoud, N. (2024). *Artificial intelligence and unemployment dynamics: an econometric analysis in high-income economies*. Technological Sustainability., DOI: 10.1108/TECHS-04-2024-0033

Massa, A. (2024, February 12). Citadel Securities says round-the-clock stock trading carries risks. *Bloomberg*. https://www.bloomberg.com/news/articles/2024-02-12/citadel-securities-says-24-7-stock-trading-holds-hidden-risks

Mateas, M. (2001). Expressive AI: A Hybrid Art and Science Practice. *Leonardo, 34*(2), 147–153. DOI: 10.1162/002409401750184717

Mateev, M., & Marinova, E. (2016). Relation between credit default swap spreads and stock prices: A non-linear perspective. *In World Finance & Banking Symposium*, University of Dubai.

Mba, C. F. (2024, July 8). Risk mitigation in banking: Tools, techniques, and best practices. Retrieved June 2, 2025, from https://www.linkedin.com/pulse/risk-mitigation-banking-tools-techniques-best-cristina-firica-mba-zniif/

McKinsey & Company. (2020). *Climate risk and response: Physical hazards and socioeconomic impacts*. https://www.mckinsey.com/business-functions/sustainability/our-insights

Meena, R., Mishra, A. K., & Raut, R. K. (2024). Strategic insights: Mapping the terrain of artificial intelligence (AI) in banking through mixed method approach. *VINE Journal of Information and Knowledge Management Systems*. Advance online publication. DOI: 10.1108/VJIKMS-01-2024-0028

Meilani, A. R., Hasibuan, N. M., & Nasution, M. L. I. (2022). Service Strategy And Implementation Of Digital Sharia Pawnshops In Increasing The Number Of Customers In Rantau Prapat. *Journal of Economics, Management. Accounting and Finance*, *3*(3). https://Doi.Org/10.53697/Emak.V3i3.579

Meola, A. (2020, January). *Distributed ledger technology & the blockchain explained*. https://www.businessinsider.com/distributed-ledger-technology-blockchain

Mercado, J. E., Rupp, M. A., Chen, J. Y. C., Barnes, M. J., Barber, D., & Procci, K. (2016). Intelligent Agent Transparency in Human-Agent Teaming for Multi-UxV Management. *Human Factors*, *58*(3), 401–415. DOI: 10.1177/0018720815621206 PMID: 26867556

Merigó et al. (2016). Bibliometric overview of business & economics research.

Metzler, D. R., Neuss, N., & Muntermann, J. (2021). Artificial Intelligence and Business Model Innovation in Incumbent Firms: A Cross-Industry Case Study. *Die Unternehmung*, *75*(3), 324–339. DOI: 10.5771/0042-059X-2021-3-324

Miau, S., & Yang, J.-M. (2018). Bibliometrics-based evaluation of the Blockchain research trend: 2008–March 2017. *30*(9), 1029-1045.

Mihet, R., & Philippon, T. (2019). The economics of big data and artificial intelligence. *International Finance Review*, *20*, 29–43. DOI: 10.1108/S1569-376720190000020006

Miller, K. C., Bordetsky, A., Mun, J. C., Maule, R. W., & Pollman, A. G. (2021). Merging Future Knowledgebase System of Systems with Artificial Intelligence/Machine Learning Engines to Maximize Reliability and Availability for Decision Support. *Military Operations Research (Alexandria, Va.)*, *26*(4), 77–93. DOI: 10.5711/1082598326477

Minsky, H. (1992). The financial instability hypothesis. The Jerome Levy Economics Institute Working Paper No. 74. https://www.levyinstitute.org/pubs/wp74.pdf

Minsky, H. P. (1986). *Stabilizing an unstable economy*. Yale University Press.

Moenjak, T. (2024b), "Retail CBDC: Digital Banknotes and a Platform for Innovation", Central Banking at the Frontier, Emerald Publishing Limited, Leeds, pp. 269-289. DOI: 10.1108/978-1-83797-130-520241015

Moenjak, T. (2024a). Central Bank Digital Currency (CBDC): Concepts, Wholesale and Cross-Border CBDC. In *Central Banking at the Frontier* (pp. 241–267). Emerald Publishing Limited., DOI: 10.1108/978-1-83797-130-520241014

Mohan, R., & Ray, P. (2022). *The roller coaster ride of non-performing assets in Indian banking*. Centre for Social and Economic Progress.

Mohsen, S. E., Hamdan, A., & Shoaib, H. M. (2024). Digital transformation and integration of artificial intelligence in financial institutions. *Journal of Financial Reporting and Accounting*. DOI: 10.1108/JFRA-09-2023-0544

Moral-Muñoz et al. (2020). Software tools for conducting bibliometric analysis in science: An up-to-date review. *29*(1).

Morgan P, Trinh L (2019) Determinants and impacts of financial literacy in Cambodia and Viet Nam. *J Risk Financ Manag* 12(1):19. Page 23 of 23DOI: 10.3390/jrfm12010019

Morgan, J. (2022). Macroprudential institutionalism: The Bank of England's Financial Policy Committee and the contemporary limits of central bank policy. In *Monetary Economics, Banking and Policy* (pp. 9-25): Routledge.

Morgan, S. (2020). Cybercrime Magazine. *Cybersecurity Ventures*, 1:6. https://cybersecurityventures.com/cybercrime-damages-6-trillion-by-2021/

Moudud-Ul-Huq, S. (2020). Does bank competition matter for performance and risk-taking? empirical evidence from BRICS countries. *International Journal of Emerging Markets*, *16*(3), 409–447. DOI: 10.1108/IJOEM-03-2019-0197

Mukti, T., Tulasmi, T., Shohiha, A., Garbo, A., & Mubasiroh, S. L. (2022). The effect of sharia financial literacy on the decision of the use of service products in the sharia pawn in Yogyakarta. *KnE Social Sciences*, 273-284.

Murakami, D., & Viswanath-Natraj, G. (2025). Cryptocurrencies in emerging markets: A stablecoin solution? *Journal of International Money and Finance*, *156*, 103344. DOI: 10.1016/j.jimonfin.2025.103344

Nadagouder, S. V., & Chandrika, M. P. (2013). Law Relating to E-Banking in India – An Outreach Challenge. *International Journal of Current Research, 5*(2), 3308–3512. http://www.journalcra.com

Naeem Azmi, S., & Akhtar, S. (2024). Does financial development and economic growth matter for services export? Cross-country evidence from OECD countries. *The Journal of International Trade & Economic Development, 34*(5), 1048–1069. DOI: 10.1080/09638199.2024.2361658

Nakashima, K., & Saito, M. (2012). On the comparison of alternative specifications for money demand: The case of extremely low interest rate regimes in Japan. *Journal of the Japanese and International Economies, 26*(3), 454–471. DOI: 10.1016/j.jjie.2012.04.001

Naseema, N., Akhtar, S., & Jha, P. (2025). Blockchain Disrupting Supply Chain Finance: Transformative Solutions and Emerging Challenges. In Anamika Pandey and Fadi Al-Turjman, Transformation of Supply Chain Ecosystems, 33-47.

Naseema, N., Akhtar, S., & Jha, P. (2025). Blockchain Disrupting Supply Chain Finance: Transformative Solutions and Emerging Challenges. In Anamika Pandey and Fadi Al-Turjman, Transformation of Supply Chain Ecosystems, 33-47. https://doi.org/https://doi.org/10.1108/978-1-83549-246-820251003

Naseema, N., Akhtar, S., & Jha, P. (2025). Blockchain Disrupting Supply Chain Finance: Transformative Solutions and Emerging Challenges. Transformation of Supply Chain Ecosystems, 33-47.

Nasir et al. (2020). A bibliometric analysis of corona pandemic in social sciences: a review of influential aspects and conceptual structure. *8*, 133377-133402.

Network for Greening the Financial System (NGFS). (2022). *NGFS climate scenarios for central banks and supervisors*. https://www.ngfs.net/en/ngfs-climate-scenarios-central-banks-and-supervisors

Newman, G. R., & McNally, M. (2005). Identity theft literature review. U.S. Department of Justice, National Institute of Justice. https://www.ncjrs.gov/pdffiles1/nij/grants/210459.pdf

News, A. P. (2025, January 20). How mega-polluters take advantage of billions in green loans. AP News. https://apnews.com/article/a28e03c7421222c58025b31ab8185272

Niger Delta Weekly. (2022). "Spotlighting the growing threat of bank robbery in the Niger Delta." https://p4p-nigerdelta.org/niger-delta-weekly-update-for-february-27-march-05-2022/

Normawati, R., Rahayu, S., & Worokinasih, S. (2021). *Financial Knowledge, Digital Financial Knowledge, Financial Attitude, Financial Behaviour And Financial Satisfaction On Millennials*. Https://Doi.Org/10.4108/Eai.6-3-2021.2305967

Nugrahanti, T. P., Lanjarsih, L., & Mutumanikam, P. R. (2024). Financial management and accounting education in improving the village local economy for MSMES in Godobangkong Vilage. *Community Development Journal: Jurnal Pengabdian Masyarakat*, *5*(4), 5891–5898. DOI: 10.31004/cdj.v5i4.30358

Nwankwo, G. O. (1992). Banking Fraud. Lecture delivered at the 5th Anniversary of Money Market Association of Nigeria.

Obidimma, E. O. C., & Ishiguzo, R. O. (2023). Artificial intelligence and cybercrime investigation in Nigeria: Addressing the legal and technical skills gaps. *African Journal of Criminal Law and Jurisprudence*, *8*, 30–36.

Odufisan, O. I., Abhulimen, O. V., & Ogunti, E. O. (2025). Harnessing artificial intelligence and machine learning for fraud detection and prevention in Nigeria. *Journal of Economic Criminology*, *7*, 100127. DOI: 10.1016/j.jeconc.2025.100127

Odum, P. (2012). *An Assessment of the Relationship Between the Credit Default Swap Market and the Stock Market*. Lund University.

OECD (2013), *Financial literacy and inclusion*: Results of OECD/INFE survey across countries and by gender.

OECD (2013b). *Financial Literacy Framework, in OECD, PISA 2012 Assessment and Analytical Framework: Mathematics, Reading, Science, Problem Solving and Financial Literacy*, OECD Publishing. doi: DOI: 10.1787/9789264190511-7-en

Oentoro, W. (2020). *Mobile payment adoption process: a serial of multiple mediation and moderation analysis*. DOI: 10.1108/BL-09-2020-0059

Ogunjobi, J. O., Oladipo, O. A., Eseyin, O., Opaola, O., & Aransiola, I. J. (2022). Exchange Rate and Agricultural Exports: Evidence From Nigeria (1981-2019). *International Journal of Innovation and Scientific Research*, *09*(04), 89–101. DOI: 10.51244/IJRSI.2022.9410

Ogunmola, G. A., & Das, U. (2024). Analyzing consumer perceptions and adoption intentions of central bank digital currency: A case of the digital rupee. Digital Policy. *Regulation & Governance*, *26*(4), 450–471. DOI: 10.1108/DPRG-09-2023-0136

Oliver Wyman. (2023). The EU banking regulatory framework and its impact on banks and the economy. https://www.ebf.eu/wp-content/uploads/2023/02/The-EU-banking-regulatory-framework-and-its-impact-on-banks-and-the-economy_30Jan-1.pdf

Olk, C., & Miebs, L. (2025). A credit theory of anti-credit money: How the cryptocurrency sphere turned into a shadow banking system. *Review of International Political Economy*, *32*(5), 1414–1441. Advance online publication. DOI: 10.1080/09692290.2025.2476738

Ololade, Y. J. (2024). SME financing through fintech: an analytical study of trends in Nigeria and the USA. *6*(4), 1078-1102.

Ololade, B. M., Salawu, M. K., & Adekanmi, A. D. (2020). E-Fraud in Nigerian Banks: Why and How? *Journal of Financial Risk Management*, *9*(3), 211–228. DOI: 10.4236/jfrm.2020.93012

Oluwatosin, R., Johnson, S. O., Femi, O., & Ogugua, C. O. (2024). Cybersecurity Dynamics in Nigerian Banking: Trends and Strategies Review. *Computer Science & IT Research Journal*, *5*(2), 336–364. DOI: 10.51594/csitrj.v5i2.761

Omodunbi, B. A., Odiase, P. O., Olaniyan, O. M., & Esan, A. O. (2016). Cybercrimes: Analysis, detection, and prevention. *Journal of Engineering Technology*, *1*(1), 37–42.

Omorogieva, M. (2017). *Nigeria: Bank Robbers on the Prowl.* Daily Champion., https://allafrica.com/stories/200706070741.html

Oni, S. A. (2012). Regulation and Supervision of Financial Institutions - the Nigerian Experience. *CBN Economic and Financial Review* 50(4), 107-129.https://dc.cbn.gov.ng/cgi/viewcontent.cgi?article=1094&context=efr

Owolabi, S. A. (2010). Fraud and Fraudulent Practices in Nigeria Banking Industry *African Research Review. An International Multi-Disciplinary Journal*, *4*(3b), 240–256.

Oxfam. (2022). Inequality kills: The unparalleled action needed to combat unprecedented inequality in the wake of COVID-19. https://www.oxfam.org/en/research/inequality-kills

Oyinbo, O., Abraham, F., & Rekwot, G. (2014). Nexus of Exchange Rate Deregulation and Agricultural Share of Gross Domestic Product in Nigeria. *CBN Journal of Applied Statistics, 5*(2), 49–64. https://dc.cbn.gov.ng/jas/vol5/iss2/3

Ozili, P. K. (2023), "Redesigning the eNaira Central Bank Digital Currency (CBDC) for Payments and Macroeconomic Effectiveness", Tyagi, P., Grima, S., Sood, K., Balamurugan, B., Özen, E. and Eleftherios, T. (Ed.) Smart Analytics, Artificial Intelligence and Sustainable Performance Management in a Global Digitalised Economy (Contemporary Studies in Economic and Financial Analysis, Vol. 110B), Emerald Publishing Limited, Leeds, pp. 189-197. DOI: 10.1108/S1569-37592023000110B012

Ozili, P. K. (2023). Central bank digital currency can lead to the collapse of cryptocurrency. In Digital Transformation, Strategic Resilience, Cyber Security and Risk Management (pp. 191-198). Emerald Publishing Limited. DOI: 10.1108/S1569-37592023000111A013

Ozili, P. K. (2022). Central bank digital currency research around the world: A review of literature. *Journal of Money Laundering Control*, *26*(4), 450–471. DOI: 10.1108/JMLC-01-2022-0012

Ozili, P. K. (2023). CBDC, Fintech and cryptocurrency for financial inclusion and financial stability. Digital Policy. *Regulation & Governance*, *25*(1), 40–57. DOI: 10.1108/DPRG-04-2022-0033

Ozili, P. K. (2023). Central bank digital currency and bank earnings management using loan loss provisions. Digital Policy. *Regulation & Governance*. Advance online publication. DOI: 10.1108/DPRG-10-2022-0119

Ozili, P. K. (2024). Determinants of global interest in central bank digital currency: The role of sustainable development and cryptocurrency. *Digital Transformation and Society*, *3*(2), 179–196. DOI: 10.1108/DTS-04-2023-0020

P A. A. N. & Akhtar, S. M. J. (2021). Determinants of financial literacy in rural India: A study of Aligarh district. *Int. J. Financ. Eng*, *8*(2).

Palupiningtyas, ., (2023). *Bibliometric Analysis of Social and Environmental Innovation Research Developments: Trend Identification, Key Concepts, and Collaboration in the Scientific Literature.*, *1*(04), 245–254.

Panico, C., Pinto, A., Anyul, M. P., & Suarez, M. V. (2014). The evolution of financial regulation before and after the crisis. *Revista Economica*, *15*(1). Advance online publication. DOI: 10.22409/economica.15i1.p54

Panos, G., & Wilson, J. (2020). Financial literacy and responsible finance in the FinTech era: Capabilities and challenges. *European Journal of Finance*, *26*(4–5), 297–301. DOI: 10.1080/1351847X.2020.1717569

Pastor, M.Jr. (1987). The effects of IMF programs in the Third World: Debate and evidence from Latin America. *World Development*, *15*(2), 249–262. DOI: 10.1016/0305-750X(87)90080-5

Patel, M. (2024). Positioning Central Bank Digital Currency in the Payments Landscape. *Fintech Notes*, *2024*(006), 1. DOI: 10.5089/9798400289118.063

Paul, J., & Rosado-Serrano, A. (2019). Gradual Internationalization vs Born-Global/International new venture models: A review and research agenda. *International Marketing Review*, *36*(6), 830–858. DOI: 10.1108/IMR-10-2018-0280

Pavlidis, G. (2020). Financial action task force and the fight against money laundering and the financing of terrorism. *Journal of Financial Crime*, *28*(3), 765–773. DOI: 10.1108/JFC-09-2019-0124

Pemer, F. (2021). Enacting Professional Service Work in Times of Digitalization and Potential Disruption. *Journal of Service Research*, *24*(2), 249–268. DOI: 10.1177/1094670520916801

Pérez-López, I. J. (2020). *De las 7 Bolas de Dragón a los 7 Reinos de Poniente: viajando por la ficción para transformar la realidad.* CopiDeporte S.L.

Pfister, C., & Valla, N. (2021). Financial stability is easier to green than monetary policy. *Inter Economics*, *56*(3), 154–159. DOI: 10.1007/s10272-021-0972-y

Piketty, T., & Saez, E. (2003). Income inequality in the United States, 1913–1998. *The Quarterly Journal of Economics*, *118*(1), 1–41. DOI: 10.1162/00335530360535135

Plotnikova, M. (2018). *Too Big to Fail or Too Small to Compete? The Impact of Basel III on Risk Taking of Large and Small Bank* [Master's Thesis, Radboud University]. https://theses.ubn.ru.nl/handle/123456789/5873

Prates, M. (2025). What critics still get wrong about stablecoins. OMFIF, September 18, 2025. https://www.omfif.org/2025/09/what-critics-still-get-wrong-about-stablecoins

Prodan, S., Konhäusner, P., Dabija, D., Lazaroiu, G., & Marincean, L. (2024). The rise in popularity of central bank digital currencies: A systematic review. *Heliyon*, *10*(9), e30561. DOI: 10.1016/j.heliyon.2024.e30561 PMID: 38756603

Puschmann, T., & Leifer, L. (2020). Sustainable Digital Finance: The Role of FinTech, InsurTech & Blockchain for Shaping the World for the Better. In: University of Zurich: Zurich, Switzerland, Stanford University: Standford....

Putri, J. K. Sugianto, & Nasution, J. (2023). The Influence of Capital, Production Costs, and Sharia Pawnshop Financing on Micro Business Income Levels in Langsa City. *Jemsi (Journal of Economics, Management and Accounting)*, 9(5), 1813–1822. https://Doi.Org/10.35870/Jemsi.V9i5.1470

Quarshie, M. A., Djimatey, R., Akhtar, S., & Nawaah, D. (2025). Maximizing financial efficiency through technological synergy: Unleashing ICT for enhanced cash management in SMEs. Journal of the International Council for Small Business, 1–31. DOI: 10.1080/26437015.2025.2461025

Quarshie, M. A., Djimatey, R., Akhtar, S., & Nawaah, D. (2025). Maximizing financial efficiency through technological synergy: Unleashing ICT for enhanced cash management in SMEs. *Journal of the International Council for Small Business*, 1–31. https://doi.org/https://doi.org/10.1080/26437015.2025.2461025

r, N., & Fainani, F. (2023). Analysis of the Position of Collateral in Financing at Sharia Pawnshops(Case Study of Sharia Pawnshop Prenduan Branch). Muqaddimah: *Journal of Economics, Management, Accounting and Business*, 1(2), 105–118. https://Doi.Org/10.59246/Muqaddimah.V1i2.189

Radelet, S., Sachs, J. D., Cooper, R. N., & Bosworth, B. P. (1998). The East Asian financial crisis: Diagnosis, remedies, prospects. *Brookings Papers on Economic Activity*, *1998*(1), 1–90. DOI: 10.2307/2534670

Rahmadanti, N. I., & Sugiarti, D. (2024). Comparative Analysis Between Sharia Pawnshops and Conventional Pawnshops in *The Economic Empowerment of Indonesian Communities* 4 1 (2024): *Proceeding of The 7th International Seminar on Business, Economics, Social Science, and Technology (ISBEST)* / DOI: 10.33830/isbest.v4i1.3394

Rahman, S., Moral, I. H., Hassan, M., Hossain, G. S., & Perveen, R. (2022). A systematic review of green finance in the banking industry: Perspectives from a developing country. *Green Finance*, *4*(3), 347–363. DOI: 10.3934/GF.2022017

Rajan, R. G. (2010). *Fault lines: How hidden fractures still threaten the world economy*. Princeton University Press.

Ramakreshnan et al. (2021). A comprehensive bibliometrics of 'walkability' research landscape: visualization of the scientific progress and future prospects. *28*, 1357-1369.

Ramasamy et al. (2015). Influence of macroeconomic variables on exchange rates. *3*(2), 276-281.

Ramnath, A. P. (2013). *Advanced Law Lexicon*, 4th ed., Nagpur; Wadhwa and Co.
Ripples Nigeria. (20220. "Panic as armed robbers raid First Bank, Zenith Bank in Kogi, escape with cash." https://www.ripplesnigeria.com/panic-as-armed-robbers-raid-first-bank-zenith-bank-in-kogi-escape-with-cash/

Rasser, M., Lamberth, M., Riikonen, A., & Guo, C. M. H. and P. S. (2019a). The American AI Century: IMPROVE GOVERNMENT READINESS. In *Center for a New American Security*.

Rasser, M., Lamberth, M., Riikonen, A., & Guo, C. M. H. and P. S. (2019b). *The American AI Century: SHAPE GLOBAL NORMS FOR AI USE*.

Reetu, & Devi, M. (2025). The evolution of financial regulation: A historical overview. International Journal of Creative Research Thoughts (IJCRT), 13(3), J728–J729. https://www.ijcrt.org/papers/IJCRT25A3128.pdf

Rehman, F. U., & Muslim, A. (2025). From Growth to Grime : How Macroeconomic Shifts Shape Bad Loans in India " Faiz Ur Rehman, Research Scholar, Department of Commerce, Aligarh Prof. *Nawab Ali Khan, Professor, Department of Commerce, Aligarh Muslim International Journal of Research.*, *12*(05), 71–88.

Reinhart, C. M., & Rogoff, K. S. (2009). *This time is different: Eight centuries of financial folly*. Princeton University Press.

Reporters, S. (2020, June 4). DPO, seven policemen killed in Kogi bank robbery. https://saharareporters.com/2020/06/04/update-dpo-seven-policemen-killed-kogi-bank-robbery

Repullo, R. (2004). Economic and regulatory capital in banking: What is the difference? *International Journal of Central Banking*, *3*(3), 87–117.

Reslow, A. (2024). Cross-Border Payments with Retail Central Bank Digital Currencies. *Fintech Notes*, *2024*(002), 1. DOI: 10.5089/9798400272035.063

Reuters. (2025, April 30). Citadel Securities flags US regulator about 24-hour trading infrastructure risks. *Reuters*. https://www.reuters.com/sustainability/boards-policy-regulation/citadel-securities-flags-us-securities-regulator-about-24-hour-trading-risks-2025-04-30

Reuters. (2025, February 19). Nigeria seeks $81.5 bln in economic losses, back tax from Binance: court document. *Reuters*. https://www.reuters.com/world/africa/nigeria-seeks-815-bln-economic-losses-back-tax-against-binance-court-document-2025-02-19/

Reuters. (2025, January 14). G20 financial stability watchdog urges broader adoption of climate transition plans. Reuters. https://www.reuters.com/sustainability/sustainable-finance-reporting/g20-financial-stability-watchdog-urges-broader-adoption-climate-transition-plans-2025-01-14/

Review, G. F. M. (2025, May 15). The complexity of clarity: Why banking needs more than simple rules. https://www.gfmreview.com/banking/the-complexity-of-clarity-why-banking-needs-more-than-simple-rules

Rey, H. (2025, September). Stablecoins, tokens, and global dominance. *Finance & Development*, 24–27. https://www.imf.org/en/Publications/fandd/issues/2025/09/stablecoins-tokens-global-dominance-helene-rey

Ricaldi, L., Finke, M., & Huston, S. (2013). Financial literacy and shrouded credit card rewards. *Journal of Financial Services Marketing*, *18*(3), 177–187. DOI: 10.1057/fsm.2013.11

Ripple Labs Inc. (2025, May 28). Written input on regulatory sandboxes. U.S. Securities and Exchange Commission. https://www.sec.gov/files/ctf-written-input-ripple-letter-regulatory-sandboxes-052825.pdf

Rodriguez, T. N. and S. (2019). *A Candle in the Dark: A FRAMEWORK FOR UNDERSTANDING APPLIED AI.*

Rodrik, D. (2020). *Why does globalization fuel populism? Economics, culture, and the rise of right-wing populism* (NBER Working Paper No. 27526). National Bureau of Economic Research. DOI: 10.3386/w27526

Rodrik, D. (2011). The globalization paradox: Democracy and the future of the world economy. *World Trade Review*, *10*(1), 409–417.

Rogoff, K. (2025). *Our Dollar, Your Problem: An Insider's View of Seven Turbulent Decades of Global Finance, and the Road Ahead.* Yale University Press.

Rohman, A., Asfahani, A., & Iqbal, K. (2023). Comprehensive Analysis of AI's Contribution to Communnity *Development Journal,* 5(4).Tahun 2024, Hal. 5891-5898P-ISSN 2721-4990l

Rolanda, I., Mulia, A. A., & Laksmiwati, M. (2023). Increasing Financial Literacy for Students at the Literacy Smart House (Rpa) Kandang Gede, Kresek, Tangerang, Banten. *Krishna,* 3(1), 126–135. Https://Doi.Org/10.36080/Kresna.V3i1.70

Romer, C. D. (2012). Fiscal policy in the crisis: Lessons and policy implications. *IMF Fiscal Forum.* https://www.imf.org/external/np/seminars/eng/2012/fiscal/

Rybnicek, R., & Königsgruber, R. (2019). What makes industry–university collaboration succeed? A systematic review of the literature. *89*(2), 221-250.

S&P Global Trucost. (2021). *Physical risk data for financial institutions.* https://www.spglobal.com/esg/

Sachdeva, M., & Saravelos, G. (2025). What do stablecoins mean for dollar dominance? Deutsche Bank Research, September 10, 2025. https://www.dbresearch.com/PROD/RI-PROD/PDFVIEWER.calias?pdfViewerPdfUrl=PROD0000000000602780

Saengchote, K., & Samphantharak, K. (2024). Digital money creation and algorithmic stablecoin run. *Finance Research Letters, 64*, 105435. DOI: 10.1016/j.frl.2024.105435

Saez, E., & Zucman, G. (2019). *The triumph of injustice: How the rich dodge taxes and how to make them pay*. W. W. Norton & Company.

Safitri, N., Permadi, I., Fathussyaadah, E., Tinggi Ilmu Ekonomi, P. G. R. I., & Sukabumi, S. (2022). Literasi Keuangan Digital, Keberlanjutan Usaha Industri Kecil Dan Menengah Serta Dampaknya Terhadap Kesejahteraan Keuangan. *Jurnal Ilmiah MEA (Manajemen, Ekonomi, & Akuntansi),* 6(3), 1203–1214. Http://Www.Journal.Stiemb.Ac.Id/Index.Php/Mea/Article/View/2478

Sahay, N. (2024). *Robots vs. Robbers: How AI is Revolutionizing Crime Fighting: Is AI the Future of Crime Prevention? Examining the Pros and Cons*. https://nehasahay-5891.medium.com/robots-vs-robbers-how-ai-is-revolutionizing-crime-fighting-c6c93ef3f5a4

Şahin, E. E., & Özkan, O. (2018). The relationship between credit default swaps, exchange rate and BIST100 index. *Hitit University Jou. of Social Sci. Inst., 11*(3), 1939–1945. DOI: 10.17218/hititsosbil.450178

Salampasis, D., Schueffel, P., Dominic, R., & Cameron, D. (2023). Central Bank Digital Currencies: Opening Pandora's Box or Paving the Future of Money? In Baker, H. K., Benedetti, H., Nikbakht, E., & Smith, S. S. (Eds.), *The Emerald Handbook on Cryptoassets: Investment Opportunities and Challenges* (pp. 283–306). Emerald Publishing Limited., DOI: 10.1108/978-1-80455-320-620221019

Salim, M., Ahsan, M. A., & Khan, P. A. J. B. A. I. J. (2025). Decoding sustainability: a tempting bibliometric review of blockchain in climate action for emerging trends and future directions.

Salim, M., Khan, M., Shamim, M. J. A.-B. J. o. F., & Management. (2022). A critical appraisal of ASPIRE scheme of India. *10*(2), 63-73.

Salim, M., Khan, P. A., Jalil, N. A., Johl, S. K., Jafar, S. H., Irfan, F., & Khan, M. J. K. S. S. (2023). Fusion of blockchain and sustainable development goals: a bibliometric analysis for future trends. 633–654-633–654.

Salim, M., Khan, P. A., Rahman, H., Asif, M., Jan, A., & Khan, M. N. (2025). Trends and Future Directions on Adoption of Blockchain Technology for SDGs in VUCA World: A Bibliometric Analysis. *Business Strategy & Development*, *8*(3), e70149. DOI: 10.1002/bsd2.70149

Samala, N., Katkam, B. S., Bellamkonda, R. S., & Rodriguez, R. V. (2022). Impact of AI and robotics in the tourism sector: A critical insight. *Journal of Tourism Futures*, *8*(1), 73–87. DOI: 10.1108/JTF-07-2019-0065

Sanusi, A. (2023). "Banks raid: Police confirm DPO, three cops killed, gun down fleeing robbers" *Punch*.https://punchng.com/benue-robbery-police-confirm-killing-of-two-suspects-condemn-officers-murder/

Sapignoli, M. (2021). Anthropology and the Ai-Turn in Global Governance. *AJIL Unbound*, *115*, 294–298. DOI: 10.1017/aju.2021.38

Sardana, V., & Singhania, S. (2018). Digital technology in the realm of banking: A review of literature. *1*(2), 28-32.

Schoenmaker, D., & Schramade, W. (2019). *Principles of sustainable finance*. Oxford University Press.

Scholtens, B. (2009). Corporate social responsibility in the international banking industry. *Journal of Business Ethics*, *86*(2), 159–175. DOI: 10.1007/s10551-008-9841-x

Sertoglu, K., Ugural, S., & Bekun, F. V. (2017). The Contribution of Agricultural Sector on Economic Growth of Nigeria. *International Journal of Economics and Financial Issues*, *7*(1), 547–552. https://www.econjournals.com/index.php/ijefi/article/view/3941

Setyowati, A. (2003). Harmadi H, Sunarjanto S. Islamic Financial Literacy and Personal Financial Planning: A Socio-Demographic Study. *J Keuang dan Perbank*. 2018;22(1):63–72.

Shaffer, K. J., Gaumer, C. J., & Bradley, K. P. (2020). Artificial intelligence products reshape accounting: Time to re-train. *Development and Learning in Organizations*, *34*(6), 41–43. DOI: 10.1108/DLO-10-2019-0242

Shampa, M. T. A., Shimu, N. J., Chowdhury, K. A., Islam, M. M., & Ahmed, M. K. J. H. (2023). A comprehensive review on sustainable coastal zone management in Bangladesh: Present status and the way forward. *9*(8).

Shao, J., Lou, Z., Wang, C., Mao, J., & Ye, A. (2022). The impact of artificial intelligence (AI) finance on financing constraints of non-SOE firms in emerging markets. *International Journal of Emerging Markets*, *17*(4), 930–944. DOI: 10.1108/IJOEM-02-2021-0299

Sheehan, M. (2023)... *AI Regulations and How They Get Made.*, *24*(24), 108–125.

Sheppard, L. R., Karlén, R., Hunter, A. P., & Balieiro, L. (2018). Report Subtitle : THE IMPORTANCE OF THE AI ECOSYSTEM FRAMEWORK FOR. *Artificial Intelligence*, (May), 2020.

Shiller, R. J. (2000). *Irrational exuberance*. Princeton University Press.

Shiller, R. J., Fischer, S., & Friedman, B. M. (1984). Stock prices and social dynamics. *Brookings Papers on Economic Activity*, *1984*(2), 457–498. DOI: 10.2307/2534436

Shin, K. S., Lee, T. S., & Kim, H. J. (2005). An application of support vector machines in bankruptcy prediction model. *Expert Systems with Applications*, *28*(1), 127–135. DOI: 10.1016/j.eswa.2004.08.009

Shleifer, A., & Vishny, R. W. (1997). The limits of arbitrage. *The Journal of Finance*, *52*(1), 35–55. DOI: 10.1111/j.1540-6261.1997.tb03807.x

Shukla, M. S., & Singh, M. P. (2014). E-Commerce: A Virtual Assistance Making Life Challenging Or Simpler. 281.

Singh, C. (2024b). *Is generative AI (arti fi cial intelligence) the next advent in the evolution of fi nance and navigating fi nancial crime and regulation ?* DOI: 10.1108/JFC-07-2024-0232

Singh, C. (2024a). Artificial intelligence and deep learning: Considerations for financial institutions for compliance with the regulatory burden in the United Kingdom. *Journal of Financial Crime*, *31*(2), 259–266. DOI: 10.1108/JFC-01-2023-0011

Singh, C., & Lin, W. (2020). Can artificial intelligence, RegTech and CharityTech provide effective solutions for anti-money laundering and counter-terror financing initiatives in charitable fundraising. *Journal of Money Laundering Control*, *24*(3), 464–482. DOI: 10.1108/JMLC-09-2020-0100

Singh, S., Srivastava, S., & Kaur, H. (2025). Greening the Portfolio: Investor Insights into Sustainable Development Opportunities in India. In *Green Horizons: Role of AI in Sustainable Finance* (pp. 237–253). Springer Nature Singapore. DOI: 10.1007/978-981-96-6495-5_13

Singh, V., & Yadav, M. (2025). User adoption of digital currency: A systematic review and future agenda using TCCM approach. *Central Bank Review*, *25*(1), 100183. DOI: 10.1016/j.cbrev.2024.100183

Single Resolution Board. (2024). Single Resolution Mechanism. https://www.srb.europa.eu/en/content/single-resolution-mechanism

Soni, H. P., Shyamsuder, C., & Prasad, K. (2023). Risk return profile of commodity derivatives: An investors perception. [Management and Administrative Professional Review]. *Revista de Gestão e Secretariado*, *14*(7), 12004–12016. DOI: 10.7769/gesec.v14i7.2389

Sood, K., & Singh, S. (2024). Multi-central bank digital currencies arrangements: A multivocal literature review. *China Finance Review International*, *14*(4), 813–841. Advance online publication. DOI: 10.1108/CFRI-09-2023-0221

Southall, R. J. R. o. A. P. E. (2016). The coming crisis of Zuma's ANC: the party state confronts fiscal crisis. *43*(147), 73-88.

Srivastava, S., Singh, S., & Kaur, H. (2025). Beyond the Bottom Line: An Impact of CO2 Emissions and R&D on Corporate Sustainability in India. In *Green Futures: Navigating the Path to Environmental Resilience* (pp. 311–326). Springer Nature Singapore. DOI: 10.1007/978-981-96-0843-0_16

Stantcheva, S. (2022). Inequalities in the times of a pandemic. *Economic Policy*, *37*(109), 5–41. DOI: 10.1093/epolic/eiac006

Statista. (2024). https://www.statista.com/statistics/893954/number-fintech-startups-by-region/

Steele, G. S. (2024), "The Miner of Last Resort: Digital Currency, Shadow Money and the Role of the Central Bank", Levine, L. (Ed.) Technology vs. Government: The Irresistible Force Meets the Immovable Object (Studies in Media and Communications, Vol. 25), Emerald Publishing Limited, Leeds, pp. 197-221. DOI: 10.1108/S2050-206020240000025008

Stephan De Spiegeleire, M. M. and T. S. (2017). *ARTIFICIAL INTELLIGENCE AND THE FUTURE OF DEFENSE: AI – TODAY AND TOMORROW* (Issue May 2024).

Stiglitz, J. E. (1999). Lessons from East Asia. *Journal of Policy Modeling*, *21*(3), 311–330. DOI: 10.1016/S0161-8938(99)00005-8

Stoner, H. NGOs in Transition: Exploring Organizational Changes and Online Work Strategies Post-COVID-19.

Stopar, K., & Bartol, T. (2019). Digital competences, computer skills and information literacy in secondary education: mapping and visualization of trends and concepts. *118*(2), 479-498.

Sukardi, B., Wijayanti, N. R., & Fachrurazi, F. (2023). *Literacy and strategic marketing to raise public awareness using Sharia pawnshops during the COVID-19 pandemic*. Qualitative Research in Financial Markets.

Sussangkarn, C. (2011). Chiang Mai Initiative Multilateralization: Origin, development, and outlook. *Asian Economic Policy Review*, *6*(2), 203–220. DOI: 10.1111/j.1748-3131.2011.01196.x

Swiss National Bank. (2023). Piloting monetary policy implementation on a DLT-based infrastructure – Issuance of digital SNB Bills (SNB Working Paper 2023-1). https://www.snb.ch

Tabassum, S., Haque, S. I., Ahsan, M. A., Salim, M., & Khan, P. A. (2025). *Assessing Employees' Engagement in Hybrid Work Arrangement: Mediating role of Employee Voice for Achieving SDG 8 and SDG 10.* Paper presented at the International Conference on Environmental, Social, and Governance (ICESG 2024). DOI: 10.2991/978-2-38476-358-0_24

Tam, D., & Fulmer, S. J. T. J. F. C. (2021). Spain. *Sociedad De Gestión De Activos Procedentes De La Reestructuración Bancaria (Sareb)*, *3*(2), 726–756.

Tan, Y., & Tsionas, M. G. (2022). Modelling sustainability efficiency in banking. *International Journal of Finance & Economics*, *27*(3), 2349–2367. DOI: 10.1002/ijfe.2349

Task Force on Climate-related Financial Disclosures (TCFD). (2017). *Final report: Recommendations of the Task Force on Climate-related Financial Disclosures*. https://www.fsb-tcfd.org/publications/

Tax Policy Center. (2023, May 11). *How did the fiscal response to the COVID-19 pandemic affect the federal budget outlook?* Urban Institute & Brookings Institution. https://taxpolicycenter.org/briefing-book/how-did-fiscal-response-covid-19-pandemic-affect-federal-budget-outlook

Teglio, A., Raberto, M., & Cincotti, S. (2012). THE IMPACT OF BANKS' CAPITAL ADEQUACY REGULATION ON THE ECONOMIC SYSTEM: AN AGENT-BASED APPROACH. *Advances in Complex Systems*, *15*(supp02), 1250040. DOI: 10.1142/S0219525912500403

Television, C. (2014). "1 Police Officer, 2 Robbers Killed in Kogi Bank Robbery." https://www.channelstv.com/2014/01/11/1-police-officer-2-robbers-killed-in-kogi-bank-robbery/

Temperini, J., D'Ippoliti, C., & Gobbi, L. (2024). Is the time ripe for helicopter money? Growth impact and financial stability risks of outright monetary transfers. *Structural Change and Economic Dynamics*, *69*, 24–36. DOI: 10.1016/j.strueco.2023.11.003

Tercero-Lucas, D. (2023). Central Bank digital currencies and financial stability in a modern monetary system. *Journal of Financial Stability*, *69*, 101188. DOI: 10.1016/j.jfs.2023.101188

Thaler, R., & Sunstein, C. (2008). Nudge: Improving decisions about health, wealth and happiness. In *Amsterdam Law Forum; HeinOnline: Online* (p. 89).

Thavorn et al. (2021). Collaboration network and trends of global coronavirus disease research: a scientometric analysis. *9*, 45001-45016.

The Economist. (2024, November 14). Why financial markets are so oddly calm. https://www.economist.com/finance-and-economics/2024/11/14/why-financial-markets-are-so-oddly-calm

The Federal Trade Commission. (2024). "Identity Theft". https://www.identitytheft.gov

The White House. (2025). Fact Sheet: President Donald J. Trump signs GENIUS Act into law. https://www.whitehouse.gov/fact-sheets/2025/07/fact-sheet-president-donald-j-trump-signs-genius-act-into-law/

Themistocleous, M., Rupino da Cunha, P., Tabakis, E., & Papadaki, M. (2023). Towards cross-border CBDC interoperability: Insights from a multivocal literature review. *Journal of Enterprise Information Management*, *36*(5), 1296–1318. DOI: 10.1108/JEIM-11-2022-0411

Thompson, S. T. (2025). Exploring banditry in Nigeria. *Security Journal*, *38*(1), 28. DOI: 10.1057/s41284-025-00477-1

Time. (2021, October 15). 'Green Swan' climate events can rock the world's economies. How banks prepare for them could save more than dollars. Time Magazine. https://time.com/6109448/world-economy-climate-change/

Tkachenko, N. (2024). Integrating AI's carbon footprint into risk management frameworks: Strategies and tools for sustainable compliance in banking sector. *arXiv*. https://arxiv.org/abs/2410.01818

Tobin, J. (1969). A general equilibrium approach to monetary theory. *Journal of Money, Credit and Banking*, *1*(1), 15–29. DOI: 10.2307/1991374

Toha, M. A., Johl, S. K., Khan, P. A., Salim, M. J. Q., & Quantity. (2025). Why diverse boards are market game-changers: driving the sustainable future from the lens of proactive eco-innovation for firm market performance. 1-30.

Toha, M. A., Khan, P. A., Irfan, F., Salim, M., & Khan, M. (2024). Unboxing eco-innovation and ESG for circular economy. In *Climate Governance and Corporate Eco-innovation: A Framework for Sustainable Companies* (pp. 353–366). Springer. DOI: 10.1007/978-3-031-56423-9_13

Tourpe, H. (2023). A Guide to Central Bank Digital Currency Product Development. *Fintech Notes*, *2023*(007), 1. DOI: 10.5089/9798400253690.063

Trinh, Q. L., Morgan, P. J., & Sonobe, T. (2020). Investment behavior of MSMEs during the downturn periods: Empirical evidence from Vietnam. *Emerging Markets Review*, 45, Elsevier BV; 2020. p. 100739.

Tsang, M. (2023). Currency crisis: Turkey in 2021. *The CASE Journal*, *19*(5), 679–698. DOI: 10.1108/TCJ-08-2022-0140

Tucci, L. (2020). "A guide to artificial intelligence in the enterprise." https://www.techtarget.com/searchenterpriseai/Ultimate-guide-to-artificial-intelligence-inthe-enterprise

Tuhkanen, H., & Vulturius, G. (2020). *Climate risk information for adaptation: Assessing the needs of financial institutions*. Stockholm Environment Institute. https://www.sei.org/publications/climate-risk-finance/

Turek, M. (2022). A new approach to sustainable financial stability and its prospects. *WSB Journal of Business and Finance*, *56*(1), 64–71. DOI: 10.2478/wsbjbf-2022-0007

U.S. Commodity Futures Trading Commission. (2024). Dodd-Frank Act Title VII. https://www.aima.org/asset/3C46E7C1-08D2-49DD-A82E9317C3EF04D7.9BDBBD0D-30E5-4C87-BF4C78D94207928E/

U.S. Department of the Treasury. (2024). Financial Stability Oversight Council. https://home.treasury.gov/policy-issues/financial-markets-financial-institutions-and-fiscal-service/fsoc

U.S. Securities and Exchange Commission (SEC). (2021). *Staff report on equity and options market structure conditions in early

Uddin et al. (2013). Network effects on scientific collaborations. *8*(2), e57546.

Uddin, S. M. M., & Akhtar, S. (2025). Convergence in efficiency and technology gap of Indian banks: implication of GFC and COVID-19. *Quality & Quantity, June*. https://doi.org/https://doi.org/10.1007/s11135-025-02195-7

Uddin, S. M. M., & Akhtar, S. (2025). Convergence in efficiency and technology gap of Indian banks: Implication of GFC and COVID-19. *Quality & Quantity*. Advance online publication. DOI: 10.1007/s11135-025-02195-7

Ukhami, E. I., & Abdulsalam, D. (2024). Globalisation and National Security: Perspectives on Cybersecurity Threats in Nigeria. *Journal of Political Discourse*, *2*(1/2), 273–286. https://www.jopd.com.ng

Ulidaman, N. (2019). Rationalization of Sharia Pawnshopsat the Ternate Sharia Pawnshop Bastiong Unit as a Non-Bank Financial Institution. *Foramadiahi: Journal of Educational and Islamic Studies,* 10(1), 90. Https://Doi.Org/10.46339/Foramadiahi.V10i1.115

Umar, M., Shahzad, F., Iqbal, A., & Tong, F. (2024). Does institutional quality matter for Central Bank digital currency adoption? *Economic Analysis and Policy*, *83*, 378–389. DOI: 10.1016/j.eap.2024.06.022

Umeaduma, C. M.-G., & Dugbartey, A. N. J. I. J. C. A. T. R. (2023). Effect of exchange rate volatility on export competitiveness and national trade balances in emerging markets. *12*(11), 57-71.

UNEP Finance Initiative. (2021). *The Climate Risk Landscape: A Synthesis of Tools and Approaches*. https://www.unepfi.org/publications/the-climate-risk-landscape/

UNEP. (2021). *Adaptation Gap Report 2021: The Gathering Storm*. https://www.unep.org/resources/adaptation-gap-report-2021

UNICEF. (2021). COVID-19 vaccine delivery: Challenges and opportunities.

United Nations Conference on Trade and Development (UNCTAD). (2021). Digital economy report 2021. https://unctad.org/publication/digital-economy-report-2021

Utami et al. (2021). Adoption of FinTech products: a systematic literature review. *16*(3), 233-248.

Van Roosebeke, B., & Defina, R. (2023), "Central Bank Digital Currencies: The Motivation", in Kim, S.-J. (Ed.) Fintech, Pandemic, and the Financial System: Challenges and Opportunities (International Finance Review, Vol. 22), Emerald Publishing Limited, Leeds, pp. 185-200. DOI: 10.1108/S1569-376720220000022009

Vanguard News. (2023, October 21). Benue bank robbery: Death toll rises as police confirm Otukpo DPO, 3 officers killed. https://www.vanguardngr.com/2023/10/benue-bank-robbery-death-toll-rises-as-police-confirm-otukpo-dpo-3-officers-killed

Vanguard News. (2024, May 20). Police parade suspect who stormed bank with fake bomb, demanded N100m. https://www.vanguardngr.com/2024/05/police-parade-suspect-who-stormed-bank-with-fake-bomb-demanded-n100m

Vanguard. (2024). "Two killed as robbers raid banks in Kogi." https://www.vanguardngr.com/2024/03/two-killed-as-robbers-raid-banks-in-kogi/

Vashkevich, A., & Basazinew, S. T. 2013. Relationship between sovereign credit default swap and stock markets: *The Case of East Asia. Umeå School of Business and Economics Master Thesis*.

Volante, L., DeLuca, C., & Klinger, D. A. (2023). Leveraging AI to enhance learning. *Phi Delta Kappan, 105*(1), 40–45. DOI: 10.1177/00317217231197475

Wagner, W. (2015). Representation in action. In Sammut, G., Andreouli, E., Gaskell, G., & Vasiner, J. (Eds.), *The Cambridge Handbook of Social Representation* (pp. 12–28). Cambridge University Press. DOI: 10.1017/CBO9781107323650.004

Walter, C. E. (2022). *The red dream: the Chinese Communist Party and the financial deterioration of China*. John Wiley & Sons.

Wamba-Taguimdje, S. L., Fosso Wamba, S., Kala Kamdjoug, J. R., & Tchatchouang Wanko, C. E. (2020). Influence of artificial intelligence (AI) on firm performance: The business value of AI-based transformation projects. *Business Process Management Journal, 26*(7), 1893–1924. DOI: 10.1108/BPMJ-10-2019-0411

Wang, C., Lu, D., Meihe, E., Mu, Y., & Peng, Y. (2025). Safe asset scarcity and multipolar international currency. *Economics Letters, 112621*, 112621. Advance online publication. DOI: 10.1016/j.econlet.2025.112621

Wang, R., Basu, A., & Clements, A. (2023). Are credit default swaps still a sideshow? How information flow between equity and CDS markets has changed since the financial crisis. *Global Finance Journal, 57*, 100849. DOI: 10.1016/j.gfj.2023.100849

Wang, W., Zhang, J., & Wang, Y. (2021). Capital Supervision, Information Disclosure and Risk-taking—Evidence from Rural Commercial Banks in China. *Emerging Markets Finance & Trade, 58*(8), 2273–2289. DOI: 10.1080/1540496X.2021.1971076

Wati, K. (2023). The Influence of Ar-Rahn Financing for Motor Vehicle Owner Book Micro Businesses on the Development of Customers' Micro, Small and Medium Enterprises at the Ahmad Yani Sharia Pawnshop, Pontianak. *Indonesian Muamalat Journal*, 3(2). https://Doi.Org/10.26418/Jmi.V3i2.68243

Weber, O. (2016). The impact of social banking on bank performance and risk: Evidence from Europe. *Journal of Sustainable Finance & Investment*, *6*(1), 1–18. DOI: 10.1080/20430795.2014.887345

Weisel, D. L. (2007). Bank Robbery. Problem-Oriented Guides for Police Problem-Specific Guides Series, Guide No. 48. U.S. Department of Justice, Office of Community Oriented Policing Services. www.cops.usdoj.gov

Welford, H. E. (2022). Revisiting the thermophilic bacterial genus Venenivibrio; physiological, phenotypic, and genotypic (re) characterisation the type strain and novel Venenivibrio isolates.

Whelan, T., & Fink, C. (2016). *The comprehensive business case for sustainability*. Harvard Business Review. https://hbr.org/2016/10/the-comprehensive-business-case-for-sustainability

Wojcik, D. (2021). Financial geography I: Exploring FinTech–maps and concepts. *45*(3), 566-576.

Wong, M.C.S., Chan, E.K.H., and Yousaf, I. (2024), "CBDCs, regulated stablecoins and tokenized traditional assets under the Basel Committee rules on cryptoassets", Journal of Financial Regulation and Compliance, Vol. ahead-of-print No. ahead-of-print. DOI: 10.1108/JFRC-03-2024-0050

World Bank Group. (2018). Conflict and Violence in Nigeria: Results from the North East, North Central and South South Zones. https://documents1.worldbank.org/curated/en/111851538025875054/pdf/130198-WP-P160999-PUBLIC-26-9-2018-14-42-49-ConflictViolenceinNigeriaResultsfromNENCSSzonesFinal.pdf

World Bank. (2020). Poverty and shared prosperity 2020: Reversals of fortune. https://www.worldbank.org/en/publication/poverty-and-shared-prosperity-2020

World Bank. (2021). *Climate Risk Country Profiles*. https://climateknowledgeportal.worldbank.org/

World Bank. (2021). Global economic prospects. https://www.worldbank.org/en/publication/global-economic-prospects

World Bank. (2022). Global economic prospects. https://www.worldbank.org/en/publication/global-economic-prospects

World Economic Forum (WEF). (2019). Central Banks and Distributed Ledger Technology: How are Central Banks Exploring Blockchain Today? Retrieved from https://www3.weforum.org/docs/WEF_Central_Bank_Activity_in_Blockchain_DLT.pdf

World Economic Forum. (2023). *Global Risks Report 2023*. https://www.weforum.org/reports/global-risks-report-2023

World Health Organization (WHO). (2022). Global vaccination coverage. https://www.who.int/news-room/fact-sheets/detail/immunization-coverage

Xue, X., Yang, X., Deng, Z., Tu, H., Kong, D., Li, N., & Xu, F. J. F. i. P. H. (2022). Global trends and hotspots in research on rehabilitation robots: a bibliometric analysis from 2010 to 2020. *9*, 806723.

Xu, Y., Shieh, C. H., van Esch, P., & Ling, I. L. (2020). AI customer service: Task complexity, problem-solving ability, and usage intention. [AMJ]. *Australasian Marketing Journal*, *28*(4), 189–199. DOI: 10.1016/j.ausmj.2020.03.005

Yang, X., ... (2025). The impact of community banks' innovation on regulatory choices. Edinburgh Research Explorer. https://www.research.ed.ac.uk/files/509090128/YangEtal2025EAPTheImpactOfCommunityBanks_Innovation.pdf

Yang, S., Hussain, M., Ammar Zahid, R. M., & Maqsood, U. S. (2024). The role of artificial intelligence in corporate digital strategies: Evidence from China. *Kybernetes*. Advance online publication. DOI: 10.1108/K-08-2023-1583

Yan, M., Hall, M. J., & Turner, P. (2012). A cost–benefit analysis of Basel III: Some evidence from the UK. *International Review of Financial Analysis*, *25*, 73–82. DOI: 10.1016/j.irfa.2012.06.009

Yanthiani, L. (2020). Moral Value Of Ijarah And Ujrah: Review Of Rahn Concept In Islam. International. *Journal of Islamic Archipelago*, *8*(1), 1–9. https://Doi.Org/10.15575/Ijni.V8i1.84. DOI: 10.15575/ijni.v8i1.8490

Yee, L., Chui, M., & Roberts, R. (2024). McKinsey Technology Trends Outlook 2024. In *McKinsey Digital* (Issue July). https://www.mckinsey.com/capabilities/mckinsey-digital/our-insights/the-top-trends-in-tech

Yin, H. (2021). The impact of competition and bank market regulation on banks' cost efficiency. *Journal of Multinational Financial Management*, *61*, 100677. DOI: 10.1016/j.mulfin.2021.100677

Young, M. (2025, September 23). Crypto liquidations hit $1.8B in a day: Final flush or more to come? Cointelegraph. https://cointelegraph.com/news/1-8-billion-leveraged-positions-liquidated-final-flush-more-to-come\

Yu, Z., Razzaq, A., Rehman, A., Shah, A., Jameel, K., & Mor, R. S. (2021). Disruption in global supply chain and socio-economic shocks: a lesson from COVID-19 for sustainable production and consumption. *Operations Management Research*, 233–248. DOI: 10.1007/s12063-021-00179-y

Yuh-Shan et al. (2023). Publication performance and trends in Total Quality Management research: a bibliometric analysis. *34*(1-2), 97-130.

Yulianto, A. (2018). *Pengaruh Literasi Keuangan Syariah Terhadap Keputusan* Penggunaan Produk atau Layanan Lembaga Keuangan Syariah. dspace.uii.ac.id; 2018. DOI Page 283DOI: 10.18502/kss.v7i10.11365

Zafar, A. (2023). Emerging markets: Anatomy, characteristics, and history. In *Emerging markets in a world of chaos: Pathways for economic growth and development* (pp. 23–110). Springer. DOI: 10.1007/978-3-031-29949-0_3

Zghal, R., Ghorbel, A., & Triki, M. (2018). Dynamic model for hedging of the european stock sector with credit default swaps and Euro STOXX 50 volatility index futures. *Borsa Istanbul Review*, *18*(4), 312–328. DOI: 10.1016/j.bir.2018.05.003

Zhao, H., Zhang, F., & Kwon, J. J. I. B. R. (2018). Corporate social responsibility research in international business journals: An author co-citation analysis. *27*(2), 389-400.

Zhu, J., & Liu, W. J. S. (2020). A tale of two databases: The use of Web of Science and Scopus in academic papers. *123*(1), 321-335.

Zhu, H. (2006). An empirical comparison of credit spreads between the bond market and the credit default swap market. *Journal of Financial Services Research*, *29*(3), 211–235. DOI: 10.1007/s10693-006-7626-x

Zivot, E., & Andrews, K. (1992). Further evidence on the great crash, the oil price shock, and the unit root hypothesis. *Journal of Business & Economic Statistics*, *10*(3), 251–270. DOI: 10.1080/07350015.1992.10509904

Zou et al. (2023). Insight into digital finance and fintech: A bibliometric and content analysis. *73*, 102221.

About the Contributors

Shakeb Akhtar is currently Lecturer in University of Technology and Applied Science, Ibra, Oman and Research Fellow in Department of Business and Communications, INTI International University, Nilai, Negeri Sembilan, Malaysia. He holds an MFC and Ph.D. in Banking and Finance from Aligarh Muslim University, India. He specializes in accounting and finance related courses and has over 10 years teaching experience in accounting and finance at both tertiary and senior high school levels. Previously he was Program Director (MBA-FS), Chair Professor, Research Coordinator and Examination cell head in School of Business, Woxsen University, Hyderabad, India. Then before that Division Chair (Area Chair) and Assistant Professor at Galgotias University, Greater Noida, India. His research interest is in banking industry, behavioral economics, and secondary data analysis techniques namely; static panel estimation, dynamic panel estimation, ARDL panel modulation and time series estimation, efficiency analysis, sustainability and SDG's with seven years of research experience. He has made significant contributions to the academic and research community, showcasing his expertise through a multitude of research papers published in prestigious journals indexed in ABDC, ABS, Scopus and Web of Science journals with 35 publication. His commitment to advancing knowledge is evident in the quality and quantity of his scholarly works. In addition to his prolific research output, Dr. Akhtar has been recognized for his thought leadership and has been invited as both a session and keynote speaker at various international conferences. His presentations reflect a deep understanding of his subject matter and a keen ability to communicate complex ideas effectively to diverse audiences. Dr. Akhtar's commitment to excellence has been acknowledged through several accolades, including Best Paper awards, underscoring the impact and significance of his research contributions. This recognition not only reflects his individual achievements but also serves as a testament to the importance of his work within the academic and professional communities. Furthermore, Dr. Shakeb Akhtar plays a vital role as a reviewer for numerous journals, contributing his expertise to ensure the quality and rigor of scholarly publications. His dedication to the peer review process underscores his commitment in maintaining high standards in academic research. Overall, Dr. Shakeb Akhtar's career is marked by a passion for knowledge creation, dissemination, and continuous learning. His multifaceted contributions, ranging from research publications and conference presentations to awards and peer review activities, showcase his outstanding commitment to advancing the academic and research landscape.

Mohsin Khan is currently serving as an Assistant Professor (Senior Grade) in the Department of Commerce at the School of Social Sciences and Languages, Vellore Institute of Technology (VIT), Vellore, Tamil Nadu, India. He holds a Ph.D. in Corporate Finance from the Department of Commerce, Aligarh Muslim University, Aligarh, Uttar Pradesh, India. His primary research interests lie in the fields of Finance and Accounts, Behavioral Finance, Sustainable Financial Goals, Sustainble Development, Social Sciences and Humanities, and Corporate Employee Cognition. Dr. Khan is proficient in accounting practices and adept at utilizing both primary and secondary data analysis techniques, including various statistical tools. He has authored more than 18 papers published in reputed international journals indexed in Web of Science, Scopus, ESCI, and ABDC (B category), accumulating over 146 citations and an h-index of 4 on Google Scholar. Additionally, he holds a patent from the Intellectual Property Rights (IPR) India. With seven years of post-Ph.D. experience in teaching and research, Dr. Khan has also contributed as a guest editor for the 'Journal of Statistics and Management Systems' (ABDC, C category). He has successfully organized more than two international conferences as an organizing secretary and has been an active member of the Board of Studies for several organizations. Dr. Khan has also edited a book entitled "Futuristic of Management" and received a seed grant project focusing on corporate employee cognition. Currently He is serving as an Editor of Book (Edited) which will be published by Emerald.

Faozi Abduljalil Gazem Almaqtari is an Assistant Professor in Accounting and the Head of the Department of Accounting and Finance at A'Sharqiyah University, Oman. He is recognized as one of the Top Scholars in Accounting in Oman for the Prior Five Years and is ranked #143 globally in Accounting on the Scholar GPS website. He holds a Ph.D. in Accounting from Aligarh Muslim University, India, and has extensive experience in academia, having served in senior teaching and research positions in Oman, Malaysia, and India. His research focuses on corporate governance, IFRS, financial performance, FinTech, AI in accounting, and sustainability. Dr. Almaqtari has a strong publication record, contributing to high-impact journals indexed in Scopus, Web of Science, ABDC, and ABS. His expertise includes financial analysis, panel data modeling, and sustainability performance evaluation. He has also served as an editor and reviewer for several international journals and has been actively involved in academic program development, conference organization, and research supervision. In addition to his academic achievements, Dr. Almaqtari has delivered keynote speeches, chaired sessions at international conferences, and conducted workshops on financial analysis and research methodologies. His work significantly contributes to advancing accounting and finance knowledge in emerging markets.

V. Selvam is a distinguished academician and dynamic leader, serving as Professor and Dean in the Department of Commerce, School of Social Science and Languages, at Vellore Institute of Technology (VIT), Vellore, India. With an illustrious career spanning 34 years in accounting and finance education, he has made significant contributions to research, mentoring, and institutional development. His research expertise lies in microfinance, insurance, women empowerment, and marketing, reflected in his impressive publication record—50 research articles, including 27 in Scopus-indexed journals. A passionate scholar, he has presented 54 papers at national and international conferences and actively participated in 15 conferences. A dedicated mentor, Dr. Selvam, has successfully guided six Ph.D. scholars and is currently supervising six more. His commitment to academic excellence is evident in his role as an organizer of six impactful workshops, fifteen thought-provoking guest lectures, and five industry visits, bridging the gap between academia and real-world business practices. With a keen interest in high-impact research, he has successfully completed a major ICSSR-funded project and authored ten insightful book chapters. His academic footprint extends globally, with research visits to Malaysia and Singapore, fostering international collaborations. Dr. Selvam's unwavering dedication to education, research, and leadership continues to inspire students and scholars, shaping the future of commerce and business studies.

Shilpa Bahl is currently Professor in School of business, Galgotias University, Greater Noida, U.P, India. She holds an MBA and Ph.D. in Finance and HR from Kurukshetra University, India. She specializes in accounting and finance related courses and has over 10 years teaching experience in accounting and finance at both tertiary and senior high school levels. Currently she is Program Chair of MBA, Time table coordinator and a member of SRC in School of Business, Galgotias University, India. Then before that Division Chair (Area Chair) and Assistant Professor at Galgotias University, Greater Noida, India. Her research interest is in banking industry, behavioral finance. He has made significant contributions to the research community by publishing in prestigious journals indexed in ABDC, Scopus and Web of Science journals.

***

Mohammad Ammar Ahsan is a Ph.D. Research Scholar in the Department of Commerce at Aligarh Muslim University. He holds a Bachelor's degree in Commerce and an MBA in Financial Management. His research interests lie in Finance and Banking, with a focus on Financial Technology, sustainability, banking performance, climate change, and the role of Information Technology in modern finance.

Mahfooz Alam is an accomplished Assistant Professor of Finance with over five years of academic experience. His research interests include sustainable finance, FinTech, financial markets, asset pricing, and Islamic banking. He holds a PhD in Finance from Aligarh Muslim University, where his thesis focused on the performance of mutual funds in India. He has held faculty positions at several universities, including ICFAI University and GLA University, and is currently a Faculty Instructor at the University of the People, USA.

Parvez Alam Khan is a distinguished academic and researcher specializing in sustainable innovation, finance, and environmental governance. He currently serves as a Lecturer at Universiti Teknologi PETRONAS, Malaysia, contributing to both research and teaching. With over 10 years of experience across academia, industry, and research, he has worked in esteemed institutions such as Woxsen University, Aligarh Muslim University, and Bloomberg (Wipro Ltd., India). Dr. Khan holds a PhD in Management from Universiti Teknologi PETRONAS, where his research explored the intersection of sustainable innovation, firm financial performance, and Sustainable Development Goals (SDGs). His expertise extends to financial technology (Fintech), ESG analysis, and corporate governance, with certifications from the University of Michigan and Bloomberg Terminal Interface. Recognized among the Top 50 Authors in Green Innovation and Top 100 in SDGs research by Google Scholar, Dr. Khan has published extensively in high-impact journals and secured multiple research grants. He has also played a pivotal role in academic leadership, serving as Secretary of ICESG 2024 and Coordinator of Final Year Projects (FYP). Beyond academia, he actively engages in consulting and training, recently providing ESG-related training to bank employees as part of a university revenue-generation initiative. His contributions reflect a commitment to bridging the gap between sustainability, innovation, and financial performance, shaping future research and policy directions.

Bilal Asghar is a dedicated researcher with a PhD in Commerce, from Aligarh Muslim University. His research interests span a broad range of contemporary business and management areas, including Leadership (Humble, Servant, and

Transformational), Innovation (Social and Green), Corporate Social Responsibility, Workplace Happiness, Supply Chain Management, and Sustainability in Organizations. Dr. Asghar has actively contributed to academic scholarship through research publications in peer-reviewed journals and presentations at international conferences. His work reflects a commitment to integrating theory with practice, addressing emerging challenges in organizational and policy contexts. He is proficient in both quantitative and qualitative research methodologies, using tools such as SPSS, AMOS, SmartPLS, MAXQDA, and R-Studio. He also effectively manages literature and references through Mendeley, Zotero, and EndNote.

K. Balaji is an Assistant Professor in Business and Management, Christ University, Bangalore. He did Ph.D. from KLU Business School, KL University,Vijayawada. He is having 12 years of teaching experience. He has to his credit 23 Research Articles published in reputed National and International Journals. He has participated and presented more than 12 papers in both National and International Seminars/Conferences and also attended more than 50 workshops/ FDPS organized by various reputed organizations. He has also participated in more than 50 seminars / webinars organized by various reputed organizations. He has also attended in 6 Short Term Training programs.He has successfully conducted 3 webinars, one 5 day FDP and one International Conference on Reimaging marketing in New Normal. He is a ratified as Assistant Professor by both JNTUH, JNTU Anantapur and Sri Venkateswara University,Tirupati. His specialized areas include, Accounting and Financial management, Marketing Management, Retailing Management, Consumer Behavior studies, Entrepreneurship and Business Laws.

Swati Bhalerao is a dedicated academic professional with over 15 years of diverse experience in industry and academia, specialising in accounting, financial management, Corporate Finance, and banking. Her research interests are exploring innovative strategies for financial planning and analysis, investigating the efficiency of banking operations, investment analysis, and corporate finance. Passionate about financial education, which includes ten research papers published in esteemed journals, is remarkable. She has mentored students and contributed significantly to academic research areas under management and discipline. As a central coordinator for All India Council for Technical Education (AICTE) approvals and head of the Intellectual Property Rights (IPR) Cell, she has a proven track record in managing University exams SPPU.

Csongor Czipf, Ph.D. Honorary Associate Professor, Assistant Professor Széchenyi István University, Győr, Hungary Gyula Kautz Faculty of Economics, Department of International Applied Economics Ongoing teaching experience at

Széchenyi István University since 1999. Appointed as Regional Economic Manager of the Piarist Order Hungarian Province in Budapest as of January 2022. Master's degree in Religious Education and Dormitory Teaching obtained from the College of Theology in Győr in 2017. Doctoral degree awarded in 2011 by Janus Pannonius University of Pécs. Research specialization: corporate evaluation from a human resources perspective. Bachelor's degree in Economics with a specialization in Comparative Economic Policy completed in 1999 at Széchenyi István College.

Basil Osayin Daudu, PhD, is a lecturer at Kogi State University, Nigeria. He received his doctorate from Nnamdi Azikiwe University, Nigeria, and he has 10 years of teaching experience. He is a certified educator and has undergone training as a Microsoft Innovative Educator. His work has appeared in over 20 academic journals and book chapters, both locally and internationally. His areas of expertise include Artificial Intelligence and African Studies (society, culture, and politics).

Piyush Dixit is currently serving as an Asst. Professor at Indira University, Pune. He has over 16 years of diverse work experience in academics and industry. His expertise covers a wide range of subjects, including Marketing Mgmt., Sales & Distribution mgmt., Product & Brand Mgmt., Retail Marketing, Consumer behaviour & Services Marketing to name a few. Prof. Piyush Dixit has published multitudinous research papers at National and International Level Journals contributing astute judgements & insights. He has also published 18 text books in Marketing, Entrepreneurship & General mgmt. allied courses in PG & UG curriculum. Prior to his academic career, he served with reputable companies such as Adidas group, Kansai Nerolac Paints & Nike Inc. where he consistently exceeded targets & received prestigious rewards and accolades. His expertise and dedication contributes remarkably to the academic excellence and student advancement.

Mehmet Levent Erdas holds a PhD in Business Administration from Suleyman Demirel University, Turkey. He started his professional career as a revenue expert with the Finance Ministry. He is currently Assoc. Prof. Dr. at Akdeniz University, Turkey, Department of Economics and Finance. His research interests include application of econometric and optimisation methods for the study of economics and finance. He published numerous research papers in that fields.

Omar Guirette-Barbosa has experience in quality systems based on ISO standards such as 9001, 17025, etc. He is a consultant on accreditation and certification issues, as well as on the application of continuous improvement tools and industrial engineering.

Rishikaysh Kaakandikar boasts an exceptional academic journey, spanning over 15 years of dedicated teaching and a year of valuable industrial experience, and currently holds the esteemed position of Associate Professor at SaiBalaji Education Society's SaiBalaji International Institute of Management Sciences in Pune. His scholarly contributions shine brightly, encompassing a remarkable portfolio of over 40 research papers in prestigious journals. A sought-after intellectual resource, He has contributed substantially to academia through guest lectures, seminars, workshops, and conferences at esteemed institutions across India. His insights have enriched the academic community and stimulated engaging discussions on various facets of his field. He is a prominent finance columnist for leading newspapers in Maharashtra, including Sakal, Lokmat, Punyannagari, and Prabhat

Harpreet Kaur is an assistant professor at Christ University within the School of Commerce, Finance, and Accountancy. Her research expertise lies in the domain of services marketing, consumer behaviour, luxury fashion marketing, and cross-cultural studies. Her scholarly pursuits primarily delve into topics such as customer retention, service selection parameters, and model development. Dr. Kaur has contributed significantly to her field, and her work has been published in numerous top marketing journals, such as the International Journal of Bank Marketing, Journal of Financial Services Marketing, etc.

Nawab Khan has been the Chairman, Department of Commerce, Aligarh Muslim University, Aligarh w.e.f. 1st July 2019 to 30th June 2022 and Dean, Faculty of Commerce, Aligarh Muslim University, Aligarh w.e.f. 17th March 2016 to 16th March 2018. Professor Khan has also been involved in the residential life of students as Provost of Sir Ross Masood Hall (Hall of Residence), during 2009-2011. He has also been the Chairman, Central Allotment Committee, Aligarh Muslim University, Aligarh. Professor Khan has been a Member of Executive Council, Academic Council, Aligarh Muslim University Court (Governing Body), Finance Committee. Professor Khan has authored 8 books (In Press 2) and published 82 research papers in the reputed National and International Peer Reviewed/Indexed in journals Scopus, ISI and ABDC. He has organized 6 National Seminars sponsored by ICSSR, NSA and UTI and 8 Workshops as Convenor in his Department. He has presented a large number of research papers in national and international seminars and conferences. He has chaired a number of Technical Sessions and delivered the Keynote and Special Addresses in a large number of national and international seminars and conferences.

Mahesh Kumar, Assistant Professor, MIT World Peace University, Pune. Qualification and Name of institution: B.E. (IT), Army Institute of Technology Pune.

M.B.A (Finance), B.R.A.B.U. Muzaffarpur. Ph.D, Manipal University Jaipur. UGC-NET-JRF(Management). All India Engineering Entrance Examination(CBSE), 2007. Broad Area of Research: Finance Sub Area of Research: Econometrics, Foreign Exchange Management, FinTech, Equity research, corporate finance, business analysis, sustainability reporting

Vikas Maheshwari has around 22 years of Capital Markets experience across managing Equities/ Fixed Income/ Derivatives Portfolios, Research, Strategies, M&A etc. He has worked across Conventional Bank, Merchant Bank and Investment companies. In the last role he worked as Head of Public Investments at Abu Dhabi Capital Group (ADCG). ADCG is a large institutional investor based out of Abu Dhabi (UAE). he managed ADCG's Capital Market Investments across Global Equities (Developed/ Emerging/ MENA), ETFs, Fixed Income, Derivatives, and Alternative Investments. He led a team of excellent and driven executives. Before joining ADCG, he was part of Treasury and Global Markets Group at First Gulf Bank (Now First Abu Dhabi Bank). I managed USD 400mn Global Macro Hedge Fund (Al Saqer Fund: Bloomberg Ticker ALSAQER UH EQUITY) that primarily invested in Global Equities, ETFs, Equity Derivatives and Fixed Income. He has also managed the USD 100mn Global Proprietary Equities/ Equity Derivatives Investments for the bank and worked extensively on strategic initiatives like M&As, Divestments, Bank Strategy etc. In his previous roles as Lead Equity Analyst at Bank of America Securities and First Global. His research reports appeared in many featured international media like Bloomberg, Wall Street Journal, Barrons', Yahoo Finance, 24 Ore Sole (Italy), Latin Finance (Brazil/Mexico), etc. He was also rated as 5 Star Analyst (highest ratings) by Starmine (an international renowned analyst rating agency) for his consistent earning projections of 2 US telecom companies.

Ameya Patil is currently Assistant Professor at MIT World Peace University, Pune with 10 years of teaching experience and 3.5 years of Industrial experience. He previously worked as an Assistant Manager with IDBI Bank and as Assistant Professor and HOD of BBA and BBA-IB at Sinhgad College, Pune. He teaches subjects related to Finance and International Business. He has authored several books and research papers related to various topics in Finance, Management and International Business. His research interest areas include stock prediction, green finance, behavioral finance and allied areas in finance and general management. He is a member of Indian Institute of Banking and Finance (IIBF) and ASCB(UK). 14 of his research works have appeared in Scopus and ABDC journals, and with reputed publishers such as Wiley, Springer, Emerald, Inderscience, IGI Global and Emerald

Krunal Purohit is a professor of SOB with a specialization in accounting and finance at Woxsen University and an expert in various fields like accounting, mutual funds and investment decisions, and economics. Dr. Krunal Purohit has published various number of articles in various journals with the topics related to mutual funds and economic concepts.

Afzalur Rahman is a professor of financial economics and sustainability at Woxsen University's School of Business (SOB). His research has made significant contributions to the existing literature. He is also a frequent session chairperson for national and international conferences held at Woxsen University.

Rama Rao is an Assistant Professor with GITAM Business School. He has two decades of teaching and research experience. published research papers in finance and marketing domains in international journals of repute. He authored a book on consumer marketing and acts as a resource person for workshops, seminars and conferences.

Mohd Salim is currently Assistant Professor in Woxsen University, Hydrabad India. He holds an MBA (Finance and Operations) and Ph.D. in Entrepreneurship from Aligarh Muslim University, India. He specializes in accounting, finance and operations related courses and has over 4 years teaching experience in accounting and finance and One year of Industry experience in Wipro Pvt. Ltd as an Financial Analyst in US municipal process using Bloomberg terminal. His research interests lie in Finance and entrepreneurship, focusing on Fintech, sustainability, climate change, and emerging technologies.

Seetha Ram is an Associate Professor with 18 years of teaching and research experience. His research interests are into behavioral finance, neuro finance, economic development linking technology. Successfully guided four scholars leading to their doctoral degree and is an active resource person for workshops, seminars and conferences on the research interest areas. He is also reviewer for journals such as JEMM, IJEM, IJPD, PLOS, AJEBA, SJASSE, Island Studies etc.

Shanu Singh is a dedicated academic professional with over 9 years of experience in commerce, finance, and accounting. She has completed B.Com (Honors), M.Com and Ph.D along with UGC-NET-JRF currently serving as an Assistant Professor at Christ University, Delhi NCR. She has previously held similar positions at institutions such as Amity University, Noida, Galgotias University, Greater Noida and AKS University, Madhya Pradesh. Shanu has significantly contributed to academic administrations and holding key role as MOODLE Coordinator and IQAC Coordinator at departmental level. She is currently holding position of IQAC Coordinator and also involved in Media coordination, class mentorship, and strategic action planning. Her academic engagements include organizing international conferences and delivering guest lectures on topics like digital marketing and fintech. Her achievements include multiple research publications in Scopus & UGC-Care listed journals and presentations at renowned conferences. Shanu has authored academic books, co-edited research-oriented books, and contributed chapters on topics ranging from banking digitalization to women's health. Furthermore, she has completed several faculty development programs and certifications in research methodology and academic quality assurance, showcasing her commitment to continuous learning and academic excellence.

Abhishek Sinha is a passionate management educator and finance practitioner with over two decades of experience across equity research, financial consulting, and management and entrepreneurial education. Currently serving as an Assistant Professor at Mahindra University, Hyderabad, he is an Entrepreneurial Finance evangelist, helping bridge the gap between theory and real-world finance. His research, case studies, and book chapters on different aspects of entrepreneurship – IPO exit valuation, startup finance, and sustainability have been published in Scopus and ABDC-indexed journals. He has also contributed to popular media by simplifying concepts on Moneycontrol.com and Outlook Business. At present, he writes Opinion Columns with Outlook Business. A certified Financial Risk Manager (FRM, GARP – US) and PhD in Finance from UPES, Dehradun, Dr. Sinha continues to nurture finance-savvy entrepreneurs by combining academic depth with hands-on experience. He is also a renowned corporate trainer specializing in storytelling as a pedagogical tool.

Surbhi Srivastava is an academician, researcher, and tax consultant. She has qualified UGC -NET exam and has done her doctorate from the University of Allahabad. Her area of interest is taxation, finance, auditing, business compliance & sustainability. She has published in international & national Scopus & Web of Science-indexed journals. She has published a book on Financial Management and has three patents related to commerce and management. She has qualified CA Intermediate exam and has done her industry articleship for 3 years. She has done statutory and internal audits of around 15 state-owned and public projects. She has been guiding UG and PG students with their research projects in the areas of finance, taxation, reporting and sustainability.

Sukirno is a Professor in Economics, Finance and Management Accounting. He serves as an editor for journals including Cakrawala Pendidikan, Jurnal Kependidikan, Economia, Jurnal Pendidikan Akuntansi Indonesia, Nominal, and

Kajian Pendidikan, Akuntansi Indonesia. He also serves as a reviewer for several national and international journals including Jurnal Pendidikan Vokasi, Harmoni Sosial Jurnal Pendidikan IPS, Sosio Didaktika, Jurnal Pendidikan Ekonomi Dinamika Pendidikan (JPEDP), Jurnal Pendidikan Akuntansi, Journal of Economic and Administrative Sciences, and Journal of Applied Research in Higher Education. He also serves as a reviewer for LPDP, Ristekdikti, and Seminar Nasional Akuntansi (SNA). He works as an assessor for national (LAMEMBA) and international accreditation board (FIBAA). He wrote a book chapter entitles Artificial Intelligence Applications in Finance: A Proposed Model at IGI Global Scientific Publishing.

Safas VP is currently pursuing a Ph.D. in Commerce at Vellore Institute of Technology, Vellore. He previously served as an Assistant Professor at Kalasalingam Academy of Research and Education (Deemed to be University). He holds a postgraduate degree in M.Com (Business Finance) from the Central University of Pondicherry. His academic interests include accounting, finance, Sustainability, business strategy, etc.

Index

A

Artificial Intelligence 5, 19, 20, 23, 84, 114, 116, 156, 162, 186, 261, 262, 265, 266, 276, 288, 289, 290, 291, 292, 293, 294, 295, 297, 298, 310, 317, 318, 319, 320, 321, 343, 345, 347, 349, 379, 396, 413, 460

Asian Financial Crisis 3, 6, 14, 22, 34, 65, 66, 67, 68, 71, 72, 75, 78, 79, 80, 81, 82, 83, 88, 106, 181

B

Banking 1, 2, 3, 5, 8, 9, 10, 13, 14, 16, 18, 19, 20, 21, 22, 23, 25, 26, 30, 34, 36, 37, 40, 42, 43, 59, 68, 69, 73, 74, 76, 81, 82, 83, 85, 86, 93, 94, 95, 96, 97, 98, 99, 100, 101, 102, 103, 104, 105, 106, 107, 108, 109, 110, 111, 112, 115, 116, 117, 118, 119, 120, 121, 122, 123, 124, 125, 126, 127, 128, 129, 130, 131, 132, 134, 136, 137, 140, 141, 142, 143, 145, 146, 149, 150, 152, 155, 157, 159, 160, 161, 162, 163, 165, 166, 167, 168, 169, 170, 171, 172, 173, 174, 176, 178, 179, 180, 181, 183, 184, 185, 186, 187, 188, 189, 190, 191, 197, 200, 202, 204, 206, 208, 209, 214, 218, 222, 230, 234, 235, 242, 243, 244, 245, 246, 249, 251, 253, 255, 256, 258, 260, 261, 265, 266, 268, 269, 271, 272, 273, 275, 276, 277, 279, 283, 288, 289, 290, 292, 293, 297, 298, 299, 301, 302, 307, 308, 309, 310, 311, 313, 314, 315, 317, 318, 319, 321, 340, 341, 342, 344, 354, 376, 405, 406, 411, 412, 413, 414, 415, 416, 417, 418, 419, 420, 421, 422, 423, 425, 426, 427, 428, 429, 430, 431, 432, 433, 434, 438, 441, 442, 444, 447, 449, 450, 453, 454, 455

Banking Regulation 95, 103, 106, 115, 116, 123, 178, 187

Bank Robbery 297, 298, 299, 300, 301, 305, 306, 307, 310, 311, 314, 315, 316, 319, 320, 321

Basel III 3, 14, 17, 74, 81, 83, 94, 96, 97, 105, 111, 112, 113, 114, 115, 119, 120, 121, 122, 123, 137, 138, 160, 179, 342

Bibliometric Analysis 260, 261, 411, 413, 414, 432, 434, 435, 436, 437, 438, 439

Biometric ATMs 314, 315, 321

Block Chain 157

C

Capital flows 1, 3, 10, 22, 24, 83, 141, 155, 197, 208, 227

Cash 30, 32, 35, 36, 37, 42, 45, 55, 60, 62, 77, 78, 81, 83, 87, 137, 138, 149, 168, 176, 188, 191, 217, 218, 220, 221, 224, 228, 237, 238, 239, 240, 241, 243, 244, 246, 247, 248, 249, 250, 253, 254, 256, 294, 298, 305, 319, 336, 380, 381, 383, 388, 389, 390, 391, 394, 395, 396, 398, 400, 401, 402, 403, 404, 408, 412, 435, 443, 445, 448, 450, 455, 456, 459

Central Bank Digital Currency 26, 38, 46, 47, 49, 51, 52, 54, 55, 56, 57, 59, 60, 62, 237, 250, 258, 259, 260, 261, 262, 263

Central Bank Independence 237, 238, 239, 241, 256

Climate Risk Assessment 379, 387

Cloud Computing 20

COVID-19 Economic Shock 65, 67

Credit Access 454

Credit Risk 13, 101, 105, 149, 155, 168, 176, 177, 179, 183, 189, 272, 275, 276, 355, 356, 357, 362, 373

D

Decision Making 21, 126, 267, 268, 272, 276, 277, 281, 326, 402, 404, 442, 449

Digital Currencies 20, 23, 29, 34, 38, 46, 52, 55, 57, 59, 113, 115, 205, 206,

219, 238, 240, 242, 244, 245, 246, 247, 251, 254, 255, 256, 257, 258, 259, 260, 261, 262, 263, 346, 429
Digital Finance 18, 30, 36, 302, 317, 415, 437, 439
Dollar Hegemony 195, 196, 197, 198, 199, 200, 222, 226

E

e-Banking Theft 297, 298, 299, 301, 310, 311, 314, 315, 321
Economy 4, 5, 6, 8, 10, 11, 16, 17, 24, 25, 27, 30, 32, 34, 35, 36, 42, 43, 45, 47, 49, 52, 53, 55, 58, 61, 71, 73, 82, 83, 85, 88, 94, 96, 105, 109, 111, 115, 118, 121, 126, 127, 128, 131, 135, 142, 143, 144, 145, 152, 155, 162, 166, 169, 175, 176, 179, 180, 182, 183, 195, 197, 199, 207, 208, 209, 211, 224, 229, 230, 233, 234, 235, 237, 238, 239, 241, 242, 244, 250, 251, 254, 256, 257, 258, 262, 288, 297, 298, 299, 303, 310, 316, 321, 329, 330, 351, 352, 353, 356, 375, 379, 380, 383, 438, 442, 445, 447, 456, 461
ESG Integration 144, 150, 158

F

Financial Crises 14, 65, 66, 68, 74, 78, 79, 81, 82, 115, 181, 191, 222, 342, 374, 430, 455
Financial Inclusion 16, 20, 29, 36, 37, 41, 43, 44, 45, 46, 52, 59, 62, 111, 119, 149, 152, 210, 211, 223, 240, 242, 243, 246, 247, 248, 249, 251, 254, 257, 260, 262, 270, 271, 272, 273, 276, 279, 285, 290, 313, 314, 317, 318, 415, 429, 432, 434, 443, 444, 445, 446, 447, 448, 449, 450, 454, 455, 456, 457, 458, 459, 460
Financial Literacy 233, 270, 276, 285, 288, 441, 442, 443, 444, 445, 446, 447, 448, 449, 450, 451, 453, 454, 455, 456, 457, 458, 459, 460, 461, 462, 463
Financial Modelling 150, 379, 381, 382, 385, 400, 401, 402, 405
Financial Performance 168, 190, 290, 318, 435, 456
Financial Privacy 255
Financial Regulation 71, 97, 119, 120, 122, 145, 233, 263
Financial Sector 61, 72, 94, 105, 127, 128, 132, 135, 136, 138, 140, 159, 160, 161, 166, 172, 173, 175, 179, 190, 191, 290, 299, 303, 311, 355, 357, 360, 369, 372, 373, 374, 444, 450
Financial Stability 1, 10, 14, 16, 27, 29, 30, 37, 43, 45, 47, 49, 54, 56, 59, 73, 76, 78, 86, 94, 95, 96, 108, 109, 112, 114, 115, 118, 119, 120, 122, 125, 127, 128, 129, 131, 135, 139, 141, 146, 159, 160, 162, 163, 166, 167, 173, 178, 179, 180, 182, 183, 187, 211, 214, 216, 219, 223, 228, 234, 238, 243, 247, 248, 253, 255, 256, 259, 260, 262, 263, 276, 311, 340, 341, 342, 343, 347, 348, 352, 353, 406, 429, 448
Fiscal Policy 29, 30, 51, 52, 59, 69, 81, 83, 84, 88, 175, 184, 209, 214, 217, 239, 244
Fiscal Policy Transmission 29, 30, 51, 52
Fraud 19, 42, 43, 53, 95, 102, 103, 112, 186, 255, 272, 278, 285, 297, 299, 301, 302, 303, 308, 309, 310, 312, 313, 314, 315, 316, 318, 319, 321, 343

G

G20 Countries 355, 357, 358, 360, 362, 373, 374, 377
Geopolitics 353
Global Financial Crisis 3, 6, 10, 14, 22, 30, 35, 43, 65, 66, 68, 72, 74, 76, 77, 78, 79, 80, 81, 82, 83, 94, 96, 105, 106, 116, 120, 137, 171, 172, 181, 184, 199, 342, 360, 412, 417, 419, 429
Global Stock Exchanges 325
Great Depression 65, 66, 67, 68, 69, 72, 74, 78, 79, 80, 81, 82, 83, 86, 87, 166
Green Banking 146, 155, 161, 416

I

International Banking 1, 2, 5, 8, 9, 10, 13, 14, 30, 93, 94, 95, 97, 103, 104, 105, 106, 107, 110, 112, 115, 116, 162
International Finance 1, 2, 5, 10, 12, 13, 14, 21, 23, 263, 293

L

Latin American Debt Crisis 65, 68, 70, 71, 78, 79, 80, 106

M

Macroeconomic Variables 165, 167, 168, 175, 189, 191
Macroprudential Policy 123
Mitigation 14, 95, 121, 128, 144, 151, 268, 276, 342
Model 7, 21, 25, 39, 40, 41, 42, 43, 44, 46, 59, 71, 74, 168, 169, 170, 171, 183, 184, 189, 190, 202, 205, 211, 218, 221, 224, 227, 237, 239, 241, 242, 244, 245, 246, 249, 257, 259, 265, 267, 268, 271, 275, 277, 285, 286, 287, 289, 290, 292, 293, 295, 311, 312, 358, 359, 360, 366, 367, 368, 377, 380, 381, 383, 388, 389, 390, 391, 392, 393, 394, 396, 400, 404, 405, 416, 435, 447, 454, 456, 458
Monetary Policy 25, 29, 30, 31, 32, 33, 34, 36, 37, 41, 43, 45, 47, 49, 58, 59, 67, 68, 69, 71, 75, 76, 86, 87, 127, 144, 162, 175, 176, 180, 181, 182, 183, 184, 214, 215, 217, 218, 221, 222, 225, 233, 239, 240, 241, 242, 247, 248, 251, 254, 256, 257, 329, 354, 445

N

Non-Performing Assets 37, 165, 166, 167, 169, 173, 174, 175, 178, 180, 184, 187, 188, 189, 191, 272, 275
North-Central Nigeria 298, 299, 305, 306, 308, 315, 321

P

Pawnshop Usage 441, 453
Policy Failures 65, 66, 68, 70, 71, 73, 82
Policy Frameworks 68, 125, 132
Policy Successes 69, 70, 72, 73

R

Regulation 2, 3, 10, 14, 17, 22, 26, 56, 66, 71, 72, 74, 81, 83, 84, 95, 96, 97, 103, 105, 106, 108, 110, 111, 113, 115, 116, 119, 120, 121, 122, 123, 127, 140, 143, 144, 145, 154, 166, 175, 178, 179, 181, 187, 195, 196, 203, 204, 211, 212, 214, 216, 218, 219, 223, 224, 228, 230, 233, 234, 235, 258, 261, 262, 263, 279, 280, 295, 319, 325, 343, 346, 353, 381, 391, 403, 406, 416, 429, 432, 445
Regulatory Compliance 57, 93, 113, 146, 179, 214, 253, 302, 311, 313, 343, 446
Risk Management 5, 10, 13, 26, 38, 40, 95, 99, 101, 111, 125, 131, 137, 138, 139, 140, 145, 146, 148, 154, 160, 163, 166, 174, 260, 262, 319, 344, 345, 352, 357, 358, 372, 373, 375, 404, 454, 455

S

Security 42, 45, 46, 53, 56, 57, 58, 94, 95, 152, 185, 186, 188, 211, 214, 224, 228, 244, 247, 249, 250, 255, 257, 262, 267, 269, 272, 278, 279, 283, 284, 294, 297, 298, 299, 300, 303, 305, 306, 307, 310, 311, 314, 315, 317, 318, 320, 321, 329, 343, 442, 445, 452, 458
Seigniorage 205, 237, 238, 242
Stablecoins 195, 196, 197, 198, 199, 200, 201, 202, 203, 204, 205, 206, 207, 208, 209, 210, 211, 212, 213, 214, 215, 216, 217, 218, 219, 220, 221, 222, 223, 224, 225, 226, 227, 228, 229, 230, 231, 233, 234, 235, 236, 259, 263, 351

Stock Market 34, 35, 68, 77, 80, 106, 275, 292, 355, 357, 358, 359, 360, 364, 367, 369, 372, 373, 374, 375, 376, 377
Sustainable Enterprises 379, 382, 384, 385, 387, 389, 390, 404, 405
Sustainable Finance 21, 24, 114, 115, 116, 125, 126, 127, 129, 130, 132, 138, 140, 141, 142, 143, 144, 146, 151, 157, 158, 159, 160, 161, 162, 163, 262, 401, 406, 436
Sustainable Financial Growth 266

T

Tax Evasion 19, 53, 237, 238, 239, 240, 241, 242, 244, 253, 256

www.ingramcontent.com/pod-product-compliance
Lightning Source LLC
LaVergne TN
LVHW081317300926
849161LV00008B/1789
* 9 7 9 8 3 3 7 3 3 7 2 5 8 *